Reader's Digest

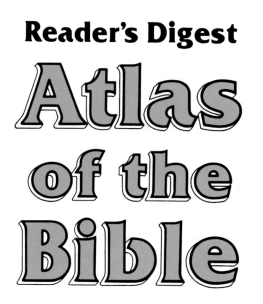

Atlas of the Bible

Reader's Digest

Atlas of the Bible

An Illustrated Guide to the Holy Land

❖

The Reader's Digest Association, Inc.
Pleasantville, New York • Montreal

Atlas of the Bible

Editor: Joseph L. Gardner
Art Editor: Richard J. Berenson
Associate Editor: Kaari Ward
Art Associate: Evelyn S. Bauer
Research Editors: Monica Borrowman
Mary Jane Hodges
Picture Researcher: Margaret Mathews
Copy Editor: Zahava Feldman
Project Secretaries: Mary A. Bradner
Ann Purdy

The editors are deeply grateful for the generous and thoughtful assistance of Prof. Harry Thomas Frank at every stage of preparation of this volume. Professor Frank researched the maps and wrote most of the accompanying texts that appear in the "Historical Atlas of Biblical Times," pages 50–208, and compiled the "Gazetteer of the Bible World" that begins on page 209. We also wish to thank the Board of Consultants, who reviewed selected portions of the volume.

Principal Adviser and Editorial Consultant

Harry Thomas Frank
Danforth Professor of Religion
Chairman, Department of Religion, Oberlin College

Board of Consultants

Denis Baly
Department of Religion
Kenyon College

Edward F. Campbell, Jr.
McCormick Theological Seminary

David Noel Freedman
Department of Near Eastern Studies
University of Michigan

Rev. Stephen J. Hartdegen
Department of Education
United States Catholic Conference

Laton E. Holmgren
General Secretary (Ret.)
American Bible Society

George MacRae
The Divinity School
Harvard University

Nahum M. Sarna
Department of Near Eastern and Judaic Studies
Brandeis University

Rabbi Marc H. Tanenbaum
National Director
Interreligious Affairs
American Jewish Committee

The acknowledgments and credits that appear on pages 244–245 are hereby made a part of this copyright page.

Library of Congress Catalog Card Number 80-53426
ISBN 0-89577-097-0
Printed in the United States of America

About This Book

The narrow land bridge between Asia and Africa—historic Palestine, today a region divided between Israel and its Arab neighbors—is among the most important geographic areas on earth. A link between the earliest civilizations of Mesopotamia and Egypt, it became the highway for conquering armies, a pawn in the power struggle waged for centuries, even millennia, by the great empires that rose and fell in the Near East. And today it is almost daily in newspaper headlines as rival nations assert their claims to the area.

The true significance of this ancient land, of course, lies outside any geographical or political considerations. For this is the Holy Land— birthplace of both Judaism and Christianity, sacred also to the followers of Muhammad. To a devout reader of the Bible, it is as familiar as his own neighborhood. He has stood with Abraham at the oak of Moreh and heard the Lord promise, "To your descendants I will give this land."* With Moses he has climbed Mount Nebo, to be shown "a good land, a land of brooks of water, of fountains and springs, flowing forth in valleys and hills . . ." He has marched with Joshua as he "defeated the whole land, the hill country and the Negeb and the lowland and the slopes . . ." He has followed Jesus along the shores of the Sea of Galilee as he gathered his "fishers of men" and accompanied him on his last, fateful journey to Jerusalem. With Paul he has set out for that blinding encounter on the road to Damascus.

Assyrian archer and shield-bearer, page 14

As these few examples attest, the Bible is a book of movement, grand and glorious events enacted against the backdrop of a land starkly, awesomely beautiful and taking the reader from "Ur of the Chaldeans" down to Egypt and across the northern rim of the Mediterranean to Greece and Italy. To provide a deeper understanding of the Bible's immortal stories, Reader's Digest has sought to place them in their proper geographical and historical context. The result, ATLAS OF THE BIBLE, is a unique reference work and a fascinating reading experience.

There are other atlases of the Bible, most of them prepared by scholars for use by other scholars. They provide needed and valuable information and have earned their places on library reference shelves or in bibliographies such as the one on page 244. The present work, however, was prepared with the general reader in mind. It is a book based on the best contemporary scholarship and with the able assistance of the scholars and theologians listed opposite. Yet the constant goal of the editors has been to make the volume as clear and precise as it is accurate and up-to-date. ATLAS OF THE BIBLE serves to explain, elucidate, and expand on what is already in the Bible but may not always be immediately comprehensible. It is designed to be read from cover to cover or to be consulted on specific points, as a companion to the Bible.

At the core of any atlas are the maps, and ATLAS OF THE BIBLE has dozens of these. But before the reader comes to the maps, he is given an extended introduction to the Bible world, a collection of special features that serves as an illustrated guide to the Holy Land.

The ancient peoples of Mesopotamia and Egypt left numerous pictorial records of how they dressed; a modern artist has based his meticulous portraits of biblical folk on these sources. Here are members

Chapter and verse of biblical citations are given on page 245.

Isaiah scroll and jars in which some of the famed Dead Sea scrolls were found, page 27

Jerusalem at the center of the world in a 13th-century wheel-pattern map, page 31

of a Semitic clan in the time of the Patriarchs, a Canaanite charioteer, a Philistine warrior, a Pharisee at prayer, a Roman legionnaire, a peasant family at the time of Jesus, and others. As readers of the Bible well know, both Old and New Testaments are rich with references to fauna and flora. Modern artists here bring to life the animals and plants of biblical times in full-color illustrations. A table of weights and measures clarifies biblical references; a selection of ancient coins is reproduced alongside.

The Bible, as the pages of this book amply demonstrate, can serve as a valid and revealing history book—quite apart from its timeless, unparalleled value as a work of faith and wisdom. The Bible also has a fascinating history of its own: how it came to be set down originally in Hebrew and Greek; when and how it was first translated into English; what are the poetic qualities of the King James Version and the scholarly merits of the Revised Standard Version. Photographs of the Dead Sea Scrolls and early manuscript and printed Bibles accompany this four-page feature.

Because of its great strategic value and unique religious significance, the Holy Land is one of the most precisely mapped areas in the world today. It has also fascinated cartographers through the ages, as revealed in a portfolio of rare and unusual antique maps.

Unlike Egypt, with its pyramids and other monuments of the Pharaohs, the Holy Land has few great material remains of its illustrious past. What it does have, however, are tells—the mounded-up, layered remains of ancient cities, towns, and fortifications, each built atop the ruins of its immediate predecessor. Probing these tells, archaeologists are painstakingly uncovering the past—and in the process finding confirmation of many Bible stories. A picture feature is devoted to one such archaeological dig, Tell el-Hesi.

The people of biblical times regarded their strange and mysterious land with awe. Within an area the size of New Jersey, there are sharp contrasts: the tumbled hills of its forbidding wilderness areas, below-sea-level lakes, fertile valleys and plains, the life-giving Jordan River, arid desert wastes, snowcapped Mount Hermon. Modern geology has an explanation for the formation of the land; four pages of present-day views of the Holy Land follow this special feature.

Concluding this extended introduction are four pages of maps—at a generous scale of one inch to eight miles—that show

An architect-surveyor plotting an excavation at Tell el-Hesi, page 36

The Great Rift Valley on a global perspective, page 39

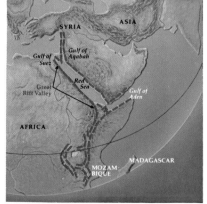

the Holy Land, north to south, in colors keyed to elevation and with more than 300 biblical sites named and located. Like most of the other maps in ATLAS OF THE BIBLE, these large-scale projections were created specifically for this volume by Reader's Digest, based on the definitive, up-to-date relief as compiled by Survey of Israel, the cartographic branch of Israel's Ministry of Labor, and used with their gracious permission.

An overview of the Holy Land as photographed from a NASA satellite serves to introduce "Historical Atlas of Biblical Times," the long, central section of this book. A narrative keyed to accompanying maps puts the beloved and well-known Bible stories within a geographical and historical framework—starting with the journey of the Patriarch Abraham from Mesopotamia to the land of Canaan and ending with the Apostle Paul's missionary journeys and the subsequent spread of Christianity throughout the Roman empire.

The maps based on the Survey of Israel relief are shown in three scales and in two color combinations. Each of these maps started with a painstakingly researched sketch and accompanying textual outline, submitted by ATLAS OF THE BIBLE's principal adviser and editorial consultant, Prof. Harry Thomas Frank. Working with Dr. Frank, staff artists and editors designed the maps and prepared comprehensive layouts. The final maps were executed by Donnelley Cartographic Services. Additional, specially commissioned maps are used to carry the story beyond the Holy Land's restricted borders, as in the Exodus story, the exile to Babylonia, and the conquests of Alexander the Great.

Adding to the illustrative variety of ATLAS OF THE BIBLE's map section are dozens of photographs showing the Holy Land as it appears today, historical artifacts, and reverent works of art throughout the centuries. Box features introduce such neighbors and enemies of the Hebrews as the Phoenicians, Philistines, Assyrians, and Babylonians and present such topics as the discovery of a long-forgotten civilization at Ebla, the life of desert nomads, and fishing in the Sea of Galilee. Working from the reports of recent archaeological expeditions and checking their preliminary sketches with the experts, artists created six dramatic reconstructions of ancient cities and buildings.

A supplementary reference tool—"Gazetteer of the Bible World"—begins on page 209. Prepared by Dr. Frank, the gazetteer lists some 900 place-names, with biblical citations and, where possible, locations cross-referenced to the large-scale maps on pages 44–47. Concluding the volume are a chronology of Bible times, a selected bibliography for further reading, a key to biblical quotations used in the volume, picture credits, and a full index.

"We came to the land to which you sent us," the spies returning from Canaan told Moses; "it flows with milk and honey . . ." It was this report that provided a vision to the wandering Hebrews and gave impetus to their struggle to win and retain the Promised Land. And as the land gave shape to the turbulent history and enduring faith of the Jews, so it was this very land that produced a humble teacher, Jesus of Nazareth, whose message of hope and love would be carried one day to the four corners of the globe. ATLAS OF THE BIBLE provides the setting for yet another retelling of this greatest story.

THE EDITORS

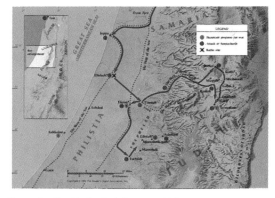
Sennacherib attacks Judah, page 140

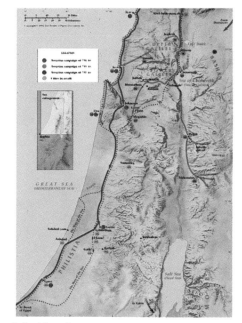
Fall of Israel, page 137

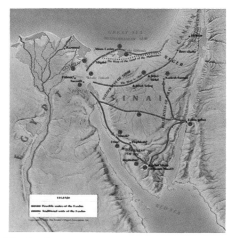
The Exodus, page 67

Contents

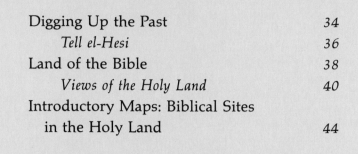

HISTORICAL ATLAS OF BIBLICAL TIMES

"In the beginning . . ."

No more deeply stirring words have ever been written than the starkly simple yet majestic and ringing phrases that open the book of Genesis. "In the beginning God created the heavens and the earth. The earth was without form and void, and darkness was upon the face of the deep; and the Spirit of God was moving over the face of the waters."

The first 11 chapters of Genesis are designated by scholars as primeval history, giving a universal setting for what subsequently is the narrative of a particular group of people, the Old Testament Hebrews. Some of the familiar events—the creation, the fall of man, the flood—are also found in the literature of other ancient peoples. One story, that of Cain and Abel, has been interpreted as a personification of the age-old conflict between the pastoral and agricultural ways of life. And, as we will later see, the story of the Hebrew Patriarchs is the story of seminomadic herdsmen settling down to become tillers of the soil. Archaeology gives us a plausible source for at least one event in the first chapters of Genesis, the building of the tower of Babel. But these dramatic occurrences are clearly beyond historical recapture. As the introduction to the world's most profound and enduring religious document, they must be received on faith. Nonetheless, the first 11 chapters of Genesis have been scrutinized as perhaps no other work, with fascinating if controversial results.

The biblical story of creation has its literary parallel in an early Mesopotamian epic that takes its name, *Enuma elish*, from the first words of the initial line, "When on high the heaven had not been named . . ." This Babylo-

The forbidden fruit of "the tree of the knowledge of good and evil" is the traditional apple in this depiction of Adam and Eve in the garden of Eden by 16th-century German artist Lucas Cranach.

nian creation story contains many details similar to those found in Genesis—a primeval chaos; the creation of light, the firmament, dry land, luminaries, and man; the gods resting after their endeavor. Yet there is a critical difference between the two works: *Enuma elish* has a number of rival deities; Genesis is dominated by one god—thus introducing at the outset the monotheistic concept that is the theme of the entire Bible.

Having found a literary counterpart in Mesopotamia for the creation story of Genesis, scholars have looked there as well for a setting for the garden of Eden. "A river flowed out of Eden to water the garden, and there it divided and became four rivers." The names of two of these rivers, the Tigris and Euphrates, persist to this day and pose no problem. However, attempts to identify the Pishon and Gihon—looking as far east as the Indus and southwest to Africa's Nile—have failed.

The Pishon is described as the river "which flows around the whole land of Havilah, where there is gold; and the gold of that land is good; bdellium and onyx stone are there." This is the only mention of the Pishon in the Bible. However, one subsequent reference to Havilah (Gen. 10:29) places it in southwestern Arabia, while another (Gen. 25:18) places it on the border of the land inhabited by Ishmael's descendants—that is, northeastern Arabia. The reference to gold and precious stones is no clue to solving this puzzle. The Gihon is described as the river "which flows around the whole land of Cush." This is the only reference in the Old Testament to the Gihon as a river, though it appears elsewhere as a spring east of Jerusalem. But the name Cush is generally used for Ethiopia.

Hebrew scholars note that Pishon and Gihon could be translated as "gusher" and "bubbler," and one authority on the book of Genesis suggests that they might be the long-forgotten names of minor tributaries to the Tigris and Euphrates. He further suggests that these four streams once converged near the head of the Persian Gulf to create a lush plain that in later memory remained the symbol of an earthly paradise.

Some students of the Bible see a further parallel between Genesis and other early Mesopotamian works, such as the Babylonian Gilgamesh epic. In one episode the hero's friend, Enkidu, is seduced by a woman who then praises him for having gained the wisdom of a god; after his fall, Enkidu—like Adam after he succumbed to temptation—needs to clothe his nakedness.

Even more striking is the comparison between the story of Noah and the great flood recounted in Gilgamesh.

At the end of 40 days Noah sent forth first a raven and then a dove to see if the waters of the great flood had subsided from the earth. When the dove returned with an olive leaf, he knew that his ordeal had ended. Venetian craftsmen of the 13th century rendered the story in mosaic.

Flemish artist Pieter Bruegel the Elder transferred the tower of Babel story to his own 16th-century northern Europe and used as a model for the massive construction the Colosseum he had observed on a trip to Rome. Bruegel's tower is a honeycomb of stepped-back tiers that pushes through the clouds and almost off the canvas at top. As an army of antlike workers swarm about the site, a king or nobleman (left foreground) makes an inspection tour of the project. The artist has also applied his fertile imagination to the rendering of construction equipment.

In the Babylonian epic, the gods decide to send a deluge to still the intolerable clamor of men which is disturbing their sleep. But first one of them chooses a man named Utnapishtim to survive the catastrophe and gives him instructions to build a boat in which to ride out the flood. He takes aboard his family and the beasts of the field and wild creatures. "With the first glow of dawn," the Gilgamesh chronicler writes, "a black cloud rose up from the horizon." Soon all is submerged in a storm so fierce that even the gods are frightened. On the seventh day, as the tempest subsides, Utnapishtim lands on a mountaintop and sends out, in succession, a dove, a swallow, and a raven to find dry land. And when he emerges from his vessel, the Babylonian hero—like Noah—offers a sacrifice for his deliverance. The mountain on which Utnapishtim landed has been placed in northern Iraq, only 300 miles southeast of Turkey's Mount Ararat.

Geological surveys of Mesopotamia indicate that, sometime in the distant past, waters of the Persian Gulf submerged sizable coastal areas. If this sudden rise of the sea level was caused by underwater volcanic activity, it could also have been accompanied by torrential rains—a combination of natural disasters that would have been commemorated in the history and legend of various peoples of the Near East, including the Hebrews.

The descendants of Noah, Genesis continues, spread over the earth. "And as men migrated from the east, they found a plain in the land of Shinar," where they made bricks to build a city. Shinar has been identified with Sumer. In this rich agricultural land between the Tigris and Euphrates rivers rose what is generally acknowledged as the world's first civilization—a network of cities built of mudbrick and dominated by step-pyramids called ziggurats that honored their gods. The identification of the tower of Babel with one such ziggurat seems inescapable. If "Ur of the Chaldeans" from which Terah took his clan is Sumerian Ur, the patriarchal clan could have preserved the memory of that city's ziggurat in the account of its origins.

As we shall see, beginning on page 50, it is with the appearance of Abraham in Genesis 11:26 that the Bible and history actually converge.

People of the Bible

In seeking to re-create the clothing worn by the people who lived in the Fertile Crescent in biblical times, modern scholars have depended heavily on various pictorial records left by the ancient Egyptians and Assyrians. Unfortunately, written descriptions are scarce, and while the Bible provides names for different articles of clothing, the terms used are often vague and confusing or seem to change in meaning from century to century.

In Egypt the fabric commonly used was linen, woven from the flax that grew abundantly in that area. The cooler, wetter climates of Mesopotamia, Syria, and Palestine, however, required warmer clothing, and linen garments were supplemented by others made from sheep's wool. In contrast to the predominantly white clothing worn by the Egyptians, the Hebrews and Mesopotamians favored bright colors and decorated their garments with fringe and tassels.

The specially commissioned illustrations on this and the following pages—presented with the ancient works of art on which they are based—depict some of the people who inhabited the biblical world over a span of two millennia, from the time of the Patriarchs down to the 2nd century A.D.

The detail above is from a famous wall painting, dating from the early-19th century B.C., found on the tomb of an Egyptian nobleman at Beni Hasan. It depicts a Semitic clan arriving in Egypt to trade black eye-paint for grain, and their apparel is probably much the same as that worn by Abraham and his family. The men's sandals are apparently made of leather thongs, while the women's and boy's low boots seem to be fashioned out of soft leather. Most of the group are wearing multicolored tunics—an example of the preference for colorful attire that marked the Hebrews' clothing in the biblical era. Excavations have shown, in fact, that some cities in later times had highly specialized weaving and dyeing industries, producing patterned fabrics by first dyeing the thread and then weaving it into cloth. As suggested in the illustration at right, shades of red, blue, yellow, and brown were among the considerable variety of colors available for use. Most coveted of all was purple, a color extracted from the murex shellfish of the eastern Mediterranean and associated with high social rank in much of the ancient Near East.

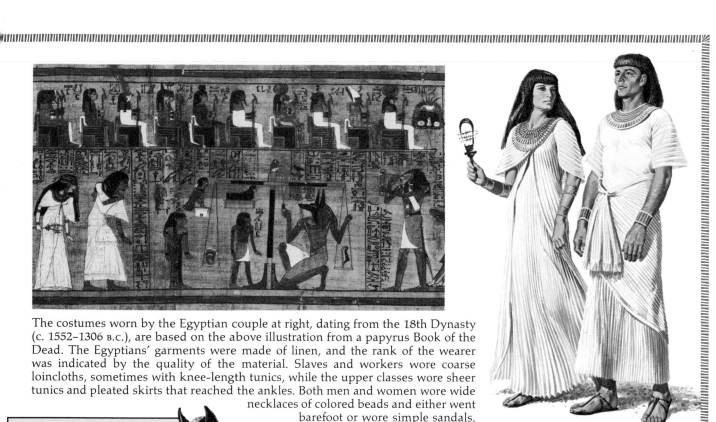

The costumes worn by the Egyptian couple at right, dating from the 18th Dynasty (c. 1552–1306 B.C.), are based on the above illustration from a papyrus Book of the Dead. The Egyptians' garments were made of linen, and the rank of the wearer was indicated by the quality of the material. Slaves and workers wore coarse loincloths, sometimes with knee-length tunics, while the upper classes wore sheer tunics and pleated skirts that reached the ankles. Both men and women wore wide necklaces of colored beads and either went barefoot or wore simple sandals.

The detail above from a 12th-century B.C. Egyptian relief shows a group of Philistines being led into captivity after the victory of Ramses III over the Sea Peoples. A typical Philistine warrior (left) was clean-shaven and wore a tasseled kilt and a crowned helmet secured with a chin strap. The distinctive headgear is thought by many scholars to have been made from feathers; others suggest it could have been fashioned from reeds, leather strips, or horsehair.

Based on a decoration from the side of a 15th-century B.C. Egyptian chariot, the Canaanite charioteer above is probably very similar in appearance to those who fought against Joshua and the Hebrew army during the conquest of Canaan in the 13th century B.C. He is protected by a close-fitting metal helmet, a coat of leather or heavy cloth covered by bronze mail, and a thick leather collar.

People of the Bible
(continued)

As befit their great empires, both the Assyrians and Persians favored heavy, richly ornamented clothing. By comparison, the garments of the Israelite king and Judean soldier are simple and, in fact, are probably not typical. The only known depictions of the Hebrews from this period are Assyrian reliefs showing them as vanquished foes—hardly an occasion for fancy attire.

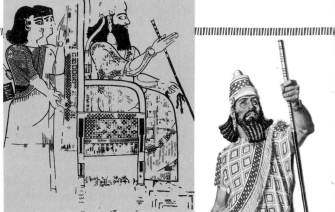

Assyria's powerful King Tiglath-pileser III (c. 745–727 B.C.) and his ministers are shown in a fresco (top) from the palace at Calah, with the modern artist's interpretation above. Assyrian kings and male commoners alike wore earrings and crimped their hair and beards with curlings irons. The royal headgear, in the shape of a truncated cone with a smaller, rounded cone at the top, was festooned with ribbons that hung down the back to waist level.

The mighty Assyrian army consisted of infantrymen, cavalry, and charioteers—the prototype of modern armored forces. The elite of the infantry were the archers, shown at left in a drawing based on a relief (above left) from the palace of Sargon II (c. 721–705 B.C.) at Dur Sharrukin. Each bowman wears a close-fitting metal helmet and a mailed vest, with a sheathed iron sword at the waist. A small, lightweight shield of woven wicker covered with leather is carried by a shield-bearer assigned to protect the archer, who would otherwise be vulnerable to enemy crossfire, especially in short-range combat.

The detail above, from a relief in Sennacherib's palace at Nineveh, depicts the conquest of the Judean city of Lachish in 701 B.C. The Judean soldier at left wears a garment resembling a modern T-shirt, a turbanlike helmet, and a heavy protective waistband. The Israelite king (far left), with his turned-up slippers, pointed cap, and long-fringed tunic, is based on the portrayal of King Jehu of Israel (c. 842–815 B.C.) on the famed Black Obelisk of Shalmaneser III, the only known contemporary depiction of an Israelite ruler.

At the heart of the imperial Persian army was the elite bodyguard known as the Ten Thousand Immortals, whose ranks included Medes and Elamites as well as Persians. Above, a 5th-century B.C. glazed-brick frieze from the royal city of Susa depicts Elamite members of the Immortals. The guardsman illustrated at right, who enjoyed such special privileges as the right to be accompanied in the field by his concubines, wears a rope headband, soft leather boots, and magnificent raiment. The base of his spear bears the insignia of his unit, a golden pomegranate.

People of the Bible

(continued)

With the conquest of the Near East by Alexander the Great in the latter part of the 4th century B.C. and the Roman occupation of the Holy Land nearly three centuries later, the clothing worn by Jews was subjected to successive waves of Greek and Roman influence. Since no contemporary pictorial representations of Jewish dress exist, the information has been culled from literary sources. Specifically, the garb of the High Priest is mentioned in Exodus 28 and in the work of the Jewish historian Josephus.

The apronlike garment worn by the High Priest (above) is the ephod and is covered in part by the breastplate, which hangs by gold chains from two stone epaulets and is inset with 12 gemstones shown at top right. The stones, set in gold and engraved with the names of the children of Israel, are of 12 different colors and symbolize the 12 tribes of the Hebrew nation.

In the time of Jesus, Jews of both sexes wore a linen undergarment and a woolen tunic that covered the body from the lower neck to well below the knees. Over these was draped a cloak that served variously as topcoat, blanket, bedroll, carpet, and even as collateral for loans—provided the borrower was allowed the use of it at night. To keep the voluminous tunic from billowing awkwardly, men and women wore belts of rope, leather, or cloth, sometimes highly decorated. Even the poorest Jews, as with the peasant family above, deemed footgear essential and wore sandals of camel hide or wood.

The Pharisee shown at prayer above wears clothing that actually differs little in its essentials from the workaday garb of the peasant family at left. However, he has added a *tallith*, or tasseled prayer shawl. Made of wool, linen, or silk but preferably of coarse, unbleached lamb's wool, this article is worn by Jews at morning prayer to this day. Attached by leather thongs to his forehead and left hand are the *tefillin*, also known by the Greek term *phylacteries*—small cases made from the skin of ritually clean animals, each containing four passages inscribed on parchment from Exodus and Deuteronomy.

The relief at right, from an altar dedicated to the Peace of Augustus in 9 B.C., depicts a religious procession by family and attendants of the emperor, the men wearing togas and the women draped in stoles. In earlier times the toga had been the basic attire for both sexes at all levels of society, differing chiefly in color and material. By the time of Augustus, however, its use was limited to men of the upper classes, like the aristocrat at left; in later years it grew fuller and more elaborate, with numerous variations in color and pattern to denote the wearer's rank.

The modern depiction of a Roman legionnaire at left is based on reliefs from Trajan's Column in Rome (detail far left), commemorating that emperor's victories in Dacia early in the 2nd century A.D., and on the iron helmet shown in the photograph above, found in Israel in 1970. Roman legionnaires wore distinctive ankle-high flexible sandals and, on the upper torso, cuirasses of segmented metal designed to allow the arms and shoulders freedom of movement. They also wore a heavy leather sword-belt and a short kilt of leather or cloth, sometimes reinforced with metal strips. Their convex rectangular shields, of leather over wood with metal reinforcements, protected virtually the entire body and on march were slung from the left shoulder.

Wild ox

Asiatic domestic ox

Donkey

Wild ass

Mule

Goat

Horse

Sheep

In the grouping above, the wild ox, or aurochs, is believed to be the ancestor of the domesticated ox, a draft, food, and sacrificial animal. Hebrews used the donkey as a riding animal, but its forebear, the wild ass, or onager, was famed for its intractability; Ishmael was termed a "wild ass of a man." Mules had to be imported, due to the biblical prohibition on hybrid breeding. The goat and the sheep (in grouping at right) were widely domesticated and are mentioned frequently in the Bible. The horse became important to the Hebrews from Solomon's time onward.

Animals of the Bible

The Bible is rich in references to the animal life of the ancient Holy Land. Most widely mentioned are the domesticated species so important to the peoples of that region. Commonly observed wild animals also find frequent mention, as well as the dangerous wild animals that menaced man and his flocks. Beyond these references to their role in everyday life, animals appear frequently in the vivid imagery of the Bible; Isaiah, for example, described the kingdom of peace as a time when "The wolf shall dwell with the lamb, and the leopard shall lie down with the kid, and the calf and the lion and the fatling together, and a little child shall lead them."

Our specific knowledge of the animals of biblical times comes from three main sources. Most important are their names in the Hebrew and Greek manuscripts, although precise translations of some Old Testament terms are perhaps lost beyond recovery. Carvings and other contemporary illustrations are a second important source. Modern archaeological investigation also supplies important clues. These drawings represent often-mentioned species.

Arabian camel

Asiatic elephant

The camel—used as a mount and a beast of burden—figured in such metaphors as the camel going through the eye of a needle.

The elephant was a weapon of war in biblical times and also a source of ivory. Following the use of war elephants by Darius III of Persia at Gaugamela, they were employed in the Near East, including the devastating attack on the Jews by the forces of Antiochus V.

Gazelle

Arabian oryx

Fallow deer

Nubian ibex

The gazelle served as a biblical simile for beauty and grace, especially in the Song of Solomon. Another member of the antelope family, the oryx was a game animal; Isaiah mentions an antelope being hunted and caught by net. The roebuck referred to in Deuteronomy 14:5 as one of the clean animals the Hebrews were permitted to eat is perhaps the fallow deer. The meat of the ibex (right), a form of wild mountain goat, was highly regarded; the game Isaac asked Esau to find may have been an ibex.

Animals of the Bible

(continued)

The lion ranged widely through the Near East in biblical times, and its majestic appearance and fierce courage served as a rich source of simile and metaphor for the Bible chroniclers. A king's wrath was "like the growling of a lion"; Judas Maccabeus was "like a lion in his deeds." The lion appears frequently in the ancient art of the region, and lion hunts were literally the sport of kings. The den of lions into which Daniel was cast—and in which the Lord protected him from harm—was a man-made stone pit built to contain captive lions.

Asiatic lion

Lioness

Cub

Wolf

Jackal

Fox

Leopard

The wolf's reputation as a plunderer of flocks appears consistently in biblical imagery. Jeremiah called the enemies of Judah wolves. "Beware of false prophets," Matthew warns, "who come to you in sheep's clothing but inwardly are ravenous wolves." Translators of the Bible have had difficulty distinguishing between terms for the jackal and the fox, probably because their similar appearance confused the biblical writers. Generally, scholars have assumed that figures of speech implying scavenging, for example, refer to jackals—"I will make Jerusalem . . . a lair of jackals"—while in the references to cunning the fox was used, such as Jesus' incisive characterization of Herod Antipas: "Go and tell that fox . . ."

Another of the big cats, the leopard, roamed the Holy Land in ancient times, and its stealth and nocturnal habits made it even more feared than the lion. In the Bible the leopard serves as a metaphor for menace. The Israelites are warned by the Lord, "like a leopard I will lurk beside the way," and Israel's external enemies, including the Babylonians, Persians, and Romans, are likened to a waiting, stalking leopard.

Syrian bear

The dove was an enduring symbol in Christian art, stemming from Matthew's description of Jesus' baptism: "the heavens were opened and he saw the Spirit of God descending like a dove . . ." The Hebrews domesticated doves, which were the poor man's sacrificial offerings. The scavenging ravens were proscribed as unclean, yet they too were under God's eye: ravens "neither sow nor reap . . . and yet God feeds them."

Rock dove

Turtle-dove

Raven

The brown bear lived in the wooded hills of the Holy Land in biblical times, and while it generally avoided man, the she-bear's fierce defense of her cubs was noted by biblical writers. "I will fall upon them like a bear robbed of her cubs" symbolized the Lord's anger. The proverb about a fool and his folly is given considerable weight with the advice that it is better even to encounter "a she-bear robbed of her cubs" than a fool. The modern frying-pan-into-the-fire image is reflected in the passage in Amos, "as if a man fled from a lion, and a bear met him."

Palestine viper

John the Baptist's condemnation of the Pharisees and Sadducees—"You brood of vipers! Who warned you to flee from the wrath to come?"—was probably an allusion to the deadly Palestine viper common to the entire region. To biblical writers vipers, or serpents, were symbols of danger, treachery, and fear, and from the serpent's condemnation in Genesis as cursed "above all cattle, and above all wild animals" their role in biblical imagery was fixed.

In Chapter 41 of the book of Job, God speaks from the whirlwind to berate Job for his questioning and to demonstrate his human frailty by asking, "Can you draw out Leviathan with a fishhook . . . ?" Many scholars interpret the passages describing the mighty leviathan that follow as in fact a description of the Nile crocodile. In addition to the crocodile's known habitat in Egypt, there is literary evidence that it was also found on the coastal plain of the Holy Land in biblical times; a town called Crocodilopolis apparently once existed to the south of Mount Carmel. Although the author of Job speaks of the great creature breathing fire and smoke, other elements of his description indicate a closer familiarity with the crocodile. The Lord asks: "Can you fill his skin with harpoons, or his head with fishing spears? . . . Who can penetrate his double coat of mail? . . . His back is made of rows of shields . . . He makes the deep boil like a pot."

Nile crocodile

Plants of the Bible

Flax

Cotton

Like other ancient peoples who learned to cultivate crops, the once-pastoral Hebrews gradually settled into communities and took up a life of farming. Little wonder, then, that about 100 different plants are referred to by name in the Bible, some of them so often that they have taken on an almost proverbial familiarity. Date palms, olive trees, grape vines, all were vital not only as sources of food, drink, fuel, and other commodities but also as basic and enduring symbols—the palm, a tree associated with Jericho and with Israel's kings, was also a ceremonial emblem of triumph; the olive branch, a token of peace; and the vine, a symbol of Israel itself. Another traditional symbol, the famed cedars of Lebanon—mentioned no fewer than 70 times in biblical passages—were prized both for their natural beauty and for their exceptional durability as building materials. Well known also are two of the plant products used in religious ceremonies, the aromatic resins frankincense and myrrh.

A great many of the plants mentioned in the Bible, though, are of a sort as commonplace today as they were then—staples like wheat, barley, and flax, along with such fruits and vegetables as figs, apricots (the apples of the Bible), beans, cucumbers, and onions. References to flowers also abound, and while not always specific or easy to translate they would certainly include such native wildflowers as tulips, hyacinths, irises, anemones, and narcissus. The plants of the ancient Near East, as shown on these pages, were much as they are today— vigorous and profuse, encompassing some 2,300 species in the Holy Land alone, and displaying as much variety and contrast as the land itself.

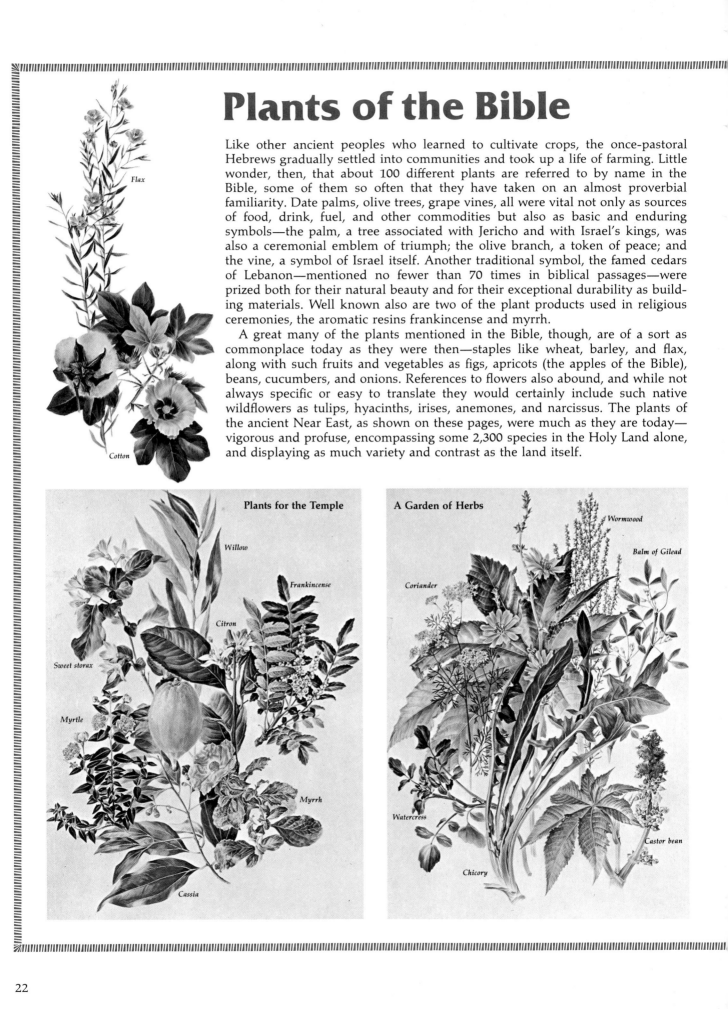

Plants for the Temple

Willow

Frankincense

Citron

Sweet storax

Myrtle

Myrrh

Cassia

A Garden of Herbs

Wormwood

Balm of Gilead

Coriander

Watercress

Castor bean

Chicory

Broad bean
Barley
Onion
Pomegranate
Olive
Wine grape
Walnut
Lentil
Cucumber
Fig
Date
Apricot

Food for Life
Fruits of the Land

Flowers of the Field
Iris
Star-of-Bethlehem
Narcissus
Hyacinth
Anemone
Dandelion
Tulip
Saffron crocus

Trees of the Lord
Acacia
Tamarisk
Holm oak
Laurel
Almond
Cedar of Lebanon
Cypress

Weights and Measures

In antiquity weights and measures were fixed in terms of common everyday things. For example, weights might be determined in grains of cereal and measures as the distance from the elbow to the tip of the finger or the width of the palm of the hand. In time stones and pieces of metal came to be used to calculate the equivalencies between different items. Probably the earliest instrument for weighing objects was the primitive balance scale with two pans suspended from the ends of a beam.

The weights and measures of biblical times were mostly based on those of Mesopotamia and Egypt. There was no single standard, and sometimes two standards prevailed. Thus a cubit has been estimated at 17.4 inches (the short, or common, cubit) and at 20.4 inches (distinguished as Ezekiel's cubit). In New Testament times a talent could mean a specific weight or any large weight or large sum of money.

OLD TESTAMENT WEIGHTS	U.S. system	Metric system
talent (60 minas)	75.558 lb	34.227 kg
mina (50 shekels)	20.148 oz	571.175 grams
shekel (2 bekas)	176.29 grains	11.423 grams
beka, ½ shekel (10 gerahs)	88.14 grains	5.711 grams
gerah	8.81 grains	0.570 grams
NEW TESTAMENT WEIGHTS		
talent (Hebrew talent)	75.558 lb	34.227 kg
pound (Hebrew mina)	20.148 oz	571.175 grams
pound (Latin libra)	0.719 lb	325.707 grams
OLD TESTAMENT MEASURES OF CAPACITY		
Dry measures		
homer, measure, cor (2 lethechs)	6.524 bu	229.892 L
lethech (5 ephahs)	3.262 bu	114.946 L
ephah, measure (3 seahs)	20.878 qt	22.986 L
measure (3⅓ omers)	6.959 qt	7.661 L
omer, 1/10 ephah (1⅘ kabs)	2.087 qt	2.297 L
kab	1.159 qt	1.276 L
Liquid measures		
measure, cor (10 baths)	60.738 gal	229.893 L
bath (6 hins)	6.073 gal	22.986 L
hin (3 kabs)	1.012 gal	3.830 L
kab (4 logs)	1.349 gal	1.276 L
log	0.674 pt	0.318 L
NEW TESTAMENT MEASURES OF CAPACITY		
measure (Hebrew bath)	6.073 gal	22.986 L
measure (Hebrew cor)	6.524 bu	229.892 L
measure (Hebrew seah)	6.959 qt	7.661 L
measure	10.3 gal	38.985 L
quart	0.98 dry qt	1.078 L
bushel (Latin modius)	7.68 dry qt	8.455 L
pot (Latin sextarius)	0.96 dry pt	0.528 L
	or 1.12 fluid pt	0.529 L
OLD TESTAMENT MEASURES OF LENGTH		
cubit (2 spans)	17.49 in	44.424 cm
span (3 handbreadths)	8.745 in	22.212 cm
handbreadth (4 fingers)	2.915 in	7.404 cm
finger	0.728 in	1.849 cm
NEW TESTAMENT MEASURES OF LENGTH		
cubit	c. 18 in	45 cm
fathom	c. 72 in	182 cm
furlong, stadia, or		
the equivalent in miles	c. 606 ft	184 m
mile	c. 4,879 ft	1,486 m

A

Currency

In earliest societies trade was conducted by simple barter: surplus movable property such as cattle and farm produce was exchanged for other desirable or necessary goods. Gradually metals—gold, silver, copper—were molded into uniform shapes and came to represent a standard value and weight. When the weight and purity of a piece of metal were guaranteed by an official stamp issued by a ruler or government, the coin was born.

The first coins are thought to have been minted in Lydia in Asia Minor at the end of the 7th century B.C. Trade brought coin currency to Greece and, soon thereafter, to other lands of the eastern Mediterranean. The biblical references to specific coins prior to the 6th century are, therefore, anachronistic. Coined money did not become common in the Near East until the 5th century B.C. Before that the Hebrew word *shekel* referred to a unit of weight that at one time was equal to 320 grains of barley. With the introduction of metals, the weight of a shekel was fixed at about 11.4 grams of silver. As minted silver became common currency, a basic silver coin was called a shekel.

Shown on these pages is a sampling of coins that were used in the Holy Land from the 5th century B.C. to the 2nd century A.D.

H

These tables are adapted from the New Oxford Annotated Bible.

A) Silver ingots and fragments of jewelry of the 7th century B.C. Before the minting of coins, pieces of metal fashioned into ingots, bars, and jewelry such as bracelets and earrings served as currency.

B) Silver tetradrachma minted in Gaza in the 5th century B.C. A replica of an Athenian coin, the obverse shows the head of the goddess Athena; the reverse, an owl. Although western Asia was under Persian control at this time, only Greek and imitation Greek coins were used.

C) Silver drachma minted in Judea in the 4th century B.C. Obverse, a bearded man; reverse, a god in a chariot holding a falcon, which may represent a Persian interpretation of the Jewish deity.

D) Gold octadrachma struck in Joppa in the 3rd century B.C. Arsinoe, wife of the Egyptian ruler Ptolemy II, appears on the obverse; the reverse depicts a double cornucopia. The Greek version of the Old Testament, the Septuagint, is believed to have been translated in Alexandria beginning in the reign of Ptolemy II (284–246 B.C.).

E) Silver shekel minted in Tyre. Obverse, the head of the Phoenician god Melqart; reverse, an eagle. The silver shekel was the most common coin in the Near East from 126 B.C. to A.D. 65. It is believed that the "thirty pieces of silver" Judas received for the betrayal of Jesus may have been Tyrian shekels. According to Jewish law, payments to the Temple had to be made in pure silver, and the Phoenician shekel qualified despite its pagan symbols.

F) Bronze prutah struck in Judea during the reign of Alexander Janneus (103–76 B.C.). Obverse, a lily with "Jonathan the king" written in old Hebrew script; reverse, an anchor with inscription "Alexander the king" in Greek.

G) Bronze sesterce minted in Rome in A.D. 71 to celebrate the Roman capture of Jerusalem the previous year. One of the many in the *Judaea Capta* series of coins issued in gold, silver, and bronze, it depicts Emperor Vespasian on the obverse and two figures on the reverse: a victorious Roman and—symbol of defeated Judea—a grieving woman under a palm tree.

H) During the Bar Kokhba Revolt (A.D. 132–35) a number of Roman coins were overstruck with Jewish symbols. On the obverse of this Judean silver tetradrachma the Temple and the word "Jerusalem" inscribed in ancient Hebrew script replaced a hated Roman design.

The History of the Bible

The scholarship that has been applied to the Bible is beyond calculation. The intense intellectual labors that have been required to trace its history, decide upon the contents, and assure faithful translations began centuries ago; no doubt they will continue as long as this cherished body of writings remains the cornerstone of Judaic and Christian thought.

The Hebrew Bible or Old Testament, the chronicle of the Lord's relationship with the people of Israel, originated as a body of oral and written traditions whose beginnings date from perhaps as early as the 12th century B.C. and whose formulation continued for a thousand years. None of the original, or autograph, documents is known to have survived. This growing collection of writings that in time would be canonized—accepted as divinely inspired—was passed on from generation to generation and century to century by scribes, or copyists; indeed, it was these faithful and dedicated scribes, working laboriously by hand, who remained the sole "transmitters" of both the Old and New Testaments until the advent of the first printed Bibles in the 15th century A.D. The earliest known manuscript copies of the Old Testament—the book of Isaiah and fragments of others—date from the first three centuries B.C. and were among the celebrated Dead Sea Scrolls, discovered in 1947 and thereafter in desert caves bordering the Dead Sea.

With the exception of a few passages in Aramaic, the Old Testament was written entirely in Hebrew. As Aramaic became a common language among Jews following the Exile (6th century B.C.), however, translations for the use of the faithful were made into that tongue. Greek was the next language to predominate in much of the ancient Mediterranean world, as a consequence of the spectacular conquests of Alexander the Great. The most famous early Greek translation of the Pentateuch, or the first five books (in Hebrew the Torah, or Law), was the Septuagint, named for the 70 elders of Israel mentioned in Exodus 24:1,9 as companions of Moses. There is a legendary belief that this translation was accomplished under the direction of 70 (or 72) Jewish scholars living in Alexandria's Jewish community. These scholars had completed the translation of the Pentateuch into Greek by about 250 B.C., and over the course of the next two centuries the remainder of the Old Testament was also rendered in Greek. At the same time, the process of canonization of the Scriptures continued. By the 2nd century A.D., or perhaps even earlier, the contents of the Old Testament had been fixed, although it remained for later Jewish scholars to establish standardized spelling, punctuation, and arrangement into paragraphs of the Hebrew text.

The Old Testament's long evolution, the relative scarcity of early documented manuscript copies, the variety (and vagaries) of its translations, and the inevitable errors and modifications made by scribes over the course of centuries are among the challenges that biblical scholarship has had to contend with. New Testament scholarship presents problems of a somewhat different sort, although they are no less intricate.

The 27 books comprising the New Testament, the portion of the Christian Bible in which the life and teachings of Jesus form the unifying thread, were originally written in Greek. The date, place of origin, and authorship are not certain for many of the books, and no autograph manuscript is known to exist. Nonetheless, the earliest (2nd century A.D.) of the large number of New Testament manuscript copies that have survived are much closer in time to the original writings than is the case with the Old Testament. The Greek Septuagint translation of the Old Testament was accepted by most early Christians. To this was added, by a process of canonization lasting until the 4th century, the books of the New Testament, thus completing the Christian Bible. (See note on books of the Bible, page 211.)

The spread of Christianity inspired additional Greek translations of the Bible and several into Latin that were alike only in their general lack of scholarship and uniformity. Augustine complained of the "infinite variety of Latin translations." To remedy the problem, in about the year 382 Pope Damasus I commissioned the leading biblical scholar, Jerome, to prepare a standard Bible in Latin. For some two decades Jerome worked at the task, utilizing Old Testament Hebrew manuscripts, previous Latin versions, the Septuagint, and New Testament manuscripts in Greek. His work, completed about 405, became known as the Vulgate ("the common version") and gained gradual acceptance as the standard Bible of the Roman Church, a status confirmed by the Council of Trent in 1546. As such, its impact on Western Christendom has been immense.

Christianity reached Britain more than a thousand years before the first translation of the complete Bible into English. Throughout the Middle Ages certain portions of the Scriptures, such as the Gospels and the Psalms, were translated into the vernacular, primarily for the benefit of the clergy in their missionary efforts, but it was not until 1382 that a complete English Bible appeared. John Wyclif was the inspiration for this radical departure.

Wyclif was himself a radical. An instructor in religion and philosophy at Oxford and rector of Lutterworth, he lashed out at the corruption and materialism afflicting the Church and at its interference in secular affairs. To Wyclif, God's word as embodied in the Scriptures, not as interpreted by the Church, should rule man's spiritual life, and to spread his doctrine he supervised the translation of the Latin Vulgate Bible into English in order to bring the Scriptures within the reach of the common man. For these beliefs Wyclif has been called the "morning star of the Reformation." The Church reacted strongly to Wyclif's teachings, condemning him as a heretic and forbidding the use of his Bible. Nevertheless, it enjoyed widespread underground use for some 150 years. At least 170 manuscript copies have survived.

In the history of the English Bible the towering figure is William Tyndale (c. 1494–1536). Tyndale's work coin-

The most spectacular modern-day biblical find was made in 1947 at Qumran on the western shore of the Dead Sea by a young Bedouin shepherd who stumbled on a cave containing what came to be known as the Dead Sea Scrolls. This and other finds in nearby caves proved to be the hidden library of a Jewish sect, thought by many to be the Essenes, and included Old Testament manuscripts a thousand years older than any previously known. The so-called Cave IV, visible at left, held a vast number of fragments. Above is a portion of the book of Isaiah scroll, written in Hebrew. At right are two of the pottery jars in which some of the leather scrolls were stored.

cided with, and was affected by, the revolutionary currents sweeping the Western world—the explosive spread of printing, the advent of humanism, the intellectual challenge of the Reformation. The time was ripe for a new English translation of the Bible, and Tyndale responded brilliantly.

Educated at Oxford and Cambridge, Tyndale was influenced by the humanist scholar Erasmus, who published the Greek New Testament along with a Latin translation and commentary in 1516. A linguist of immense skill—he was adept at no fewer than seven languages—Tyndale first applied his scholarship to the New Testament, which he began translating secretly in London. Fearing the wrath of the Church, he went to Germany in 1524, where he was influenced by Martin Luther, whose great translation of the New Testament into German had been published two years earlier. By 1525 Tyndale was in Cologne supervising the first printing of his New Testament, which he based on medieval Greek manuscripts. Threatened with arrest by the authorities, he fled with the printed sheets to Worms, where the work was completed. Thousands of copies were smuggled into England. Tyndale was promptly condemned as "the murderer of truth" and charged with the "advancement and setting forth of Luther's abominable heresies." Church authorities bought as many copies as they could find and publicly burned them. Tyndale had meanwhile turned to translating the Old Testament, which he based on both manuscript and printed versions of the Hebrew text. He began its publication with the Pentateuch in 1530 but did not live to see his work completed. He was betrayed in Antwerp, judged a heretic, and in 1536 was strangled and his body burned at the stake.

Tyndale's scholarly fame rests not only on the fact that his work was the first in English to be based on Hebrew and Greek sources but on the magnificence of his translation as well. The richness of his language and style would serve as the model for subsequent English translations.

Henry VIII's break with the Roman Church signaled a veritable flood of English Bibles. Within little more than three decades after Tyndale's death, half a dozen new versions went to the press. Miles Coverdale's 1535 Bible had the distinction of being the first complete printed English version. He drew from Latin, the German translations of Luther and Zwingli, and the unfinished work of Tyndale. Two years later, in 1537, a friend of Tyndale's named John Rogers (who published under the pseudonym "Thomas Matthew") completed the publication of Tyndale's work, supplemented by Coverdale's translation of those books of the Old Testament that Tyndale had not finished before his death. In 1539 Richard Taverner, an English layman, offered his own translation, which followed Tyndale-Rogers closely in the Old Testament but reflected his considerable skill in Greek in his rendering of the New Testament. That same year there appeared the so-called Great Bible, a massive work physically, with pages 15 by 9 inches. It was essentially the Tyndale-Rogers translation as edited by Miles Coverdale and bore the authorization of the king, who ordered that copies should be placed in

Early Bibles

No book has appeared in as many languages and editions as has the Bible. According to the American Bible Society, the entire Bible has been translated into 273 languages, while at least parts have been published in 1,412 additional languages. The society's library in New York, devoted exclusively to manuscript and printed Bibles and related works, has 38,600 volumes on its shelves, making it the largest such collection in the world. A few examples from this remarkable repository are shown here.

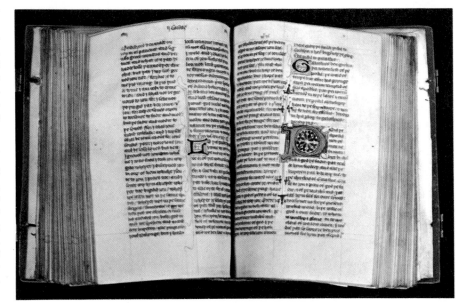

Before the 15th-century invention of printing, the copying and illuminating (adding ornamental designs) of Bibles was a painstaking labor of love—often carried out by monks in Europe's cloistered monasteries. The late-13th-century manuscript of the Vulgate at top was made for an English earl; the Wyclif manuscript Bible at right dates to 1440.

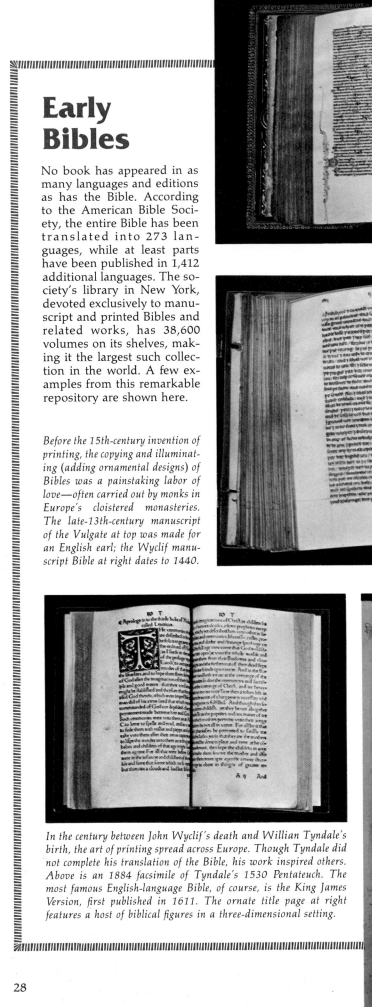

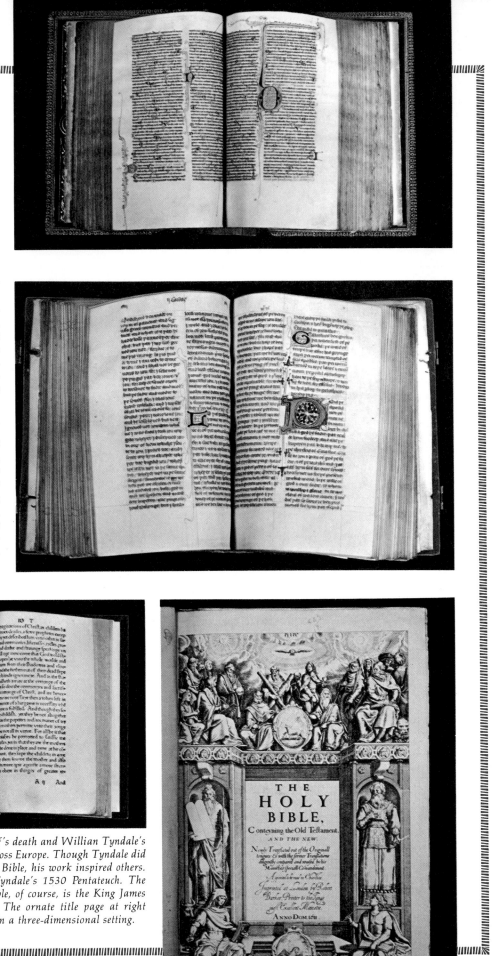

In the century between John Wyclif's death and Willian Tyndale's birth, the art of printing spread across Europe. Though Tyndale did not complete his translation of the Bible, his work inspired others. Above is an 1884 facsimile of Tyndale's 1530 Pentateuch. The most famous English-language Bible, of course, is the King James Version, first published in 1611. The ornate title page at right features a host of biblical figures in a three-dimensional setting.

The History of the Bible (continued)

every church in England. An official revision of the Great Bible, known as the Bishops' Bible, appeared in 1568.

If the Great Bible belonged to the clergy, the Geneva Bible belonged to the common man. It took its name from the site of its publication in 1560, for many English scholars had fled to Geneva when the fiercely Catholic Queen Mary took the English throne. Printed in a handy size and utilizing easy-to-read Roman type instead of the ornate Old English type, the Geneva Bible was a great popular success in England where the Protestant Elizabeth I now ruled. Its publishing life included some 140 editions. It was the Bible of Shakespeare, of John Bunyan, and of the Pilgrims when they sailed to the New World in 1620.

The Roman Church continued to resist putting a translated Bible into the hands of the people, for fear its authority would be undermined. As a Catholic cleric complained in 1540: "The heretics want the Bible to be the authority, but only on condition that it shall be for them to interpret it. We have no controversy with the heretics about the Bible, but about the meaning of the Bible. . . . We say that the meaning is to be discovered in the perpetual agreement of the Catholic Church. They continue to spread the Bible abroad among the illiterate." Bowing at last to necessity, the Roman Church authorized an English translation. Known as the Douay Bible, for the town in France where the work was undertaken, it was based on the Latin Vulgate and published in 1609–10. It remained, like its Vulgate predecessor, a work intended primarily for the clergy.

Even as the Douay Bible was being prepared for the press, a group of scholars was hard at work in England preparing the most famous of all English translations, the King James Version. The name is well deserved, for James I was very much the father of the deed. In 1604 he decreed "that a translation be made of the whole Bible, as consonant as can be to the original Hebrew and Greek, and this to be set out and printed without any marginal notes and only to be used in all churches of England in time of divine service." He followed up his decree by appointing "certain learned men to the number of four and fifty for the translating of the Bible" and stipulating a rigorous review process of their work. James' "learned men" included distinguished Oxford and Cambridge scholars and clerics from both the Anglican and Puritan denominations. For seven years they labored, and in 1611 the King James Version received its first printing. In their preface, the editors modestly stated their goal: "We never thought from the beginning that we should need to make a new translation, nor yet to make of a bad one a good one—but to make a good one better, or out of many good ones, one principal good one, not justly to be excepted against; that has been our endeavour . . ." History has adjudged them too modest; the King James Version has been acclaimed "the noblest monument of English prose."

The creators of the King James Version drew on all previously published English translations (including the Catholic Douay Bible), some Latin versions, and even on Luther's German translation, and they consulted the best Hebrew and Greek texts available to them. But their chief inspiration was William Tyndale. In the New Testament, for example, so greatly did they admire Tyndale's achievement that fully a third of his rendering was adopted without change, and the balance owes its basic language structure to his 1520's translation. What made the King James so notable was the extraordinary character of its language. As the biblical scholar Sir Frederic Kenyon wrote in 1936: "It was the good fortune of the English nation that its Bible was produced at a time when the genius of the language for noble prose was at its height, and when a natural sense of style was not infected by self-conscious scholarship." The rolling cadences were particularly effective when read aloud from the pulpit, helping to make the King James Version a much-loved treasure for millions for two and a half centuries.

By the latter half of the 19th century, however, a growing number of scholars and churchmen began to call for a revision of the King James. In part this was due to the discovery of earlier, superior Hebrew and Greek manuscript copies that made revision desirable on the grounds of accuracy. But even more important was the changing nature of the English language itself. Not only had many of the common usages of the King James become archaic in the years since 1611, but some of the wording had come to mean something entirely different. The King James translators, for example, had used "allege" for "prove" (Acts 17:3); "conversation" for "behavior" or "conduct" (2 Cor. 1:12); "prevent" for "precede" (1 Thes. 4:15); "reprove" for "decide" (Is. 11:4); "communicate" for "share" (Gal. 6:6). Thus, in these and numerous additional instances the meaning of passages no longer reflected what translators of previous centuries had intended. In 1870 the Church of England appointed a committee of 54 (symbolically, the same number of "learned men" as King James had appointed) English scholars and churchmen of various denominations to the task of a major revision. The new Bible was published in 1881–85 as the English Revised Version. In 1901 the American Standard Version appeared, presenting the preferences in interpretation and language of American scholars.

Biblical scholarship is never a static discipline. The 20th century has seen the discovery of many important ancient manuscripts as well as improvements in the techniques of textual criticism. In 1952 there appeared the Revised Standard Version of the Bible, undertaken with the intention of embodying "the best results of modern scholarship as to the meaning of the scripture," yet reflecting full respect for the magnificence of the King James Version. Unless otherwise noted, the Reader's Digest ATLAS OF THE BIBLE takes quotations from *The New Oxford Annotated Bible With the Apocrypha* (Revised Standard Version), edited by Herbert G. May and Bruce M. Metzger and published in 1977. In respectful tribute to the King James editors, May and Metzger say in their preface: "Truly (good Christian Reader) we never thought from the beginning, that we should need to make a new Translation, nor yet to make of a bad one a good one . . . but to make a good one better."

The Holy Land in Maps

When Joshua charged his men, "Go up and down and write a description of the land," he may have been ordering a map to be made. The later account of David's census in 2 Samuel 24:1–9 and 1 Chronicles 21:1–6 suggests to some the use of a map by the census takers. However, no Hebrew maps from so early a period exist nor did the ancient civilizations that contended for the strategic land bridge between Asia and Africa leave any cartographic representations of the Holy Land. The earliest surviving geographic records of the region are the locations of towns plotted by Ptolemy of Alexandria in the 2nd century A.D. and an early-4th-century gazetteer compiled by Eusebius of Caesarea.

During the thousand years that the accomplishments of Ptolemy and Eusebius were largely forgotten in the West, the Holy Land—as the birthplace of both the Jewish and Christian faiths—continued to fascinate cartographers. Palestine was centrally featured in most medieval representations of the known world; indeed, on some, where symbolism was the primary purpose of the cartographer, Jerusalem was portrayed as the literal center of the world (opposite).

Despite the growing number of pilgrimages to the Holy Land after the 4th century, advances in cartography tended to be more artistic than geographically reliable. The preoccupation with illustration is apparent in the map commissioned by the 15th-century German cleric Bernhard von Breydenbach (pages 32–33), in which the urge to depict biblical landmarks predominated over any attempt to portray geography accurately.

It was not until the 18th century that the cartography of Palestine began to assume realistic proportions, due in part to the invention of instruments for measurement and surveying. When Napoleon launched his campaign in the Near East in 1798, for example, his army was accompanied by a corps of scholars who surveyed and mapped Egypt and Palestine. The map they produced (a section of which is shown on page 32) was a landmark in modern Holy Land cartography.

The growing sophistication of biblical scholarship and the parallel increase in archaeological study of the Holy Land in the 19th century pointed up the continuing gaps in cartographic knowledge of the region. One of the first projects commissioned by the London-based Palestine Exploration Fund after its founding in 1865 was a full-fledged survey of Palestine. Led by Lts. C. R. Conder and H. H. Kitchener of the Royal Engineers, fieldwork took six years. Drawn to a scale of one inch to the mile, the finely detailed work was published in 26 sheets in 1878 (detail on page 33). Its careful rendering of place-names has remained authoritative to the present.

The high cartographical standards set by the Conder-Kitchener survey have been maintained in the 20th century. Since the British mandate over Palestine in the between-wars period, British, American, and Israeli surveys (including, since World War II, the use of aerial photography) have produced maps of great accuracy and remarkably minute detail. The Holy Land is thus one of the most precisely mapped areas in the world today.

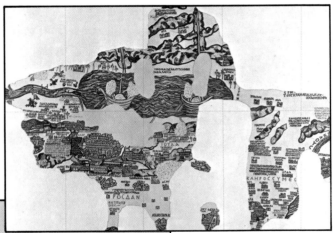

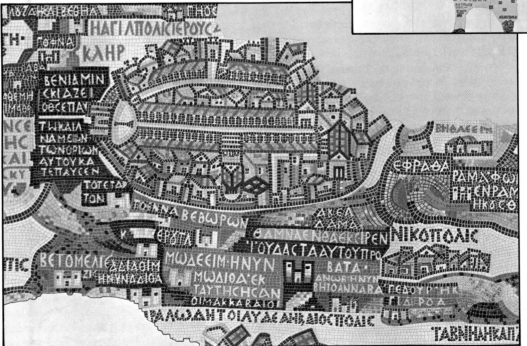

The earliest-known cartographic representation of the Holy Land is the mosaic fragment above, found in 1884 among the ruins of a Byzantine church at Medeba, east of the Dead Sea. Made about A.D. 560 and labeled in Greek, it puts east at the top. Jesus' baptism is placed where the Jordan River empties into the Dead Sea (top left). At left is a detail of Jerusalem. Inside what is today the Damascus Gate (far left) is the pillar from which all distances in the Holy Land were measured. The main thoroughfare bisecting the city is flanked by colonnades. At lower center is the Church of the Holy Sepulchre.

This wheel-pattern map, from a Latin manuscript dating to about A.D. 1250, pictures Jerusalem as the center of a world presided over by Jesus. Asia is at top, Europe at lower left, and Africa at lower right. The seven-mouthed Nile joins the Mediterranean at lower center, and the Red Sea really is red. The Jordan flows through the Sea of Galilee (with fish) and empties into the Dead Sea just to the left of the Red Sea.

The Holy Land in Maps (continued)

The detailed panorama at right is the central section of a map prepared by a Dutch painter named Erhard Reuwich, who accompanied the German churchman Bernhard von Breydenbach on a pilgrimage to the Holy Land in 1483. The walled city of Jerusalem completely dominates Reuwich's scene, although other biblical sites are also represented pictorially. At the upper right is Bethlehem, with the Dead Sea beyond. At the upper left is the Sea of Galilee. Mount Carmel is in the left foreground, with a stream winding from its heights to the coast. The carefully drawn vessel in the left foreground docks at the Mediterranean port of Jaffa (Joppa). Within Jerusalem the Dome of the Rock (Mosque of Omar) is prominent. Beyond the open square to the right of the mosque, the domes of the Church of the Holy Sepulchre are marked with double crosses. Near the center of the long wall in the foreground is the Golden Gate, through which Jesus entered the city on Palm Sunday.

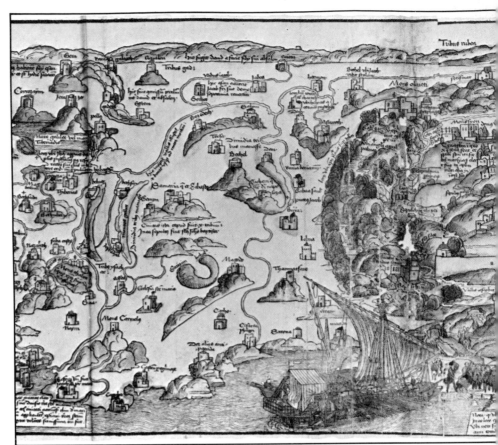

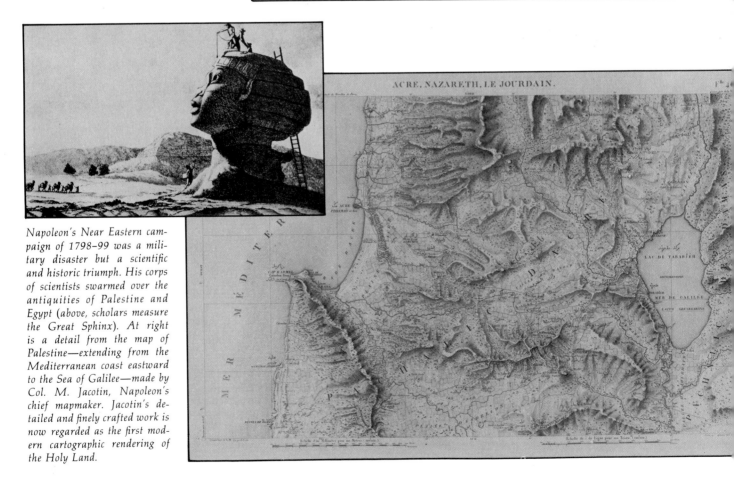

Napoleon's Near Eastern campaign of 1798–99 was a military disaster but a scientific and historic triumph. His corps of scientists swarmed over the antiquities of Palestine and Egypt (above, scholars measure the Great Sphinx). At right is a detail from the map of Palestine—extending from the Mediterranean coast eastward to the Sea of Galilee—made by Col. M. Jacotin, Napoleon's chief mapmaker. Jacotin's detailed and finely crafted work is now regarded as the first modern cartographic rendering of the Holy Land.

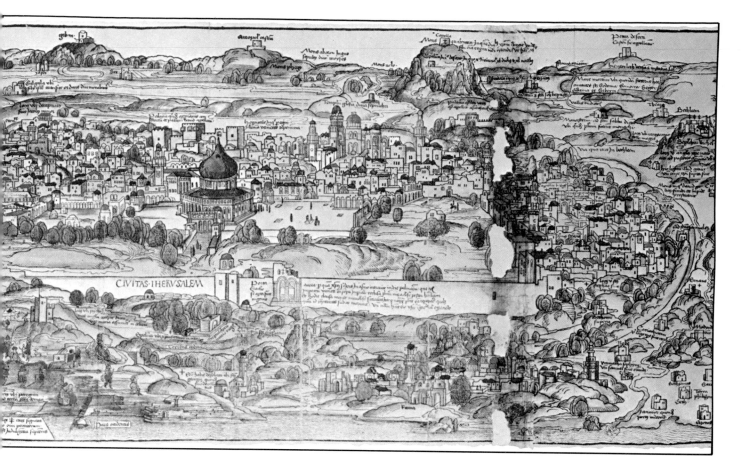

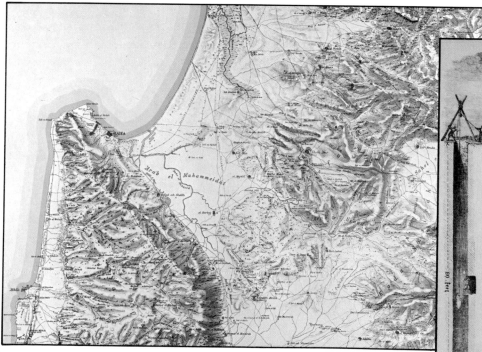

Since Jacotin's survey of Palestine was limited to the areas traveled by Napoleon's army, it remained for the Palestine Exploration Fund to sponsor the first complete survey of the region. Enduring bouts of malaria and attacks by local habitants, British Army cartographers labored at their task from 1871 to 1877. The detail of their work above covers part of the area of Jacotin's map opposite. At right, the cover of the fund's quarterly depicts intrepid explorers descending an 80-foot shaft to the base of Jerusalem's Temple platform.

Digging Up the Past

The ancient history of the Holy Land as derived from the Bible is a tantalizing patchwork, sometimes rich and detailed in texture, sometimes frustratingly vague, sometimes even contradictory. A primary tool in unraveling the mysteries and filling in the gaps is the science of archaeology. First applied to the ancient Near East some 150 years ago "for the illustration and defense of the Bible," as one sponsoring group put it, archaeology has furnished an increasingly sophisticated framework within which to examine the long course of biblical history.

Unlike such monumental, highly visible works of the ancient world as the pyramids of Egypt or the Parthenon of Athens, the material remains of past millennia in the Holy Land are generally buried beneath the ground. One of the unique topographical features of the Near East landscape is the large number of mounds, or tells, long believed to be simply natural hillocks. Only within the course of the last century have archaeologists demonstrated that in fact these tells are man-made, containing a rich record of the past. The first serious, biblically oriented topographical study of the region was undertaken in 1838 by the American scholars Edward Robinson and Eli Smith, who identified scores of historic sites in the Holy Land. Other expeditions, supported by such newly founded organizations as the Palestine Exploration Fund (1865) and the American Palestine Society (1870), soon followed. But the mystery of the tells was not fully solved until 1890, when the Englishman W. M. Flinders Petrie laid the foundations for modern archaeological science.

A veteran Egyptologist, Petrie spent six weeks at Tell el-Hesi (Eglon?), some 16 miles northeast of Gaza. He proved conclusively that the tells were in fact the mounded-up, layered remains of ancient cities and towns and fortifications, one built atop the ruins of its predecessor, each in turn the victim of abandonment and collapse or of destruction such as that described in Joshua 8:28—"So Joshua burned Ai, and made it for ever a heap of ruins, as it is to this day." At the Tell el-Hesi site, Petrie established two key elements of archaeological study that have endured to the present day—the principle of "stratigraphy," or the decipherment of the various layers of ruins; and "ceramic typology," the technique of dating the layers by means of the pottery or potsherds (pottery fragments) discovered by careful excavation in the strata. "There are no coins and no inscriptions to serve to date any of the levels," Petrie said of Tell el-Hesi. "How then can we read history in a place if there is not a single written document? How can we settle here what the date of anything is, if not a single name or date remains? This is the business of archaeology. Everything is a document to the archaeologist. His business is to know all the varieties of the products of past ages, and the date of each of them. When our knowledge is thus developed, everything teems with information. Nothing is so poor or so trivial as not to have a story to tell us. The tools, the potsherds, the very stones and bricks of the wall cry out, if we have the power of understanding them."

Petrie theorized that Tell el-Hesi was the ancient biblical city of Lachish, but later investigators have tentatively identified it as Eglon. The site continues to be studied intensively; the photographs on the following two pages depict the work of the Joint Archaeolological Expedition that began a systematic probe of the tell in 1970 under sponsorship of the American Schools of Oriental Research and a consortium of educational institutions.

Following Petrie's pioneering work, other tells began yielding up their secrets. The American George Reisner, working at Samaria in 1908–10, further refined Petrie's new techniques. The British mandate over Palestine following World War I brought political stability to the region and ushered in a golden age of archaeology. Dozens of expeditions ranged across the area. Some of the sites they investigated were obscure, some rich in biblical historiography. A massive 14-year undertaking plumbed the history of the famous fortress-city of Megiddo, scene of many battles in biblical times, and it was announced that the fabled walls of Jericho had been found (a claim later disputed). Important new undertakings continued in the period after World War II, utilizing ever-more sophisticated methods and expanding archaeology into a truly modern interdisciplinary science.

One of the great modern archaeologists, Kathleen Kenyon, described the dilemma of her profession: "It must be remembered that all excavation is destruction. The evidence concerning an ancient site is contained in the layers of soil comprising its floors, and those which lie above and beneath them. Once these layers have been disturbed, the evidence is disturbed, and has been destroyed altogether unless it has been properly observed, recorded and subsequently made public." Only after the meaning of a layer has been established can the layer be removed and the excavation process continued into the next, older layer. As archaeologists say, "The answer lies below."

After a site has been selected and surveyed, test trenches are dug and the sides carefully smoothed. Layers are thus revealed by means of their varied color and texture. Perhaps stone or brick walls are uncovered as trenching continues in a gridlike pattern. In that event, trenches are cut at right angles to the wall, in order to pinpoint the location of the original floor and of any man-made debris. Full field records are kept of all findings, including description and location. Plans and drawings are made, and photographs are taken. It is a slow and painstaking process—the noted Israeli archaeologist Yigael Yadin has estimated that the proper excavation of the site of Hazor could take hundreds of years—calling for careful planning, direction, and teamwork. In recent years the frequent replacement of unskilled local labor by student volunteers to do the excavating has greatly increased the professionalism of the typical "dig"—and coincidentally produced a new generation of archaeologists with invaluable on-site training. Gone are the days when a battalion of laborers would sink great shafts into historic ground, as Capt. Charles Warren of the Royal Engineers did in 1867 to probe the base of Jerusalem's walls, in the process destroying or hopelessly jumbling remnants of the city's long past.

The second of the archaeological techniques pioneered by Petrie was the analysis of objects found during excavation, most notably pottery. Not only was pottery common everywhere in the ancient world, but to the good fortune of archaeology its pieces are all but indestructible. In work carried out at Tell Beit Mirsim between 1926 and 1932, the eminent American archaeologist W. F. Albright classified pottery development from the third millennium to the early-6th century B.C. The changing styles and methods of pottery-making have proved invaluable for dating the successive waves of peoples who inhabited tell sites. The finding of "foreign" pottery and other objects indicates the extent of commerce and trade, or perhaps the occupation of the site by an invading army. The discovery of tablets or inscriptions not only assists in dating a site but contributes to the decipherment of the languages of the region throughout history; like the textual criticism of biblical manuscripts, such findings shed new light on interpretations of the Bible.

Since World War II there has been a striking expansion of archaeology. Such varied disciplines as anthropology, zoology, botany, architecture, geology, and geography are now being applied to the digs, broadening the analysis of discoveries. The technique of radiocarbon dating (which utilizes the known decay rate of carbon 14 in formerly living organisms) has been borrowed from nuclear physics, and computer programming and data processing promise to ease the burden of record keeping and promote the comparative analysis of different sites.

Archaeology has confirmed and in fact expanded on many areas of biblical history. The Philistines, for example, are only one of the many peoples mentioned in the Bible whose history and culture have begun to take clearer form through excavations at such sites as Ashdod and at Gezer, where levels 11 through 13 of a total of 26 have been identified as Philistine. The essential facts of the Exile of the Jews in the 6th century B.C. have been confirmed; archaeologists have found evidence of the destruction and depopulation of virtually every site in Judah in this period. The wealth and power of Israel in Solomon's time, long thought by some to be exaggerated in the Bible, have not only been confirmed but may actually have exceeded the descriptions in 1 Kings and 2 Chronicles. The size and wealth of such cities as Megiddo and Hazor at this time are evidenced by the elaborate water systems and great double walls and gates that have been uncovered. As a consequence of these and many other discoveries, scholars have gained new respect for the biblical chroniclers. Many gaps in our knowledge remain, and many seeming discrepancies are still unexplained, but thanks to archaeology, further investigations may answer many of the questions and resolve many of the riddles. If the bricks and stones of the Holy Land can indeed cry out, as Flinders Petrie believed, we now have the means of understanding them.

Archaeological Sites

Dan
Hazor
Acco
Capernaum
Sea of Galilee
Tiberias
Megiddo
Taanach
Caesarea
Beth-shan
Pella
Dothan
Samaria
Tirzah
Gerasa
Zarethan?
Shechem
Succoth?
Aphek
Joppa
Shiloh
Rabbah
Mezad Hashavyahu
Bethel
Ai
Jericho O.T.
Mizpah?
Jericho N.T.
Gezer
Gibeon
Gibeah
Ashdod
Beth-shemesh
Jerusalem
Ramat Rahel
Qumran
Heshbon
Ashkelon
Herodium
Medeba
Mareshah
Beth-zur
Eglon?
Lachish
Gaza
Dibon
Debir?
En-gedi
Dead Sea
Masada
Beer-sheba
Arad
Bab edh-Dhra
Aroer
MEDITERRANEAN SEA
Jordan River

Ramat Matred

Copyright © 1981 The Reader's Digest Association, Inc.

Sites listed alphabetically below show modern names in parentheses.
T. = Tell (mound)   Kh. = Khirbet (ruin)

Acco (T. el-Fukhkhar)
Ai (Kh. et-Tell)
Aphek (Ras el-Ain)
Arad (T. el-Milh)
Aroer (Kh. Arair)
Ashdod (Isdud)
Ashkelon (T. Asqalan)
Bab edh-Dhra
Beer-sheba (T. es-Saba)
Bethel (Beitin)
Beth-shan (T. el-Husn)
Beth-shemesh (T. er-Rumeila)
Beth-zur (Kh. et-Tubeiqa)
Caesarea
Capernaum (T. Hum)
Dan (T. el-Qadi)
Debir? (T. Rabud)
Dibon (Dhiban)
Dothan (T. Duthan)
Eglon? (T. el-Hesi)
En-gedi (Ein Jidi)
Gaza (el-Ghazza)
Gerasa (Jerash)
Gezer (T. Jazer)
Gibeah (T. el-Ful)
Gibeon (el-Jib)
Hazor (T. el-Qedah)

Herodium (Kh. el-Fureidis)
Heshbon (Hisban)
Jericho O.T. (T. es-Sultan)
Jericho N.T.
  (T. Abu el-Alayiq)
Jerusalem (el-Quds)
Joppa (Yafa)
Lachish (T. ed-Duweir)
Mareshah (T. Sandahannah)
Masada
Medeba
Megiddo (T. el-Mutesellim)
Mezad Hashavyahu
Mizpah? (T. en-Nasba)
Pella (Kh. Fahil)
Qumran (Kh. Qumran)
Rabbah (Amman)
Ramat Matred
Ramat Rahel
Samaria
Shechem (T. Balata)
Shiloh (Kh. Seilun)
Succoth? (T. Deir Alla)
Taanach (T. Tinnik)
Tiberias
Tirzah (T. el-Farah)
Zarethan? (T. es-Saidiya)

Tell el-Hesi

At the Tell el-Hesi site near Gaza, W. M. Flinders Petrie pioneered modern archaeology nearly a century ago. Today it is the scene of an ongoing "dig" by the Joint Archaeological Expedition utilizing new scientific techniques and enlisting investigators from several disciplines. These photographs depict the painstaking efforts required to uncover the secrets of Tell el-Hesi.

An overall view of the acropolis portion of Tell el-Hesi is reproduced at the top of the opposite page. Excavation fields are on the summit and the south slope of the mound. The acropolis was occupied from c. 2000 B.C. down to the Hellenistic period (4th to 1st century B.C.)—and as recently as the 1948 and 1956 Arab-Israeli conflicts, when it served as a military post. At the right is a close-up of the south-slope field, showing the grid pattern of excavation that uncovered the mud-brick walls of an elaborate fortification dating from the Israelite period. Piers slope into the surrounding ground, perhaps a form of erosion control. Intervening catwalks or "balks" of soil are left in order to analyze the strata uncovered. Above is an on-site field conference to examine newfound evidence. Former expedition director John E. Worrell is at lower center; at the right is his successor, D. Glenn Rose. Two volunteer workers stand by. Each bit of new evidence must be evaluated, recorded, and, if significant, photographed before the excavation continues. At the top of this page, architect-surveyor Bishara Zoughbi maps the architecture revealed by excavation of Tell el-Hesi's acropolis.

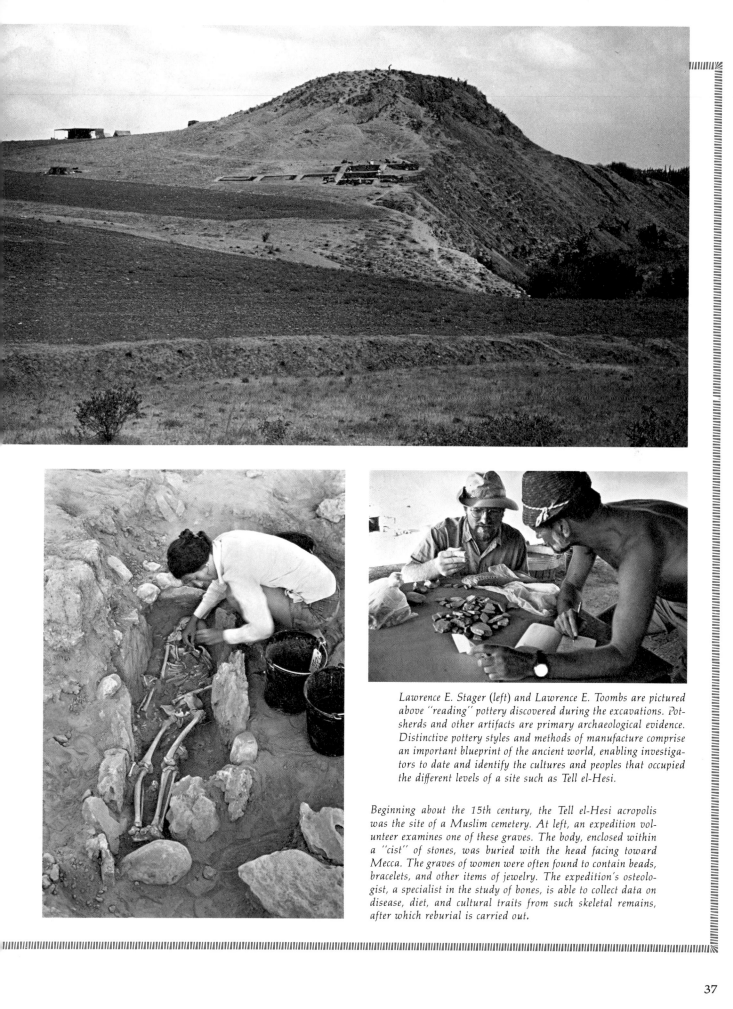

Lawrence E. Stager (left) and Lawrence E. Toombs are pictured above "reading" pottery discovered during the excavations. Potsherds and other artifacts are primary archaeological evidence. Distinctive pottery styles and methods of manufacture comprise an important blueprint of the ancient world, enabling investigators to date and identify the cultures and peoples that occupied the different levels of a site such as Tell el-Hesi.

Beginning about the 15th century, the Tell el-Hesi acropolis was the site of a Muslim cemetery. At left, an expedition volunteer examines one of these graves. The body, enclosed within a "cist" of stones, was buried with the head facing toward Mecca. The graves of women were often found to contain beads, bracelets, and other items of jewelry. The expedition's osteologist, a specialist in the study of bones, is able to collect data on disease, diet, and cultural traits from such skeletal remains, after which reburial is carried out.

Land of the Bible

"Thou didst set the earth on its foundations,
   so that it should never be shaken.
Thou didst cover it with the deep as with a garment;
   the waters stood above the mountains.
At thy rebuke they fled;
   at the sound of thy thunder they took to flight.
The mountains rose, the valleys sank down
   to the place which thou didst appoint for them."

Thus the psalmist, writing more than 2,500 years ago, described the creation of the world. Modern geological theory offers striking confirmation of that explanation. Water did once cover the land, the mountains rose, the valleys sank.

For millions of years, for instance, the Holy Land itself was a sea bottom. Sediment composed of shells of tiny sea animals was compressed to form the brilliant white limestone Solomon would quarry to build the Temple in Jerusalem. During the age of the dinosaurs hard limestone and dolomite mountains were thrust upward from the sea. Finally, some 26 million years ago the recognizable landforms of the Holy Land as we know them began to emerge.

Several factors went into this shaping of the land. Torrential rains filled a great inland sea 200 miles long between the central ridge and the Transjordan highlands to the east. The Mediterranean Sea made inroads as its strong currents carried sand from the Nile's mouth to scour the coastal lowlands and deposit dunes that today reach far inland. Volcanic activity and the erosion of wind and water left varied soils in the valleys and sunken plains. During a phase of gradual climatic change, rainfall lessened until it failed to keep pace with the rate of evaporation, and the inland sea shrank into three separate bodies of water—Lake Huleh, the Sea of Galilee, and the Dead Sea—linked by the Jordan River.

The most dramatic event in the Holy Land's geological calendar, overlapping these changes, began some 20 million years ago. According to the geological theory of plate tectonics, shifting of the subsurface plates on which continents rest creates massive fractures in the earth's crust. A complex of such fissures, called the Great Rift Valley, is the deepest and most spectacular scar on the planet's land surface. It stretches 4,000 miles, from Syria in the north through the Jordan valley and the Red Sea to Mozambique in eastern Africa. In the Holy Land the massive granite block that forms the Transjordanian face of the fracture was tilted upward, creating the sheer cliffs of the eastern plateau. To the west the mountain ranges buckled and heaved into what we know as the Judean and Ephraim plateaus. A web of smaller faults tributary to the Great Rift was formed. The Jordan valley sank, becoming the deepest land trench on the globe; today the Dead Sea is some 1,300 feet below sea level.

The peoples of biblical times looked on this awesome and dramatic landscape with a sense of wonder. As George Adam Smith wrote in his classic *The Historical Geography of the Holy Land:* "the sense of space and distance, the stupendous contrasts of desert and fertility, the hard, straight coast with the sea breaking into foam, the swift sunrise, the thunderstorms sweeping the length of the land, and the earthquakes . . . were symbols of the great prophetic themes." This land spoke to them of God's providence and judgment and majesty, for it was, in the words of the psalmist, "the place which thou didst appoint for them."

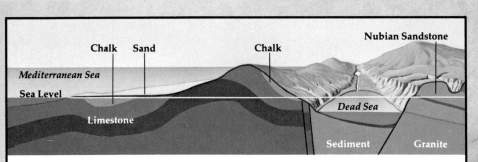

This schematic cross section of the Holy Land reveals typical landforms as well as the composition and distribution of rocks. West of the Dead Sea, plate pressure has pushed up layers of limestone laid down during periodic flooding. Pockets of chalk form the Judean moat on the coastal plain, but where the central hills slope steeply to the east such chalk has been eroded down to the harder limestone bedrock, thus forming deep-cut wadis. East of the Dead Sea the rigid granite plate, overlaid in places with Nubian sandstone, was tilted upward by the Great Rift upheaval to form the eastern plateau. The floor of the Dead Sea is a dropped wedge layered with the sedimentary deposits of eons.

The Great Rift Valley is shown on the global perspective at left. Much of the subterranean activity of this massive crack in the earth's crust, created by the shifting of continental plates beneath Africa and Asia, took place in the distant past though minor movements continue to this day. At its northern end the Great Rift forms the below-sea-level Jordan valley. The Red Sea fills another section of the 4,000-mile-long trench; the gulfs of Suez, Aqabah, and Aden fill lateral branches. This fault activity also split off the island of Madagascar from the African mainland.

Mt. Hermon

Lake Huleh

Yarmuk River

Sea of Galilee

Jezreel Valley

Yabis River

Jabbok River

Saddle of Benjamin

Jordan River

Jerusalem

Wilderness of Judea

Ghor Plain

Judean Hills

Dead Sea

Arnon River

Jordan Valley

Eastern Plateau

Sea Level

Ghor Plain

A topographic map of the Holy Land in biblical times is sectioned east-west and north-south to show its relation to sea level. The region's major geographic features are the sandy coast and chalk plains; the upwarped limestone hills that, east of the watershed, drop steeply through the eroded Wilderness of Judea; the Jordan valley portion of the Great Rift fault; and the eastern plateau tilting toward the desert. From the foot of Mount Hermon in the north the Jordan River flows into the basin of Lake Huleh and drops rapidly (900 feet in 10 miles) into the Sea of Galilee. Doubled in volume by the entry of its major tributary, the Yarmuk, the Jordan twists and turns through the Ghor Plain (floor of the ancient inland sea), formed of marls and marked by arid, tumbling badlands, streambeds, and wadis, which carry water only seasonally. Hinge, or lateral, faults north of the Dead Sea form the Saddle of Benjamin and the Jezreel valley. The Jordan finally enters the Dead Sea, a landlocked salt lake that is the lowest body of water on earth. Prevailing westerly winds from the Mediterranean Sea deposit most rainfall west of the watershed.

39

Views of the Holy Land

Although barely the size of New Jersey, the Holy Land exhibits a remarkable diversity of geographical features and extremes of temperature and rainfall. The photographs on these two pages were taken in the northern part of the region. Those on the following two pages, revealing a very different view of the Holy Land, are scenes in the latitude of the Dead Sea. (The sites of the eight photographs are indicated on the locator map at right.)

In many areas, variations in terrain and climate are abruptly drawn within remarkably short distances. From the mild, flat seacoast, hills rise to 2,600 feet at temperate Jerusalem, just 34 miles away. The land to the east then drops sharply; Jericho is only 15 miles distant but 800 feet below sea level, with a tropical climate that in summer can be enervating. A few miles farther east, the Transjordan plateau is 4,000 feet higher than Jericho and receives snowfall in winter. North-south contrasts are equally vivid; from the parched Jordan valley, where temperatures reach 110 degrees, the snowcapped peaks of Mount Hermon are clearly visible. Adequate rainfall west of the watershed line causes the land to bloom and be fruitful. Rain, sometimes in torrents, also falls in the eastern plateau. The watershed is likewise a dividing line between the cool Mediterranean breezes and the hot, often violent desert winds. Thus it is not surprising, wrote George Adam Smith, that in this land of stark contrasts so many different peoples "sustained their own characters in this little, crowded province through so many centuries."

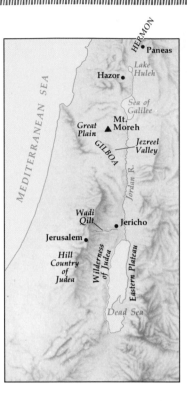

Above, headwaters of the Jordan gush from rocks at the foot of Mount Hermon, a ridge of limestone so porous that snow water from its heights seeps to the base. After coursing through the Huleh basin, the Jordan plunges into the Sea of Galilee (right), at 680 feet below sea level the world's lowest freshwater lake. Some 13 miles long with a maximum width of 8 miles, it is no more than 150 feet deep.

The perspective of this photograph is northeastward across the Huleh basin, toward snowcapped Mount Hermon. The road in the foreground curves around the mound of Hazor. The lush farmland vista shown here is the culmination of eons of change. Millions of years ago the region was covered by a great inland sea. Climatic changes reduced this sea to the more modest dimensions of Lake Huleh, which continued to shrink steadily in size due to evaporation. In New Testament times the basin's alluvial soils were intensely cultivated; Josephus reported that "no part lies idle." But already, silting from erosion of the surrounding foothills was turning it into a freshwater swamp fed by the Jordan and bordered by great stands of papyrus. Centuries later, in the 1950's, the Israelis drained the swamp to reclaim the land, and once again it bloomed as it had in biblical times. The small blue area in the center, just above the belt of trees, is all that remains of ancient Lake Huleh.

Southwest of the Sea of Galilee the mounded Hill of Moreh—seen here from the heights of Mount Gilboa—is an outcropping amid a flow of volcanic basalt. The foothills sheltering Nazareth are on the horizon at upper left. The Jezreel valley (center) is a transverse fault that slopes from the Great Plain into the Jordan valley rift to the west. The "Vale of Jezreel," a collapsed basin filled in with rich red and black loam, was a historic invasion route. It was here that Gideon campaigned against the oppressing Midianites and here that Jehu marched against the Omrides.

This spectacular aerial view shows the watered slopes of the hill country of Judea southwest of Jerusalem and west of the watershed line. Once heavily timbered, the land was ravaged by erosion, but as early as biblical times farmers began terracing the hillsides to counter the destructive effects of the rains. The green cultivated areas are wadi floors, across which walls have been built to counter erosion.

Views of the Holy Land *(continued)*

From the barrens of Qumran can be seen the Moab cliffs on the eastern shore of the Dead Sea. At the left is a green oasis, watered by the alluvial delta of a wadi. Evidence of 30 lake levels has been found in shore terraces. Fed by the Jordan but with no outlet, the level of the saline Dead Sea is maintained by evaporation, so intense at times that it forms a thick blue haze over the surface of the lake.

Above is the lunar landscape of the Wilderness of Judea, a place of desperate refuge for David and the rebel Maccabeans. It "glowed and beat with heat like furnaces," one awed observer wrote, producing a "sense of living next door to doom."

The deep-cut Wadi Qilt angles out of the Judean hills near Jericho and into the Dead Sea (background). Herod channeled its seasonal water flow to his palaces in Jericho, and both Jesus and the Roman Tenth Legion followed its course to Jerusalem.

Biblical Sites
in the Holy Land

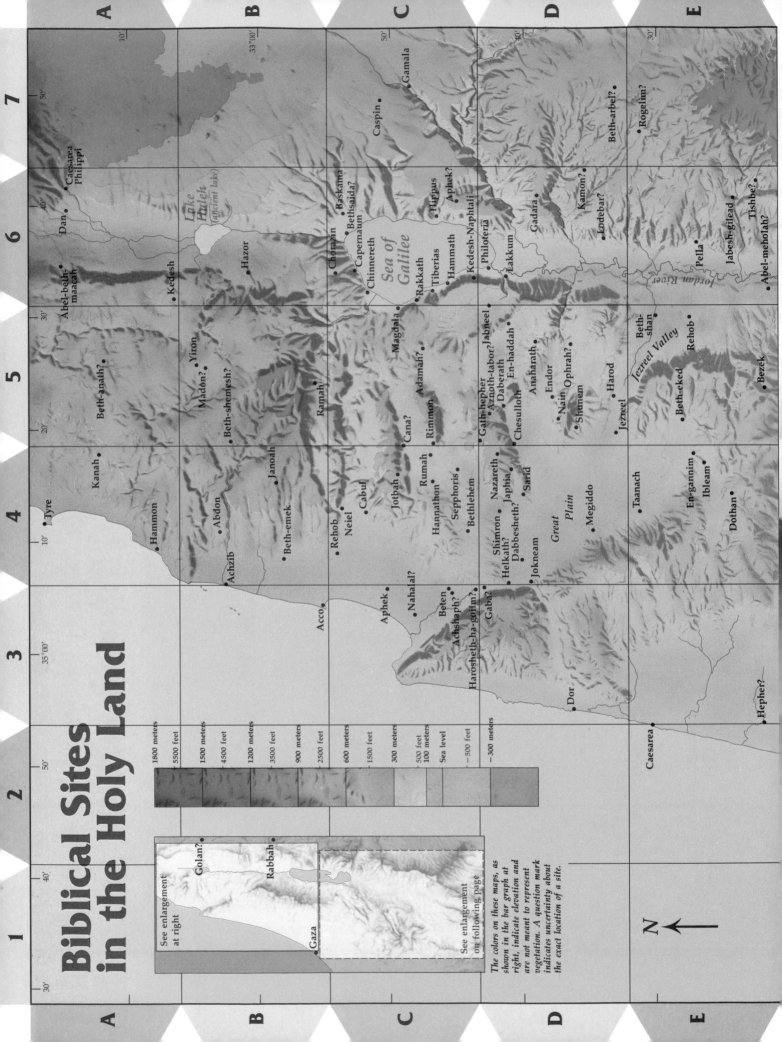

See enlargement at right

See enlargement on following page

The colors on these maps, as shown in the bar graph at right, indicate elevation and are not meant to represent vegetation. A question mark indicates uncertainty about the exact location of a site.

1800 meters	5500 feet
1500 meters	4500 feet
1200 meters	3500 feet
900 meters	2500 feet
600 meters	1500 feet
300 meters	500 feet
100 meters	Sea level
	–500 feet
–300 meters	

N

Golan?
Rabbah
Gaza

Tyre
Kanah
Hammon
Abdon
Achzib
Beth-anath?
Madon?
Yiron
Beth-shemesh?
Janoah
Beth-emek
Kanah
Ramah
Rehob
Neiel
Cabul
Jotbah
Cana?
Rimmon
Rumah
Hannathon
Sepphoris
Bethlehem
Nazareth
Japhia
Sarid
Shimron
Dabbesheth?
Helkath?
Jokneam
Gaba?
Gath-hepher
Aznoth-tabor?
Jabneel?
Daberath
Chesulloth
En-haddah
Anaharath
Endor
Nain
Ophrah?
Shunem
Harod
Jezreel
Megiddo
Great Plain
Taanach
En-gannim
Ibleam
Dothan

Acco
Aphek
Nahalal?
Beten
Achshaph?
Harosheth-ha-goiim?
Dor
Caesarea
Hepher?

Caesarea Philippi
Dan
Abel-beth-maacah
Kedesh
Hazor
Lake Huleh (ancient lake)
Baskama
Bethsaida?
Bethsaida
Chorazin
Capernaum
Chinnereth
Rakkath
Tiberias
Hammath
Magdala
Adamah?
Gamala
Caspin
Hippus
Aphek?
Kedesh-Naphtali
Philoteria
Lakkum
Sea of Galilee
Gadara
Kamon?
Lodebar?
Beth-arbel?
Rogelim?
Pella
Jabesh-gilead
Tishbe?
Abel-meholah?
Jordan River
Beth-shan
Rehob
Beth-eked
Bezek
Jezreel Valley

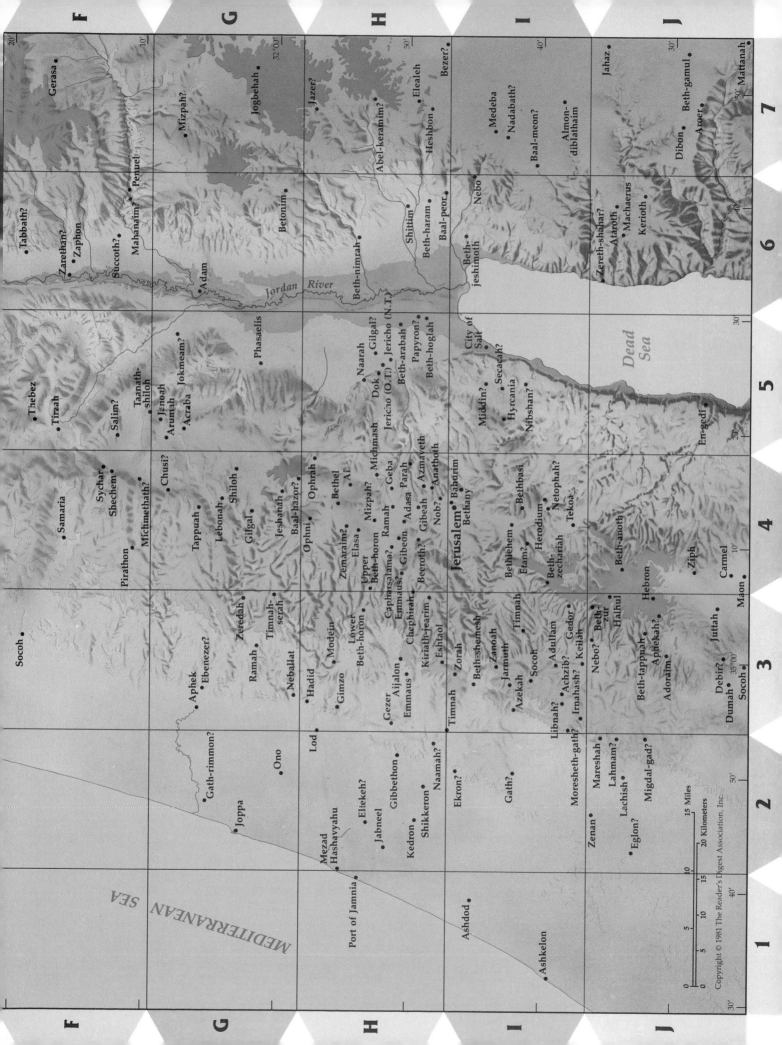

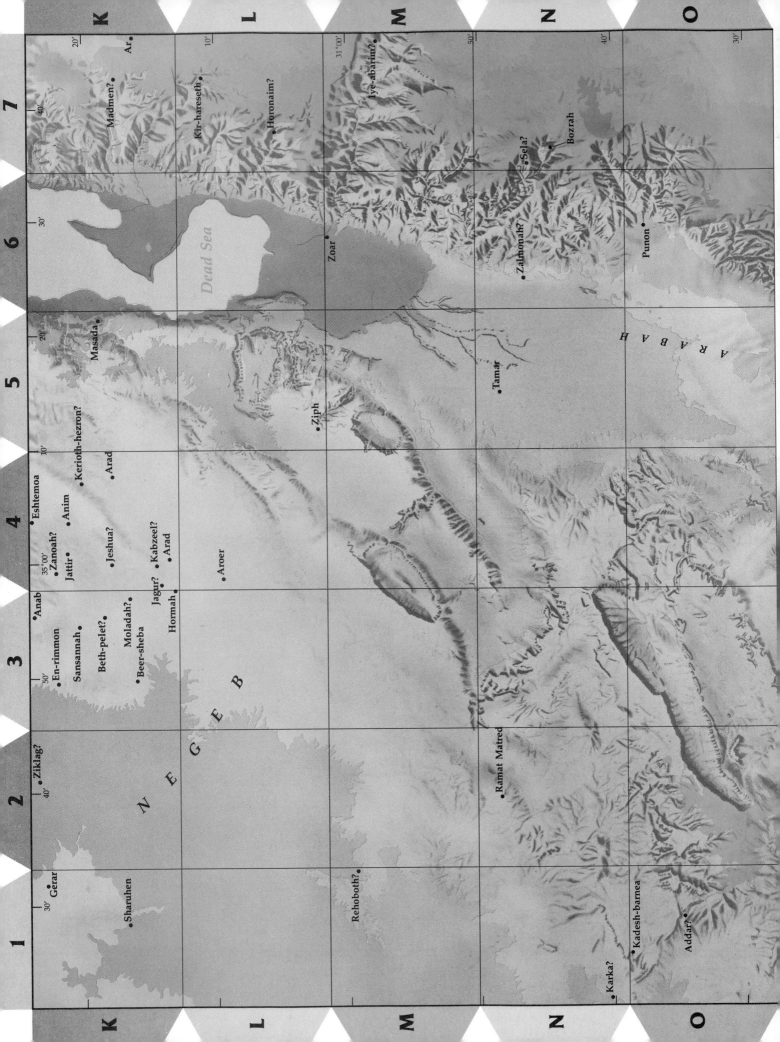

Petra

•Jotbathah

•Abronah?

Ezion-geber
•

P Q R S T

15 Miles

20 Kilometers

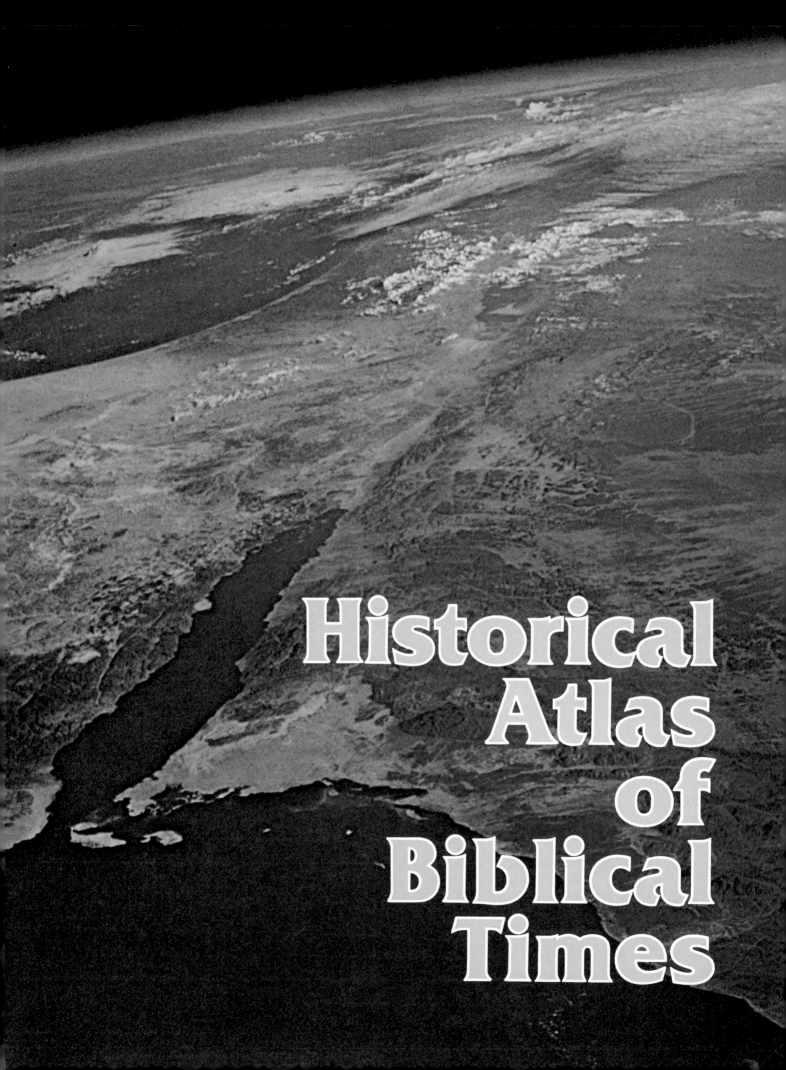

Historical
Atlas
of
Biblical
Times

World of the Patriarchs

With Abraham and his descendants—Isaac, Jacob, and Joseph—the people of the Bible step into the pages of history. The Patriarchs of Israel are the earliest biblical figures that can, with any degree of confidence, be placed in a specific geographical and historical context.

These forefathers of the Israelite nation, whose stories are told in Genesis 11–50, lived sometime between 2000 and 1500 B.C. (see chronology on page 242). Their world encompassed a vast panorama of the ancient Near East, the great arc of land stretching for some 1,200 miles from Mesopotamia in the east to Egypt in the west. Encircled by towering mountains, forbidding deserts, and terrifying seas, this Fertile Crescent was virtually self-sufficient both culturally and economically—though some manufactured goods were traded for the raw materials of lands beyond. It was dominated by two mighty river systems: the Tigris and Euphrates in Mesopotamia and the Nile in Egypt.

The word "Mesopotamia" means "between rivers." The Tigris and Euphrates rise less than 100 miles apart in the Turkish highlands. The Tigris, 1,150 miles long, tumbles swiftly from its headwaters onto the plains of southern Mesopotamia. The Euphrates takes a meandering course of some 1,700 miles until it joins the Tigris, 120 miles before disgorging into the Persian Gulf. Although less turbulent than the Tigris, it holds its own terrors. It causes terrible floods, and where it traverses the hard, nearly impervious soil of the southern plains, it can suddenly shift its course with disastrous results. In midvalley the two rivers come within 30 miles of each other and then separate again to flow in a southeasterly direction for about 200 miles before their eventual union. Here the soil can be fertile, but the climate is one of extremes: in winter temperatures drop below freezing, while in summer they soar to over 100°F in the shade and dust storms hang like thick fog in the heat. Rain is infrequent in this low-lying plain, which stretches monotonously to the horizon. To the north and east, however, between the Tigris River and the Zagros Mountains, the rich, red-brown loam is watered by tributary rivers and by occasional rainfall. Although the hills are beautiful when they are carpeted with flowers after the rains, in summer the land is soon burned brown by the sun, and the winters are even more severe than in the plain.

In Egypt, at the opposite end of the Fertile Crescent, the Nile is regular and dependable, a far more benign river than either the Tigris or the Euphrates. Fed by monsoon rains that fall on the Ethiopian highlands to the south, the Nile swells with its annual flood from June through October, bringing life to the virtually rainless valley and providing natural fertilizer in the form of the thick volcanic silt it has borne from thousands of miles upstream.

As it winds northward through the boundless sands of the Egyptian desert, the river creates scenes of striking beauty. Near the first cataract, sandstone cliffs in warm hues of yellow, brown, and red are reflected in the rippling water. Elsewhere, the river slides endlessly through the "black land," a grayish-black alluvial plain. Then comes the "red land," where deserts stretch behind sandstone and limestone cliffs tracing the valley edge. Downriver the cliffs retreat, the alluvial plain widens, and the blue of the Nile contrasts brilliantly with the green and black of its banks, the red of the desert, and the ever-changing colors of the hills, while the omnipresent sun casts dark shadows along the limestone cliffs. Then the plain widens even more, driving the desert back 6 to 9 miles, especially along the western bank, for almost 200 miles of the river's length. In Lower Egypt, the Nile has deposited a fan-shaped delta 100 miles long and 150 miles across at its widest point. And while the river unites Upper Egypt, here in the Delta it divides the country: in ancient times seven major branches of the Nile (today there are only two) and numerous smaller waterways cut through the deep, black soil.

It was at these two extremes of the Fertile Crescent, along the two great river systems, that the earliest urban civilizations on earth appeared. They first evolved in southern Mesopotamia, which has been called the cradle of civilization. From perhaps as early as the fifth millennium B.C. the area had been inhabited by peoples who lived in villages scattered across the plain between the Tigris and Euphrates. These early settlers developed basic irrigation techniques that allowed them to grow grains and fruits. They also engaged in fishing and cattle raising and mastered the skills of weaving, pottery making, carpentry, and masonry. Then, about 3500 B.C., a non-Semitic people called the Sumerians, who are generally believed to have originated in central Asia, arrived on the scene. Genesis 11:2 preserves what may be a reference to the coming of the Sumerians: "And as men migrated from the east, they found a plain in the land of Shinar [Sumer] and settled there."

These newcomers devised an intricate network of irrigation canals and dikes that enabled them to sustain an ever-larger population. Out of this growth emerged a new, more complex civilization. As villages gave way to cities over the next few centuries, the Sumerians developed a political and social system based on the city-state. By 3000 B.C. the plain was green with wheat and barley and dotted with cities: Ur, Nippur, Erech, Eridu, Lagash, and Kish.

The Sumerians built their cities out of what they had at hand in their virtually treeless, stoneless land: mud. With this humble material, which they fashioned into bricks and let dry in the sun, they constructed massive walls around their cities as protection both against one another (for the Sumerian cities long remained politically autonomous and constantly warred with each other for supremacy) and against their foreign enemies, marauding mountain tribesmen and insistent desert nomads, who perennially threatened. Within their city walls they built towering, step-pyramid structures called ziggurats to honor their many gods. A remarkable, inventive people, the Sumerians were the first to use the arch and the wheel, the latter for fashioning pottery and for transportation. They sculpted images of their gods and rulers

Mesopotamian landscape: in a marshy delta of the Tigris and Euphrates rivers graceful boats are used to move goods and people. Similar craft made of reeds plied these waters more than 6,000 years ago, when this valley supported one of the earliest civilizations on earth.

The earliest-known system of writing, called cuneiform, was invented in Sumeria in the third millennium B.C. A nation of traders, the Sumerians introduced their word symbols throughout the Near East, where cuneiform became widely used because it was adaptable to a diversity of languages. At right is a cuneiform prism giving a list of the Sumerian kings.

This gypsum statuette from Mesopotamia, discovered in a Sumerian temple, dates to about the third millennium B.C. It represents a worshiper holding a libation cup used in religious ceremonies. The coiffure, the wavy beard, and the fringed dress are believed to be typical of the day.

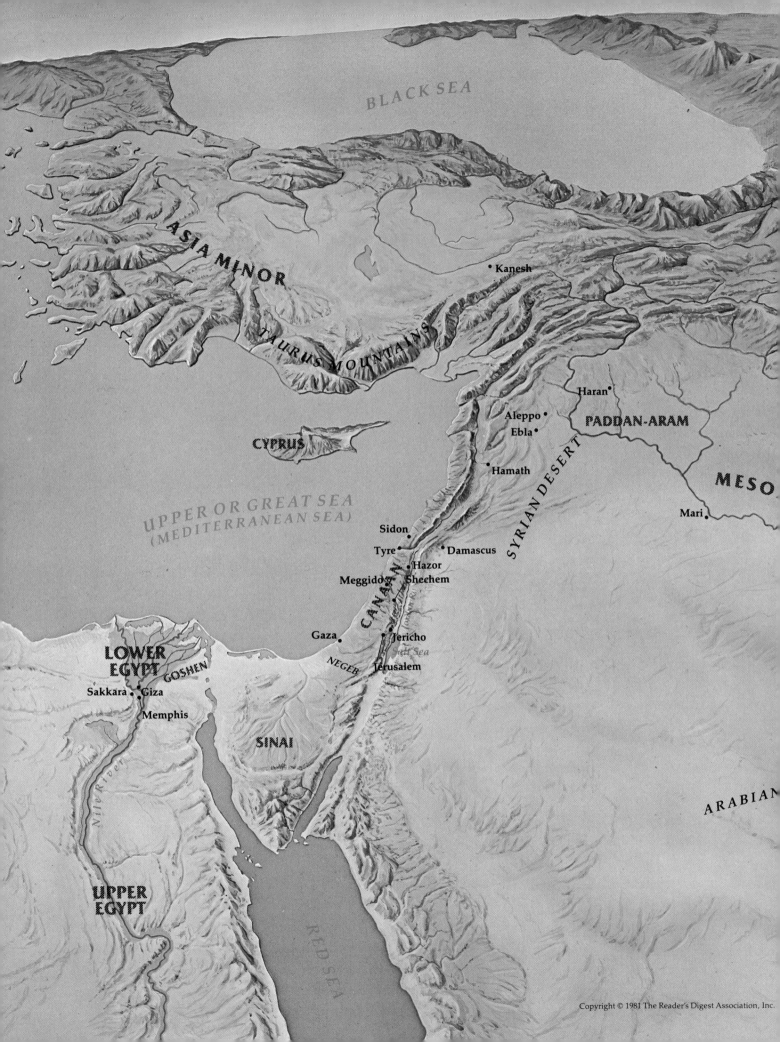

BLACK SEA

ASIA MINOR

•Kanesh

TAURUS MOUNTAINS

Haran•

Aleppo•   PADDAN-ARAM

Ebla•

CYPRUS

Hamath•   MESO.

UPPER OR GREAT SEA
(MEDITERRANEAN SEA)

SYRIAN DESERT

Mari•

Sidon•

Tyre•   •Damascus

•Hazor

Meggido• •Shechem

C
A
N
A
A
N

Gaza•   •Jericho

Salt Sea

LOWER
EGYPT   GOSHEN

NEGEB   Jerusalem

Sakkara •Giza

Memphis   SINAI

ARABIAN

Nile River

UPPER
EGYPT

RED SEA

CAUCASUS MOUNTAINS

ARARAT MOUNTAINS

CASPIAN SEA

...OTAMIA

Tuttul

AKKAD

Babylon • Kish

BABYLONIA

• Nippur

Tigris River

ZAGROS MOUNTAINS

• Lagash

Euphrates River

• Erech   SUMER

Ur •

• Eridu

DESERT

LOWER SEA
(PERSIAN GULF)

from stone, and they understood the complex technology of alloying tin with copper to make bronze and then working it into usable tools. In mathematics they originated a system of numerical notation, based on 10's and 6's, which persists to this day in the way we tell time and in the division of the circle into 360°.

The Sumerians' crowning achievement, however, was the development of a complete system of writing, called cuneiform, using wedge-shaped marks impressed onto clay tablets. This was the beginning of written history. For the first time mankind could pass on to future generations the accumulated wisdom of the past. And on their surviving clay tablets, the Sumerians have bequeathed us a remarkable body of literature: myths, epic tales, hymns, the earliest known law code. These writings convey a picture of a people with a love of life tempered by a deep sense of insecurity and helplessness in the face of the harsh and unpredictable forces of nature. Long before the story of Noah was written down in the Bible, the Sumerians wrote about a great flood that destroyed mankind.

Soon after the distinctive Sumerian culture evolved, the spark of civilization flared again, at the southwestern end of the Fertile Crescent, in Egypt. The Egyptians figured out how to use the Nile's annual flood to irrigate their valley, and they planted wheat, barley, and other crops in a green swath 600 miles long but nowhere more than 13 miles wide. In the Delta they grew vegetables, fruit, flax, and grapes. They grazed sheep, goats, and cattle, particularly in the hospitable land of Goshen in the eastern Delta. On the river, boat traffic moved easily, carried northward by the current and southward by prevailing winds.

Egypt was far more isolated geographically than Sumer, a fact that played an important role in determining the character of the country and its culture. There was no constant threat from outside as there was in Mesopotamia. The Egyptians built no large walled cities like those of Mesopotamia, and for a long time they did not even have a standing army. Yet early, perhaps as early as 3100 B.C., Upper and Lower Egypt were forged into a single political state, highly centralized, efficient, and powerful. Whenever political stability waned, natural conditions encouraged unity and unity bred strength.

The Egyptians were the first to build monumental stone structures. The pyramids seem the essence of ancient Egypt: massive, changeless, seemingly rooted in

Egyptian landscape: a farmer works the rich black soil of the Nile valley. Agricultural methods have scarcely changed since ancient times. People today depend on the Nile's annual flood to deposit mineral-rich silt over the land and to fill the channels of the extensive irrigation systems. The plow, which appears in pictures as early as the Old Kingdom (2664–2180 B.C.), is still pulled by cattle as in the photograph above.

Symbolic of the Egyptian belief in the afterlife, the great pyramid complex at Giza—honoring Pharaohs Mycerinus, Chephren, and Cheops—has crowned the desert sands for some 45 centuries. Constructed so perfectly of sandstone and rock that no mortar was needed, the pyramids have lost their outer coating of limestone; only Chephren's tomb (at center) retains such vestiges at its peak. The three satellite tombs in front of Mycerinus' pyramid (in the foreground) belong to the Pharaoh's immediate family. Chephren's tomb appears larger than the Great Pyramid of Cheops behind it, because it is built on higher ground. Scholars still question the significance of their placement.

eternity. Nothing rivals these royal tombs, especially the 3rd-Dynasty (c. 2664–2615 B.C.) step-pyramid of Djoser at Sakkara and the three great 4th-Dynasty (c. 2614–2502) pyramids at Giza. Even today these colossal tombs impress us as awesome feats of engineering. The largest, the Great Pyramid of Cheops at Giza, covers 13.1 acres and rises to a height of 481.4 feet. It consists of 2,300,000 quarried stones averaging 2½ tons each, and the nine granite slabs that roof the king's burial chamber weigh about 45 tons apiece.

The Egyptians devised the world's first solar calendar of 365 days, dividing the year into twelve 30-day months plus 5 feast days. No ancient people matched them in medical skill: they gleaned a knowledge of anatomy from their practice of mummifying their dead, and they were able to perform delicate surgery on the living. They also developed a complicated system of writing, at first using pictographs, which evolved into hieroglyphics. While their literature is less varied and rich than that of the Sumerians, the Egyptians wrote medical treatises and extensive religious texts and endlessly extolled their kings on the walls of temples and palaces. The Egyptians have captured human imagination through the centuries, as people have looked in awe upon their tombs and temples covered with pictures of their love of life and their confidence—so different from the Sumerians—in the changelessness and dependability of their material and spiritual world.

King Narmer is shown smiting a prisoner held by the hair. This palette of about 3100 B.C. may celebrate the unification of Upper and Lower Egypt, often associated with Narmer.

Linking Mesopotamia and Egypt was Canaan, a fertile land bridge that narrows to 40 miles between the Mediterranean Sea and the Jordan River. Here hills and valleys break up the terrain. With no major rivers, its fields, vineyards, and orchards were wholly dependent upon seasonal rains, which usually start in October, increase in December, and continue into April. Rainfall ranges from 10 inches a year in the south to about 23 inches in the central highlands and 30 inches in the highest parts of Galilee in the north. But the rains tend to be concentrated in short periods and are consequently often too heavy. Violent storms pour over the hills, eroding the landscape and washing away the thin, precious layer of topsoil. (Indeed, the Egyptians spoke of the rains of Canaan as the Nile falling from the sky.) In good years the Great Plain of Galilee would yield two crops, and abundant crops would also flourish in the narrow central valleys. In other years, however, dreaded famine would overtake the land.

Canaan's historic role was as a highway linking Egypt and Mesopotamia. Along the Mediterranean coast and along the highlands across the Jordan River ran two major international trade routes: the Way of the Sea following the coast, and inland the King's Highway. Canaan's walled cities—such as Megiddo, on the vital coastal route, or Shechem, at an important interior crossroads—owed their wealth not only to the fertility of surrounding fields but also to these trade routes. Most of Canaan,

Prof. Paolo Matthiae (top left) discusses the treasures of Ebla at Tell Mardikh—site of an ongoing excavation since 1964. Many unique artifacts have been found, but the most exciting discoveries are the state archives (above), containing more than 16,000 cuneiform tablets (most, however, are fragments). Not only have tablets like the ones at left revealed a new language called Eblaite, but they have given scholars new clues to the understanding of ancient Sumerian.

Ebla: A Lost Civilization Discovered

A long-forgotten city of ancient Syria, Ebla is emerging from the rubble of a massive tell nearly 200 miles north of Damascus to claim a place among the ancient civilizations of Mesopotamia and Egypt.

An Italian archaeological team under Paolo Matthiae began digging at the site in 1964, but it was 10 years before they were able to establish that Ebla was the center of one of the largest inhabited areas of the Near East in the third millennium B.C., with a population of up to 260,000. The city of Ebla boasted a royal palace and an immense state archive—the oldest known in history. From preliminary studies of the cuneiform tablets found in the archives, scholars have determined that Ebla was a leading economic center. Far-reaching trade links have been identified with Kanesh in Asia Minor to the north; Mari and Tuttul to the southeast on the Euphrates River; and possibly Hazor, Tyre, and Megiddo to the south. But Ebla lay in the path of the expanding Akkadian empire and was destroyed about 2250 B.C. Rebuilt and destroyed at least twice more, Ebla became no more than a footnote to history—until the recent archaeological finds.

Most intriguing of these is the discovery of a new Semitic language designated Eblaite by the former team epigrapher, Giovanni Pettinato. Eblaite, which has ties primarily with Akkadian and also with other Semitic languages, has led some scholars to speculate about Ebla's connections with people and events of the Old Testament. At one point it was announced that, among the thousands of tablets, references had been found to the five Cities of the Plain named in Genesis 14:2. Claims were made that other biblical names appeared in the archives. While the debate continues, painstaking archaeological work is uncovering the life of a great city that rose, thrived, and fell more than 4,000 years ago.

World of the Patriarchs *(continued)*

however, was little more than hinterland for much of its history, politically important only when major powers to the northeast and southwest were weak.

Here geography tended to divide, not unite, and political unity eluded the Canaanites as city fought against city and as newcomers arrived adding to the confusion. The Negeb to the south and the plains across the Jordan supported large numbers of wandering shepherds. These nomads constantly raided the exposed fringes of the settled areas, occasionally venturing farther into the interior. But other nomads, pastoral and more peaceful, abandoned the burning deserts and swarmed over Canaan looking for a home where they could cultivate grapes and olives, even occasionally planting their own fields of barley and wheat, while finding good grazing lands for their flocks. Among them was Abraham.

By the time of Abraham and the other Patriarchs the lands of the Near East were already ancient, with long and illustrious histories. While the people were beginning to have commercial contacts with distant lands, they were almost self-sufficient. They also usually—but not always—had enough military strength to maintain themselves in the presence of pressure from both mountain people and desert tribes who were ever seeking to secure the more fertile valleys for themselves. The patriarchal period and that immediately preceding it was a time when that strength failed. It was an age of turmoil, at least for much of Mesopotamia and Canaan. Shifting nomads overran once mighty cities. In Canaan, where there had been substantial urban development after 3000 B.C., nomadic invaders (probably Semitic peoples known as the Amorites) destroyed cities and brought chaos to the land. The dawn of the second millennium saw the gradual return to political stability as the newcomers settled down and built new cities. Beginning about this time, too, the Egyptians seem to have exercised some political control over Canaan, particularly the coastal plain around Gaza.

The Sumerians were also the victims of outside pressure. Weakened by rivalries and intermittent warfare among city-states vying for supremacy, Sumer was ripe for the taking by nomads from the north. A Semitic people under King Sargon the Great seized power in the 24th century B.C. and created the Akkadian dynasty, the world's first true empire, which came to rule not only Sumer but all of Mesopotamia and at times perhaps reached out as far as the Mediterranean. The Akkadians assimilated the Sumerian culture and religion and ruled for nearly 200 years. In the 22nd century B.C. they in turn were overthrown by the Gutians, barbarians from the Zagros Mountains who took over Sumer but seem to have exercised a loose control over its cities. Not much is known from this period, but by the 21st century the Sumerians had broken loose from Gutian dominance to establish the 3rd Dynasty of Ur.

Although this 3rd Dynasty was to last only a little more than a century (c. 2060–1950), it brought a cultural and political renaissance that spawned new building and literary activity. But it never succeeded in holding the cities together under a firm central government. Old rivalries flared again as the city-states struggled with each other for political and commercial advantage, and this paved the way for the ascendance of Amorite dynasties already entrenched in Mesopotamia. By the end of the 18th century, the land was under the control of the Babylonian empire and its great king Hammurabi. Yet the cultural legacy of Sumer lived on in Babylonia, and literature and the sciences continued to flourish. Hammurabi is celebrated today for his famous law code, which was derived largely from the earliest-known compilation of laws, those enacted by Ur-Nammu, the founder of Ur's 3rd Dynasty. Hammurabi's Code antedates by several centuries the biblical laws of Moses.

According to Genesis 11:27–31, the original home of Abraham and his family was the city of Ur, in Mesopotamia. He perhaps lived there at the time when the Sumerian civilization was enjoying its final heyday, and Ur was its leading city and the capital of the ruling dynasty. Founded more than 1,500 years earlier, the prosperous city was situated on the banks of the Euphrates, where sailing vessels laden with goods from distant lands could pull up to the wharves. Carefully tended, irrigated fields surrounded the massive walls, and above them loomed the renowned ziggurat of Ur, which rose in three tiers from a base 200 by 150 feet to a height of 70 feet, topped by a shrine to the city's patron deity, the Sumerian moon god, Nanna.

Abraham, his father Terah, his wife Sarah, and his nephew Lot left Ur, Genesis tells us, "to go into the land of Canaan."* As the clan departed on their fateful journey, they may well have looked back for a last view of the proud city on the river, its great temple towering over its walls. (Today the ruins of this ziggurat, in what is now southern Iraq, are the largest tangible legacy of the Sumerians. The Euphrates long ago shifted its course away from the city, leaving it in dust, and the ziggurat is a lonely heap of mud bricks in a desert wasteland.)

Abraham and his clan probably followed the course of the Euphrates as they traveled toward the northwest, with their tents and their flocks, until they reached the region known as Paddan-aram, where the Mesopotamian desert rises to meet the mountains of Anatolia. A wide-open steppe, deeply etched by wadis, the southern portion of Paddan-aram has enough rain (eight inches a year) for grasses and even for crops. In the northern portion, rainfall increases to 10 inches, sufficient for a modest settled population. When the sojourners reached the caravan center of Haran, some 600 miles northwest of Ur, they settled down. And here Terah died, leaving his son Abraham as the head of the clan.

It was at Haran that the Lord commanded Abraham, "Go from your country and your kindred and your father's house to the land that I will show you," and also promised him, "And I will make of you a great nation, and I will bless you, and make your name great . . ."

So Abraham, with Sarah and Lot and the rest of his clan, set forth again, this time southward toward Canaan, 400 miles distant. They traveled slowly, pitching their tents here and there, staying as long as pasturage held out for the flocks, occasionally even planting their own fields of barley or wheat for a season or two, but always moving on again as they drew ever nearer the Promised Land.

Chapter and verse of biblical citations are given on page 245.

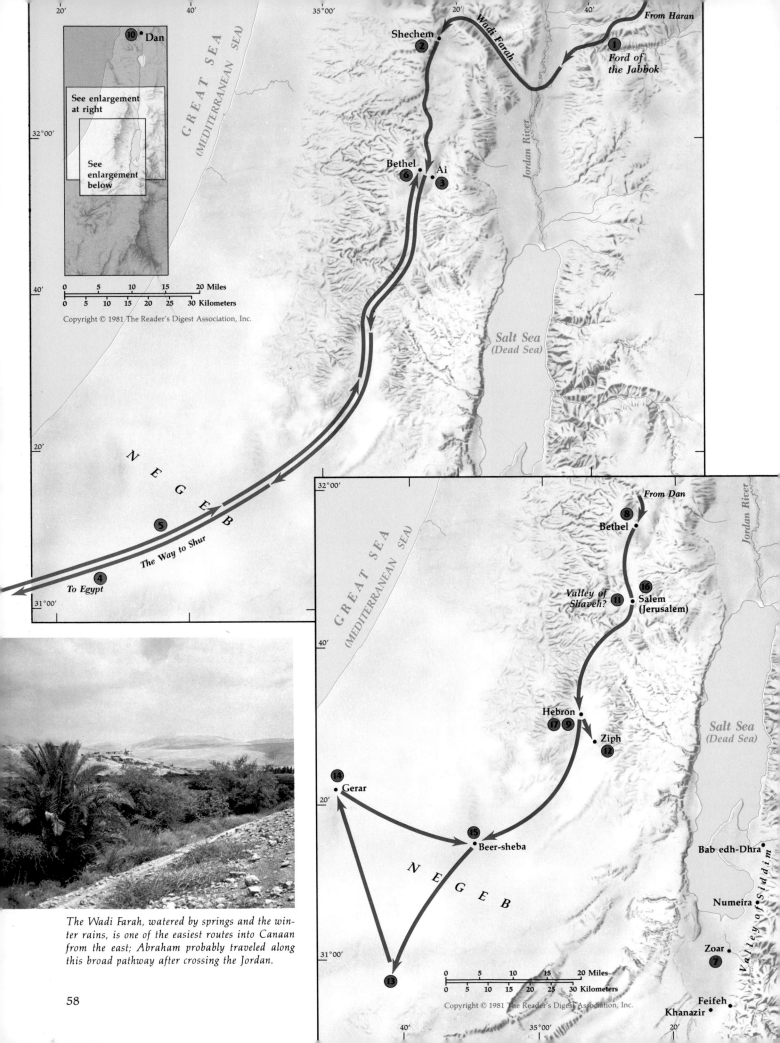

Inset map (top left)

10 Dan

GREAT SEA (MEDITERRANEAN SEA)

See enlargement at right

See enlargement below

32°00'

40'

0   5   10   15   20 Miles
0   5   10 15 20 25 30 Kilometers

Copyright © 1981 The Reader's Digest Association, Inc.

Main map (upper)

From Haran

Wadi Farah

35°00'   20'   40'

Shechem 2

1 Ford of the Jabbok

Jordan River

Bethel 6   Ai 3

Salt Sea (Dead Sea)

N E G E B

5

4

The Way to Shur

To Egypt

31°00'

20'

Lower map

32°00'   40'

From Dan

Bethel 8

GREAT SEA (MEDITERRANEAN SEA)

Valley of Shaveh? 11   16 Salem (Jerusalem)

40'

Hebron 17 9   Ziph 12

Salt Sea (Dead Sea)

Gerar 14

15 Beer-sheba

N E G E B

Bab edh-Dhra

Numeira

Valley of Siddim

13

Zoar 7

0   5   10   15   20 Miles
0   5   10 15 20 30 Kilometers

31°00'

Feifeh

Khanazir

35°00'   20'

40'

Copyright © 1981 The Reader's Digest Association, Inc.

The Wadi Farah, watered by springs and the winter rains, is one of the easiest routes into Canaan from the east; Abraham probably traveled along this broad pathway after crossing the Jordan.

58

Abraham in the Land of Canaan

From the heights east of the Jordan, a number of narrow passes can be seen leading up into the mountains across the valley. The most inviting—and most used today as in antiquity—is the well-watered Wadi Farah. It is likely that Abraham descended to the ford of the Jabbok (1, map at left, above) before crossing the Jordan and entering Canaan—for this is the route later taken by his grandson Jacob when he returned from Haran. Abraham, no doubt, stopped at the oases in the valley, nearly 800 feet below sea level. From these depths he, with his family and flocks, would have ascended 2,300 feet in just under 23 miles, to the oak of Moreh at Shechem (2). And there, after the Lord promised to give the land to his descendants, Abraham built his first altar in Canaan.

Abraham did not tarry in the vales that converge upon Shechem but instead moved south along the watershed that forms a natural north-south route through the land. Not for the last time, he was attracted to the rolling hills "with Bethel on the west and Ai on the east" (3), and there he built a second altar. With few towns and no large cities in the area, the brush-covered and forested hills provided ample food for his animals. Water, however, was scarce, and a severe famine drove Abraham far south into Egypt, probably along the Way to Shur (4), a direct and open route through the Negeb that has been a favorite of nomads from the dawn of history.

Fearing the Egyptians would kill him for his beautiful wife, Sarah, Abraham had her pose as his sister. But after Sarah was taken into Pharaoh's house, the Lord afflicted the Egyptian ruler with plagues. Learning the cause of his misery, Pharaoh ordered the Hebrew Patriarch to leave. And Abraham, by now "very rich in cattle, in silver, and in gold," began his journey north with Sarah and with Lot, his brother's son.

Again passing through the Negeb (5), Abraham returned to the Bethel region (6) and pitched his tents once more in the peaceful hills. But strife between his herdsmen and those of Lot shattered the pastoral calm, and the two decided to part lest the anger of their men spread to them. Given a choice of land, Lot went south of the Salt Sea in the direction of Zoar (7, map at left, below) and "moved his tent as far as Sodom." Thus did Abraham's kinsman come into the region of the five Cities of the Plain (see page 60) in the Valley of Siddim.

For the second time Abraham journeyed south from Bethel (8), this time to the oaks of Mamre at Hebron (9), at the high point of the central mountain ridge where the hills fall away gently to the desert at Beer-sheba. At Mamre he received word that kings of the north had attacked the Cities of the Plain and that Lot had been taken captive. With 318 trained men Abraham followed these kings to Dan (10, on locator), then known as Laish. There he attacked at night, routing the kings and chasing them "to Hobah, north of Damascus." Lot, his goods, women, and people were rescued.

As he was returning to Hebron, apparently along the mountain ridge route he now knew so well, Abraham was met at the Valley of Shaveh (11) by the king of Sodom. Melchizedek, king and priest of nearby Salem (Jerusalem), brought out bread and wine for the two men and blessed Abraham and thanked God, "who has delivered your enemies into your hand!"

At Hebron once more, Abraham and Sarah grew increasingly sad. Despite God's repeated promise of an heir, the couple not only remained childless but Sarah was well past childbearing age. So, after the custom of the times, Sarah brought her maid, the Egyptian Hagar, to Abraham that there might be an heir. And Hagar bore a son, Ishmael. When the boy was 13, three men came to Abraham's tent one day, saying that in the spring Sarah would have a son. After feasting them in typically gracious nomadic fashion, Abraham showed them the way to Sodom, probably going with them toward Ziph (12), from which two routes lead through the rocky gorges down to the Salt Sea. There the Lord revealed to Abraham his intention to destroy Sodom and Gomorrah but said he would spare them if 10 righteous men were found in Sodom. The next morning, however, when Abraham came again to the place where he had stood before the Lord and looked toward Sodom and Gomorrah, he saw smoke—"like the smoke of a furnace"—rising from the valley. Warned by angels, Lot escaped though his disobedient wife perished.

South of Hebron the hills arc westward, embracing a triangular depression extending from Beer-sheba to the coast. Through this semiarid area, dominated by the city of Gerar, ran the major trade routes between Egypt and Canaan. And this now became the arena of Abraham's activity—perhaps as a donkey caravaneer bringing such produce of Canaan as salt, potash, wine, and olives south to exchange for the cotton and linen goods of Egypt. He dwelt in the desert (13) between Kadesh and Shur and sojourned at Gerar (14). Despite an initial dispute with Abraham, Abimelech, king of Gerar, allowed the Patriarch to pitch his tents and graze his flocks east of the city. It was somewhere between Gerar and Beer-sheba that Isaac was born, fulfilling God's promise. In the midst of her joy, however, Sarah caused Hagar and Ishmael to be driven into the desert, where they were likely to die. Yet God preserved the fugitives—and Ishmael's descendants became nomads in the southern wilderness.

Because of conflict over water rights between Abraham's and Abimelech's servants, Abraham left the Gerar area and went to Beer-sheba (15), an oasis embracing a number of wells clustered in the desert. There God put him to a supreme test: "Take your son . . . and go to the land of Moriah, and offer him there as a burnt offering . . ." In the painful moment of affirming his faith at Moriah, traditionally identified with the Temple Mount at Jerusalem (16), Abraham was told to spare Isaac.

When Sarah died, Abraham purchased the cave of Machpelah at Hebron (17) in which to bury her. He, too, was eventually laid to rest there. And thus the cave of Machpelah became the burial place of the Patriarchs of Israel and is hallowed to this day by Jews, Christians, and Muslims.

Cities of the Plain

Writing at about the time of Jesus, the Jewish historian Josephus noted that it was possible to see the remains of ancient cities south of the Dead Sea. Since at least the 1st century B.C., historians have placed the biblical Cities of the Plain—Sodom, Gomorrah, Admah, Zeboiim, and Bela (Zoar)—in that region. Later scholars speculated that earthquakes destroyed the cities and their remains lay beneath the shallow waters of the southern Dead Sea. Then in 1924, W. F. Albright discovered an Early Bronze Age site—Bab edh-Dhra—in the southeastern Dead Sea area. Digging there in the 1960's, Paul Lapp found a large city and a nearby cemetery. Since 1973 two American archaeologists, Walter Rast and Thomas Schaub, have located four additional settlements of that era—known by their recent Arabic names: Numeira, es-Safi, Feifeh, and Khanazir. Excavations at Bab edh-Dhra and Numeira have led Rast and Schaub to propose that these might be two of the biblical cities. Environmental surveys reveal that the land at the southern end of the Dead Sea was more fertile in the third millennium B.C. and that there was enough water to support a sizable agricultural economy. The fortress cities would have offered refuge in times of crisis. Bab edh-Dhra, the largest of them, most likely served as the major city in relation to the others. It could well contain the ruins of ancient Sodom, with the ruins of the neighboring city of Gomorrah possibly being at Numeira. Both sites met a violent end about 2350 B.C.—nearly four centuries before the earliest date currently suggested for the life of Abraham. Such a memorable event as the sudden destruction of these cities would have become firmly lodged in the traditions of the area and could have found its way into the Abraham narrative.

Salt-encrusted tree stumps rise from the waters of the Dead Sea (top), suggesting the pillar of salt into which Lot's wife was turned. Excavations at Bab edh-Dhra, in the southeastern area of the sea, have yielded some of the best examples of Early Bronze Age pottery (left) dating to 3200–3100 B.C. In addition the impressive circular burial houses (above) are singular features at Bab edh-Dhra—no similar structures have been found at other Near Eastern sites. Compared with the common burial practices of the time—placing bodies in natural or artificially cut caves—the careful construction of the charnel houses indicates a wealthy population.

Isaac, Jacob, and Joseph

Isaac was a man of the desert, a pastoral nomad who moved from place to place, occasionally growing crops and constantly seeking water for his flocks. This "son of the Promise," this joy of Abraham's old age, was born to Sarah in the desert, somewhere between Gerar and Beer-sheba (1, map on page 63). And there in the northwestern Negeb he lived most of his life, scarcely venturing more than 50 miles from his place of birth. So far as we know, he only left the area when, as a child, he was nearly sacrificed by his father at Moriah (2) in the central highlands. Following the death of his mother, Isaac dwelt at Beer-lahai-roi (3), an oasis on the caravan route to Egypt and the place where an angel had comforted Sarah's pregnant maid, Hagar, when she fled from her mistress's cruelty. It was there that Rebekah, Isaac's bride, was brought to him, riding a camel, and there that their twin sons, Esau and Jacob, were born.

The Negeb, like most desert in the Holy Land, is rocky with some sandy stretches. When springs and wells run dry, famine threatens to bring economic ruin to herdsmen. In antiquity the fertile fields of Egypt, nourished by the Nile, offered haven from such disaster, and Isaac—as his father had before him—looked in that direction when famine struck. At Gerar (4), however, Isaac heeded God's command not to go to Egypt.

The Gerar region, dotted by abundant wells, lay between the true desert and the area of permanent settlement. Although flash floods erode deep gullies in winter, and the summer winds blow dust storms across the crumbled, sunburnt earth, this southern steppe is not inherently barren. The soil—yellow-brown loess—is essentially the same as in the more fertile areas to the north and has been sporadically cultivated throughout history. By supplementing the 6 to 10 inches of annual rainfall with an elementary irrigation system, the pastoralist can successfully cultivate crops.

When Isaac reopened the wells that Abraham had dug and sowed crops, he "reaped in the same year a hundredfold." He became so rich and powerful that Abimelech, feeling threatened, ordered him away. Going only as far as the Valley of Gerar (5), probably to the southwest of the town, Isaac once more found water for his flocks. But the herdsmen of Gerar disputed with Isaac's herdsmen over wells to which Isaac gave the names Esek ("contention") and Sitnah ("enmity"). Isaac then dug a third well, naming it Rehoboth ("room"), for at last he seems to have found a place to graze his flocks in peace. Nonetheless, Isaac left Gerar and went to the oasis of Beer-sheba (6), where the Lord again renewed his covenant with the Patriarchs.

Unlike Isaac, who lived in a corner of the Negeb, his son Jacob knew the vast sweep of the Near East from the steppeland of Paddan-aram beyond the Euphrates in the north to the lush Nile Delta in the south—a distance of nearly 600 miles. Born deep in the desert, at Beer-lahai-roi (7), Jacob, the younger of twin sons, "was a quiet man, dwelling in tents," whereas his older brother, Esau, was drawn to the robust life of a desert hunter.

Returning tired and hungry from the field one day, Esau traded the birthright of the elder son for some bread and a pottage of lentils Jacob was boiling. Later at Beer-sheba (8), Rebekah helped her favorite son, Jacob, deceive the aged, nearly blind Isaac into bestowing his blessing upon her second-born son. Cheated by his brother of both birthright and blessing, Esau plotted to kill Jacob. To escape Esau's wrath and also to find a wife among his mother's people, Jacob journeyed north toward Haran, to his ancestral home in Paddan-aram.

Making his way up the central mountain watershed, he came to a place in those rolling hills that had attracted his grandfather Abraham. In a dream Jacob saw a ladder reaching to heaven, with angels ascending and descending on it. And the Lord appeared to him and renewed the promise of the land made to his grandfather and father. When he awoke, Jacob set up a pillar, anointed it, and called the place Bethel (9), "house of God."

We do not know Jacob's route from Bethel toward Haran. It is likely that he crossed the Jordan near Adam and climbed the easy slope of the heavily eroded yet verdant Jabbok valley, finally reaching the King's Highway on the high plains. If so, he went past Damascus, already ancient, and by Hamath along the western edge of the great steppe, and through Aleppo, astride the trade route. At length he would have crossed the Euphrates into the grasslands of Paddan-aram (see map on pages 52–53). There, by chance, he met his cousin Rachel at a well as she came to water her father's flock. She ran to tell her father, Laban, who graciously received the son of his sister Rebekah.

Laban offered his nephew work and wages. But Jacob asked instead to serve Laban seven years as the price of marrying Rachel. Tricked into marriage with Leah, Laban's older daughter, Jacob worked another seven years as the price for Rachel. He then continued for six more years as a herdsman to his father-in-law, becoming a rich man in the process. At length, afraid Laban would oppose his departure, Jacob fled while his father-in-law was away with his flocks.

Laban pursued Jacob and his slow-moving herd and in seven days overtook him in the hill country of Gilead. Angry scenes were followed by reconciliation and an uneasy covenant of peace. Laban returned home, and Jacob went to meet his brother, Esau.

From Mahanaim (10), dominated by the scarred limestone cliffs of the narrow Jabbok valley, Jacob sent messengers to Esau in far-off Edom (Seir), seeking peace—only to learn that his brother was approaching with 400 men. As a precaution, Jacob divided his people and goods, speculating, "If Esau comes to the one company and destroys it, then the company which is left will escape." Jacob then sent gifts to his brother and prayed. That night he wrestled with a stranger until the breaking of day—after which the man said to him, "Your name shall no more be called Jacob, but Israel, for you have striven with God and with men, and have prevailed." At sunrise Jacob limped past Penuel (11), for

Isaac, Jacob, and Joseph *(continued)*

his thigh had been put out of joint as he wrestled.

At this point Jacob encountered his brother's company. But to his great relief Esau greeted him kindly, and the long-separated brothers embraced and wept tears of joy. As Esau returned to Edom, Jacob went to Succoth (12), deep in the Jordan valley, and built a house and booths for his cattle in this hot, humid place. But he soon moved on, crossing the Jordan into Canaan and making his way up the Wadi Farah to Shechem (13). There he bought land and erected an altar.

Now tragedy struck. Jacob's daughter, Dinah, was raped by Shechem, son of the Hivite prince Hamor. In revenge two of her brothers killed the prince and his son, massacred the men of Shechem, and plundered the city. Fearful of reprisal, Jacob took his clan to Bethel (14), where he built an altar. Then, retracing the footsteps of Abraham, Jacob continued down the central mountain route. Near Bethlehem Rachel died while giving birth to Benjamin, Jacob's 12th son. After more than 20 years Jacob was reunited with Isaac at Mamre (Hebron, 15), and when Isaac died, Jacob and Esau buried him in the cave of Machpelah there. Then Esau "went into a land away from his brother Jacob. For their possessions were too great for them to dwell together."

At the birth of her first child, Joseph—Jacob's 11th son—Rachel had declared, "God has taken away my reproach." It was clear that "Israel [Jacob] loved Joseph more than any other of his children, because he was the son of his old age; and he made him a long robe with sleeves." Joseph's robe was luxurious in comparison to the shepherd's simple mantle made of tough goat's hair, soft camel's hair, or occasionally leather. It is little wonder that Joseph's rough-clad brothers resented the 17-year-old favorite of their father.

Jacob was a rich man with large flocks. In the dry season the sheep and goats and cattle had to be herded to water and pasturage—a job that fell to Joseph's brothers. It was a heavy responsibility, for not only did the animals have to be watered daily, but each had to be watched lest it get lost in the rocky hills or become entangled in the thornbushes. And, of course, the flocks had to be protected from jackals, foxes, lions, bears, and other predatory beasts, particularly at night.

Jealousy filled the hearts of Reuben and his brothers as they moved northward with the herds in search of pasturage. Joseph would have an easy time of it in his father's tents at Mamre while they endured the heat of the day, the cold of the night, and a monotonous diet of goat's milk, olives, raisins, and occasionally bread and cheese. And Joseph had been haughty, flaunting his fine robe at them and saying that someday they would bow down before him.

"Go now, see if it is well with your brothers, and with the flock," said Jacob to his son Joseph. So young Joseph left Hebron (16) and went north along the mountain route so clearly defined by the watershed on one side and by deep valleys on the other—past Bethlehem, Jerusalem, and Bethel, places now hallowed by family memories. The way was dangerous, for at a number of places the path skirted steep hillsides with their many boulders and scraggly bushes—excellent hiding places for robbers.

And then at Lebonah the hills opened to the valley floor, which led up to Shechem (17). Joseph sought his brothers in vain in the fields below the twin sentinels of Mount Gerizim and Mount Ebal until a man approached him with news that they had gone north toward Dothan.

To follow them there, Joseph climbed the hills once more and came to the beautiful Plain of Dothan (18). But there his brothers seized him roughly and threw him into an empty cistern.

In the growing season the plain resembles the undulating sea as the wind passes gently through the heavy heads of ripening barley and other grains. But within weeks of harvest it is a flat, empty stretch of land populated only by grazing sheep and goats and the shepherds who watch over them. Occasionally, a caravan passes through the area along a branch of the Way of the Sea, one of the great Near Eastern trade routes.

When Joseph's brothers noticed an Ishmaelite caravan approaching, they saw a chance not only to get rid of Joseph without killing him but also to make a little profit. They brought Joseph out of the pit and sold him into slavery for 20 shekels of silver. They then took Joseph's robe, ripped it, stained it with goat's blood, and laid it before their father at Hebron. Jacob was grief-stricken, for he believed that a wild beast had devoured his son. But Joseph was even then on his way to Egypt (19).

Thirteen years later, at the age of 30, Joseph became Grand Vizier of Egypt—unknown to his sorrowing father, who was back in Beer-sheba. When famine arose in the land, Jacob said to his sons, "I have heard that there is grain in Egypt; go down and buy grain for us there, that we may live, and not die." Joseph gave them grain and, after a series of complicated plots to test them, revealed his identity. When the truth was known, Joseph asked his brothers to bring Jacob to be reunited with him in Egypt. And Jacob and his people came to dwell "in the best of the land; . . . in the land of Goshen." There the Hebrew shepherds grazed their flocks amid peace and plenty and served Pharaoh with gladness. The dark days of bondage were a long way off.

"Behold, your father is ill." Thus was Joseph summoned to the bedside of Jacob. He brought his sons, Manasseh and Ephraim, before his father to receive the deathbed blessing—seeing to it that Manasseh, the firstborn, was in position to have Jacob's right hand laid on him. But Jacob crossed his hands, blessing Joseph's sons but giving Ephraim precedence over his older brother. He then blessed each of his 12 sons, and "when Jacob finished charging his sons, he drew up his feet into the bed, and breathed his last, and was gathered to his people."

At Joseph's command, physicians embalmed Jacob's body, a procedure that took 40 days. After another 70 days of mourning, Joseph returned Jacob's body to Canaan—to Hebron and the cave of Machpelah, where Jacob was buried next to Abraham and Isaac.

Joseph lived on in Egypt, where the descendants of Jacob "multiplied and grew exceedingly strong." When he died, his body too was embalmed and laid in a coffin. Generations later, according to tradition, Joseph's bones were taken along in the Exodus from Egypt and buried at Shechem since Hebron was then in enemy hands.

62

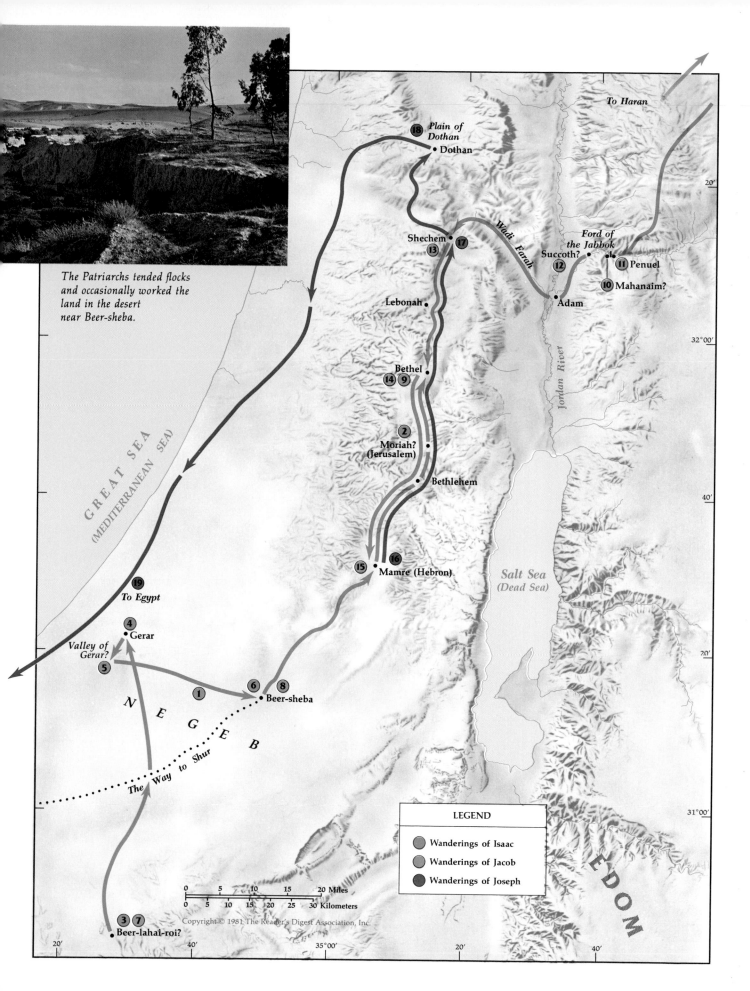

The Patriarchs tended flocks
and occasionally worked the
land in the desert
near Beer-sheba.

To Haran

⑱ Plain of
Dothan
• Dothan

Wadi Farah

Shechem ⑬ ⑰

Ford of
the Jabbok
Succoth? ⑫ ⑪ Penuel
⑩ Mahanaim?

Lebonah •

Adam •

Jordan River

Bethel
⑭ ⑨ •

②

Moriah? •
(Jerusalem)

Bethlehem •

GREAT SEA
(MEDITERRANEAN SEA)

Salt Sea
(Dead Sea)

⑮ ⑯
• Mamre (Hebron)

⑲
To Egypt

④
• Gerar

Valley of
Gerar?
⑤

N E G E B

① ⑥ ⑧
• Beer-sheba

The Way to Shur

EDOM

LEGEND

⭘ Wanderings of Isaac

⭘ Wanderings of Jacob

⭘ Wanderings of Joseph

0   5   10   15   20 Miles

0 5 10 15 20 25 30 Kilometers

Copyright © 1981 The Reader's Digest Association, Inc.

③ ⑦
• Beer-lahai-roi?

Ramses II: Pharaoh of the Exodus?

It is likely that at the time the Hebrews went forth from Egypt in the Exodus the land was ruled by the powerful Ramses II, third king of Egypt's 19th Dynasty. Ramses' long reign (c. 1290–1224 B.C.) is one of the most celebrated in ancient Egypt's history, mainly because he was an indefatigable builder with a grand plan. Ramses was responsible for nearly half of Egypt's temples that have survived, many of them created to glorify his achievements.

In the early part of his reign, Ramses was very much the warrior-king, vigorously continuing the efforts of his father, Seti I, to reclaim and hold Egypt's Asiatic empire.

(The dimensions of that empire appear on the map below.) The primary threat to the Pharaoh's imperial hegemony came from the Hittites to the north. Syria was Ramses' battleground with this threatening people, and about 1286 B.C. the two forces came face to face at Kadesh. Ramses boasted that he won the combat virtually singlehanded, although there is evidence that the battle was inconclusive. In any event, nearly two decades later he made a lasting peace with the Hittites, and to seal the bargain married the daughter of the Hittite king. In the meantime he had also waged a successful campaign against rebellious towns in Canaan. The hostilities ended, Ramses devoted the rest of his life to building projects memorializing his reign in stone.

Pharaoh Seti I initiated the campaign to regain Egypt's lost glories, a policy his son, Ramses II, continued. Seti is pictured above in a wall relief at a temple in Karnak, driving his war chariot over the bodies of his defeated enemies. Below is a cartouche (an oval frame enclosing a royal name in hieroglyphs) of Pharaoh Ramses II, from a temple at Abydos.

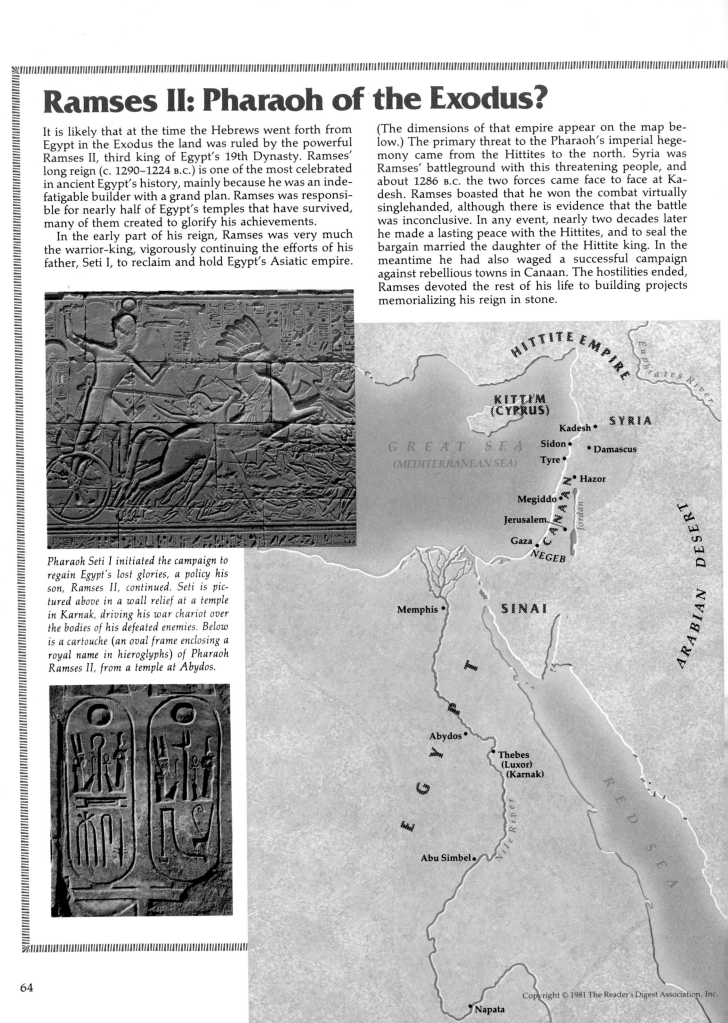

64

Perhaps the most remarkable of Ramses II's building projects are the temples at Abu Simbel, carved into the sandstone cliffs overlooking the Nile. At left is the exterior of the larger of the two temples, its entrance guarded by colossal statues of Ramses II, each 67 feet high. Ramses is shown (above) on an interior wall, smiting a foe. In a monumental engineering project, completed in 1966, the huge temples were cut away from the rock and moved to higher ground to save them from the rising waters of the Nile's new Aswan High Dam.

This painting from a tomb at Thebes shows in detail captive workmen manufacturing bricks, a task forced on the Hebrews by Egypt's Pharaohs. At left, water is drawn from a pool. Clay is kneaded (center) with short hoes and poured into brick molds (top right) under the watchful eye of a seated overseer. The bricks are then stacked in the sun to dry and harden (top center) before they can be used.

The Exodus

"Now there arose a new king over Egypt, who did not know Joseph." Thus Exodus, compressing some 400 years of Egyptian history into a single sentence, describes a portentous event in the life of the Hebrews. About 1750 B.C. the Hyksos, a foreign people, infiltrated Egypt, established themselves in the Delta, and eventually ruled the entire land for more than a century. Under them Joseph had risen to the influential post of Grand Vizier to the Pharaoh. However, with the expulsion of the Hyksos about 1550 B.C. and the return to native rule, the royal favor Jacob's descendants had enjoyed came to an end. During Egypt's 18th Dynasty the Hebrews were little more than despised pastoralists settled among other aliens, "wretched Asiatics" and "sand dwellers" as the Egyptians scornfully called nomads who moved in and out of the Nile Delta.

With the coming of the kings of the 19th Dynasty, about 1306 B.C., the Egyptians began to build great treasure cities—Pithom and Raamses—near the Hebrew settlements in the eastern Delta, the land of Goshen (1). The Hebrews were pressed into labor gangs and forced to serve as fieldhands and makers of brick and mortar for the Pharaoh's building program. Bondage was unspeakably harsh. Yet the powerless Hebrews managed to escape the grip of the most powerful ruler on earth, probably early in the reign of Ramses II (c. 1290–1224 B.C.). Led by the visionary Moses, they began their journey out of Egypt and toward the Promised Land.

Exodus tells us that there were "about 600,000 men on foot, besides women and children" in the caravan. This would mean a total of some 2½ million people, and perhaps even more. Such a large number is diffi-

"Stretch out your hand over the sea, that the water may come back upon the Egyptians . . ." Thus the Lord spoke to Moses—a famous scene depicted in an early-14th-century manuscript.

cult to accept. Where would that many people have obtained food and water to sustain them and their flocks during their wanderings through a desolate land? It is probable that this figure actually represents the population of the Hebrew kingdoms in the 10th century B.C. Whatever their actual number at the time of the Exodus, the Hebrews left Egypt. But where did they go? The route of the Exodus is not known for certain and probably never will be.

It is likely that a number of Hebrew groups left Egypt by different routes at different times and that their adventures were later combined into a single biblical narrative. This has given rise to various theories about the route of the Exodus. Yet on one thing most scholars now agree: after the Hebrews left Succoth (2), they crossed the Sea of Reeds and not, as it appears in the English text of Exodus, the "Red Sea." The confusion apparently arose when the Hebrew term *Yam Suph*, meaning

"Sea of Reeds," was incorrectly translated as "Red Sea."

What scholars do not agree on is the location of the Sea of Reeds. According to some, it was situated in the area of Lake Timsah (3), north of the Bitter Lakes. Others believe it to be the freshwater swamps (4) east of Raamses, where papyrus reeds grow, hence giving rise to the ancient Egyptian name for the area, Papyrus Marsh. Still others identify it with the lake the Greeks called Sirbonis (5), another body of water with reeds. In such marshy areas pursuing Egyptian chariots might easily have met the disaster so vividly described in Exodus.

There is further disagreement among scholars as to the subsequent route taken by the Hebrews in crossing the Sinai peninsula, a triangular land mass that is about 230 miles long and, at its northern end, 150 miles wide. Four possibilities have been suggested.

After leaving Succoth, Exodus tells us, the Hebrews moved toward the wilderness but then turned back and encamped "in front of Pi-ha-hiroth, between Migdol and the sea, in front of Baal-zephon . . ." Scholars who identify Lake Sirbonis as the marshy Sea of Reeds think that the Hebrews made good their escape along the narrow strand of sand (6) between the lake and the Great Sea. Migdol was considered the northernmost town in Egypt, as the book of Ezekiel twice indicates, and if classical Mons Casius is Baal-zephon ("Lord of the North") it fits Exodus' description of being "by the sea." Other sites mentioned in the biblical narrative, however, are difficult to place along this route. It was also an inhospitable way, with little drinking water and much treacherous quicksand. Furthermore, the northern route would eventually have taken the Hebrews along the so-called Way of the Land of the Philistines (although the Philistines did not settle there until later). And Exodus says: "When Pharaoh let the people go, God did not lead them by way of the land of the Philistines, although that was near."

A second possible route of the Exodus was the Way to Shur (7). It led eastward from Succoth and Pithom directly across the desert and on to Beer-sheba and Hebron but bypassed Kadesh-barnea, which was the focus of the Hebrews' later desert wanderings. If this route was taken, then either Jebel Yeleq, a massive yellowish mountain rising 3,566 feet above sea level, or the 2,920-foot-high Jebel Helal might be the traditional Mount Sinai. The Way to Shur was one of the most traveled caravan routes between Egypt and Canaan, but it was avoided by armies because of its lack of sufficient water—the same reason it might have been shunned by the Hebrews.

A third alternative that has been suggested for the He-

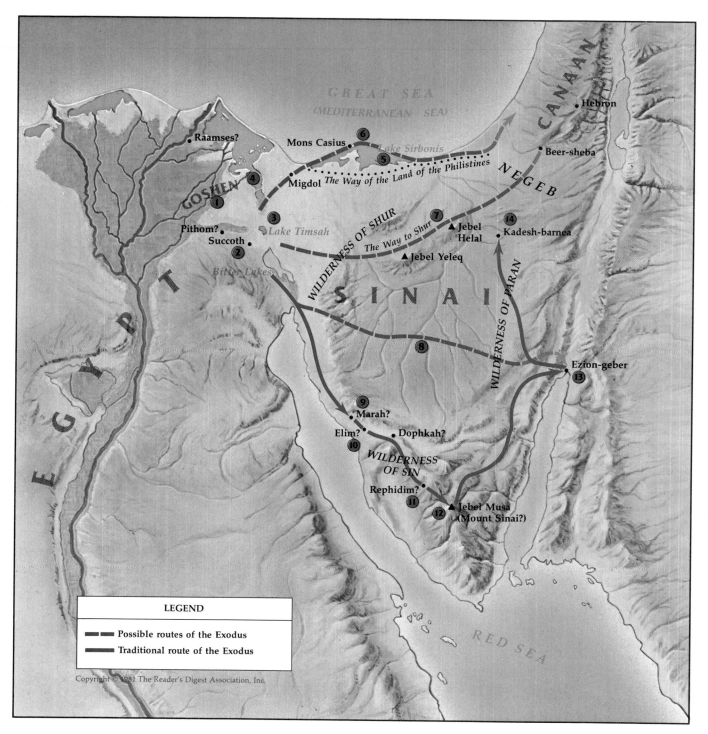

LEGEND

- - - Possible routes of the Exodus
─── Traditional route of the Exodus

Copyright © 1981 The Reader's Digest Association, Inc.

brews' escape was the Arabian trade route (8) across the middle of the Sinai toward Ezion-geber. Egyptian and Arabian merchants carried their goods over this harsh, virtually waterless route. While perhaps a useful road for those seeking profit, it was hardly suitable for large numbers of nomads moving slowly as a group.

The traditional route of the Exodus, favored by many scholars, goes south-southeast along the way that leads to the old Egyptian turquoise and copper mines in western Sinai. After making their getaway by the Sea of Reeds, the Hebrews traveled south through the Wilderness of Shur. In three days they came to the oasis of

Marah (9), which means "bitter"—and indeed the water there proved unfit for drinking. According to Exodus, Moses made the water sweet, and the people and the flocks quenched their thirst. They went farther south to Elim (10), where they camped among abundant springs and shady groves before entering the Wilderness of Sin.

As they plunged ever deeper into the arid, mountainous Sinai, the land became more desolate and barren. Fantastic rock formations rose everywhere above narrow, twisting valleys. The steep mountains, first red and brown sandstone and then bronze-red granite, terrifying yet beautiful in the heat of the day, stood silent watch as

The Exodus (continued)

the straggling band of men, women, and children made its way across the boulder-strewn sand. Occasional stands of scrub brush, and here and there a tamarisk tree or an acacia, marked the landscape. For the most part, water was scarce. Soon, however, food began to run out, and the disgruntled people remembered the lush fields of Egypt, once so hateful to them but now the object of bitter longing. Even the harsh days of bondage looked good compared with their miserable present and uncertain future. Beyond the turquoise mines at Dophkah (Serabit el-Khadim), at Rephidim (11), the fierce Amalekites—the scourge of the desert—attacked the Israelites. Moses appointed a younger man to be warrior chieftain, and Joshua—mentioned for the first time in the Bible—succeeded in driving off these raiders.

Safe again, the people of Israel moved slowly into the uplands of southern Sinai, where they came to Mount Sinai, traditionally identified with Jebel Musa (12), or "Mountain of Moses." Though not the highest mountain in the area, Jebel Musa's great peaks, rising to 7,500 feet, are nonetheless impressive. A perennial natural water source and fair pasturage nourished the people and their beasts, and the mountain walls offered protection against further attacks. In that stark setting, amid the grandeur of soaring granite mountains, now occurred the event that constituted Israel as the people of God. According to Exodus, it was there that the Lord entered into an everlasting covenant with his people, revealing to Moses the divine commandments and laws.

The association of Mount Sinai with Jebel Musa came about only in the 4th century A.D., when the Emperor Constantine's mother, Saint Helena, is said to have built a chapel and tower at the foot of the mountain to commemorate the place where Moses saw the Burning Bush. Two centuries later Emperor Justinian (527–565) recognized Jebel Musa as a holy place by building a fortress monastery to protect the monks of his new church dedicated to the Virgin Mary. It was rededicated to Saint Catherine about the 10th century, when the relics of the martyred saint were brought to the church. The Koran, too, identifies Mount Sinai with Jebel Musa. Whether Muhammad was relating an independent tradition, was influenced by Justinian's claim, or depended on Jewish legends now lost to history is not certain. Further, 1 Kings 19 tells of the prophet Elijah's pilgrimage to a holy mountain far south of Beer-sheba—perhaps Jebel Musa.

In the spring—one year after the Hebrews fled from Egypt—they set out from Mount Sinai and went into the Wilderness of Paran, which gives way to the Negeb.

By whichever route they came, the Hebrews eventually encamped in the hills and valleys around the oasis of Kadesh-barnea. Possibly, as stated in Numbers 33:35, they wandered as far east as Ezion-geber (13). Although Deuteronomy 1:2 says that it takes 11 days to go from the holy mount to Kadesh-barnea (14), a distance of about 150 miles, surely this would refer to pilgrims traveling unencumbered. Nomadic families following their flocks would have moved infinitely slower. The crossing of the Sinai ended, the Hebrews were nearly within sight of Canaan. There, on the threshold of the Promised Land, Moses sent 12 spies into Canaan.

Life in the Desert

As the Hebrews, led by Moses, journeyed through the barren valleys, spectacular limestone hills, and the multi-colored granite mountains of the Sinai wilderness, the way of life they adopted was probably similar to that of the Bedouins who inhabit the region today.

Said to be descendants of the outcast Ishmael, the Bedouins have adhered to an unchanging life-style for centuries. Living in tents made of camel's hair, herding their flocks, hunting game, and occasionally raiding neighboring tribes, these nomads do not wander aimlessly but travel within clearly defined territories. They may stay days, weeks, or a season in one area before moving on in search of new pasturelands. The Bedouins' diet is meager by Western standards. They gather what they can from the land—dates, figs, and water from oases—and supplement this with camel's milk and flour or roasted grain. Meat is reserved for special occasions such as feasts. However, according to desert tradition, they share whatever they have, for to refuse hospitality to a stranger in the harsh, trackless desert is an offense against their god, Allah.

Having come to terms with the desert and learned to read its signs, a Bedouin can feel a sandstorm brewing in the air, locate an oasis, and trace his way through the seemingly featureless landscape with astonishing accuracy.

Amid the wastelands and rocky mountains of the Sinai peninsula, verdant oases offer not only relief but sustenance to travelers. Stately date palms, evergreen acacias, flowering tamarisks, and other forms of plant life crowd around these sparkling water sources.

Jebel Musa—"Mountain of Moses"—located in the southern end of the Sinai peninsula, is the traditional Mount Sinai where Moses received the Ten Commandments from the Lord. Its red granite peak in the foreground, capped with a chapel, reaches an impressive height of 7,500 feet.

What wealth the Bedouins possess is carried with them; for safekeeping, gold coins are sewn onto a woman's veil (above). Long, flowing robes and head garments not only protect the Bedouins from the scorching desert sun but absorb perspiration to regulate body heat.

The camel—the ship of the desert—provides the Bedouin with many necessities of life. Besides serving as an indispensable means of transportation, it is a source of food and material for clothing and shelter. Even camel dung is used, as fuel for fires.

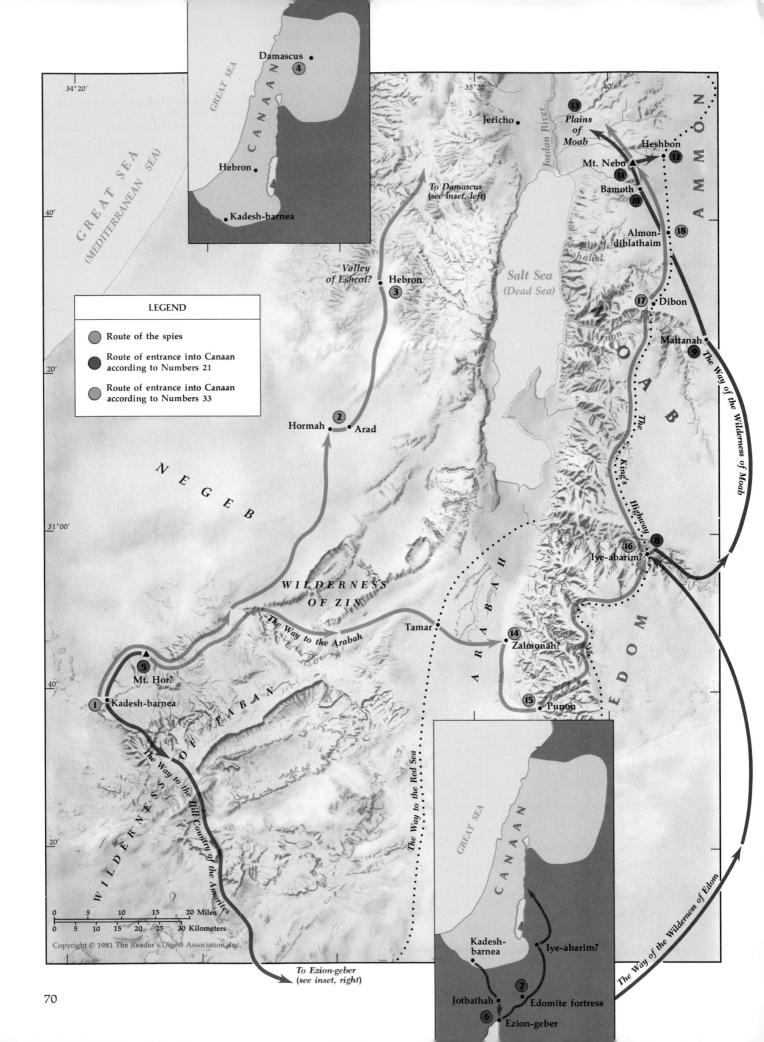

LEGEND

Route of the spies

Route of entrance into Canaan according to Numbers 21

Route of entrance into Canaan according to Numbers 33

GREAT SEA (MEDITERRANEAN SEA)

Damascus ④

CANAAN

Hebron

Kadesh-barnea

To Damascus (see inset, left)

Valley of Eshcol? Hebron ③

Jericho

Jordan River

Plains of Moab ⑬

Mt. Nebo ▲ ⑪

Heshbon ⑫

Bamoth ⑩

AMMON

Almond-diblathaim ⑱

Nahaliel

Salt Sea (Dead Sea)

Dibon ⑰

M O A B

Arnon

Mattanah ⑨

The Way of the Wilderness of Moab

Hormah ● Arad ②

The King's Highway

N E G E B

WILDERNESS OF ZIN

The Way to the Arabah

Tamar

A R A B A H

Zalmonah? ⑭

Iye-abarim? ⑯ ⑧

E D O M

Mt. Hor? ▲ ⑤

Kadesh-barnea ①

WILDERNESS OF PARAN

The Way to the Hill Country of the Amorites

Punon ● ⑮

The Way to the Red Sea

The Way of the Wilderness of Edom

0 5 10 15 20 Miles
0 5 10 15 20 25 30 Kilometers

Copyright © 1981 The Reader's Digest Association, Inc.

To Ezion-geber (see inset, right)

GREAT SEA

CANAAN

Kadesh-barnea

Iye-abarim?

⑦

Jotbathah

Edomite fortress

⑥ Ezion-geber

70

Wanderings of the Hebrews

"Go up into the Negeb yonder, and go up into the hill country, and see what the land is, and whether the people who dwell in it are strong or weak . . ." With these words Moses sent Joshua of Ephraim, Caleb of Judah, and one man from each of the other 10 tribes on a spy mission into the land of Canaan. Among other things, they were to bring back word of a likely invasion route.

To the northwest lay the open coastal routes shunned by pastoral nomads such as the Hebrews. To the east is some of the most forbidding and desolate land in the Negeb. The shortest and easiest route for Moses' spies—and the one used throughout the centuries by desert peoples—led northeast from Kadesh-barnea (1) toward Hormah and Arad (2) and then into the highlands around Hebron (3). This major route was well watered, an open road running up into what appeared to be the virtually defenseless gentle southern slopes of the hill country.

Moses' spies did not stop at Hebron but went to the northern limit of Canaan beyond Damascus (4, on inset at top), and as far north as "Rehob, near the entrance of Hamath." The reconnaissance thus covered the full extent of the Promised Land and more. The natural target of any invasion from the south, however, was the high tableland that rises to over 3,300 feet just north of Hebron. But the Hebrews saw there the great walls of fortified cities and brought back terrifying tales of the descendants of Anak, a tall people beside whom the spies "seemed to ourselves like grasshoppers." Nonetheless, the lure of the land was irresistible.

It was late summer when the spies set off, the time of ripening of pomegranates, figs, and grapes. From the Valley of Eshcol near Hebron they cut a single cluster of grapes so heavy it had to be carried on a pole between two men. Even today this area is famous for the extraordinary grapes that grow on heaped stones because trellises cannot bear the weight of the fruit clusters. The pastoralist might grow an occasional crop of grain, but fruit was a delicacy to people from the desert and its cultivation a symbol of the settled life. Little wonder the spies said that the land they had seen "flows with milk and honey."

Caleb and Joshua urged immediate invasion, but the people were dissuaded by the fear of the other spies, lamenting that they would rather have died in Egypt or in the wilderness. And the Lord granted them their wish, telling Moses that his people would wander 40 years in the wilderness: a year for every day the spies had spent in Canaan. Therefore, no one who was over 20 at the time—save Caleb and Joshua—would enter the Promised Land. Then, despite Moses' warning that the "Lord is not among you," a determined group set out to invade the hill country. The result was defeat and disaster as the Amalekites and Canaanites stopped the Hebrews before Arad and pursued them back into the desert beyond Hormah—though later accounts turn this rout into a Hebrew victory.

After the people of the hill country chased the invaders "as bees do," the Hebrews pitched their tents in the northern Sinai. Archaeological surveys show that, while this area was occupied both earlier and later, there were few if any permanent settlements there in the 13th century B.C., the time of Moses—a situation that favored the Hebrews. The area around Kadesh-barnea is capable of supporting a large group of nomads over a long time. There are a number of strong springs nestled beneath cliffs, and the wide, shallow wadis can be dammed to trap winter rains for the growing of modest crops. Even after the spectacular spring carpet of grass and flowers has yielded to the tans and browns of summer, the watercourses retain sufficient amounts of underground moisture in shallow wells to quench the endless thirst of man and beast.

It was at Kadesh-barnea that Miriam, the sister of Moses and Aaron, died and was buried. And it was there too, perhaps, that Moses struck the rock with his rod to provide water—but failed to credit the Lord with the miracle and for this was later denied entrance into the Promised Land. From Kadesh-barnea, the multitude moved to biblical Mount Hor (5), possibly Jebel Madurah, along the route earlier taken by the spies. There Aaron died.

Deterred by the rout at Arad from making another thrust north, perhaps prevented by the arrival of the Philistines along the coast from invading Canaan from the west, the Hebrews took the only route left to them: a penetration of the heartland of Canaan from the east. But how did they get from Mount Hor to their striking point on the Plains of Moab north of the Salt Sea? There are few more difficult or disputed questions in biblical geography than this. Two different routes are given in Numbers, and the story is repeated with some variations in Deuteronomy.

Numbers 20–21 (possibly echoed in Deuteronomy 2) makes it clear that the Edomites and Moabites refused to allow Moses and his people to pass through their

Towering cliffs, some nearly 2,000 feet high, outline the northern shore of the Gulf of Aqabah, once dominated by the settlement of Ezion-geber. Coral reefs, sudden squalls, and numerous islands made the waterway treacherous for the small, unwieldy ships of ancient times.

The vine is used in biblical literature as the symbol of the Hebrews' conquest of the Promised Land. Psalms 80:8 reads, "Thou didst bring a vine out of Egypt; thou didst drive out the nations and plant it."

Rolling green hills, covered with vineyards and orchards, constitute one of the three major geographical areas of Israel. A land of contrasts, the fertile hills shelter valleys such as the one shown at right and can abruptly give way to treeless plains or to barren desert.

lands—and that they had the power to back up their refusal. As a result, the Hebrews were forced to move through the terrible Wilderness of Paran, possibly as far south as Ezion-geber (6, on the lower inset map). But it would seem from Numbers 33 that the Hebrews moved directly east from Mount Hor to Zalmonah (14). This would have taken them along the Way to the Arabah, a major trade route with spectacular views. The problem of the two routes in Numbers is further complicated because some of the sites mentioned cannot be identified.

Very likely these are independent traditions summarizing the experiences of different groups at different times; indeed, we know that the people of Israel set out "by stages." Archaeological surveys suggest that the kingdoms of Edom and Moab came into being east and southeast of the Salt Sea late in the 13th century B.C. Numbers 33, which depicts the people of Edom and Moab as unable to prevent large clans of nomadic shep-

herds from crossing their land with devouring flocks, fits an earlier historical situation than Numbers 20–21, where the Hebrews have to avoid established kingdoms there. Some scholars find further evidence in the Conquest Narrative (Joshua and Judges), written after the people entered Canaan, that the wilderness wanderings and the invasion of Canaan involved more than one group of people. They have suggested that biblical writers later blended several traditions into a single story of the people of Israel. In so doing they sought to simplify a complicated historical and geographical process.

Whatever route the Hebrews followed, the passage from Kadesh-barnea to the borders of Moab took 38 years, a sojourn spent in seasonal encampments near oases and wells or watercourses where these migrants grew crops while tending their flocks. When the short growing season ended, they took their animals farther afield in search of water and food, always working together as

The Promised Land

To the Hebrews, who spent 40 years in the harsh wilderness of the Sinai, Canaan was a land "flowing with milk and honey"—the long-sought Promised Land. "Honey" (most likely date syrup) and "milk" express the two forms of agricultural economy in Canaan—cultivation of the soil and the grazing of livestock. A pastoral people, the Hebrews were already experienced in the care and tending of flocks. Extensive agriculture and the growing of fruits, however, represented luxuries to these pastoralists, who had long lived on a simple diet, gleaning what they could from the desert and the occasional oases. Indeed, after investigating the land, the spies sent by Moses returned triumphantly with a cluster of grapes so large "they carried it on a pole between two of them."

Deuteronomy 8:7–8 tells us that Canaan was "a good land, a land of brooks of water, of fountains and springs, flowing forth in valleys and hills, a land of wheat and barley, of vines and fig trees and pomegranates, a land of olive trees and honey." Of the seven products listed above, grapes, olives, and grain were basic to Canaan's economy. Grapes were eaten fresh, dried for raisins, or made into wine. The olive, too, was eaten fresh, but its primary value was as a source of oil. Grains such as wheat and barley formed a staple of the diet.

The Hebrews were not the first to find Canaan an inviting land. In the 20th century B.C. the Egyptian fugitive Sinuhe had taken refuge in Canaan, describing the land enthusiastically: "It was a good land . . . Figs were in it, and grapes. It had more wine than water. Plentiful was its honey, abundant its olives. Every [kind of] fruit

The red, juicy pulp of the pomegranate was made into drinks, while juice from its rind provided a fine leather dye.

was on its trees. Barley was there, and emmer [wheat]. There was no limit to any [kind of] cattle."

However, compared with the lush Nile Delta and much of the Tigris and Euphrates river valleys, Canaan had but sparse vegetation. In Deuteronomy 11:10–11, the Hebrews are warned that the land would not be like Egypt, "where you sowed your seed and watered it with your feet, like a garden of vegetables"; rather it would be a land that "drinks water by the rain from heaven." Canaan was a land limited to hills and valleys that were dependent on unpredictable rainfall—not at all like the great plains of Egypt and Mesopotamia where the lands were well watered by its mighty rivers and irrigation systems. It would be a land of toil, thus echoing the words of the Lord in Genesis 3:19, "In the sweat of your face you shall eat bread."

Since farming was so much a part of the ancient Hebrews' life, it is no wonder that agriculture became entwined in their religion. Throughout the Bible religious ideals are frequently presented in agricultural terminology. In Amos 9:15, for example, the restoration of Israel is portrayed as follows: "I will plant them upon their land, and they shall never again be plucked up out of the land which I have given them." Some of the most familiar agricultural metaphors can be found in the New Testament parables of Jesus, as in Mark 4:31–32, comparing the kingdom of God to a grain of mustard seed, "the smallest of all the seeds on earth; yet when it is sown it grows up and becomes the greatest of all shrubs, and puts forth large branches, so that the birds of the air can make nests in its shade."

a family, a clan, and a tribe. After a season, a year, or a few years they would move on.

"From Mount Hor they set out by the way to the Red Sea, to go around the land of Edom," it is written in Numbers 21:4. The Way to the Red Sea ran down the entire western length of the Arabah, the 110-mile-long valley stretching south from the Salt Sea to the Gulf of Aqabah and bounded by the steep limestone scarps of the southern Negeb on the west and the wall of sandstone mountains of Edom on the east. In midvalley it is strewn with rocks lying on a thin crust of gravel. The upper reaches of the watercourses that scar the hills are rough and full of boulders, but their lower margins form alluvial fans of sand mixed with loess and clay marked by scattered vegetation starkly punctuating the barren landscape. The Arabah narrows near midpoint to an average width of about four miles. Rainfall is less than one inch a year, and the watercourses are short and often

empty year to year. Expanses of sand frequently give way to salt flats. Only south of the oasis at Jotbathah do the sand dunes alternate with sediments of sand and loess, where enough vegetation can grow to support flocks—at least during the rainy season.

Would the Hebrews have taken the Way to the Arabah from Kadesh-barnea to Tamar and then turned south along the entire length of the Way to the Red Sea? It is doubtful that their extensive flocks could have survived any length of time in such an arid landscape. More likely, they followed the Way to the Hill Country of the Amorites, which went from Kadesh-barnea across the Wilderness of Paran to Ezion-geber. Even today a dirt track traces this ancient route. While it is hardly an easy path, it is smoother than many others in Sinai, since it avoids both the mountains to the northeast and the deep ravines and heavily eroded valleys that mark the landscape to the southwest. As it draws within 30 miles of

Wanderings of the Hebrews (continued)

the Gulf of Aqabah, it begins to rise from 1,800 feet to more than 3,000 feet. A track turns east, however, avoiding the high ground and joining the Way to the Red Sea north of Jotbathah. It would have been possible for the Hebrews to reach Ezion-geber by these broad paths that cut through the wilderness.

Proceeding north from Ezion-geber and following the oases and wells along the King's Highway, the Hebrews could travel only about 50 miles before coming to a wall of mountains rising 4,600 to 5,600 feet. Archaeological surveys indicate that this southern border of the Edomite heartland was heavily fortified at the time. A strong Edomite fortress (7, on lower inset) guarded the steep pass through which the King's Highway came as it ascended to the Edomite plateau. A few miles northeast another tumble of walls is silent witness today to Edomite efforts to prevent people from outflanking the main fortress and entering through another pass. A line of fortresses extending north kept unwanted groups along the desert fringes as they bypassed Edom along the Way of the Wilderness of Edom. For the Hebrews this meant a further detour east, adding to their already long journey.

According to this first itinerary, the Hebrews, after skirting Edom, turned west down the valley of the Zered, encamping first at Oboth (site unknown) and then at Iye-abarim (8). This would have taken them back to the King's Highway within Moab. But this attempt to enter Moab apparently failed and the Hebrews once again turned back to the desert, perhaps moving along the Way of the Wilderness of Moab. This eventually brought them to the Arnon, a river coursing down a spectacular fault canyon $2\frac{1}{2}$ miles wide. The Lord provided water at Beer ("well," site unknown) as the Hebrews turned northwest toward their destination, the Plains of Moab. At Mattanah (9) they entered the land of Sihon, king of the Amorites. After crossing the shallow upper reaches of the Nahaliel, they proceeded to Bamoth (10) and the heights of Pisgah, among which rises Mount Nebo (11).

Sihon's refusal to allow Israel to pass through his lands proved disastrous to him and his Amorite and Ammonite subjects, for the Hebrews slew him in battle and took his capital of Heshbon (12) and his lands north of it. Thus the tribes of Reuben and Gad came into possession of much of the Transjordan region as the Hebrews encamped at last on the Plains of Moab (13), east of the Jordan and opposite Jericho.

"And they set out from Mount Hor," says Numbers 33:41, "and encamped at Zalmonah." Zalmonah (14) is on the eastern side of the Arabah—about 60 miles from

From the top of Mount Nebo southeast of the Plains of Moab, Moses looked across the Jordan toward Canaan. But the aged prophet was not allowed to join his people as they entered.

Mount Hor across some of the most rugged, desolate, and taxing ground in the entire land. This itinerary suggests that the Hebrews followed the Way to the Arabah, which runs along a plateau skirting the northern edge of the highest land in the Wilderness of Paran. To the southwest the jagged peaks rise 3,200 feet above sea level before the land falls off into the Arabah. Sparse vegetation marked numerous watercourses, but as the Hebrews entered ever more deeply into the Wilderness of Zin the effects of its drainage of the eastern slopes of the Negeb became more pronounced and food and water for the flocks more abundant. To their left, on the northern edge of the Wilderness of Zin, the gentle incline created spurs running down into the valley. But to their right, on the south, the harder rock presented a badlands appearance as steep cliffs dropped abruptly to the valley floor and many forbidding canyons cut into the cliff face.

Only briefly in winter is it possible even for nomadic shepherds to exist on these barren hills south of the Wilderness of Zin, and we can be almost certain that the Hebrews were not tempted to linger here. Instead, they came to the depths of the hot, arid Arabah, probably near Tamar, an oasis and route junction some 900 feet below sea level. Passing the deeply incised wadis that point toward the great body of salt water to the north, they crossed the valley at the most convenient place and came to Zalmonah (14) on the eastern side of the rift valley. Now they turned south under the Transjordan heights and entered the hills along the way that led to the broad bay of the valley at Punon (15).

From Punon the Hebrews began to climb those eroded and exceedingly steep ways that brought them onto the broad eastern plateau, 3,200 to 3,600 feet above sea level, and to the King's Highway, one of the most famous caravan routes in antiquity. Thus they reached Iye-abarim (16), at the ford of the Zered, inside Moab's border with Edom. Continuing north along the King's Highway, the Hebrews crossed the Arnon and encamped at Dibon (17), the most important Moabite town in the region, later assigned to the tribe of Gad. Beyond, at Almon-diblathaim (18), a route branched off of the King's Highway and ran northwest through increasingly populated hill areas down to the Plains of Moab across from Jericho.

Having taken his people to Canaan's borders, Moses ascended Mount Nebo to be offered a panoramic view of the land promised to the Patriarchs. His mission complete, and prevented from entering the Promised Land, Moses died and was buried in an unknown spot. And Israel, on the eve of the long-anticipated invasion, "wept for Moses in the plains of Moab thirty days."

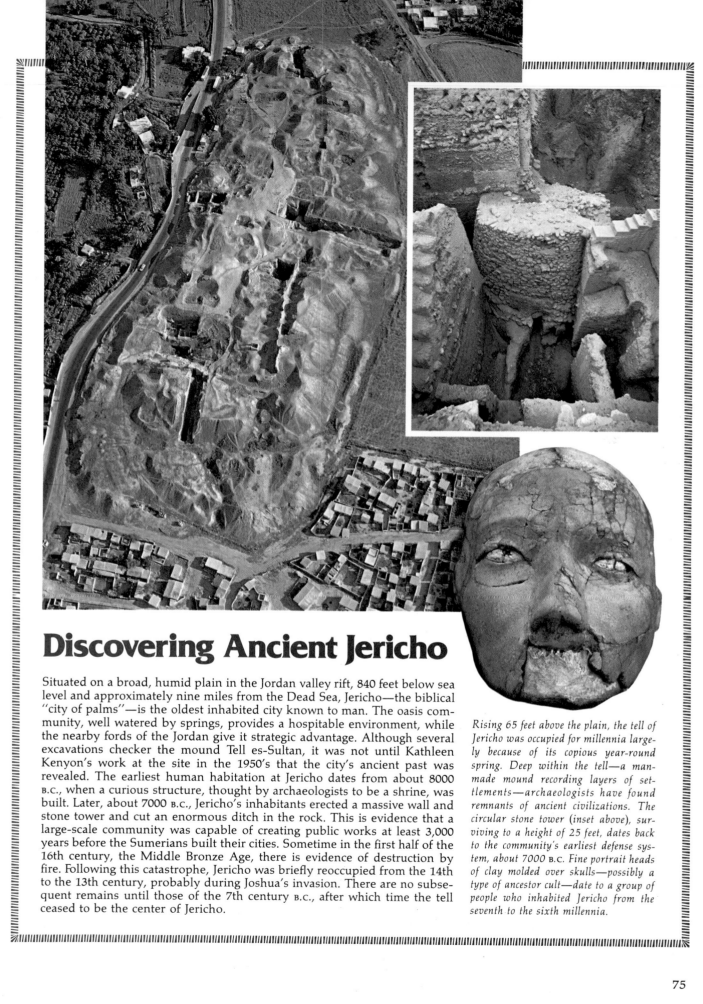

Discovering Ancient Jericho

Situated on a broad, humid plain in the Jordan valley rift, 840 feet below sea level and approximately nine miles from the Dead Sea, Jericho—the biblical "city of palms"—is the oldest inhabited city known to man. The oasis community, well watered by springs, provides a hospitable environment, while the nearby fords of the Jordan give it strategic advantage. Although several excavations checker the mound Tell es-Sultan, it was not until Kathleen Kenyon's work at the site in the 1950's that the city's ancient past was revealed. The earliest human habitation at Jericho dates from about 8000 B.C., when a curious structure, thought by archaeologists to be a shrine, was built. Later, about 7000 B.C., Jericho's inhabitants erected a massive wall and stone tower and cut an enormous ditch in the rock. This is evidence that a large-scale community was capable of creating public works at least 3,000 years before the Sumerians built their cities. Sometime in the first half of the 16th century, the Middle Bronze Age, there is evidence of destruction by fire. Following this catastrophe, Jericho was briefly reoccupied from the 14th to the 13th century, probably during Joshua's invasion. There are no subsequent remains until those of the 7th century B.C., after which time the tell ceased to be the center of Jericho.

Rising 65 feet above the plain, the tell of Jericho was occupied for millennia largely because of its copious year-round spring. Deep within the tell—a man-made mound recording layers of settlements—archaeologists have found remnants of ancient civilizations. The circular stone tower (inset above), surviving to a height of 25 feet, dates back to the community's earliest defense system, about 7000 B.C. Fine portrait heads of clay molded over skulls—possibly a type of ancestor cult—date to a group of people who inhabited Jericho from the seventh to the sixth millennia.

Invasion and Conquest of Canaan

Encamped at Abel-shittim (1) on the Plains of Moab and secure in their grip on much of Ammon and Gilead, the Hebrews prepared to invade the Promised Land.

What most likely were the experiences of various invading groups that spanned years—even centuries—are compressed into a single biblical epic found in the books of Joshua and Judges. According to this unified Conquest Narrative, Joshua first sent two spies across the Jordan River to gather intelligence. Nearly five miles from the river, in the hot, dusty valley 840 feet below sea level, lay Jericho (2). This oasis city and the hills behind it were the spies' objectives. Their report on the low morale of the people about to be attacked was encouraging to the Hebrews, who moved out early in the morning to cross the shallow, muddy Jordan.

It was spring, a time when surging waters of the river in flood can undermine the steep marl cliffs at Adam, 18 miles to the north. Twice within the 20th century the collapse of these cliffs has blocked the river there—once for more than 21 hours—and the riverbed farther south has dried up. When Joshua launched his invasion, such a providential stoppage of waters at Adam allowed the Hebrews to cross the Jordan on dry ground.

Once safely across, the Hebrews gathered at Gilgal (3), which Joshua made his base for extending his authority over the immediate region and for his impending thrust into the central highlands. At Gilgal, 12 stones (one for each of the tribes)—taken from the dry Jordan riverbed during the crossing—were erected as a memorial to the miraculous passage. Here, too, all males born during the years of wandering were brought into the covenant with the Lord by circumcision as they prepared for holy war.

Joshua's siege and capture of Jericho is one of the best-known battles of antiquity. On six successive days

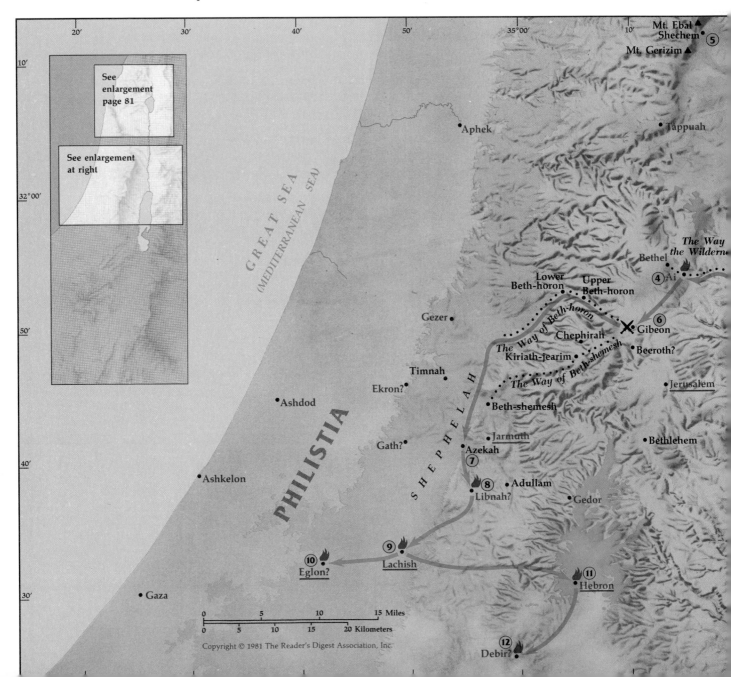

the Hebrews marched once around the walled city. And on the seventh day, after making seven circuits of the city, seven priests blew their seven trumpets of rams' horns, the people shouted, and the wall collapsed. Entering the city, the Hebrews massacred the inhabitants and seized their treasure for "the house of the Lord."

Extensive archaeological work at Jericho in the 1950's revealed no walled city in the 13th century, the time of Joshua's invasion. At best there was a minor settlement with few or no fortifications to protect it. Jericho's life as a walled city came to an end 300 years earlier as a result of violent destruction, perhaps the work of prior invaders. But whatever kind or size of settlement at Jericho in the time of Joshua, it would have been taken by the Hebrews in order to secure the water sources in the valley floor north of the Salt Sea before they began probing the routes into the central highlands.

There are three routes to the interior from the Jericho area. All follow ridges high above the spectacular, deep gorges that are characteristic of this desolate wilderness,

which rises from the depths of the Jordan valley to 2,700 feet above sea level around Jerusalem. The southernmost route runs south-southwest toward Bethlehem. The second and the shortest route goes to Jerusalem and has been the most heavily traveled throughout the centuries. But like the way to Bethlehem, it presents hazards for an army; it is a difficult climb, without shade—and worse, without water. There is broom, thistle, and some scrub grass, but the overwhelming impression is one of desolation, which is the meaning of the biblical name for the area, Jeshimon. Joshua chose the northernmost route, the Way of the Wilderness, which enters the hills west of Jericho and twists northwestward toward Ai. Though no easy route, it is not as difficult as the other two since once the plateau is reached the desert gives way to vegetation. More important, this way leads directly onto the broad, boulder-strewn, moorland plateau north of Jerusalem. Control of this plateau has always been vital to those contending for the land.

In the biblical account, the route of the Hebrews into the highlands was blocked by the fortified city of Ai (4). Again, Joshua sent scouts to assess the situation. Their report of a small defense force that could be easily routed proved incorrect, as the Hebrew frontal attack was repulsed with a loss of 36 men. The Hebrews then discovered that one of their number had taken plunder at Jericho for himself, thus bringing the Lord's wrath upon the entire army. By putting the man and his family to death, the army was cleansed. Joshua then resorted to a stratagem that drew Ai's defenders into the open north of the city while an ambush force entered Ai from the west. And another town was put to the torch and its inhabitants massacred.

Again archaeologists have been unable to confirm a particular episode in the Conquest Narrative. There was no town on the site of Ai in the 13th century. An important city existed there much earlier but came to an end about 2400 B.C. Not until after 1200 was the site resettled, and then only a rude, unfortified village grew up among the old ruins. The answer to this problem may lie in the name Ai, which means "ruin," for this place was a conspicuous ruin for much of antiquity. Perhaps local stories of how such devastation came to be were recited at the shrine at Bethel, a mile and a half away. When the Conquest Narrative began to take shape, these local stories may have been incorporated into the epic of Israel.

It is clear that the Hebrews under Joshua did not have to take Shechem (5) by force, though this important city 20 miles due north of Ai controlled a vast area of the central hill country. The Shechemites were of mixed ancestry and may have originated in the movement of peoples that earlier brought Abraham to Canaan. While not a part of the Exodus group, they may have had affinities with the invading Hebrews and thus been eager to enter into a covenant with them. This may explain the gathering of "sojourner as well as homeborn" between Mounts Gerizim and Ebal, the twin peaks guarding the pass at Shechem, for the blessing of Israel.

It was also by treaty that the Hebrews gained control over the vital plateau around Gibeon (6), to the southwest of Ai. Four cities in this strategic 10-by-12-mile area—

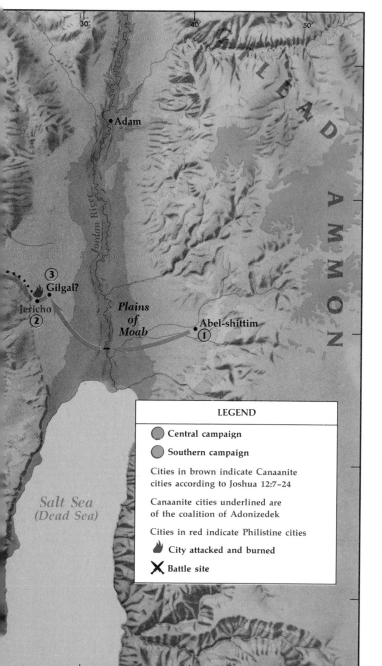

LEGEND

- Central campaign
- Southern campaign

Cities in brown indicate Canaanite cities according to Joshua 12:7-24

Canaanite cities underlined are of the coalition of Adonizedek

Cities in red indicate Philistine cities

- City attacked and burned
- Battle site

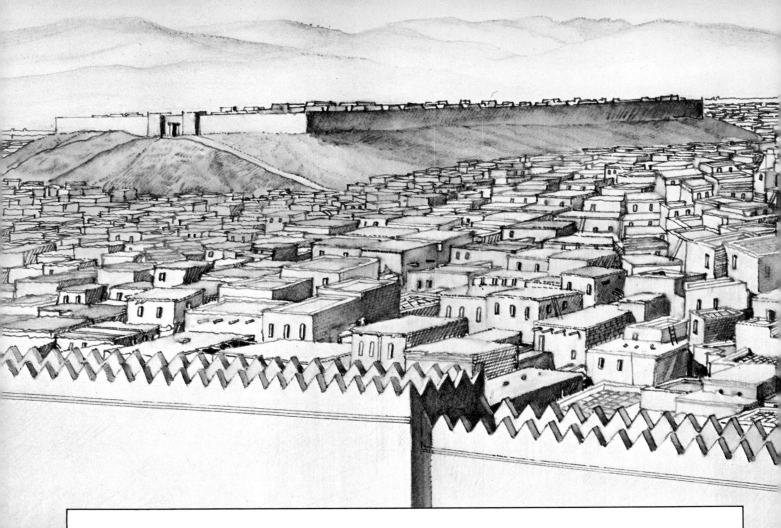

Hazor: Fortress-City of the Canaanites

The largest city of Canaan and long a major political and commercial center, Hazor supported a population of between 30,000 and 40,000 by the late-13th century B.C. This artist's rendering, based on the discoveries in the late 1950's and 1960's of a team led by the Israeli archaeologist Yigael Yadin, shows the walled city as it might have looked to Joshua and his men. In this southwest view from in front of one of the massive gates in the outer wall, the upper city can be seen rising above the plateau over which the lower city sprawled. The upper city covered about 15 acres and was surrounded by its own wall—a defensive line established a thousand years earlier when the city was confined only to the tell.

For generations after its destruction by Joshua, the once-proud city remained a scene of desolation. Only simple dwellings and tents occupied the site until the 10th century B.C., when King Solomon rebuilt a portion of the upper city as a royal garrison from which his troops could control the northern approaches. Solomon's Hazor was itself destroyed by fire, to be replaced in the 9th century by an impressive new city probably built during the reign of Israel's king Ahab. At length, Hazor's history as a Canaanite and then as an Israelite city came to an end with its destruction by the Assyrians in 733 B.C. While modest settlements later appeared there, the vestiges of its past eminence would remain buried and forgotten for 27 centuries.

Invasion and Conquest of Canaan (*continued*)

Gibeon, Beeroth, Chephirah, and Kiriath-jearim—had formed a federation that was governed, not by a king, but by elders. These people were Hivites, not Canaanites. Their elders now approached Joshua at Gilgal and tricked him into thinking that they had come from a far country, and thus were not an enemy. As a result, the men of Israel entered into an alliance with the Hivites sealed by solemn oath. When Joshua discovered the deception, he kept his oath. He spared the lives of the Hivites but made them "hewers of wood and drawers of water for the congregation and for the altar of the Lord . . ."

The Hebrews had gained access to the routes leading west into the Shephelah, the low hill country bordering the coastal plain. With the invasion threat now extended across the waist of the land, it is no wonder that a coalition of Canaanite kings arose to oppose any further westward movement by the Hebrews. Adonizedek, king of Jerusalem, summoned the rulers of Hebron, Jarmuth, Lachish, and Eglon to join him in an assault on Gibeon.

The besieged Gibeonites promptly invoked their alliance with Joshua. After a night march from Gilgal, the Hebrews attacked and quickly defeated the Canaanites. The biblical account stresses the wonderment and gratitude of the Hebrews for the Lord's intervention at Gibeon—sending hailstones that took more lives than did the Israelite swords and making the sun and moon stand still "until the nation took vengeance on their enemies." Retreat down the Way of Beth-horon became rout as the Hebrews pursued the Canaanites to Azekah (7) and Makkedah (site unknown). Joshua's victory was absolute: the land had been cut in two and the central campaign successfully concluded.

In the swift second phase of the conquest, the southern campaign, the Hebrews took advantage of their breakthrough into the Shephelah to sweep down the strategic valley south of Azekah. From this two-to-three-mile-wide valley two important routes lead eastward back into the central hill country. At its northern end, the Way of Beth-shemesh takes a steep, rocky path to-ward Jerusalem. Control of this obviously important route was hotly contested and played a major role in subsequent Israelite history. At the southern end of the valley, a second route ran through heavy forests for much of the way from Lachish to the 3,000-foot-high tableland around Hebron. Joshua now led the people of Israel down this valley for what appear to have been lightning-quick assaults on Libnah (8), Lachish (9), and Eglon (10). Turning eastward, he destroyed Hebron (11) and Debir (12). "So Joshua defeated the whole land . . . [and] returned, and all Israel with him, to the camp at Gilgal."

Archaeological work at several of these sites, particularly Lachish and Debir, shows signs of destruction in the time of Joshua. But some scholars are hesitant to attribute the damage to Joshua. According to Judges 1:10-15, Caleb and his Judahites were still campaigning in this area after the death of Joshua. It is also possible that some of the larger cities of the Shephelah and nearby areas were assaulted not only by the Hebrews but also by raiding Philistines or even by Egyptians.

The arena for the third phase of the Hebrews' violent assault upon the land was the fertile, well-watered hills and abundant forests of Upper Galilee far to the north. Hazor (13, on map opposite) was the chief city of the area. Situated along the Way of the Sea, $8\frac{1}{2}$ miles north of Lake Chinnereth and beside the swamps extending 5 miles south of Lake Huleh, Hazor had enjoyed sporadic periods of prosperity for more than 1,500 years before the arrival of the Hebrews. At the time Joshua beheld its deep moat, massive walls, and great gates, its circuit encompassed a citadel and lower city of 205 acres, making it by far the largest city in Canaan.

Hazor's domination of the north, however, had been increasingly challenged by the growing numbers of Hebrews who were settling in the hills, steadily encroaching upon Hazor's lands, and eroding the great city's strength. To counter the Hebrew threat, Jabin, king of Hazor, summoned his allies from Canaanite cities throughout

This 13th-century B.C. sanctuary at Hazor is thought to predate the Hebrews' arrival there. The seated statue, the row of miniature stelae, and the offering table in the foreground most likely honored the moon goddess. The lion figure was probably part of a doorjamb.

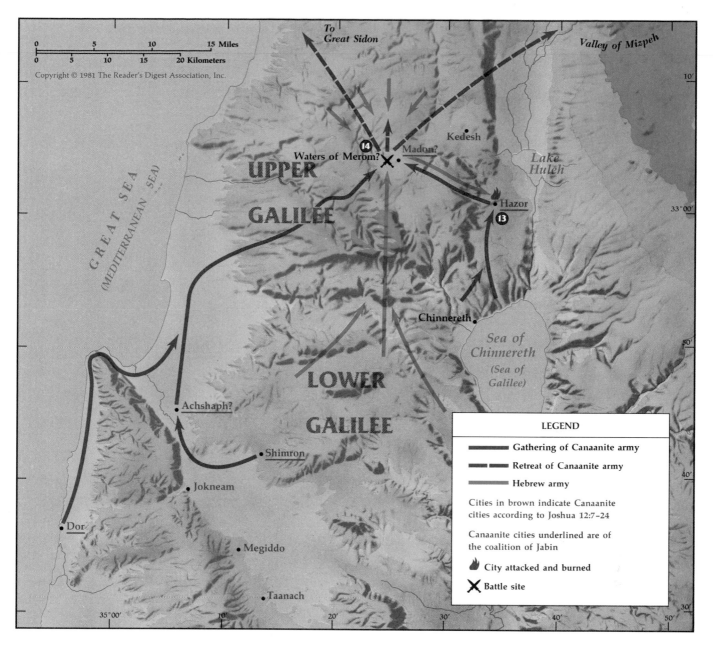

LEGEND

━━━━ Gathering of Canaanite army

━ ━ ━ Retreat of Canaanite army

━━━━ Hebrew army

Cities in brown indicate Canaanite cities according to Joshua 12:7–24

Canaanite cities underlined are of the coalition of Jabin

🔥 City attacked and burned

✗ Battle site

Upper and Lower Galilee and from along the coast to gather at the waters of Merom (14). The heavily armed Canaanite warriors were secure in their belief that the Hebrew hill fighters could not cope with massed horses and chariots.

But Joshua too gathered his forces from Upper and Lower Galilee for a surprise attack on the Canaanite army encamped in the narrow defiles and heavy sycamore and oak forests at Merom. With no room to maneuver, the chariots were useless. Amid great confusion the Hebrews hamstrung the horses and set the chariots ablaze. The Canaanites fled into the forest and through the valleys, but the Hebrews cut off the escape route back to Hazor and, indeed, all of the routes south, which left the northern routes toward Sidon (the great Phoenician seaport to the northwest) and the Valley of Mizpeh. With the forces of the kings of the Canaanite confederation in disorderly flight, Joshua

and his men turned back from pursuing the enemy and came to Hazor, which was without defenders. The Hebrews took Hazor and set it afire after slaughtering the inhabitants.

Archaeological work at Hazor in the 1920's and 1950's confirms the biblical narrative. In the 13th century the city was destroyed by fire, almost certainly the work of Joshua, and was not rebuilt until the time of Solomon. Rude huts and perhaps transient tent settlements occupied the site for the next two centuries. This is not surprising for a pastoral people, who had no urban tradition prompting them to rebuild this once-mighty city.

The Hebrew Conquest Narrative ends with a list of the conquered Canaanite cities, leading one to think that virtually all the cities fell before Joshua and his conquering armies. But the Narrative also mentions land remaining to be conquered, underlining again the complexity of the Hebrews' arrival in the Promised Land.

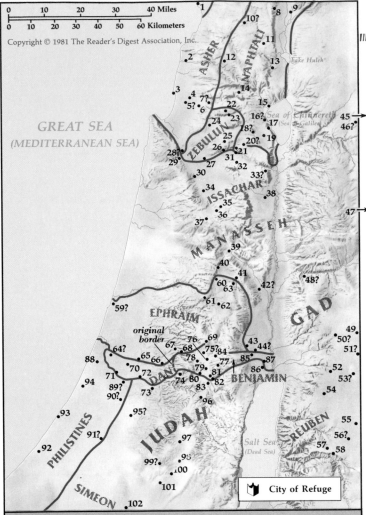

Copyright © 1981 The Reader's Digest Association, Inc.

GREAT SEA
(MEDITERRANEAN SEA)

Tribal areas (according to Joshua 13–19) are indicated above; numbers refer to the cities listed below, with the Levitical cities (according to Joshua 20–21 and I Chronicles 6:54–81) in brown.

1. Tyre	35. Beth-haggan	69. Bethel
2. Abdon	36. Ibleam	70. Gibbethon
3. Acco	37. Dothan	71. Shikkeron
4. Rehob	38. Beth-shan	72. Timnah
5. Mishal?	39. Tirzah	73. Beth-shemesh
6. Kabul	40. Shechem	74. Kiriath-jearim
7. Hukkok?	41. Taanath-shiloh	75. Mizpah?
8. Abel-beth-maacah	42. Jokmeam?	76. Ramah
9. Dan	43. Naaran	77. Almon
10. Beth-anath?	44. Gilgal?	78. Gibeon
11. Kedesh	45. Ashtaroth	79. Gibeah
12. Beth-shemesh	46. Golan?	80. Waters of Nephtoah
13. Hazor	47. Ramoth-gilead	81. Anathoth
14. Ramah	48. Mahanaim?	82. En-shemesh
15. Chinnereth	49. Rabbah	83. Jerusalem
16. Karthan?	50. Jaazer?	84. Geba
17. Hammath	51. Mephaath?	85. Jericho
18. En-gannim?	52. Heshbon	86. Beth-hoglah
19. Jabneel	53. Bezer?	87. Beth-arabah
20. Heleph?	54. Medeba?	88. Jabneel
21. Daberath	55. Jahez	89. Ekron?
22. Jotbah	56. Kedemoth?	90. Gath?
23. Kanah	57. Dibon	91. Eglon?
24. Hannathon	58. Aroer	92. Gaza
25. Gath-hepher	59. Gath-rimmon?	93. Ashkelon
26. Chisloth-tabor	60. Michmethath	94. Ashdod
27. Sarid	61. Tappuah	95. Libnah?
28. Helkath?	62. Shiloh	96. Bethlehem
29. Jokneam	63. Janoah	97. Hebron
30. Megiddo	64. Eltekeh?	98. Juttah
31. Kishion	65. Gezer	99. Debir?
32. Endor	66. Aijalon	100. Eshtemoa
33. Jarmuth?	67. Lower Beth-horon	101. Jattir
34. Taanach	68. Upper Beth-horon	102. Beer-sheba

Tribal Areas and Levitical Cities

When Joshua was "old and advanced in years," the Lord commanded him to "allot the land to Israel for an inheritance"—even though much of Canaan remained to be conquered, including the powerful Philistine cities along the coast.

The tribes of Israel, who came to possess land on both sides of the Jordan, traced their origin to the 12 sons of Jacob. The people of Joseph were now two tribes, the descendants of his sons Manasseh and Ephraim. Since Reuben, Gad, and half of the tribe of Manasseh had received portions east of the Jordan from Moses, it remained for Joshua to assign land west of the Jordan to Judah, Ephraim, Benjamin, Simeon, Zebulun, Issachar, Asher, Naphtali, Dan, and the remaining half-tribe of Manasseh. The tribe of Levi, whose members were to devote themselves to religious duties, received no territory. Instead, they were given 48 cities (see map siting 41 at left) and their pasturelands. Six of the 48 were designated as cities of refuge. There persons who had unwittingly committed homicide could seek sanctuary from the victim's relatives until proper judgment was rendered.

The question of the tribal borders is one of the most difficult matters to resolve in the historical geography of the Bible. Joshua 13–19 may indicate that a city belongs to one tribe, whereas Joshua 20–21 places it in the territory of another. Moreover, Joshua 13–19 seems to combine two lists, one of borders and the other of towns, and these may come from different times. For example, only borders are given for Ephraim and Manasseh, while only towns are given for Simeon. Some northern tribes have both, but Issachar's border is incomplete. Reuben, Gad, and the half-tribe of Manasseh east of the Jordan are vaguely described. The southern border given for Judah is actually the limit of Canaan.

Borders are an elusive matter and subject to change. For example, Simeon's inheritance was in the midst of the tribe of Judah and appears to have been absorbed by the more powerful Judahites fairly early. The tribe of Dan, unable to establish itself in its assigned territory, eventually migrated far to the north and seized the city of Laish (Leshem), renaming it Dan. The land originally allotted to Dan was divided among Benjamin (note the original western limits of Benjamin on the map), Ephraim, the Philistines, and probably Judah.

Many scholars view the tribal areas listed in Joshua as administrative districts of a later period—from the time of David or, more probably, Solomon. However, we also know that in the 12th and 11th centuries B.C. Canaan was in great confusion following the collapse of Egyptian control. Many people were making claims to various areas—among them the tribes of Israel. The struggles of these tribes with other peoples and with each other are the subject of the next phase of Israelite history, the period of the Judges.

Struggles of the Judges

Throughout much of the 12th and 11th centuries B.C., the period of the Judges, Canaan was in a state of anarchy. Although the Hebrew tribes laid claim to the entire country, they had not succeeded in subjugating all the people living there. The city-states of Canaan, now only nominally under Egyptian sovereignty, were divided by hill and valley; thus geography encouraged political disunity, a chronic Canaanite malady made worse by the constant influx of new peoples. The Hebrews also came into conflict with some of these other newcomers, particularly the Philistines, as well as with the long-established Ammonites and Moabites in the Transjordan and with marauding Midianite and Amalekite nomads from the eastern and southern deserts. And, occasionally, the tribes fought among themselves. But when the land had rest from war, the Hebrews mingled peacefully with their neighbors and sought to learn from them the art of farming as they slowly abandoned their ancient pastoral way of life.

"In those days there was no king in Israel; every man did what was right in his own eyes." Thus Judges describes the chaotic situation among the Hebrew tribes at a time when there was no central authority. In periods of crisis, however, certain tribal leaders—who are said to have "judged" Israel—were called forth by the Lord to deliver the people from their enemies. Ehud, Deborah, Gideon, Jephthah, and Samson—some of the most important of these deliverers from the time of the death of Joshua to the kingship of Saul—became folk heroes to the people, and stories about them are full of grand, legendary elements. At the same time, their adventures illustrate the regional fragmentation of the Hebrews as they struggled to settle in the land.

Ehud. Ever since the Hebrews seized the Plains of Moab (1, map on following page) during their invasion of Canaan, the Moabites had sought to reassert their claims there. With the help of the Ammonites and the Amalekites, they succeeded in reconquering the plains, even capturing "the city of palms" (Jericho, 2) across the Jordan. Moabite influence reached into the Saddle of Benjamin (3), an area of gentle hills, deeply scarred wadis, and rich grazing lands from which the Hebrews brought tribute to Eglon, king of Moab, at Jericho.

The Israelites had endured Moabite domination for 18 years when a left-handed Benjaminite named Ehud contrived a clever plot as he joined others bringing tribute to Eglon. Rather than returning home with his people, Ehud left them at Gilgal (4) and went back to Eglon's palace, where he told the Moabite that he had a secret message for him. After the king's retainers left "his cool roof chamber," Ehud slew Eglon with a long two-edged sword he had concealed beneath his clothes on his right side, where it would have gone undetected by the royal guards. Escaping to the hill country of Ephraim (5), Ehud rallied the Hebrews for an attack on the leaderless foe. As the terrified Moabites fled across the humid plain and came to the fords of the Jordan (6), they found their

escape route in Hebrew hands and were slaughtered. This defeat apparently put an end to the Moabite hold on the Jericho area and brought 80 years of peace.

Deborah. In a major northern conflict the Hebrews who had settled in the forests and valleys of Galilee were pitted against the area's Canaanite inhabitants. The references to Jabin of Hazor (1) in the narrative suggest either that the story of Deborah belongs before Joshua's destruction of Hazor or that Jabin, a famous king, was later introduced into the story. At any rate, according to Judges, King Jabin had been able to maintain control of the region for 20 years despite Hebrew pressure. Then Deborah—a prophetess who lived between Ramah and Bethel (2)—summoned Barak of the tribe of Naphtali and told him to gather 10,000 men at Mount Tabor (3) to challenge Sisera, the general of Jabin's army. The Hebrews assembled in relative safety at Kedesh-Naphtali (4), where men from Ephraim and Manasseh joined them. From there they moved to the slopes of Mount Tabor. Sisera's force—including 900 iron chariots—was drawn up at Harosheth-ha-goiim (5), to the west of the Hebrews but cut off from them by hills and valleys. For the poorly armed men from the hills to engage the well-trained, heavily armed Canaanites and their dreaded chariots in open battle on the plain was to court disaster. Nonetheless, the Hebrews advanced across the fields as the Canaanite horses drew their chariots forward.

The two armies met in a swampy area (6) "by the waters of Megiddo." This was the basin of the Kishon, a small stream that inland from the seacoast is dry for most of the year. But when heavy rainstorms sweep in from the Mediterranean, the shallow Kishon overflows its banks, flooding the plain and making it virtually impassable. Now the rains fell on Canaanite and Hebrew alike. Chariots quickly bogged down in the mud, depriving the Canaanites of their fearsome weapon. As the Hebrews swarmed over his immobilized chariots, Sisera panicked and fled on foot to the oak in Zaanannim (7), near Kedesh-Naphtali—there to meet death in the tent of Heber, with whom King Jabin of Hazor was supposed to be at peace.

The Hebrew victory is celebrated in the "Song of Deborah," the earliest extensive fragment of Hebrew literature, which includes this verse:
"From heaven fought the stars,
    from their courses they fought against Sisera.
The torrent Kishon swept them away,
    the onrushing torrent, the torrent Kishon.
March on, my soul, with might!"

Gideon. Although Barak and Deborah had broken Canaanite control in the southern hills of Galilee, no ruler rose to fill the void—thus leaving the region open to marauders from the eastern deserts. The narrow Jezreel valley (1), a rich and well-watered vale leading up from the Jordan, provided easy access to fertile lands for the Midianites and the Amalekites. For seven years they

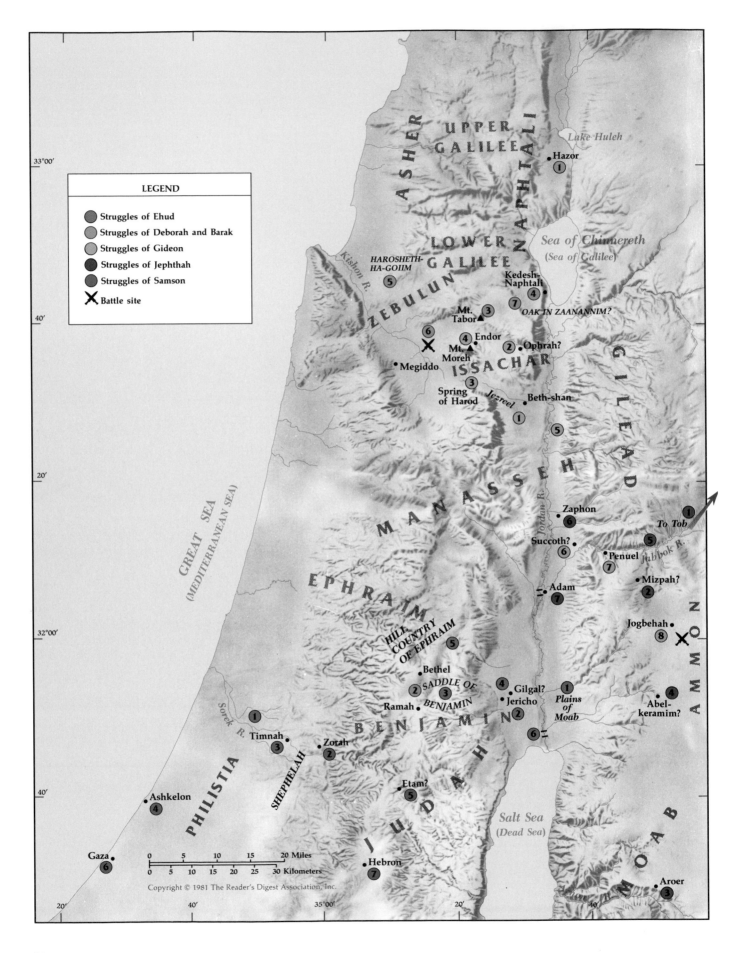

LEGEND

Struggles of Ehud
Struggles of Deborah and Barak
Struggles of Gideon
Struggles of Jephthah
Struggles of Samson
✗ Battle site

Lake Huleh

ASHER

UPPER GALILEE

NAPHTALI

Hazor ①

Sea of Chinnereth
(Sea of Galilee)

LOWER GALILEE

HAROSHETH-
HA-GOIIM ⑤

Kishon R.

ZEBULUN

Kedesh-
Naphtali ④

⑦ OAK IN ZAANANNIM?

Mt.
Tabor ③

⑥ Endor
Mt. ④
Moreh ② Ophrah?

ISSACHAR

GILEAD

Megiddo

③
Spring
of Harod
Jezreel ① Beth-shan

MANASSEH

⑤

Jordan R.

Zaphon ⑥

To Tob ①

Succoth? ⑥

Penuel ⑦

Jabbok R.

⑤

Mizpah? ②

EPHRAIM

Adam ⑦

Jogbehah ⑧

GREAT SEA
(MEDITERRANEAN SEA)

HILL
COUNTRY
OF EPHRAIM

⑤

AMMON

Bethel

② SADDLE OF ③ BENJAMIN

④ Gilgal? ①

Jericho ②

Plains
of Moab

Abel-
keramim? ④

Ramah

BENJAMIN

⑥

Sorek R. ①

Timnah ③

Zorah ②

J U D A H

Etam? ⑤

Salt Sea
(Dead Sea)

PHILISTIA

SHEPHELAH

Ashkelon ④

MOAB

Gaza ⑥

0   5   10   15   20 Miles
0   5   10 15 20 25 30 Kilometers

Hebron ⑦

Aroer ③

33°00'

40'

20'

32°00'

40'

20'

40'   35°00'   20'   40'

Judges *(continued)*

preyed on the tribes of Manasseh, Asher, Zebulun, Naphtali—and probably Issachar, though it is not mentioned in this story. Finally, the Lord chose Gideon of Ophrah (2) to deliver his people. He was the youngest son of the least important family in the tribe of Manasseh.

When Gideon called on the Hebrews of the area to make a stand against these raiders, 32,000 men came forth. From among them Gideon chose only 300, giving each man a trumpet made from a ram's horn and a clay jar containing a torch. In three groups of a hundred each they left their camp at the spring of Harod (3), crossed the narrow neck of the valley in the dead of night, and took positions on three sides of the enemy camp near Endor (4). At Gideon's signal the raiders blew their horns, broke their jars, and shouted, "A sword for the Lord and for Gideon!" Taken by surprise, the enemy fled in panic toward the Jordan, their only escape route.

Gideon called upon the men of Ephraim to block the Jordan crossings, probably the easy fords (5) below Bethshan. But his failure to seek aid earlier had allowed many Midianites to escape, and Gideon urged his men forward in pursuit of the enemy beyond the river. At Succoth (6) and Penuel (7) his hungry troops asked for food, but the local inhabitants refused to help because they feared Midianite reprisals. Beyond Jogbehah (8), Gideon and his men surprised the enemy, who were at ease in their camps. After Midianite Kings Zebah and Zalmunna fell into Gideon's hands, the Hebrew leader took revenge on Succoth and Penuel and then slew the Midianite rulers. The victorious Hebrews sought to make Gideon king but he refused. Instead, he asked that each man give him the gold earrings taken as spoil from the enemy. From this booty the hero made an ephod, perhaps some type of image, but it proved to be "a snare to Gideon and to his family." Nonetheless, Gideon's victory had brought 40 years of peace.

Jephthah. East of the Jordan the Ammonites had been pressuring the Hebrews of Gilead for 18 years in an attempt to recover territory earlier lost to the Hebrews. They had even crossed the Jordan to raid Judah, Benjamin, and Ephraim. The elders of Gilead turned to the son of a harlot, the mighty warrior Jephthah, an exile dwelling in the land of Tob (1).

After returning to Mizpah (2) and accepting leadership of the Hebrews, Jephthah sent word to the Ammonite king, urging him to give up his hostile actions. When the king continued to press his claims, Jephthah decided to attack. He vowed before the Lord that, if victorious, he would offer as a burnt sacrifice whoever first came from his house to greet him on his return. In the ensuing campaign Jephthah defeated the Ammonites from as far south as Aroer (3) on the rim of the Arnon River gorge, to Abel-keramim (4), thereby securing the western grazing lands of the Ammonites, including the lands running northward beyond the Jabbok (5). As the victorious Jephthah came home to Mizpah, his joy turned to grief when his daughter, his only child, "came out to meet him with timbrels and with dances." The heartbroken father did as he had vowed.

Now the contentious Ephraimites crossed the river and confronted Jephthah at Zaphon (6), demanding to know why they had not been summoned for the attack on the Ammonites. Perhaps they claimed rights to the area; perhaps they came seeking revenge or booty. Whatever the reason, they made the mistake of threatening Jephthah, who attacked them in force and drove them in disarray toward the fords of the Jordan at Adam (7). There the Ephraimites found Jephthah's men demanding a password, "Shibboleth," before allowing anyone to cross the river. Since the men of Ephraim apparently could not make the *sh* sound, they pronounced the word as "Sibboleth," were easily recognized, and immediately slain by their fellow Hebrews.

Samson. The Shephelah, a distinct area of low hills and narrow glens separating the Philistine coastal plain from the heights of Judah, was an arena of continuing conflicts between the Hebrews and the Philistines. It was in the broad and lovely Sorek valley (1) that Samson singlehandedly took on the Philistines. Despite their legendary nature, the many stories about this great folk hero clearly reflect the frustrating struggles of the Hebrews in their efforts to secure the area. Indeed, Samson's tribe, Dan, failed to establish itself there and eventually migrated far to the north.

Samson's birth was foretold by an angel who appeared to Manoah and his barren wife in Zorah (2), saying that Samson would be a Nazirite, a person dedicated to God by taking special vows.

Samson was different from the other Judges in that he relied on his own great physical strength in contests with the enemy rather than lead others into battle. Moreover, he spent most of his short life tormenting his Philistine neighbors and in riotous living with Philistine women.

Samson's earliest love was a woman of Timnah (3), the daughter of a Philistine. Once on his way to see her he had slain a lion with his bare hands, and at their wedding celebration he proposed a riddle about this lion for the Philistine guests to solve. Failure to do so would cost them 30 linen garments and 30 festal garments. When his wife of seven days betrayed the answer to her countrymen, Samson was furious. He went down to Ashkelon (4), where he killed 30 Philistines, taking their festal garments to pay his wager at Timnah. Upon returning to Timnah, he found that his bride had been given to his companion.

At the time of the wheat harvest, Samson took his revenge. He caught 300 foxes, turned them tail to tail, attached a torch to each pair, and let them loose in the fields. Not only the crops but the slow-growing olive groves burned. When the Philistines killed Samson's wife and father-in-law in retaliation, Samson "smote them hip and thigh with great slaughter" and then fled to Etam (5) in the hills of Judah. Fearing the Philistines who came seeking Samson, the Judahites got the fugitive to agree to be bound and surrendered to his enemies. But as the Philistines came for Samson, "the ropes which were on his arms became as flax that has caught fire, and his bonds melted off his hands. And he found a fresh jawbone of an ass, and put out his hand

Judges (continued)

and seized it, and with it he slew a thousand men."

Another of Samson's adventures involved the men of the Philistine city of Gaza (6), who lay in wait for him at the city gate while he visited a harlot there. Samson not only eluded his would-be captors but took with him the doors of the gate of the city, carrying them to "the top of the hill that is before Hebron" (7)—a distance of nearly 40 miles.

Once more in the Sorek valley, Samson fell in love with Delilah. Their love story is one of the most famous in history. The Philistines persuaded Delilah to try to entice from Samson the secret of his great strength. Three times she tried, and three times she failed, for he misled her with his answers. But Delilah persisted, until he was "vexed to death" and told her, "A razor has never come upon my head; for I have been a Nazirite to God from my mother's womb. If I be shaved, then my strength will leave me, and I shall become weak, and be like any other man." And so, as Samson slept upon her knees, Delilah had his locks shaved off and called the lords of the Philistines. The weakened hero was easily taken. At Gaza once more, he was blinded, made to wear bronze fetters, and put to work at the prison grindstone. Eventually, after Samson's hair had grown long again, he was brought out on a feast day to be made sport of in the great temple of Dagon, one of the chief deities of the Philistines. Samson called upon God and avenged himself. Pulling down the two middle columns, he collapsed the house on top of himself as well as on more Philistines "than those whom he had slain during his life."

The Minor Judges. Five minor judges are mentioned in the Bible. Though they "judged Israel," they are not called deliverers, and little is known about them. In some cases we know the name of the town where they lived or where they were buried. For others, only a general area is suggested, if that. Tola, son of Puah, lived and was buried at Shamir (site unknown) "in the hill country of Ephraim." Jair the Gileadite was buried in Kamon in Gilead. Ibzan of Bethlehem, like Jair, had 30 sons. Elon the Zebulunite was buried in Aijalon of Zebulun, somewhere in the Great Plain. Abdon the son of Hillel the Pirathonite was from Ephraim, from Pirathon, where he had 40 sons.

Aside from the major deliverers already discussed, there were two other judges who were also deliverers, but their exploits have not been preserved in detail. Othniel of Debir in Judah was the first of the deliverer-judges. This son-in-law of the famous Caleb delivered the people of southern Judah and was so famous that he is mentioned in Judges 1:13 and 3:9–11, in Joshua 15:17, and in 1 Chronicles 4:13 and 27:15. But what were his exploits of valor, and who was his opponent, the mysterious Cushan-rishathaim?

Of Shamgar we are told only that he "killed six hundred of the Philistines with an oxgoad" and that he delivered Israel. The song in Judges 5 says that in his time "caravans ceased and travelers kept to the byways." The locale of his activity is unknown. Some think he was in the Great Plain in the north, but others place him in the Shephelah.

Excavations at Ashdod (above) have revealed that it was the site of an important trading center in the Canaanite period. This settlement was set afire in the 13th century B.C., possibly by the Sea Peoples on their sweep toward Egypt. Later the Philistines built Ashdod, one of their five major cities, at the same site. As an important religious center, it contained a shrine of the god Dagon, a powerful warrior figure. The clay statue in the shape of a throne (at left) was unearthed in the ruins of Philistine Ashdod. It represents a goddess whom the excavators whimsically named Ashdoda.

The Philistines

For almost 200 years the Philistines were Israel's troublesome neighbors in the land of Canaan, imperiling the very existence of the emerging nation. These people, whose name in our language has become synonymous with materialism, were one of a loose confederation of tribes known collectively as the Sea Peoples. According to biblical tradition, the Philistines came from the island of Caphtor, frequently identified with Crete, but many historians now believe they originated in Anatolia. Forced from their homelands by famines that plagued Asia Minor at the end of the 13th century B.C., they pushed into Syria and Canaan and launched attacks on Egypt before occupying the southern coast of Canaan in the 12th century.

The Philistines are first mentioned in the inscriptions of Ramses III, Pharaoh of Egypt (c. 1183–1152), who recorded their invasion on the walls of his temple at Medinet Habu. These elegantly carved bas-reliefs tell how the Sea Peoples advanced by land and sea, bringing with them their women, children, and possessions—entire tribes moving irresistibly south, looting and burning towns and villages on their way. Finally, in a series of pitched battles, this human wave was stopped and defeated at Egypt's door.

Forced to retreat, many of the Sea Peoples moved back up the coast of Canaan. One group, the Philistines, eventually came to dominate the southern coastal plain from their five major cities: Gaza, Ashkelon, and Ashdod, which controlled the strategic overland coastal trade route, the Way of the Sea, and Gath and Ekron farther inland. The armies of the Philistines soon came into conflict with the Israelites over possession of the hill country. The Philistines proved to be a worrisome foe be-

The Philistine pottery group shown above (from left to right, a "beer jug," a "stirrup jug," and a bowl) is embellished with geometric patterns and an elegantly stylized bird. The style of decoration reflected a cultural mix that combined Aegean, Cypriot, Egyptian, and Canaanite elements.

cause of their political sophistication, their military organization, and above all, their superior weapons. While the Israelites were still fighting with copper and bronze, the Philistines had learned the art of working iron—a secret they jealously guarded from the Hebrews. As a result, according to 1 Samuel, "there was no smith to be found throughout all the land of Israel." Thus, when the Israelites, who were poorly armed and poorly organized, went out to do battle with their enemy near Ebenezer in the second half of the 11th century B.C., the result was predictable disaster. The Hebrews were soundly beaten, though this gave them the impetus to unite under a single leader. The Philistines were subdued though not eliminated by King David in the 10th century.

Although they survived in their cities for 300 years more, by the 7th century B.C. the Philistines had been absorbed by the conquering Assyrians. During that period they occasionally harassed the Hebrew states, but the Philistine confederation was never to rise again.

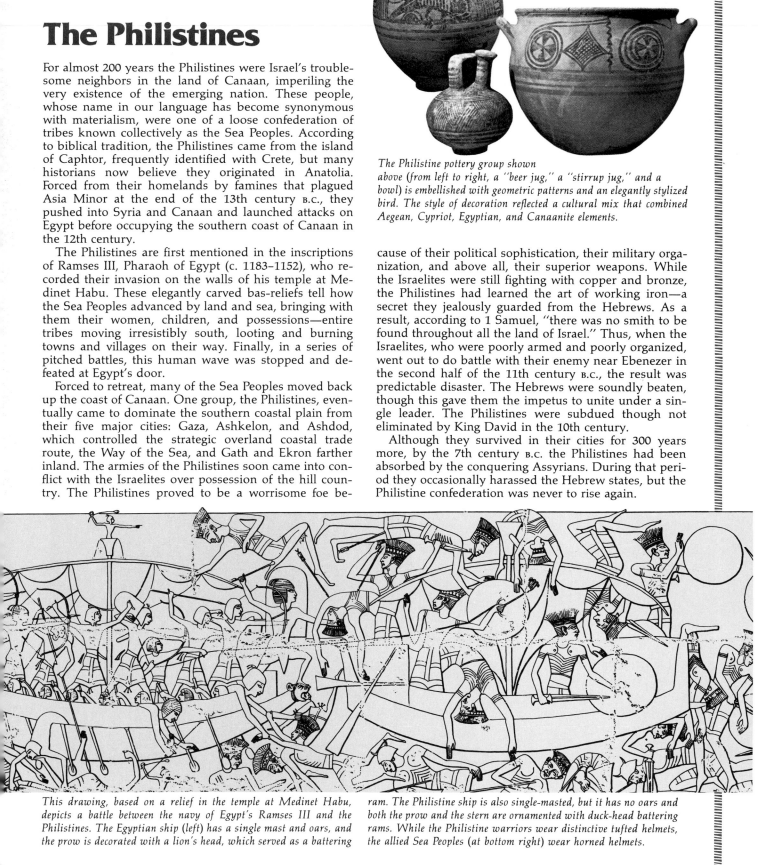

This drawing, based on a relief in the temple at Medinet Habu, depicts a battle between the navy of Egypt's Ramses III and the Philistines. The Egyptian ship (left) has a single mast and oars, and the prow is decorated with a lion's head, which served as a battering ram. The Philistine ship is also single-masted, but it has no oars and both the prow and the stern are ornamented with duck-head battering rams. While the Philistine warriors wear distinctive tufted helmets, the allied Sea Peoples (at bottom right) wear horned helmets.

The Ark Captured

War between the Hebrews settling in the hill country and the Philistines establishing themselves on the coast was inevitable as both groups grew and extended their power. Tensions had long existed, as is made clear in the stories of Samson's struggles with the Philistines. But some time in the 11th century B.C., toward the end of the period of the Judges, mounting hostility- erupted into open warfare. In the course of this conflict, many Hebrews became aware of the need for a central authority as they were forced to abandon their tribal sectionalism in face of the powerful Philistine threat. The outcome of the first full-scale clash between the Hebrews and the Philistines, the battle of Ebenezer, underlined the futility of a divided people fighting a highly organized foe.

The Philistines had spread northward along the coast from their original area of settlement in Philistia (1). Now they gathered their forces at Aphek (2), a strategically important juncture where the westerly branch of the Way of the Sea converged with the easterly branch, thereby skirting the springs along the Yarkon River (3)

and the marshy Plain of Sharon to its north, an area through which neither caravans nor armies could pass. About two miles east of Aphek, the Hebrews were encamped at Ebenezer (4), blocking access to a ridge route leading into the heartland of Ephraim and to Shiloh (5), an important shrine of the Hebrews where the ark of the covenant was housed. Since the time of the Exodus, the ark, a specially built wooden chest that contained the Ten Commandments, had been the most sacred object of the people of Israel. It had accompanied the Hebrews throughout their wanderings and represented their covenant with the Lord.

The Philistines attacked the Hebrews near Ebenezer. In a pitched battle the Hebrews suffered defeat, but they were not driven from Ebenezer. Hoping to rally their forces and inspire courage among the warriors, the elders sent for the ark, which was brought down under the care of Hophni and Phinehas, the two sons of the aged and blind Eli, a priest at Shiloh and the spiritual leader of the Hebrews at the time. But when the battle was joined once

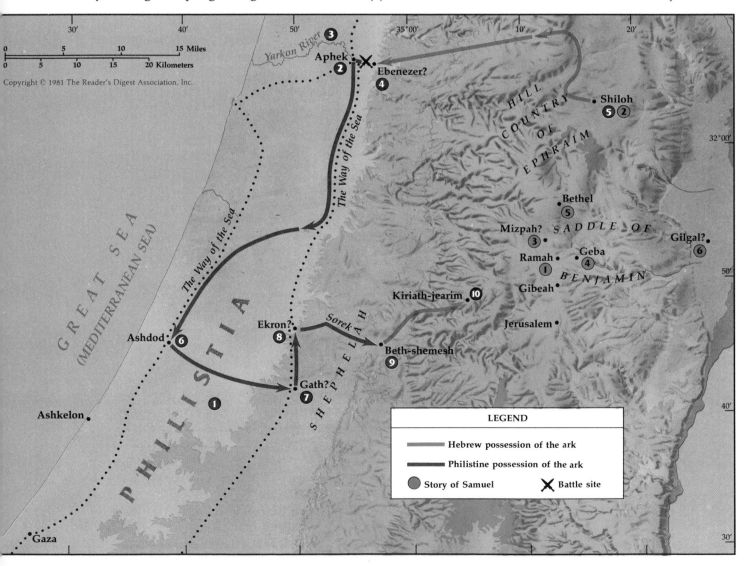

more, the Philistines—despite their fear of the power the ark might hold—succeeded in routing the Hebrews and slaughtering a great number of them, including Eli's two sons. Still worse, the ark was captured by the enemy. When the terrible news of all that had happened reached Eli at Shiloh, the old man fell over backward, broke his neck, and died. His daughter-in-law, who was expecting Phinehas' child, went at once into labor and bore a son. She named him Ichabod, which means "there is no glory," for she said, "The glory has departed from Israel, for the ark of God has been captured."

The joyous Philistines took this great spoil of victory southward to Ashdod (6) and placed it in the temple of Dagon, one of their chief deities. But the next morning joy turned to terror when they found the image of Dagon toppled to the ground. To make matters worse, the Ashdodites were afflicted with tumors. (The tumors were probably an outbreak of the bubonic plague, later known to be carried by rodents—and we are told in Samuel that mice ravaged the land.) The troubled lords of the Philistines (the rulers of their five principal cities, Gaza, Ashkelon, Gath, Ekron, as well as Ashdod) gathered together and brought the ark to Gath (7), but again tumors broke out among the people. When the ark was taken to Ekron (8), "a deathly panic" spread throughout the city as tumors appeared there also. On the advice of priests and diviners, the Philistine lords prepared to send the ark out of their territory where for seven months it had brought them nothing but disaster.

From Ekron an important route ran eastward through the Sorek valley into Hebrew territory. Along this way the ark moved slowly in a driverless cart hitched to two cows. Also in the cart was a small box containing a guilt offering: five golden images of tumors and five golden images of mice—one of each for the five Philistine cities. The Philistines hoped these gifts would rid their land of the plague. As the cart approached Beth-shemesh (9), on the border of Philistine territory, the Hebrews who were reaping their wheat harvest in the nearby fields saw it and rejoiced. And when the cart reached the field of Joshua, they split it into firewood, set it aflame, and sacrificed the cows as a burnt offering of thanksgiving. But the ark had unhappy consequences for the men of Beth-shemesh, some of whom were killed because they had dared look into it.

With the shrine at Shiloh in ruins in the wake of the Philistine victory at Ebenezer and their subsequent drive into the highlands, the ark was taken into the hills to Kiriath-jearim (10). It remained there for some 20 years until King David brought it to his new capital at Jerusalem.

Samuel

Even before Samuel was born, his mother, Hannah, vowed to dedicate her son to the service of the Lord. When the child was weaned, he was taken from his birthplace in Ramah (1, on map opposite) to the shrine at Shiloh (2), where he served under the priest Eli. As Samuel grew, "all Israel from Dan to Beer-sheba" came to know that he was a prophet of the Lord.

After the battle of Ebenezer—with Eli dead, Shiloh in ruins, and the Philistines reaching deep into the highlands—spiritual leadership of the Hebrews passed to Samuel. Samuel's first concern was with the faith of his

people, and so he called them to Mizpah (3), where they confessed their sins and he prayed to the Lord for them. When the Philistines heard of the Hebrew gathering, they attacked Mizpah. But "the Lord thundered with a mighty voice," throwing the Philistines into confusion, and they were easily routed. Yet before long the Philistines were back in force at Geba (4), in a position to dominate the major eastern approach through the Saddle of Benjamin into the highlands; only with great difficulty did the Hebrews later drive them from this area.

Although this was an uneasy period in the history of the Hebrews, with the ebb and flow of strife in the highlands and in the bordering Shephelah, the situation was apparently stable enough to allow Samuel to make a yearly circuit from his home in Ramah to Bethel (5), Gilgal (6), and Mizpah. On his tour of these towns he rendered judgments in disputes and administered justice.

As Samuel grew old and his sons proved unworthy successors, the people looked with increasing apprehension to an uncertain future. Centralized government with power in the hands of a strong leader who could act swiftly and decisively against the enemy seemed to many their only hope for survival. And thus the elders of Israel said to Samuel, "now appoint for us a king to govern us like all the nations." When Samuel's warnings of potential abuses of kingly power fell on deaf ears, the Lord commanded him to fulfill the people's wish and find a king. Samuel's divinely inspired choice of a ruler fell upon Saul of Gibeah, a warrior who could lead men but whose power base was weak and who might thus be restrained. Although Saul came from an insignificant family of the tribe of Benjamin, the smallest of the tribes, there was no more handsome man than he in all Israel, and "from his shoulders upward he was taller than any of the people." With this imposing figure begins the tumultuous history of monarchy in Israel.

This 10th-century B.C. limestone altar from Megiddo stands 22 inches high and was probably used by priests of Samuel's time for burning incense. The horns symbolize divine power; their shape may have evolved from bull figures worshiped by the early Canaanites.

Saul, Israel's First King

The crisis that brought Saul to power was the increasing tempo of the Hebrews' conflict with the Philistines, especially in the Saddle of Benjamin, just northeast of his home at Gibeah (1). Not seeking to occupy or rule the entire land, the Philistines nonetheless were attempting to expand their power while containing Israelite growth. Unwittingly, however, these efforts produced the very situation they wished to avoid—the unification of the Hebrew tribes under a single leader.

Saul's abrupt rise to kingship is twice related in 1 Samuel. Sent to recover his father's asses, Saul and a servant wandered through the hill country of Ephraim. Returning empty-handed, they entered Ramah (2), where they decided to seek advice on their humble quest from the prophet Samuel. Unbeknown to Saul, the Lord had told Samuel only the day before, "I will send to you a man from the land of Benjamin, and you shall anoint him to be prince over my people Israel." To his surprise, Saul was greeted warmly and feasted. Early the next morning Samuel took him aside, anointed him with a vial of olive oil, and pledged, "you shall reign over the people of the Lord and you will save them from the hands of their enemies round about."

In another account of how Saul became king, Samuel called together the tribes of Israel at Mizpah (3) in order to meet their demand and select a king publicly by lot, a time-honored method of determining the will of God. The lot fell upon the reluctant Saul, and the people proclaimed him with shouts of "Long live the king!" When he returned home to Gibeah, he was accompanied by "men of valor whose hearts God had touched." Yet others doubted that the untested Saul could save them from the Philistine threat. He soon had a chance, however, to prove his mettle in battle—but against the Ammonites rather than the Philistines.

The Ammonite leader Nahash laid siege to the Israelite town of Jabesh-gilead (4), far to the north across the Jordan. As his grim condition for agreeing to a peace treaty, Nahash demanded the right eye of every man in the town. Winning a seven-day respite, the desperate Jabeshites sent out couriers seeking aid for their cause. At Gibeah, Saul learned of their plight as he was returning with his oxen from the fields, "and his anger was greatly kindled." As a call to war, he cut a yoke of oxen to pieces, which he sent throughout Israel with the admonition, "Whoever does not come out after Saul and Samuel, so shall it be done to his oxen!" The people answered his call "as one man," assembling at Bezek (5), on the route from Shechem to Beth-shan. It was a momentous occasion, with all the Hebrew tribes joining together against a common foe.

Saul's military prowess was soon apparent. In a swift nighttime march, he led his forces across the Jordan and through the Wadi Yabis (6) to the verdant valley below besieged Jabesh-gilead. At dawn he thrust three attacking columns into the unsuspecting Ammonite camp. The surprise was complete; the victory, total. The slaughter continued "until the heat of the day." The deliverance of Jabesh-gilead made Saul's reputation as a battle commander. He could now turn his attention to a more serious threat: the Philistines, whose knowledge of iron smelting and access to good ore gave them weapons superior to those of the Israelites.

At the ancient shrine of Gilgal (7), Saul was reaffirmed as king. Less than 15 miles away, at Geba (8) and Michmash (9), the Philistines were astride the strategically vital pass that led to the Hebrew-dominated highlands. Saul raised a fighting force of 3,000 men, taking 2,000 with him as he advanced on Michmash and assigning the balance as a reserve at Gibeah under his son Jonathan. This impetuous prince attacked and defeated the Philistine garrison at Geba. Saul heralded the victory throughout the land, seeking to rally more Hebrews to his cause. Alerted to the danger, the Philistines collected their scattered outposts into a powerful united force of chariots, horsemen, and infantry "like the sand on the seashore in multitude." His army disintegrating around him, Saul had withdrawn to Gilgal. Deserters hid in tombs and cisterns and in the numerous caves of the limestone hills.

With battle imminent, Saul waited with increasing concern for Samuel to arrive, as he had promised, to entreat God's favor with a burnt offering. Finally, Saul offered the sacrifice himself. At that moment, Samuel appeared and denounced the king for presuming to take over the priestly role. Saul's kingdom would not continue, Samuel warned; instead God would seek "a man after his own heart." With that he abandoned Saul and went to Gibeah.

Nevertheless, Saul advanced to Geba with the 600 men still remaining to him. Across the valley the Philistines held Michmash in strength, sending out raiding parties in three directions to pillage the countryside and to improve their tactical positions. Saul did not attack but moved to Gibeah, about five miles away. However, the bold Jonathan decided on a sortie of his own. Taking only an armor-bearer with him, he set out to scout the enemy positions. A Philistine outpost on a rocky crag challenged him. Scrambling up the hillside on all fours, Jonathan and his armor-bearer threw themselves savagely on the enemy, killing about 20. News of this sudden and fearful stroke swept through the Philistine camp, sending it into confusion and panic. Seeing the Philistine ranks "surging hither and thither," Saul seized the moment to launch an assault with his entire army. The slaughter was great as the routed Philistines fled their camp in disorder. Now the Israelite deserters who had earlier gone into hiding emerged from tombs, cisterns, and caves to join the pursuit, so that it seemed that the land itself had risen up against Israel's enemies. The Philistines rushed westward along the Way of Beth-horon (10) and past Aijalon (11), the quickest route to Philistia. The countryside was littered with their corpses. Only on the borders of Philistia did the Israelites break off the pursuit.

The spectacular victory secured the highlands—the heart of Saul's kingdom—for the Hebrews. From this base Saul went on to do battle with Israel's enemies on

The Way of Beth-horon—a route running through the hills of Judah—
provided an expedient escape homeward for the Philistines as they
fled from Saul after their defeat at the battle of Michmash.

LEGEND

⬤ The story of Saul

▬ Philistine raiding parties

▬ Flight of Philistines

✕ Battle site

every hand, ranging eastward across the Jordan and into the desert to the south, and "wherever he turned he put them to the worse." It was on one of these campaigns that Saul again roused Samuel's anger.

In battle with the Amalekites, a people of the southern desert, Saul captured the Amalekite king, Agag. While Agag's followers were all slain, he himself was spared, as were the best of the Amalekite flocks and oxen, and carried off by the victors to Gilgal. There Samuel furiously denounced Saul for refusing to destroy everyone and everything: "Because you have rejected the word of the Lord, he has also rejected you from being king." Saul's repentance was unavailing. When Agag was brought before Samuel, the Amalekite was cheerful, saying, "Surely the bitterness of death is past." "As your sword has made women childless," Samuel replied, "so shall your mother be childless," and the unyielding prophet forthwith hacked the king to death.

With that, Samuel returned to Ramah and Saul to Gibeah, less than three miles away. At the Lord's command, Samuel filled his horn with oil and went south to Bethlehem (12), disguising his true mission for fear that Saul might attempt to kill him. In Bethlehem he found David, youngest son of Jesse, and anointed him Israel's king.

Saul and David: Rivals for Power

David is a towering figure in Israel's history, and his life—especially his early life—was the subject of legendary stories seeking to glorify this great king who rose from humble beginnings. History and legend became intermixed. We do not know, for example, precisely how David first came to Saul's attention, for the Bible contains two differing accounts.

Following his break with Samuel, Saul—according to 1 Samuel 16—suffered periods of what might be termed extreme melancholia, when an "evil spirit" overtook him as a sign of God's disfavor. His servants suggested employing a skilled lyre player to soothe him during these times of depression. David of Bethlehem, already a young man of some reputation, not least as a musician, was brought to Saul, and his lyre playing had the desired effect: "Saul was refreshed, and was well, and the evil spirit departed from him." David entered the grateful king's service, employed not only as a musician but as Saul's personal armor-bearer, carrying his heavier equipment such as his shield and being responsible for his safety in battle. The later verses of 1 Samuel 17, however, suggest that David first came to Saul's attention on the battlefield, at the confrontation with the giant Goliath during renewed struggles with the Philistines.

The Philistines were once again contending with the Hebrews, this time in the Shephelah. They were established in force between Socoh and Azekah (1), prepared to strike into the highlands of Judah. Alert to the threat, Saul placed his army in a blocking position in the nearby Valley of Elah (2), with low-lying hills on each side. Both armies were in naturally strong positions, and neither made an immediate move to attack. Their battle lines faced each other in stalemate.

There was a tradition among ancient armies that individual combat might decide the outcome of such a military standoff. Each side would send forth a single warrior; the survivor's army would be declared the victor, the loser's would relinquish its position. The Philistines, exercising this option, sent a champion who was truly fearsome—mighty Goliath of Gath.

This enormous man—"whose height was six cubits and a span" (that is, about 10 feet) and whose spear shaft "was like a weaver's beam"—came forth from the Philistine camp every day for 40 days, daring Saul's army to send a champion to meet him in single combat. His challenge went unanswered. "All the men of Israel, when they saw the man, fled from him, and were much afraid." Not David, however; greatly angered at this defiance of the army of the living God, he determined to take up the challenge. Saul offered him his own armor and sword, but David was not used to such weapons and refused them. Armed only with his shepherd's sling and a handful of stones from a nearby streambed, he sallied forth. Goliath was disdainful and taunted him. David sprinted forward, whipped his sling round and round, and released a single stone. It struck the giant squarely in the forehead. Goliath fell, and David snatched up the Philistine's own sword and beheaded him. Seeing their

champion killed, the Philistines took to their heels, pursued by Saul's men. The flight ended only when the vanquished found haven behind the gates of the fortified cities of Gath (3) and Ekron (4).

Young David was now a great hero to the Israelites, winning triumph after triumph in the king's service. "And the women sang to one another as they made merry,

> 'Saul has slain his thousands,
> and David his ten thousands.'"

He formed a close friendship with Saul's son Jonathan and even wed the king's daughter Michal, after demonstrating his worthiness by killing 200 Philistines. But the seeds of tragedy had been sown. "An evil spirit from God rushed upon Saul," making him intensely jealous of David, "and he raved within his house." On three occasions the king hurled his spear at David as the youth sought to soothe him with his lyre. By now "Saul was David's enemy continually." Learning of a plot, Michal warned her husband, "If you do not save your life tonight, tomorrow you will be killed." With her help, David fled from his house in Gibeah (5), leaving a dummy figure in his bed to deceive the king's agents. So began David's odyssey, which would take him far from his home to escape Saul's vengeance.

David went first to Ramah (6) to seek the aid of Samuel, who had anointed him Israel's future king. Three times messengers sent to take David were caught up instead in the "prophesying," or ecstatic dancing, of Samuel's followers and failed to return. Then Saul himself came to Ramah, and he too was deflected from his mission by a frenzy in which, transported, he tore off his garments and fell to the ground. David returned to Gibeah and pleaded with his friend Jonathan to intercede in his behalf. They arranged a signal. If Jonathan determined that his father was "well disposed toward David," he would shoot three arrows for his servant to recover in the field where David was hiding. If it was still unsafe for David to return, he would shoot the arrows far beyond the servant. The news was unfavorable, the arrows passed beyond the servant, and David fled once more. Hungry and without weapons, he went to Nob (7), where he convinced the chief priest of that important shrine that he was on a secret mission for Saul. He was given holy bread and was armed with Goliath's sword, which had been brought there as tribute.

David now decided on a bold stratagem: to seek sanctuary among Israel's foremost enemies, the Philistines. Descending the highlands of Judah, he reached the city of Gath (8). The servants of Achish, Gath's king, were suspicious of him, questioning why this famous slayer of Philistines should seemingly change sides. Realizing that he had put himself in grave danger, David feigned madness, and the disgusted Achish sent him away. David went about 10 miles southeast through the Shephelah to Adullam (9), near the scene of his victory over Goliath. In this rugged no-man's land between the Philistines and Saul's domain, he made a fortified camp. Secure on

In natural hideouts like the cave of Adullam, shown above, David and his followers maintained their watch for the armies of the jealous Saul.

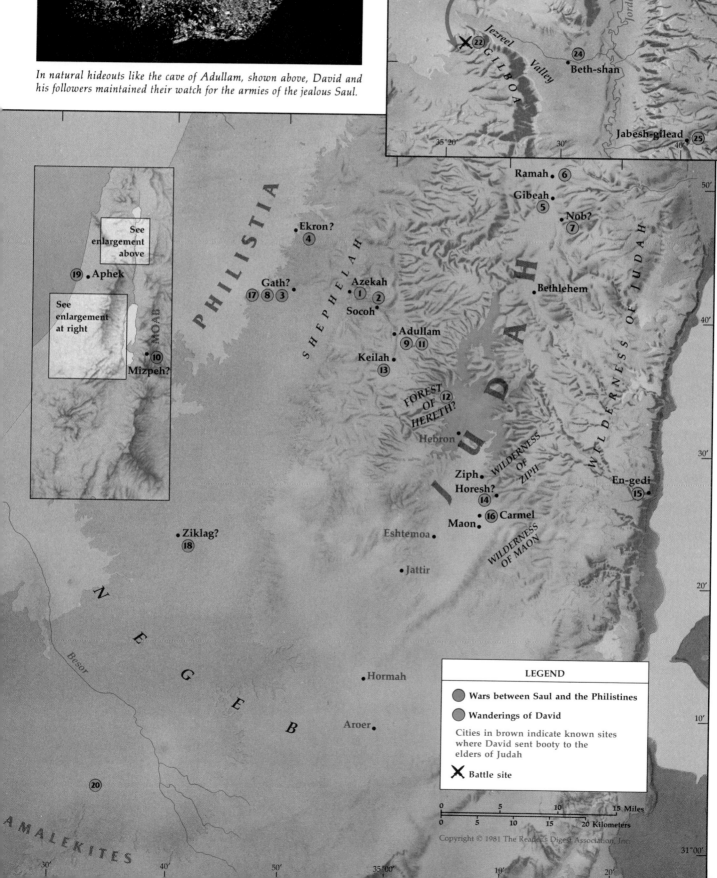

Sea of Chinnereth
(Sea of Galilee)

Copyright © 1981 The Reader's Digest Association, Inc.

Endor (23)

MOREH

Shunem (21)

Jezreel Valley

GILBOA

✕ (22)

Beth-shan (24)

Jordan River

40'

32°30'

Jabesh-gilead (25)

35°20'   30'   40'

Ramah (6)
Gibeah (5)
Nob? (7)

Ekron? (4)

PHILISTIA

See enlargement above

Aphek (19)

See enlargement at right

MOAB

Mizpeh? (10)

SHEPHELAH

Gath? (17)(8)(3)

Azekah (1)(2)
Socoh

Bethlehem

Adullam (9)(11)

Keilah (13)

FOREST OF HERETH? (12)

Hebron

JUDAH

WILDERNESS OF JUDAH

Ziph (16)
WILDERNESS OF ZIPH

Horesh? (14)

Maon
Carmel (16)

Eshtemoa

WILDERNESS OF MAON

En-gedi (15)

Ziklag? (18)

N
E
G
E
B

Jattir

Besor

Hormah

Aroer

50'

40'

30'

20'

10'

LEGEND

● Wars between Saul and the Philistines

● Wanderings of David

Cities in brown indicate known sites where David sent booty to the elders of Judah

✕ Battle site

AMALEKITES

(20)

0   5   10   15 Miles
0   5   10   15   20 Kilometers

Copyright © 1981 The Reader's Digest Association, Inc.

30'   40'   35°00'   10'   20'

31°00'

Saul and David (continued)

steep heights, with an adequate water supply and many concealing caves, he could not be easily surprised by his enemies. He was joined there by his brothers and members of his clan, and also by "every one who was in distress, and every one who was in debt, and every one who was discontented." From this band of the disaffected he formed an outlaw army of 400 adventurers. He took other precautions. Fearing for the safety of his family, he accompanied his parents on the long journey across the Salt Sea to Mizpeh (10, on locator) in the kingdom of Moab and left them there in the protection of the Moabite king. He then took refuge first at his "stronghold" (11) near Adullam and then in the Forest of Hereth (12), a more strategic location.

When David heard that the Philistines were fighting against Keilah (13), which belonged neither to Judah nor to the Philistines, David and his little army fell on the Philistine besiegers and routed them. But to David's surprise, the people of Keilah showed no gratitude for their deliverance; indeed, he learned that they intended to betray him to Saul's advancing army. Once more David fled, this time to Horesh (14), in the Wilderness of Ziph. In this area—less a wilderness than an upland plateau—David established himself. But the people of Ziph sought out Saul and told him of David's whereabouts. Pursued by Saul's 3,000-man army, David hurried south into the Wilderness of Maon. "Saul went on one side of the mountain, and David and his men on the other side of the mountain; and David was making haste to get away from Saul, as Saul and his men were closing in . . ." For David the end seemed near when, providentially, a courier arrived to warn Saul that the Philistines were raiding to the north. The king turned back to meet the crisis. Reprieved once more, David reached the relative safety of En-gedi (15) on the shore of the Dead Sea.

After he had disposed of the Philistine threat, Saul resumed his relentless pursuit of David. In the rugged hills and valleys near En-gedi, he entered a cave where David and some of his followers were hiding. David could have killed the king then and there; instead, he stealthily cut off a piece of Saul's robe as evidence that he had spared his life. Later, David shouted across the hills to Saul, telling him of his action, showing him the piece of robe, and bowing down to the earth in respect for the monarch. Saul, momentarily remorseful, returned to Ramah, and David went to the stronghold near Adullam.

At this point Samuel died and was buried at Ramah. Maybe because of this, David once more shifted his base, back to the Wilderness of Maon. It was at nearby Carmel (16) that David had a dispute with the merchant Nabal and later married his widow, Abigail.

Once more the Ziphites told Saul of David's whereabouts, thus setting the stage for a final confrontation between the two. The king and his army camped at the edge of the Wilderness of Ziph, preparing to trap David. At night, as Saul slept amid his troops, David and a companion crept unseen into the camp. The companion offered to kill the sleeping monarch, but David stayed his hand. "As the Lord lives," he said, "the Lord will smite him; or his day shall come to die; or he shall go down into battle and perish." He was content to slip

away with Saul's spear and personal water jar. Once safely clear of the camp, he shouted out what he had done, displaying the spear and water jar as proof that again he had spared the king's life. Again Saul was contrite and broke off the chase.

Yet in his heart David knew the truce could not last. He adopted a new and more aggressive strategy. As he had done earlier, he sought sanctuary at Gath (17), among the Philistines. This time, however, he took his whole army with him, which now numbered 600 veteran warriors. When Saul learned that David had turned to Gath, "he sought for him no more." David asked Achish, the king of Gath, for a Philistine settlement where he might rule and serve as the king's vassal. Perhaps because he was now dealing from a position of armed strength, David's request was granted. He was given the town of Ziklag (18) in the Negeb. There he remained for 16 months, playing a deadly game with the Philistines. Achish had intended that David and his army should strike at Philistia's enemies in the Judah foothills and on the rim of the Negeb. Instead, David raided deep into the Negeb against the Amalekites and other peoples there. These were particularly bloody raids, for to deceive Achish David "smote the land, and left neither man nor woman alive" to tell the tale.

When the Philistines mustered their forces at Aphek (19, on locator) in preparation for a showdown battle with Israel, David faced a dilemma. To join the Philistine host in battle would make him a traitor to his people. To refuse would reveal his game of deception. Fortunately for David, he did not have to make the choice. Achish's fellow Philistine rulers mistrusted the renowned commander David and feared that he might turn his strong force of Hebrew mercenaries on them at a critical point in the coming battle. So David and his men were sent back to Ziklag, and the Philistines turned northward, anticipating a decisive battle with Saul.

Returning across the arid, dusty land to Ziklag, David discovered that the Amalekites had taken revenge for his earlier raids on them by burning the town and carrying off the families and belongings of his men. David's bitter men turned on him and almost stoned him, but he calmed them and organized a pursuit. They caught up

The lovely valley of Jezreel, which sweeps up to the mountain range of Gilboa, shown in the distance, became the scene of a bloody battle as the Israelites suffered a disastrous defeat at the hands of the Philistine forces. Among the men who "fell slain on Mount Gilboa" were Saul and his three sons Jonathan, Abinadab, and Malchishua.

with the camel-borne raiders at their desert camp (20) deep in the Negeb, beyond the Besor, and exacted a savage vengeance, smiting them "from twilight until the evening of the next day." All the captives and all the booty were recovered. Eyeing kingship, David shrewdly distributed spoils among the elders of southern Judah.

Meanwhile, the Philistines had advanced to do battle with the Israelites. From their assembly point at Aphek they marched northward, following the Way of the Sea, and then turned eastward into the Jezreel valley (map at top of page 93). At the head of the valley, in the shadow of Mount Moreh, they made their camp at Shunem (21). Saul positioned his army on nearby Mount Gilboa (22) to the south, probably at the springs on the northwestern edge of the mountain. When Saul observed the enormous size of the enemy force, "he was afraid, and his heart trembled greatly." All his efforts to discern God's will as to the course of the impending battle went unanswered. In desperation, he sought out a medium to give him a sign, contrary to his own decree against such practices. By night, in disguise, he secretly journeyed northward to Endor (23), where he pleaded with the medium (or witch) of Endor to conjure up the spirit of Samuel. The woman did as Saul bid. But in death, as in life, Samuel brought no comfort to Saul. He prophesied only disaster: "and tomorrow you and your sons shall be with me; the Lord will give the army of Israel also into the hand of the Philistines."

In his previous struggles with the Philistines, Saul's battlefield skills and the inspirational feats of Jonathan and David had won the field for the Israelites. This time the Philistines were not to be denied. Even though their feared war chariots were largely neutralized by the rugged terrain of Gilboa, they determined to use their advantage in numbers to take Saul's position by storm. Their attack was probably not in the direct line from Shunem but instead farther around to the south, where gentler slopes and shallow wadis would have permitted easier access to the left flank of Saul's army—and at the same time cut off his line of retreat. Saul's defenses were overwhelmed, and he and his men fled in rout up Mount Gilboa's sides. Among the rocks and brush on the heights—the "fields of disaster," as David would call

them—the pursuit was relentless. Brave Jonathan, who had pledged to support David, fell in the onslaught, while two of Saul's other sons, Abinadab and Malchishua, were also killed. The king himself was gravely wounded by a Philistine archer. He pleaded with his armor-bearer to kill him, lest the enemy "come and thrust me through, and make sport of me." When the terrified man refused, "Saul took his own sword, and fell upon it."

The next day, when the Philistines went over the field of their victory, they discovered the bodies of Saul and the three princes. They were beheaded and stripped of their armor, which was placed as a victory offering in the temple of Ashtaroth at Beth-shan (24). Saul's head was taken to the temple of Dagon there. The mutilated corpses were fixed to the walls of the city, and messengers hastened to Philistia "to carry the good news to their idols and to the people." Reports of the defeat and the humiliation of the bodies of Saul and his sons quickly spread through Israel At night a courageous band of men from Jabesh-gilead (25), a town east of the Jordan whose inhabitants Saul had once delivered, went to Beth-shan, spirited away the bodies, and carried them back for ritual burning.

With the defeat of Saul's army at Gilboa, the Hebrews lost control over the region bordering the Jezreel valley, abandoning their cities and fleeing. The terrible news of the disaster and its aftermath reached David at Ziklag in the desert three days after his return from crushing the Amalekites. "Then David took hold of his clothes, and rent them; and so did all the men who were with him; and they mourned and wept and fasted until evening for Saul and for Jonathan his son and for the people of the Lord and for the house of Israel . . ." David's intense grief moved him to compose one of the most beautiful laments in all literature, which begins:

"Thy glory, O Israel, is slain upon
    thy high places!
How are the mighty fallen!"

David the King

The death of Saul, about 1000 B.C., endangered the Israelite monarchy, threatening a return to the political anarchy of an earlier day. At issue was the succession to the kingship. The critical contest was between David and Ish-bosheth, the surviving son of Saul, and for a short time it looked as if there might be two kingdoms rather than one.

Ish-bosheth claimed to be king of "Gilead and the Ashurites and Jezreel and Ephraim and Benjamin and all Israel," that is, all of Saul's kingdom except Judah. But it was a hollow boast. He was actually a puppet ruler, dependent on the loyalty of Abner, commander of Saul's army. And the fact that he was forced to establish his court at Mahanaim (1, lower map opposite), in Gilead east of the Jordan, shows that much of Saul's old kingdom had fallen to the Philistines. In the meantime, David established his own power base. Following the period of mourning after Saul's disastrous defeat at Gilboa, he was commanded by the Lord to abandon Ziklag (2, upper map) in the Negeb for Hebron (3, lower map), the chief city in Judah and the burial place of the Patriarchs of Israel. There the elders anointed him "king over the house of Judah," and there he would rule for more than seven years.

A "cold war" was soon raging between the house of David and the house of Saul, represented by Ish-bosheth and Abner. David's initial tactics in the power struggle involved persuasion and politics. For example, he sent messengers far to the north to Jabesh-gilead (4, upper map)—a strategic location outflanking Mahanaim—carrying his blessings to the people for their rescue of the bodies of Saul and his sons and inviting them to transfer their loyalty to him now that their ruler was dead. But nothing came of this effort.

At Gibeon (5, lower map) in Benjamin, strategically situated on the major east-west route into the highlands, units of the two armies came face to face. Abner himself headed Ish-bosheth's troops, while Joab, David's chief lieutenant, led the contingent from Judah. The fighting men glowered at one another across the "pool of Gibeon." (Probably this was part of the remarkable water system unearthed by archaeologists in the late 1950's and shown in the photograph on the opposite page. Eighty feet below the town, and safe within rock walls, it offered the people of Gibeon a secure water supply in times of siege.) In an attempt to defuse the explosive situation, Abner proposed that a dozen men from each force "arise and play." Such wrestling matches were designed to settle disputes without bloodshed. But soon swords flashed, men fell to the ground, and a fierce fight ensued. Joab's troops gained the upper hand and Abner and his men fled across the hills.

Asahel, the young brother of Joab, set out in pursuit of the enemy commander. Abner begged him: "Turn aside from following me; why should I smite you to the ground? How then could I lift up my face to your brother Joab?" But the hot-blooded Asahel rushed after him heedlessly, and the veteran warrior killed him. With a

despairing message to Joab—"Shall the sword devour for ever? Do you not know that the end will be bitter? How long will it be before your people turn from the pursuit of their brethren?"—Abner retreated to Mahanaim, probably passing Michmash and the fords of the Jordan near Adam. Grieving and bitter, Joab buried his brother in the tomb of his father at Bethlehem (6). "And Joab and his men marched all night, and the day broke upon them at Hebron."

In the "long war between the house of Saul and the house of David," Ish-bosheth's fortunes waned while David's position grew stronger and stronger. Before any showdown on the battlefield, however, Ish-bosheth and Abner quarreled. The king angrily challenged his commander for taking one of Saul's concubines, an act he regarded as a signal that Abner was laying claim to royal power. Furious, Abner determined to switch allegiance and support David's rule over all Israel and Judah, from Dan (7, upper map) in the far north to Beer-sheba (8) in the Negeb. He made efforts to undermine Ish-bosheth, particularly in Benjamin, by asserting that David offered the best hope of deliverance from the hand of the Philistines. Ish-bosheth, remote in Mahanaim across the Jordan, had been betrayed. Under promise of safe-conduct from David, Abner and 20 of his men then came to Hebron, where the king prepared a feast for them. Abner made a secret agreement with the aspiring king and "went in peace."

When he returned from a raiding expedition, Joab was angered to learn of the covenant between David and Abner. Without telling David, Joab recalled Abner to Hebron and murdered him in revenge for the death of his brother Asahel—and also to eliminate a potential rival for the command of David's army. The deed endangered David's standing with the elders of the northern tribes, for Abner had been under royal protection. David convincingly disclaimed responsibility for the killing by staging a great funeral for Abner and acting as the chief mourner. The sorrowing king followed the bier and wept at the commander's grave.

Abner's murder rocked Ish-bosheth's court at Mahanaim. Two army captains who were brothers, Rechab and Baanah, were emboldened to take matters into their own hands. Slipping past the dozing doorkeeper, they found the king in his bedchamber taking a midday nap and assassinated him. Expecting great rewards, they took Ish-bosheth's head and traveled through the night to deliver it to David. From Mahanaim (9, lower map) they crossed the fords of the Jordan and traveled hurriedly south through the Jordan valley (10) to Hebron (11). David's response was an object lesson for regicides as well as a demonstration of his enduring respect for Saul and his family. The two assassins were executed, their hands and feet cut off, and their corpses hanged in a public place for all to see.

Then the elders of all the northern tribes came to David at Hebron, saying, "Behold, we are your bone and flesh." They entered into a solemn covenant before the

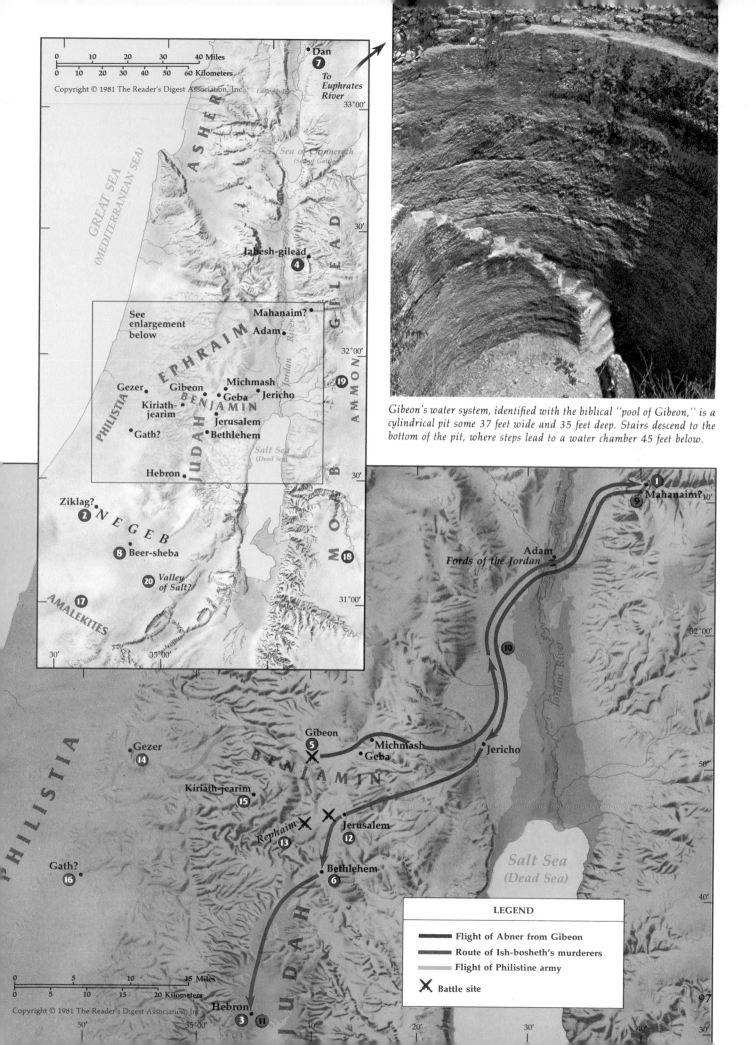

Scale (top-left map)

0   10   20   30   40 Miles
0   10   20   30   40   50   60 Kilometers

GREAT SEA (MEDITERRANEAN SEA)

ASHER

GILEAD

Dan ● **7**

To Euphrates River

Lake Huleh

Sea of Chinnereth (Sea of Galilee)

33°00'

30'

Jabesh-gilead ● **4**

Mahanaim? ●

Adam ●

Jordan River

EPHRAIM

BENJAMIN

See enlargement below

Gezer ●   Gibeon ●   Michmash ●   Geba ●   Jericho ●

Kiriath-jearim ●

PHILISTIA   **JUDAH**

Gath? ●

Jerusalem ●   Bethlehem ●

AMMON

19

32°00'

MOAB

Hebron ●

Salt Sea (Dead Sea)

30'

Ziklag? ● **2**

N E G E B

8 ● Beer-sheba

20 Valley of Salt?

18

AMALEKITES **17**

31°00'

30'   35°00'   30'

Photo caption

Gibeon's water system, identified with the biblical "pool of Gibeon," is a cylindrical pit some 37 feet wide and 35 feet deep. Stairs descend to the bottom of the pit, where steps lead to a water chamber 45 feet below.

Main map (bottom)

1 Mahanaim? **9** 10'

Adam   *Fords of the Jordan*

10

32°00'

Jordan River

Gibeon **5**   ● Michmash   ● Geba   ● Jericho

BENJAMIN

Gezer ● **14**

Kiriath-jearim ● **15**

PHILISTIA

Rephaim **13** ✕   ✕   Jerusalem **12**

Gath? ● **16**

Bethlehem ● **6**

JUDAH

Salt Sea (Dead Sea)

50'

40'

Hebron **3** **11**

0   5   10   15 Miles
0   5   10   15   20 Kilometers

50'   35°00'   10'   20'   30'   40'   30'

Legend

LEGEND

—— Flight of Abner from Gibeon
—— Route of Ish-bosheth's murderers
—— Flight of Philistine army
✕ Battle site

David the King (continued)

Lord and anointed 37-year-old David—now "King David"—ruler of all Israel. He would reign over a united kingdom for 33 years, or until about 961.

Hebron was too far south and too closely identified with Judah to remain David's capital. Jerusalem (12), some 20 miles to the north along the central ridge route and easily accessible from several directions, had much to recommend it as capital of a united Israel. Located on a rocky, triangular-shaped spur, it was guarded on two sides by deep valleys. A dependable spring made its own water supply secure, while in the surrounding limestone mountains there were few water sources to support an attacking army. The slopes around the city were rich in olives and grapes. Perhaps most important, Jerusalem was neutral ground as far as the two parties that had contended for power were concerned. Indeed, it was not even under Israelite control but had remained an enclave occupied by a people called the Jebusites.

David and his army laid siege to Jerusalem. The Jebusites taunted him from the walls, crying, "You will not come in here, but the blind and the lame will ward you off." Their bravado was not matched by their military skill. They neglected to guard the tortuous tunnel and the vertical shaft that gave the Jebusites access to water in times of siege. While David directed a diversionary assault on the walls, Joab and a picked force entered the watershaft and slipped into the city. Thus Jerusalem became the "city of David."

The Philistines, who had doubtless watched with satisfaction as the Hebrew tribes warred among themselves, now became alarmed. They did not relish a united Israel under a cunning leader like David. Marching into the Judah highlands, they approached Jerusalem through the wild and difficult Valley of Rephaim (13). Suddenly David's army sprang at them "like a bursting flood" and sent them reeling. Doggedly, the Philistines regrouped and came once again through the Valley of Rephaim, this time alert for an ambush. David had a different surprise ready for them. He sent his troops on a concealed flank march through a balsam forest and they fell on the

rear of the Philistine columns, taking a heavy toll and blocking the direct line of retreat down the valley. The enemy struggled through the rugged country to the north, hotly pursued all the way to Gezer (14) in the land of the Philistines. A triumphant David had beaten back the enemy not just once, but twice.

With Jerusalem secure, David set about consolidating his power. He brought the ark of the covenant from Kiriath-jearim (15), where it had been for 20 years since its return by the Philistines. Along the way, the oxen pulling the cart that carried the ark stumbled and the ark began to sway. When one of the drivers, Uzzah, put out his hand and steadied the sacred object, he was struck dead on the spot. Filled with fear, David "was not willing to take the ark of the Lord into the city of David; but David took it aside to the house of Obed-edom the Gittite." Only after three months passed and he heard that the ark had blessed the household of Obed-edom did David bring it into Jerusalem. This was an occasion for great rejoicing. Caught up in the joy and frenzy of the moment, David—dressed only in a linen ephod, which was probably a kind of loincloth—danced with all his might. His wife Michal, watching the king from the window, despised him in her heart, for she said he had uncovered himself before the eyes of his servants' maids "as one of the vulgar fellows shamelessly uncovers himself!"

The bringing of the ark to Jerusalem was a masterful stroke, for it gave Jerusalem ties with Israel's most sacred past and forever riveted it in the people's memory as the "holy city." David also established an efficient bureaucracy and paid particular attention to strengthening Israel's army. But he kept his own private army, which had been with him since the days of adventure in his flight from Saul and was utterly loyal.

David made relentless war on Israel's enemies and potential enemies. He took the offensive against the Philistines, for a time even holding their stronghold of Gath (16). In the Negeb he attacked his old nomadic enemies, the Amalekites (17, upper map). In a series of campaigns east of the Jordan, he subdued the Moabites (18) and the Ammonites (19). He crushed the Edomites in the Valley of Salt (20).

It was during the wars with the Ammonites that the story of David and Bathsheba unfolded. Late one spring afternoon, as the king was walking about on the roof of the royal house in Jerusalem, he caught sight of a beautiful woman bathing. He sent for her, and from their meeting Bathsheba conceived a child. But since she was married to Uriah the Hittite, David formed a plan whereby Uriah would be placed in the front lines and sent into the fiercest fighting. Predictably, Uriah was slain in the heat of battle and David married Bathsheba. But for his sin, the son she bore him was struck down by the Lord. Later David and Bathsheba would have a second son, who was called Solomon.

David's reach extended far to the north as well, gaining trading privileges in the region of the Euphrates River. In the wake of these victories, booty and tribute poured into Jerusalem. During his long reign King David had created a great empire, but in doing so, he had overextended Israel's resources to hold such a vast domain.

This inviting waterfall and pool are part of the oasis of En-gedi. Located on the western shore of the Dead Sea, these spring-fed waters provide pleasure to travelers today much as they did in ancient times.

Much of the Wilderness of Judah is an endless sea of rock. In his flight from Saul, David and his loyal followers trekked these furrowed hills to find shelter in the wilderness near En-gedi. The ancient Hebrew words for this type of lifeless terrain are jeshimon *and* tsia, *meaning "desolation" and "wasteland." In the Bible the land around En-gedi is also referred to as the Wildgoats' Rocks.*

The Revolt of Absalom

David was a great king. But as he grew old and became remote from the everyday affairs of his kingdom, his third son, Absalom, took advantage of the situation to raise the flag of revolt.

The seeds of the rebellion were sown 11 years earlier, when Amnon, David's firstborn son and heir to the throne, raped his half sister Tamar. Though angry, David failed to take action. After waiting two years, Absalom, who was Tamar's full brother, took matters into his own hands and ordered his servants to kill Amnon. Absalom then fled north, taking refuge for three years with his maternal grandfather, the king of Geshur (1). Finally, Joab persuaded David to allow Absalom to return to Jerusalem (2), for he saw that the king pined for his son. Yet another two years passed before David and Absalom were personally reconciled.

Absalom was handsome and talented—born to rule. His mother was a princess, and he had inherited much of his father's daring and cunning. No sooner was he in his father's good graces than he set about to undermine the old king's authority and usurp the crown. He not only affected the royal manner by riding in a chariot and having 50 men run before him, but more important, he stood by the city gate and told all who came to seek judgment before David that if only he were king, justice would be quickly served. When anyone attempted to bow down to him, Absalom held out his hand, raised him up, and kissed him. And "so Absalom stole the hearts of the men of Israel."

After four years of careful plotting, Absalom felt strong enough to reach boldly for the throne. Under the pretense of fulfilling an old vow, Absalom went to Hebron (3) with 200 followers, who were in the dark about his motives. Once there, he had himself anointed king, as his supporters throughout the land rose and proclaimed, "Absalom is king at Hebron!"

When David heard about this, he decided that he was in no position to make a direct military stand against his son and fled from Jerusalem (4) with his household and a band of faithful soldiers. The fugitive king and his men took the most direct route to the east, through the Wilderness of Judah toward the fords of the Jordan near Jericho. There he knew he could cross safely and continue north into Gilead, which was still loyal to him.

David was by no means willing to yield the throne to his son. Even as he was fleeing, the wily king sent a trusted adviser named Hushai back to Jerusalem, which had in the meantime been occupied by Absalom and the men of Israel. Hushai's task was to pretend allegiance to Absalom and offer the young man poor advice so that David would have time to make good his escape and regroup his forces. While an officer named Ahithophel counseled Absalom to pursue David at once, before the king had time to recover his strength, Hushai recommended that Absalom wait and gather a decisive force for the strike against David. The old king, Hushai said, was still the "expert in war."

Not knowing whose advice Absalom would follow, Hushai sent word to David not to spend the night at the fords but to cross the Jordan quickly lest he and his men be "swallowed up" by Absalom's forces. By dawn David's party was safely across the fords of the Jordan (5), making its weary way toward Mahanaim (6). In the Transjordan the exhausted refugees were given beds and food by David's loyal subjects in Gilead and Ammon— by Shobi from Rabbah (7), by Machir from Lodebar (8), and by Barzillai from Rogelim (9).

Since Absalom had heeded Hushai's advice to delay the pursuit, David had time to muster his forces and regroup the men into three powerful contingents. Upon learning that his counsel had been ignored, Ahithophel "saddled his ass, and went off home to his own city. And he set his house in order, and hanged himself . . ." When Absalom's newly gathered army—led by David's nephew Amasa after Ahithophel committed suicide— crossed the Jordan into Gilead, David was ready for war. He sent forth his battle-hardened soldiers, but not before he warned their leaders, "Deal gently for my sake with the young man Absalom."

The two armies met in the heavily wooded Forest of Ephraim (10). Absalom's men were hardly a match for David's veterans. As the battle spread over the wooded land, the number of casualties mounted; even more became hopelessly lost in the trackless forest. Fearing for his life, Absalom fled on his mule, but his hair caught fast in the thick branches of a great oak. While he hung there helpless, Joab and his armor-bearers killed this ambitious young man who could not wait for the throne to come to him.

Distraught over the death of his son, David returned to the Jordan, where many from Judah came to pay homage to the king they had so lately opposed. With this triumphant company of Judahites, David crossed to Gilgal (11), the ancient shrine where much earlier the Hebrews under Joshua had consecrated themselves after walking across the dry riverbed into the Promised Land. When the men of Israel arrived, they angrily demanded to know why they had been denied the honor of bringing David across the Jordan. In this increasingly tense atmosphere the revolt begun by Absalom played out its final scene.

Sheba, a Benjaminite from the hill country of Ephraim (12), was among the Israelites at Gilgal. He rallied the men, and said:

"We have no portion in David,
     and we have no inheritance in the son of Jesse."
Sheba withdrew to the north, leaving David with only his Judahite followers. Because he was angry with his commander Joab for killing Absalom, David sent Amasa, Absalom's one-time commander, to summon troops for the eventual fight with Sheba. But when Amasa was gone too long, Joab, Joab's brother Abishai, and all the mighty men of David—the king's personal guard—went in pursuit of Sheba. When Amasa met this group at Gibeon (13), he was brutally murdered by Joab, who contin-

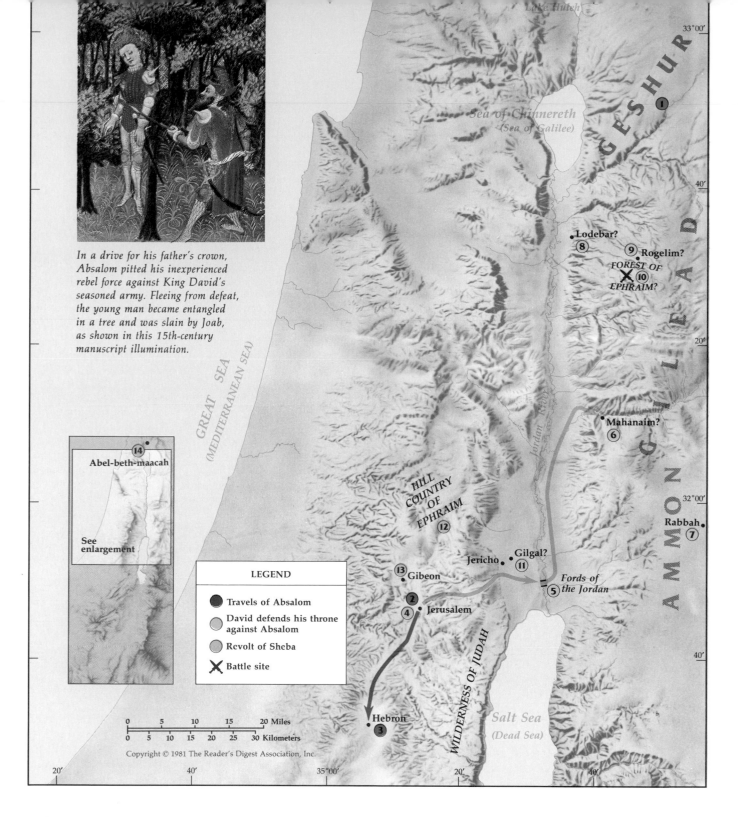

In a drive for his father's crown, Absalom pitted his inexperienced rebel force against King David's seasoned army. Fleeing from defeat, the young man became entangled in a tree and was slain by Joab, as shown in this 15th-century manuscript illumination.

GESHUR

Lake Huleh

Sea of Chinnereth
(Sea of Galilee)

GREAT SEA
(MEDITERRANEAN SEA)

Lodebar?
⑧

Rogelim?
⑨

FOREST OF
✕ ⑩
EPHRAIM?

GILEAD

Mahanaim?
⑥

Jordan River

AMMON

HILL
COUNTRY
OF
EPHRAIM
⑫

Rabbah
⑦

Jericho
Gilgal?
⑪

⑬ Gibeon

Fords of
⑤ the Jordan

② Jerusalem
④

WILDERNESS OF JUDAH

Salt Sea
(Dead Sea)

Hebron
③

LEGEND

● Travels of Absalom

● David defends his throne against Absalom

● Revolt of Sheba

✕ Battle site

⑭
Abel-beth-maacah

See
enlargement

| 0 | 5 | 10 | 15 | 20 Miles |
| 0 | 5 | 10 | 15 | 20 | 25 | 30 Kilometers |

Copyright © 1981 The Reader's Digest Association, Inc.

33°00'
40'
20'
32°00'
40'
20'
40'
35°00'
20'
40'

ued to pursue Sheba all the way to Abel-beth-maacah (14, on locator) and besieged the city. To save their own lives, the townspeople cut off Sheba's head and threw it over the wall to Joab, who thereupon lifted the siege and returned to Jerusalem. The revolt of Absalom had been stilled, and the events that began with the rape of Tamar had come to an end.

In his declining years, as David's health failed and his ability to govern was seriously impaired, the question of a successor became critical. David was aware that the potentially dangerous situation could easily erupt into civil war. Naturally Adonijah, the fourth and oldest surviving son of David, was scheming to succeed his father. But Bathsheba, once David's mistress and now his wife, persuaded the king to name their second and surviving son, Solomon, king over Israel and Judah.

Shortly after Solomon was anointed, David "died in good old age, full of days, riches, and honor." His 40-year reign (c. 1000–961 B.C.) had come to an end, and the golden age of Israel was about to begin.

Solomon's Empire

"Solomon in all his glory"—the phrase has rung down through the ages. The most splendid prince ever to rule in Israel, King Solomon was a monarch quite different from his two predecessors. Whereas Saul had held court under a tamarisk tree, Solomon ruled amid the opulence of a vast palace. Whereas David had installed the ark of the covenant in a tent in his new capital, Jerusalem, Solomon built a magnificent shrine there to hold it. Israel had come a long way from the pastoralism of the Patriarchs, and the nation was ultimately to pay a great price for the transformation.

Although Solomon is a famous figure in history, surprisingly little is known about him. Practically all the Bible tells us of his early life is that he was the second son of King David and Bathsheba. According to 1 Kings, his rise to power was engineered by his ambitious mother through a palace intrigue. As a result, Solomon was anointed while his father lived, so far as is known a singular occurrence in the history of the Israelite monarchy. Yet it was a wise move, for Israel was without a dynastic tradition, a fact that might otherwise have resulted in a bitter and bloody struggle for the succession.

When the old king finally died, Solomon ruthlessly removed members of the palace inner circle who represented an imminent threat to his power. Among these was David's eldest surviving son, Adonijah, whose earlier attempt to have himself declared king had failed. "So the kingdom was established in the hand of Solomon."

From his father, Solomon inherited an empire that stretched from Egypt north to the area around Kadesh—but his sphere of influence reached to the Euphrates. Solomon moved at once to secure his far-flung domain. His policy of seeking judicious alliances—often sealed by a royal marriage, as with the daughter of the Pharaoh—paid off handsomely. During his long, peaceful reign, from about 961 to 922 B.C., the king devoted his efforts to the cultural and economic development of the land. He established a successful maritime industry, the first in Israel's history, which engaged in luxury trade with East Africa and probably the Arabian peninsula. He worked to expand the natural resources and create agricultural settlements so necessary for the nation's prosperity. He reorganized the tax structure, dividing the country into districts. But most of all he showed himself to be an avid builder as he poured the riches of his empire into ambitious projects.

The special object of Solomon's passion for building was, of course, Jerusalem (1). On the little plateau just north of David's city, Solomon constructed his grand palace with its adjoining royal chapel, after the fashion of the times. But his chapel was more than a place of worship, it was the focus of Israelite life, for to it Solomon brought the ark of the covenant. (A reconstruction of Solomon's Temple appears on pages 108–109). The palace was no less magnificent, with splendid royal apartments and three large public buildings: the House of the Forest of Lebanon, the Hall of Pillars, and the Hall of the Throne, where six steps led up to the great ivory throne overlaid with the finest gold, for "silver . . . was not considered as anything in the days of Solomon."

As part of Solomon's grand plan, he used forced labor to build fortified military bases guarding the heartland of his kingdom: Hazor (2), commanding the routes from the north; Megiddo (3), commanding the major pass through the Mount Carmel range; Gezer (4), at the entrance to the most direct route from the coast to the Judah highlands and Jerusalem; and Lower Beth-horon (5). Baalath, a fifth city, may have been Kiriath-jearim (6) and, if so, was yet a third fortified base guarding the western borders. (Solomon was understandably concerned about the approaches leading to his domain. The Egyptians may have already reasserted authority over Philistia—which would explain the Pharaoh's gift of Gezer as part of the dowry for Solomon's Egyptian wife.) Below the Salt Sea, Tamar (7) helped establish control over a restless vassal, Edom, and served to guard the routes leading to the copper mines of the Arabah and to the port of Ezion-geber (8).

To ensure the success of his spectacular building program, Solomon had solicited the help of Hiram, king of Phoenician Tyre (9). Hiram furnished Solomon with architects, masons, and carpenters (the Phoenicians had a well-earned reputation as skilled builders) and with building materials, especially cypress wood and cedar from the mountains of Lebanon. In exchange, Solomon agreed to provide Hiram with 125,000 bushels of wheat and more than a million gallons of olive oil annually. For some years, things went well.

Solomon also entered into a joint commercial venture with Hiram and his seamen to exploit maritime trade possibilities. Israel already dominated the Way of the Sea and the King's Highway, two of the most lucrative avenues of commerce in the ancient world (inset at right). With his merchant fleet based at Ezion-geber at the head of the Gulf of Aqabah, Solomon sent ships down the Red Sea to fabled Ophir (although the location of Ophir is unknown, some scholars identify it with Somaliland in East Africa, while others place it on the Arabian coast). When the merchant-sailors returned from their three-year-long voyages, they brought back gold, silver, ivory, peacocks, and even pet apes. In addition, Ezion-geber also served as a major center of the Arabian caravan route. Thus Solomon controlled trade between Asia and Africa as well as the spice trade from Arabia. He became a rich middleman between the potentates to the north and the Egyptians, exchanging costly Egyptian chariots for the majestic stallions of Kue (ancient Cilicia in Asia Minor). And there is little doubt that the journey of the Queen of Sheba (modern Yemen in the Arabian peninsula) to Jerusalem to visit its famous merchant prince was prompted by commercial considerations.

Solomon paid particular attention to the Negeb, constructing a network of small forts to protect the caravan routes and establishing agricultural settlements in an early and partly successful attempt to make the desert bloom. Since agriculture was the basis of the economy in the land, Solomon took steps to encourage and expand

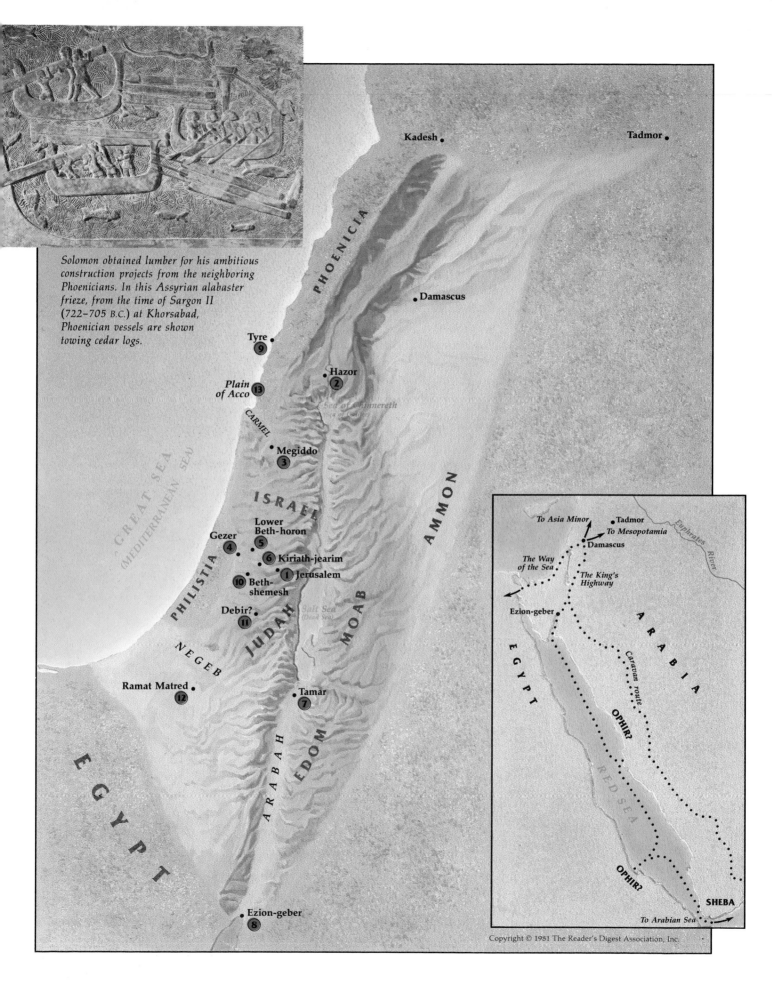

Solomon obtained lumber for his ambitious
construction projects from the neighboring
Phoenicians. In this Assyrian alabaster
frieze, from the time of Sargon II
(722–705 B.C.) at Khorsabad,
Phoenician vessels are shown
towing cedar logs.

Kadesh

Tadmor

PHOENICIA

Damascus

Tyre
9

Plain
of Acco 13

Hazor
2

CARMEL

Sea of Chinnereth
Sea of Galilee

Megiddo
3

ISRAEL

GREAT SEA
(MEDITERRANEAN SEA)

Lower
Beth-horon
Gezer   5
4
6 Kiriath-jearim
1 Jerusalem
10 Beth-
shemesh

AMMON

PHILISTIA

Debir?
11

Salt Sea
(Dead Sea)

JUDAH

MOAB

NEGEB

Ramat Matred
12

Tamar
7

EDOM

ARABAH

EGYPT

Ezion-geber
8

To Asia Minor   Tadmor
To Mesopotamia
Damascus

The Way
of the Sea
The King's
Highway

Euphrates River

Ezion-geber

EGYPT

ARABIA

Caravan route

OPHIR?

RED SEA

OPHIR?

SHEBA

To Arabian Sea

The Queen of Sheba

There are no known contemporary likenesses of the queen of Sheba, though her beauty is legendary. The head of this young woman, carved of alabaster, with hair of plaster and eyes of lapis lazuli, was created sometime in the first millennium B.C., possibly in the time of the queen of Sheba. It is from the Timna cemetery of Qataban, a neighboring kingdom of Sheba.

The queen of Sheba has captured the imagination of men for 3,000 years, and she lives on in literature, music, and art. The poet William Butler Yeats extolled her learning; the composer Handel celebrated her in the baroque cadences of his oratorio *Solomon*; and artists from Piero della Francesca to Hans Holbein, Tintoretto, and Rubens have sought to capture her mystery, grace, and elegance. Above all, it is the romantic link between King Solomon and the queen of Sheba that has aroused the most intense interest. Yet we know little of that romance—if romance indeed it was.

The original story of Solomon and the queen of Sheba is told in 13 verses of 1 Kings 10. According to the biblical account, the queen, hearing reports of Solomon's great wisdom, "came to test him with hard questions." Satisfied that his knowledge and riches surpassed her every expectation, "she gave the king a hundred and twenty talents of gold, and a very great quantity of spices, and precious stones." It seems that Solomon too was captivated, for he "gave to the queen of Sheba all that she desired, whatever she asked . . . So she turned and went back to her own land, with her servants."

Who was this beguiling woman, and where did she come from? According to the 1st-century A.D. Jewish historian Flavius Josephus, she was the queen of Egypt and Ethiopia. However, most modern scholars agree that the kingdom of Sheba (or Saba) was located in southwestern Arabia on the east shore of the Red Sea, roughly in present-day Yemen, and that the primary purpose of the queen's visit was commerce. Archaeological findings reveal the kingdom of Sheba to have had a highly developed culture supported by a lucrative trade in frankincense and myrrh—gum resins extracted from the bark of trees. Sheba was situated on the caravan routes leading north and east to Syria, Asia Minor, and Mesopotamia and west toward Egypt. The queen of Sheba would have been very much interested in establishing good relations with Solomon, who not only controlled a vital link in this overland route but whose merchant fleet traded with Arabian ports and sailed down the coast of East Africa, bringing back gold, silver, jewels, ivory, and exotic goods. It would have been to the queen's advantage to take samples of her own wares to Solomon and discuss trade agreements with him.

Whatever the reason for their meeting, the story has been embellished over the centuries. In some legends the queen is an alluring temptress, in others an evil sorceress. She has also been given some bizarre physical characteristics. Jewish legends represent her as the female demon Lilith; in Islamic stories she has the foot of an ass; in French gothic sculpture she is web-footed. The legends of Ethiopian origin hold that Ethiopia's kings are direct descendants of Menelik, a child born of the union of Solomon and the queen.

While it is unlikely that the facts of this ancient encounter will ever be known, the story of Solomon and the queen of Sheba continues to be one of the most popular in biblical literature.

---

this necessary resource. Archaeology has revealed that Beth-shemesh (10), Debir (11), and Ramat Matred (12, ancient name unknown) were major centers of agricultural activity in the time of Solomon. Of these, Ramat Matred is particularly important, for it shows Solomon's attempt to develop agriculture in the southern desert. He was successful, and future rulers sought to emulate his success in establishing control of the area.

Like the burgeoning desert, the nation as a whole was transformed as Solomon developed potential sources of wealth. A vastly expanded and well-organized government bureaucracy employed many, as did the huge military machine with its newly established strike force of 1,400 chariots and 12,000 horsemen. Tribute and trade greatly added to Israel's growing wealth in material goods. Many became rich. The arts flourished. The stories of Israel's earliest traditions—the Patriarchs, the Exodus, the conquest of Canaan—were shaped into a national epic in which God was seen as guiding the destiny of his chosen people, while heroic tales of David brought glory to the ruling dynasty. Music flourished in the new Temple, and the king—not unlike some other ancient potentates—gained a reputation for collecting and writing wisdom sayings, among them, perhaps, the book of Proverbs, traditionally attributed to Solomon.

But there was a price to be paid. Debts to Hiram began to pile up, until after 20 years Solomon was forced to cede 20 cities north of Mount Carmel and much of the land in the Plain of Acco (13) in repayment. This was not conquered land but a part of Israel itself, and the loss was bitterly resented by the people.

Solomon's insatiable need for revenue to pay for his

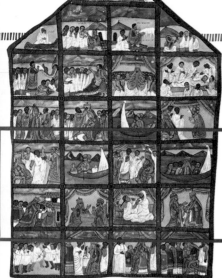

The Ethiopian version of the legend of Solomon and Sheba is depicted frame by frame in the sheepskin painting at left. In the detail below, the first row shows an emissary sailing past the pyramids to Solomon's court, followed by the queen; the second row illustrates the meeting between the monarchs. The story can be traced to the Kebra Nagast ("Glory of the Kings"), compiled by the monk Yeshaq in the 14th century to establish Ethiopia's claim as the true successor to Israel.

In Yeshaq's account, Solomon was so impressed with the visiting queen that he determined to beget a child by her. He wooed her with a feast, then invited her to share his chamber. She accepted on the condition that he would not take her by force, and he agreed, provided that she take nothing without his permission. That night, thirsty from the spicy foods, she took a drink of water. Solomon accused her of breaking her oath and seduced her. The queen returned to her own land and gave birth to a son, who was called Menelik, or Ibn al-Hakim, "son of the wise man." When he was grown, he visited Solomon, studied the Hebrew faith, and was anointed king of Ethiopia.

For centuries Ethiopian royalty has boasted of this link. The 1955 revised constitution of Ethiopia stated that the royal line "descends without interruption from the dynasty of Menelik I, son of the Queen of Ethiopia, the queen of Sheba, and King Solomon of Jerusalem."

massive construction program and his expensive life-style led him to divide "all Israel" (that is, the northern tribes) into 12 tax districts. His primary purpose was to make tax collection more efficient, with each district providing enough revenue annually to support the royal household for one month. According to 1 Kings 4:22, that meant a daily supply of 195 bushels of fine flour, 390 bushels of meal, 10 fat oxen, 20 pasture-fed cattle, 100 sheep, "besides harts, gazelles, roebucks, and fatted fowl." That Judah was probably exempt from such heavy taxation added fuel to the smoldering fire of discontent in the north.

For some time Solomon had had to resort to pressed labor gangs to carry out his building projects. David may have enslaved conquered peoples, but Solomon empressed first his Canaanite subjects and then his own countrymen from the northern tribes. There was also religious opposition to shrines honoring the gods of Solomon's foreign wives, which the king had allowed to be built just east of Jerusalem. His manner of living, including his harem of 700 wives and 300 concubines, placed additional financial burden on the people. But the anger went much deeper. Many bitterly resented Solomon's policies, which they saw as an attack on the old social order and a breakdown of traditional patterns of life. Here lay the seeds of future political division.

Finally, under all these pressures, the governmental structure began to fall apart. Though Israel's territory was still impressive in size, Solomon had lost control of the area immediately south of the Euphrates and gained an enemy in Damascus. After a 40-year reign, Solomon died about 922 B.C. and his splendid kingdom died with him.

David and Solomon's Jerusalem

"For the Lord has chosen Zion;
  he has desired it for his habitation:
  'This is my resting place for ever;
  here I will dwell, for I have desired it.' "

These verses from Psalms clearly underline the unique and powerful role that the city of Jerusalem played in the religious life of ancient Israel. Not just a place but a symbol, an idea, the Holy City provided a focal point and binding force that helped the Jews to preserve their identity over a long and tumultuous history. And in time—because both Jesus and Muhammad were identified with Jerusalem—the city became a center of devotion for Christians and Muslims as well.

Originally, Jerusalem became part of Israel's life for the most practical of reasons: King David's need for a capital of his united kingdom (see page 98). Compared with the city as it appears today, or even as it appeared in the time of Jesus (see reconstruction on pages 184–185), the Jebusite town taken by David and his troops was an extremely modest place. As indicated on the map at right, the city of David was confined to 11 or 12 acres on the southern spur of the Ophel ridge, with a population that could scarcely have exceeded 2,500. Nevertheless, the site had already been inhabited for some 2,000 years and was prominent enough to have been listed in Egyptian documents dating as far back as the 19th century B.C. The name "Jerusalem" is derived from *yeru*, meaning "foundation of" and from the name of the ancient god of the evening star, Shalem. And in one of the early Bible stories told in Genesis 14:18, the Patriarch Abraham is offered bread and wine by the Canaanite king of Salem, a place identified with Jerusalem.

David's first priority, it must be remembered, was to strengthen and enlarge his kingdom, but he seems not to have completed all his planned improvements in the new capital. The Bible tells us that David "built the city round about from the Millo [perhaps terraces on the eastern slope] in complete circuit; and Joab repaired the rest of the city." From this and other accounts it has been inferred that he upgraded the city's defenses, making repairs in the walls (especially on the north side, where the terrain made it vulnerable), rebuilding the Jebusite citadel, and erecting barracks for his troops. The Bible says also that he built "houses for himself"—though, given the limited space within the walls, David's residences can hardly have been of palatial proportions. (Solomon, in any event, seems to have found these wanting—to judge from the time and expense he subsequently lavished on his own palace.) David's principal contribution to the new capital, of course, was to bring the ark of the covenant there from its previous resting place at Kiriath-jearim. The ark was installed in an ornamental tent in

The ark was the holiest object to the Hebrews, but its exact appearance remains a mystery. This depiction, an ornate chest on wheels, is from a 3rd-century A.D. synagogue in Galilee.

accordance with Mosaic tradition—and with that, the city of David became the religious as well as the political capital of a land that was fast becoming a major power in the Near East.

If David had little time for architectural pursuits, Solomon delighted in ambitious building projects. Inheriting the empire created by his father, and the great wealth it produced, King Solomon transformed Jerusalem into a capital worthy of a large and vigorous kingdom. The centerpiece of the city was the palace complex, including Israel's first Temple, built on Mount Moriah, the site of the threshing floor David had purchased from the Jebusite Araunah for his altar of burnt offerings. Solomon first had to extend the city walls northward to enclose the area and construct a roughly rectangular stone platform to serve as a foundation. Completion of the Temple alone reportedly took seven years; the adjacent royal compound—which included separate palaces for Solomon and his most important wife, the Pharaoh's daughter, and various ceremonial and administrative quarters—required an additional thirteen.

With these undertakings, Solomon dramatically changed the face of Jerusalem. Its area was enlarged to about 32 acres, almost three times its earlier size, and the population grew to perhaps 4,500 or 5,000—not counting the settlements that inevitably sprang up outside the walls of any thriving commercial center. And indeed, for much of Solomon's 40-year-long reign Jerusalem served to control an unprecedented volume of trade between Egypt and Mesopotamia and the increased commercial traffic between Phoenicia and Solomon's bustling gateway to the Red Sea, Ezion-geber, and the ports of Africa and Arabia.

Finally, though, in surveying Solomon's impact on the nature and the history of Jerusalem, all else pales in comparison with his construction of the Temple (see reconstruction on pages 108–109). David had taken the momentous step of bringing the ark to Jerusalem but, on the Lord's command given to him by the prophet Nathan, had stopped short of building a permanent shrine to house it. It fell to Solomon, then, to complete the process of making Jerusalem Israel's Holy City, and in creating an official home for the ark—the symbol of God's sacred covenant with his chosen people—he inevitably made that place different from all other places.

In building the Temple, Solomon had to overrule lingering ideas that the ark should have no fixed home at all, that to give it one was to cast aside an old and venerable tradition. But, in effect, Solomon was establishing a new tradition. The days of tribal wandering were over for the Hebrews. Israel at last had come of age as a nation.

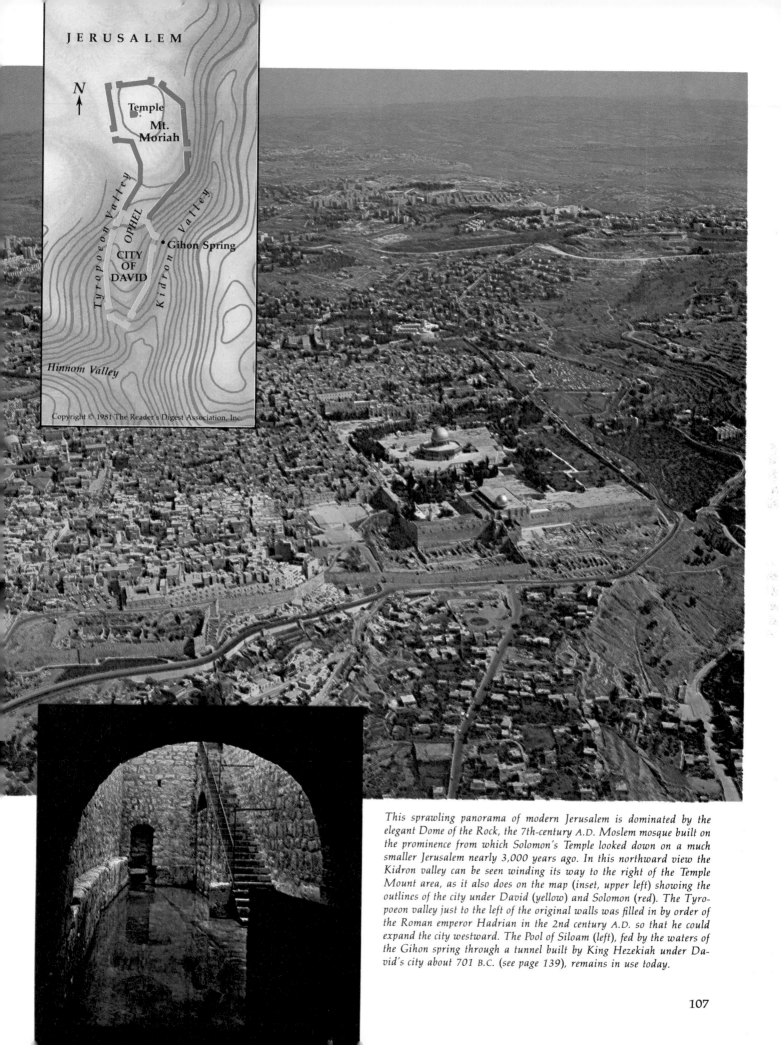

JERUSALEM

N

Temple
Mt. Moriah

Tyropoeon Valley

OPHEL

CITY OF DAVID

Kidron Valley

• Gihon Spring

Hinnom Valley

Copyright © 1981 The Reader's Digest Association, Inc.

This sprawling panorama of modern Jerusalem is dominated by the elegant Dome of the Rock, the 7th-century A.D. Moslem mosque built on the prominence from which Solomon's Temple looked down on a much smaller Jerusalem nearly 3,000 years ago. In this northward view the Kidron valley can be seen winding its way to the right of the Temple Mount area, as it also does on the map (inset, upper left) showing the outlines of the city under David (yellow) and Solomon (red). The Tyropoeon valley just to the left of the original walls was filled in by order of the Roman emperor Hadrian in the 2nd century A.D. so that he could expand the city westward. The Pool of Siloam (left), fed by the waters of the Gihon spring through a tunnel built by King Hezekiah under David's city about 701 B.C. (see page 139), remains in use today.

107

Then he made the molten sea; it was round,
ten cubits from brim to brim, and
five cubits high . . . It stood upon
twelve oxen, three facing north,
three facing west, three facing
south, and three facing east . . .

2 Chr. 4:2–4

. . . and he set the sea on the
southeast corner of the house.

1 Kg. 7:39

He made an altar of bronze,
twenty cubits long, and twenty
cubits wide, and ten cubits high.

2 Chr. 4:1

In front of the house he made two pillars thirty-five cubits high,
with a capital of five cubits on the top of each. . .
He set up the pillars in front of the temple, one on the south,
the other on the north; that on the south he called Jachin,
and that on the north Boaz.

2 Chr. 3:15–17

He lined the walls of the house on the inside with boards of cedar; from the floor of the house to the rafters of the ceiling, he covered them on the inside with wood; and he covered the floor of the house with boards of cypress.
1 Kg. 6:15

He carved all the walls of the house round about with carved figures of cherubim and palm trees and open flowers . . .
1 Kg. 6:29

And he made for the house windows with recessed frames.
1 Kg. 6:4

. . . and he made the ceiling of the house of beams and planks of cedar.
1 Kg. 6:9

For the entrance to the inner sanctuary he made doors of olivewood . . .
1 Kg. 6:31

In the inner sanctuary he made two cherubim of olivewood, each ten cubits high. . . . And he overlaid the cherubim with gold.
1 Kg. 6:23, 28

For the cherubim spread out their wings over the place of the ark, so that the cherubim made a covering above the ark and its poles.
1 Kg. 8:7

The Temple of Solomon

The gleaming limestone Temple built by King Solomon and dedicated about 950 B.C. was a monument of noble proportions—roughly 180 feet long, 90 feet wide, and 50 feet high. One entered from the east through a doorway flanked by 40-foot bronze pillars. A vestibule led into the large main sanctuary, illuminated by small windows near the ceiling. No stone could be seen anywhere inside the Temple, since the floor was of cypress and the ceilings were coffered throughout. Past the shewbread table at the center of the room and directly behind the incense altar, steps led up to the most sacred place in the Hebrew world: the windowless Holy of Holies, entered just once a year by the High Priest. Outside the entrance were a 15-foot-high altar for burnt offerings and an immense bronze bowl called the molten sea, holding water that may have been used for ritual cleansing.

This reconstruction is based on biblical evidence (such as the superimposed quotations) and on contemporary archaeological findings elsewhere; there is no comparable information about Solomon's palace, which would have been adjacent to the Temple.

Divided Monarchy

Soon after Solomon was buried at Jerusalem (1), the united kingdom he had inherited from David split in two. Solomon's son Rehoboam, recognized as king by the elders of Judah, traveled north to Shechem (2), where the elders of "all Israel" had gathered. They refused to confirm his accession to the throne unless he abandoned his father's repressive policies. Although his older counselors urged leniency, Rehoboam listened instead to the young men about him and pledged an even heavier yoke: "My father chastised you with whips, but I will chastise you with scorpions." The elders of the north rejected the arrogant young king with virtually the same words that the Benjaminite Sheba had used earlier in rejecting Rehoboam's grandfather, David:

"What portion have we in David?
We have no inheritance in the son of Jesse.
To your tents, O Israel!
Look now to your own house, David."

The elders went further and anointed their own king: the Ephraimite Jeroboam, a rebel against Solomon, now returned from his refuge in Egypt. From this point forward the monarchy was divided into two kingdoms, each with its own ruler (see chronological table of kings below.)

The powerful state crafted by Saul, David, and Solomon divided roughly along the tribal lines that had existed since the time of Joshua. "All Israel"—the northern tribes of the central hills, the Great Plain, the area of Galilee, and the Transjordan—were ruled from Shechem by Jeroboam. From Jerusalem the proud Rehoboam controlled only Judah, Simeon, most of Benjamin (see map on page 82), a small portion of Philistia, a desert strip down to Ezion-geber, and perhaps parts of Edom.

Conquered areas broke away from both kingdoms. The king of Damascus consolidated his position in Syria, and Ammon and Moab in the Transjordan gained their independence. The situation in Edom is less clear, but certainly Judah did not hold the entire area nor perhaps very much of it. In the west the Philistines reasserted themselves around Gibbethon.

Solomon's economic empire, already in trouble during his lifetime, collapsed. Monopolistic income from the lucrative trade routes—the Way of the Sea and the King's Highway—came to an end, as of course did tribute from the former conquered territories. The great trading en-

The Kings of Judah and Israel

David and his son Solomon ruled a united kingdom for more than 70 years. Following the latter's death about 922 B.C., the kingdom split in two: Judah confirming Solomon's son Rehoboam as king; the northern tribes choosing the rebel Jeroboam to rule Israel. The Lord had promised (2 Samuel 7:16) that the house of David, father to son, would rule in Judah forever. The dynasty lasted through 19 generations until Jerusalem fell to the Babylonians in 587. The single exception was the Omride princess Athaliah, who usurped the throne in 842 and reigned for five years. However, a son of the assassinated Ahaziah was spared the purge of both royal houses that followed the revolt of Jehu in 842. As King Joash, he restored the house of David to Judah's throne. Only as the southern kingdom neared its end did the succession prove irregular—with Josiah being followed, in turn, by two sons (Jehoahaz and Jehoiakim), then a grandson (Jehoiachin) taken into exile, and finally a third son, Zedekiah, who was blinded and led in chains to Babylon, where he died.

In Israel, however, there was little or no single dynastic succession—assassination and coup d'etat being the rule in the northern kingdom. Jeroboam's son Nadab was assassinated by Baasha; Baasha's son Elah, by Zimri—who under siege committed suicide after a week on the throne. The house of Omri lasted little more than three decades; that of Jehu—Israel's most durable—nearly a century. In the two decades before the fall of Samaria to the Assyrians in 721, five kings ruled Israel, with only one son (Pekahiah) succeeding his father (Menahem).

Biblical writers used different and often conflicting chronological systems. The dates in the table at right are based on the proposals of the late biblical scholar W. F. Albright.

David (c. 1000-961)
Solomon (c. 961-922)

JUDAH		ISRAEL
Rehoboam (922-915)		(922-901) Jeroboam
Abijam (915-913)		
Asa (913-873)		(901-900)* Nadab
		(900-877) Baasha
		(877-876)* Elah
		(876)** Zimri
Jehoshaphat (873-849)		(876-869) Omri
		(869-850) Ahab
		(850-849) Ahaziah
Jehoram (849-842) m. Athaliah		(849-842)* Jehoram
	Queen of Judah	
Ahaziah (842)*	(842-837)*	(842-815) Jehu
Joash (837-800)*		
		(815-801) Jehoahaz
Amaziah (800-783)*		(801-786) Jehoash
		(786-746) Jeroboam II
Uzziah (783-742)		
		(746-745)* Zechariah
		(745)* Shallum
		(745-738) Menahem
Jotham (742-735)		(738-737)* Pekahiah
		(737-732)* Pekah
Ahaz (735-715)		(732-724) Hoshea
Hezekiah (715-687)		(721) FALL OF SAMARIA
Manasseh (687-642)		
Amon (642-640)*		
Josiah (640-609)		
Jehoahaz (609) Jehoiakim (609-598)		
Jehoiachin (598-597) Zedekiah (597-587)		* = assassinated ** = suicide

FALL OF JERUSALEM (587)

terprises with Egypt, Kue, Sheba, and Africa diminished if they did not end altogether as fraternal strife and sporadic warfare with neighboring peoples sapped the energies of the two petty succession states.

Rehoboam's intention to reunite the country by force was foiled by the opposition of religious conservatives already antagonistic to the monarchy—and probably by the sober realization that Israel was militarily stronger than Judah. Moreover, the people of the north, resentful of Solomon's policies, were now ready to defend their independence. The people of Judah were less anxious to fight—though they were forced to contend for a defensible border with Israel.

The line separating the two kingdoms ran roughly along the traditional boundary between Ephraim and Benjamin. To the northwest, however, it left Gezer (3), Aijalon, and the vital Way of Beth-horon in Judah's hands. It then passed south of Bethel (4) and ran eastward through Benjamin down to the Jordan valley below Jericho (5), which had been seized by Israel. This border was intolerable to Rehoboam since it left Jerusalem, his capital, vulnerable. There was "war between Rehoboam and Jeroboam continually" as the rival monarchs struggled for the strategic plateau north of Jerusalem.

After Rehoboam's death, his son Abijam (known also as Abijah) wrested Bethel and the surrounding hill country from Israel. But Baasha, who assassinated Jeroboam's son and successor, Nadab, and seized Israel's throne, not only retook this area from Abijam's son Asa but drove as far as Ramah (6)—only 5½ miles from Jerusalem.

In a masterful counterstroke, Asa allied himself with Ben-hadad of Damascus, who obligingly invaded Israel in the north, overrunning Dan (7), Abel-beth-maacah (8), Hazor (9; although the Bible does not mention Hazor, archaeological evidence reveals signs of destruction from this time), and Chinnereth (10). As Judah's king had anticipated, Baasha withdrew Israel's troops from his southern border in order to meet the threat from Syria. Seizing this opportunity, Asa attacked, captured Ramah, and dismantled the unfinished fortress there. With the stones and timbers of Ramah, Asa fortified Geba (11) and Mizpah (12) against Israel. Digging at Mizpah, archaeologists have found remains of a massive wall with distinctive inset salients that seems to have formed a part of Asa's fortifications commanding the northern approaches to Jerusalem. Bethel and its immediate area remained Israelite, however, and the Judahites had to live with the threat of a potential enemy only 10 miles from their capital.

In population and resources Israel (see map on next page) was by far the stronger of the two kingdoms, and its geography enriched it. Jeroboam originally made Shechem (1) his capital but soon moved to the more easily defended town of Tirzah (2). His eastward-looking foreign policy was underscored by the fortification of Penuel (3), a move in Israel's long struggle to control a portion of the King's Highway (4). But the Way of the Sea (5) was more important to Israel, since it bisected the northern kingdom. Along this great road passed caravans and goods, men and ideas, armies and ambition.

Israel's geography immersed it in the international life of the time—for better or for worse. There was trade and

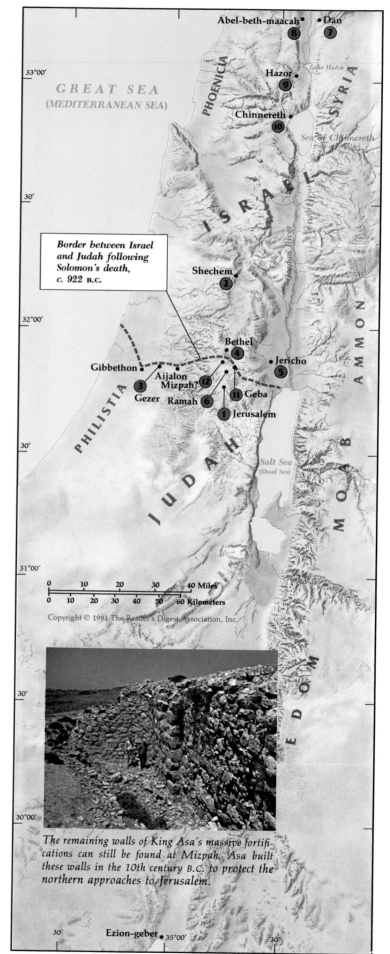

The remaining walls of King Asa's massive fortifications can still be found at Mizpah. Asa built these walls in the 10th century B.C. to protect the northern approaches to Jerusalem.

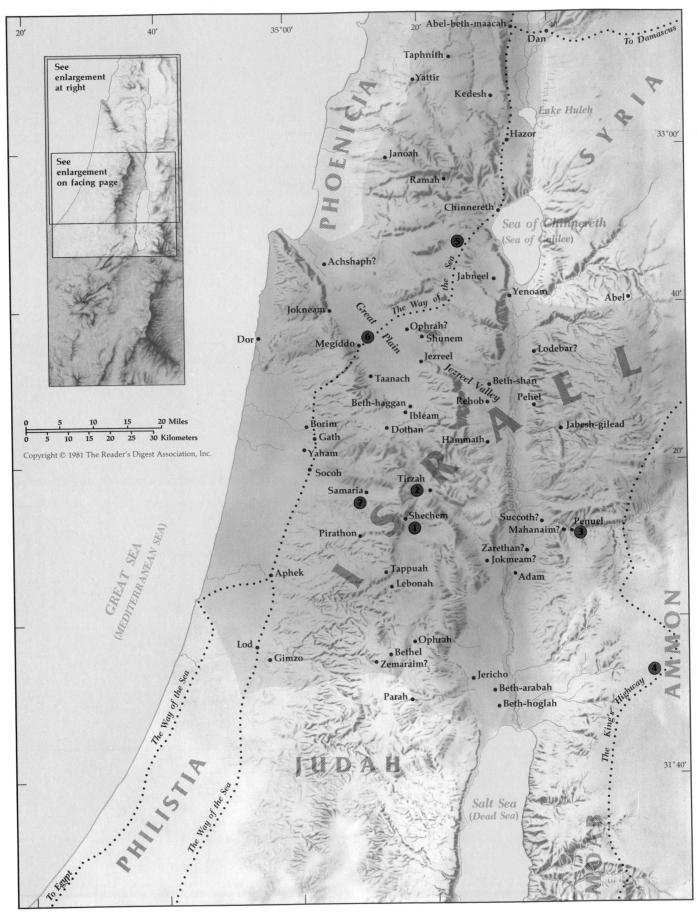

20'
40'
35°00'
20'
40'

Abel-beth-maacah

Dan

To Damascus

PHOENICIA

Taphnith

Yattir

Kedesh

Lake Huleh

SYRIA

Hazor

33°00'

Janoah

Ramah

Chinnereth

Sea of Chinnereth
(Sea of Galilee)

⑤

40'

Achshaph?

Jabneel

Yenoam

Abel

Jokneam

The Way of the Sea

Great Plain

Ophrah?

Shunem

Lodebar?

Dor

Megiddo ⑥

Jezreel

Beth-shan

Taanach

Jezreel Valley

Rehob

Pehel

Beth-haggan

Ibleam

Borim

Dothan

Hammath

Jabesh-gilead

Gath

Yaham

Socoh

Tirzah

Samaria ⑦

②

Shechem ①

Succoth?

Mahanaim?

Penuel ③

Pirathon

Zarethan?

Jokmeam?

ISRAEL

Aphek

Tappuah

Lebonah

Adam

AMMON

Lod

Ophrah

Gimzo

Bethel

Zemaraim?

Jericho

④

Parah

Beth-arabah

Beth-hoglah

The King's Highway

31°40'

JUDAH

GREAT SEA
(MEDITERRANEAN SEA)

Salt Sea
(Dead Sea)

The Way of the Sea

PHILISTIA

To Egypt

See enlargement at right

See enlargement on facing page

0   5   10   15   20 Miles
0   5   10   15   20   25   30 Kilometers

Copyright © 1981 The Reader's Digest Association, Inc.

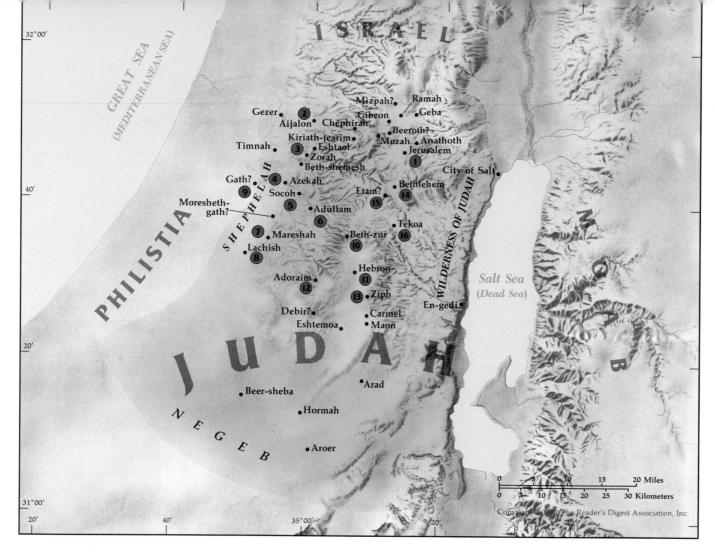

a measure of prosperity, but when an expansionist ruler sat on the throne in Egypt or in Assyria, Israel was likely to feel the tread of hostile feet. And the Great Plain (6) was another kind of highway that struck southeastward from Phoenicia, on the northern coast, into Israel's very heart. This too brought prosperity as Phoenician goods and skilled workmen poured into Israel, especially after about 875 B.C. when King Omri built his new capital at Samaria (7) and oriented his economic policies northwestward. There was no military threat here, but foreign ideas in religion, politics, and economics clashed with Israel's traditional ways to produce violent strife that ripped apart society and fostered political instability. Out of these conflicting forces came Jezebel and Elijah as well as Elisha and the terrible revolt of Jehu.

Its position astride the way from Asia to Africa thrust Israel into the international arena. On the surface at least, the kingdom was cosmopolitan and urbane. It was always involved in geopolitical intrigues, and ultimately Israel was swept into alliances against far stronger powers and was destroyed in the Assyrian maelstrom.

In contrast Judah (see map above) was a landlocked stump removed from important trade routes and, indeed, from much international commerce and intercourse. Its fiercely contested border with Israel too often cut it off from the north, while the Salt Sea effectively blocked eastward expansion. To the south lay the desert, while on the west the scrub-covered hills of the Shephelah

formed another natural barrier. David's dynasty provided political stability for nearly 400 years, while the Temple in Jerusalem (1) and an ongoing tradition of prophetic reformers ensured religious continuity. Yet Judah was a relatively poor, conservative, withdrawn nation until it became involved in anti-Babylonian alliances around 600 B.C.—and this spelled the end for the southern kingdom.

The heartland of Judah was well defined by the fortifications of Rehoboam, carried out either near the beginning of his reign or more likely in preparation to defend his land against an attack by the Egyptian Pharaoh Shishak. In 2 Chronicles 11:5–10 there is mention of 15 "cities for defense" built by Rehoboam. By fortifying Aijalon (2), Zorah (3), Azekah (4), Socoh (5), Adullam (6), Mareshah (7), and Lachish (8), he sought to secure the four western passes into the hills. (Gath, 9, occupied by Judahites, lay in the coastal plain.) At Beth-zur (10) and Hebron (11) he fortified the southern end of the central ridge route that ran north-south through the center of his kingdom. Adoraim (12) and Ziph (13) were strategically placed on the western and southeastern approaches to Hebron. Bethlehem (14) and Etam (15) blocked the ridge route nearer Jerusalem as well as forming, with Tekoa (16), a defensive perimeter against enemies approaching from the east.

Rehoboam's efforts to defend his truncated kingdom against a hostile thrust from the south were soon proved to have been in vain.

113

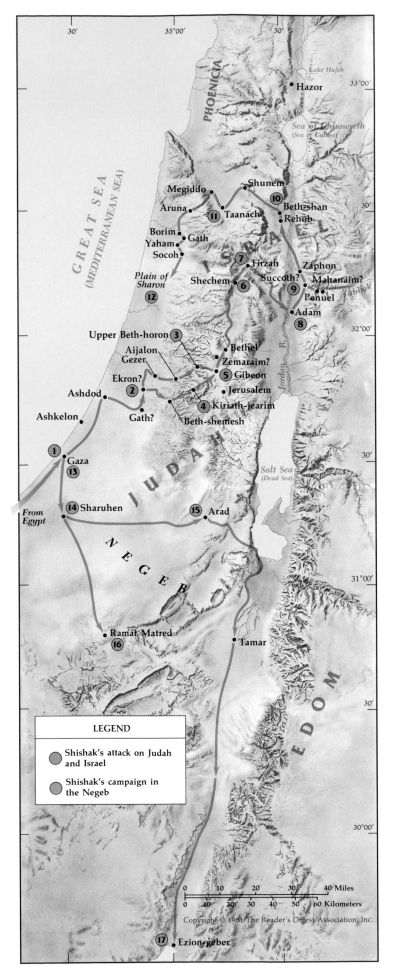

Copyright © 1981 The Reader's Digest Association, Inc.

Egypt Invades

In the fifth year of Rehoboam's reign in Judah (c. 918 B.C.), Pharaoh Shishak (Sheshonk I), the Libyan founder of Egypt's 22nd Dynasty, invaded the Hebrew kingdoms.

Having sheltered the rebel Jeroboam when he fled Solomon's wrath, Shishak might have been expected to support Jeroboam's assumption of power over the northern kingdom. But the Pharaoh's intention—perhaps even in allowing the fugitive to return and make his claim at Shechem—was always to weaken the northern neighbor that had come to dominate trade in the land bridge with Asia and thus thwart Egypt's imperial ambitions in that direction. With Solomon's kingdom now divided, Shishak struck, further weakening the two succession states and gaining control of the all-important trade routes.

The brief notices of Shishak's invasion in the Bible (1 Kings 14:25–28 and 2 Chronicles 12:1–12) give the impression that the Pharaoh's objective was Jerusalem and that Rehoboam surrendered the treasures of the Temple and the palace (including Solomon's gold shields) in exchange for Shishak's sparing Jerusalem from destruction. But the Bible also notes that the Egyptian army consisted of 1,200 chariots and 60,000 horsemen and that Shishak took "the fortified cities of Judah," which suggests something more than a strike at Jerusalem and Solomon's considerable treasure of gold.

Fortunately, we have Shishak's own account of this military expedition, found in the Temple of Amon at Karnak. This inscription, listing more than 150 places captured, shows that Shishak attacked not merely Judah but also the settlements of the Negeb and the northern kingdom of Israel, including the Transjordan. Moreover, widespread archaeological discoveries support the Egyptian account of the invasion. Burns still to be seen on walls and gates, as well as destruction debris lying on ruined houses and shops, reveal the ferocity of the Egyptian onslaught. It is thus possible to trace the path of destruction, even 3,000 years after the blow fell upon the Hebrew kingdoms.

Advancing into the Philistine plain, the Egyptians came to Gaza (1) and there divided their army in two. One strike force went south and east into the Negeb, while the other went northward. The Egyptians' northern force did not, however, penetrate Judah along a single route. From Ekron (2) one unit of Shishak's army went north and then turned eastward along the Way of Beth-horon, through Upper Beth-horon (3), while a second group was smashing into the central hill country eight miles south along the Way of Beth-shemesh through Kiriath-jearim (4)—the route along which the Philistines had once returned the ark of the covenant. The two columns joined forces at Gibeon (5), less than six miles northwest of Jerusalem. It would seem that Rehoboam, his fortified cities now smoldering heaps, came to Gibeon to exchange his father's wealth for the safety of Judah's capital.

Moving north along the central ridge route, the Egyptian army entered the kingdom of Israel at a vulnerable point. There were no large, fortified cities to anchor a defense line; indeed, there was hardly any defense line at

Pharaoh Shishak proudly inscribed the southern wall of the temple of Amon at Karnak (left) with the names of more than 150 cities that had fallen before him during his military sweep of Israel and Judah. The ravaged cities of Megiddo and Gezer are among those listed, and archaeological excavations attest to their destruction during Shishak's time. Jerusalem, however, was spared the Egyptian onslaught because of the heavy tribute paid by Rehoboam. The wall relief shows the god Amon in the center holding ropes to captured kings while other captives kneel in submission before him.

all. For all their border problems with Judah, the Israelites had never been overly concerned about the potential power of the rival kingdom to the south. And perhaps thinking of Shishak as an ally, Jeroboam had apparently not taken seriously the possibility of an Egyptian invasion. But now the Egyptian army found itself among the unprotected vineyards and orchards of the hill country.

Neither the earlier fortifications of David and Solomon nor the defensive measures of Rehoboam could stop the Egyptian juggernaut. Solomon's engineers had favored the casemate wall (a double wall with connecting cross walls) as a means of nullifying the effects of a battering ram. Such city walls from Solomon's time have been found at Gezer, Hazor, and Megiddo. Archaeologists have also uncovered the distinctive triple-chambered gates—the work of Solomon's military engineers—at each of these sites. Although these were the latest developments in city defenses, Shishak's army smashed through the casement walls at Gezer and Megiddo as destruction levels there show. Interestingly, the Bible speaks of no battles; the Egyptian inscription at Karnak merely lists the places captured. What had become of the armed forces Solomon had amassed and equipped so well?

The Egyptians passed Shechem (6)—which archaeology shows was destroyed about this time—and struck Tirzah (7), the new capital of Israel. But, as excavations reveal, the damage there was less than at many other places, and Tirzah soon recovered. East of Tirzah the Wadi Farah offered the Egyptians a broad highway down to the fords of the Jordan at Adam (8). Here the invaders crossed to the east bank, going northward to Succoth (9) and then up the valley of the Jabbok to Mahanaim and Penuel, perhaps because Penuel was a royal city of Israel or merely to destroy Israelite power in the Transjordan.

The invincible Egyptian army retraced its route down the Jabbok valley and moved relentlessly north, destroying Zaphon before recrossing the river and entering the Jezreel valley at Beth-shan (10). Rehob, Beth-shan, and Shunem all fell. At the southern edge of the Great Plain, Taanach (11) was destroyed and burned, as excavations confirm. And five miles away at Megiddo, Solomon's great city was stormed, burned, and rebuilt as an Egyptian base guarding the main route of the Way of the Sea as it passed through the Carmel range. A fragment of a stele commemorating Shishak's capture of Megiddo has been found there.

At this point Shishak turned homeward and went down the Way of the Sea—though his work of destruction was not done. He reduced the towns along the way—among them Aruna, Borim, Gath, Yaham, and Socoh—as he seized control of the trade route not only in the northern valleys but also in the Plain of Sharon (12) and all the way down the coast back to Philistia.

Meanwhile, the Egyptian army that had marched from Gaza (13) into the Negeb took Sharuhen (14), which excavators think may have been refortified as an Egyptian garrison to control movement between the Negeb and the coast. Shishak's list of sites in the Negeb contains about 70 names, most of them settlements established in the time of Solomon. Few of these sites can be identified today, but enough is known to indicate that Egyptian activity was concentrated in the southern Negeb and to suggest that Shishak's objective here was the establishment of Egyptian control over the trade routes with Arabia, including Sheba.

The Egyptians scoured the entire Negeb south of Arad (15), which appears to be the northernmost site attacked by this prong of the invasion. Fortresses such as Arad and agricultural settlements such as Ramat Matred (16) are shown by archaeology to have been destroyed at this time. The Egyptians were not interested in resettling the Negeb, only in ending Judah's hold on the area. To this end they seem also to have struck close to Edom, ending Judah's firm hold on that region. Finally, the excavations at Ezion-geber (17) tell us that the Solomonic town there was put to the torch about this same time. It is not likely that this important port and center of Arabian trade would have escaped Shishak's attention.

Having laid waste to so much of the two kingdoms, the Pharaoh was forced to return home to quell internal disturbances. If Shishak was not able to reestablish Egypt's Asian empire, he at least guaranteed in this devastating campaign that there would no longer be a strong power on Egypt's northeastern frontier.

The Phoenicians: Seafarers and Craftsmen

Israel's northern neighbors, the Phoenicians, were the merchants, craftsmen, and seafarers of the eastern Mediterranean. Descendants of earlier Canaanites, they settled along the coast and about 1200 B.C.—after the Sea Peoples ravaged the area—established themselves in a loose confederation of city-states. Occupying a narrow strip between the mountains to the east and the sea to the west, the Phoenicians built their communities on islets or rocky promontories that provided natural harbors on both their northern and southern shores. The cities of Sidon and Tyre, Arvad and Byblos, studded the seacoast like jewels, inspiring envy in their neighbors and competition among themselves. But the Hebrew prophet Ezekiel predicted doom for vainglorious Tyre at the hands of strangers, saying to the city: "and they shall draw their swords against the beauty of your wisdom and defile your splendor."

The Phoenicians developed a flourishing sea trade as well as a vigorous shipbuilding industry. Although the arable land was limited, it was fertile and well irrigated by mountain streams. Fig, olive, and palm trees abounded; wheat and grapes flourished; sheep and goats grazed the hillsides. Fish and shellfish were plentiful, and the region was famous for the murex, from which the Phoenicians extracted a highly prized purple dye. From the mountains came marble, lignite, and iron as well as a fine sand that was used in the manufacture of glass. And, of course, there were the magnificent forests of Lebanon, renowned throughout the Near East for their pines, cypresses, and particularly cedars. And Solomon used cedars of Lebanon, provided by King Hiram of Tyre, in the building of his Temple.

The extent to which Phoenicia's trade had developed at the height of its power is apparent from the tribute it paid to the Assyrian kings, who later began to expand into the region. On an expedition into Phoenicia about 876 Ashurnasirpal II records that he received "silver, gold, lead, copper, vessels of bronze, garments made of brightly colored wool, linen garments, a great monkey, and a small monkey, maple-wood, boxwood, and ivory . . ." Much of the tribute mentioned above was undoubtedly local handicraft, but the Phoenicians imported copper from Cyprus; gold and linen from Egypt; ivory from India; copper, tin, and iron from Spain; precious stones from Arabia; wool from Syria; horses from Anatolia; and slaves and peacocks from Africa.

The Phoenicians were skilled artisans, noted for their fine work in ivory and metal, as well as first-rate carpenters, masons, and architects. They also raised the craft of glassmaking to a fine art and have even been credited with the invention of glassblowing. Their major cultural contribution, however, seems to have been the development of the alphabet. Although they continued to use cuneiform, the Phoenicians had an alphabetic script as early as the 15th century B.C. Consisting of 22 consonants, it was the basis for Hebrew, Arabic, Syriac, and various other Near Eastern alphabetic scripts. It was also adopted by the Greeks, spread throughout western civilization, and is the foundation of the English alphabet.

Phoenicia reached its zenith with the colonization of Mediterranean lands early in the first millennium B.C. By 900 it had expanded into Cyprus, Sicily, Sardinia, Africa, and Spain and by 814 had founded the city of Carthage. Although Carthage would survive until it was sacked by Rome in 146, the independence of the great city-states of Phoenicia ended with the Assyrian conquests. The fall of Tyre to the Babylonian king Nebuchadnezzar in 573 bore out the prophecy of Ezekiel; and the glory of Phoenicia was at an end. The Babylonians, in turn, succumbed to the Persians in the year 539, and in 332 Alexander the Great—having conquered Tyre—incorporated the remnants of Phoenician culture into his Hellenistic empire.

To merchants like the Phoenicians the introduction of coinage was a boon. The first Phoenician coins were struck at Tyre around the middle of the 5th century B.C. The Tyrian shekel above sports a dolphin and a murex, the mollusk used to make purple dye. At right, waves dash against the rocky coastline.

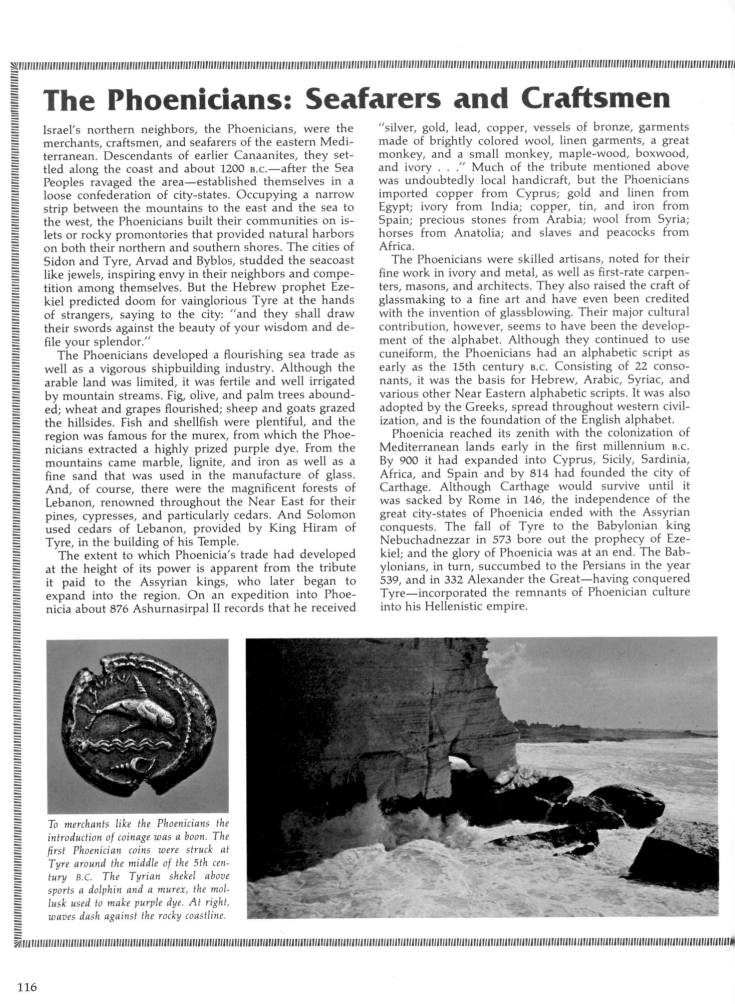

As they colonized the Mediterranean, the Phoenicians took their gods with them. The figure with upraised arms on the stele above is the Carthaginian goddess Tanit, or Astarte, as the Phoenicians called the mother-goddess of their homeland. The dolphin, a fertility symbol, attests to her fecundity.

The Phoenicians derived much of their artistic inspiration from other peoples, as is evident from the stylized figures borrowed from Egypt and the Aegean horses on the 7th-century silver-gilt ceremonial bowl at right.

The baked clay model below, from the 5th or 4th century, is a trireme, a Phoenician warship with three banks of oars, a fierce battering ram, and a row of shields to protect the oarsmen on the upper deck. Ships like these may have been 120 feet long with 170 oarsmen. The Phoenicians were master sea traders whose colonies dotted the Mediterranean. Navigating by the stars, they were able to travel by night; their trading and exploratory voyages took them around Africa and into the Atlantic, perhaps as far north as the British Isles.

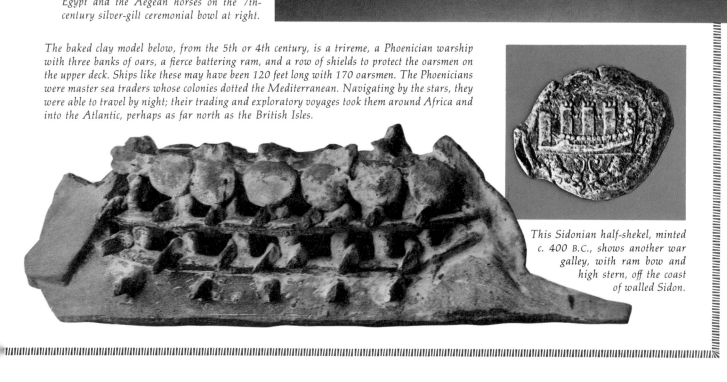

This Sidonian half-shekel, minted c. 400 B.C., shows another war galley, with ram bow and high stern, off the coast of walled Sidon.

Wars of Israel and Judah

In the half century following the death of Solomon, wars and political instability progressively weakened the northern kingdom of Israel. By the time of King Baasha's death (877 B.C.) parts of Upper Galilee had been devastated by the Syrians, and most of Benjamin at Israel's southern border was in the hands of Judah. Baasha's son, Elah, reigned for less than two years before he was assassinated at his capital Tirzah (1) by an ambitious chariot commander known as Zimri. The usurper ruthlessly slaughtered Baasha's family, just as Baasha had eliminated the family of Jeroboam 24 years earlier. The Israelite army, which was fighting the Philistines around Gibbethon (2), where the borders of Israel, Judah, and Philistia met, proclaimed their commander, Omri, king and marched on Tirzah. After the city fell to Omri, Zimri withdrew to the citadel of the palace and burned down the house on himself. Israel had its third king in a week, but Omri had still to contend with the followers of another challenger, one "Tibni the son of Ginath," before securing the throne.

Although he reigned for only seven years, Omri founded an extraordinarily capable dynasty. Decades after its fall, the kings of Israel were still called sons of Omri. The Omrides not only brought profound political and religious change to the northern kingdom, they succeeded in relegating the kings of Judah to a secondary role. Moreover, the only queen ever to reign in her own right in either land was an Omride princess, Athaliah, who ruled Judah for five years, the one break in the house of David's long control over the southern kingdom.

Once in power, Omri sought to revive Solomon's policies, emphasizing peace and expanded trade with Israel's neighbors. This brought stability and prosperity—but also religious opposition to state policy. In his foreign dealings, Omri sealed a political alliance with the Phoenicians by marrying Israel's crown prince, Ahab, to Jezebel, daughter of the king of Tyre. (Later Ahab would follow his father's example as royal matchmaker by marrying his daughter, Athaliah, to Judah's crown prince, Jehoram.) As another indication of this new orientation, Omri moved his capital nine miles to the west of Tirzah, to an isolated hill he bought from a man named Shemer—from whom the city of Samaria (3) derived its name. Like Solomon's Jerusalem, Samaria was built by Phoenician architects and masons, and fragments of Samaria's palace walls are among the finest to survive from antiquity.

Succeeding to the throne in 869, Ahab continued his father's work. At Samaria he finished the "ivory house," an opulent palace on which the prophet Amos later

Samaria, Israel's capital, was built with the help of Phoenicians. These artisans were known for their delicate ivory carvings, such as this 9th-century B.C. miniature plaque of a sphinx.

poured scorn. Built on the summit of the hill, the royal quarters were isolated from the rest of the city by a light casemate wall. This barrier between king and people was a far cry from the Israelite ideal of a monarch who had been anointed from among his brethren.

Major rebuilding was also undertaken at Megiddo (4), Hazor (5), and doubtless elsewhere in the land. At Megiddo the city wall was restored and the gate strengthened. A small, sturdy palace was constructed along with a huge stable complex capable of sheltering some 500 horses. Today the remains of these stables are mute evidence of Ahab's strengthening of Israel's armed forces, especially its mobile strike force: the chariot corps. At Hazor a strong fortress was constructed over most of the acropolis. The old Solomonic casemate walls, which had proved ineffective against Syrian attackers, were repaired and filled in to make a solid fortification. To ensure adequate water for this fortress, a tunnel was dug down to the water table near the southern edge of the mound. This remarkable water system—found by excavators in 1968—is 100 feet deep; its 15-foot-high sloping tunnel has 80 steps ranging up to 16½ feet in width.

These and other preparations that Ahab undertook for the defense of his realm may well have followed an invasion of Israel by the Arameans of Damascus. In the 9th century B.C. Syria under the Arameans had replaced the Israel of David and Solomon as the dominant power in the region. Now, in a campaign about which we know very little, the leader of the alliance of Aramean kingdoms, Ben-hadad (the throne name of successive rulers of Damascus), drove deep into Israel. We do not know the route Ben-hadad and his large army took to lay siege to Samaria in the heart of Israel or what havoc they caused on the way. But the Syrian assault was unsuccessful, and Ahab won a great victory.

The following spring, however, Ben-hadad was back. This time Ahab blocked the Syrians before they crossed the Jordan. At stake was control of Aphek (6), a strategic point east of the Sea of Chinnereth, where an important route leads up to the Bashan plateau and Damascus. The actual battle may have been fought south of the town, perhaps as far south as the Yarmuk valley. For seven days the two armies remained encamped opposite each other, until the smaller Israelite force successfully attacked. The Syrians fell back to the town, where many, including Ben-hadad, were forced to surrender. When Ben-hadad agreed to restore cities the Syrians had earlier captured from Israel and to allow Israelite merchants to open bazaars in Damascus, Ahab freed him—much to the disgust of those

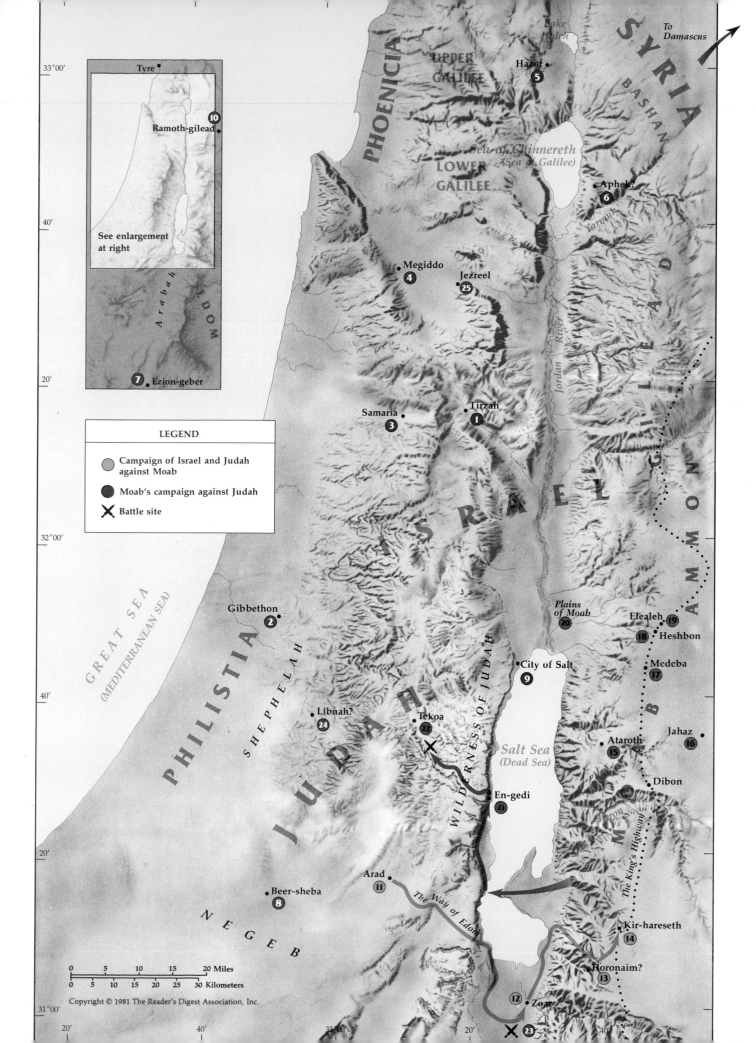

Wars of Israel and Judah (continued)

religious leaders who wanted the Syrian king dead.

Israelite interest in the Transjordan was not confined to the area contested with Damascus. Ahab was anxious to retain Gilead as an integral part of Israel and to hold Ammon and Moab. He failed with Ammon but succeeded for a time in keeping King Mesha of Moab a vassal of Israel and in maintaining Israelites in Moabite territory north of the Arnon River.

Meanwhile, Judah under Asa and his son, Jehoshaphat, was resurgent. The southern kingdom reestablished authority over Edom and much of the other territory it had lost in Shishak's invasion half a century earlier. Archaeology shows that Ezion-geber (7, on locator) was rebuilt at this time; ruins of the period bear similarities to contemporary buildings at Megiddo. In imitation of Solomon's Red Sea ventures, a merchant fleet was based at the Gulf of Aqabah port. New Judahite settlements in the Negeb seem to have been built west of Beer-sheba (8). The Wilderness of Judah also saw new settlements such as the City of Salt (9), and attempts at agriculture were carried out in the forbidding hills just west of there.

In 859 Shalmaneser III came to the throne of Assyria. With massive military might he crossed the Euphrates and pushed through northern Syria all the way to the Great Sea, where, he said, "I washed my weapons." This superpower to the northeast caused Ahab and Ben-hadad to forget their local conflicts and to join with a number of other princes to oppose a potentially fatal threat. The Bible does not mention this coalition, saying only that "For three years Syria and Israel continued

without war" with each other; nor does it tell of the battle fought with Assyria at Qarqar (see map on page 130) on the Orontes River in 853. But, as we learn from Shalmaneser's annals, Ahab put 2,000 chariots in the field—more than half of the coalition's total. "They rose against me for a decisive battle," said the Assyrian, who went on to describe a plain covered with enemy corpses. Although Shalmaneser claimed a victory, the battle was a draw, with staggering losses on each side. But the coalition had meant only to stop the Assyrians. And, indeed, it was more than four years before the Assyrians came again in force.

During this respite, Ahab renewed his Syrian wars—with terrible consequences for Israel. Gilead, with its well-watered, heavily forested uplands, was Israelite. Bashan's basalt and limestone plateaus were Syrian. The natural division between Gilead and Bashan was not the Yarmuk River but the limestone plateau that extends south of the river to the foothills of Gilead. The area was much disputed. There the strategic crossroads of Ramoth-gilead (10, on locator) became the focus of battle.

Jehoshaphat of Judah was allied with Ahab of Israel, and the two kings tried a ruse. Jehoshaphat was dressed in royal robes to draw Syrian fire, while Ahab entered the fray in disguise. Ben-hadad had told his chariot commanders to seek out only Ahab in the battle. When the Syrians discovered it was Jehoshaphat and not Ahab at the head of the troops, they broke off the pursuit. But a stray arrow struck Ahab "between the scale armor and the breastplate." Fearing that his troops would retreat in panic if they saw their king leave the field, the bleeding

It is likely that King Ahab of Israel rebuilt Solomon's city of Hazor in the first half of the 9th century B.C. At the highest point of the city a rectangular citadel, 70 feet by 82 feet with walls 6½ feet thick, crowned the massive fortress. A number of administrative buildings crowded nearby, including a splendid storehouse whose pillars—perhaps supporting a second story—are still in place, as seen above. It probably held military stores for the garrisons guarding the main route from the north into Israel.

The grandeur of Ahab's Hazor is evident in the reconstructed proto-Aeolic capitals and monolithic lintel of the doorway at left, now in the Israel Museum at Jerusalem. At one time they graced the entrance to the courtyard of the citadel.

Ahab was propped up in his chariot and stayed on the battlefield until evening, when he died. As the combined armies of Israel and Judah withdrew, Ahab's body was taken to Samaria for burial. There his bloody chariot was washed beside the pool of the city, "and the dogs licked up his blood, and the harlots washed themselves in it . . ."

Ahaziah succeeded his father, Ahab, as king of Israel but reigned only two years. In a freak accident, Ahaziah fell through the latticework of a second-story palace window at Samaria, was severely injured, and soon died. In 849 Jehoram succeeded his unfortunate brother on the Israelite throne. (In a curious coincidence, Judah was to have a king named Jehoram in the same years—Jehoshaphat's son and brother-in-law to Jehoram of Israel.)

Even before the events of Ramoth-gilead, Mesha of Moab had withheld from Israel his annual tribute of rams' wool and lambs—a sure sign of rebellion. Then, as 2 Kings 1:1 and 3:5 tell us, Mesha took advantage of the succession crisis following the death of Ahab to revolt. But the Bible does not describe Mesha's campaign. The king's own account of his victories is inscribed on a stele found at Dibon, the famous Moabite Stone.

According to 2 Kings 3:4–27, Jehoram set out to subdue the rebellious Moabites. He marched south from Samaria to be joined by Jehoshaphat and his vassal, the king of Edom. The combined army went by Arad (11) and down the Way of Edom, where after a seven-day march through waterless tracks they arrived at Zoar (12), the men and their animals suffering from terrible thirst. The prophet Elisha, accompanying the army, prophesied victory over Moab and said the Lord would provide water out of regard for the godly Jehoshaphat. The next morning the wadis were filled with water, probably the runoff from fortuitous rains in the mountains of Edom.

After moving north along the shore of the Salt Sea, the Israelite-Judahite army turned eastward to reach the high plateau and thus outflank Mesha's defenses on Moab's southern border. It seems there was a battle near Horonaim (13), after which Mesha retreated along the King's Highway to the stronghold of Kir-hareseth (14), where he was besieged. Moabite attempts to break the siege failed, and in desperation Mesha took his son, the crown prince, up to the ramparts of this towering fortress and there sacrificed him in the sight of the besieging army. This gruesome spectacle seems to have created panic among the Israelites and Judahites, who lifted the siege and withdrew.

The Moabite Stone makes no reference to Jehoram's campaign. Rather, it lists the cities that fell before the Moabites, including such old Israelite centers as Ataroth (15) and Ahab's strongpoint Jahaz (16). With Israelite captives, boasts Mesha, "I cut beams for Qarhoh . . . I built Aroer, and I made the highway in the Arnon [valley]; I built Beth-bamoth . . . I built Bezer . . . with fifty men of Dibon . . ." Mesha had, in fact, taken the whole of the tableland around Medeba (17), Heshbon (18), and Elealeh (19), as well as the scarplands to the west, leading down to the Plains of Moab (20).

Mesha also attacked Judah. Joined by Ammonites and Edomites, the Moabites waded across the Salt Sea at a

A popular type of fortification since before King Solomon's time was the casemate wall (a section of Samaria's casemate wall is shown above). It consisted of a line of parallel walls broken into "rooms" by shorter intersecting cross walls. During siege this type of reinforced wall could withstand the blows of battering rams better than a single, solid line of fortification; in peacetime the compartments served as storerooms.

shallow point and seized the important oasis of En-gedi (21). Moving up into the hills, they passed through the Wilderness of Judah and came into the Wilderness of Tekoa (22), where they ran into Rehoboam's old line of fortifications. There the Judahites fought fiercely at the very edge of their densely settled, fertile lands, and the battle went well for them. For reasons we do not know, the Moabites and Ammonites turned on the Edomites, and Mesha's coalition broke up near Tekoa.

Judah was saved, but yet another disaster soon befell the reeling country. Edom revolted. In a battle south of Zoar (23) the Edomites repulsed Jehoshaphat's son, Jehoram of Judah. Worse for Judah, the Edomites regained the rich copper mines of the Arabah (see locator) and also Ezion-geber. At this lowest point in Judah's fortunes, Libnah (24) in the Shephelah revolted.

Meanwhile, Jehoram of Israel renewed warfare with Syria near Ramoth-gilead. Wounded in the fighting, he journeyed to Jezreel (25), the summer palace of the Israelite kings, to recuperate. There Jehoram was visited by his nephew, Ahaziah, who had just become king of Judah. The scene was set for the final, bloody chapter in the saga of the Omrides.

The Prophet Elijah

Elijah is one of the towering figures of the Old Testament, ranking in Israel's memory with Abraham, Moses, and David. Long after he was gone, devout believers held that Elijah would return to herald the coming of the Messiah. Early Christians viewed John the Baptist as an Elijah figure, a precursor of Jesus. Today in the Jewish Passover feast a cup of wine is set on the table for Elijah, and at a prescribed moment in the ceremony the door is opened for the prophet to enter.

The Elijah stories in 1 and 2 Kings are a legendary cycle, weaving together his miraculous adventures and historical events in the time of the Omrides. Thus we have brief glimpses of the great prophet rather than a chronological narrative of his life, making it impossible to establish with certainty the exact order of events or their precise location. This rough man of the desert fringe—spare, solitary, rudely clothed in hair shirt and leather—seemed to appear and disappear at will, leaving his supporters mystified and his opponents perplexed.

We know the historical background of Elijah's career. In 869 B.C. Ahab succeeded his father, Omri, on the throne of Israel and continued the policy of developing peaceful economic contacts with Israel's neighbors. He encouraged skilled foreign laborers, particularly Phoenicians, to come to Israel and guaranteed toleration to all. But Ahab's queen, Jezebel, daughter of a Phoenician king, was zealous for her own god, Baal Melqart, and was not satisfied, as Solomon's foreign wives had been, with a temple to her deity in the capital. Instead, Jezebel established 450 prophets of Baal and 400 prophets of Asherah as prophets to the royal household and succeeded in according them official status. While the majority of the people went "limping with two different opinions," some welcomed the cult, but many resisted. Those who defied the queen faced reprisals, and possibly even death. As Israelite places of worship were attacked and altars to the God of Israel destroyed, many Israelite prophets fled to the hills and hid in caves.

In this 15th-century manuscript illumination Elijah arrives for the Passover feast seated on a donkey; behind the prophet rides a family of four.

This internal crisis was heightened when the stern, forbidding Elijah—a champion of the Israelite God—came forth from Tishbe (1) across the Jordan. He was determined to challenge the king and his foreign queen. When the implacable religious opponents, Elijah and Jezebel—each with fanatical and unswerving beliefs—confronted one another, the result was disaster for the Israelite state. At the new capital, Samaria (2), Elijah foretold of an awful famine by which God would bring judgment upon the land: "As the Lord the God of Israel lives, before whom I stand, there shall be neither dew nor rain these years, except by my word." And at the command of the Lord, Elijah fled from Samaria and hid "by the brook Cherith, that is east of the Jordan" (3). In one of the most charming of the Elijah stories, the prophet was said to have been fed by ravens at the Cherith and to have drunk from the brook—until it, too, dried up.

Again at the Lord's command Elijah made a journey, this time to the Phoenician city of Zarephath. There he is said to have performed miracles: ensuring that the food supply of the widow with whom he was staying would not run out and reviving her son whose "illness was so severe that there was no breath left in him."

In the third year of the drought, the word of the Lord came to Elijah, "Go, show yourself to Ahab; and I will send rain upon the earth." Meanwhile, Ahab had been searching the land for Elijah and found him with the aid of Obadiah (chief of Ahab's household, who had been hiding 100 Israelite prophets in caves). Coming to meet Elijah, the king said, "Is it you, you troubler of Israel?" Undaunted, Elijah turned the king's words back upon him, accusing Ahab of troubling the nation "because you have forsaken the commandments of the Lord and followed the Baals." And he challenged the king to summon the prophets of Baal and Asherah "who eat at Jezebel's table" for a contest to determine whose god was the true god.

Ahab did as asked, and the people of Israel gathered as two altars were set up on Mount Carmel (4). One altar was for the prophets of Baal; the other for Elijah. A pyre and a dismembered bull were placed on each. All morning and into the afternoon the ecstatic Baal worshipers danced about their altar, crying aloud, cutting themselves with swords and lances until the blood gushed upon them, and pleading with their god to send down fire to consume the sacrificial offering. But there was no word from Baal, only sarcasm from Elijah. Finally, the solitary prophet had his altar doused with water three times. As he prayed to the Lord, an all-consuming fire fell upon the altar. At Elijah's command the prophets of Baal were seized and taken down to the brook Kishon (5), where they were killed.

Back on the mountain, Elijah bowed to the ground and seven times sent his servant to look toward the sea, where at last he saw "a little cloud like a man's hand" rising from the waters. As the sky grew black with clouds, Ahab mounted his chariot and rode toward Jezreel (6), but Elijah "ran before Ahab to the entrance of Jezreel."

Furious, Jezebel threatened to kill Elijah within the day. The prophet fled south—perhaps by the quickest and safest route, along the Way of the Sea (7)—into southern Judah, to Beer-sheba (8) on the edge of the Negeb. There he left his servant and went into the desert, where the despondent prophet—thinking he alone was faithful in all Israel—asked God to let him die. But while Elijah was asleep under a broom tree an angel came and comforted him, providing food and drink.

Penetrating deeper into the desert, Elijah went "forty days and forty nights to Horeb the mount of God." Though Mount Horeb cannot be located with certainty, tradition identifies it with Jebel Musa (see map on page 67). As Moses before him had done, Elijah talked with God. While the prophet lamented Israel's faithlessness, storm, earthquake, and fire passed by, but he heard no word from the Lord. Then "a still small voice" spoke to the prophet, and the message was one of political revolution: Jehu son of Nimshi was to be anointed king of Israel, thus overthrowing the house of Ahab. Hazael was to be anointed king of Damascus, bringing a new dynasty to that land. And finally, Elisha son of Shaphat was to be anointed prophet in Elijah's place to carry out these deeds. "And him who escapes from the sword of Hazael shall Jehu slay; and him who escapes from the sword of Jehu shall Elisha slay." Only the 7,000 Israelites who had not bowed to Baal were to be spared. This story of Elijah can be placed in the time of Israel's Syrian wars and the contest previously described between Ahab and Ben-hadad.

The storm of rebellion and horror did not come to Israel while Ahab lived, though the king's conflict with Elijah was increasing. At Jezreel, the summer capital of Israel at this time, Ahab had offered to buy the vineyard of Naboth, an Israelite whose land was next to the royal gardens. But Naboth adamantly refused, citing the Hebrew principle that the land of the fathers remained forever the possession of the sons. Rebuffed, the king returned to his palace. But Jezebel, who cared little for Israel's faith or for its traditions, had Naboth falsely accused of cursing the king and God and then stoned to death—whereupon Ahab seized the vineyard. Elijah came to denounce Ahab and prophesy the downfall of his dynasty, saying that dogs would lick his blood and "eat Jezebel within the bounds of Jezreel." Hearing these words, the king repented and mourned his deeds.

When death on the battlefield at Ramoth-gilead removed Ahab's strong hand from Israel's government, it proved only a matter of time before the forces unleashed during his reign brought the kingdom low. When his son and successor Ahaziah, a worshiper of Baal, fell from the second story of the palace at Samaria and lay ill, he sent messengers to inquire of Baal-zebub, god of Ekron (9), whether or not he would recover. Elijah intercepted the messengers, perhaps on the road from Samaria toward the coast, and there turned them back with an answer for the doomed young ruler: "You shall not come down from the bed to which you have gone, but you shall surely die."

It was also time for Elijah to depart. With Elisha, whom he had recruited as his successor at Abel-meholah

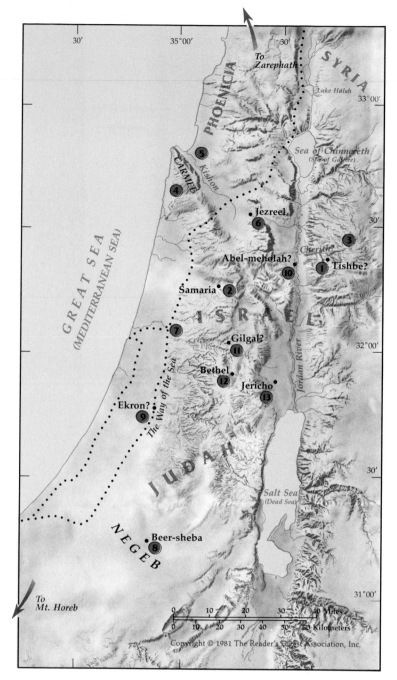

(10), the prophet set out on his last journey. Despite Elijah's repeated attempts to leave his young follower behind, the devoted Elisha remained at his side as they journeyed from Gilgal (11) to Bethel (12) to Jericho (13). At the Jordan, Elijah rolled up his mantle and struck the water so that it parted, allowing the two to pass over on dry ground. Asked to confer a double share of his spirit upon his successor, Elijah promised Elisha it would be so "if you see me as I am being taken from you." And as the two were talking, a chariot of fire drawn by horses of fire separated them and took Elijah in a whirlwind to heaven.

After rending his garments in grief, Elisha picked up Elijah's mantle and returned to the banks of the Jordan. There he repeated the miracle of parting the waters and crossed to Jericho on dry land. The sons of the prophets, members of an ecstatic guild, bowed down to him, saying, "The spirit of Elijah rests on Elisha."

Elisha and the Revolt of Jehu

Anointed to complete the work of Elijah, Elisha nonetheless stood in sharp contrast to his revered predecessor. Miracles are also attributed to Elisha: making the waters of the spring at Jericho wholesome; feeding 100 men with a small amount of food; making an axe head to float; breathing life into a dead child. But while the older prophet had been a forbidding, solitary figure, Elisha worked closely with the sons of the prophets, those groups of ecstatic prophets that appeared throughout the land from before the time of Saul. Elisha, too, was an ecstatic. Indeed, it was in a musically induced trance that he prophesied abundant water for the combined army of Israel and Judah as it made its way through the wilderness and southeast of the Salt Sea toward Moab.

Elisha's presence on that campaign indicates that he was a public figure in Israel, deeply involved with both domestic and foreign affairs of state. Whereas Elijah had been an outright opponent of Ahab's, Elisha became an adviser to Jehoram, Ahab's son. This is curious, for Elijah had bequeathed to Elisha a terrible enmity toward the house of Omri. Yet Elisha appears to have supported the Omrides for several years, until he at last took up Elijah's mission.

Although Elisha seems to have had some sort of base on Mount Carmel (1), he was often in or around the capital of Samaria (2). He was apparently there when Jehoram received a plea from the Syrian king Ben-hadad to cure his commander, Naaman, of leprosy. If we read this story in the context of the renewed wars between Syria and Israel, it is clear why Israel's king saw in this peculiar request an excuse for Ben-hadad to pick a quarrel. In this tense situation Elisha asked Jehoram to send the soldier to him and directed the dubious Naaman to wash himself clean in the Jordan.

Despite Elisha's wondrous cure of Naaman, Israel and Syria were soon at war again. Informed by his prophetic knowledge of Syrian plans, Elisha warned the king of Israel to avoid an ambush. When the Syrians sought to seize the prophet at Dothan (3), he prayed that they be blinded, and thus brought them to Samaria. On another occasion Samaria, besieged by the Syrian army, faced starvation and the people were being reduced to cannibalism. But Elisha predicted that within 24 hours food would be plentiful. At dusk four straying lepers found the Syrian camp abandoned. Jehoram thought it was a trick to get the people to leave the city and sent out scouts, who found that the Syrians had fled beyond the Jordan, littering the way with garments and equipment. Quantities of food had been left behind in the camp.

Whatever historical core lies behind these stories of Elisha's miraculous deliverance of Israel, he was certainly deeply involved in the politics not only of Israel but also of Damascus. In the end, in carrying out the Lord's mission as given to Elijah, Elisha was directly responsible for the overthrow of the royal houses in both capitals. Elisha himself went to Damascus, where King Ben-hadad lay ill. When the king heard that the man of God was in his capital, he sent his servant Hazael with gifts for Elisha and with the question: "Shall I recover from this sickness?" Elisha sent a false message to Ben-hadad and encouraged Hazael to seize the throne, which he did after smothering Ben-hadad in his sickbed.

Since the death of Ahab the fortunes of Israel had waned, mostly because of ill-fated military adventures in the Transjordan. When Jehoram renewed open warfare with Syria near Ramoth-gilead (4, on locator), he was wounded in the fighting and, as previously mentioned, withdrew to Jezreel (5), the summer palace of the Israelite kings. There he was joined by the Queen Mother, Jezebel, and by his nephew, Ahaziah, who had just become king of Judah.

The year was 842 B.C., and at Ramoth-gilead, among the disgruntled chariot corps—so proud at the battle of Qarqar a decade earlier—was a commander named Jehu. Deeply angered by Omride policies, the dissident religious group now joined the army in a plot. Elisha sent one of the sons of the prophets to anoint Jehu as king with instructions to strike down the entire house of Ahab. The Omrides were thus to be destroyed as the house of Jeroboam and the house of Baasha had been earlier. Jehu and his men set out down to the Jordan and up into the Jezreel valley past Beth-shan (6).

The summer palace was situated on the western slopes of the valley, with a vista stretching down toward the Jordan. A watchman spied the company of Jehu and warned the king. Two messengers sent by Jehoram to ask if Jehu was coming in peace were seen by the watchman to join the approaching group. Then Jehoram and his nephew, Ahaziah, each in his own chariot, rode out from the summer palace to meet Jehu. They encountered him in the vineyards that Ahab, aided by Jezebel, had seized from Naboth. "Is it peace, Jehu?" asked Israel's king. "What peace can there be," replied the rebel, "so long as the harlotries and the sorceries of your mother Jezebel are so many?" As he turned his chariot in flight,

Separating the hills of Galilee from Samaria is the beautiful Jezreel valley. The town of Jezreel, located at the foot of Mount Gilboa, became the site of the summer palace of Israel's kings.

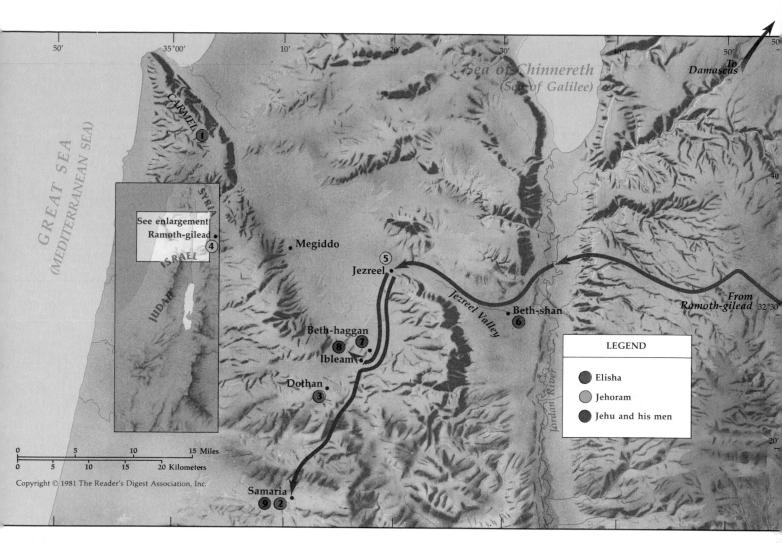

Jehoram was struck by an arrow of Jehu's that pierced his heart.

Jehu and his men pursued the young king of Judah past Beth-haggan (7) and at the ascent of Gur (8), near Ibleam, they wounded him. Ahaziah managed to bring his chariot to Megiddo but died there and was later buried in the tomb of his fathers in Jerusalem.

Meanwhile, Jezebel had painted her face and adorned her head and was looking out the palace window when Jehu entered Jezreel. "Is it peace, you Zimri . . . ?" she said, in reference to the assassin of King Elah. "Throw her down," Jehu commanded two of Jezebel's palace servants, and they did so "and some of her blood spattered on the wall and on the horses, and they trampled on her." Later, after eating and drinking, Jehu gave orders that Jezebel be properly buried, for she was, after all, the daughter of a king. But they found only her skull, feet, and palms of her hands. Fulfilling Elijah's awful prophecy, dogs had eaten the Queen Mother's corpse.

The deaths of Jehoram, Ahaziah of Judah, and Jezebel were but the beginnings of Jehu's purge. The new king taunted the elders of Samaria to choose one of the remaining 70 sons of Ahab to be their leader and come forth to do battle with him. Instead, the elders murdered all 70 and sent their heads in baskets to be piled outside the gate of Jezreel. After slaying "all that remained of the house of Ahab in Jezreel," Jehu advanced on Samaria (9) in the company of religious supporters. En route he met 42 kinsmen of Ahaziah and had them killed, too.

In Samaria Jehu continued the slaughter. He called together all the people, saying: "Ahab served Baal a little; but Jehu will serve him much." The king's irony went undetected as the priests and followers of Baal assembled in the temple to the god, where Jehu offered the requisite sacrifices—and then had them put to the sword. And the house of Baal was turned into a latrine.

In Jerusalem Queen Mother Athaliah, daughter of Ahab, seized the empty throne for herself and ruled Judah as a usurper from 842 to 837. But Joash, Ahaziah's young son, was hidden by members of the family in a bedchamber so that one day the house of David might rule again over the southern kingdom.

In Israel the man whom Elisha had chosen to be king was an unrelieved disaster for the country. Soon Jehu would bow with his face to the ground before Shalmaneser III, king of Assyria.

Elisha outlived Jehu's bloody reign, but his public career was virtually over. During the reign of Jehu's grandson, Jehoash (Joash, 801–786), the prophet fell ill and died, with the king weeping and repeating the words Elisha had said when Elijah was taken to heaven: "My father, my father! The chariots of Israel and its horsemen!"

125

Under the Assyrian Sword

The end of the Omride dynasty in 842 B.C. found Israel and Judah seriously weakened by religious unrest at home and by decades of sporadic warfare with Syria and the kingdoms of the Transjordan. Edom, Moab, and Ammon had regained their independence, and much of the Negeb was lost. Moreover, the revolt of Jehu in Israel spelled the end of the alliances that the Omrides had carefully built with Phoenicia and with Judah.

Israel had been especially affected by the extraordinary level of violence accompanying Jehu's revolt. Archaeological work at various Israelite sites from this period suggests that the standard of living declined. At the same time Damascus under the usurper Hazael (842–806) was growing in power. Taking advantage of the turmoil in Israel, Hazael exerted such great pressure upon Israelite Gilead that Jehu finally and unwisely appealed for relief to the Assyrian king Shalmaneser III.

The battle of Qarqar in 853 had convinced the rulers of the petty states between Mesopotamia and Egypt that they could at least stop the Assyrians from marching south. According to his own annals, Shalmaneser III had crossed the Euphrates to campaign in the Carchemish area before turning south along the Aleppo-Hamath-Qarqar trade route (see map on page 130). Three times—in 849, 848, and 845—Ben-hadad of Damascus had sought to bring together a coalition to oppose Assyria, but there is no mention of Israel in these battles. Although Ben-hadad and his allies were defeated each time in northern Syria, the Assyrians did not move any farther south because of pressure from enemies on the northern border of their vast empire. In 841, while Assyria was thus occupied elsewhere, Ben-hadad's successor, Hazael, launched a major attack against Gilead. It was this attack that brought Jehu's appeal to Shalmaneser. The Assyrian ruler hardly needed urging for a strike at Damascus, and his army reached the city's walls, destroyed the surrounding gardens, but did not succeed in breaching the stout ramparts of the Syrian capital.

A subsequent event provides us with our only contemporary picture of an Israelite monarch. In his annals Shalmaneser tells us what happened after he left Damascus with his army: "I marched as far as the mountains of Ba'li-ra'si which is a promontory [at the side of the sea] . . . At that time I received the tribute of the inhabitants of Tyre, Sidon, and of Jehu, son of Omri." A monument recording this scene, the so-called "Black Obelisk" of Shalmaneser III, contains a number of scenes depicting kings bringing tribute to the Assyrian. On one panel Jehu is shown on his hands and knees, his head to the ground, before Shalmaneser. The inscription reads: "The tribute of Jehu, son of Omri. Silver, gold, a golden bowl, a golden vase, golden cups, golden buckets, tin, a staff for the royal hand (?), puruhati-fruits." The scene reveals how far Israel's fortunes had declined since the glory days of Ahab, little more than a decade earlier.

Where did Jehu's submission to Shalmaneser take place? It is possible that the Assyrian army turned southwest from Damascus to invade Israel, causing the damage to Hazor (1) that is dated to this period. Shalmaneser could then have cut across the country to strike a blow at Libnath (2), where archaeologists have also uncovered a level of destruction from this time. This route suggests Mount Carmel, a conspicuous promontory by the sea, as the site of the scene depicted on the Black Obelisk. From Carmel the Assyrians most likely turned north along the coast to Tyre (3) and Sidon, soon reaching the Dog River (north of modern Beirut). Inscriptions carved into a rock there depict a number of kings, and some scholars suggest that Dog River was the site of Jehu's obeisance. At any rate, it would seem that Jehu's tribute had bought time for his beleaguered kingdom.

But it was also the internal problems of Assyria that saved Israel, Damascus, and the other petty kingdoms of the area. The rebellion of one of Shalmaneser's sons and strife with formerly subject peoples in the mountains beyond the upper Tigris removed Assyrian pressure on the southwest. Seizing this opportunity, Hazael sent his armies not merely into Gilead (4) but all the way down the King's Highway to Aroer (5). According to 2 Kings 10:32–33, Hazael was victorious "from the Jordan eastward, all the land of Gilead, the Gadites, and the Reubenites, and the Manassites, from Aroer, which is by the valley of the Arnon, that is, Gilead and Bashan."

Hazael next crossed the Jordan and drove toward the sea, but we have no clear record of the battles that seem to have taken place. Jehoahaz, Jehu's son and successor, saw his army reduced to "fifty horsemen and ten chariots and ten thousand footmen." Hazael had destroyed the rest "like the dust at threshing" and allowed Jehoahaz little more than an internal police force. It was probably the Syrians who at this time inflicted further damage on Ahab's once-brilliant Hazor (6), since that fortress had long been a thorn in Damascus' side. At any rate, Hazael and his army drove down the coast—doubtless by the Way of the Sea—to capture Gath (7). They were now in an ideal position to attack Judah through the defiles of the Shephelah that lead up into the hills.

Judah was once more ruled by the house of David. Ahaziah's son, Joash, had been brought to the throne at the age of seven when the priest Jehoiada led a coup d'etat that overthrew and killed Queen Athaliah, the Omride usurper. When Syrian king Hazael turned from Gath and "set his face to go up against Jerusalem" (8), 2 Kings 12:18 tells us that Joash (also called Jehoash) sent a tribute of the votive gifts of his fathers and "all the gold that was found in the treasuries of the house of the Lord and of the king's house." However, 2 Chronicles 24:23–25 mentions a battle that left the princes dead and the king wounded. While recovering, Joash was assassinated; he was succeeded by his son, Amaziah, in 800.

The assassins of Joash were avenging the king's death sentence against the priest Jehoiada's son, Zechariah, who had accused Joash of forsaking the Lord. But it was not without significance that the assassins were an Ammonite and a Moabite, traditional enemies of Judah. With Israel and Syria once more distracted by the powerful Assyrian threat, Amaziah moved to reclaim Edom.

Amaziah's army encountered the Edomites in the arid wastes of the Valley of Salt (9) and defeated them, inflicting heavy losses. Judah's king took quick advantage of the situation to move southeastward into the glowing red Edomite hills and take Sela (10) by storm, thus securing the rich copper mines in the region. We are not told by what route the Judahite army reached Sela. But a road to Edom ran between two great barren depressions that on a map look like giant footprints in the Negeb. At Tamar there is a strong spring and abundant water, and from there the route crosses the hot Arabah to reach the Edomite hills by way of Punon. This was a chief highway to Edom, and if this was the way he went, then Amaziah would have secured not only the copper mines but an important trade route as well.

In the flush of his successes in Edom, Amaziah sent messengers to Israel's king—Jehu's grandson, Jehoash—seeking a face-to-face meeting and suggesting that Jehoash's daughter be given in marriage to his son. One of the issues between the two monarchs was the matter of Israelite mercenaries whom Amaziah had hired for his Edomite adventure but whom he had sent home before the battle in the Valley of Salt. As they returned to Israel, these disappointed warriors fell upon certain cities of Judah, killing and looting. If Amaziah wished to settle this matter and to reestablish peaceful relations between Judah and Israel, it did not come about. Jehoash gave a surly reply to what he regarded as Amaziah's haughty demand, calling Judah a thistle and Israel a cedar and warning Amaziah to be content with his Edomite victory. When Amaziah pressed the matter, war broke out.

It is likely that the Israelites moved west from Samaria (11) and south along the Way of the Sea in order to invade Judah at its vulnerable western approaches. The two armies met at Beth-shemesh (12), where Amaziah was captured. Without army or king to defend it, Jerusalem (13) fell, and the Israelites pulled down great stretches of its northern wall while the rest of the city, including the Temple and palace, was looted. When the invaders withdrew, they took hostages as well as booty to Samaria. Amaziah, however, was released.

Urged on by the aged and dying Elisha, Jehoash renewed war with Damascus by destroying the Syrian base at Aphek (14). He thereby removed a military threat to Israel and provided a springboard from which his son, Jeroboam II, would eventually capture Damascus.

In Judah, however, the state's fortunes seemed less promising. Amaziah ruled in his ruined capital for several more years but made little recovery from the debacle of his war with Israel. In this dispirited atmosphere unrest increased. When at length Amaziah heard that there was a plot against him, he fled to the fortress city of Lachish (15) near the border with Philistia. But he was unable to escape the assassins who had followed him there. Amaziah's body was taken back to Jerusalem for burial as his 16-year-old son, Uzziah, came to the throne in 783. Few would have guessed that this lad would reverse the severe decline in the fortunes of Judah and lead it to unprecedented power and prestige at the very time that Israel was enjoying a renaissance under Jeroboam II.

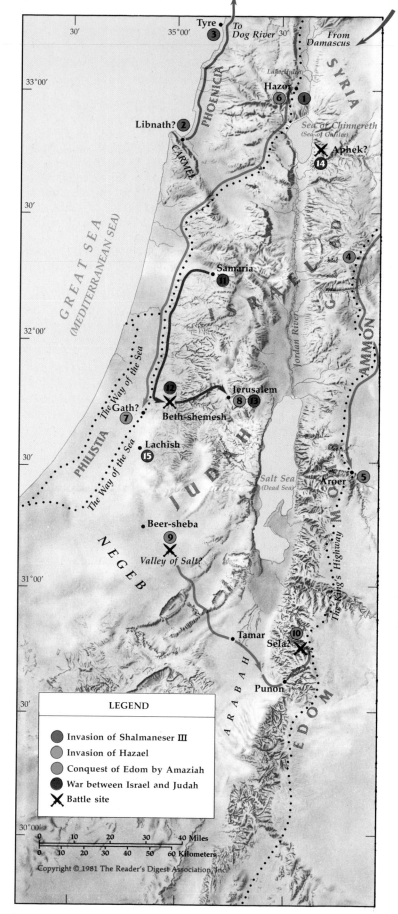

LEGEND

- Invasion of Shalmaneser III
- Invasion of Hazael
- Conquest of Edom by Amaziah
- War between Israel and Judah
- X Battle site

Copyright © 1981 The Reader's Digest Association, Inc.

Renaissance of the Two Kingdoms

The fortunes of Israel and Judah changed dramatically for the better in the second decade of the 8th century B.C. Syria, so recently a serious threat to both Israel and Judah, had not recovered from the most recent battering it had received from Assyria, the assault about 806 B.C. of Adad-nirari III, who had captured Damascus and levied an enormous tribute before being called home to deal with a revolt in the north. At the death of Adad-nirari in 784, the Assyrian empire was plunged into nearly half a century of turmoil that forestalled any further adventures in the west. Moreover, Egypt had not been an important political or military factor in the area since the late-10th-century invasion of Shishak.

At this opportune moment outstanding kings appeared in Israel and Judah, and each was to have a long reign. Jeroboam II, son of Jehoash of Israel, came to the throne in Samaria (1) in 786 and ruled for 40 years. Uzziah (Azariah) succeeded his ill-fated father, Amaziah of Judah, as king at Jerusalem (2) in 783 and ruled for 41 years. During their reigns both kingdoms enjoyed periods of unprecedented expansion and prosperity.

The energetic and able Jeroboam II moved quickly to press the advantage against Damascus that his father had seized at Aphek (3). He scored major military victories, about which, unfortunately, very little is known. The only written source is Amos 6:13, where there is a brief reference to the capture of two cities. We have, therefore, to depend upon our knowledge of the geography of the region and of military tactics of the time to reconstruct Jeroboam's strategy. It is clear that he moved against Lodebar (4), which controlled a crucial plateau and an important route into the interior of the Bashan-Gilead area. This was a necessary first step for a strike at long-disputed Ramoth-gilead (5, on locator), some 25 miles to the east. The only other site mentioned in Jeroboam's assault against Syria is Karnaim (6, on locator), today a ruin, on a major route running northward from Ramoth-gilead toward Damascus. With both Aphek and Ramoth-gilead in his hands, Jeroboam could have advanced on Karnaim from the west and south simultaneously. But his offensive swept far beyond the southern edge of the Bashan plateau and carried into Damascus and even beyond. When it was over, the Israelites had extended their authority to Lebo-hamath, on the northern reaches of the kingdom that David and Solomon had once ruled.

With the forests and fields of Gilead restored to Israel, with the Syrian threat momentarily removed, and with tribute pouring in from conquered peoples, Israel enjoyed a prosperity it had scarcely known as a separate kingdom. The population grew and, as archaeological evidence shows, spilled beyond the walls of the cities. Discoveries also reveal a high level of craftsmanship. At Megiddo (7), an important administrative center of the kingdom, excavators at the turn of this century found a magnificent seal bearing the image of a roaring lion and the words "Shema, servant of Jeroboam." Shema was probably the governor of the region and this may have been his official seal. It has remained for later archaeologists working at Megiddo to show just how prosperous that great city, with its many public buildings and fine stone houses, was at the time of Jeroboam II.

Indeed, archaeologists working at Hazor (8) have uncovered evidence of some of the finest Israelite houses from antiquity, which date to Jeroboam's reign. Over the ruins of much of Ahab's storehouse there, shops, workshops, and houses arose during Israel's 8th-century renaissance. These were of a high architectural standard, requiring skilled workmanship. One house had a courtyard of some 30 feet by 26 feet, flanked by two large rooms and three smaller ones. Other houses had two stories, with their well-built stairs still in place after more than 2,700 years. The household goods found in these houses also attest to some wealth and a high standard of workmanship. A wide variety of well-made pottery was in use, as were bowls and millstones fashioned out of the native basalt. The most opulent find was an ivory cosmetic spoon, its handle beautifully carved in an inverted palmette design of a type well known in the ancient Near East of the time. The back of the bowl is carved in the shape of a woman's head, and two doves appear to be entangled in the woman's hair. Finer ivory objects from this time have been discovered but only in royal palaces.

In the wake of an earthquake that damaged Hazor in the middle of Jeroboam's reign, probably about 760, fine new houses arose on the site, leaving no doubt about the level of material well-being in Israel during the last half of this great monarch's reign. But something else can be seen in the ruins of Hazor. Although normal life resumed after the earthquake, considerable modifications were made to the fortifications. Buildings near the edge of the mound were demolished in order to strengthen the city wall, which was now designed with offsets and insets to provide positions for flanking fire against attackers. A strong rectangular tower measuring 33 feet by 23 feet was added to the strategic northwestern corner of the mound. And the defenses of the city gate were increased. There was clearly unease in Israel as the Assyrian giant once more began to stir.

Others, too, were growing uneasy in those times of prosperity. Two years before the great earthquake an extraordinary man—a Judahite who had come north to the shrine at Bethel (9)—started preaching a message of doom upon Israel. He was Amos of Tekoa, the first of the great "ethical prophets." According to Amos 3:15, "the houses of ivory shall perish"—which scholars interpret as a reference to the ivory carvings and inlays in Jeroboam's palace on the summit of Samaria's hill. (Early in this century, archaeologists found what had remained of the palace after the Assyrians had looted and destroyed it; traces of its opulence and superior workmanship were still evident.) Amos pointed to the social ills that prosperity had brought to the land: the exploitation of the poor by the rich, bribery and lack of justice in the courts, the decline of morals, the problems of wine and

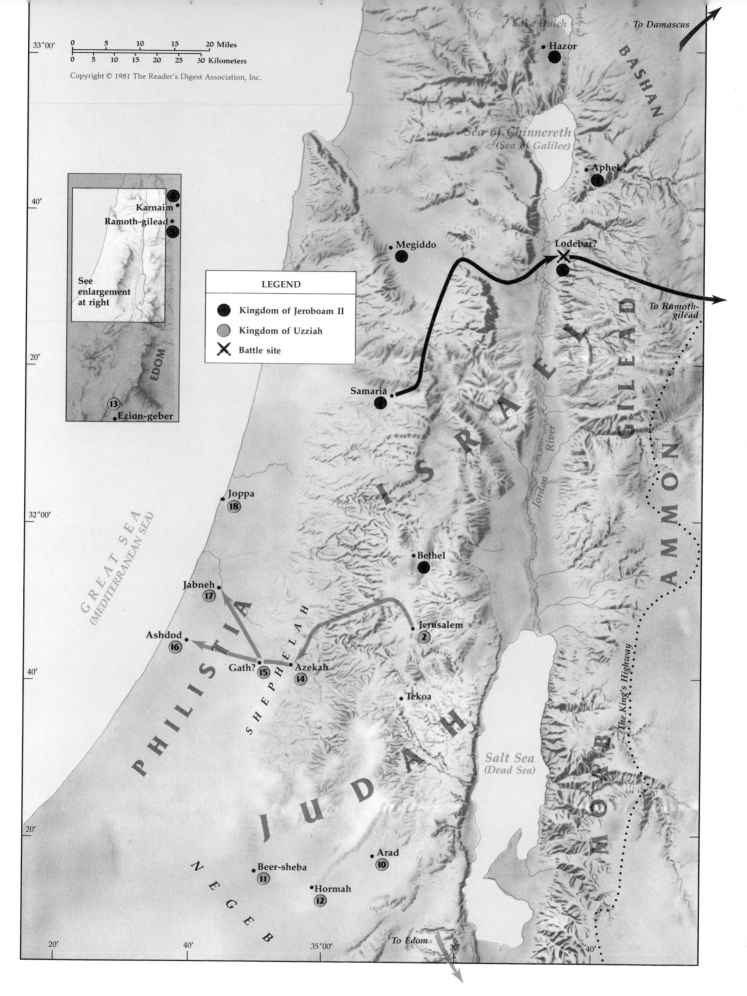

5   10   15   20 Miles
0 5 10 15 20 25 30 Kilometers

Copyright © 1981 The Reader's Digest Association, Inc.

Lake Huleh

To Damascus

BASHAN

Hazor

Sea of Chinnereth
(Sea of Galilee)

Aphek?

40'

Karnaim
Ramoth-gilead

Megiddo

Lodebar?

See
enlargement
at right

EDOM

20'

Ezion-geber

LEGEND

● Kingdom of Jeroboam II

● Kingdom of Uzziah

✕ Battle site

To Ramoth-
gilead

Samaria

GILEAD

AMMON

The King's Highway

Jordan River

ISRAEL

Joppa
(18)

32°00'

Bethel

GREAT SEA
(MEDITERRANEAN SEA)

Jabneh
(17)

Jerusalem
(2)

Ashdod
(16)

SHEPHELAH

Gath?
(15)

Azekah
(14)

Tekoa

40'

Salt Sea
(Dead Sea)

MOAB

JUDAH

20'

Arad
(10)

NEGEB

Beer-sheba
(11)

Hormah
(12)

To Edom

20'   40'   35°00'   20'   40'

The Mighty Assyrians

By the 8th century B.C. the Assyrian empire—the prophet Hosea's "vulture . . . over the house of the Lord"—already had a tradition of conquest and exploitation hundreds of years old. As early as 1100, the Assyrian ruler Tiglath-pileser I had grandiosely referred to himself as "king of the world" (he controlled much of Mesopotamia, if only temporarily), and a long line of successors sought to follow his example. During most of the 9th century, Assyria flourished under a series of strong rulers who repeatedly attacked westward and exacted tribute from a number of states, Israel among them. With the advent in 745 of the forceful Tiglath-pileser III, Assyria embarked on a new and unprecedented epoch of empire building.

The primary agent for this was the vaunted Assyrian army. Large and well organized, with skilled commanders, seasoned troops, and an unparalleled reputation for brutality, it was the most powerful fighting force of its age. A key ingredient in the Assyrians' military success was their mastery of siege warfare. Records such as the relief (right) commemorating the siege of Lachish, from the palace of Sennacherib at Nineveh, illustrate some of their methods, including a key piece of equipment: the siege engine. Wooden towers mounted on wheels, these could be pushed up a log ramp to the wall of a besieged city, carrying archers and iron-headed battering rams.

By such military tactics—and by a policy of transporting defeated peoples to far corners of its empire—Assyria extended its reach across a larger domain than had any earlier nation. In the first half of the 7th century the empire attained its greatest dimensions (see map at left), climaxing in 663 with the seizure of Thebes, the capital of Egypt. But the historical tide soon turned. Egypt broke free, and for most of his reign Assyria's king Ashurbanipal (668-27) was forced to contend with mounting pressure at both ends of the empire. This put a great strain on Assyria's resources, and within 15 years of Ashurbanipal's death the once-invincible giant had been brought to its knees—supplanted by another whose name would reverberate through the annals of biblical life: Babylonia.

Ashurbanipal, shown hunting in the detail from a relief above, ruled Assyria at the time of its greatest expansion. A scholar as well as a warrior, he amassed a library of clay tablets.

strong drink, superficial piety, and the corruption of worship at the hallowed sanctuaries. Time had run out for Israel, an overripe summer fruit bearing the seeds of rottenness, and the judgment of the Lord had been pronounced. "For lo, I will command, and shake the house of Israel among all the nations as one shakes with a sieve . . ."

Hosea, a younger contemporary of Amos', was from Israel, but we do not know his hometown. Less stern than the Judahite who was so vociferously condemning the nation, Hosea wept over his native land and implored God to pity the people and to spare them. But Hosea clearly saw the growing cloud in the northeast and the coming judgment and exile. "A vulture is over the house of the Lord, because they have broken my covenant," he said, referring to Assyria as the vulture and to Israel's infidelity to God and the social ills which Amos had also seen.

In the south, meanwhile, Uzziah had restored to Judah some of the glory it had not seen since the days of Solo-

mon. An extraordinary administrator, Uzziah set about systematically to exploit the economic resources of his kingdom. He had new cisterns dug to support his large herds and encouraged agriculture according to what the soil of the region would yield: grains in the valleys and on the plains, and vineyards on the hillsides.

One of Uzziah's more remarkable achievements was his expansion of the work begun by Jehoshaphat in imitation of Solomon's scheme for placing military-agricultural settlements in the Negeb to secure control over the trade routes in that forbidding but spectacular land. This renewed activity in the Negeb was carefully planned and well executed. Major and minor fortifications were built to a standard military design—with casemate walls and no fewer than eight towers—at junctions of major routes and at strategic places along the way. Agricultural villages were founded at many of these fortresses, but the sites were chosen for their military value and not for their agricultural promise. Obvious places such as Arad (10), Beer-sheba (11), and Hormah (12) were refortified.

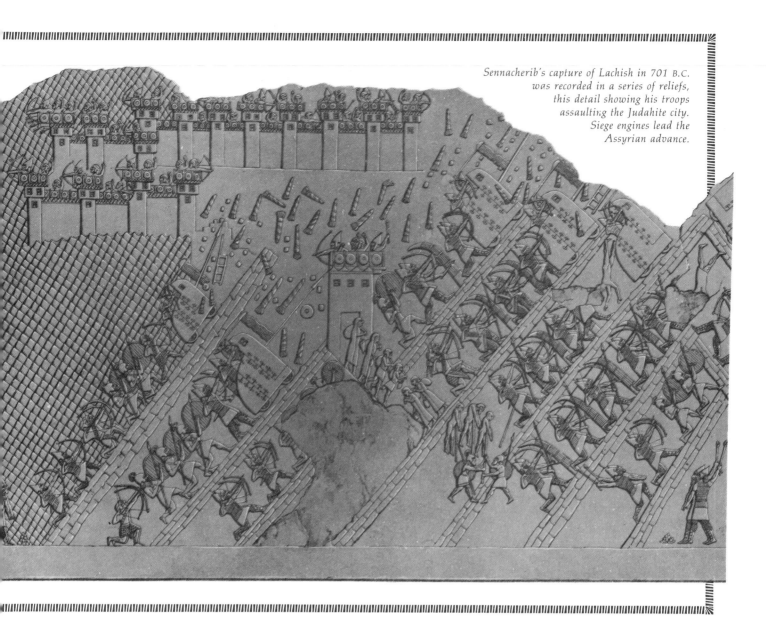

But there were other "towers in the wilderness," as 2 Chronicles 26:10 calls them. Archaeologists have found many but certainly not all of these.

Uzziah also strengthened the fortifications of Jerusalem. He built wooden structures atop towers and battlements to protect his men while they shot arrows and hurled great stones at the enemy. He also reorganized and reequipped the army of Judah with "shields, spears, helmets, coats of mail, bows, and stones for slinging." At the forefront of this efficient fighting force were the revitalized "mighty men of valor," an elite strike force that traced its origins to King David's personal guard.

With his new army Uzziah not only secured the Negeb but renewed his father's attack on Edom, retaking territory all the way down to Ezion-geber (13, on locator), which he rebuilt as a major port and an important town on the Arabian caravan route between Egypt and Damascus. Uzziah's desire for a port on the Great Sea led to an attack on Philistia. He secured the Shephelah

for Judah and built a fortress at Azekah (14). The defenses of Gath (15), Ashdod (16), and Jabneh (17) were destroyed and Gath and Jabneh were incorporated into Judah, along with some of the area formerly controlled by Ashdod. Finally Uzziah extended his authority to the port of Joppa (18), which along with securing the always troublesome and vulnerable western approaches to the hill country of Judah had been a major objective of his military offensive.

We also hear of a military action "against the Arabs that dwelt in Gurbaal, and against the Meunites." Gurbaal is unidentified, but the Meunites have sometimes been seen as the people of the Edomite desert who could have threatened Judah's control over the southern end of the King's Highway. While Uzziah did not control that famous route farther north, the Ammonites who did paid tribute to him. Nothing is said about Moab in this time. But the Moabites could hardly have been a threat to this king of Judah whose fame "spread even to the border of Egypt, for he became very strong."

131

Caught in the Maelstrom

Israel was plunged into political chaos with the death of Jeroboam II in 746 B.C., as three kings mounted the throne in Samaria in a single year. After a reign of only six months, Zechariah, Jeroboam's son, was struck down at Ibleam (1) by an assassin, who thus brought an end to the century-long dynasty of Jehu. Zechariah's murderer and successor, Shallum, held power for only a month when he in turn was killed by Menahem of Tirzah. A glimpse of Menahem's character and of the opposition he faced in solidifying power can be seen in his merciless sack of Tappuah (2), where "he ripped up all the women in it who were with child." By such measures he succeeded in gaining control over Israel, which so recently enjoyed great power and prestige but was now seriously weakened.

In that same year, 745, Tiglath-pileser III (also called Pul in the Bible) came to the Assyrian throne and by his superior administrative and military abilities launched that fearful empire upon its greatest period of expansion (see page 130). Moreover, he brought a fateful change to Assyrian imperial policy. No longer were campaigns undertaken merely to secure booty, slaves, tribute, and commercial advantage; now conquered areas were to be incorporated into the Assyrian empire. The native leadership was to be deported, and conquered peoples from elsewhere settled in the newly captured regions.

Struggling without success to duplicate their feat of 853, when they had checked Assyrian imperial ambitions on the field at Qarqar, the petty states to the west repeatedly hurled a multinational force against the advancing Assyrians. The annals of Tiglath-pileser III identify the leader of this effort as "Azriau from Iuda"—none other than Uzziah (Azariah) of Judah. Leprous and failing in his old age, this great monarch sought to rally his fellow kings against the potentially fatal power from the northeast. It was a futile undertaking. Assyria's vast resources of men and matériel made inevitable the ultimate achievement of its insistent imperial ambitions. Soon almost every ruler in the area was paying tribute to Assyria, including Rezin of Damascus, Hiram of Tyre, and even Zabibe, the queen of Arabia.

Menahem of Israel was among those paying tribute to Tiglath-pileser—apparently with the hope that it not only would keep Assyrian soldiers out of Israel but also would help confirm his shaky claim to the royal throne. But the tribute was so enormous—a thousand talents of silver—that Menahem resorted to exacting 50 shekels of silver from each wealthy man in the land. Even though Menahem was able to hold power for seven years, the manner of his coming to the throne, his exactions from the landowners, and his accommodating attitude toward Assyria contributed to this monarch's widespread unpopularity. His son, Pekahiah, had hardly ascended the throne when he was assassinated by Pekah in a military coup d'etat led by Gileadites. This signaled a significant—and fatal—turn in Israel's foreign policy.

Israel and Syria, so often bitter enemies in the recent past, joined forces as Pekah allied himself with Rezin in yet another attempt to form a defensive coalition against Assyria. But Jotham of Judah, Uzziah's son, who had served as coregent during his father's waning years and who now reigned alone, would have none of it. Isolated in their hills, the Judahites hoped that the storm would pass by. When Jotham died in 735 his son, Ahaz, was pressed anew by Pekah and Rezin. In the face of Ahaz's refusal to join their anti-Assyrian alliance, Pekah and Rezin determined to invade Judah, remove Ahaz, and replace him with "the son of Tabeel" (otherwise unidentified), who would bring Judah into the coalition. When Ahaz heard that Israel and Syria had made common cause against him, "his heart and the heart of his people shook as the trees of the forest shake before the wind."

For about a century and a half, until the fall of Israel in 721, the city of Samaria served as the capital of the northern kingdom. The site, on the top of the hill of Samaria, which is seen in the distance, was easily defensible, a factor that most likely influenced Omri in his decision to build a city there. Archaeological evidence has shown that Samaria must have been one of the wealthiest cities in Israel at that time, with a fine royal palace and palace walls. In the ruins was found a group of more than 500 fragments of ivory carvings of exquisite workmanship.

In this time of uncertainty and declining power Israel and Judah lost control of the Transjordan to Syria as Rezin sent his armies far down the King's Highway to extend his authority to Ezion-geber (3). But that authority was scarcely firm, and Syrian domination over much of the Transjordan, and especially the southern portions, was short-lived as native control asserted itself.

Rezin also dispatched an army to Israel in order to join forces with Pekah to bring pressure on Judah. It is possible—even likely—that they came along the direct route through Aphek (4) and by Lodebar (5), once more in Syrian hands. Since the aim of Pekah and Rezin was to terrify Judah and overthrow Ahaz, the combined army invaded Judah directly across the northern border and in heavy fighting lay siege to Jerusalem (6). In this campaign a large amount of booty was taken, as were numbers of Judahite captives. These people—hungry, thirsty, naked, and thoroughly wretched—were first brought to Samaria (7). But the prophet Oded denounced Israel, saying that the nation had sinned enough without adding this transgression. After certain chief men of the country joined their objections to those of Oded, the captives were fed, given drink and clothing, their wounds attended to, and taken to Jericho (8). Perhaps in this incident we see internal opposition to Pekah and his policies. If so, this was of little comfort to the king in Jerusalem.

Ever more desperate and on the verge of panic, Ahaz considered an appeal for help to Tiglath-pileser. In this crucial moment he was confronted by Isaiah, one of the greatest prophets of ancient Israel. "Take heed, be quiet, do not fear," said the prophet, "and do not let your heart be faint because of these two smoldering stumps of firebrands." Judah's hope of salvation lay in its trust in the Lord. The childless royal line would continue, for the young queen would bear a son whose name was to be Immanuel, "God is with us." Moreover, Zion, the holy hill of God in Jerusalem, was inviolable, in Isaiah's view. And even if Jerusalem did fall, a righteous remnant would remain. A true assessment of the strength of those "smoldering stumps," Israel and Syria, would show them to be less of a threat to Judah than the fearsome Assyrians with their unlimited ambitions. Thus Isaiah advised the king.

But the Israelites and Syrians pressed hard against Jerusalem. And in that critical moment some of Judah's ancient enemies struck. Edom not merely regained its freedom but seized the whole of the Arabah (9) with its mineral resources down to Ezion-geber. As Judah's defenses fell apart in the south, Edomite raids reached into the Negeb (10). In the west the Philistines not only recovered what had been lost to Uzziah but took Beth-shemesh (11), Socoh (12), Timnah (13), Aijalon (14), and Gimzo (15). Thus the entrances to two of the most important and vulnerable of the western approaches to Judah—the Way of Beth-horon and the Way of Beth-shemesh—were held by Judah's enemies and were thereby denied to Ahaz. Moreover, the Philistines took Gederoth (16) and made raids into the Negeb (17), looting and destroying Uzziah's network of military-agricultural settlements.

Under pressure from every direction, the king of Judah made a fateful appeal to Tiglath-pileser.

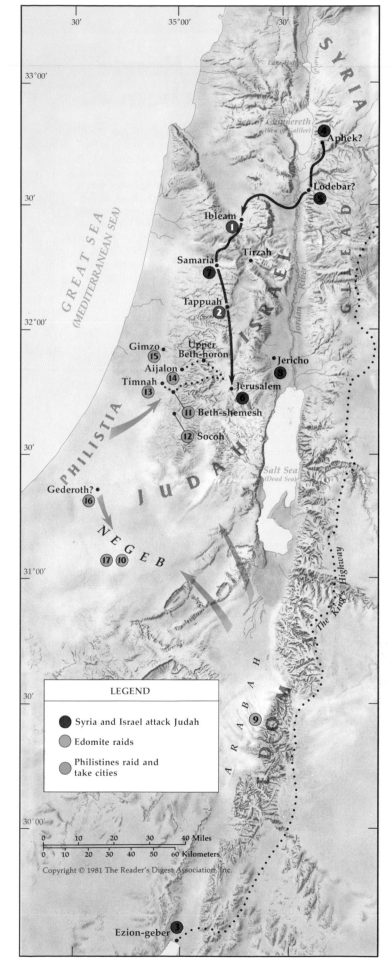

LEGEND

● Syria and Israel attack Judah

● Edomite raids

● Philistines raid and take cities

Copyright © 1981 The Reader's Digest Association, Inc.

The Fall of Israel

The appeal of King Ahaz of Judah to Tiglath-pileser III had immediate and far-reaching consequences. As the prophet Isaiah had warned, the Assyrian ruler needed little encouragement. Indeed, Tiglath-pileser had already laid plans to crush the power of Syria and incorporate it into his empire. Knowing that Egypt would oppose his designs, he intended to block any possible interference from the south. The plan called for three military campaigns, which would neutralize Egypt, isolate Syria, and then destroy the power of Damascus.

Israel seems not to have figured in Tiglath-pileser's scheme except insofar as it was necessary for him to cross Israelite territory en route to sealing off Egypt. Pekah's alliance with Rezin of Damascus, however, had placed Israel in more peril than the shortsighted Israelite king could have realized. By the time Tiglath-pileser had accomplished his aims in the three successive campaigns of 734, 733, and 732 B.C., Israel lay mortally wounded.

In 734 the Assyrian army started down the coast along the Way of the Sea toward the Brook of Egypt, Egypt's traditional northeastern frontier. Beyond Tyre (1) and Acco (2) it faced the problem of getting safely past Mount Carmel. At one point, only a few hundred yards separate the steep promontory from the sea. Without control of the surrounding region, it was an unacceptable military risk to lead an army, however powerful, through that narrow passage. Therefore, the Assyrians made a 10-mile detour inland to the first major pass through the Carmel range. What damage they may have inflicted on Israel with this glancing blow we do not know. They entered the range at Jokneam (3), emerged east of Dor (4), and once more joined the main branch of the Way of the Sea southward, thereby avoiding sieges of the major inland strongholds.

We know that Tiglath-pileser assaulted Gezer (5) on this campaign, although it is not clear why he chose to destroy this fortress. Perhaps its proximity to the eastern branch of the Way of the Sea—only five miles distant—was viewed as a threat. Archaeologists working at Gezer have found ample evidence of the destruction; excavated remains of houses from this period bear dramatic witness to a great fire. The old Solomonic gate, rebuilt but still sturdy and in use, was finally destroyed at this time. A relief on the wall of Tiglath-pileser's palace at Nimrud confirms the siege and capture of Gazru, or Gezer.

After conquering Gaza (6), Tiglath-pileser marched to the Brook of Egypt, where he sought to establish himself in strength in order to contain his potential southern rival. Tiglath-pileser's short-term success was perhaps as much due to the weakness of Egypt at this time as to the might of Assyria. When Egypt caused difficulties for Tiglath-pileser's successors, it was in the form of encouraging local uprisings and sending ineffective armies to try to reestablish Egyptian control over the Gaza area.

The next year, 733, the Assyrians returned to strike a blow aimed squarely at Israel with the apparent intention of reducing Galilee, taking Gilead, and thus cutting off Syria from the west and south. Pekah was now to suffer the consequences of his anti-Assyrian alliance with Rezin. Long lines of warriors marched past towering Mount Hermon (9,232 feet) as they emerged from the pass between the Lebanon and Anti-Lebanon mountains and began to descend into the great rift valley near the Israelite fortresses of Ijon and Abel-beth-maacah (7), which they swiftly reduced. This route, important today as in antiquity, clings to the foothills of Galilee because of Lake Huleh and the area's extensive swamps. Commanding this approach to the heartland was Hazor (8), a massive citadel crowning the 130-foot-high mound.

Archaeological work at Hazor has shown that Assyrians stormed the citadel from the eastern and relatively less steep side of the mound. On that side the destruction was so severe that only foundations below floor level were left; everywhere else on the mound the ferocity of the assault is also much in evidence. Floors of the military buildings and houses were strewn with debris. Only a few important artifacts remained in the ruins, illustrating the thoroughness of the Assyrian soldiers as they looted. Finally Hazor was burned. The still-black ash layer is three feet thick over the mound. This is some of the most dramatic evidence of destruction that has been found in excavations anywhere in the land.

While we cannot be certain of the movements of the Assyrian army, it appears that, at Hazor, Tiglath-pileser divided his forces into three strike groups. He sent the first into Upper Galilee along the well-traveled route by Kedesh (9) and through Janoah (10), both of which were destroyed, and down to the coast at Acco (11). Subsequently, this force turned southward, this time passing between Mount Carmel and the sea. As it moved past Dor (12), we lose track of it. Perhaps the army went down to reinforce the garrisons along the Brook of Egypt.

The second and third strike groups moved south of Hazor to Chinnereth (13), where they parted, one moving south and east through Pehel (14) and Jabesh-gilead. A part of this second group took the route past Mahanaim (15) as the Assyrians fanned out through Gilead.

In following a branch of the Way of the Sea into Lower Galilee, the third group came up from the rift by the extinct volcano at Adamah and continued westward through the central lateral valley of Lower Galilee, destroying the towns of Rumah, Kanah, Jotbah, and Hannathon (16). From Hannathon a valley leads south to the Great Plain, across which stood Megiddo (17).

Controlling the Wadi Ara, a major passage through the Carmel range and the one traced by the Way of the Sea, Megiddo had long been a fortress. It was also at this time one of the most important cities in Israel, the administrative center for much of the northern part of the kingdom. Megiddo was now assaulted, most likely by the strike group that had passed through Lower Galilee but perhaps augmented by detachments from the army that had marched through Upper Galilee and come down the coast. Although heavily fortified for many centuries, Megiddo had gained an offset-inset wall at some point in the Israelite period—probably at the time of

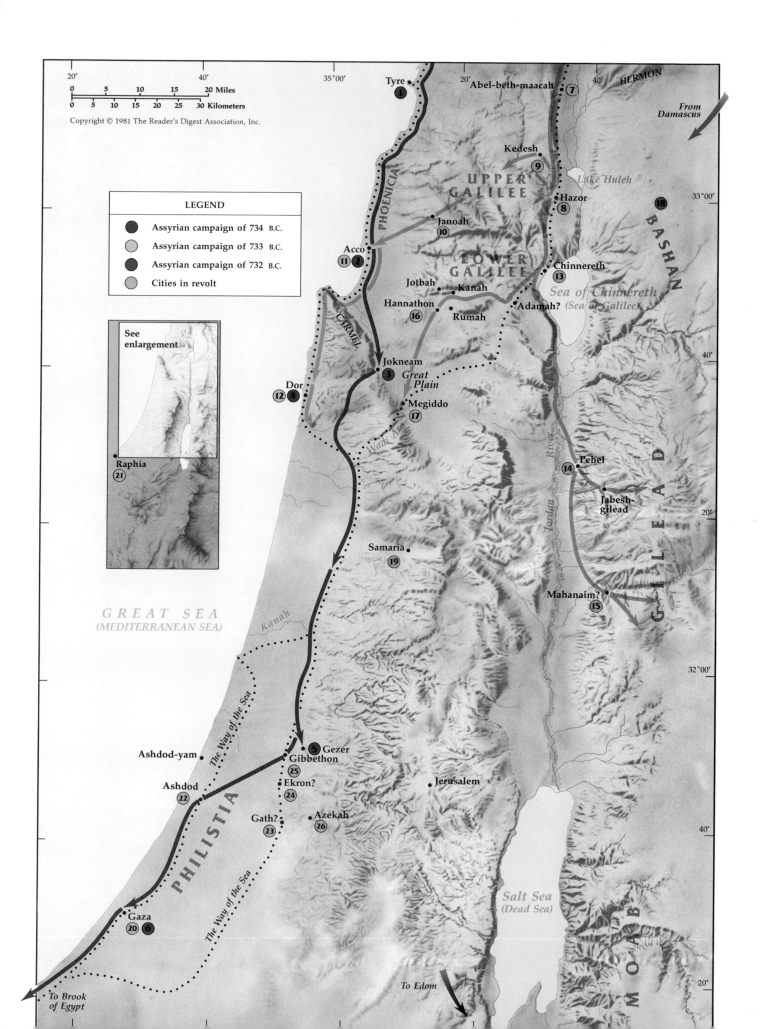

20' 40' 35°00' 20' 40' HERMON

0 5 10 15 20 Miles
0 5 10 15 20 25 30 Kilometers

Copyright © 1981 The Reader's Digest Association, Inc.

Tyre
①

Abel-beth-maacah ⑦

From Damascus

Kedesh
⑨

UPPER GALILEE

Lake Huleh

Janoah
⑩

Hazor
⑧

⑱

33°00'

B A S H A N

LEGEND

● Assyrian campaign of 734 B.C.
○ Assyrian campaign of 733 B.C.
● Assyrian campaign of 732 B.C.
● Cities in revolt

PHOENICIA

LOWER GALILEE

Chinnereth
⑬

Acco
⑪ ②

Jotbah   Kanah

Hannathon
⑯   Rumah

Adamah?

Sea of Chinnereth
(Sea of Galilee)

See enlargement

CARMEL

Jokneam
③ Great Plain

40'

Dor
⑫ ④

Megiddo
⑰

Wadi Ara

Pehel
⑭

Jordan River

G I L E A D

Jabesh-gilead

20'

Raphia
㉑

Samaria
⑲

Mahanaim?
⑮

GREAT SEA
(MEDITERRANEAN SEA)

Kanah

32°00'

Ashdod-yam

Gezer
⑤ Gibbethon
㉕

The Way of the Sea

Ekron?
㉔

Jerusalem

Ashdod
㉒

PHILISTIA

Gath?
㉓

Azekah
㉖

40'

The Way of the Sea

Salt Sea
(Dead Sea)

M O A B

Gaza
⑳ ⑥

To Brook of Egypt

To Edom

20'

The Fall of Israel (continued)

Ahab—to provide flanking fire against attackers. Within these walls were many large public buildings, two sizable stable complexes, and extensive residential areas with well-built stone houses.

Evidence of the Assyrian destruction at Megiddo is not so dramatic as at Hazor—perhaps because the Assyrians rebuilt most of the city and in the process removed much of what had stood before. But the extent of Tiglath-pileser's assault of Megiddo can be measured by the fact that the Assyrians rebuilt the city on an entirely different plan. Blocks of houses along straight streets intersected at right angles and were oriented differently from those of Israelite Megiddo. Rebuilt Megiddo became the administrative center of a new Assyrian province named Magiddu. Isaiah called this province Galil-ha-goiim (district or region of the foreigners), and we know it today as Galilee. The whole of the northern part of the kingdom of Israel was annexed to the Assyrian empire. At the same time, the coast south of Mount Carmel down to the brook Kanah was annexed as the province of Dor.

In Samaria, meanwhile, Pekah was struck down in a conspiracy led by Hoshea, who became the last king of Israel. According to Tiglath-pileser's annals, Hoshea had Assyrian assistance in his successful plot. Events would prove that Hoshea and his supporters in Samaria were not as pro-Assyrian as might have appeared. But for the moment this coup d'etat preserved a sense of independence for the reduced kingdom of Israel—though it should have been clear that the northern state was not to survive.

Israel had lost all pretense of claim to Gilead, and its territory west of the Jordan had been reduced by more than half. Its resources were meager, and much of what was left had to be used to pay tribute to Assyria. The sense of independence was purely an illusion. Assyria was on three sides of what was left of Israel. The routes from the north to Samaria were wide open, with no major fortifications intact between the Great Plain and the capital. It would take but a single mistake to end the life of the country, and Hoshea was to make that mistake when Tiglath-pileser died.

On his third drive south, in 732, Tiglath-pileser finally stormed and captured Damascus, making Syria a province of his empire and deporting large numbers of people. Moving south of Damascus, the Assyrian armies secured Syrian Bashan (18).

At this time Ahaz of Judah, who had sent the Assyrian king tribute that he had stripped from the Temple, the royal palace, and the palaces of the princes of Judah, was ordered northward to Damascus to bow before his rescuer, Tiglath-pileser. And, says 2 Chronicles, the king of Assyria "afflicted him instead of strengthening him." It was while he was in Damascus that Ahaz saw an altar and had a copy of it made. Already, in previous times of crisis, Ahaz had offered worship to any deity he thought might aid him. Now, following the custom of worshiping the divinities of the vassal's lord, Judah's king placed the altar to a foreign god in the Temple in Jerusalem, removing the altar to the Lord from its place of prominence. To Ahaz and his advisers, subservience was the only course offering the promise of survival.

Tiglath-pileser III died in 727. As happened so often in antiquity when a strong king died, conquered people on the fringes of his empire revolted. Israel was no exception. While pretending loyalty to the new Assyrian ruler, Shalmaneser V, Hoshea sought help from the king of Egypt. Upon receiving assurances from the weak Pharaoh—who was probably Tefnakht of the 24th Dynasty—Hoshea withheld tribute from Shalmaneser. This was an open declaration of rebellion. Too late Hoshea realized his mistake: he had touched an Assyrian raw nerve, the potential threat of Egypt. Shalmaneser moved against Israel, and Hoshea was taken prisoner—perhaps while en route to the Assyrian king to make amends. As thousands of people from the towns and villages of Israel crowded behind the walls of Samaria (19), the Assyrians came and laid siege to the city.

If the Assyrian soldiers had little trouble getting to Samaria, they found this city on its solitary hill exceedingly difficult to take. The siege lasted three years, one of the longest recorded sieges in antiquity. And though Shalmaneser died and was replaced by Sargon II, the change in monarchs made little difference to Israel.

During the siege, suffering increased daily and desperation mounted by the hour, until the Assyrians finally breached the walls and took the city. The year was 721. After two centuries the northern kingdom of Israel had come to an end. In his annals Sargon boasts of taking away as booty 27,290 inhabitants of Samaria, scattering these people to Upper Mesopotamia and Media. He also brought into Israel peoples conquered elsewhere, placing an Assyrian governor over them and requiring the customary tribute. He had, in fact, combined what was left of Israel with the province of Dor and annexed it to his empire as the province of Samaria. The newcomers, in time, merged with the remaining Israelites to become the Samaritans of the New Testament.

In a footnote to this sad history, Sargon tells of revolts that broke out at Hamath, Damascus, Samaria, and Gaza. This was in 720 and seems to have been inspired by the king of Hamath (one of the Syrian kingdoms), but the Egyptians were also involved. Sargon acted swiftly to put down these rebellions, routing an Egyptian army that had come to the aid of Gaza (20). Continuing south, Sargon took Raphia (21, on locator); he tore down the walls, burned the city, and sent more than 9,000 of its inhabitants into exile.

Yet again—in 713 or 712—the Egyptians managed to stir up trouble, with Ashdod (22) as the center of rebellion. This time it seems that Judah (under its new king, Hezekiah) as well as Edom and Moab joined the revolt. Isaiah strongly opposed Judah's involvement, and Judah along with Edom and Moab withdrew before extensive damage to their kingdoms was done. Ashdod and its port, Ashdod-yam, fell and the area was made into the Assyrian province of Ashdod. Gath (23), Ekron (24), and Gibbethon (25) were other targets of Assyrian vengeance. Azekah (26), which controlled the Way to Bethshemesh and thus access to Jerusalem, was also taken. The Assyrians apparently thought that sooner or later something would have to be done about Judah. It proved to be sooner rather than later.

Sennacherib Attacks Judah

Shortly after Sargon II destroyed Israel, the Assyrian ruler faced rebellion at the far end of his empire as a Chaldean prince named Merodach-baladan succeeded in establishing Babylonian independence. The struggle there was to drag on for perhaps as many as 12 years. In pulling troops out of Samaria and the surrounding territories to deal with his problems to the east, Sargon risked secession attempts in his newly conquered provinces along the Great Sea. And, as we have seen, such revolts did flare up, in 720 B.C. and in 713-12. Hezekiah of Judah, who wanted to reverse his father's pro-Assyrian policies, apparently joined the anti-Assyrian forces in 713-12, signaling what was to come.

Sargon was ultimately able to suppress these challenges to his authority at opposite ends of his extensive empire. Coming to the throne in 704, his son and successor, Sennacherib, proved to be a less vigorous ruler, devoting the first years of his reign to beautifying his capital of Nineveh. At about the same time, long-dormant Egypt was reasserting itself under the kings of the 25th (Ethiopian) Dynasty.

Taking advantage of this situation, Hezekiah withheld tribute and made extensive preparations for full-scale rebellion against Assyria. The Bible tells us how he readied Jerusalem (1, map on the following page) for the anticipated attack. A spectacular remnant of these preparations is the water tunnel under the city that the king had dug from the Gihon spring in the Kidron valley in order to provide adequate water in time of siege. This tunnel runs about 1,750 feet through solid rock, which was chipped away piece by piece by hand using iron tools. It varies in width between 3 and 11 feet and in height between 4 and 16 feet and still functions, pouring its clear waters into the Pool of Siloam. At the same time, Hezekiah sought to deny water to an attacking army. The limestone hills around Jerusalem have but few large springs, which the Judahites endeavored to stop or foul as the invader approached.

Unfortunately, the Bible does not say where and how Hezekiah strengthened defenses elsewhere. But in light of geography and of subsequent events we can gain a clear idea of what was required. While ancient enemies might make sorties from the east or south, a major attack from the Assyrians would not come from those directions where the Wilderness of Judah and the Negeb formed effective frontiers. North of Jerusalem the border with the Assyrian province of Samaria lay barely 10 miles away, but to bring a large army over the deeply scarred Samarian hills would have been difficult. Nonetheless, the plateau north of Jerusalem was clearly a vulnerable point and could not be neglected.

To the west the Shephelah, that area of low-lying hills, scrub brush, and small valleys between coastal plain and central highlands, offered a forward line of defense. A would-be conqueror breaking through a tough line of fortifications there would be confronted with yet another natural line upon which the stubborn defenders of Judah could make a stand: the compact mountain range that guards the heartland of Judah and contributed to the kingdom's insularity. Judah was hardly impregnable, but its geography gave numerous natural advantages to the defenders.

But there were also serious defensive problems for Hezekiah. Relatively easy access to central Judah is provided by a series of defiles slashing through the Shephelah, most notably the Way of Beth-shemesh (2), a broad approach to Jerusalem. Subsequent events show that Hezekiah concentrated fortifications here and that Sennacherib had difficulty dealing with them. Rehoboam's old line of fortifications along Judah's northern frontier (see map on page 111) was doubtless the anchor for Hezekiah's military preparations. But, judging from Sennacherib's claim that he destroyed 46 cities and walled forts in Judah, we can be sure that Hezekiah took advantage of his country's geography to turn Judah into a stronghold bristling with fortifications at every strategic point.

In addition to strengthening his fortifications, Hezekiah prepared for war in other ways. He raided into Edom (3, on locator), in order to secure his southern frontiers. He standardized equipment in Judah's army and re-armed his soldiers, taking special care to see that vast stores of darts and shields were ready. Hezekiah also undertook a religious revival, combining a return to traditional religious values with a renewed nationalism. On the basis of his religious reforms, the king appealed to Samaria and Galilee to join in the rebellion, but his overtures met a mostly negative response.

Hezekiah also looked for support to others who were anti-Assyrian. He received ambassadors from the resurgent Merodach-baladan, who had renewed the Babylonian rebellion against Sennacherib, and formed an alliance with King Sidqa of Ashkelon (4). Other Philistine rulers at Ashdod and Gaza—with recent painful memories of Assyria's might—hesitated to commit themselves. Because Padi, king of Ekron (5), was loyal to Sennacherib, his subjects seized him and sent him to Hezekiah, who imprisoned him at Jerusalem. When Pharaoh Shabako of Egypt promised military aid, Hezekiah signed a treaty with him—despite Isaiah's warning that "the protection of Pharaoh [shall] turn to your shame, and the shelter in the shadow of Egypt to your humiliation." Ammon, Moab, and Edom may have been involved in Hezekiah's coalition. If so, they backed off quickly when Assyrian armies appeared.

By 702 Merodach baladan's rebellion in Babylonia was again under control, and Sennacherib turned at once to deal with the coalition of restive vassals forming around Hezekiah. In 701 the Assyrians came down the coast in massive force, first striking the Phoenicians. Luli, king of Tyre (6, on locator), fled to Cyprus, while Tyre and its inland town of Uzu were so thoroughly devastated that the great port, when rebuilt, lost its place of commercial prominence.

The Assyrian army was not again distracted as it moved swiftly down the Way of the Sea toward Philistia and western Judah. Ashkelon's dependency, the port of

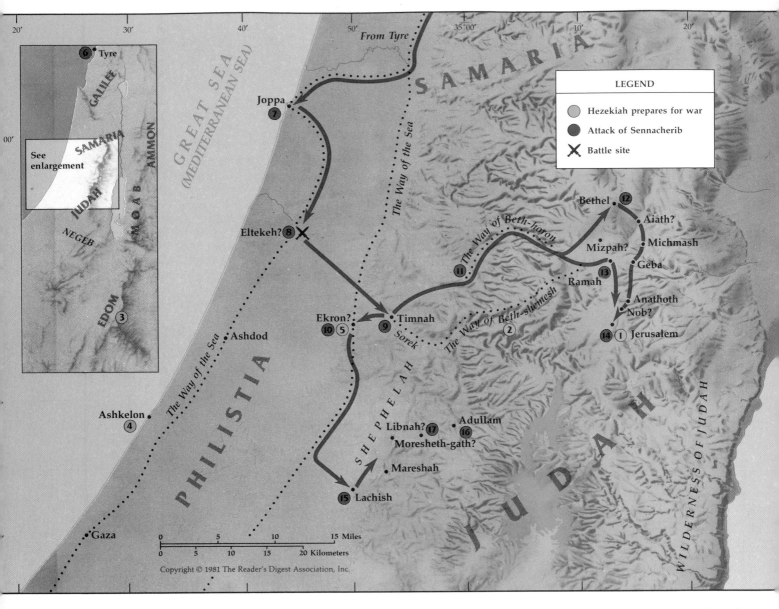

Joppa (7), was the first target; it fell with ease. But suddenly Sennacherib faced an Egyptian army strengthened by the presence of bowmen, chariots, and cavalry from Ethiopia. The armies collided at Eltekeh (8), with the Assyrians scoring a great victory. After taking and destroying Eltekeh, however, Sennacherib failed to follow up his advantage and allowed the Egyptians to retreat unharassed. Instead, the Assyrian ruler advanced on Timnah (9) and Ekron (10), not as a prelude to a direct thrust into the central highlands through the Sorek valley and the Way of Beth-shemesh, but rather to punish those who had cooperated with Hezekiah in removing and imprisoning King Padi of Ekron. The Assyrian plan for reducing Judah now began to unfold.

One army went up the Way of Beth-horon (11) to strike at Jerusalem from the north. This force fought its way onto the plateau north of the capital after making a wide arc through Bethel (12), Aiath, Michmash, Geba, Anathoth, and Nob. Part of the army captured Ramah (13), which cut off Mizpah, anchor of Hezekiah's north-

ern defenses. Not wishing to waste men, matériel, and time in attacking Mizpah, the Assyrians simply isolated it. Sennacherib surrounded Jerusalem (14) with earthworks to prevent anyone from leaving the city. Hezekiah was shut up in his capital, boasted Sennacherib, "like a bird in a cage."

While the king of Judah was thus cut off from directing the defense of his realm, the other army under Sennacherib himself set about to storm the strong cities and walled forts in the Shephelah. The key to these western defenses was Lachish (15), the largest mound in the country and one of the most strongly fortified. If Lachish could be taken, Sennacherib could move steadily northward through the Shephelah, attacking city after city. And this is what he did—though Lachish did not prove an easy victory. In his annals Sennacherib speaks of using earthworks, tunnels, breaches, and sappers in his operations. Archaeological work at Lachish confirms the ferocity of the Assyrian assault, with fire being used extensively as a weapon of offense. Moreover, burial pits in which the Assyrians cast their victims after the fall of the city have been found; one contained 1,500 bodies.

At the same time they were besieging Lachish, the Assyrians took Adullam (16) and continued to cause havoc around Jerusalem. The country was being systematically devastated—city, town, village, and field. Many deserted Judah's army, and even Isaiah, who had earlier opposed submission to Assyria, encouraged Hezekiah to give up before it was too late. Negotiations were opened, but Sennacherib's terms were severe. In response to Hezekiah's gift of silver and gold—some of it stripped from the Temple—Sennacherib sent one of his ministers, the Rabshakeh, to Jerusalem to negotiate the surrender of the capital and to conduct a little psychological warfare. For when the Assyrian envoy stood outside the walls of the city, he abandoned Aramaic, the diplomatic language of the day, and spoke to the defenders of the walls in Hebrew. He told them how hopeless their situation was and how Hezekiah had caused both political and religious trouble. Speaking on behalf of the king of Assyria, he said, "Make your peace with me and come out to me; then every one of you will eat of his own vine, and every one of his own fig tree, and every one of you will drink the water of his own cistern." But stony silence greeted his words, and Isaiah now urged Hezekiah to stand fast in the face of this mortal threat. God would deliver Jerusalem.

If Isaiah believed that God hovered like a bird over sacred Jerusalem, protecting it, Micah of Moresheth-gath took a different view. This great prophet represented the feelings in western Judah, where heavy blows had repeatedly fallen on the people because of policies made in Jerusalem. Micah threatened the destruction of the corrupted capital stone by stone, until grass grew in the streets.

When the Rabshakeh returned to his master, Sennacherib was at Libnah (17), Lachish having fallen. Moresheth-gath and Mareshah, west and south of Libnah, also fell before the relentless foe. According to the plan of Sennacherib, the Shephelah was slowly being laid waste.

Subsequent events are not clear. Sennacherib seems to have gone up to Jerusalem, either to join his forces already there or with reinforcements. Suddenly, mysteriously, the Assyrian army was decimated. "And that night the angel of the Lord went forth, and slew a hundred and eighty-five thousand in the camp of the Assyrians," 2 Kings 19:35 tells us, "and when men arose early in the morning, behold, these were all dead bodies." The 5th-century B.C. Greek historian Herodotus speaks of mice invading the field and causing the Assyrian army to withdraw. The reference to mice suggests to some that plague—the scourge of ancient armies—had broken out in the Assyrian camp.

Sennacherib ruled Assyria for 20 years after this campaign, and some scholars interpret the biblical text as referring to a second attack on Hezekiah's Judah, about 689. It was this later invasion, they theorize, that ended with the miraculous deliverance of Jerusalem. But the Assyrian records are silent about a second campaign. From these sources we do learn that Hezekiah sent the massive tribute demanded by Sennacherib to Nineveh. Sennacherib tells us what it contained: "30 talents of gold, 800 talents of silver, precious stones, antimony, large cuts of red stone, couches [inlaid] with ivory, chairs [inlaid] with ivory, elephant-hides, ebony wood, box-wood [and] all kinds of valuable treasures, his [own] daughters, concubines, male and female musicians. In order to deliver the tribute and to do obeisance as a slave he sent his [personal] messenger."

Hezekiah received congratulations for his resistance from Merodach-baladan, who had renewed his rebellion against Assyria. But there was little cause for rejoicing. Sennacherib boasted of driving 200,150 people—"young and old, male and female"—out of their homes and seizing "horses, mules, donkeys, camels, big and small cattle beyond counting." Not only had the strong cities and walled forts of Judah fallen, but the countryside with its small villages had been devastated. It would be several decades before the southern kingdom recovered from so basic a disruption of its life.

End of Judah

Death spared Hezekiah further humiliation at the hands of the Assyrians. His son and successor, Manasseh, whose 45-year-reign (687–42 B.C.) was the longest in Judah's history, adopted a policy of abject submission to Assyria. He paid tribute to Sennacherib and his successors, worshiped their divinities in Jerusalem, and even provided troops for their successful assaults on Egypt—which ultimately was made an Assyrian vassal.

Popular resentment against Manasseh's rule grew steadily. Looking solely at his religious policies, biblical writers considered him to have been the worst king Judah ever had. Yet he had little choice; nor did his son, Amon, who continued his father's policies for two years until he was struck down by assassins and was succeeded in 640 by his eight-year-old son, Josiah.

But the Assyrian rulers had overextended themselves,

and by the second half of the 7th century they could no longer govern their far-flung territories. Egypt broke away, and Babylonia—always a problem for Assyria—again revolted, this time with the support of Media. As Assyrian troops were withdrawn from the provinces to meet the Babylonian threat, a power vacuum developed in the land bridge between Africa and Asia.

By 628, when Josiah was 20 years old, Judah had become politically free by default. For a brief moment—the brightness of a candle before the flame goes out—Judah enjoyed national expansion and prosperity on a scale unseen since the days of Uzziah more than a century earlier. Freed from Assyria, Josiah pressed for sweeping religious reforms supported by the prophet Zephaniah, who condemned the religious practices that had flourished under Manasseh and urged Judah to purify itself

End of Judah (continued)

and its worship. Another prophet, the young Jeremiah, added his voice in support of the king's reforms.

The religious reformation and the outpouring of patriotic fervor, following decades of subservience to Assyria, not only united Judah internally but also fostered an expansion of its borders. Josiah was able to push Judah's frontiers farther into the Negeb, but we do not know to what extent. Since we later hear of Edom harassing Judah in the Negeb and Nebuchadnezzar of Babylon wresting part of the Negeb from Judah, it is likely that Josiah held a sizable amount of territory in the south. In the west, archaeologists working along the coast at a site known today as Mezad Hashavyahu (1) have unearthed clear evidence that Josiah pushed out to the Great Sea. A fort from the time of Josiah has been uncovered there, and in it were found inscriptions making it clear that the site was in Judah's hands at the time.

The Bible tells us that Josiah extended his kingdom northward to include Ephraim (2), Manasseh (3), and Naphtali (4), which suggests that much of the old Assyrian provinces of Samaria and Megiddo were annexed to Judah. (One of Josiah's wives, in fact, came from Rumah, west of the Sea of Chinnereth.) The city of Megiddo (5) was rebuilt by Josiah to serve as administrative headquarters for his new northern domains. We do not know why Assyrian Megiddo declined, but archaeological work shows a general if modest reconstruction of the city at the time of Josiah. The homes were small, more suited to village life than to a city, but it was hardly the stronghold it had been before its destruction by Tiglath-pileser, although there was a large palace-fortress.

Nineveh fell to the Babylonians in 612, and the book of Nahum—an exultant poem on the destruction of the Assyrian capital—shows the joy Assyria's enemies felt. The event, however, also heralded disaster for Judah. The hard-pressed Assyrians fell steadily back toward northern Syria. By 609 their situation was desperate as the Babylonians massed for a fatal blow. Pharaoh Neco of Egypt, seeing a chance to reassert his country's claims to empire in Asia and not wanting a strong Babylonia to replace a weakened Assyria, rushed northward along the Way of the Sea to aid the Assyrians.

Neco had assured Josiah that he meant no harm to Judah but only wished to move rapidly through his kingdom. His route would take him by Megiddo, through Galilee and by ruined Hazor (6). For reasons that are not clear, Josiah refused the Egyptians passage and attempted to block their way at the pass through Mount Carmel that leads to Megiddo. As events were soon to prove, Egypt had designs on the old Assyrian provinces of Samaria and Megiddo, and perhaps Josiah was aware of this.

Little is known about the battle of Megiddo except its outcome and consequences. The Egyptians destroyed Judah's army with apparent ease and, after leveling the small fortress of Megiddo, hurried north. Although disguised so that his royal person would not be recognized, Josiah was wounded on the field of battle and taken to die in Jerusalem (7). Judah virtually died with him. The nation's grief was profound, and Jeremiah poured out his lamentations for this 39-year-old king who had brought religious and political unity to the nation.

Meanwhile, far to the northeast at Haran, Neco and his Assyrian allies were routed by the Babylonians. Neco fell back to Riblah in Syria and summoned Jehoahaz—who had succeeded to his father Josiah's throne only three months earlier—to appear before him. He deposed the young king and replaced him with his brother, Jehoiakim. We may also assume that Egypt seized those northern territories that Judah had taken under Josiah.

Egypt's dreams of reestablishing its ancient Asian empire were short-lived. In 605 Nebuchadnezzar defeated Neco at Carchemish, and in the following year he advanced southward to the coastal plain of Philistia, seizing the territory claimed by Egypt. In a letter found by archaeologists in Egypt, the king of Ashkelon (8) appeals for help to the Pharaoh, noting that the Babylonians were coming to attack him—and that they were already in Aphek (9).

By pledging himself vassal to Nebuchadnezzar, Jehoiakim spared Judah from attack during this campaign. But when Neco of Egypt and Nebuchadnezzar of Babylonia fought to a draw in 601, Jehoiakim rebelled. Not yet ready to tie up his armies in the central hill country, Nebuchadnezzar satisfied himself with ordering his vassals in Ammon, Moab, and Edom to attack Judah.

Under Jehoiakim the religious reforms of Josiah collapsed. General morality declined as corruption in high places increased. The king's lack of concern for his people was reflected in his enlarging the royal palace at Ramat Rahel with pressed labor gangs. Jeremiah condemned the deteriorating situation in the country and denounced Jehoiakim for his "vermilion" house (archaeologists have found red painted stones in the excavations at Ramat Rahel). The king, in turn, personally cut up one of Jeremiah's writings, expressing his bitter feelings toward this prophet who would not support his king. But Jeremiah would give him no word of comfort and continued to pour contempt upon the false prophets who spoke of peace and well-being in such times.

In the latter part of 598 Jehoiakim died, perhaps by assassination. Jeremiah had already condemned him, saying: "With the burial of an ass he shall be buried, dragged and cast forth beyond the gates of Jerusalem." Jehoiachin, the 18-year-old son of Jehoiakim, came to the throne in a moment of supreme crisis, for Nebuchadnezzar was marching south to take revenge on Judah.

Once again, we know little of the actual attack, only its consequences. We are merely told that Jerusalem (10) was besieged and that Nebuchadnezzar came from Babylon to be present at the assault. Neither surviving Babylonian texts nor archaeology adds anything to this knowledge. Some think that Lachish (11) and Debir (12) were taken by storm at this time, but we cannot be sure. In any case, the entire Babylonian campaign was swiftly concluded. After he had been on the throne three months and 10 days, Jehoiachin surrendered his capital to Nebuchadnezzar in 597. Leaders of the anti-Babylonian government—including the king—were deported.

The situation in Jerusalem was confused. Texts found in Babylon show that Jehoiachin was well treated in captivity, and many in Judah thought that he would return to deliver them. Instead Nebuchadnezzar—after taking portions of the Negeb and of the strategic Shephelah away from Judah—installed Jehoiachin's 21-year-old uncle, Zedekiah, on the throne of a reduced kingdom. Many felt that Zedekiah—destined to be Judah's last king—did not hold clear title to the throne. Indeed, archaeological discoveries reveal that agents of the king still referred to themselves as "stewards of Jehoiachin." Anti-Babylonian feelings ran high, and the well-intentioned but weak Zedekiah was simply carried along by the popular tide. When in 595–94 there was a brief flare of rebellion within Babylonia, Jerusalem became the center of an intrigue involving Edom, Moab, Ammon, and to the north, Tyre (13) and Sidon. Jeremiah spoke out strongly against this turn of events and was viewed as a traitor by the nationalists. Zedekiah—ever unsure of himself—repeatedly sought out Jeremiah for advice, most of which he rejected.

In 589, supported by Egyptian promises, Zedekiah openly rebelled against the king of Babylon. Early the next year the Babylonians were once again before the walls of Jerusalem. In a repeat of the campaign of Sennacherib, Nebuchadnezzar sealed off Jerusalem with siege works and set about systematically to devastate the entire country. A look at the accompanying map shows how widespread this destruction was. From Gibeah (14) to Arad (15), from Eglon (16) to En-gedi (17), Judah was set ablaze. (Excavations at these sites and at Lachish, Beth-shemesh, Debir, Beth-zur, and Ramat Rahel vividly illustrate how thorough was the destruction.)

A poignant reminder of Babylon's irresistible onslaught comes from the excavated gate at Lachish, where a series of hasty dispatches written on potsherds have been found. A signal post had been set up to relay messages between Lachish (18) and Azekah (19), the last-remaining fortresses outside the capital. To the anxious commander of Lachish, the officer in charge of the signal post writes: "We are watching for the signals of Lachish, according to all the indications which my lord hath given, for we cannot see [the signals of] Azekah." Only Lachish and Jerusalem were left.

The ruins of Lachish still show the ferocity of the Babylonian assault. The fires against the walls were so intense that the mortar between the stones melted and ran down the entrance road in streams, where, solidified, it can still be seen. Great, gaping holes were torn in the walls. And then only Jerusalem was left.

A forlorn hope for Judah was kindled in the summer of 588 when an Egyptian army approached along the coast, probably as the result of an appeal by the commander of the Judahite army. But Nebuchadnezzar repelled this relieving force somewhere south of Gaza (20), and the siege of Jerusalem dragged on into the spring of 587. While Judah was dying, Edom attacked in the Negeb.

The book of Lamentations paints vivid pictures of the horrors in Jerusalem: "How lonely sits the city that was full of people! . . . In the street the sword bereaves . . . my flesh and my skin waste away . . . The tongue of the nursling cleaves to the roof of its mouth for thirst; the children beg for food, but no one gives to them. . . . The hands of compassionate women have boiled their own children; they became their food . . ."

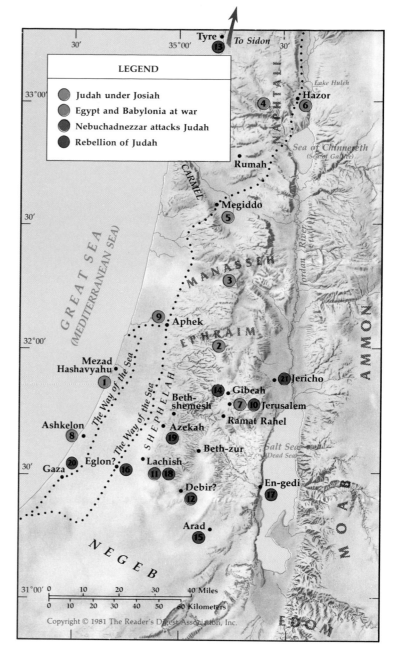

LEGEND
- Judah under Josiah
- Egypt and Babylonia at war
- Nebuchadnezzar attacks Judah
- Rebellion of Judah

Copyright © 1981 The Reader's Digest Association, Inc.

Jeremiah urged Zedekiah to surrender the city, but the king refused for fear he would be handed over to his Judahite enemies who had already gone over to the Babylonians. In the summer of 587 the city's food supply ran out. About the same time, the Babylonians finally succeeded in breaching the walls. At night Zedekiah and some of his men fled through the southeastern gate of the city toward Jericho (21), perhaps hoping to reach Ammon, which, unlike others in the abortive coalition, had remained faithful to its word to Zedekiah. But the hapless king was captured on the plains of Jericho and taken northward to Nebuchadnezzar at Riblah in Syria. There Zedekiah's sons were killed before his eyes. Then he was blinded, put in chains, and deported to Babylon.

About a month later Nebuzaradan, captain of Nebuchadnezzar's bodyguard, arrived in Jerusalem, rounded up thousands for deportation to Babylonia, and put the city to the torch. The captain "left some of the poorest of the land to be vinedressers and plowmen," but Judah—some 400 years after David's kingship—was no more.

Exile in Babylonia

The Babylonian victory over Judah in 587 B.C. was total. At site after site in the hill country archaeologists have found uniform evidence of massive destruction and burning, not merely of military installations but also of commercial and residential quarters. Once-splendid Jerusalem (1, on inset) lay uninhabitable among its ashes, some of the people apparently finding shelter in nearby caves. Many places, such as Debir (2), were never occupied again. To the south in the Negeb and to the north at Bethel (3) and beyond, however, there was no disruption to life, for these areas had been annexed by Babylonia a decade earlier and thus escaped the storm of 588–87.

Thousands died in the vain defense of Judah; others succumbed to starvation or disease. Many Judahites hid in wilderness areas, while a few fled east into Ammon and Moab and even south to Edom seeking refuge. Some found asylum in Egypt (4, on large map), Babylonia's enemy. After their victory, the Babylonians executed a number of the leading political, military, and religious figures and subsequently deported to Babylonia (5) most of the remaining leaders along with their families. It is difficult to know how many were exiled. According to Jeremiah, the largest deportation took place when more than 3,000 families had been taken away along with King Jehoiachin—an event that occurred in 597. In 587 the number deported may have been just over 830 families, with another 745 families following them into exile in 582. The total would thus have been about 4,600 families, or perhaps some 18,000 people.

The deportation to Babylonia was but one phase in the eventual dispersal of the Jewish people, for many voluntarily fled the land. Taken together, the deaths, flights, and forced exiles reduced the population of Judah to almost half the approximately 250,000 people who lived there at the start of the century. Since the Babylonians failed to resettle other peoples in Judah—as the Assyrians had done in Samaria following their conquest of the kingdom of Israel in 721 B.C.—and since the ruined economy of the region contributed to a still further outpouring of people, the population of Judah within half a century stood at less than 20,000.

The Babylonians established a local government at Mizpah (6, on inset), Jerusalem no longer being suitable, and named Gedaliah, a member of one of the most distinguished families of Jerusalem, as governor. Gedaliah encouraged people not to fear the Babylonians but to return to the land, pay tribute to the foreign king, and "gather wine and summer fruits and oil, and store them in your vessels, and dwell in your cities that you have taken." From their hiding places in the hills and the wilderness as well as from Ammon, Moab, and Edom refugees drifted back. Good harvests aided Gedaliah's attempt to reestablish an orderly life in the land.

In 582, just as Gedaliah was experiencing some success in restoring the fortunes of Judah, he along with some of his Jewish associates and some Babylonian officials were murdered by Ishmael, leader of a band of nationalists in league with the Ammonite king. In the ensuing confusion many Judahite army officers and others who had returned to the land at Gedaliah's heeding fled to Egypt, lest they become targets of Babylonian vengeance. When the prophet Jeremiah advised against such a flight, they forcibly took him with them to Tahpanhes (7, on large map), on the frontier of Egypt. For a third time in 15 years many families fled just before the Babylonians ordered another deportation.

Little is known of Judah's history for the next half century, as the center of Jewish life shifted elsewhere. Doubtless some of the "remnant of Judah"—Jews as they were now called—stayed in Ammon, Moab, and Edom, and others were likely to be found in Samaria and Galilee. But the major centers of the early Jewish Diaspora—the spreading abroad of the people of Judah—were in Egypt and Babylonia.

The Jewish community in Egypt would grow in size and influence until it came to play an important commercial and, occasionally, political role under the Ptolemies, who ruled from the 4th to the 1st century B.C. In the period immediately after the fall of Judah, however, Jewish communities were found mostly in Lower Egypt, particularly in the eastern Delta where centuries earlier Jacob had settled with his sons to avoid a different kind of disaster. But some 500 miles from the Great Sea, at the first cataract of the Nile, on the island of Yeb (8), there was a military colony whose recovered documents show that its members held unusual religious beliefs for Jews—including worship of a female deity.

Babylonia became the most important and influential

In this 14th-century miniature from a Latin Bible, Jeremiah strikes a mournful pose outside Jerusalem as he laments the destruction of the city at the hands of the Babylonians and the deportation of its people.

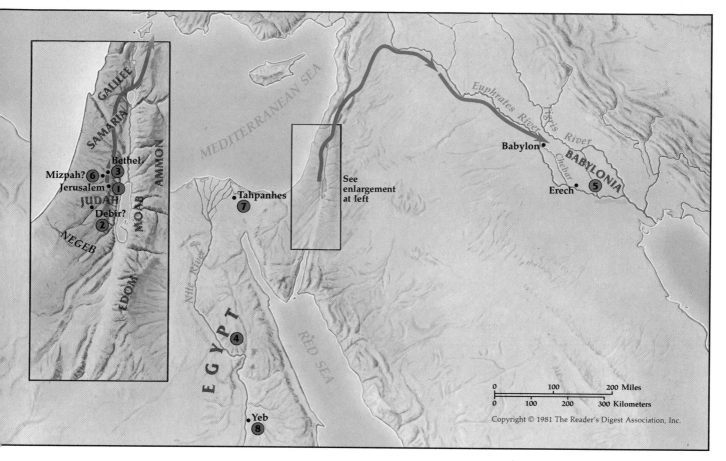

center of Jewish life and thought during the Exile, and we know more about it than about the early Diaspora communities in Egypt. After the fall of Samaria in 721, the Assyrians took many Israelites into exile and scattered them throughout much of their vast empire, where they vanished from history—the so-called 10 lost tribes. The Babylonian policy of settling the remnant of Judah in Babylonia itself, mostly in villages and towns along the Chebar River (actually an irrigation canal), ensured the survival of the Jewish people. The canal, the famous "waters of Babylon," ran through the heart of lower Mesopotamia from Babylon to Erech, a distance of more than 100 miles.

Not only were the exiled Jews allowed to live together in communities, they were also given the right to farm and engage in other useful work. The picture is one of a relatively benign exile in which many Jews eventually became wealthy. Tablets found near the Ishtar Gate in Babylon indicate that even in exile Jehoiachin was called king of Judah and that he received food supplies from the royal storehouse.

Writing from Jerusalem, Jeremiah urged the exiles in Babylonia to take full advantage of their situation: "Build houses and live in them; plant gardens and eat their produce. Take wives and have sons and daughters; take wives for your sons, and give your daughters in marriage, that they may bear sons and daughters; multiply there, and do not decrease." In Jeremiah's view—shared by most theologians and prophets of the time—the Exile was the punishment God had been threatening to visit

upon his wayward people; nonetheless, the exiles should maintain hope for the coming day of redemption. But bitterness and despair consumed some:

"By the waters of Babylon,
 there we sat down and wept,
 when we remembered Zion.
On the willows there we hung up our lyres.
For there our captors required of us songs,
 and our tormentors, mirth, saying
 'Sing us one of the songs of Zion!'
How shall we sing the Lord's song
 in a foreign land?"

The real threat to the Jewish community was the ease with which its members could be assimilated into Babylonian life; doubtless many broke with their traditional ways and disappeared into the society around them. To prevent this and to preserve their identity, the religious Jews of Babylon faithfully observed the Sabbath and circumcised their males—practices that set them apart from their new neighbors. It was also a period of intense literary activity, as old traditions were rethought, rewritten, and preserved.

The Jewish communities in Babylonia were made up of the religious and political elite, for these were precisely the people whom the Babylonians wished removed from Judah. And from these people came impulses to preserve old ideas while producing new institutions. It was eventually from Babylonia that Ezra came to Jerusalem, bringing back the Law—one of the most significant events in the history of the Jews.

145

Brief Glory of Babylon

Against the long span of Near Eastern history, the Babylonian renaissance of the 7th and 6th centuries B.C. can be described as meteoric: dramatic, brilliant, and brief. By the time Assyrian king Ashurbanipal died in 627, the population of Babylonia included large numbers of Chaldeans, nomads who had settled there over a period of centuries and who had long chafed under Assyrian rule. The turmoil following Ashurbanipal's death encouraged their ambitious leader Nabopolassar—Babylon's first Chaldean king—to declare his independence in 626. During the years of intermittent warfare that ensued, the Assyrians grew steadily weaker—particularly after the Babylonians joined the Medes in a coalition against them. In 612 these allies destroyed Assyria's famed capital, Nineveh—an event described with understandable glee by the prophet Nahum.

Such jubilation, however, proved to be shortsighted. Subsequent Babylonian victories over the retreating Assyrians and their newfound Egyptian allies left no one capable of halting the Babylonian advance to the shores of the Mediterranean. Within a remarkably short time Babylon possessed an empire nearly as large as that built up by Assyria over a span of centuries. Nabopolassar's son, Nebuchadnezzar, proved more than equal to the task of governing such a domain during his long reign (c. 605–562). He was as capable of brutality as any Assyrian conqueror—as evidenced by his destruction of Jerusalem in 587 and the merciless treatment of the captured king Zedekiah. But he also showed tolerance toward the Jews deported to Babylonia, allowing them a large measure of freedom and treating their former king, Jehoiachin, less as a prisoner than as guest of the court.

But the power and glory of Nebuchadnezzar's Babylonia was not destined long to outlive him. In the seven years following his death in 562 the throne was occupied by three successors before it was seized by Nabonidus. His erratic reign of some 17 years would provide the final chapter in the empire's short history, for Babylon no longer possessed the unity or the will to defend itself.

A major new threat appeared in the person of Cyrus, king of the Persians, whose campaign against his Median overlords had upset the entire structure of power in the Near East. Ironically, Nabonidus had at first welcomed and supported Cyrus as a useful source of trouble for the Medes, whom he considered the chief threat to his own security. What he could not have anticipated was the stunning speed and magnitude of Cyrus' success: by about 550 the Medes had been conquered; within a scant few years thereafter Cyrus' domain reached westward to include Asia Minor. It was inevitable that he should soon turn his gaze toward Babylonia; in 539 he did. Brushing aside a paltry resistance, the Persians reached the gates of the capital and entered unopposed. The Babylonian era was over; for the next two centuries the world of the Bible would belong to Persia.

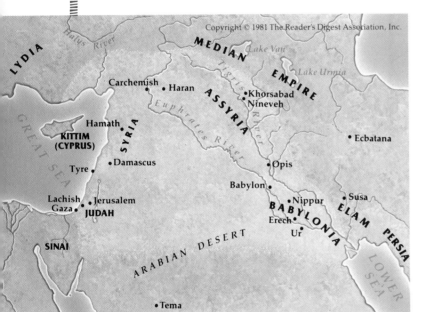

The new Babylonian empire was almost as large as Assyria's had been at its peak. After the collapse of Assyria, the Medes were occupied in extending their empire northwestward. This left Babylon free to rule as much of the Fertile Crescent as it could conquer. Nebuchadnezzar took full advantage of the opportunity, and by the early-6th century his domain reached from the Persian Gulf (Lower Sea) to the Mediterranean (Great Sea).

A crowning achievement of Nebuchadnezzar's reign was his transformation of the city of Babylon into a cultural, political, and economic hub of the empire. The reconstruction above shows the massive Ishtar Gate in the foreground, guarding the northern entrance to the city. The gate was decorated with enameled-brick reliefs of bulls and drag-ons, while the walls of the avenue approaching it depicted a procession of snarling lions, one of them shown at left. Just inside to the right are the fabled Hanging Gardens, cultivated on the terraces of the king's palace. Beyond them rises the seven-storied ziggurat, sometimes identified with the biblical Tower of Babel.

The Return

By the middle of the 6th century B.C. momentous events were occurring in the Near East. And in the course of these events the hopes of the survivors and descendants of Judah to return to Jerusalem were fulfilled.

The ancient civilizations of Egypt and Mesopotamia had run their magnificent course and were in rapid decline. The last king of Babylon, Nabonidus, introduced religious practices that cost him the allegiance of his subjects. Increasing conflict with the priests in Babylon was one reason why he moved his royal residence to Tema, an oasis far to the southwest in the Arabian desert. His son, Belshazzar—whose feast is the subject of Daniel 5—ruled as his deputy in Babylon. Moreover, Persian armies, which had taken over the Median empire and extended it to include all of Asia Minor, were now poised on the Babylonian frontier. In late summer of 539 the Persians struck and, in a decisive battle at Opis on the Tigris River, destroyed the Babylonian army. Within weeks Babylon itself fell without opposition. By command of Persian king Cyrus, the invading troops respected the city's inhabitants and their property. When Cyrus himself entered the conquered city 18 days later, multitudes lined his way and hailed him as deliverer from Nabonidus' oppressive and unpopular rule. To an anonymous Jewish prophet in exile, this was the hand of the Lord at work:

> "Who stirred up one [Cyrus] from the east
> whom victory meets at every step? . . .
> I, the Lord . . ."

This prophet saw Cyrus as the anointed one sent to redeem God's chosen people—and they were not disappointed. One of the most enlightened monarchs of antiquity, Cyrus abandoned the Assyrian and Babylonian policies of brutality and deportation of conquered peoples for a program of toleration and restoration. In 538 he issued an edict allowing Jews to return to Yehud (as the Persian province of Judah was called) and to rebuild the Temple of Jerusalem. As twice reported in the book of Ezra (Ezra 1:2–4 and 6:3–5), the edict directed that the Temple be rebuilt in part with funds from the royal treasury. Holy vessels taken from the Temple by Nebuchadnezzar were to be returned.

For the Jews in exile, redemption had come. In their unalloyed joy they spoke of the heavens singing, the depths of the earth shouting, and the mountains breaking forth in song because of what the Lord had done. The reality of the return, however, would be sobering.

The literary evidence for the return to Judah is unclear, since "the Chronicler" (the writer of 1 and 2 Chronicles, Ezra, and Nehemiah) probably confused the first and second returns and seems to have had little concern for chronology, passing over long periods of time—70 or even 120 years—without comment. But it appears that, as soon as they could, a small group of Jews—fired by religious zeal—set off from the Nippur region in Babylonia, bound for Jerusalem. They were probably led by Sheshbazzar, "prince of Judah," who was a son of Jehoiachin, the Judahite king exiled to Babylonia in 597. We do not know by which route they returned or how long it took them to make the journey. The shortest passage across the Syrian desert would have been about 600 miles. More likely they took the trade route through Aleppo, which would have made their journey nearly 1,000 miles long.

When the returning exiles finally arrived in the hills of Judah and beheld Jerusalem (1) from the surrounding heights, their joy must have mixed with bitter sorrow at the appalling sight. The city still lay in ruins, its walls demolished and its tumbledown buildings silent reminders of the ferocity of the Babylonian attack half a century earlier. The task of rebuilding was beyond the means of these faithful few.

There were other problems, too. While Sheshbazzar is called governor of Judah, it seems that the Samaritans claimed authority over Jerusalem and were unsympathetic to the resettlement of Judah. Moreover, the returned Jews refused to allow the Samaritans to help in the rebuilding because they considered them religiously unclean. (The Samaritans were descendants of the survivors of Israel who had intermarried with foreigners brought in by the Assyrians after the destruction of the northern kingdom two centuries earlier.) There was even opposition from the Jews of Judah who had not been in exile and understandably claimed the land they lived on. To make matters worse, a succession of crop failures left many destitute, although a few managed to profit from the difficulties of others. The harsh realities of day-to-day existence brought an end to the work on the Temple before much more than the foundation had been laid. Then we hear no more of Sheshbazzar, who, being in his sixties, may have soon died.

At some point, but no later than 522, a second group of Babylonian Jews came to Jerusalem and then settled "each to his own town." The lists of these towns in Ezra 2:2–35 and Nehemiah 7:6–38 indicate that the returning Jews established themselves in an area roughly 40 miles (east to west) by 30 miles (north to south) in the hill country of Judah. On the east they extended into the Jordan valley around Jericho (2), while to the west they penetrated the coastal plain, settling in Lod and Ono (3). To the north they reached beyond the old border of Judah to Bethel (4). In the south they held the strategic site of Beth-zur (5) but were cut off from Hebron, which was in the hands of the Edomites. Although their area was small, the Jews controlled vital approaches to the highlands. Yet they could not be secure until Jerusalem, the leading city and place of ultimate refuge, was refortified.

The second group of returning exiles was led by Zerubbabel, grandson of Jehoiachin and nephew of Sheshbazzar. He was the civil governor, while Joshua son of Jehozadak was the high priest and spiritual leader of the tiny community—probably no more than 20,000 people all told. About this time two other important persons appeared: the prophets Haggai and Zechariah. Nearly 20 years after the first return, only the foundation of the Temple had been completed. "Is it a time for you yourselves to dwell in your paneled houses," cried Haggai, "while this house [the Temple] lies in ruins?" The famines and poverty were punishment for their indolence in rebuilding the Lord's house, he said. Haggai also prophesied the overthrow of kingdoms and the elevation of Zerubbabel as the chosen one of the Lord of hosts. Such talk had a whiff of sedition about it, as did the night visions of Zechariah whereby he urged greater efforts to rebuild the Temple and Jerusalem, foretelling both renewed prosperity for the cities of Judah and the ultimate ingathering of all the scattered people to Zion. Under such fervent urgings, the altar was restored (although worship seems never to have ceased completely at the Temple site) and a religious celebration held as work on the Temple began once more.

The messianic zeal of Haggai and Zechariah may have been related to international events. When Darius I came to the throne of Persia in 522, there were nationalistic revolts at many places in the enormous empire that then stretched from Asia Minor and Egypt in the west to India's frontier in the east. But Darius moved quickly to control his vast domain, reorganizing the empire into 20 satrapies, each supervised by a representative of the king. The fifth satrapy included all the land between northern Syria and the border of Egypt as well as the island of Cyprus. It was called Abar-nahara, or "beyond the river" (that is, west of the Euphrates), and was governed from Damascus. Yehud was a subdivision of the satrapy.

As work on the Temple began in earnest, opposition surfaced once more. Before long the governor of Abar-nahara, Tattenai, came to Jerusalem to learn by what authority the Jews were rebuilding their Temple. He allowed work to continue while inquiry was made to the Persian court. In the royal archives a scroll was found containing Cyrus' decree—which Darius reconfirmed. Tattenai was ordered not to interfere with the rebuilding of "this house of God on its site." Moreover, he was told to underwrite the project from royal revenues.

With this aid and under the stern urging of the prophets, Zerubbabel led the effort to complete the Temple. Poor though it was, the finished Temple was rededicated in 515 amid great joy—72 years after its destruction by the Babylonians. Unlike the Temple of Solomon, this shrine was not the focus of a nation. Prayers were offered for the Persian king and his sons—a daily reminder that, while the restored community had weathered its

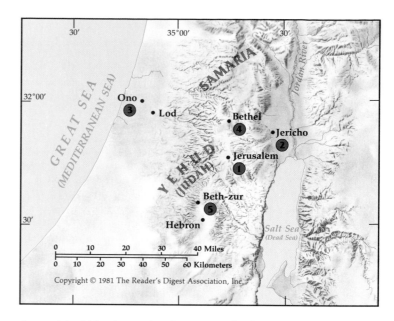

Copyright © 1981 The Reader's Digest Association, Inc.

first crisis, Yehud was firmly a part of a huge empire.

When Zerubbabel left the scene, hope of reestablishing the royal line of Judah came to an end. For the next 70 years or so—until the coming of Nehemiah—we know very little of the life of this little community. The prophet Malachi urged the people to be loyal to the covenant and condemned the priests for corrupting worship. Yet the religious life of the Jews steadily deteriorated as mixed marriages and increasing commercial contacts with non-Jews threatened to produce assimilation. The people of the community, isolated and defenseless on the hilltops around Jerusalem, endured a relatively poor and perilous existence under the leadership of high priests, who also assumed a measure of local political power. If the community survived, it was not by much. Its extravagant hopes had been dampened by harsh reality. Once the Temple was rebuilt, there seemed little to motivate the people to further unified action.

In time news of the sorry plight of the Jews of Yehud reached the ears of Nehemiah in Susa, where he was a high official—cupbearer to the king of Persia. A pious Jew, he asked permission to journey to Yehud and rebuild the fortifications of Jerusalem. Not only was Nehemiah granted his wish, he was named governor of the faraway province.

Reconstruction and Reform

In the century following their return, the Jews witnessed dramatic changes taking place all around them. Among other things, the area was opening up to greatly expanded international trade, particularly with Greece. Phoenicians held sway down the coast from Acco (1, map on page 151) to Gaza (2), but most of the ports also became homes for colonies of Greek merchants. Dor (3) is a good example of this growing cosmopolitan mixture. A part of the Persian empire's fifth satrapy, Dor was ruled by Phoenicians, but in the mid-5th century B.C. its large

community of Greek merchants apparently qualified it for membership in the Attic sea alliance. Many Attic pottery vessels have been found at Dor, indicating a close commercial connection with Greece. Such pottery has also been found at Acco, Gaza, and Ashdod (4). Gaza became a royal Persian fortress—as did Acco, Hazor (5), and Lachish (6)—and served Cyrus' son and successor, Cambyses, when he invaded and conquered Egypt in 525.

Gaza was developing another role, one that would expand for several centuries, bringing prosperity to this

Reconstruction (continued)

ancient port. To the east, in what had been Edom, people from northwest Arabia were establishing themselves. Later known as Nabateans, they would become one of the great commercial peoples of antiquity, with Gaza as their main western port. The Babylonian invasions of the 6th century had destroyed effective government in Edom and Moab and allowed these desert nomads to infiltrate and eventually rule an area from southern Syria to Edom as well as much of the Negeb and even western Sinai. From Petra (7) the Nabateans eventually controlled the King's Highway as well as the east-west caravan routes from Arabia through Ezion-geber (8) to Gaza and Egypt. The heyday of these people would come later, but already they were driving the Edomites (later known as Idumeans) into the Negeb and what had been southern Judah. Settling in the desert south of Beer-sheba (9), the Edomites established themselves in the relatively lush tableland and hills around Hebron (10), which became one of their chief cities.

In the Transjordan the Tobiads had control of much of the area northeast of the Salt Sea, previously contested by Israel and Moab, and ruled the Persian province of Ammon. Beyond Jerusalem (11), in what had once been the heartland of the northern kingdom of Israel, the Samaritans ruled a province of the fifth satrapy—and claimed authority over Yehud. The Tobiads and Samaritans, moreover, saw themselves as the true preservers of the ancient faith of Israel, and they had many close contacts with Jews in and around Jerusalem. Thus when Nehemiah first came to Jerusalem as governor of Persian Yehud, probably about 445 B.C., he found the small Jewish community there surrounded by peoples competing for a place in the developing new era—and he also found the people demoralized and divided.

Scholars disagree on the chronology of Ezra and Nehemiah. Although the biblical text indicates that Ezra came before Nehemiah, there is general scholarly recognition that the texts of Ezra and Nehemiah have suffered a severe dislocation, making it impossible to know the exact sequence of events. Most likely Nehemiah came first and Ezra appeared briefly toward the end of Nehemiah's second term as governor of Yehud. Together these two pivotal figures restructured—and preserved—the Jewish community.

A high Persian official, Nehemiah arrived in Jerusalem with a military escort as well as with a group of other Babylonian Jews. He immediately recognized the pressing need to make Jerusalem secure and, on his third night in the city, secretly walked around the walls to determine for himself exactly what rebuilding had to be done. Work on the walls, he decided, would begin at once. Summoning the inhabitants, he said: "You see the trouble we are in, how Jerusalem lies in ruins with its gates burned. Come, let us build the wall of Jerusalem, that we may no longer suffer disgrace." To procure a labor force and also to repopulate the stricken city, Nehemiah instituted a levy on the four administrative districts of the province which the Persians had taken over from the Babylonians. Many people volunteered to move to Jerusalem and help with the rebuilding of the city.

The wall was divided into sections, with groups from different villages and outlying areas responsible for given stretches. Within the remarkable time of only 52 days the wall was secure. The battlements, revetments, and gates required another 28 months before they were finished. Archaeologists have found parts of Nehemiah's wall, indicating workmanship of great haste and enclosing an area substantially reduced from the Jerusalem of the monarchical period.

Even though Nehemiah had authority from the Persian king to rebuild Jerusalem's fortifications, he faced a concerted opposition. Tobiah, governor of Ammon, had family connections with the High Priest in Jerusalem, and Sanballat, governor of Samaria, became allied by marriage to the family of Jerusalem's High Priest. Geshem the Arab ruled the emerging desert peoples from northwestern Arabia to western Sinai, including the Negeb, part of southern Yehud, and Edom. These three powerful rulers, along with the people of Ashdod, tried various means to undermine Nehemiah and bring his work in Jerusalem to a halt. The refortification of Jerusalem was a particular threat to Sanballat's claims over Yehud; a strong Jerusalem would be a safe base for a political rival. For his part, Tobiah ridiculed Nehemiah and his compatriots, saying, "Yes, what they are building—if a fox goes up on it he will break down their stone wall!" Together these two men sought to use relatives and friends within the city to strike fear in Nehemiah, while other attempts were made to undermine the morale of the workers. A determined Nehemiah dismissed these efforts easily. But when the Arabs, Ammonites, and Ashdodites began to terrorize outlying Jewish villages and even raid around Jerusalem, Nehemiah had to act. With characteristic decisiveness he brought Jewish villagers into Jerusalem, where he divided his crews into shifts. Some—armed with "spears, shields, bows, and coats of mail"—stood guard while others worked. And each of the workers labored with a sword girded to his side. By such tactics and under heavy pressure from his enemies, Nehemiah and his people rebuilt the walls of Jerusalem to provide the first requirement for stabilizing the life of the community: physical safety.

Twelve years after he came to Jerusalem, and perhaps unable to get his term extended, Nehemiah returned to Susa. He had provided safety and brought about certain economic reforms to prevent the rich from preying on the poor, but he hardly considered his work finished. Within a year or so he had persuaded the king to reappoint him governor of Yehud. Upon returning, he undertook vigorous if somewhat uncoordinated religious reforms: providing adequate funds for the Temple and its officials by strict collection of tithes; enforcing Sabbath observance by stopping business activity on that day; opposing marriages with foreigners to the extent of physically assaulting the offenders.

Although Nehemiah brought security and a degree of political and economic stability to the community, his sporadic religious reforms did not affect the inner life of the people. It remained for a priest named Ezra to provide the spiritual restructuring that Nehemiah's attempts lacked. Also a Jew from Babylonia, Ezra secured royal authority over Jewish religious affairs in the satrapy of Abar-nahara. In April—probably 428—he set out for Jerusalem carrying contributions from Babylonian Jews for the Temple, silver and gold from the king, and the Law. Traveling by the fastest route across the desert and without military escort, Ezra arrived in Jerusalem in four months, in August. Two months later, on the eve of the Feast of Tabernacles, he and his associates read the Law from a wooden platform in one of Jerusalem's public squares. Aramaic was widely spoken in the Persian empire, and the Phoenicians, Nabateans, Tobiads, and Samaritans all spoke various dialects of Aramaic, as did the Jews of Yehud. Aramaic translations of the Hebrew text of the Law, as well as explanations, were given section by section from dawn to midday. The next day the feast was celebrated with solemnity and joy.

Abuses nonetheless continued, and in December Ezra, "weeping and casting himself down before the house of God," made public confession of the sins of the people, prominent among which was mixed marriages. Acknowledging that they had broken faith with the Lord, a spokesman for the people proposed a covenant whereby Jews would put away their foreign wives and children born of such liaisons. A proclamation summoned Jews throughout the land to gather three days later in Jerusalem—under threat of property forfeiture and banishment. Once more Ezra came before the people to accuse them. Standing in a heavy rain in a square by the Temple, the crowd answered as one: "It is so; we must do as you have said." Ezra selected a panel of elders to investigate marriages, and when it reported three months later, all mixed marriages were dissolved.

Within a year of his coming to Jerusalem, Ezra's work was finished. The Law that he read to the people and by which they reconstituted themselves was either the Torah or the core of what became the Torah, the five books of the Law of Moses—Genesis, Exodus, Leviticus, Numbers, and Deuteronomy. Little wonder that the rabbis honored this priest who appeared on the stage for a brief, crucial moment, saying that Ezra restored the Law.

Nehemiah is reported to have been the first to place his seal on the covenant of Ezra. Then both men pass from view. According to one tradition, Ezra died and was buried in Jerusalem. But in southern Iraq a grave said to be that of Ezra is still shown. Did he return to Babylonia? And what happened to Nehemiah? Perhaps he went back to Susa at the end of his second term as governor. In any event, the work of these two men was completed; the community in Yehud was safe for the moment, and Judaism had the Law, the great monument by which it has maintained itself throughout the ages.

With the reforms of Ezra and Nehemiah in the second half of the 5th century B.C., the historical narrative of the Old Testament ends. We know almost nothing of Jewish history until shortly before the outbreak of the Maccabean revolt in the 2nd century B.C. Indeed, as one historian has written, "no period in Israel's history since Moses is more poorly documented." However, with the rise and fall of new empires—especially those of Greece and Rome—the land bridge between Asia and Africa continued to be the battleground of the mighty.

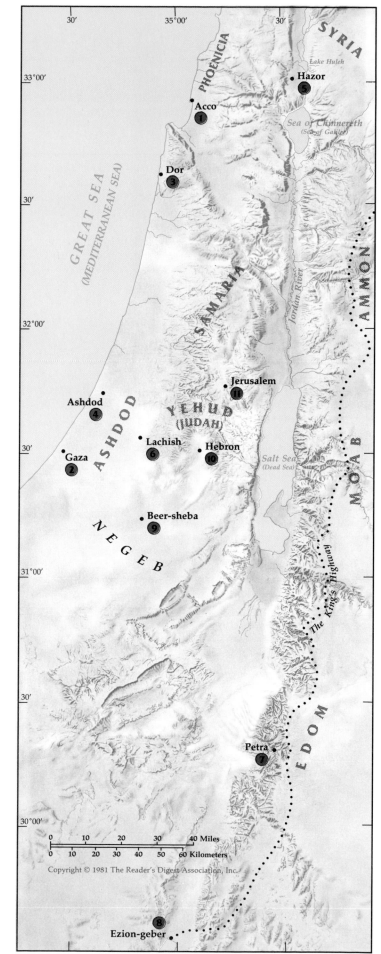

Copyright © 1981 The Reader's Digest Association, Inc.

Alexander the Great

"He advanced to the ends of the earth, and plundered many nations. When the earth became quiet for him, he was exalted, and his heart was lifted up. He gathered a very strong army and ruled over countries, nations, and princes, and they became tributary to him." In these words 1 Maccabees sums up the brief, dramatic career of Alexander the Great. One of the most famous conquerors of history, Alexander skirted the mountain fastness of Judah en route to Egypt but nonetheless changed forever the course of Jewish history.

Alexander's spectacular rise to power began in 336 B.C. at age 20 when he succeeded to the Macedonian throne upon the assassination of his father, Philip II. He promptly revealed his military skill as he brought the restive Greek states under Macedonian control. In 334 he led his army across the Hellespont (1, on lower map), determined to drive the Persians out of Asia Minor. At Issus (2) he won a surprising victory against the Persian host of Darius III although his men were outnumbered three to one. He now stood in triumph astride the crossroads of empire. "For the future," he told the vanquished Darius, "whenever you send to me, send to me as the king of Asia . . ." Before continuing his Asian campaign, however, he needed to secure his southern flank—and so put his army on the road to Egypt.

To break Persian naval control of the eastern Mediterranean, he plotted the capture of the enemy's main fleet base at Tyre (3, on upper map). Fortress Tyre was in fact two cities, one on the mainland and the other on an island half a mile offshore. While Alexander's military fame rests primarily on his innovative use of powerful infantry phalanxes and swift cavalry, Tyre called forth his considerable talents as a military engineer.

Lacking the naval strength for an amphibious assault on the island stronghold, Alexander conceived the imaginative notion of constructing a great mole, or causeway, to carry his besieging army across the 2,500-foot intervening sea barrier (see inset). His first operation was to capture mainland Tyre and raze the city in order to obtain rubble for the mole. Timber was brought from the forests of Lebanon and quarries established to supply additional stone. As the advancing 200-foot-wide causeway came within range of the fortress, the defenders opened fire with catapults, raining missiles, molten lead, and red-hot sand on the Macedonians. Undaunted by this fierce resistance, Alexander pressed on.

At last the causeway was completed. The Macedonians smashed at the stout walls with their great siege catapults and battering rams, to little effect. The siege

In 333 B.C. Alexander and his army defeated King Darius III of Persia at the pivotal battle of Issus; the 23-year-old commander is shown in this mosaic fragment found at Pompeii.

was now in its seventh month. Alexander had been gathering a fleet of his own, and he planned a massive combined assault. While his phalanxes and siege artillery attacked from the causeway, amphibious forces probed for an opening from the flanks. In severe fighting, a breach was finally made in the walls. Utilizing bridging ramps in the manner of modern-day landing craft, reinforcements poured ashore to exploit the breakthrough. Bitter battles filled the streets of Tyre, but the Macedonians soon gained the upper hand. An estimated 8,000 of the defenders were slain, and Alexander had 2,000 captives put to death. The city's remaining population was sold into slavery. Most of the fortress was leveled, ending Tyre's usefulness as a Persian fleet base.

Alexander now advanced southward along the coast, overrunning Acco (4) and swinging inland at Strato's Tower (5). Using cavalry to put down any opposition in the central highlands, the Macedonians returned to the coastal route, taking Azotus (6) and Ashkelon (7). At Gaza (8), the historic gateway to Egypt, the triumphant procession was brought up short. Batis, the Persian commander of the garrison, sought to block Alexander's advance until reinforcements arrived from Egypt or from Darius to the east.

Like Tyre, Gaza was a formidable military obstacle. The high-walled fortress was located atop a steep rise, making it invulnerable to the usual siege tactic of advancing towers up to the walls from which to fire down upon the defenders within. Alexander hit upon the idea of creating his own high ground from which to attack. His indefatigable troops were put to work building an immense ramp to carry the siege machinery up to a height level with the fortress. Battering rams and catapults were soon pounding the walls, which were further weakened by diggers undercutting the foundations. At last a breach was made, and the Macedonian infantry, using scaling ladders to clamber over the rubble, broke into the city. To a man, Batis and his troops fell in savage street fighting, and the city was sacked.

It was after Gaza's fall, according to tradition, that Alexander journeyed to Jerusalem to meet with the High Priest. Whether this is legend or fact is uncertain, but in any event Jerusalem was effectively under Alexander's control. Late in 332 he took his all-conquering army into Egypt. The Persians gave up this remote outpost of their empire without a fight, and at Siwa (9, on lower map) Alexander proclaimed himself Pharaoh by divine right. He had already personally laid out the site of Alexandria, destined to become one of the great centers of Greek, or Hellenistic, culture and indeed one of the great cities of the ancient world. He would eventually found a dozen or more cities bearing that name, as he pursued his goal of putting the stamp of Greek culture on the diverse people he was conquering.

The seizure of Tyre and Gaza and the occupation of Egypt gave Alexander the assurance that his southern flank was secure. He now resumed his march of conquest eastward, where Darius was reassembling his Persian host in the Tigris River valley. In the spring of 331, the Macedonian army retraced its route along the eastern Mediterranean coastline. During the conqueror's absence in Egypt, the Samaritans had revolted against their governor; in revenge, Alexander ordered the destruction of Samaria (10, on upper map). At this time, too, a Macedonian expeditionary force may have penetrated as far as Jericho. Arriving at Tyre (11), Alexander turned his army northeastward through Syria, marching toward "the ends of the earth."

Alexander's unprecedented 14,000-mile route of conquest took him as far as India. At Gaugamela (12, on lower map), he routed Darius and his hordes, shattering the Persian empire, and Persian power, forever. To reinforce that victory, he went on to take Darius' capitals at Babylon (13), Susa (14), and Persepolis (15), where he captured intact the immense Persian treasury and burned Darius' great palace. Now fully possessed by his dream of conquest, Alexander resumed his eastern campaign. In 326, in a battle on the banks of the Hydaspes (16), he defeated perhaps the most skillful foe he ever faced, the Indian king Porus. At last, pressured by his war-weary army, Alexander the Great ended his odyssey and turned back, having laid claim to most of Asia (the extent of Alexander's empire is shown in yellow). But he would never reach his homeland; at Babylon, in 323, he took a fever and died. He was only 32 years old. With him died his soaring ambition of world conquest.

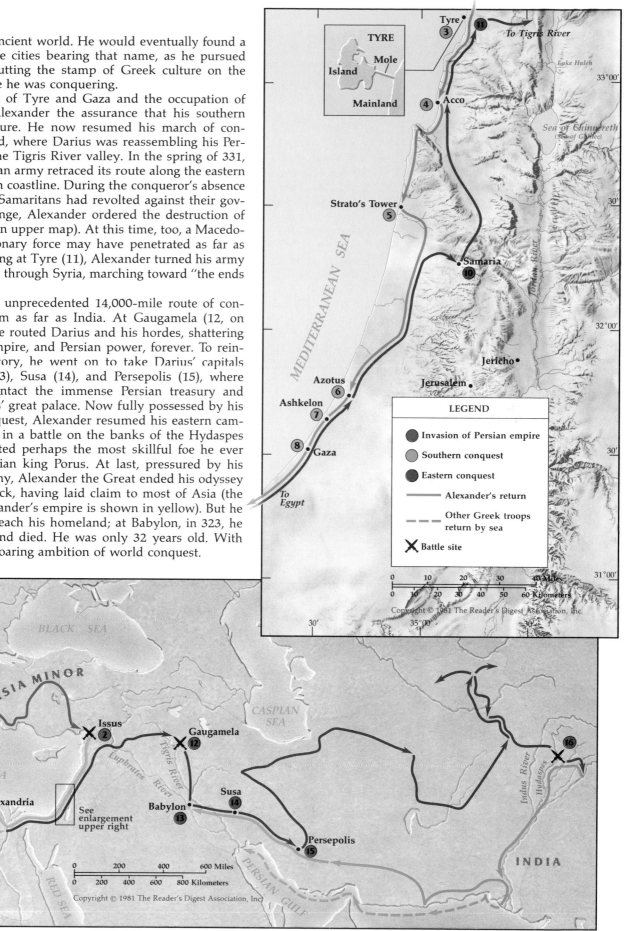

LEGEND
● Invasion of Persian empire
● Southern conquest
● Eastern conquest
— Alexander's return
--- Other Greek troops return by sea
✕ Battle site

Copyright © 1981 The Reader's Digest Association, Inc.

Ptolemies Versus Seleucids

Following the death of Alexander the Great, his Macedonian generals scrambled among themselves to carve up his vast empire. According to 1 Maccabees, "They all put on crowns after his death, and so did their sons after them for many years." Between 320 and 301 B.C., southern Syria and the lands down to the border of Egypt changed hands five times as rival rulers contended for strategic harbors that would give them domination of the eastern Mediterranean. First to seize the area was Ptolemy I, who had established himself in Egypt. Before long he was challenged by his former comrade-in-arms Antigonus "the One-Eyed," who pushed southward from Asia Minor along the coast toward Egypt, conquering Tyre (1), Joppa (2), and Gaza (3). In 312, while Antigonus was occupied in Asia Minor, Ptolemy defeated Antigonus' son, Demetrius, at Gaza, forcing him back through Syria to his base in Asia Minor. Antigonus countered by leading a large army into the disputed area and driving out Ptolemy's forces. As Ptolemy and his men retreated southward they destroyed Joppa and Gaza as well as the fortified cities of Acco (4, later called Ptolemais) and Samaria (5), lest the enemy use them as forward bases.

In 311 Antigonus sent Demetrius to attack the Nabateans in the south at Petra (6), seeking to gain control of the lucrative Arabian spice trade and the developing resources of the southern Salt Sea (now called Lake Asphaltitis). But these Arabs—masters of the desert and secure in their fortress of rose-red rock—repulsed the Macedonians with heavy losses.

Meanwhile, the struggle between Ptolemy and Antigonus waxed and waned. Finally, Ptolemy made common cause with other former comrades-in-arms from Alexander's army, including Seleucus, who was seeking to establish a western base in Syria. Even without Ptolemy's battlefield assistance, this coalition crushed Antigonus at Ipsus in Asia Minor in 301. In the division of spoils following the battle, Seleucus received the province of Syria, which included Judea (as the Greeks called Judah). He soon discovered, however, that Ptolemy had already appropriated his new province. Two decades of defending Egypt's gates against invasion from the east had convinced Ptolemy of the strategic importance of the land bridge between Africa and Asia. Unwilling to fight his friend and ally, Seleucus did not press his claim to the buffer zone. Thus Judea passed under Ptolemaic Egyptian rule.

Ptolemaic "Syria and Phoenicia" (as the area was then called) enjoyed almost a century of prosperity despite conflicts between the successors of Ptolemy and Seleucus. The conservative administration that ruled the land from Alexandria turned it into a defensive zone, organized along Hellenistic lines. Military garrisons were posted at strategic sites and crossroads, and military colonies were established along the frontiers.

Times were changing—with new Greek names given to ancient cities: for example, Ptolemais (Acco), Scythopolis (Beth-shan), Philadelphia (Rabbah). The coastal plain, which was of particular interest to the Ptolemies, was reorganized into small administrative units. Military galleys protected the sea lanes over which trade passed with growing tempo. The fortress at Samaria continued as administrative center for the central highlands, just as Jerusalem remained the focus of the province of Judea. There the High Priest held a measure of civil authority under Ptolemaic officials, probably paying an annual tribute for the privilege. Yet there was no concentrated attempt on the part of the Egyptian rulers to alter the patterns of life or to influence the religious practices of the Jews in Judea. So long as the taxes (which were high) were paid and the status quo maintained, the Ptolemies were satisfied. In 219, however, that status quo was shattered.

The successors to Seleucus had not been as passive as he in accepting Ptolemaic control of Syria and Phoenicia. Beginning in 276 they had waged three fierce but inconclusive wars with the Macedonian rulers of Egypt over the disputed territory. In a fourth war (219-17), however, Antiochus III ["the Great"] forced his way down the coast, capturing Tyre (7) and Ptolemais (8) and besieging Dora (9). Driving eastward beyond the Sea of Galilee, he seized additional cities while some simply opened their gates to him. Allied with the Nabateans, he took Philadelphia (10) and sent his cavalry back across the Jordan. Making his headquarters at Ptolemais, he spent the winter solidifying his gains and recouping his forces, readying himself for the test sure to come against the main Egyptian army.

In the spring of 217, Antiochus III advanced along the Way of the Sea through Gaza (11) to Raphia (12). Ptolemy IV and his massive army—replete with war elephants—approached across the sands from Egypt. In the ensuing clash the Egyptians prevailed, driving Antiochus back to Syria. Ptolemy IV marched through the country in victorious procession as far as the northern borders of his realm, a royal tour intended to demonstrate that Judea and Phoenicia were once again securely in the hands of the Ptolemies.

Preoccupied with affairs elsewhere in his vast domain, Antiochus III did not renew his quarrel with the Ptolemies until about 203. Once more he pushed down the coast. City after city surrendered to him, and only at Gaza (13) did he finally meet determined resistance. At length Gaza fell to his siege, but the delay won time for the Ptolemies to gather their host for a counterattack. With Scopas (a Greek and one of the most highly regarded generals of the time) in command, the Ptolemies pushed the Seleucids back in fierce fighting. After securing Jerusalem (14), Scopas advanced northward in the rain and cold of winter along the central mountain route, reestablishing Ptolemaic authority over the area. Antiochus retreated to the pleasant, rugged, well-watered hills at Paneas (15) below Mount Hermon and in 198 prepared for a showdown battle. Scopas attacked in strength, only to be sent reeling back in defeat. He and the remnants of his command fled to Sidon (16) on the coast, where they were besieged and starved into surren-

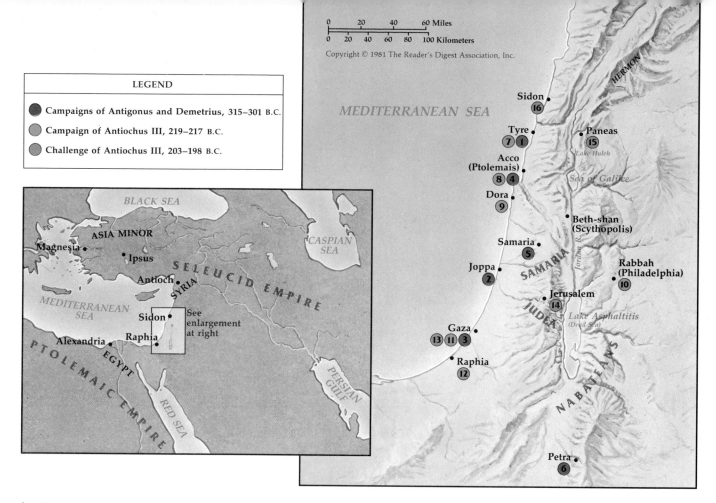

LEGEND

● Campaigns of Antigonus and Demetrius, 315–301 B.C.

● Campaign of Antiochus III, 219–217 B.C.

● Challenge of Antiochus III, 203–198 B.C.

der. In a triumphal tour of his own, Antiochus reversed much of Scopas' line of march. The Seleucids renamed the conquered province "Coele-Syria and Phoenicia." *Coele* means "hollow," a reference to the great valley of southern Syria, which lies between Mount Hermon and the coastal range.

We have little detailed information about the effects of this heavy fighting on the land and its people. We do know that villages as well as cities suffered and that the economy was disrupted. Jerusalem and the Temple were damaged, for the Egyptians defended the citadel and there was rioting in the streets between Ptolemaic and Seleucid followers. Some of the Jewish Tobiad faction remained loyal to the Ptolemies, and the last of the Tobiad line, Hyrcanus, would later commit suicide during the reign of Antiochus IV.

Despite the century of relative prosperity under Ptolemaic rule, pro-Seleucid sentiment had remained strong among the Jews of Jerusalem. In 198 Antiochus III issued a decree providing that materials for rebuilding the Temple could be brought into Judea without the usual customs duties. Taxes imposed by the Ptolemies on the High Priest and various city officials were suspended, and taxes on other citizens were canceled for three years. Other benefits granted the Jews included the right "to have a form of government in accordance with the laws of their country." To the Seleucids this was simply a formality granted to peoples within their empire to encourage loyalty by promoting local customs. To the Jews it meant far more, including a reconfirmation of the High Priest as head of the community with certain—but ill-defined—political powers. It was in fact the High

Priest who carried out the rebuilding of Jerusalem and the Temple.

For three decades the Jews prospered under Seleucid rule; at the same time the seeds of serious discord were sown. While the position of the High Priest was strengthened, there were differing understandings of what this meant in political terms. Further conflict would arise over the rulers' active encouragement of Hellenization, for the Seleucids saw themselves as the heirs of Alexander the Great, entrusted with his vision of uniting all peoples within the framework of Greek culture. These policies would produce an explosive conflict between the Jews and the Seleucids in the next generation.

In 192, six years after his successes in Coele-Syria, Antiochus III crossed into Greece after subduing large areas of Asia Minor. In a fundamental strategic mistake, he allied himself with Hannibal of Carthage, the enemy of the rising power of Rome and its fearsome legions. Having secured the western Mediterranean after the Second Punic War with Carthage, Rome was free to look eastward. After the Roman Senate declared war on Antiochus, Publius Scipio Africanus, the celebrated victor over Hannibal, crushed the Seleucid army at the battle of Magnesia in Asia Minor in 190. Imposing extraordinarily harsh terms, the Romans forced Antiochus to disarm much of his remaining force, abandon his territories in Asia Minor, and pay a staggering tribute. The vast Seleucid empire was already showing signs of internal stress and dissolution, and Magnesia accelerated the process. But before this splendid empire finally collapsed, there was an attempt to seize Egypt—and a subsequent war with the Jews of Judea.

Maccabees: Flag of Revolt

The 30 years' peace following the battle of Paneas was shattered in 167 B.C. by an outbreak of violent religious persecution in Jerusalem (1). The new Seleucid ruler, Antiochus IV—pursuing his father's ambitions in Egypt but checkmated by the Romans—turned in wrath upon his restless vassal Judea. Having previously looted the Temple, Antiochus now proscribed Judaism, perhaps misled by the local Hellenized Jews into thinking that the people would accept his edict. Such Jewish practices as circumcising males, observing the Sabbath, and adhering to dietary laws were forbidden. A cult of the Olympian Zeus replaced worship of the God of Israel in the Temple—the famous "abomination of desolation" of the book of Daniel. Every settlement in the land was ordered to worship Zeus and other foreign deities. A new fortress, called the Akra, was erected in Jerusalem, to serve as the Seleucid stronghold amid the storms of Jewish rebellion for the next quarter century.

Jews refusing to abandon their traditional faith were killed or enslaved. Many fled into the hills or the wilderness. Those who remained were subjected to bloody persecution. Less than 20 miles from Jerusalem, at Modein (2), however, a Jewish priest named Mattathias Hasmoneas created an incident that triggered revolt. When a king's agent arrived to confirm that the village was offering the proper homage to foreign gods, Mattathias not only killed a fellow Jew attempting a pagan sacrifice at the altar but slew the royal officer as well. With his five sons (John, Simon, Judas, Eleazar, and Jonathan), Mattathias fled into the Gophna Hills (3), an area of heavily forested ridges and valleys.

Jews throughout the land rallied to Mattathias, especially the Hasidim, the "Pious Ones," who dedicated themselves to the Law. They had been steadily losing power to the Hellenizers, those who were encouraging Greek culture among the people of Judea. Village after village rose against the Syrian Greeks. Mattathias designated Simon, "wise in counsel," to head the rebellion, but the old man astutely chose his third son, Judas, to be military commander, for he "has been a mighty warrior from his youth." Already Judas was called Maccabeus ("the hammer"), a name that would be applied to the mounting rebellion. When Mattathias died in 166, the revolt had not yet produced major fighting, but virtually the whole of Judea except the large towns and walled cities was under rebel control.

Judas skillfully prepared his followers for guerrilla warfare. They knew the land, its hills and valleys, its forests and rocky enclaves, and they drew their support from the local populace. By day they blended with the villagers or hid in the hills and forests. By night they struck pro-Syrian settlements and ambushed enemy patrols. Judas' fame spread; ever more of the people rallied to his banner, and as in the case of David of old, songs were sung in his praise:

> "He was like a lion in his deeds,
> like a lion's cub roaring for prey."

Judas' guerrilla bands harassed traffic along the roads, threatening to sever the two main arteries to Jerusalem, the Way of Beth-horon (4) from the coast, and the central ridge route (5) from Samaria. As this menace grew, the Hellenized Jews in Jerusalem appealed to Apollonius, the Seleucid governor of Samaria with authority over Judea. Apollonius gathered what was essentially a civilian militia force—probably Macedonian settlers—and advanced along the ridge route toward Jerusalem. Near Lebonah (6), Judas sprang an ambush and routed the loyalist force. Apollonius was slain and Judas took his sword "and used it in battle the rest of his life." His guerrillas captured many weapons in this action, greatly increasing their strength.

Four times more the Syrians sought to restore communications with Jerusalem. An army of regular soldiers under Seron, military commander of Coele-Syria, followed a road through the coastal plain, turning inland toward Jerusalem. At Upper Beth-horon (7), Judas again achieved surprise, sending his irregulars rushing headlong down a hillside into the heavily armed enemy column as it toiled up the slopes. The Syrians fled in disorder, leaving behind the bodies of Seron and 800 of his men.

In the spring of 165 Antiochus IV tried once more, ordering his chief minister, Lysias, to dispatch a large army into Judea "to wipe out and destroy the strength of Israel and . . . to banish the memory of them from the place . . ." Under Nicanor and Gorgias, this force advanced cautiously from the north and established a base camp at Emmaus (8). Learning that Judas was at Mizpah (9), Nicanor planned to take a leaf from the enemy's book and launch a surprise attack of his own. He directed Gorgias to advance with 6,000 men against the Jewish camp by night. Thanks to his superb military intelligence—a product of his grass-roots support—Judas was quickly informed of this move and executed a flanking maneuver that brought him south of Emmaus. At Mizpah, Gorgias found what appeared to be a hastily abandoned camp and scoured the hills for fugitives. Finding none, he marched back to his base. But upon reaching the brow of a hill overlooking Emmaus, Gorgias saw a pillar of smoke rising from the direction of the camp. In his absence, Judas had fallen on Nicanor's force, mauled it, and sent it fleeing in several directions. Seeing the triumphant Jewish army arrayed in battle formation, Gorgias' Seleucids became greatly frightened and they too fled the field.

Smarting from this third successive defeat, Lysias now took personal command of a fourth attempt to open the routes to Jerusalem. He elected to follow a course that looped toward Jerusalem from the south, through friendly territory. At Beth-zur (10), however, some 16 miles from Jerusalem, Judas again exercised his talent for choosing the terrain in which to offer battle. The area's hills and narrow ravines handicapped the Syrian formations, and Judas' slashing attacks were fearfully effective. Lysias was routed, with the loss of 5,000 men.

"Behold, our enemies are crushed," said Judas; "let us

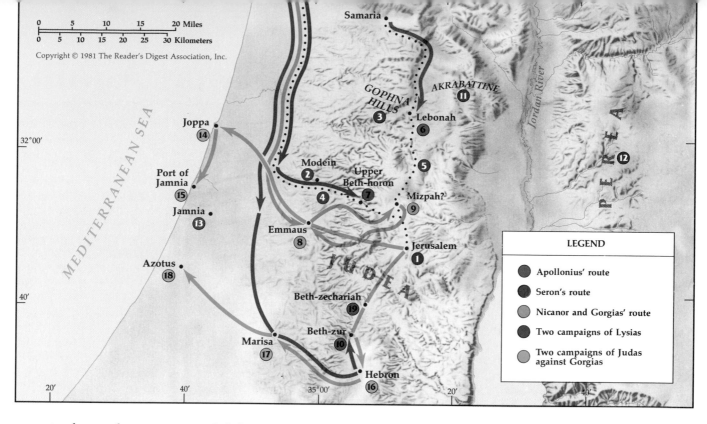

go up to cleanse the sanctuary and dedicate it." In Jerusalem his army took the Temple Mount, and "Judas detailed men to fight against those in the citadel [Akra] until he had cleansed the sanctuary." In December of 164 the Holy House was rededicated and the lamps of the eternal light were lit once more to the glory of the God of Israel. This moment has ever since been celebrated by Jews as the festival of Hanukkah.

For the next two years the Seleucids were occupied by events far removed from Judea. Antiochus IV had died, and Lysias held effective power as regent for the nine-year-old king, Antiochus V. Simon and Judas used this breathing space to strengthen their position, lifting pressure on Jewish settlements in the Akrabattine (11), striking across the Jordan at enemies of the Jews who inhabited Perea (12), and rescuing stranded Jewish communities in Gilead to the northeast and in Galilee to the north.

In the south, however, Joseph and Azariah, two of Judas' commanders, were less successful. Contrary to orders, they invaded the coastal plain near Jamnia (13), where Gorgias was governor. They proved no match for the Syrian general and lost some 2,000 men, nearly one-tenth of all the available trained forces. Judas moved swiftly to prevent further disaster. First he burned Joppa (14) and the port of Jamnia (15). In his second campaign he destroyed Hebron (16), routed Gorgias at Marisa (17), and advanced to the walls of Azotus (18), collecting enormous booty before withdrawing.

In 163—with Judas besieging the Akra in Jerusalem—Lysias appeared with the strongest force yet assembled in the continuing effort to put down the rebellion. According to 1 Maccabees, it included 100,000 infantry, 20,000 cavalry, and 32 war elephants—which the Jewish army had not faced in battle before. Lysias retraced his southern approach toward Jerusalem. Profiting from his previous mistakes, he was determined not to let Judas seize the initiative and fight on ground of his own choosing. Instead, the Syrian wanted to force a battle on open ground, where his superiority in numbers, war elephants, and swift cavalry would be effective.

Judas had heavily fortified Beth-zur, site of his previous victory over Lysias, but the powerful Syrian siege machines battered through its defenses. Judas withdrew soldiers from the siege of the Akra in Jerusalem to take up a position in Beth-zechariah (19). The Syrians marched smartly forward in frightening numbers, and "When the sun shone upon the shields of gold and brass, the hills were ablaze with them and gleamed like flaming torches." The war elephants, carrying archers in wooden towers, proved to be the decisive battle element. Maddened by wine and mulberry juice and urged on by their Indian drivers, the great beasts charged into the Jewish ranks. Judas' brother, Eleazar, bravely darted beneath one of the elephants, drove his sword into its vitals—and was crushed by the stricken beast. Such Jewish heroism and futility marked the battle. The formidable Syrian infantry and cavalry swept the field. To save what was left of his army, Judas fled to the safety of the Gophna Hills.

Before he could turn his victory at Beth-zechariah into conquest of Judea, Lysias learned that there was a challenge to his regency in Syria. Pressed by the need to return to Antioch, he proposed a compromise peace to the Jews of Jerusalem. He would grant them religious freedom if they would evacuate their stronghold on the Temple Mount. The bargain was struck. For many Jews, the goal of the rebellion—religious freedom—had been achieved; the Hasidim, for example, abandoned the struggle and would support no more fighting. But Judas, at the lowest point in his fortunes and now without these strong supporters, was determined to continue the rebellion. He sought nothing less than complete political independence for Judea.

Maccabees: Independence Again

In the year 162 B.C. Antioch, the Syrian capital, witnessed the opening of a long and bloody fratricidal struggle for the Seleucid throne between heirs and supposed heirs of Antiochus IV and his brother Seleucus IV. Seleucus' son, Demetrius I, took the opening round in the royal battle, deposing and slaying both his cousin Antiochus V and the young king's protector, Lysias. It was in this atmosphere of dynastic strife that the Jewish rebels in Judea would recover their political independence.

From his base in the Gophna Hills (1, on lower map opposite), Judas was once again attempting to block the routes to Jerusalem (2). When the High Priest he had installed at Jerusalem asked for help against this renewed Maccabean threat, Demetrius sent Nicanor back to Judea. In a show of strength, Nicanor led 3,000 men out of Jerusalem to the Way of Beth-horon—and stumbled into an ambush laid by Judas at Capharsalama (3). As Nicanor retreated to Jerusalem, Judas and his guerrilla band won new support.

Nicanor made a second attempt to open the Way of Beth-horon, marching out of Jerusalem to Lower Beth-horon (4), where he met reinforcements coming up from Lydda (5). As he was returning to Jerusalem at the head of this combined force, Nicanor was again taken by surprise, this time at Adasa (6). The Jews struck from the south, to cut the Syrians off from Jerusalem. Nicanor himself was the first casualty, and when his soldiers saw him fall, they panicked. Their disordered flight over 22 miles of mountainous terrain to the fortress of Gazara (7) was a brutal rout. Aroused by Judas' trumpets, the local villagers fell upon the weary Syrian stragglers and killed them by the score.

The Maccabean revolt was rekindled; once more Judas was a force to be reckoned with. The Romans, ever anxious to do anything to discomfit the Seleucid empire, formed an alliance with Judas. Before hearing of this, however, Demetrius had ordered his best field commander, Bacchides, to Judea with an elite unit. Bacchides traced a route straight through the heart of the country to Jerusalem. Judas did not offer battle to such a host; indeed, many of his men lost heart, and desertions ran high.

In 161 Bacchides set up a base at Beeroth (8), from which he could move directly against the vastly outnumbered rebel forces encamped at Elasa (9). Although the guerrilla strategy Judas had developed dictated that he avoid pitched battle, he apparently concluded that in this instance it would be best to meet the enemy head on. Urged by his troops to withdraw and fight another day, Judas replied: "Far be it from us to do such a thing as to flee from them. If our time has come, let us die bravely for our brethren, and leave no cause to question our honor." Judas hurled his tiny force at the wing of the Syrian army led by Bacchides himself and for a time drove it before him. But the odds against him were too great. The other Syrian wing pressed relentlessly against the rear of Judas' command. Caught between the two massive forces, the Jewish army was crushed and Judas

killed. "And all Israel made great lamentation for him; they mourned many days and said,

'How is the mighty fallen,
the savior of Israel!' "

The few surviving guerrillas fled southward into the Wilderness of Tekoa (10, on upper map), where the Maccabean rebellion remained alive. Its military leader was now Jonathan, youngest of Mattathias' sons. At the beginning, the rebels were reduced to a life of virtual banditry in order to survive. Then, gradually, they picked up support and strength. By 156 Jonathan had a well-trained force established at Bethbasi (11) on the desert's edge near the populated areas—and near the main north-south route to Jerusalem.

Because Judea had been quiet for two years, it must have come as a shock to Bacchides when the Hellenized Jews of Jerusalem begged him to return from Antioch to counter the renewed rebel threat to the city. Bacchides laid siege to Bethbasi with a powerful force. As his older brother Simon skillfully conducted the fortress defenses, Jonathan ranged through the countryside, harassing Bacchides' supply lines. Frustrated by these classic guerrilla tactics, Bacchides angrily turned on the Hellenizers in Jerusalem, accusing them of dragging his crack army into a military quagmire, killed many of them, and threatened to return to Antioch. But when Jonathan proposed peace, Bacchides agreed to negotiate. The fighting ceased, prisoners were exchanged, and Bacchides went home. Jonathan now gave up the sword in favor of politics, establishing an opposition government at Michmash (12).

The tide of events was running his way, a trend accelerated by the continuing dynastic struggle in Antioch. In 153 Alexander Balas (the "Alexander Epiphanes" of 1 Maccabees 10:1) arrived in southern Syria, claiming to be the son of Antiochus IV. Even though he was known to be an impostor, other rulers supported him against Demetrius I in hopes of weakening the Seleucid empire. In the meantime, Jonathan was extending his authority over the Judean countryside. Desperate for friends, Demetrius granted Jonathan royal authority "to recruit troops, to equip them with arms, and to become his ally." Jonathan promptly moved his government to Jerusalem. Except for garrisons at Beth-zur and at the Akra in Jerusalem, the Syrians evacuated the country.

The pretender Alexander Balas was not to be outdone. He offered the high priesthood to Jonathan, who accepted it. For the next decade Jonathan successfully played off one rival for the Seleucid throne against the other, all the time strengthening his own position in Judea. When Alexander Balas made a dynastic marriage with Cleopatra, daughter of Ptolemy VI of Egypt, Jonathan was not only invited but received with honor. Many of the political aims of the Maccabean revolt had now been achieved. If Judea was not completely free, it was at least a self-governing part of the Seleucid empire.

After the death of Demetrius I in battle against Alexander Balas, his son Demetrius II had taken up the father's quarrel. He now allied himself with Egypt militarily and dynastically, obtaining not only weapons but even Cleopatra, whom Ptolemy VI retrieved from the increasingly ineffective Alexander Balas.

Demetrius II determined to punish Jonathan for his alliance with Alexander and sent an army south under Apollonius, whom he had appointed governor of Coele-Syria. But the attempt failed. Moreover, Jonathan marched to the coast, where he took Joppa (13), evaded a Syrian ambush south of Jamnia (14), and defeated the Syrians at Azotus (15). The Jewish hero went on to lay siege to the Akra in Jerusalem in an attempt to win final separation from the Seleucid empire. The Hellenizers' usual appeal to Antioch for military aid did not bring results this time, for Demetrius II, beset by troubles elsewhere, was anxious to end his Judean problems. At Ptolemais (16), Demetrius met Jonathan and turned over much of Samaria to him, ending the annual tribute and confirming Jonathan in all his offices.

By 143 there was a new figure in the Seleucid dynastic struggle. Alexander Balas had been assassinated, but one of his generals, Trypho, had Alexander's minor son proclaimed king as Antiochus VI. At first, Jonathan sided with Demetrius II in the renewed conflict, even sending 3,000 men to Antioch to quell an uprising in the Syrian capital. When Demetrius reneged on his past promises, however, Jonathan switched allegiance to Trypho. He was rewarded with new concessions on the strategically vital coastal plain. With that area secured, he opened a campaign to gain the cities of Upper Galilee. The operation nearly ended in disaster when forces loyal to Demetrius ambushed the Jewish army at the Plain of Hazor (17). Rallying from the brink of defeat, Jonathan drove the enemy from the field. He went on to do battle far to the north, in Hamath, raiding widely and securing great booty.

Trypho, nourishing plans to overthrow his puppet king, Antiochus VI, embarked on a course of treachery in his dealings with Jonathan. On the promise of turning over the city of Ptolemais, he lured Jonathan and his 1,000-man honor guard to that city. Once inside the gates, Jonathan was taken captive and his men slaughtered. Trypho and his invading army followed the coastal route in order to attack Judea from the south, but near Adora (18) his path was blocked by a heavy snowstorm. Giving up his campaign, he crossed the Jordan and moved northward. Near Bascama (19) he had Jonathan put to death.

The final act of the Maccabean revolt now began. After Trypho murdered Antiochus VI and claimed the throne for himself, Simon resumed his brother's daring game of playing off the rival kings one against another. His price this time—exacted from Demetrius—was full independence. He was in a position of strength, and Demetrius agreed to his demand. In the spring of 142 Judea became politically independent, "and the people began to write in their documents and contracts, 'In the first year of Simon the great high priest and commander and leader of the Jews.' " It had been 25 years since Mattathias Hasmoneas triggered the Maccabean rebellion in the village of Modein.

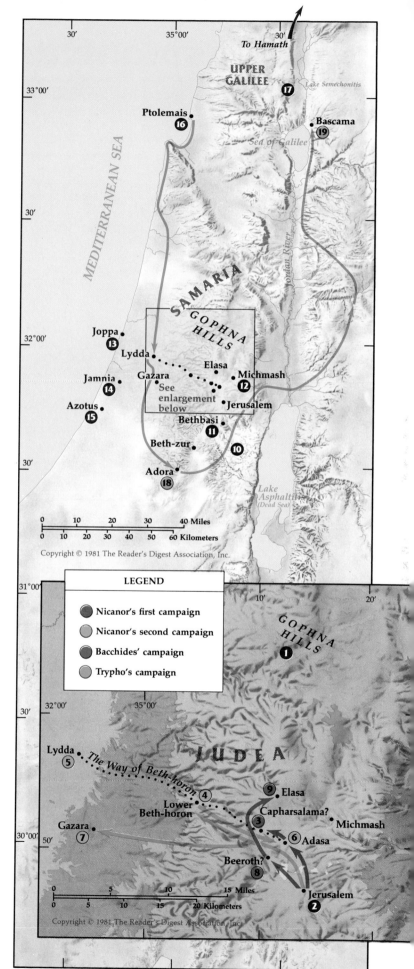

Copyright © 1981 The Reader's Digest Association, Inc.

LEGEND

Nicanor's first campaign
Nicanor's second campaign
Bacchides' campaign
Trypho's campaign

Copyright © 1981 The Reader's Digest Association, Inc.

The Hasmonean Dynasty

With political independence at home and the continuing weakness of the Seleucid empire, Simon moved to consolidate his gains. He took Joppa (1) and its harbor "and opened a way to the isles of the sea." Gazara (2), guarding approaches to two of the major western passes to Jerusalem (3), was conquered and its Gentile population expelled; the site was turned into a Jewish military base, with John Hyrcanus, Simon's son, as governor. In 141 B.C. the besieged Syrian garrison in the Akra in Jerusalem finally surrendered, and rejoicing Jews entered this hated symbol of foreign domination.

The people recognized Simon as High Priest, confirming him in the office with its temporal powers and hereditary rights previously conferred by the Seleucid rulers. The Roman Senate—ever anxious to weaken the Seleucids—guaranteed the Jews unrestricted rights to their lands. One group of Jews regarded Simon's priesthood as profaning both the holy office and the Temple. They withdrew to Qumran (4), on the northwestern shore of Lake Asphaltitis, built a monastery, and lived a sectarian existence emphasizing scriptural study and ritual purity as they looked toward the coming of a messiah. From these people came the famous "Dead Sea Scrolls," in one of which they called Simon (or one of the other Hasmoneans) "the Wicked Priest." Yet the vast majority of those in Judea prospered under Simon and "tilled their land in peace."

In 139, however, Antiochus VII, who would prove to be the last strong Seleucid king, attempted to reassert his rights in certain Judean cities. The aged Simon dispatched his sons Judas and John Hyrcanus to meet the threat, and their army defeated the Syrians at Kedron (5). However, probably in the year 134, Simon and two of his sons, Mattathias and Judas, were treacherously murdered at the fortress of Dok (6) near Jericho. The assassin was Simon's son-in-law, probably in league with Antiochus. Simon was the last of the five Hasmonean brothers to meet a violent death.

Forewarned that he, too, was marked for assassination, John Hyrcanus hastened to secure Jerusalem, where he became High Priest by hereditary right. Antiochus besieged him there for a year. The city held out, but Hyrcanus was forced to pay tribute for Joppa and Gazara to the Seleucids. Yet this reverse proved temporary. When

Antiochus VII was killed in battle in 129, the Seleucid empire went into its death throes. In the subsequent power vacuum, Hyrcanus began to expand Judea's borders, accelerating the rise of the Hasmonean kingdom.

Other links to the sea were established with the takeover of Jamnia (7) and Azotus (8). Also, the city of Medeba (9) in the Transjordan was reduced after a long siege; thus a portion of the King's Highway connecting Damascus and the Red Sea came under Jewish control, with important economic advantages. By 125 Hyrcanus had annexed part of Samaria and all of Idumea. The conquest of Idumea meant that the easy southern approaches to the hill country of Judea—which the Seleucids had used repeatedly—were secure. The people in these territories were forced to accept Judaism as a means of ensuring their loyalty. (Among the converted were the ancestors of the future king of Judea, Herod the Great.) In 108 Hyrcanus embarked on a second campaign in Samaria. Shechem (10) was taken and leveled, ending the long history of that famous site where Abraham had built his first altar in the Promised Land. After a year-long siege, the city of Samaria (11) also fell and was destroyed.

However, serious internal divisions began to appear toward the end of Hyrcanus' 30-year reign. There was growing conflict between the Sadducees, the aristocratic priestly faction supporting the royal house, and the Pharisees, a religious group devoted to strict observance of the Law. Hyrcanus sought to suppress the Pharisees, but he died before the full fury of this struggle broke over the land. In his will he sought to resolve the conflict by removing secular power from the high priesthood: his oldest surviving son, Aristobulus, was to receive the holy office, but Hyrcanus' widow was to rule the state. Aristobulus promptly put his mother in prison, where she starved to death. Secure in the seat of power, he continued his father's expansionist policies. He made a swift conquest of Galilee and Judaized the region as Hyrcanus had done in Idumea. Aristobulus died in 103, after only a year in power, but all the mountain and hill country west of the Jordan was again in Jewish hands.

Aristobulus was the first to take the royal title and style himself "king." Although the Pharisees objected, saying that only a descendant of David could take this

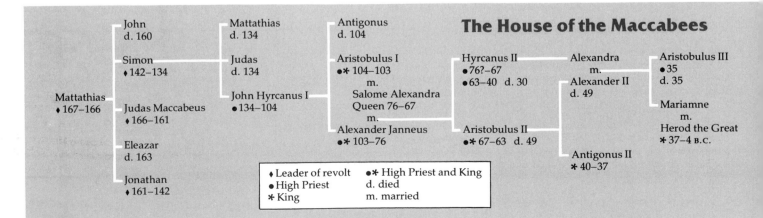

title, he had brushed aside their objections. Worse was to come under Alexander Janneus, who succeeded his brother in 103.

Janneus launched a series of military campaigns that would add sizable territories to the kingdom, until it would approach the size of King David's domain. The achievements of his 27-year reign stemmed not from his skill as a field commander—he never won a major battle—but from his persistence and stubborn resolution.

Janneus' opening campaign was against the port city of Ptolemais (12). His besieging army was driven away by a force under the Egyptian Ptolemy Lathyrus, king of Cyprus, who stormed down the coast "ravaging Judea with impunity." When Ptolemy reached the border of Egypt, however, he was attacked by land and sea by his mother, Cleopatra III. She not only defeated her son but nullified his conquests by forming an alliance with Janneus. She then withdrew to Egypt. After campaigning east of the Jordan, Janneus marched against the cities of the southwest coast, which the defeat of Ptolemy and the withdrawal of Cleopatra had left virtually defenseless. Only Gaza (13) resisted stubbornly, but in 96 it too fell, after a long and costly siege. The capture of Gaza put the entire coast, from Mount Carmel to Rhinocorura (on the Egyptian border) in Jewish hands, with the exception of Ascalon and the area around it. In the southeast Janneus added to the areas earlier secured by Hyrcanus. Along the east shore of Lake Asphaltitis he gained cities ranging from Libba (14) in the north to Zoar (15) in the south. Lake Asphaltitis became a Jewish sea.

In the meantime, however, Janneus' relations with the Pharisees were steadily deteriorating. His mercenary soldiers clashed with Jewish groups, and his civil administration, based on Hellenistic models and with many Greek civil servants, was widely opposed. The fact that he inscribed his coins "Alexander the King" in Greek as well as Hebrew was seen by many as symbolic of his homage to Hellenization. In 90 the Pharisees openly rebelled, and Judea was soon embroiled in civil war. Janneus' attempts to negotiate failed when the Pharisees demanded his death as their price for peace. They called on Syrian troops to come to their aid, and there were pitched battles between the two sides. After six years of conflict, the Pharisees were finally suppressed. The Jewish historian Josephus estimated the cost of the civil war at "no fewer than fifty thousand Jews."

Having survived the civil war and a subsequent Syrian threat, Janneus resumed his expansionist moves. For three years he campaigned south and east of the Sea of Galilee. Pella (16), in the Transjordan, was leveled and its Gentile population expelled. Hippus (17), Philoteria (18), and Gamala (19) fell, and the Sea of Galilee, with its important fishing industry, became another Jewish sea.

Surprisingly little is known of the internal organization of Janneus' kingdom. The five divisions that he inherited—Judea, Idumea, Samaria, Galilee, and Perea—were ruled by civil governors, but the conquered Greek cities were under military rule. There were upward of 20 major military fortresses scattered across the area, including such spectacular desert fortresses as Masada (20); Machaerus (21), guarding the troublesome south-

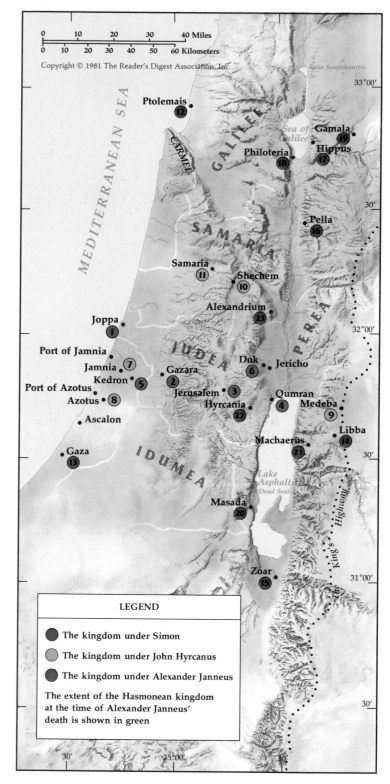

LEGEND

● The kingdom under Simon

● The kingdom under John Hyrcanus

● The kingdom under Alexander Janneus

The extent of the Hasmonean kingdom at the time of Alexander Janneus' death is shown in green

eastern border; Hyrcania (22), the dreaded state prison in the Wilderness of Judea; and Alexandrium (23), controlling traffic in the Jordan valley.

In 76, while conducting a siege east of the Jordan, Alexander Janneus succumbed to his habitual heavy drinking. At his death, the Hasmonean kingdom was at its greatest territorial limits (shown in green). Yet internally the nation was deeply divided. Forces that had been cruelly repressed would rise up again within a generation and help bring an end to Hasmonean rule.

161

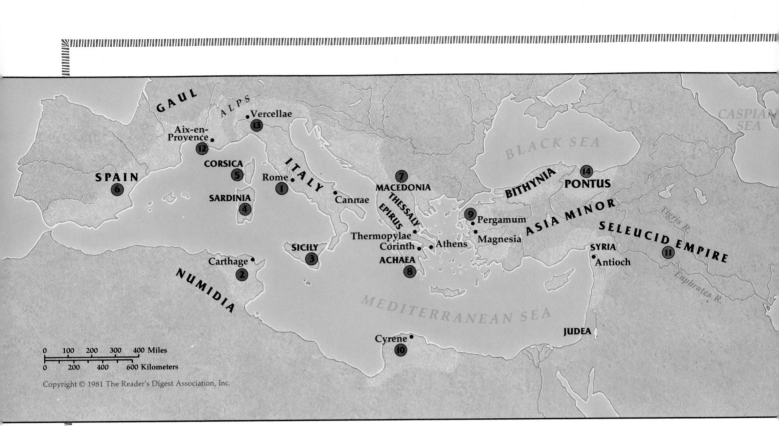

The Rise of Rome

From its modest start as a dusty village on central Italy's Tiber River in the 8th century B.C., Rome grew at an ever-accelerating pace until it finally became the colossus of the ancient world. By the 1st century B.C., its expansionist drive would bring it into direct confrontation with the Hasmonean kingdom under Alexander Janneus.

It was Rome's good fortune, during its rise to world domination, to be able to confront its foes one at a time rather than collectively; in the end it always proved equal to the task of defeating or absorbing successive enemies, gaining strength with each victory. From its base on the Tiber, Rome (1) reached out north and south until, by the year 270 B.C., it dominated the Italian peninsula. From this power base, the Roman republic looked for other worlds to conquer.

Growing military sophistication—achieved in part by the adoption of the most effective tactics and weaponry of its foes—made Rome's legions strong enough by the 3rd century B.C. to face their greatest test. The challenge came from Carthage (2), the maritime power on the African coast in present-day Tunisia. Rome's chief prize in the First Punic War (264–41) were the islands of Sicily (3), Sardinia (4), and Corsica (5), which were organized administratively into Rome's earliest provinces. In the Second Punic War (218–201) with the Carthaginians, however, Rome's army was pushed to the brink of defeat by the military genius of Hannibal, who made his celebrated march over the Alps to carry the battle to the walls of Rome itself. At Cannae in 216 Hannibal inflicted a crushing reverse on Roman arms, killing some 25,000 soldiers and capturing 10,000 more. Yet with the resil-

iency and ruthlessness that marked every step of its imperial climb, Rome rallied and renewed its forces. In Scipio Africanus it found a general who was a match for Hannibal. When the fighting ceased, the imperial forces were in command of resource-rich Carthaginian Spain (6). With typical thoroughness, Rome ended the Third Punic War (149–46) by utterly destroying the city of Carthage. The region became the Roman province of "Africa." Yet even before the menace of Carthage was removed forever, the Romans had already turned eastward.

One expansionist strategy that stood Rome in good stead was "divide and conquer." The first stage of most of its imperial ventures was marked by promises, threats, attempts to undercut the rival government, and lip-service "alliances." The second stage against a softened-up foe featured the mailed fist. This strategy was used against the two great eastern powers, the successor states of Alexander the Great—Philip V's Macedonia, and Antiochus III's Seleucid empire.

Rome was careful to take on these empires one at a time. Macedonia (7) was the first target. After fomenting rebellion among Philip's subject Greek and Aetolian peoples, Rome defeated the Macedonians in Thessaly in 197. Thus was Greece "liberated" from the Macedonian yoke, or so the victors claimed. In time, the confederation of Greek city-states known as the Achaean League was goaded into revolting against its Roman protector and crushed. Epirus was devastated and 150,000 citizens enslaved. Corinth was sacked and its treasures carried off. Southern Greece became the Roman province of Achaea (8).

Antiochus did not await his turn to be attacked but rashly took the offensive and was crushed at Thermopylae and Magnesia. The Romans, with apparent generos-

Pompey, whose idealized bust appears at right, was quick to add to his laurels in competition with another rising soldier, Julius Caesar, shown at left. Though the two men, along with Crassus, formed the First Triumvirate in 60 B.C., they remained rivals, eventually leading Rome into civil war. The relief at center, from the 1st-century A.D. Column of Trajan, illustrates the type of close combat that most often ended in victory for Rome.

ity, awarded Asia Minor to their new allies, then set out to subvert these client states. They were so successful with Pergamum (9) that its tormented ruler, Attalus III, simply bequeathed his kingdom to Rome in 133. (A similar fate awaited Cyrene (10) in North Africa.) Soon Asia Minor was firmly in the Roman orbit. Rome then set about hastening the collapse of what remained of the failing Seleucid empire (11) by inciting revolts among its restless subject peoples, including the inhabitants of Judea.

In Rome itself the fruit of the imperial adventures was often bitter. The Roman republic became republican in name only, for the Senate was dominated by indolent aristocrats who indulged in massive corruption. Maneuvering for power went on between the Optimates, who supported the Senate, and the Populares, who appealed to citizen assemblies. Gaius Gracchus, elected ruling tribune on a reform platform, could not effect his program and was overthrown by the Optimates in 121.

The army now came to the forefront of the chaotic Roman political scene, dooming the republic to ultimate overthrow. Under the generalship of Gaius Marius, the army became thoroughly professionalized. The soldiers were ambitious volunteers rather than the ragged peasant militia who left their plows to serve the state. They were well trained and fully equipped but poorly paid; their livelihood depended on booty, and often their loyalty was less to the state than to the generals who could lead them to that booty.

In 105 "Marius' Mules" campaigned successfully in North Africa, where the Numidian king Jugurtha was captured, displayed in chains at Marius' triumph in Rome, and then executed. Marius then turned to the German barbarians, defeating them at Aix-en-Provence (12) in Gaul and at Vercellae (13) in Italy.

Marius, however, proved to be a better general than a politician, and he failed to end the turmoil in Rome. A challenger, Sulla, emerged from among Marius' staff. At the head of his veteran legions, he marched on Rome and overturned the government to favor the aristocratic Optimates. He then turned to deal with the most serious revolt yet to strike the Roman provinces in the east. In 88 King Mithradates of Pontus (14) incited the wholesale slaughter of Romans who had settled in the conquered provinces, killing some 80,000 in a single day. In two hard-fought wars, Sulla ruthlessly put down the Mithradatic revolt. Former loyal allies were not spared his vengeance. To Athenians who protested the sacking of their city and the slaughter of the citizens, Sulla replied, "I have come not to learn ancient history, but to punish rebels." He returned to Rome and in 82 was elected dictator by the cowed Senate. Four years later, in comfortable retirement, he died in his bed.

In the year 70 the rich businessman Crassus and the general Pompey, a youthful associate of Sulla's, became the ruling consuls. Pompey's rise to power had been rapid. He was a vigorous soldier, already known as "the beardless executioner" for the aggressive way he had carried out his mentor's orders. In just three months he rid the Mediterranean of the piratical bands that had been persistently preying upon Roman commerce. He then moved to put down yet another revolt by Mithradates in the east.

Styling himself "the Great," Pompey extended the Roman presence from the Caspian Sea to the Euphrates River, adding the provinces of Bithynia and Pontus to the growing empire. In 64 he took Antioch in Syria, bringing down the final curtain on the already weakened Seleucid empire. With his powerful army behind him, Pompey now turned southward, toward Judea.

The Coming of the Romans

Upon Alexander Janneus' death in 76 B.C., he was succeeded by his widow, Salome Alexandra. Hyrcanus II, their eldest son, became High Priest. There were no territorial changes in the Hasmonean kingdom during Alexandra's nine-year rule. Bountiful harvests brought prosperity to Judea and made possible extensive exports of wheat, olive oil, balsam, figs, and wine. Heeding her husband's deathbed advice, Alexandra made peace with the Pharisees, turning over much of the kingdom's internal affairs to them. While the Sadducees thus lost power—indeed many were executed by Pharisee courts—they still had to be reckoned with. Civil war, which had rent the country during Janneus' reign, was to erupt again after Alexandra's death, as her two sons contended for the throne.

Alexandra had increased the mercenary force but staffed it with Jewish officers, ensuring—or so she thought—the army's loyalty. However, many of these officers had Sadducee leanings, hoping for a renewal of the expansionist policies that would require a strong army. They favored Alexandra's second son, Aristobulus II—described by the historian Josephus as "a man of action and high spirit"—over the weak and indolent Hyrcanus. Complaining that he had no role in the kingdom, whereas his brother was High Priest, Aristobulus asked his mother for command of the fortresses. Unaware that he was making preparations to fight for the throne, Alexandra handed over a number of small strongholds to him. When she fell ill, Aristobulus, supported by the officer corps, rebelled—not against her but to prevent the throne from passing to Hyrcanus. Within two weeks, 22 Judean fortresses had gone over to Aristobulus.

Alexandra soon died, leaving the throne to Hyrcanus. Aristobulus promptly marched against his older brother, defeated him at Jericho (1), and sent him fleeing for Jerusalem (2). There Hyrcanus surrendered and renounced the throne in favor of Aristobulus, asking only to be left free to enjoy his revenues. Fatefully, the opportunistic Antipater, who had ruled Idumea during the two previous reigns, intervened, convincing many leading Jews that Aristobulus had no lawful right to the throne. He secured a safe haven for Hyrcanus in Petra (3, on smaller map), capital of the Nabatean king Aretas.

Hyrcanus promised Aretas a dozen cities (printed in red) east and south of Lake Asphaltitis in exchange for an army to challenge his brother. The bargain was struck. The Nabatean forces defeated Aristobulus and drove him into the fortified Temple Mount in Jerusalem (see detail on opposite page). Many of the pretender's mercenaries defected, as did the general population of the city. Only the priestly party remained loyal to Aristobulus. Yet his position on the Temple Mount was exceedingly strong. The eastern slope drops some 400 feet to the floor of the Kidron valley. To the west is the Tyropoeon valley. On the south is the steep-sided Ophel ridge—where David's city had stood so long ago. Only on the northwest was there a narrow spit of land and rock, but it was guarded by a fortress. Without catapults

and battering rams, Aretas could not force the position. Instead, he decided to besiege the fortress.

This was the situation when Rome's Pompey the Great entered the Judean stage in 65. One of his lieutenants, Scaurus, reached Jerusalem and was importuned by envoys of the rival brothers. Assessing the situation and realizing that Aristobulus would be difficult to root out of his fortress, Scaurus ordered the Nabateans to lift the siege or be declared enemies of Rome. They did so and withdrew eastward, but at Papyron (4), in a marshy area near the mouth of the Jordan, the pursuing Aristobulus fell on them and inflicted a resounding defeat. Fresh from his victory, Aristobulus began to court Pompey's favor. As tribute, he sent him a splendid golden vine, which was eventually placed in the temple of Jupiter Capitolinus in Rome. But now Antipater appeared before the Roman commander on behalf of Hyrcanus. Pompey postponed a decision and ordered the contending brothers to come to Damascus (5, on smaller map). Even as they arrived to plead their cases, yet a third delegation of Jews arrived in Damascus, opposing both would-be kings and asking the Romans to abolish the monarchy entirely and return Judea to its ancient custom of rule by priests. Pompey suspended final decision as he marched south to campaign against the Nabateans.

Rashly, Aristobulus left Pompey and hastened to the mountaintop fortress of Alexandrium (6), perhaps intending to use it as a base to incite rebellion. Pompey would have none of it. Abandoning the Nabatean campaign, he put his legions on the march for Judea. He came down from the Transjordanian heights, bypassed Pella, and crossed the Jordan near Scythopolis (7) to reach Coreae (8) just below the mountain fortress of Alexandrium. After lengthy negotiations, Aristobulus gave up the fortress and withdrew to Jerusalem. Pompey and his army followed. At Jericho (9), Aristobulus came before Pompey and offered to surrender Jerusalem and pay tribute, but his followers inside the capital barred the gates. Pompey arrested Aristobulus and marched on Jerusalem (10).

From the safety of their walls the populace of Jerusalem saw the plumed helmets and red capes of thousands of Roman troops standing out clearly against the brown hills, the sun glistening from their spears. The city was in turmoil. Aristobulus' men withdrew into the fastness of the Temple Mount (11, see detail), destroying the bridge (12) to the upper city, and prepared to fight. Hyrcanus' supporters opened the city gates (13) to the Romans. When the defenders of the Temple Mount refused his offer to bargain, Pompey ordered siege weapons brought from Tyre on the seacoast, and prepared for an assault.

Methodically, the Romans went to work. Soldiers fanned out over the hills to cut trees and began construction of great timber and earthen ramps for a two-pronged attack, through the fortress to the northern wall and against the western wall. As work on the ramps progressed, catapults and battering rams were inched forward. Resistance from the fortress was fierce, at times bringing the siege operations almost to a halt. The Ro-

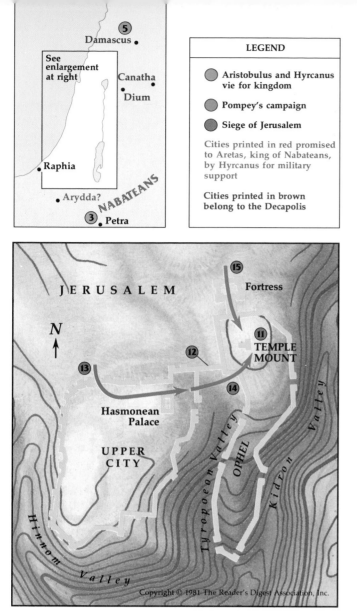

LEGEND

- Aristobulus and Hyrcanus vie for kingdom
- Pompey's campaign
- Siege of Jerusalem

Cities printed in red promised to Aretas, king of Nabateans, by Hyrcanus for military support

Cities printed in brown belong to the Decapolis

mans made their greatest progress on the Sabbath, when Jewish law forbade the defenders to fight unless attacked. Finally the siege machines were in position to hammer at the great limestone walls. The battle raged on. In the third month of the siege—in September or October of 63—breaches (14 and 15) were made in the walls and the legions poured through, followed by Hyrcanus' men. Thousands of the defenders went down under Roman or Jewish swords. Many hurled themselves to their deaths from the walls, and others died in their burning dwellings rather than surrender. In all, some 12,000 of Aristobulus' men died. Roman losses were light. Pompey and some of his men went into the Holy of Holies, where only the High Priest was permitted to enter, but they did not disturb the Temple treasury or the works in the Temple itself. Indeed on the day following the massacre, Pompey ordered the Temple cleansed and customary sacrifices resumed.

Pompey confirmed Hyrcanus as High Priest but did not give him the royal title. The Roman conqueror then set about dismantling the kingdom so laboriously assembled by John Hyrcanus I and Alexander Janneus. While there were other changes in the region—the vestiges of Seleucid power were removed, and the Hellenistic cities in the area were freed of their oriental overlords—the losses to the Jews were the most devastating. All the Greek cities taken by the Hasmonean kings, including Gaba, Samaria, Scythopolis, Hippus, Dium, Pella, Gerasa, and Marisa, were made free cities under the Roman governor of Syria. The entire coast was detached from Judea, and with it the cities of Dora, Strato's Tower, Apollonia, Arethusa, Joppa, Jamnia, Azotus, Gaza, and Raphia.

Pompey recognized that the Lydda-Gazara area was predominantly Jewish and did not detach it from Judea. He also accepted the Judaization of Galilee and of Perea as far south as Machaerus. And while western Idumea around Marisa was detached, eastern Idumea centered on Adora remained a part of Judea.

Thus was the work of the Hasmoneans undone. The kingdom was not only reduced radically in size but was divided in two, with Samaria separating Judea and Galilee. To the northeast was the Roman-created league of 10 cities (shown in brown), the famed Decapolis: Damascus, Canatha, Dium, Hippus, Abila, Gadara, Scythopolis, Pella, Gerasa, and Philadelphia. They, like Judea itself, fell under the domination of a foreign governor.

Struggles for Judea

Pompey's dismemberment of the Hasmonean kingdom produced neither peace nor stability. Instead, Judea was plunged into a quarter century of unceasing turmoil. Contending factions struggled for power and legitimacy—and especially for Roman military backing, a process complicated by Rome's own internal power struggles. Finally, out of the chaos and confusion, there rose a king of Judea, Herod the Great.

Although Pompey dispatched Aristobulus and his family as captives to Rome after Jerusalem's fall in 63 B.C., his action did not prevent continued efforts to overthrow the puppet regime of Hyrcanus and Antipater. Aristobulus' son, Alexander, escaped his captors and raised the banner of revolt. In 57 he returned to his country, collected 10,000 infantry and 1,500 cavalry, and captured the fortresses of Alexandrium (1), Hyrcania (2), and Machaerus (3). He also attempted to refortify Jerusalem (4), but the Romans in the city stopped him. The Roman governor of Syria, Gabinius, came with a talented young soldier, Marc Antony, to quell the rebellion. Defeated in battle near Jerusalem with huge losses, Alexander fled to the Alexandrium fortress, where he was besieged by Gabinius and Antony and forced into surrender. The Romans then destroyed the three fortresses.

In an attempt to solidify Roman rule, Gabinius reorganized Judea into five districts, each separately governed from a provincial center: Judea (Jerusalem), the Jordan valley (Jericho), Perea (Amathus), Galilee (Sepphoris), and probably Idumea (Adora). The plan was short-lived, but it stripped Hyrcanus of political power.

In 56 Aristobulus escaped from Rome, reached Judea, and raised another armed force. The Romans drove him and his inexperienced troops in bloody retreat across the Jordan and into the ruins of the Machaerus fortress. Aristobulus surrendered, and again found himself a prisoner on the way to Rome. Undeterred by his father's failure, Alexander once more attempted to incite rebellion, and once more Gabinius brought him to battle. Near Mount Tabor (5) the rebel army was crushed, with a loss of 10,000 men. Roman military power was too strong to be overthrown, and an enforced peace settled over the land.

Judea now became a pawn in the growing struggle for power in the Roman empire. In 60 the three contenders, Pompey, Crassus, and Julius Caesar, had formed the uneasy alliance known as the First Triumvirate. Five years later Crassus arrived in Syria as governor, seeking to enrich himself and to pursue glory in the Parthian wars. He proceeded to rob the Temple in Jerusalem, taking not only 2,000 talents from the treasury

but also the sacred golden vessels and other artifacts from the sanctuary, valued at an additional 8,000 talents. Before his greed further damaged Judea, Crassus died in battle against the Parthians. The surviving contenders, Pompey and Caesar, were soon at each other's throat. Their struggle would profoundly affect Judea.

At first, Hyrcanus and Antipater (whose behind-the-scenes manipulation was making a mere figurehead of Hyrcanus) favored Pompey's cause. Caesar's supporters sought to counter this by releasing Aristobulus from prison in Rome and sending him with two legions to Judea, but Pompey's agents nipped the plan in the bud by poisoning Aristobulus. Then his son, Alexander, was beheaded in Antioch on Pompey's direct order. Antipater, eager to accommodate the Romans on any terms, soon found an opportunity to switch sides. After being defeated by Caesar at the battle of Pharsalus in 48, Pompey fled to Egypt, where he was assassinated. When Caesar subsequently became embroiled in a difficult fight in Egypt, Antipater brought him 3,000 much-needed reinforcements. It was a move with important consequences for Jews throughout the empire. The grateful Caesar championed Jewish rights in Judea and elsewhere, setting a pattern that future emperors would follow. For his part, Antipater was rewarded with Roman citizenship, exempted from taxes, and confirmed in a position of political power while Hyrcanus was reconfirmed as High Priest and named ethnarch, a high political title but in this case one without real power. Antipater went about the land urging submission to Rome and tightening his grip on the reins of power. He appointed his eldest son, Phasael, governor of Jerusalem, and his second son, Herod, governor of Galilee.

A situation that promised stability suddenly became highly unstable. Caesar was assassinated in 44, and one of his killers, Cassius, soon came to Syria and imposed heavy new taxes on Judea. Those cities that could not raise the required sums saw their male citizens sold into slavery. An already grave state of affairs took a turn for the worse when Antipater was poisoned at a banquet. A new generation now took up the struggle for the Judean throne. On the one side was Antigonus, youngest of the murdered Aristobulus' sons; on the other, the Idumeans Herod and Phasael, sons of the slain Antipater. The two Idumeans allied themselves with the Romans, but their rule was unpopular with the people. In 40 the Parthians invaded Judea in force; they overran the country and made it possible for Antigonus (who had bribed them with the promise of 1,000 talents and 500

As part of Herod the Great's building program, this modest mountain was transformed into the grand fortress of Herodium. The hill's crown was raised and a costly aqueduct built.

women to make him king) to enter Jerusalem in triumph.

Under the pretext of opening peace negotiations, the Parthians seized Phasael and Hyrcanus and imprisoned them on the coast north of Ptolemais. Herod, however, avoided the trap and escaped from Jerusalem. He set out on a long odyssey that would eventually bring him back to Judea and power.

Rebuffed by the Nabateans and refusing the hospitality of the Egyptians, he pressed through a dangerous winter voyage across the Mediterranean to Rome. He was greeted by Antony, who persuaded the Senate to declare Herod king of Judea and brand Antigonus an enemy of Rome for his defection to the Parthians. Yet, in fact, Herod was a king without a country. Antigonus had been installed on the Judean throne by the Parthians. Phasael was dead and Hyrcanus deliberately mutilated, disqualifying him ever to resume his post as High Priest. Never daunted by adversity, Herod sailed for the east and landed at Ptolemais (6) early in 39. When the Roman commander in the region, bribed by Antigonus, offered no help, Herod raised a mercenary army and moved into Galilee. Turning south, he took Joppa (7), then moved inland through Idumea to secure Masada (8), where his family had stayed behind, and to take the fortress of Oresa (9).

Unable to sustain a siege of Jerusalem, Herod struck at Jericho (10) and then moved through Samaria by an unknown route to take up winter quarters in Galilee. There, in a snowstorm, he took Sepphoris (11) and killed Jewish brigands in caves near Arbela (12). However, continuing to be frustrated by the lack of cooperation from the Roman generals, he traveled to Samosata on the Euphrates to plead directly with Antony. Pledged the certain support of Sosius, the newly appointed Roman governor of Syria, Herod returned to Judea in the year 38 to renew his attack. His route took him down the Jordan valley to Jericho (13).

Antigonus now made the error of challenging Herod with only half his army, under the Greek general Pappus. At Isana (14), Pappus was routed. The following spring, Herod advanced to the gates of Jerusalem (15). Sosius arrived with a strong army, and siege operations were begun. It was a bitter struggle, with hand-to-hand combat, tunnels and countertunnels under the works, and sallies by Antigonus' men to burn the siege machinery. After 40 days the outer walls fell to the combined forces of Herod and Sosius, and 15 days later the inner fortifications were breached. The Temple and the upper city were taken by storm, with terrible slaughter. Surrendering, Antigonus threw himself at Sosius' feet to plead for his life. Sosius laughed at him, called him "Antigone" (the feminine of his name), and put him in irons. The Roman soldiers began to plunder and kill as reward for their efforts. Only after paying bonuses to each soldier and a huge sum to Sosius could Herod persuade the Romans to withdraw from the bleeding city, taking Antigonus with them. He was beheaded in Antioch at Herod's urging and on Antony's order.

It was 26 years since Pompey had taken Jerusalem, and the breaches he had made in the walls were gaping once again. Herod would rebuild the walls—and much more.

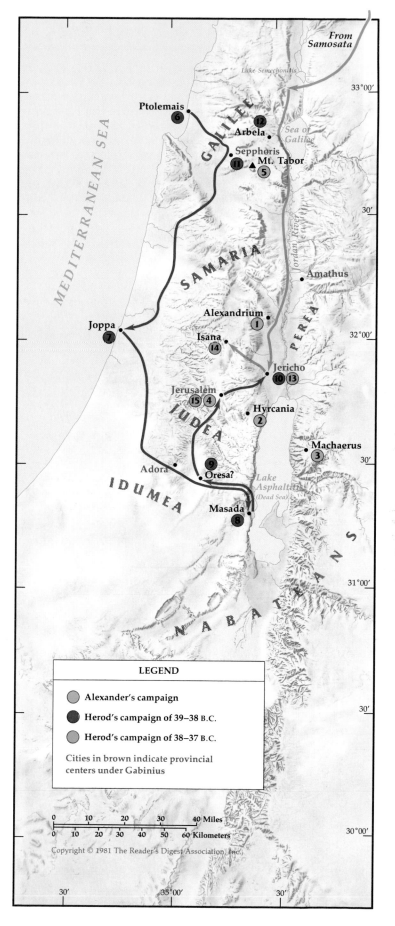

LEGEND

🔵 Alexander's campaign

⚫ Herod's campaign of 39–38 B.C.

🔵 Herod's campaign of 38–37 B.C.

Cities in brown indicate provincial centers under Gabinius

0   10   20   30   40 Miles

0   10   20   30   40   50   60 Kilometers

Copyright © 1981 The Reader's Digest Association, Inc.

Herod the Great

When the Romans marched out of Jerusalem (1) in 37 B.C., they left 36-year-old Herod master of Hyrcanus II's old kingdom (Judea, Galilee, Perea, and most of Idumea) plus areas recently granted him by the Roman Senate (Samaria, the Jamnia-Azotus region, and the rest of Idumea). But his patron, Marc Antony, was under the influence of Cleopatra VII, last and most famous of the Ptolemaic queens of Egypt. Intent on reestablishing the Ptolemaic empire, she pressed Antony for both Judea and the land of the Nabateans. He granted her the coastal region, thereby depriving Herod of access to the sea. Later, Antony added Nabatean areas and Herod's extensive plantations at Jericho (2) to her holdings, and Herod had to pay rent for use of his own plantations.

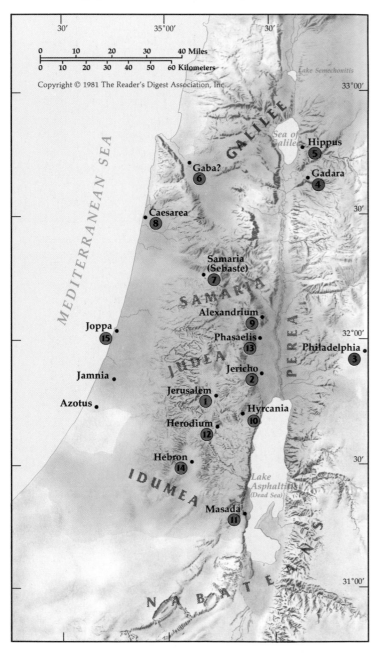

When civil war broke out between Antony and Octavian (later Caesar Augustus) in 32, Herod offered to help Antony but was ordered to campaign against the Nabateans. After a disastrous defeat at Canatha (off map), Herod avoided open battle to raid and plunder the land. About this time (spring of 31), a severe earthquake struck the area. Although Herod's army, camped in the open, was spared, upward of 30,000 perished in Judea alone. Expecting Judea to be helpless, the Nabateans resumed the war. Near Philadelphia (3), however, Herod handed them a crushing defeat and returned to Jerusalem in triumph. A short time later Antony was defeated by Octavian at Actium. Displaying the diplomatic skills of his father, Antipater, Herod adroitly switched sides.

When the inevitable command came for Herod to present himself before Octavian, he had old Hyrcanus II—"mild and moderate in all things"—put to death lest Octavian be tempted to restore the Hasmonean dynasty. Taking precautions to secure his family, Herod nervously set off for Rhodes and his interview with the victor of Actium. His fears proved groundless. Octavian realized that Herod was an important client king and confirmed his royal status. Further, after the suicides of Antony and Cleopatra, he restored to Herod the coastal regions and the city of Jericho as well as Gadara (4), Hippus (5), and Gaba (6). (Later, Augustus awarded Herod large areas in the Transjordan.) Herod's realm (shown in green) approached in size that of the Hasmonean golden age. But domestic tragedy began to threaten Herod's rule. In 29 he had his beloved wife, Mariamne (the granddaughter of Hyrcanus), executed for suspected adultery. In his grief he turned to drink and dissipation and fell seriously ill. Alexandra, a Hasmonean princess and his mother-in-law, attempted to seize power, but Herod recovered and had her put to death. Having secured firm control of his kingdom, Herod concentrated on his massive building program, whose stupendous remains are still to be seen. In a time of economic prosperity, there were extensive tax revenues for his projects.

He was already restoring Jerusalem militarily. The siege-battered walls had been rebuilt, and a massive new fortress, the Antonia, had been constructed. It featured four great towers and was guarded on three sides by steep inclines faced with smooth stones, making it one of the strongest posts in the east. Herod also built a theater and a hippodrome in the city and an amphitheater on the plain nearby. Here this Hellenistic king, who ruled over a kingdom of Jews and Gentiles, held musical concerts and athletic events. (Herod's love of athletics would be demonstrated in the year 12 when he underwrote the Olympic games in Greece and was named the games' "perpetual president.") A splendid new royal palace rose in Jerusalem. It contained immense banquet halls and lavish bedchambers. Rare stone decorated the walls, and silver and gold objects were everywhere. Circular cloisters opened onto long walks through magnificent gardens bordered by canals and pools with an abundance of bronze statuary.

In 27 Herod undertook to rebuild and enlarge Samaria (7), which was a day's march from Jerusalem, into a center for control of the countryside and as a place of refuge. The city was encircled by a wall two miles long. An enormous Corinthian-style temple rose over the ruins of the palace of Omri and Ahab. The 14 steps leading up to the entrance remain today; before the steps stood a statue of the emperor, the limbless torso of which survives. Herod renamed the city Sebaste, the Greek equivalent of Augustus, to whom it was dedicated. It was a Gentile city, and according to Josephus, "a first-class fortress."

A more grandiose scheme was the construction of a new port city Herod called Caesarea (8), also in honor of the emperor, on the sandy Mediterranean shore at the site of Strato's Tower. (See reconstruction on pages 196–197.) There were construction projects everywhere. He refurbished fortresses at Alexandrium (9), Hyrcania (10), and Masada (11; see also reconstruction on pages 170–171). He ordered new fortresses erected at Herodium (12), the place where he had fought off his pursuers on his flight from Jerusalem in 40, and at Jericho. North of Jericho he built the new city of Phasaelis (13), named for his fallen brother. At Hebron (14) he raised an immense shrine over the cave of Machpelah, the burial place of the Patriarchs. Constructed of the massive stones characteristic of his structures, it illustrates how the engineers used insets to break the monotony of vast walls without compromising their strength.

The project for which Herod is best remembered, however, is his rebuilding of the Temple in Jerusalem. Although he dedicated the Temple in 18, the full realization of his grand plan took 84 years. The platform for the complex was a marvel, extending out over the surrounding valleys. The Royal Portico at the southern end of the platform bespeaks the magnificence of the design: more than 800 feet long, it had 162 Corinthian columns, the tallest 100 feet high. The Temple stood within a series of great courts. Unfortunately, ancient writings do not give us an exact description, but (according to Josephus) "The expenditure devoted to this work was incalculable, its magnificence never surpassed." The enormous steps leading up to the southern entrance have recently been uncovered. A staircase led down to the Tyropoeon valley and its public gardens with walks and

Massive walls, the work of Herod's stonemasons, enclose the traditional burial site of the Patriarchs. Minarets and crenelations were added later.

pools. Parts of the garden have also been found.

Administratively, Herod operated an efficient and repressive police state. The kingdom was divided into five *merises* (Judea, Idumea, Samaria, Galilee, and Perea) and 22 toparchies, each with its administrative center. The Greek cities each had a governing council, but the two major Jewish cities—Jerusalem and Joppa (15)—were not governed along Hellenistic lines. To many Jews, however, Herod was a foreigner, without a claim to the throne.

Herod's family troubles dominated his declining years. He grew paranoid and had two of his sons executed for allegedly plotting against him. "I would sooner be Herod's pig than his son," Augustus is reported to have said. In about the year 5 B.C. Herod became grievously ill and had to be carried about on a couch. In his palace at Jericho he failed in a suicide attempt. As he neared death, he had a third son executed for treason. His will named three of his surviving sons to succeed him.

Herod died in the spring of the year 4 B.C. Archelaus saw to it that the funeral was splendid. Soldiers in battle armor accompanied the corpse robed in purple and wearing a crown of gold as it was borne into the hills and through the Judean wilderness to Herodium, where he was buried. But before Herod's death, there occurred an event—unrecorded at the time—that was to have momentous consequences: the birth of Jesus.

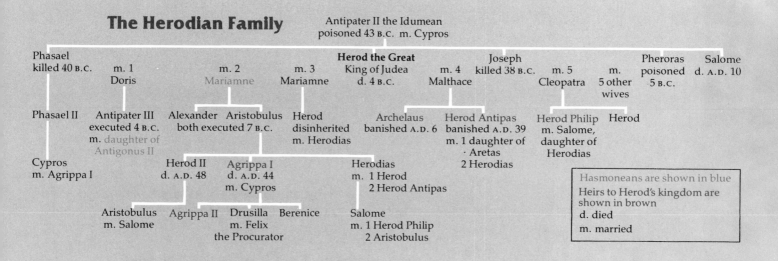

Masada:
Palace-Villa of Herod

A boat-shaped rock some 1,900 feet long and 650 feet wide, Masada stands in dramatic isolation above the Dead Sea's western shore. In the 1st century B.C. Herod the Great turned this remote outcropping into a walled fortress, including this extraordinary palace-villa—excavated and partially reconstructed by Israeli archaeologist Yigael Yadin in 1963–65. Herod built his villa on three terraces jutting out from the narrow north face of the rock, from which sheer cliffs drop breathtakingly away to the shore 1,300 feet below. Separated from the main palace and a complex of service buildings by a wall, the upper tier provided a personal retreat for Herod. Steps hollowed through the cliffs lead to the two lower terraces, largely man-made with massive retaining walls. Columned pavilions provided ample dining and lounging space for the enjoyment of an incomparable view.

V. Lazzaro

Birth of Jesus

Long recognized as eloquent confessions of faith in Jesus of Nazareth, the four Gospels—Matthew, Mark, Luke, and John—are not biographies in the modern sense. The writers show little interest in a detailed chronology; the geographic setting of many events is unclear. The earliest Gospel (perhaps written by John Mark in Rome following the death of Peter about A.D. 64) and the latest Gospel (sometimes attributed to a disciple of the Apostle John and dated to A.D. 90–100) begin with Jesus' baptism by his cousin John. The cherished stories of the birth and early life of Jesus appear only in the Gospels of Matthew (perhaps based on a collection of Jesus' sayings handed down from the Apostle Matthew) and Luke (who has been identified with "the beloved physician" of Colossians 4:14).

"Now when Jesus was born in Bethlehem of Judea in the days of Herod the king," writes Matthew—thus placing the Nativity before Herod's death in the year 4 B.C. But Luke tells us that the birth occurred at the time Augustus ordered a census "when Quirinius was governor of Syria." In A.D. 6 the emperor dispatched Quirinius to Syria at the same time Coponius was named first governor of Judea, and the two did indeed conduct a census. Yet Jesus would have had to be at least 10 years old by that date. Some scholars propose that Quirinius served an earlier term in Syria, from 10 to 7 B.C. Perhaps it was this period to which Luke refers.

A third clue to the date of the Nativity is the Star of Bethlehem. Chinese sources record a comet in 12 B.C. and a stellar explosion, or nova, in 5 B.C., either of which could have been the celestial guide to the three wise men seeking Jesus. Another explanation was proposed early in the 17th century when the German astronomer and mathematician Johannes Kepler observed the conjunction of the two planets Saturn and Jupiter within the constellation Pisces. Kepler remembered an ancient Hebrew tradition that the Messiah would appear when these two planets moved so close to one another that they appeared to be a single large star. Checking astronomical tables, Kepler found that Saturn and Jupiter had three such space rendezvous in the year 7 B.C.—on May 29, September 29, and December 4.

Could the "wise men from the East"—possibly astrologers in Babylonia—have observed the May 29 conjunction and seen it as a sign of the coming of the Messiah? Perhaps they waited until after the hot summer to start out along the caravan route to Judea, choosing the September date as an auspicious beginning for their journey. This would have brought them to the Bethlehem area toward mid-November, a time of the year when there still could have been, as Luke writes, "shepherds out in the field, keeping watch over their flock by night."

December 25 has been celebrated as the date of Jesus' birth only since the 4th century, when the Christian holiday came to supplant a Roman festival. And the system of numbering years from the supposed birth of Jesus has been used only since the 6th century. It is at least a possibility, reasoning from Kepler's original hypothesis, that Jesus was born in late autumn of the year 7 B.C.—though we will never know for certain.

Luke intertwines the birth narrative of Jesus with that of Jesus' cousin, John the Baptist. According to this account, a priest named Zechariah and his barren wife, Elizabeth, both advanced in years, came to Jerusalem (1). There Zechariah had the honor of performing the incense ceremony at the Temple, and in this holy shrine the angel Gabriel appeared and promised Zechariah a son, who "will turn many of the sons of Israel to the Lord their God . . . and make ready for the Lord a people prepared."

Six months later Gabriel "was sent from God to a city of Galilee named Nazareth" (2). There he announced to the virgin Mary that she would conceive a child and

"He will be great, and will be called
    the Son of the Most High;
and the Lord God will give to him the throne
    of his father David,
and he will reign over the house of Jacob
    for ever;
and of his kingdom there will be no end."

And Mary, having been told by the angel that Elizabeth had also conceived, rose and went "into the hill country, to a city of Judah" to see her kinswoman. This home of John the Baptist is not identified in the Gospels, but tradition has long located it at Ain Karim (3), a village in a strikingly attractive valley just under five miles west of Jerusalem. When Elizabeth heard Mary's greeting, the baby in her womb leaped for joy and she exclaimed: "Blessed are you among women, and blessed is the fruit of your womb! And why is this granted me, that the mother of my Lord should come to me?" Mary replied with a beautiful poem whose opening words are familiar: "My soul magnifies the Lord, and my spirit rejoices in God my Savior, . . ."

In this scene from a medieval stained-glass window, the three sleeping wise men are cautioned by an angel not to return to Jerusalem and tell a jealous King Herod where they have been.

When Elizabeth's child was born he was named John, meaning "the Lord has been gracious." We know nothing else about his life until he appeared along the banks of the Jordan River baptizing and proclaiming the coming of the kingdom of God.

Meanwhile, Mary and her husband, Joseph, went from Nazareth (4) to Bethlehem (5) in Judea to be enrolled in the Roman census because Joseph was of the house and lineage of David. Bethlehem, the city of Da-

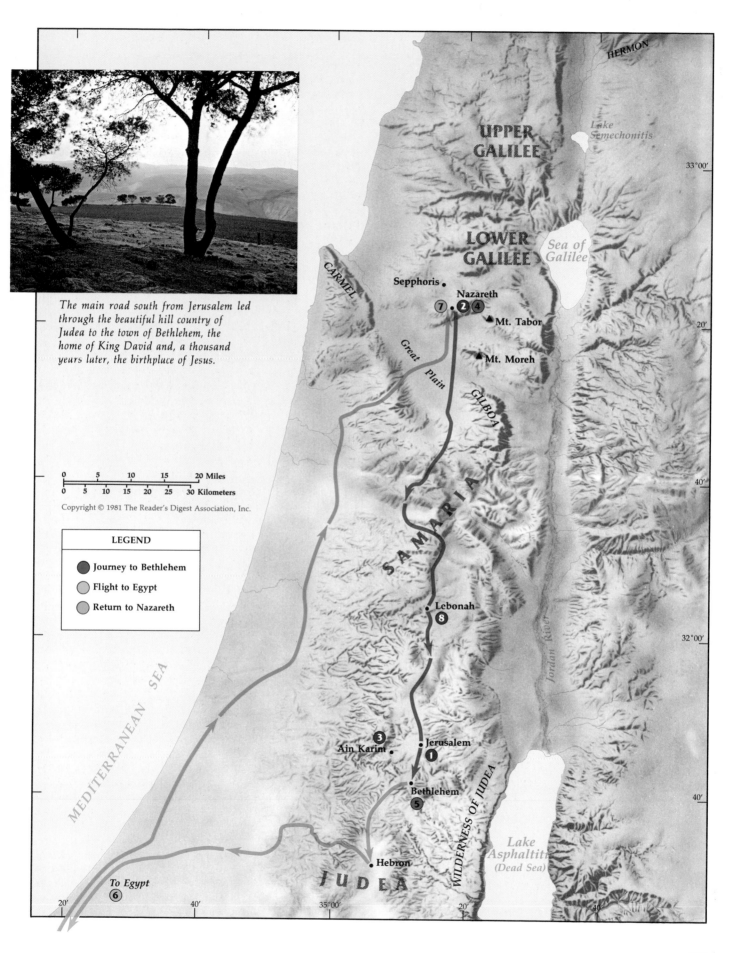

The main road south from Jerusalem led through the beautiful hill country of Judea to the town of Bethlehem, the home of King David and, a thousand years later, the birthplace of Jesus.

HERMON

Lake Semechonitis

UPPER GALILEE

LOWER GALILEE

Sea of Galilee

33°00'

CARMEL

Sepphoris

Nazareth ⑦ ② ④

Mt. Tabor

Great Plain

Mt. Moreh

GILBOA

20'

0   5   10   15   20 Miles
0   5   10   15   20   25   30 Kilometers

Copyright © 1981 The Reader's Digest Association, Inc.

40'

SAMARIA

LEGEND

● Journey to Bethlehem
○ Flight to Egypt
● Return to Nazareth

Jordan River

Lebonah ⑧

32°00'

MEDITERRANEAN SEA

Ain Karim ③

Jerusalem ①

Bethlehem ⑤

WILDERNESS OF JUDEA

40'

Lake Asphaltitis (Dead Sea)

To Egypt ⑥

Hebron

JUDEA

20'   40'   35°00'   20'   40'

Birth of Jesus (continued)

vid's birth and early life, was an important village on the north-south ridge route between Jerusalem and Hebron. Surrounded by verdant fields and lush olive groves, it boasts a setting justifying its name, "house of bread." Yet from the hard limestone on which Bethlehem stands, the stark Wilderness of Judea drops off swiftly to the east. Clearly visible are the barren mountains beyond the narrow blue stripe of the Dead Sea—14 miles away and 3,750 feet lower in elevation.

The inns of Bethlehem were always filled with travelers going to and coming from Jerusalem, five miles to the north. During the census the village would have been even more crowded. Thus Jesus was born in a stable—probably a cave where animals were usually kept—and laid in a manger. The traditional site of this cave, mentioned in Christian writings of the 2nd century, was incorporated into a 4th-century church built by Constantine. Rebuilt by Justinian in the 6th century, the basilica is one of the oldest churches in the world.

Luke tells us that an angel proclaimed the birth of Jesus to shepherds in nearby fields, and they hurried to Bethlehem to see this wonderful child. It is also Luke who recounts Jesus' circumcision on the eighth day, as is required by Jewish law; and his formal naming: *Yehoshuah* (Joshua) in Hebrew but *Jesus* in English, which means "the Lord saves." When Mary and Joseph took him to the Temple in Jerusalem to present him to the Lord—as required by Jewish law for the firstborn—and to offer a sacrifice of thanksgiving, two devout persons, Simeon and Anna, blessed God and gave thanks for the child. Simeon said:

"Lord, now lettest thou thy servant depart in peace,
   according to thy word;
 for mine eyes have seen thy salvation . . ."

Matthew does not tell of such a journey to Jerusalem but instead relates the story of the "wise men from the East." Their inquiries in Jerusalem as to the whereabouts of a new "king of the Jews" alarmed Herod, who tried to trick them into telling him where the infant could be found. Going on to Bethlehem, the wise men found the infant Jesus with his mother, worshiped him, and "opening their treasures, they offered him gifts, gold and frankincense and myrrh." But warned in a dream of Herod's true motives, they avoided Jerusalem on their return to their own land.

Joseph, likewise warned, fled with Mary and the child, Jesus, into Egypt (6), the traditional country of refuge since the time of Abraham. Thus Jesus was safe from Herod's rage, who, Matthew says, ordered the death of all male children in and around Bethlehem two years old or younger in order to eliminate a potential rival. Although Christian and Muslim traditions name 19 places in the Delta and Upper Egypt as having been visited by the Holy Family, there is no biblical evidence for such identification.

"Rise, take the child and his mother," Joseph was commanded in a dream, "and go to the land of Israel, for those who sought the child's life are dead." They nonetheless bypassed Judea, where Archelaus had succeeded his father, Herod, and came to Galilee, "and dwelt in a city called Nazareth" (7).

Nazareth sits in a basin 1,300 feet above sea level on the southernmost of the lateral ridges of Lower Galilee. To the south lies the Great Plain with the constant movement of commerce winding eastward past Mount Tabor, that singular massive hill rising out of the plain. The hills of Samaria are easily visible, as is Mount Moreh to the southeast and the great ridge of Gilboa beyond that. Westward the Carmel range can be seen, with the Mediterranean Sea shining on the horizon. Northward, four miles away, is the hill dominated in Jesus' day by the Gentile city of Sepphoris. But in the distance to the northeast—more than 50 miles away—the snowy heights of Mount Hermon tower above all.

There is a single spring—today called Mary's Well—in the limestone at Nazareth, but the annual rainfall of 25 inches amply nourishes the surrounding hills covered with citrus and olive groves. And the elevation, combined with the pleasant dry wind, makes the temperature 10 to 20 degrees cooler than in the coastal plain and much pleasanter than that of the hot, humid lakeshore of the Sea of Galilee, 16 miles away and 695 feet below sea level.

Nazareth was a small Jewish village, one of many in predominantly Gentile Galilee. There was a synagogue there, and Jesus along with the other boys of the village would have heard stirring stories of the great heroes of Israel's faith. Sadly, little if anything of Jesus' Nazareth remains. It was obliterated by Muslim fanatics in early medieval times, and the modern town sprawling over the hills has placed any substantial remains beyond the archaeologist's spade, although pious tradition identifies several holy places. Yet the geography is sufficient to recover a sense of the pleasant setting in which Jesus "grew and became strong, filled with wisdom; and the favor of God was upon him." And Jesus' later sayings reflect his keen observation of the land where he grew up, for he speaks of lilies of the field, of sowing and reaping, of the shepherd's care for his flock, and of nets thrown into the Sea of Galilee being filled with fish of every kind.

At the age of 12 (again Luke is our guide) Jesus—as was customary among Jewish boys of that time and place—was taken to Jerusalem by his parents to celebrate Passover. There in the midst of extensive construction still going on to complete Herod's spectacular plan, Jesus would have seen the soaring, white and gold sanctuary with pilgrims crowding its incense-shrouded courtyards. After the feast was over, his parents—thinking him among their kinsmen and friends on the way back to Galilee—journeyed for a day, probably coming to the steep Ascent of Lebonah (8). As they camped for the night, they discovered their son was missing. Returning to Jerusalem, they found him among the learned teachers in the Temple, "listening to them and asking them questions; and all who heard him were amazed at his understanding and his answers." When his parents admonished him for causing them anxiety, he replied: "Did you not know that I must be in my Father's house?" But he went back to Nazareth—three days journey—and we hear no more of him until he came to John and was baptized in the Jordan River.

The Nativity

Few subjects, spiritual or secular, have inspired so many works of art over so long a period of time as has the story of the Nativity. The only biblical description of Jesus' birth, found in the Gospel of Luke, is well known and brief: "And she gave birth to her first-born son and wrapped him in swaddling cloths, and laid him in a manger, because there was no place for them in the inn." An early tradition added an ox and an ass to the scene, as in the mosaic above. It was common for artists to incorporate various non-biblical details in their portrayals of Gospel stories. Thus, for example, the mosaic at right, depicting the Holy Family's Flight into Egypt, includes a fourth person, mentioned nowhere in the biblical narrative.

Above, this celebrated 5th-century mosaic of the Nativity adorns Rome's Church of Santa Maria Maggiore. Below, the Flight into Egypt was one of many biblical scenes executed in mosaic on the dome of the Florence Baptistery in the late-13th and early-14th centuries.

The Holy Land After Herod

The land in which Jesus of Nazareth was growing to maturity—though nominally ruled by the successors of Herod—was but a remote eastern outpost of Rome's Mediterranean empire. As specified in his last will, Herod's kingdom was divided into three main political areas following his death in 4 B.C. Archelaus—Herod's son by a Samaritan wife—was to reign as king in Jerusalem (1) over Judea, Idumea, and Samaria. His territory included the Hellenistic cities of Sebaste (2) and Caesarea (3). Herod Antipas, Archelaus' younger brother, was to be tetrarch of Galilee and Perea—territories separated by the cities of the Decapolis. Their half brother Philip—son of Cleopatra, one of Herod's Jewish wives—was to be tetrarch of the mainly Gentile areas north and east of the Sea of Galilee. Continuing well beyond this map, it was a large but relatively poor area.

Salome, Herod's sister, received Jamnia (4), Azotus (5), Phasaelis (6), and Herod's palace in the free city of Ascalon (7). The Hellenistic cities of Gaza (8) on the coast and Gadara (9) and Hippus (10) beyond the Jordan were placed directly under the governor of Syria, the highest ranking Roman official in the east.

This division into so many seemingly distinct political units suggests a fragmented kingdom. In reality, Roman rule would give the area unity if not necessarily stability. But nothing about this division could be done until the emperor Augustus ratified Herod's will.

After seven days of mourning, Archelaus went up to Jerusalem, where the populace was protesting his late father's execution of two rabbis. His attempt at pacification miscarried, and he was forced to call out troops to quell rioting in which 3,000 of his subjects were killed. Not even Herod's repressive rule had seen such an outrage. When he sailed from Caesarea for Rome to have his father's will ratified, Archelaus left Philip behind to rule in an explosive situation. Antipas soon appeared in Rome to press his claims—under a previous will—to be sole ruler of his father's domains. Later Philip arrived to support Archelaus and, incidentally, to safeguard his own interests.

Because rioting continued in Jerusalem and even spread to the countryside, Varus, Roman governor of Syria, came in force to control the unrest. Returning north, he left a legion behind to maintain order. But his chief financial officer, Sabinus, inflamed matters more by trying to seize Herod's treasure, ostensibly to hold it for the emperor. Archelaus' soldiers successfully resisted Sabinus and the situation grew tense. At the Feast of Pentecost, as pilgrims flocked to Jerusalem from Galilee, Idumea, Perea, and elsewhere, serious fighting broke out in the streets of the city. Many of Herod's veterans went over to the rebel force, while Roman soldiers and 3,000 auxiliaries, mostly from Sebaste, tried to subdue them.

Spontaneous uprisings now occurred throughout the country. In Judea 2,000 of Herod's seasoned soldiers forced loyal troops led by Achiab, Herod's cousin, out of the plains into the hills while a shepherd named Athronges proclaimed himself king and waged guerrilla warfare. In Galilee one Judas, in the words of Josephus, "became an object of terror to all men." He and a large number of other brigands seized Sepphoris (11) and plundered the city, including the royal palace. Men led by Simon, a former slave of Herod's, burned the splendid palace at Jericho (12), where the old king had died, and were likely responsible for the destruction of the royal residence at Beth-ramatha (13). At length Simon was tracked down and beheaded. But violence continued in Perea, with the palace at Amathus (14) also being burned.

As brigandage, terror, and anarchy spread, Varus' response was swift. With the two remaining regular legions stationed in Syria and with four cavalry troops, he came to Ptolemais (15), where he was joined by a considerable body of Nabatean infantry and cavalry sent by Aretas IV, who had hated Herod.

Varus sent troops under his son's command to drive rebels from western Galilee. They took Sepphoris, sold its inhabitants into slavery, and burned the city. Meanwhile, Varus proceeded to Sebaste (16) with the main body of his army. Sparing this loyal city, he made camp some 11 miles south, at Arus (17), a strategic village within striking distance of Jerusalem. As Varus moved toward Jerusalem, the Nabateans looted and burned Arus and, farther south, the village of Sappho (18). Emmaus (19) was burned on Varus' orders.

As the Roman legions approached Jerusalem (20), the Jews working on the unfinished defenses scattered and Varus easily entered the city to relieve the Romans under siege within its walls. The governor's troops went everywhere in the land, seeking rebels. Many who were captured were released, but 2,000 were crucified. Persuaded by Achiab, a force of 10,000 men surrendered to Varus without battle. Most were pardoned, but the ringleaders were sent to Rome, where Augustus let most of them go except for those who were related to Herod.

Augustus, who had procrastinated in the face of competing claims by Archelaus and Antipas and a delegation of Jews who wanted direct Roman rule, at last announced his decision. He confirmed Herod's will but denied Archelaus the royal title until he should prove himself worthy. He was, however, to be ethnarch, a title higher than tetrarch, which was given to his brothers.

His prestige badly damaged by being denied the kingly title, Archelaus returned to Jerusalem, where he reigned just under 10 years. Herod's son, who was of Idumean and Samaritan extraction and Roman in education, proved to be an oppressive ruler. In A.D. 6 a delegation of Jews and Samaritans charged Archelaus with cruelty toward his subjects in express violation of Augustus' orders. Summoned by the emperor to Rome, Archelaus was deposed and banished to Gaul. Samaria, Judea, and Idumea were united as the Roman province of Judea.

Antipas, on the other hand, brought peace and prosperity to Galilee and Perea and ruled for almost 43 years before he, too, was deposed. After the downfall of his elder brother Archelaus, Antipas took the name Herod and is mentioned thus 24 times in the New Testament.

Perea had long been a center of Jewish life, and Galilee—though largely Gentile—had a significant Jewish population. Antipas came to Jerusalem for the great Jewish festivals, and his coins bore no images that would offend his Jewish subjects. Not only did the Pharisees support Antipas, but a new aristocratic sect—the Herodians—emerged in his support. The Herodians were pro-Roman, but having seen the results of direct Roman rule in Judea after Archelaus, they wished to be ruled indirectly through a native prince.

Antipas rebuilt the leading cities of Galilee and Perea, which had been destroyed in the uprisings and the subsequent War of Varus. Sepphoris was renamed Autocratoris (Greek for "emperor"), while Beth-ramatha in Perea was first renamed Livias, in honor of Augustus' wife, and later Julias, when Livia was adopted into the Julian clan on the death of Augustus. It was the administrative center for Perea. But for his capital, Antipas built a magnificent new city at the famous warm springs on the western shore of the Sea of Galilee. Under construction for perhaps nine years, it was dedicated in A.D. 18 and named Tiberias (21) for the emperor. Its great palace had a gold roof and housed numerous precious objects. The sports stadium held as many as 10,000 people (out of a population of perhaps 30,000 to 40,000). Although builders discovered an ancient cemetery on the site—rendering the city unclean under Jewish law—a segment of the population was Jewish.

It was Antipas, as we shall see, who ordered the execution of John the Baptist and later interrogated Jesus on the eve of his crucifixion. Some 10 years later—in A.D. 39—Antipas ran afoul of the new emperor, Caligula, and was also deposed and banished to Gaul.

Of Herod's three successors, Philip had the most uneventful reign. He inherited the rugged north with its towering mountains, rough steppeland, and broad plateaus. He ruled his predominantly Gentile population with what the historian Josephus called a "moderate and easygoing disposition." In the beautiful, lush regions at the headwaters of the Jordan River, he enlarged Paneas, made it his capital, and called it Caesarea Philippi (22) to distinguish it from Herod's great port; it is mentioned by this name in the New Testament. Near where the Jordan flows into the Sea of Galilee he turned the fishing village of Bethsaida (23)—the home of Jesus' disciples Peter, Andrew, and Philip—into a town which he called Julias in honor of Augustus' daughter. Here Philip was buried after a reign of 37 years. He had lived out his life quietly within his own domain, enjoying his last years with his wife, Salome—the same Salome who had danced for Antipas and called for the head of John the Baptist.

While Antipas and Philip ruled to the north, Judea remained peaceful under the first three Roman governors. The center of government was shifted from Jerusalem to Caesarea, a city with direct connections to Rome by sea. No legions were stationed in Judea. There were only local auxiliaries—about 3,000 men—mostly drawn from non-Jewish Sebaste and Caesarea. However, when Valerius Gratus, the first of Tiberius' governors, came to Judea in A.D. 15, he deposed the High Priest, Annas, who

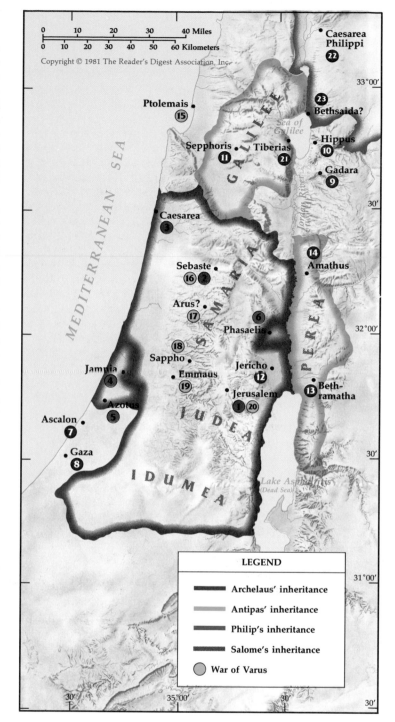

LEGEND

Archelaus' inheritance
Antipas' inheritance
Philip's inheritance
Salome's inheritance
○ War of Varus

had been installed earlier in a gesture of conciliation. Three years later, however, Annas' son-in-law, Joseph Caiaphas, was given the office.

In A.D. 26, matters in Judea took a serious turn for the worse with the coming of Pontius Pilate as governor. Violence was met with violence, and executions were not uncommon. Caiaphas was a faithful ally of Pilate's in seeking to prevent the kind of outburst that would bring the full weight of Rome down on the Jews once more. In his 10 years in Caesarea, Pilate came to be widely disliked and was eventually removed on a charge of maladministration. A minor figure in Roman history, Pilate was nonetheless to win unending notoriety as the man who authorized the execution of Jesus of Nazareth.

Jesus in Galilee

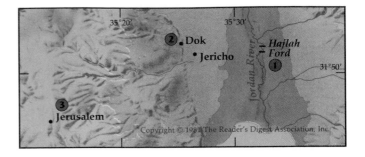

Copyright © 1981 The Reader's Digest Association, Inc.

Mark and John begin their Gospel narratives with John the Baptist—an extraordinary personage, Mark tells us, who "appeared in the wilderness, preaching a baptism of repentance for the forgiveness of sins." This "man sent from God," John testifies, "was not the light, but came to bear witness to the light."

John the Baptist came from the hill country of Judea, but much of his ministry was along the eastern banks of the Jordan River—in Perea, an area ruled by Antipas. His urgent call to prepare for the imminent coming of the kingdom of God alarmed not only Antipas but also the religious authorities in Jerusalem.

The date of Jesus' baptism by John is not known, although many place it in A.D. 26—the same year Pontius Pilate came to Caesarea as governor of Judea. The site of Jesus' baptism is equally unclear. John says it took place in "Bethany beyond the Jordan," an unidentified site, though Christian tradition since at least the 6th century has named the Hajlah ford (1, on smaller map at top of the page) east of Jericho.

After his baptism, Jesus "was led up by the Spirit into the wilderness to be tempted by the devil." The "wilderness" seems to mean the desolate hills above Jericho, and it is there that Christian tradition has hallowed a prominent mountain—the site of the ancient fortress of Dok (2)—as the place where the devil showed Jesus the kingdoms of the world. The devil also took Jesus to Jerusalem (3), "set him on the pinnacle of the temple," and challenged him to throw himself down and call for rescue by angels. But Jesus put the devil behind and returned to Galilee to take up his own ministry.

Meanwhile John had criticized Antipas' marriage to Herodias, because she had previously been married to and borne a child by one of his brothers. For such impertinence, the historian Josephus relates, John was ar- rested and shut up in the fortress at Machaerus (4, on locator opposite). While Antipas was there at a great banquet, his young stepdaughter Salome danced for him. So taken was Antipas, he promised her anything she wanted. Carefully coached by her mother, Herodias, she asked for the head of John the Baptist.

After John's arrest, Jesus came forth in Galilee, saying, "The time is fulfilled, and the kingdom of God is at hand; repent, and believe in the gospel." Luke suggests that Jesus taught in many synagogues and also relates the story of Jesus' rejection by his home synagogue at Nazareth (5, on larger map opposite) before shifting his ministry to the shores of the Sea of Galilee.

It was here that Jesus gathered his first disciples. Si- mon Peter and his brother Andrew—fishermen from Bethsaida (6)—were called while casting their net into the sea. "Follow me," said Jesus, "and I will make you fishers of men." No location is given for this summons; but where streams empty into the lake, men still wade into the waters casting their nets to catch fish feeding close to the shore. And another pair of brothers, James and John, the sons of Zebedee, were called while mend- ing fishing nets. And Jesus called Philip, also from Beth- saida. Cana (7) was the home of Simon, another of Jesus' apostles, and also of Nathanael, whom Philip brought to Jesus. Later Jesus called others including Matthew, a tax collector in Capernaum (8). Since Capernaum was the

One of the geographical puzzles that intrigues students of the New Testament concerns the site of Je- sus' baptism. The only biblical reference, in the Gospel of John, identifies the site as "Bethany be- yond the Jordan," which an early tradition placed southeast of Jeri- cho and was so located on the 6th- century Medeba map (see page 30). Although there is no historical evidence to confirm the tradition, this tranquil stretch of the Jordan River just north of where it empties into the Dead Sea is often sought out by pilgrims to the Holy Land. Shown in the inset is a 5th-century mosaic of the baptism, from the dome of the Baptistery of the Orthodox in Ravenna, Italy.

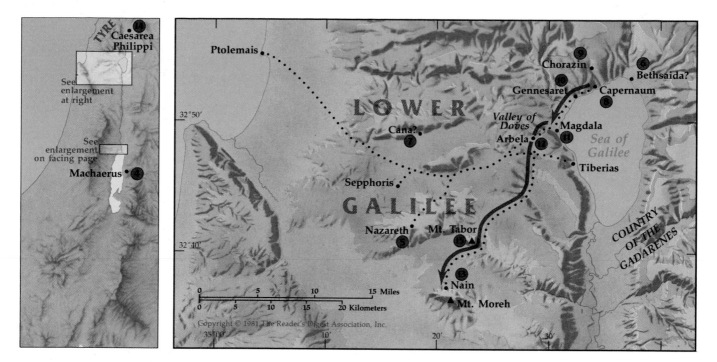

first town on the lakeshore inside the realm of Antipas as one came from Bethsaida, which lay inside the territory of the tetrarch Philip, Matthew may well have been an agent for collection of duties.

Jesus confined his preaching and healing largely to a tiny area around the Sea of Galilee, mostly in the Jewish villages along the western shore and in the hills of Lower Galilee. Capernaum is 20 miles from Nazareth, where Jesus grew up. From Bethsaida, where Jesus healed a blind man, to the country of the Gadarenes southeast of the Sea of Galilee, where he cured two demoniacs, is about 15 miles by road. Yet even with so small an arena we can at best gain only an impression of Jesus' ministry, for the Gospels provide no connected chronology, and events and sayings are more often than not reported without geographical context. While Matthew, Mark, and Luke give roughly parallel accounts, they are not in total agreement. John's Gospel seems to follow a chronology of its own, reporting events not mentioned in the other three. Consequently it is impossible to make a coherent narrative of this period in Jesus' life or to reconstruct any plausible itinerary for his travels through Galilee and the adjacent regions.

Originally a small Jewish fishing village, Capernaum had grown to become an important town on the route from Philip's tetrarchy to that of Antipas. It lay on a narrow plain—the black basalt hills rise hardly 750 feet from the shore. Yet the stony beach at Capernaum was the scene of constant activity as boats from other Jewish fishing villages stopped there because the richest fishing grounds in the lake lay between Capernaum and Bethsaida. It was Capernaum that became the center of Jesus' Galilean ministry, so much so, Mark says, that there Jesus was "at home."

Although Jesus withdrew at times for prayer and reflection, it became increasingly difficult to do so as his fame spread. On one remarkable occasion, as he taught in a house at Capernaum, four men brought a paralytic to be healed. Unable to get through the crowd, they went up onto the roof, removed part of it, and lowered the pallet bearing their friend into the presence of Jesus. On another occasion, we are told by Mark, "the whole city was gathered together about the door" of the house where Jesus was staying. The most famous instance of Jesus' preaching to the multitudes was when he went up on a mountain and began to teach the people, saying:

"Blessed are the poor in spirit,
for theirs is the kingdom of heaven. . . ."

We do not know where the Sermon on the Mount took place. Yet tradition has hallowed various sites for this profound body of teaching, and today, just south of Capernaum on a prominent hill overlooking the lake, there is an Italian nunnery on what is known as the Mount of the Beatitudes.

People even came to Capernaum by boat from Tiberias and elsewhere around the lake seeking Jesus. And Jesus went out from Capernaum to teach in the synagogues of other towns. We are not told the itinerary of this or any of the other journeys of Jesus in Galilee, but we know he visited Chorazin and Bethsaida.

Two miles north of Capernaum, as one follows the difficult route up a steep watercourse, lay the village of Chorazin (9) on a rocky eminence offering a superb view of the Sea of Galilee 885 feet below. Sitting partly in a ravine and partly on a rocky outcropping, the village was dominated by a synagogue. Today extensive and striking remains of a 3rd-century synagogue built of the black basalt of the region sit in the midst of long-unused streets lined with the tumble of ancient shops and houses. The stones of the synagogue are richly ornamented and bespeak some wealth. Among these ruins was found a "seat of Moses" bearing an inscription in Aramaic, the language Jesus spoke. Here the teacher of the Law would have sat. While the seat of Moses at Chorazin is from a later time than that of Jesus, it recalls his words: "The scribes and the Pharisees sit on Moses' seat; so practice and observe whatever they tell you, but not what they do; for they preach, but do not practice."

Fishing in the Sea of Galilee

"Follow me, and I will make you fishers of men." So said Jesus to Simon Peter and Andrew, his first two disciples—an encounter depicted in the mosaic above. The Sea of Galilee figured prominently in Jesus' early ministry, to be sure, but no more so than it did in the everyday life of the Holy Land. Fish was a far more important staple food than meat for most of the population, and the Sea of Galilee was the principal source. Some 13 miles long and up to 8 miles wide, the large lake was productive enough not only to supply fresh fish for the surrounding region but also to support a thriving industry in Capernaum and other shore towns where large quantities of fish were salted and dried for shipment throughout the Roman empire.

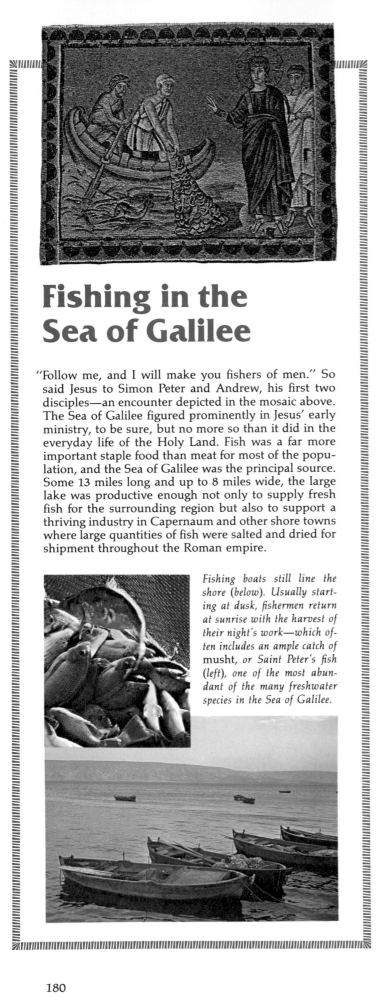

Fishing boats still line the shore (below). Usually starting at dusk, fishermen return at sunrise with the harvest of their night's work—which often includes an ample catch of musht, or Saint Peter's fish (left), one of the most abundant of the many freshwater species in the Sea of Galilee.

Jesus in Galilee (continued)

Bethsaida, a fishing village enlarged, embellished, fortified, and renamed Julias by Philip while Jesus was still a small child, has not been firmly identified. There is neither clear tradition nor archaeological evidence to guide us. It probably sat near the confluence of the Jordan River and the lake some three miles from Capernaum.

Jesus also went up from the lakeshore to the Jewish villages in Lower Galilee. Geography suggests the route that he would have taken. From Capernaum he followed the lakeshore southward through Gennesaret (10) to Magdala (11), the home of Mary Magdalene. Since the building of Tiberias, Magdala had lost much of its importance, but it still supported a large fishing industry. Westward the path turned up the extraordinary rift leading 860 feet up from the lakeshore to the basalt plateau dominated by the extinct volcano known now as the Horns of Hattin. This rift, called the Valley of Doves, is narrow, steep, and dangerous. Sheer cliffs punctuated by caves tower on both sides; the northern wall rises to over 320 feet above sea level while the southern side soars to almost 600 feet above sea level—or almost 1,300 feet above the surface of the Sea of Galilee.

At the top of this climb Jesus would have seen the village of Arbela (12)—where perhaps he ministered—and the extensive wheat fields running from the village to the slopes of Hattin. From Arbela an easy route traversed the fields and shortly joined the main road from Tiberias to Ptolemais. From this well-traveled route, spurs ran to Sepphoris and Nazareth. But Jesus could have made directly for Nain (13). At some point he was certainly in this small village nestled on a plateau on the lower northern slopes of Mount Moreh, for it was there he raised a widow's son from the dead. He seems also to have been once more in Cana—scene of his first miracle, related only by John, of changing water into wine at a wedding feast—for at Cana he healed the son of an official of Antipas.

We know that Jesus did not always work alone. According to Luke, he "appointed seventy others, and sent them on ahead of him, two by two, into every town and place where he himself was about to come." He also commissioned the Twelve Apostles to go and preach in the towns and villages of Galilee but sternly commanded them to take nothing for their journey and to "shake off the dust from your feet" as a testimony against those places that did not receive them.

But always Jesus and his disciples returned to the lakeshore and Capernaum. The crowds sought him out, and so did Antipas, who, hearing of Jesus' miracles, feared he was John the Baptist come back from the dead and wanted to see him. Nonetheless, Jesus continued his work. When his disciples returned from their journey through Galilee, Jesus sought to take them to a lonely place where they could rest for a while. But people saw their boat departing and ran along the shore, so that when Jesus arrived a great throng was waiting for him. In one of the best known of the miracle stories, "he welcomed them and spoke to them of the kingdom of God," and near the end of the day, when his disciples reminded him that the people had no food, Jesus fed the multitude of 5,000 with five loaves and two fish. Then he sent his disciples away by boat and, dismissing the crowds, "went up on the mountain by himself to pray." When evening came the boat was far out on the lake, but the disciples were having difficulty making headway in the rough seas, "for the wind was against them." Just before dawn Jesus came "walking on the sea" toward the boat and, calming the disciples' fears, got into the boat with them. And when they landed at Gennesaret, people recognized Jesus and brought the sick to him that they might be healed.

On another occasion Jesus and his disciples sailed in one of their fishing boats toward "the country of the Gadarenes." The winds coming over the hills west of the Sea of Galilee sometimes sweep down onto the lake stirring up sudden storms. The Valley of Doves often acts as a funnel, trapping the violent westerly winds and causing them to swirl over the surface of the shallow lake. Although this can occur in summer, it is more common in winter. "And a storm of wind came down on the lake," says Luke "and they were filling with water, and were in danger." Jesus—asleep in the boat—was awakened by the experienced but frightened fishermen with the news that they were perishing. But Jesus "rebuked the wind and the raging waves; and they ceased, and there was a calm."

Jesus' activity was not restricted to Galilee. He visited Jerusalem on several occasions (see page 182) and also undertook a journey to "the region of Tyre [see locator on page 179] and Sidon," from which many people had come to hear him. It is not clear how far north or west Jesus went. Part of the region of Tyre extended across Upper Galilee, and it may be that Jesus ministered there, but we cannot be sure. Mark says that he returned "through the region of the Decapolis," east of the Jordan, but it is difficult to understand why he would have taken such a roundabout route home. Matthew reports simply that when Jesus returned to Galilee from the district of Tyre, he went up into the hills, where "great crowds came to him, bringing with them the lame, the maimed, the blind, the dumb, and many others, and they put them at his feet, and he healed them."

Eventually the crowds began to desert Jesus. He had failed to live up to the hopes of the people for a nationalistic messiah who would drive out the Romans. And although some of the Pharisees of Galilee befriended him, others argued with him, constantly wanting to know the source of his authority. Now, at a crucial point in his Galilean ministry, Jesus withdrew with his disciples to the district around Caesarea Philippi (14, on locator). Here beneath the slopes of Mount Hermon, in this lovely area watered by the cold, rushing streams that converge to form the Jordan River, Jesus closely questioned his fol-

Only two partly excavated ruins remain today from Capernaum: a once-splendid 4th-century synagogue (above) and the foundation of a 5th-century church said to mark the site of Peter's house. Though not from Jesus' time, they are reminders of the town's religious significance.

lowers as to what people thought of him and his mission. And they answered him by saying that some thought he was John the Baptist returned from the dead, others thought he was Elijah, while still others identified him as "Jeremiah or one of the prophets." But Simon Peter confessed that "You are the Christ, the Son of the living God." And from that time on Jesus began to tell the disciples how he must suffer, be rejected, be killed, and rise again.

Six days later Jesus, taking only Peter, James, and John with him, went up a "high mountain apart" and was transfigured before them. Elijah and Moses appeared and talked with the radiant Jesus. And a voice was heard from heaven, saying, "This is my beloved Son, . . . listen to him." No location is given in the Gospels for this intense religious experience. But a "high mountain apart" suggested to early pilgrims Mount Tabor (15), and by the 6th century three churches stood on the summit of that isolated hill—one for each of the booths the disciples wished to make for Jesus, Elijah, and Moses.

And even though Jesus continued his ministry in Galilee, more and more he instructed his disciples privately and told them how he must die and after three days rise, but they did not understand this. At some point—we do not know when— friendly Pharisees came to Jesus, saying, "Get away from here, for Herod [Antipas] wants to kill you." Jesus ordered them to tell "that fox" that he must first finish his work in Galilee. "Nevertheless," said Jesus, "I must go on my way today and tomorrow and the day following; for it cannot be that a prophet should perish away from Jerusalem."

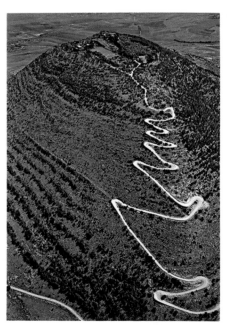

Hairpin turns mark the ascent to the isolated peak of Mount Tabor, long identified as the "high mountain apart" on which Peter, James, and John witnessed Jesus' transfiguration.

Jesus' Journeys to Jerusalem

"Three times in the year you shall keep a feast to me." Thus did the Law of Moses prescribe the three great Jewish festivals: Passover, Pentecost, and Tabernacles. To observe those feasts properly, male Jews were to present themselves in the Temple at Jerusalem. Since it was nearly impossible for Jews throughout the Diaspora to come to Jerusalem three times a year, making the great pilgrimage was the dream of a lifetime. Within the land itself, however, Jews had greater opportunity to journey to Jerusalem.

Commercial travelers and religious pilgrims were frequently on the roads, but journeys were hardly undertaken for pleasure as they were difficult, dangerous, and—except for the rich—long, since most went on foot. Travelers had to carry their provisions with them or be prepared to buy food in the villages (though it was not always available, and even water was sometimes jealously guarded). Danger was an ever-present companion, particularly for the lonely traveler who might suddenly fall "among robbers, who stripped him and beat him, and departed, leaving him half dead"—as in the Good Samaritan tale. Throughout its ancient history the Holy Land was plagued by highwaymen, and it was no different in Jesus' day as one Roman governor after another made safe passage along the routes a major, if unobtain-

able, goal. It was therefore not unusual for Jews coming to Jerusalem from Babylonia to travel in large caravans; even within the province of Judea men traveled in groups, as we learn from the Gospels.

"It was the custom of the Galileans at the time of a festival to pass through the Samaritan territory on their way to the Holy City," Josephus wrote. He is therein identifying the direct route that entered the hills of Samaria at Ginae (1) and, winding its way southward past Mount Gerizim, came up to Jerusalem (2) by the ancient north-south ridge route. Yet direct as this route was, it was often avoided by Jews, so great was the enmity between Jew and Samaritan. Only a few years after the time of Jesus, the inhabitants of Ginae fought with Jewish pilgrims from Galilee, killing a number of them. This was an outbreak of the deep hatreds that existed in the land and had added to the dangers along the roads as Jesus went back and forth between Galilee and Jerusalem.

The Gospel of John reports that Jesus was in Jerusalem on at least five occasions during the years of his ministry. According to John, Jesus went up to Jerusalem for Passover soon after the call of his first disciples and the miracle at Cana. Perhaps he traveled the central ridge route.

On his return to Galilee, Jesus would most likely have retraced his path through the heart of Samaria. As he walked along the broad, hot (it was in the springtime) valley floor north of the Ascent of Lebonah (3), he saw the low-lying hills to the east and the gradually rising heights to the west. Then Mount Gerizim came into view. Passing under its heights, he came to Sychar (4), near the ruins of ancient Shechem. Where two important routes come together by Jacob's Well he sat down, weary from his journey. When a woman of Samaria came to draw water from the well, Jesus talked with her. Pointing out the rugged crags of Mount Gerizim towering above them, she said, "Our fathers worshiped on this mountain; and you say that in Jerusalem is the place where men ought to worship." Looking beyond both the sacredness of Mount Gerizim to the Samaritans, where their temple had stood, and the sacredness of the Temple in Jerusalem to the Jews, Jesus replied, "true worshipers will worship the Father in spirit and truth . . ."

Back in Galilee (5) Jesus resumed his teaching and healing, but shortly, according to John 5:1, he returned to Jerusalem for a "feast of the Jews." This otherwise unidentified occasion is thought by some to be Pentecost, a single-day celebration 50 days after Passover, marking the completion of the wheat harvest. John 7 tells of a private visit of Jesus to Jerusalem for the Feast of Tabernacles (or Booths), the third of the great pilgrimage feasts. An autumnal festival, it celebrated the ingathering of fruit, grapes, and olives. It also reminded Jews of the wilderness wanderings in the time of Moses and of God's bounty. Jesus could not keep his presence secret, however, and was soon teaching in the city.

Whatever way Jesus traveled on this third journey, the land looked very different than it had in the spring, when he had come to Jerusalem for Passover. Gone were the

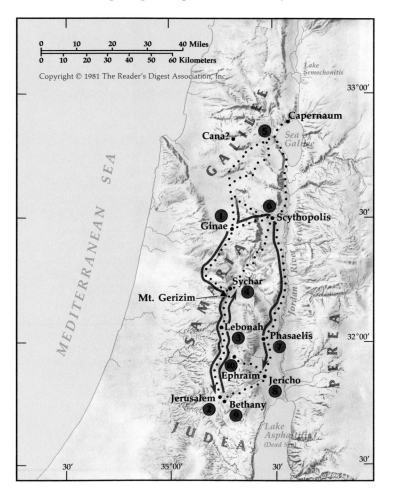

carpets of flowers—"the lilies of the field"—that covered the valleys and green hillsides. Now a gentle wind rustled through the dry weeds and the trees, upturning the white undersides of the olive leaves. The thorns and thistles, cruel in any season, tore at the toughened feet of travelers who strayed from the beaten paths.

It is possible that Jesus never again returned to Galilee and had an extended ministry in Jerusalem, Jericho, and the area beyond the Jordan north of Lake Asphaltitis. This ministry may have lasted from autumn's Tabernacles to Passover the next spring.

Jesus was certainly in Jerusalem in December for the Feast of Dedication. This is the minor festival of Hanukkah, celebrating the rededication of the Temple and the relighting of the sacred lamps by Judas Maccabeus in 164 B.C. Jerusalem would have been ablaze with light as not only the Temple but also the houses were illuminated by lamps and torches during this eight-day festival. It was cold, and Jesus may even have seen snow on the Judean hills.

The extensive section of Luke 9:51–18:34, where most of the well-known parables are preserved, has long been thought by some scholars to belong to a Perean ministry of Jesus. While it is probably incorrect to assign all of this material to such a ministry, it appears that Jesus did return to Perea, the scene of John the Baptist's activity beyond the Jordan. John 10:40–42 speaks of such a ministry: "He went away again across the Jordan to the place where John at first baptized . . . and there he remained." It is equally possible that Jesus returned to Galilee after Tabernacles and made separate journeys at Hanukkah and for Passover the following spring.

Luke 9:51–56 suggests that Jesus went through Samaria on his last, fateful journey to Jerusalem. But this impression may be corrected by Mark 10:1, 46, Matthew 19:1, 20:29,

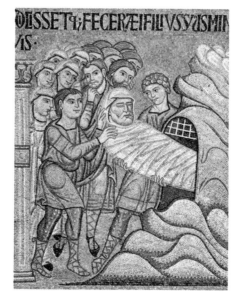

An act of Jesus' that caught the imagination of the public—and devotional artists in later times—was his restoration of life to Lazarus after four days in the tomb at Bethany. The depiction here is a 12th-century mosaic from the renowned Basilica of Saint Mark in Venice.

and Luke 18:35 where Jesus leaves Galilee for the last time and arrives at Jericho after ministering in "the region of Judea and beyond the Jordan." Perhaps deterred by the Samaritans near Ginae, he turned eastward on the route toward Scythopolis (6) and then south along the Jordan River route. Around Phasaelis (7), some 12 miles north of Jericho, Jesus would begin to pass through rich date palm plantations until he reached the ancient oasis of Jericho (8). Turning west he would have gone up to Jerusalem through the Wilderness of Judea.

He continued his ministry in Jerusalem and to the east down toward the Jordan valley. But after the raising of Lazarus at Bethany (9), opposition from the religious authorities in Jerusalem—especially from Joseph Caiaphas, the High Priest—caused Jesus to withdraw to "the wilderness, to a town called Ephraim [10]; and there he stayed with the disciples."

Six days before Passover—if we follow the chronology of John—Jesus came once more to his friends Mary, Martha, and Lazarus in Bethany. There he was anointed with costly ointment to the dismay of Judas, who lamented that it could have been sold for 300 denarii, 10 months wages, which could have been given to the poor. But Jesus brushed aside the complaint, saying, "The poor you always have with you, but you do not always have me."

The next day Jesus, seated on an ass, descended from the Mount of Olives and rode toward Jerusalem. Along his path people spread their garments and waved palm branches. "Hosanna!" they shouted. "Blessed is he who comes in the name of the Lord!"

Seeing the panorama of the Holy City spread before him, Jesus wept and said: "For the days shall come upon you, when your enemies . . . will not leave one stone upon another in you; because you did not know the time of your visitation."

183

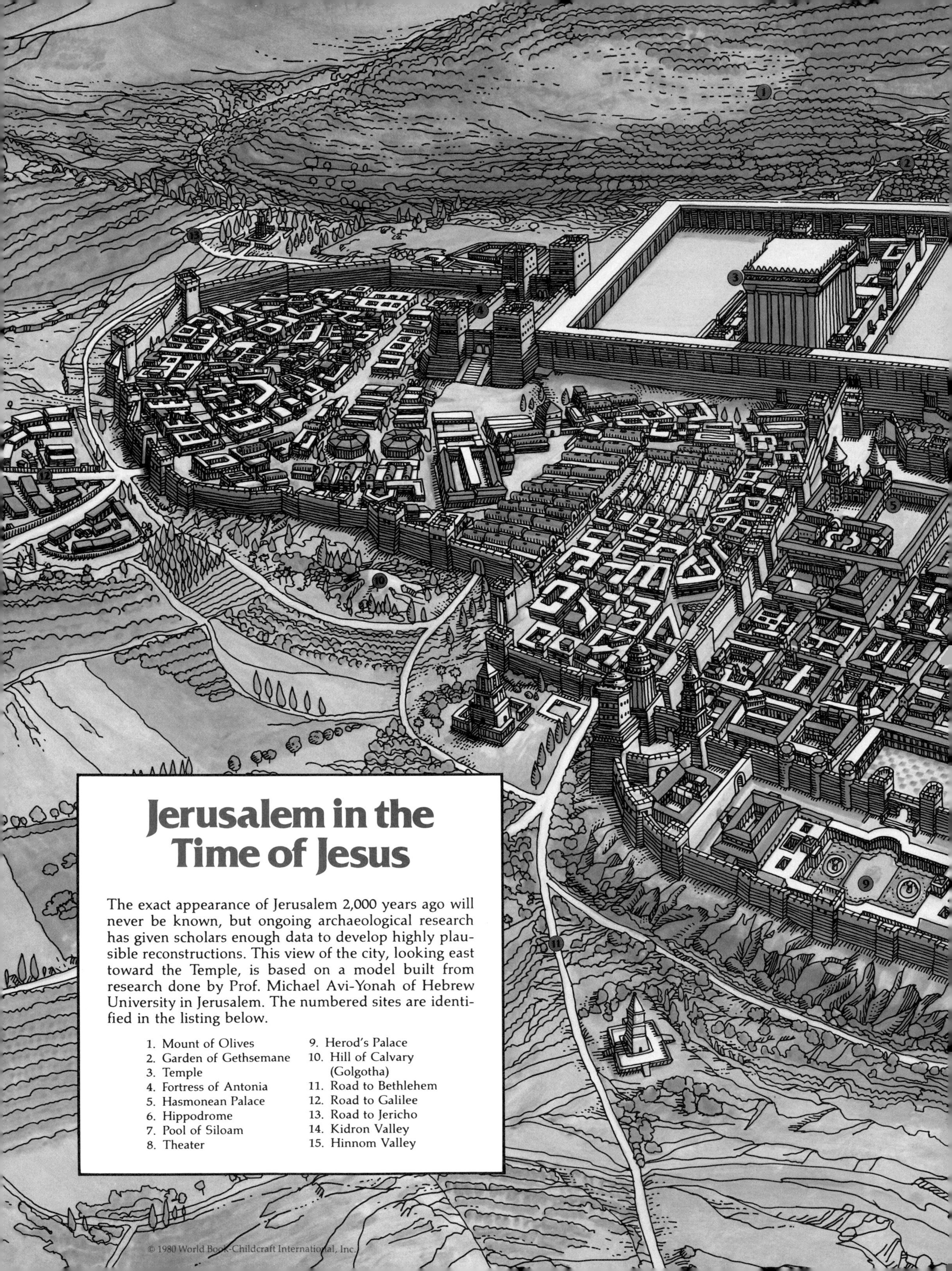

Jerusalem in the Time of Jesus

The exact appearance of Jerusalem 2,000 years ago will never be known, but ongoing archaeological research has given scholars enough data to develop highly plausible reconstructions. This view of the city, looking east toward the Temple, is based on a model built from research done by Prof. Michael Avi-Yonah of Hebrew University in Jerusalem. The numbered sites are identified in the listing below.

1. Mount of Olives
2. Garden of Gethsemane
3. Temple
4. Fortress of Antonia
5. Hasmonean Palace
6. Hippodrome
7. Pool of Siloam
8. Theater
9. Herod's Palace
10. Hill of Calvary (Golgotha)
11. Road to Bethlehem
12. Road to Galilee
13. Road to Jericho
14. Kidron Valley
15. Hinnom Valley

Death of Jesus

As Jesus came over the brow of the Mount of Olives on that first Palm Sunday, the glorious city created by Herod the Great rose before him on the heights across the Kidron valley. After a descent into the valley, there was the slow winding climb up to the Golden Gate (1), through which Jesus entered the sacred precincts of the Temple (2). Despite the cries of "Hosanna!" still echoing in his ears, he could have been under no illusions as to the ultimate reception awaiting him. As it was already late in the day, he "looked round at everything" and returned with the Twelve Apostles to Bethany.

The next day, following Mark's chronology, Jesus was back in the sacred precincts. In the Court of the Gentiles (3) he "overturned the tables of the money-changers and the seats of those who sold pigeons." He stopped those who were using the Temple courts as a shortcut to carry goods from one section of Jerusalem to another. "Is it not written," Jesus cried, " 'My house shall be called a house of prayer for all the nations'? But you have made it a den of robbers." The authorities who heard this began to seek a way to destroy him because of his growing influence with the people.

On Tuesday Jesus was again in the Temple courts, answering questions and teaching. When the chief priests, scribes, and elders challenged his authority, Jesus turned their question back on them by asking about the authority of John the Baptist. After they refused to answer him, Jesus said, "Neither will I tell you by what authority I do these things." To the Pharisees and Herodians who sought to entrap him with a politically explosive question about Roman taxes he said, "Render to Caesar the things that are Caesar's, and to God the things that are God's." To a scribe's question about which was the greatest commandment, Jesus replied that the first and greatest commandment

The Jerusalem that Jesus knew was a densely populated city with a maze of winding streets and narrow passageways much like this one in the Old City of present-day Jerusalem.

was to love God totally and the second was to "love your neighbor as yourself." He also warned the people against the ostentatious piety of the scribes and their questionable morality.

Wednesday Jesus was in Bethany, where he was anointed with costly ointment by a woman in the house of Simon the leper—an event almost identical to the one John describes as occurring four days earlier. Anointing was preparation for burial, as Mark notes, and also the designation of a king, a major point in John's account of Jesus' passion and death. It was apparently on this day that Judas arranged to betray his master.

Thursday was spent in preparation for Passover. In the evening Jesus came once more into the city with his disciples to eat the traditional meal with them. We do not know where the Last Supper took place, but ever since the Middle Ages an upper room in a Crusader-period building on Mount Zion has been designated as the site (4).

After the meal, Jesus crossed the Kidron with his disciples and came to the Mount of Olives, "as was his custom." There in the cold evening he withdrew into the garden of Gethsemane seeking strength in prayer and surrendering himself to the will of God. Christian tradition has always placed Gethsemane on the lower slopes of the Mount of Olives—though today the Roman Catholic and Russian Orthodox churches hallow different sites. Both claims are ancient, but neither has the force of proof. It is not surprising that Jesus was habitually in this area, for the Kidron and the slopes of the mount thronged with poorer pilgrims who camped there during the great Jewish festivals. The place, in any case, was well known to Judas, who now approached with a band of Temple police as Jesus prayed and his disciples slept. He greeted his friend and master in the time-honored Oriental manner—with a kiss—thereby identifying Jesus as the one to be seized.

Jesus was taken to the house of the High Priest, Joseph Caiaphas. There religious leaders headed by Annas, Caiaphas' father-in-law and a former High Priest who still wielded power, questioned Jesus. Almost certainly this interrogation took place in a fashionable section of the upper city. Recent excavations have revealed large and beautiful houses of the rich—villas in the Roman style, with mosaic-covered floors in sumptuous rooms around courtyards. The furnishings were often imported and were of the finest quality. We know that Ananias, High Priest from A.D. 48 to 58, lived in the upper city and may assume that Caiaphas did also. But where? In A.D. 808 a visitor to Jerusalem wrote of a church of St. Peter's Tears on Mount Zion. Today a handsome church on the eastern slope of the mount is called St. Peter of the Cockcrow, for it was in the courtyard of the house of Caiaphas that Peter denied Jesus three times before cockcrow. However, there is another tradition, going back to the Pilgrim of Bordeaux in A.D. 333, that places the house of Caiaphas (5) higher up on Mount Zion. Israeli excavations there in 1971–72 showed the area to have been one of wealthy homes in the time of Jesus. The excavators concluded that their work tended to support the 4th-century identification of the place of Jesus' interrogation.

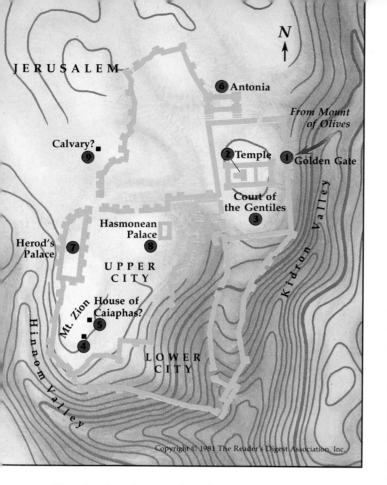

JERUSALEM

N

6 Antonia

From Mount of Olives

Calvary? 9

2 Temple   1 Golden Gate

Court of the Gentiles 3

Hasmonean Palace 8

Herod's Palace 7

UPPER CITY

Mt. Zion   House of Caiaphas? 5

4

LOWER CITY

Hinnom Valley

Kidron Valley

Copyright © 1981 The Reader's Digest Association, Inc.

Shortly after dawn—when Roman governors normally began their official duties—the chief priests came to the praetorium to proffer political charges against Jesus. Where did this fateful confrontation take place? Since the early-4th century, there has been a nearly unbroken tradition that Jesus was haled before Pontius Pilate at the Fortress Antonia (6). The First Station of the Cross is there, and the Via Dolorosa goes from the Antonia to the Church of the Holy Sepulchre, hallowed as the place of

Jesus' death, burial, and resurrection. But some scholars favor Herod's western palace (7) as the location of Pilate's trial of Jesus, pointing out that Josephus says Roman governors occasionally stayed there.

Luke tells us that Pilate, after listening to the charges against Jesus, asked if he was not a Galilean and thus belonging to the jurisdiction of Herod Antipas. Since Antipas was in the city for the holidays, Pilate sent Jesus to him—most likely at the Hasmonean palace (8). Antipas had long wanted to see his famous subject and now joined his soldiers in mocking Jesus; "then, arraying him in gorgeous apparel, he sent him back to Pilate." The Roman governor at last gave in to the demands of "the chief priests and the rulers and the people" that Jesus be crucified.

The site of Calvary—Golgotha—is also a matter of debate. Since 335 a church has marked the present site of the Church of the Holy Sepulchre, identified as Calvary (9). While it is now well within the walls of Jerusalem's Old City, in the time of Jesus it was a small hill (about 14 feet high) just outside the western walls. British excavations in the mid-1960's showed that the area was not merely outside the city walls during the time of Jesus but had no structures on it. Thus it may well have been a garden, as John says.

On the Sunday after Jesus' cruxifixion the electrifying news spread among his followers not only that his tomb was empty but that he was risen from the dead and had appeared to Mary Magdalene and others. That evening he appeared to his disciples as they were gathered together behind locked doors out of fear for their safety. "Peace be with you," he said and showed them his pierced hands and feet. Other appearances were reported in Jerusalem, in nearby Emmaus, and in Galilee before—in the presence of his disciples—he was taken up into heaven. Today a small Crusader chapel on the Mount of Olives commemorates the Ascension.

These two scenes from the Last Supper show, at left, Jesus and his disciples reclining at table in the traditional manner at Passover as Judas dips his hand in the dish; and at right, Jesus washing their feet.

The illustration is part of the Rossano Codex, a parchment manuscript of the Gospels preserved in Rossano, Italy. Scholars believe the work to be of Syrian or Byzantine origin, probably dating from the 6th century.

Early Spread of the Gospel

Fifty days after the Passover that ended with the crucifixion of Jesus, his followers were gathered in Jerusalem for the Feast of Pentecost when "suddenly a sound came from heaven like the rush of a mighty wind, and it filled all the house where they were sitting. . . . And they were all filled with the Holy Spirit . . ." At once these unlettered Galileans went into the streets of Jerusalem to proclaim the good news about Jesus, and in response to Peter's Pentecost sermon some 3,000 people were baptized. This was the beginning of the spread of Christianity as related in Acts of the Apostles.

The numbers of baptized grew day by day, but so did opposition to the new religion. When Peter and John went up to the Temple for prayer at 3 o'clock one afternoon, they healed a cripple who was begging at the Beautiful Gate. A crowd gathered and they began to preach—an act for which they were promptly arrested. Held overnight, the two apostles were brought before the council the next day and told to cease speaking or teaching in the name of Jesus. But Peter and John spoke boldly: "Whether it is right in the sight of God to listen to you rather than to God, you must judge; for we cannot but speak of what we have seen and heard." Although further threatened, the two were released.

Some time later the apostles were in Solomon's Portico, that long colonnade which, pierced only by the Golden Gate, ran the length of the Temple platform. There Peter and the others were healing the sick when they were arrested on orders of the Sadducees. Miraculously they were brought out of prison and at daybreak the next day were once more teaching in the Temple. Arrested again, they were immediately brought before the council, where their courage and defiance enraged some of its members. But the learned Pharisee Gamaliel counseled caution: "let them alone; for if this plan or this undertaking is of men, it will fail; but if it is of God, you will not be able to overthrow them."

Yet feelings against the followers of Jesus ran high, and not everyone heeded such sage advice. Stephen, one of the seven newly chosen deacons of the Jerusalem church, proclaimed his new faith in the synagogue of the Freedmen, apparently a synagogue of Diaspora Jews. But his words enraged the people, who dragged him out of the city and stoned him to death—the first martyr of Christianity. Stephen's death touched off a general persecution of the followers of Jesus in Jerusalem, and many fled—taking the message with them to Cyprus, Antioch,

A 5th-century ivory panel shows three mourning women being met by an angel at the empty tomb; above, Jesus ascends into heaven, clasping God's hands as an amazed disciple looks on.

Damascus, and other places beyond Judea. While we cannot be entirely sure of the chronology of those early days of the Christian church, the gospel seems already to have spread into Samaria and along the coastal plain.

Philip, another of the seven deacons, went from Jerusalem (1) to "a city of Samaria" (2) and there enjoyed enormous success in preaching the gospel. This city is unnamed in Acts, and many have taken it to be Sebaste. But Sebaste was a Hellenistic city, and it is doubtful that the gospel was at this time being widely proclaimed to Gentiles with any great success. Peter and John came to assist Philip, and the three preached the gospel in many Samaritan villages before returning to Jerusalem.

Philip did not long remain in Jerusalem. An Ethiopian eunuch, a high official in charge of the treasury of Queen Candace of Ethiopia, had come to Jerusalem to worship and was returning home. Commanded by an angel to go meet this man, Philip went "toward the south to the road that goes down from Jerusalem to Gaza." The quickest route from Jerusalem (3) ran to Beththter (4) and then down through the Valley of Elah—where David fought Goliath—under the lee of the hill on which the ancient city of Azekah once stood, and there it turned south down the interior valley of the Shephelah to reach Betogabris (5), which had replaced Marisa as the chief city of western Idumea. At this important junction, travelers would have gone south by the massive mound of Lachish and then southwest across the coastal plain to Gaza (6). It may well have been somewhere on this plain that Philip drew near to the chariot of the Ethiopian and heard him read from Isaiah: "As a sheep led to the slaughter . . ." When Philip explained to him that this passage spoke of Jesus, the eunuch believed. He was baptized in water by the roadside and, rejoicing, continued on his way through Egypt to Ethiopia, but Philip went to Azotus (7) and "passing on he preached the gospel to all the towns till he came to Caesarea." (8)

Initially restricted to Jews and proselytes to Judaism, the gospel was beginning to be proclaimed to Gentiles as well. Peter "went here and there among them all." When he came to the ancient, strategic crossroads at Lydda (9) amid fields and plantations, he healed the crippled Aeneas. The disciples at Joppa (10), hearing that Peter was nearby—a little over 10 miles away—sent for him to come to the old port because Dorcas, a woman "full of good works and acts of charity," had died. Peter shut himself in a room with the dead woman, prayed, and

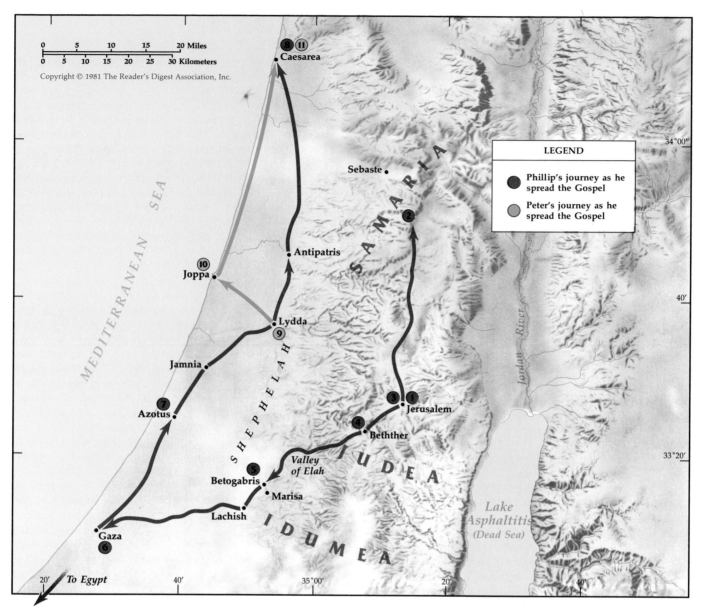

LEGEND

Phillip's journey as he spread the Gospel

Peter's journey as he spread the Gospel

brought her back to life. He remained in Joppa for many days, living in the house of a tanner named Simon.

At Caesarea there was a devout Roman soldier named Cornelius who had attached himself to the synagogue as a "God-fearer," one who studied the Law but who was neither circumcised nor obeyed the dietary regulations. In a vision he was told to send to Joppa for Peter.

Meanwhile, Peter also had a vision. About midday he had gone to the roof of Simon's house to be alone for prayer. He saw something descending "like a great sheet, let down by four corners upon the earth." In it were all kinds of animals, reptiles, and birds. Commanded by a voice to kill and eat, Peter objected that they were unclean; that is, forbidden by Jewish law. "What God has cleansed, you must not call common," said the voice.

As Peter pondered the meaning of this vision, the messengers from Cornelius arrived. The next day Peter and some of his companions went with them to Caesarea (11). There Cornelius asked "to hear all that you have been commanded by the Lord." Now Peter knew the meaning of his vision on the rooftop in Joppa, and he said, "Truly I perceive that God shows no partiality, but in every nation any one who fears him and does what is right is acceptable to him." And while Peter was telling Cornelius and his friends about Jesus, "the gift of the Holy Spirit [was] poured out even on the Gentiles."

News of this astounding happening preceded Peter to Jerusalem, where he faced severe criticism for even going to Cornelius and eating with him. While Peter seems to have calmed the fears of those in Jerusalem who believed that Jesus' message was for Jews only, other news came from Antioch. Some who had fled the persecution that arose on the death of Stephen had converted non-Jews in Antioch. The Jerusalem church selected Joseph Barnabas, a Cypriot Jew descended from the tribe of Levi, to go to Antioch to investigate. But he approved of what he found and "exhorted them all to remain faithful to the Lord with steadfast purpose." To aid him in the work at Antioch, Barnabas sought out the most remarkable of the new converts: Saul of Tarsus.

The Conversion of Saul

A consenting witness to the stoning of Stephen, the ardent young Pharisee Saul of Tarsus had enthusiastically joined in the subsequent persecution of Jesus' followers in Jerusalem. Thus while devout men buried Stephen with great lamentation, Saul "was ravaging the church, and entering house after house, he dragged off men and women and committed them to prison."

Saul, whose Greek name was Paul, had been born into a strict Jewish family at Tarsus in Cilicia but he also inherited his father's Roman citizenship. Following in his father's footsteps as a Pharisee, Saul came to Jerusalem when he was judged worthy to begin studying under the renowned Rabbi Gamaliel. There, he tells us in Galatians, "I advanced in Judaism beyond many of my own age among my people, so extremely zealous was I for the traditions of my fathers." It was this zeal—and a fear that the message of Jesus was undermining his ancient faith—that led Saul to such fierce opposition to the gospel. But, as we have seen, this only brought about the spread of the gospel to Cyprus, Antioch, Damascus, and other places beyond Judea and Samaria.

In Jerusalem (1) Saul—"still breathing threats and murder against the disciples of the Lord"—secured authority from the High Priest to go to Damascus and root out any followers of Jesus found in the synagogues there. He hurried north, by what route we cannot be sure. But however he went—perhaps north along the ridge route turning off at Sychar to Scythopolis (2) and by Hippus—eventually he came to the heights east of the Sea of Galilee and crossed the dark basalt plateau before Damascus (3). As he approached the ancient city, he had a blinding vision. "Saul, Saul, why do you persecute me?" a voice called out. Asking who it was, Saul heard the momentous words, "I am Jesus, whom you are persecuting; but rise and enter the city, and you will be told what you are to do." His companions led the blinded Saul into Damascus, where he remained for three days "without sight, and neither ate nor drank." In a vision the Lord commanded the disciple Ananias to lay his hands on Saul to restore his sight. As "something like scales fell from his eyes," Saul rose and was baptized.

When Saul began to proclaim Jesus as the Son of God in the synagogues of Damascus, there was confusion among the Jews who knew of his earlier persecution of the disciples in Jerusalem. And in time, Saul's persistence led to a Jewish plot to kill him. But he escaped his would-be assailants by having himself lowered over the city wall in a basket. He fled southward, according to Galatians, "into Arabia"; that is, into the realms of King Aretas of the Nabateans (4). After three years, he came again to Jerusalem (5).

The disciples were at first reluctant to accept Saul as one of them, but he was soon "preaching boldly in the name of the Lord" and earning the enmity of Jerusalem's Hellenists. He fled to Caesarea (6) to take ship for his home in Tarsus (7), remaining there until Barnabas brought him to Antioch (8). The two labored together for a year, the church grew, "and in Antioch the disciples were for the first time called Christians."

Later, when famine arose in Judea, the church in Antioch sent Barnabas and Paul (as we can now call him) to Jerusalem with relief for the brethren. Whether this visit occurred before or after another outbreak of persecution against the young Christian community in Jerusalem cannot be determined. Serious persecution broke out under Herod Agrippa I, whose patrons, the emperors Caligula and Claudius, had given him most of the kingdom of his grandfather, Herod the Great. Despite the fact that he had been educated in Rome, Agrippa was strongly pro-Jewish, which may have prompted his attempt to suppress the growing Christian community in Jerusalem. At Passover the Apostle James was killed "with the sword" and Peter was seized and put in prison under heavy guard. With James dead and Peter to be brought to trial after Passover, Agrippa had struck at the leadership of the community, thinking he would thereby destroy it. But the night before his trial Peter, who "was sleeping between two soldiers, bound with two chains," was miraculously delivered from the prison. He fled to the home of Mary, the mother of John Mark, and hid there before escaping from the city and going to a safe place. Agrippa's soldiers failed to find Peter, and the king returned to Caesarea. According to Josephus, it was during a public spectacle in the amphitheater there, in A.D. 44, that the king was gripped by an intense pain and died shortly afterward. Christians saw his untimely death as God's vengeance for his persecution of the church.

Paul's Missionary Journeys

From among the leaders of the Antioch church, Barnabas and Paul were chosen to spread the gospel westward. Taking John Mark with them, The Acts of the Apostles relates, the two sailed from Seleucia Pieria (1, on smaller map, page 193), across a Mediterranean that was now a Roman lake, to Cyprus.

Fleeing the recurrent disasters of their homeland, Jews had settled throughout Rome's eastern empire and may have comprised 20 percent of its population. There had been a Jewish community on Cyprus since the late-4th century B.C., and Christians had arrived there even before Paul. Of Paul's activities in Salamis (2)—the largest city on the island and an important port—we know only that he and his friends "proclaimed the word of God."

They then went "through the whole island as far as Paphos" (3), the Roman administrative center on the southwestern coast. Two roads connected these Cypriot cities: one ran along the southern coast; the other went through the mountainous interior. We do not know which way the missionaries went or how long they took, since they were intent on making converts.

At Paphos the Roman governor, Sergius Paulus, summoned the missionaries to hear what they were preaching. With the governor was "a Jewish false prophet, named Bar-Jesus," who Paul prophesied would be struck blind. "Immediately mist and darkness fell upon him and he went about seeking people to lead him by the hand." Seeing this, Sergius Paulus was converted.

From Paphos "Paul and his company" sailed to the coast of Asia Minor, to the fertile but hot and humid plain of Pamphylia, a narrow, low-lying strip between the sea and the

The Apostle to the Gentiles makes a sign of benediction in this 12th-century mosaic from the Cathedral of Monreale in Sicily; Paul stopped on the island during his voyage to Italy.

towering Taurus Mountains. The missionaries apparently did not preach at Perga (4), their first stop and one of the chief cities of the region—perhaps because Paul's "bodily ailment" forced him to abandon this unhealthy plain and move up the steep road into the cool highlands of Pisidia to the north. At Perga, John Mark left them and returned to Jerusalem.

The Pisidian highlands presented wild yet beautiful vistas with lofty peaks, numerous valleys traced by flowing rivers and, occasionally, sizable lakes. Its inhabitants were rustic, quarrelsome, and often unruly, and the area was infamous as a haven for robbers and illegal slave traders. When Paul later spoke of the perils of his journeys and being "in danger from rivers, danger from robbers," he may well have been recalling his days in these highlands. At Antioch in Pisidia (5), Paul went to the synagogue on the Sabbath and was

asked if he had "any word of exhortation for the people." Hardly needing the invitation, Paul recalled the mighty acts of God in history including the resurrection of Jesus in fulfillment of ancient promises to Israel. Some listeners asked Paul and Barnabas to return the following Sabbath, while others—Jews and converts—went with them to hear more. Before a great crowd in the synagogue the next Sabbath, however, the Jews contradicted Paul and reviled him. Now a momentous event occurred. Quoting Isaiah—"I have set you to be a light for the Gentiles, . . ."—Paul turned to the Gentiles of Antioch, many of whom received him gladly. But his Jewish opponents "stirred up persecution against Paul and Barnabas" and drove them out of Pisidia.

Leaving the mountains and descending through hills to the east, Paul and Barnabas came to Iconium (6). An important commercial center on the road from the Roman province of Asia to Syria, Iconium had attracted a sizable Jewish community. True to his maxim, "to the Jew first," Paul went to the synagogue in Iconium, where the events of Antioch repeated themselves. People were divided in their opinions, with Jews and Gentiles on both sides of the issue—some supporting Paul, others opposing him. But Paul and Barnabas were able to remain there "for a long time" until they learned of a plot "to molest them and to stone them." They fled south some 25 miles to Lystra (7). Like Antioch and Iconium, Lystra was part of the Roman province of Galatia. It sat in a small valley among low hills just below the massive Taurus Mountains.

Paul's healing of a cripple at Lystra created a sensation, and word spread through the town: "The gods have come down to us in the likeness of men!" The missionaries were scarcely able to dissuade the people from offering a sacrifice to them, but the mood changed abruptly when zealous Jews from Antioch and Iconium arrived. Paul was stoned and dragged out of town, being left for dead. With help from friends he was able to rest in the city overnight before starting off with Barnabas for Derbe (8), a frontier town some 50 miles away at the limits of effective Roman control. There they preached in peace and made many converts.

Now the two retraced their steps, encouraging the new Christians at Lystra, Iconium, and Antioch "to continue in the faith." Toward the end of his life, as Paul reflected upon his work and remembered "my persecutions, my sufferings," he connected these with this first missionary journey through Asia Minor.

Back on the Pamphylian plain, "when they had spo-

Paul's Missionary Journeys (continued)

ken the word in Perga," they went to Attalia (9), for two centuries the main port through which goods from the region flowed toward Syria and Egypt. There they found a ship bound for Seleucia Pieria. Paul later wrote: "Three times I have been shipwrecked." But we know of only one occasion—and that was on his voyage to Rome. Whether his return to Syria was uneventful or not, such journeys were not without hazards.

After having been away for perhaps as much as two years, Paul and Barnabas returned to the church at Antioch (10) in Syria "and declared all that God had done with them, and how he had opened a door of faith to the Gentiles." Word of this eventually reached the church in Jerusalem, where some were disturbed that converts had not been circumcised and made to keep the laws of Judaism. When men from Jerusalem came to Antioch to press the point, Barnabas and Paul argued with them. A crisis had been reached in the life of the infant church. Paul, Barnabas, and some others were appointed to go to Jerusalem to lay their case before the apostles and elders. Passing through Phoenicia and Samaria they reported the conversion of Gentiles, to the joy of many who heard them.

In Jerusalem (11) the issue was joined as certain Christians "who belonged to the party of the Pharisees" insisted that no one could be Christian unless circumcised and observant of Jewish laws. Peter and James, leaders of the Jerusalem church, supported Paul and Barnabas. But to keep harmony they urged that Gentile converts "abstain from what has been sacrificed to idols and from blood and from what is strangled and from unchastity." Judas Barsabbas and Silas were chosen to go with Paul and Barnabas to Antioch and inform the church there of the decision. Nothing was mentioned about other ritual laws or circumcision or any similar "yoke upon the neck of the disciples," as Peter called them.

After some days in Antioch (12, on larger map opposite), Paul suggested to Barnabas that they visit the brethren they had met on their missionary journey "and see how they are." Barnabas wanted to take John Mark, but Paul refused the services of one who had withdrawn from the earlier mission "and had not gone with them to the work." As Barnabas went off to Cyprus with John Mark, Paul chose Silas as companion on this second missionary journey, and together they went by land along the highway that led into Cilicia. At Tarsus (13), Paul's home, the route turned directly north into a spectacular gorge through the Taurus Mountains some 4,000 feet above sea level—the famous Cilician Gates. Geography dictated that this well-plied route continue north, avoiding the high mountains before it could turn west toward Derbe, Lystra, and Iconium. In these familiar places Paul told of the decision of the apostles and elders in Jerusalem. At Lystra (14), Timothy—son of a Jewish-Christian mother and Greek father—joined the missionaries. He would be Paul's faithful companion throughout most of the rest of the apostle's life.

At this point Paul apparently intended to follow the main route westward into the Roman province of Asia, of which the great city of Ephesus was the capital. But "having been forbidden by the Holy Spirit to speak the word in Asia," they went north from Antioch in Pisidia through western Galatia and Phrygia (the actual route being unknown) toward Bithynia, but again "the Spirit of Jesus did not allow them." Having traveled over a hundred miles north, the three missionaries turned west to Troas (15). But this was not merely idle wandering, for later Paul revisited some of these areas, "strengthening all the disciples" he had previously enlisted there.

The busy harbor of Troas was an open door to Macedonia. And so it proved for Paul. In Troas he had a vision of a man beseeching him, saying, "Come over to Macedonia and help us." It was also in Troas, apparently, that the Gentile Luke joined Paul, Silas, and Timothy—for at this point (Acts 16:10), the author of Acts of the Apostles, Luke, begins to speak of "we." (This was the same Luke who would later write one of the four Gospels.) The missionaries sailed from Troas northwest to the mountainous island of Samothrace, where the ship was anchored for the night. The next day Paul set foot in Europe at Neapolis, the port for the city of Philippi (16). Named for Philip of Macedon, Alexander's father, Philippi prospered from its place on the great Roman road that ran across Macedonia to Dyrrhachium, from which ship passage could be made to Italy.

Paul found no synagogue in Philippi, but on the Sabbath he went outside the city to a place of prayer by the river. There he spoke to a group of women, including Lydia, Paul's first convert in Europe.

On the way to the place of prayer, Paul exorcised a slave girl "who had a spirit of divination and brought her owners much gain by soothsaying." Seeing they had lost hope of profit from the girl, her owners haled Paul and Silas before the authorities. Under mob pressure, the magistrates tore the clothing from the two and ordered them beaten with rods and thrown into prison.

About midnight, as Paul and Silas were "singing hymns to God, and the prisoners were listening to them," an earthquake damaged the jail, making escape possible. Knowing he would be blamed for the loss of his prisoners, the jailer was about to kill himself, when Paul called out that they had not fled. The grateful jailer and his family were converted and baptized that very night. The next day the magistrates sent word to release the men, but Paul refused to leave, saying that he was a Roman citizen and had been humiliated. The frightened magistrates came to apologize but asked them to leave the city.

Luke remained in Philippi (Acts returns to a third-person narrative), but Paul, Silas, and Timothy set off southwestward. Passing through Amphipolis and Apollonia, they came to the most important city in Macedonia, Thessalonica (17).

For three weeks Paul—"as was his custom"—was in the synagogue debating the Scriptures and seeking to show that Jesus was the Christ. Some were persuaded, but others stirred up a rabble mob and attacked the house of Jason, where Paul and the others had been staying. Failing to find them, they brought Jason and his

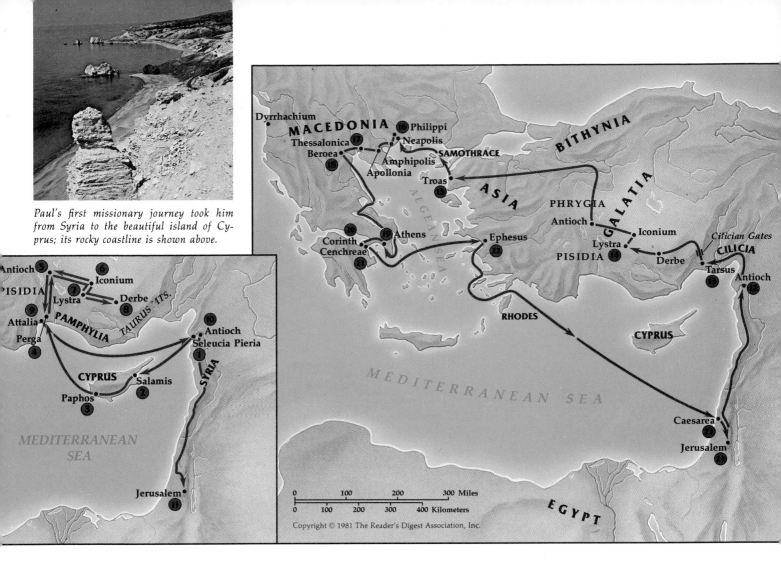

Paul's first missionary journey took him from Syria to the beautiful island of Cyprus; its rocky coastline is shown above.

Copyright © 1981 The Reader's Digest Association, Inc.

friends before the authorities, saying that they acted against Caesar's decrees by proclaiming another king, Jesus. Although Jason and his friends were released, Paul, Silas, and Timothy quietly left town. At Beroea (18) they found a synagogue where Jews "received the word with all eagerness, examining the scriptures daily to see if these things were so." When Paul's enemies from Thessalonica pursued him to Beroea, he set out by sea for Athens (19), leaving Silas and Timothy behind.

While waiting for his companions in the ancient center of Greek culture, Paul became provoked as he saw a city full of idols. He argued in the synagogue and was daily in the agora, that splendid marketplace, speaking to anyone he met. Epicurean and Stoic philosophers took him to the Areopagus, a small hill below the famous Acropolis of Athens where the traditional council of the city—by then more honorary than powerful—debated new ideas among themselves or with any thinker who came by. They wanted to know about the "strange things" Paul had been saying. He addressed them eloquently, even quoting Greek poets. But when he spoke of the resurrection of the dead, some mocked him, while others said they would hear more of this another time. So Paul—having made a few converts in Athens but having founded no church there—left before his friends arrived from Beroea and went west to Corinth (20), one of

the greatest commercial centers of the empire. Here Paul found friends in Aquila and his wife, Priscilla, who had recently come to Corinth to pursue their profession as tentmakers "because Claudius had commanded all the Jews to leave Rome." Every Sabbath Paul was in the synagogue, where he persuaded many, including Crispus, the ruler of the synagogue. When Silas and Timothy arrived, he was preaching to Jews, but soon he turned to the Gentiles of the city. Paul enjoyed a great success, staying in Corinth 18 months. Here he began another aspect of his ministry: writing letters to Christian churches in other places. From Corinth he wrote twice to the Thessalonians, and these are the earliest extant epistles of Paul.

At length Paul set out for Syria, accompanied by Aquila and Priscilla. At Cenchreae (21), the port of Corinth on the eastern side of the isthmus, Paul took ship through some of the lovely Greek isles and across the Aegean to Ephesus (22).

Paul left his two friends there but first went into the synagogue. Asked by Jews to remain with them longer, he promised to return "if God wills" and found a ship bound for Caesarea (23) more than 600 miles away. After landing, he went to greet the church at Jerusalem (24) and then returned to Antioch in Syria.

The story of Paul's third missionary journey begins abruptly in Acts: "After spending some time there [Anti-

The World of Paul

The broad and rapid spread of Christianity across the Roman world was remarkable in many ways—not least because it had originated at the fringes of empire, in the ancestral homeland of the Jews, and had roots firmly planted in a minority religion, Judaism. Few men could have been better suited than Paul—educated as a Pharisee but also exposed to the Hellenistic culture of his native Tarsus—to bridge the gap between Judaic traditions and the larger Gentile world. It was natural that so much of Paul's missionary work should be focused on such places as Ephesus, Corinth, and other cities, which, like Tarsus, were cosmopolitan trading centers with large, diverse populations, places where new ideas and beliefs were more likely to be tolerated. It was natural, too, that he should not limit his proselytizing to the Jewish communities in those cities but reach out for converts among the Gentiles, who proved increasingly receptive to a faith that set high moral standards for its followers—standards conspicuously absent in much of Roman society.

The semicircular, open-air theater at Ephesus, built into a hillside facing the harbor half a mile away, was large enough to accommodate 24,000 spectators. It was here that rioters against Paul's evangelism gathered at the instigation of the silversmith Demetrius.

och (1, map on page 198)] he departed and went from place to place through the region of Galatia and Phrygia, strengthening all the disciples." But the grave conflicts related in Paul's letter to the Galatians may have prompted this journey. The legalistic Christians of the Jerusalem church had reasserted themselves. Paul had openly confronted the vacillating Peter, accusing him of insincerity and of not being "straightforward about the truth of the gospel." For Paul the theological issue was clear: "I live by faith in the Son of God . . . for if justification were through the law, then Christ died to no purpose." But his opponents did not agree and were making their way through Asia Minor, challenging Paul's authority and seeking to change the practices of the churches there. Thus Paul hurried north. The struggle for the freedom of the gospel, as he saw it, would take place in the hills and valleys, along the plains and seacoasts of Asia Minor.

Paul retraced the steps of his second missionary journey through the Cilician Gates and continued into the interior of Asia Minor before reaching Ephesus (2). Along with Alexandria in Egypt and Antioch in Syria, Ephesus was one of the three major cities of the eastern empire: a port from which routes ran through river valleys eastward. Paul made use of this strategic position by sending his assistants up the valleys to evangelize while he worked in Ephesus. He also used the sea lanes to dispatch letters and, on occasion, assistants to churches around the Aegean.

For more than two years Paul taught in Ephesus, "a wide door for effective work." Yet there were adversaries; "beasts at Ephesus," he called them. Moreover, as he complained, there was "the daily pressure upon me of my anxiety for all the churches." Concern with the legalistic faction in the Jerusalem church and its effect upon the churches of Asia Minor and Greece was

Still standing after more than two millennia, these 7 huge stone pillars—nearly 24 feet high and 6 feet in diameter—are all that remain of the original 38 that ringed the great temple of Apollo in Corinth, which was already six centuries old when Paul preached here.

Paul's final journey—to face trial in Rome—began at the port of Caesarea, provincial capital of Judea, which boasted an enormous man-made harbor 20 fathoms deep. Built under Herod the Great, the city was supplied with fresh water from foothills to the northeast by a 13-mile-long aqueduct (opposite), half of it a subterranean tunnel and half running aboveground on massive stone arches. The harrowing sea voyage ended at Puteoli, Italy's principal seaport; the 1st-century wall painting at right depicts the scene that probably greeted Paul—a large, busy harbor, its piers supported by distinctive Roman arches and adorned with statues atop tall columns.

a constant theme on this third journey. Meanwhile, some of the Corinthian Christians seemed to have gone to the other extreme by turning the gospel of freedom into a license for moral anarchy. So serious was the situation that he sent Timothy and then another trusted helper, Titus, to Corinth and ultimately went there himself.

By a curious turn of events, it was Paul's success that led to his leaving Ephesus. For centuries the city had been a pilgrim center, drawing worshipers to the magnificent temple of the fertility goddess Artemis, which was one of the seven wonders of the ancient world. Those who came frequently took away silver, marble, or terra-cotta replicas of the shrine and statues of the multibreasted goddess. As Paul's converts abandoned their former worship, business fell off. At length, the silversmiths and other craftsmen met to hear one Demetrius blame Paul for the decline of their liveli-

hood. His denunciation of Paul triggered a riot, and shouts—"Great is Artemis of the Ephesians!"—echoed through the city.

Two Macedonian assistants of Paul, Gaius and Aristarchus, were dragged into the massive theater with its 24,000 seats overlooking the harbor. Paul's friends restrained him from going among the crowd, which was at last dispersed by the town clerk, a person of authority. He told the mob that they could be charged in the Roman courts with rioting. The Christians were not sacrilegious nor had they blasphemed Artemis, he argued. If the craftsmen wanted redress for a loss of business, they should seek relief in the courts.

Paul had already resolved to visit the churches of Macedonia and Achaia and then return to Jerusalem; the riot brought this plan into effect. As Paul set out for Troas (3)—by land or sea we do not know—he was weary of heart and body. From there, perhaps, he sailed to

195

Caesarea: Outpost of Empire

The Caesarea through which Paul passed on at least three occasions was among the grandest of Herod the Great's legacy of municipal improvements in the Holy Land. Unlike his ambitious construction projects at Samaria and Jerusalem, Caesarea was an altogether new city—and the kingdom's first true seaport. Since there was no natural harbor on the sandy coastline, Herod built a 200-foot-wide breakwater (bottom right) to offer docking vessels protection from the prevailing currents from the southwest. Cargo was stored in 100 vaulted warehouses. To the north a semicircular seawall enclosed a yacht basin, whose entrance was flanked by

colossal statues. In laying out Caesarea, Herod imposed a modern grid system. At the intersection of the two principal streets, he created a typical Roman forum, with such monumental buildings as a temple to Augustus Caesar, the patron for whom Herod prudently named his spectacular maritime city. A long colonnaded street led south to an amphitheater, still in use today. An aqueduct (top left) brought fresh water from springs beneath Mount Carmel, 13 miles away, while underneath the city lay an ingenious sewer system that was flushed by the tides and onshore currents. Completed in 9 B.C. after a decade of construction, Caesarea boasted a population of 40,000 in the 2nd century A.D. The ongoing Joint Expedition to Caesarea Maritima, led by Robert J. Bull, has uncovered three acres and projected a city of 8,000 acres.

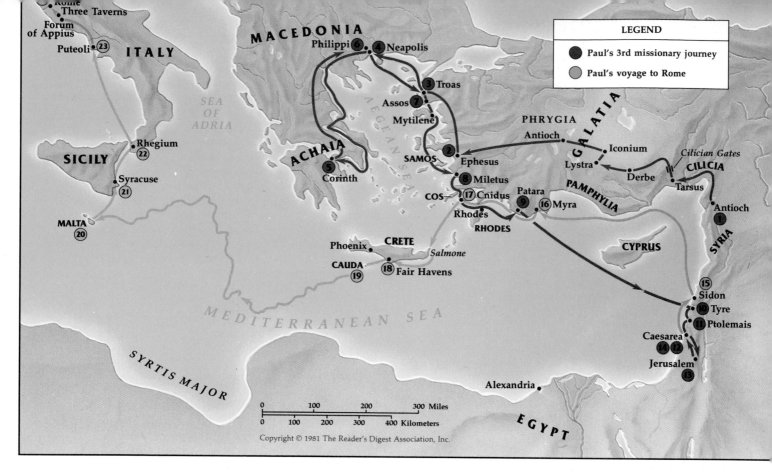

Neapolis (4), and "when we came into Macedonia," he says, "our bodies had no rest but we were afflicted at every turn—fighting without and fear within." Paul's mood changed when Titus appeared with news that the Corinthians had accepted needed discipline. Even so, he hurried on to Corinth (5) to counter the influence of persons from Jerusalem who had come questioning his authority.

We know little of Paul's activity in Corinth on this visit, except that his mind was fixed on going to Rome. It was apparently from Corinth that winter that he wrote to the Christians at Rome, expressing the hope that he would see them before taking up a mission to Spain.

With the coming of spring the sea lanes were safe from storms once more, and Paul found a ship bound for Syria—probably a Jewish pilgrimage ship going east for Passover. But when a plot was discovered against Paul's life, the sea voyage was abandoned, and he went through Macedonia by road, celebrating Passover at Philippi (6). After this he sailed to Troas, the lengthy journey (five days) suggesting a local cargo vessel. He stayed a week at Troas and on Sunday gave a sermon lasting until midnight in a third-floor room where Christians had gathered. A young man sitting in a window went to sleep, fell out, and was "taken up dead." But Paul went down and reassured the others, saying, "Do not be alarmed, for his life is in him."

Paul then went overland to Assos (7), while his friends sailed there. He joined the ship at Assos, which stopped at Mitylene and Samos en route to Miletus (8). Paul had purposely bypassed Ephesus because he was anxious to reach Jerusalem. Yet he summoned the elders of the Ephesian church to Miletus for a touching farewell before he sailed for Cos, then Rhodes, and Patara (9). There Paul's party changed to a cargo vessel bound for the Phoenician coast. Sailing within sight of Cyprus on their left, they came at last to Tyre (10).

During a seven-day stopover in Tyre, Paul took the opportunity to seek out Christians, who warned him not to go to Jerusalem. After a day with the Christians at Ptolemais (11), Paul and his company came to Caesarea (12), where he stayed in the house of Philip, one of the seven deacons of the Jerusalem church. Warned again not to go to the Holy City, Paul replied, "I am ready not only to be imprisoned but even to die at Jerusalem for the name of the Lord Jesus." All efforts to dissuade Paul failed, and he went to Jerusalem (13).

Paul told the elders of the Jerusalem church what "God had done among the Gentiles through his ministry." While they rejoiced in his tidings, the elders urged Paul to show Jewish Christians that he still honored Jewish traditions. The next day Paul went to the Temple for the purification rites. But Jews from the Ephesus region cried out against him, accusing him wrongly of defiling the Temple by bringing along a Gentile of that city. In the ensuing riot Roman soldiers narrowly prevented the mob from beating Paul to death and took the apostle to the Fortress Antonia.

When the Roman commander heard of a plot to kill his prisoner, he ordered a large detachment of infantry and cavalry to take Paul to Caesarea (14) under cover of night. There Paul remained in custody for two years.

Upon arriving in Caesarea as governor in the summer of A.D. 60, Porcius Festus received a request from the religious authorities in Jerusalem to send them the pris-

198

oner Paul. But Paul invoked his right as a Roman citizen to be tried in Rome. "I appeal to Caesar," said the apostle. "You have appealed to Caesar," said the governor; "to Caesar you shall go."

The 2,000-mile voyage to Rome began calmly enough. Julius, a centurion of the Augustan Cohort, was directed to take the prisoner to the imperial capital. Accompanied by Aristarchus—another survivor of the riot at Ephesus—and also possibly by Luke, Paul was taken aboard a ship bound for Asia Minor. At the first port of call, Sidon (15), Julius allowed Paul to visit friends. Avoiding the open seas, the ship passed under the lee of Cyprus. Not wishing to continue along the coastal route, Julius found an Egyptian vessel with a cargo of wheat bound from Myra (16) to Italy. With its heavy load and 276 people aboard, the ship made headway with difficulty, hugging the shore until it arrived at Cnidus (17). Here the captain had to decide between fighting the winds through the Greek islands or making for the open sea around Crete. He chose the latter and sailed past Cape Salmone at the eastern tip of the island but had difficulty reaching Fair Havens (18) on the southern coast.

As it was now late in the season, with storms a possibility, Paul advised that they winter there. But Fair Havens was not a suitable anchorage, and the captain, the owner of the ship, and the centurion selected Phoenix, a good harbor some 50 miles to the west. They set forth in gentle south winds, being careful to stay near shore. "But soon a tempestuous wind, called the northeaster, struck down from the land; and when the ship was caught and could not face the wind, we gave way to it and were driven." Due south of Phoenix, but 30 miles off course, the sailors managed to get the ship momentarily under control in the protected lee of the island of Cauda (19). Fearing that they would be blown across the sea onto the Syrtis Major, the dreaded shallows off the North African coast, they lowered the sails, but still the wind drove them southwestward. The next day they began to dump cargo. The violent storm raged for several days; seeing neither sun nor stars, the travelers abandoned all hope of being saved. But Paul advised them to take heart, for an angel had told him he would stand before Caesar.

About midnight of the 14th night, as the battered ship drifted between Achaia and Sicily, "the sailors suspected that they were nearing land." Soundings proved that they were moving into ever-shallower waters. As sea anchors were cast from the stern, the hapless sailors prayed for day to come. When the crew tried to abandon ship, the centurion and his soldiers cut the empty lifeboat adrift. Just before dawn Paul urged all of them to strengthen themselves with food, since they had eaten little in the 14 days.

At dawn they made out land, which none recognized. Casting off their anchors and loosening the ropes that tied the rudders, they hoisted sail and made for a bay with a beach. But the ship struck a shoal and the bow stuck fast as the furious surf began to break up the stern. The centurion kept his soldiers from killing the prisoners and ordered those who could swim to jump into the sea. Others were to hold fast to pieces of the disintegrating vessel. Thus the voyagers reached Malta (20).

The shipwrecked company spent three months on Malta, but when the weather began to turn—perhaps by early March—another Egyptian grain ship gave Julius and his captive passage to Italy. After a voyage of some 100 miles it put in for three days at Syracuse (21), a once-magnificent Greek city on Sicily but now the somewhat diminished Roman capital of the island. In favorable wind the ship sailed north, touching Italy at Rhegium (22). Three days later it dropped anchor at Puteoli (23), Italy's great commercial port.

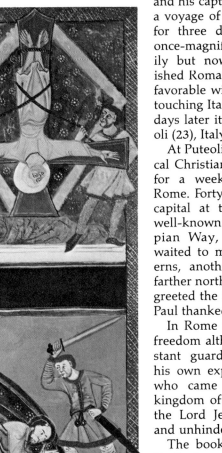

Although the Bible is silent on the matter, early traditions held that both Peter and Paul were martyred in Rome—Peter by crucifixion on an inverted cross, Paul by beheading—as in this illumination from a 10th-century Psalter.

At Puteoli, Paul was received by local Christians, with whom he stayed for a week before setting off for Rome. Forty-three miles south of the capital at the Forum of Appius, a well-known way-station on the Appian Way, Christians from Rome waited to meet Paul. At Three Taverns, another way-station 10 miles farther north, other Roman Christians greeted the apostle. "On seeing them Paul thanked God and took courage."

In Rome (24), Paul enjoyed much freedom although he was under constant guard. He had lodgings "at his own expense, and welcomed all who came to him, preaching the kingdom of God and teaching about the Lord Jesus Christ quite openly and unhindered."

The book of Acts concludes with Paul's two-year residence in Rome. Some think he was tried, released, and carried out his old dream of evangelizing Spain. A letter from Clement of Rome at the end of the 1st century suggests this. According to this view, he returned to Rome and was retried, found guilty, and beheaded. But others think he never left Rome and perished in Nero's persecution of A.D. 64.

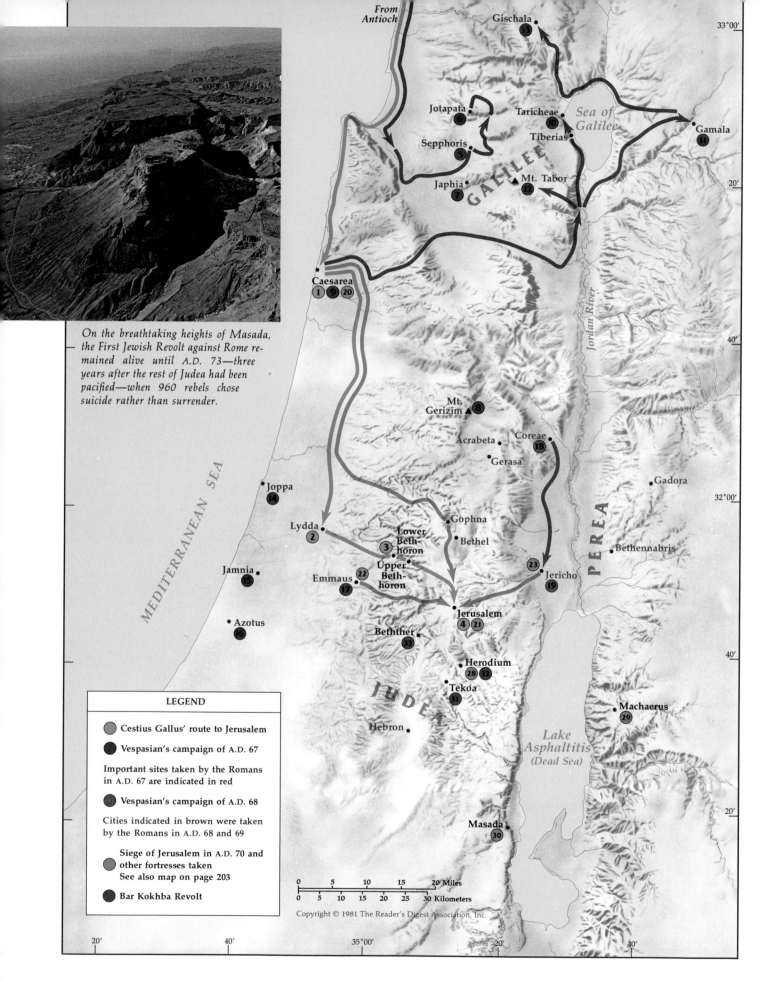

On the breathtaking heights of Masada, the First Jewish Revolt against Rome remained alive until A.D. 73—three years after the rest of Judea had been pacified—when 960 rebels chose suicide rather than surrender.

From Antioch

Gischala 13

Jotapata 6

Taricheae 10

Sepphoris 5

Tiberias

Sea of Galilee

Gamala 11

Japhia 7

GALILEE

Mt. Tabor 12

Caesarea
1 9 20

Jordan River

Mt. Gerizim 8

Acrabeta

Coreae 18

Gerasa

Gadora

MEDITERRANEAN SEA

Joppa 14

32°00′

Lydda 2

Gophna

Bethel

PEREA

Bethennabris

Lower Beth-horon 3

Jamnia 15

Upper Beth-horon

Emmaus 22 17

23

Jericho 19

Azotus 16

Jerusalem 4 21

Bethther 33

Herodium
28 32

Tekoa 31

Machaerus 29

JUDEA

Lake Asphaltitis (Dead Sea)

Hebron

Masada 30

LEGEND

- Cestius Gallus' route to Jerusalem
- Vespasian's campaign of A.D. 67
  Important sites taken by the Romans in A.D. 67 are indicated in red
- Vespasian's campaign of A.D. 68
  Cities indicated in brown were taken by the Romans in A.D. 68 and 69
- Siege of Jerusalem in A.D. 70 and other fortresses taken
  See also map on page 203
- Bar Kokhba Revolt

0   5   10   15   20 Miles
0 5 10 15 20 25 30 Kilometers

Copyright © 1981 The Reader's Digest Association, Inc.

33°00′

20′

40′

32°00′

40′

20′

20′   40′   35°00′   20′   40′

Revolts Against Rome

No portion of their world empire was more troublesome to the Romans than Judea. Even in times of apparent peace, underground revolt seethed continuously among the Jews, threatening to erupt into open conflict with their conquerors. Following the death in A.D. 44 of the Judean king Herod Agrippa I, grandson of Herod the Great, tensions rose steadily throughout the region. Each Roman procurator subsequently sent to rule the province seemed more corrupt, oppressive, and contemptuous of Jewish religious practices than the last. Extremists known as Zealots preached a holy war against Roman oppression with growing boldness. Bands of *sicarii*, or "dagger men," roamed about Jerusalem, kidnapping or assassinating Romans and Jews suspected of collaborating with the Romans. Judea was on the verge of revolt.

The fatal spark was struck by the cruel procurator Gessius Florus, who in the spring of 66 requisitioned a heavy tribute of gold from the Temple treasury. When the people gathered to protest this desecration, Florus turned his troops loose on the populace of Jerusalem. As many as 3,600 were killed. The city exploded. Rebels surged through the streets, gaining control of the Temple area. Other insurgents stormed the arsenal at Masada on Lake Asphaltitis, capturing its stock of arms and carrying them back to Jerusalem. Florus fled the city; the Roman military garrison was besieged and massacred; by August all of Jerusalem was in rebel hands and rebellion had spread throughout the land.

Cestius Gallus, the Syrian military governor whose responsibilities included Judea, set out from Antioch with a veteran legion to suppress the uprising. Marching down the coast, the Romans passed through Caesarea (1) and turned inland via Lydda (2) and Beth-horon (3). After suffering sharp losses to guerrilla attacks, Cestius reached Jerusalem (4). The chances of the small band of defenders holding off such a powerful force seemed slight, but unexpectedly Cestius broke off besieging operations and retreated the way he had come. The jubilant rebels pursued him closely. Eventually Cestius made good his escape, but not before losing all his siege artillery, most of his baggage, and his entire 400-man rear guard. It was a startling victory for the Jews. Dividing the country into seven military districts, they prepared to defend themselves against a renewed Roman offensive sure to come.

When news of the Jewish revolt reached Rome, the emperor Nero ordered his foremost general, Vespasian, to take the field. A deliberate and careful commander, Vespasian made his first target Galilee. With three infantry legions, a siege train, cavalry, and a corps of engineers, Vespasian began his advance in the spring of 67 and took Sepphoris (5) without battle. Galilee's military commander, Josephus (the future Jewish historian), was unable to challenge the Roman host in open battle and retreated into the fortress of Jotapata (6), where the defenders managed to hold out for 47 days before they were overwhelmed. Josephus, however, survived—to witness as a prisoner the entire war and later as a Roman citizen to write about it. Meanwhile, Vespasian had put down revolts at Japhia (7) and Mount Gerizim (8) to the south. From the military headquarters he had established at Caesarea (9), Vespasian next moved to suppress an outbreak at Taricheae (10). This left three centers of rebellion in the north: Gamala (11), Mount Tabor (12), and Gischala (13). When these three were taken, Galilee was firmly in Roman hands. Vespasian also moved to secure the coast, taking in turn Joppa (14), Jamnia (15), and Azotus (16).

In 68 the Roman commander launched a methodical campaign to isolate Jerusalem. The district of Perea east of the Jordan was conquered. In the west Emmaus (17) was taken and a legion garrisoned there. Entering the Jordan valley from the north through Coreae (18), Roman columns took Jericho (19), where a second garrison was stationed. Meanwhile, in Jerusalem various Jewish factions began fighting among themselves for control of the rebellion.

The overthrow and suicide of the emperor Nero brought operations in Judea to a temporary halt as Vespasian prudently withdrew to test the imperial winds. Eventually he himself was declared emperor. Sailing for Rome in the spring of 70, he left his capable son, Titus, in charge of the campaign against Jerusalem. From Caesarea (20), Titus marched rapidly southeastward with two legions and camped before the walls of Jerusalem (21). He was joined there by the legions that had been stationed at Emmaus (22) and Jericho (23). Counting cavalry and auxiliary forces, he had perhaps 80,000 men.

Titus faced a formidable task. Jerusalem was the most heavily fortified city of that time. Steep-sided valleys made its walls impregnable to assault on three sides; only from the north could an attacking army approach. A series of walls and towers provided three successive lines of defense. The Jews, who faced death or enslavement if defeated, had put aside their fratricidal conflicts to defend their stronghold with fanatic ardor. It was soon evident that they had no intention of accepting Titus' surrender demand or of waging a static defense. Jewish strike forces sallied forth to attack the Roman siege towers as they neared the outer wall (24, map on page 203) from the west. Only with great difficulty were the battering rams emplaced. Volleys of missiles were exchanged, with the Jews making use of the catapults captured from Cestius four years earlier. Casualties were heavy on both sides. On May 25 the attackers succeeded in hammering a breach in the outer wall. Roman infantry poured through and took control of the northern quarter know as Bezetha (New City).

Five days later a breach was made in the second wall (25). Again the legionnaires rushed forward; only this time they found themselves in a labyrinth of narrow streets and alleyways. Assailed from all directions, they were hurled back beyond the wall. The defenders' victory was only temporary, however; by early June the second wall was breached again, this time for good.

The walls enclosing the Temple and the upper and

Revolts Against Rome *(continued)*

lower cities were the most formidable barrier of all. Postponing an all-out assault, Titus turned to starvation tactics. A certain amount of food had been smuggled into the city almost nightly during the siege. But now the Romans sealed off Jerusalem completely with a wall of their own, made of earth and some five miles in circumference. From the outset of the siege those attempting to get through the encircling lines had been caught and crucified. Sometimes the daily executions reached 500; the crosses were never bare. Inside the city starvation and disease claimed a mounting toll. Bodies filled the streets and were stacked in houses. Thousands of corpses were thrown from the walls into the valleys below.

Titus now focused his attention on the Antonia (26), the great fortress Herod had built next to the Temple. The rams pounded away until, on July 24, Roman troops broke through, driving their foes before them in close fighting. When the great timbered gates of the Temple withstood the rams, they were set afire. Soon the fighting—and the fires—raged everywhere within the Temple complex. Before long the Temple, one of the wonders of the Roman world, was nothing more than a smoldering ruin.

The surviving rebels made a last-ditch stand within Herod's palace (27). The battering rams resumed their rhythmic work. When the legionnaires at last broke into this refuge, they found only corpses. Herod's palace and the rest of the upper city were put to the torch. Jerusalem was a city of the dead.

After the Romans took the Jewish strongholds at Herodium (28, map on page 200) and Machaerus (29), one final, grim act remained to be played in the Jews' revolt against Rome. The largest group of surviving Zealots had taken refuge at Masada (30), Herod's former mountaintop fortress and palace-villa overlooking Lake Asphaltitis. Flavius Silva, the new procurator of Judea, set forth to stamp out this last ember of rebellion.

Taking Masada required engineering skills of a high order. Silva's first move was to build a wall around the base of the mountain, to prevent the Zealots from escaping or receiving aid. He then erected a great earthen ramp to raise his siege machinery to the height of the fortress walls. Month by month the ramp grew until it reached 300 feet up the cliff face. A platform and siege tower were built atop the ramp, as mount for an iron battering ram. In May of 73 the ram broke through the main wall. The defenders retreated behind a secondary defense line of timber and earth. The Roman troops set fire to this barrier and soon gained the Zealots' last sanctuary. They found that nearly every occupant of Masada—almost a thousand men, women, and children—had committed suicide rather than submit to the Roman yoke. Only two women and five children evaded the death pact. After seven bloody years, the war was over.

Following the destruction of the Temple and much of Jerusalem in the war of 66–73, and that conflict's fearful toll among the Jewish revolutionaries, an uneasy peace took effect in Judea. Even though the military power of the rebels had been broken, their religion remained a strong and unifying force. In the villages and towns of their homeland and in the Jewish communities scattered throughout the Mediterranean world (the Diaspora), the teachings and practices of their ancient faith continued. And, as had been the case before the revolt against the Romans, a Jewish underground flourished. Many Jews continued to believe that a messianic leader would come to restore their rule of the land, and they plotted to be ready for that day.

Under the emperor Trajan (98–117), the Roman empire reached its maximum size. While Trajan was off fighting the Parthians, in pursuit of his expansionist policy, a series of rebellions against Roman rule occurred in Jewish communities in Mesopotamia, in Cyrene on the southern Mediterranean coast, on the island of Cyprus, and in Alexandria in Egypt. The response of the Romans was immediate and devastating. The uprisings were put down with great bloodshed, and Jewish religious practices were severely repressed.

Midway through the reign of Trajan's successor, Hadrian (117–38), however, there was a rush of hope among Jews that better times were ahead. Visiting Judea in the years 130 and 131, Hadrian seemed to suggest that he favored the rebuilding of Jerusalem and restoration of the Temple. The hopes of the Jewish population were soon dashed. Rather than a new Jerusalem and Temple dedicated to the God of the Jews, the emperor revealed that instead he would rebuild the city as a Roman colony, to be renamed Aelia Capitolina. Its centerpiece would be a temple erected to the worship of the Roman god Jupiter.

As the impact of Hadrian's decision spread, the faithful once again raised the banners of revolution against Rome. Their leader was Simon bar Kokhba (or Simeon ben Kosiba), a man many regarded as a messiah come to lead them to independence and triumph over the pagans—though there is doubt among historians that Bar Kokhba saw himself in such a role. In any event, he proved to be a dedicated and inspiring leader who gave his name to a revolt that rocked the Roman world.

Unlike the earlier generation that had rebelled against Rome, the Bar Kokhba rebels were better prepared to do battle with the world's leading military power. There was none of the bitter infighting that marked the Zealot leadership during the first war. The Jews had accumulated arms and hidden them in strategic locations throughout the country and had developed tactics for a campaign of guerrilla warfare. Rather than allowing themselves to be trapped in great fortresses where Roman skill in engineering and siege warfare made their eventual defeat inevitable, they had established numerous fortified "fall-back" positions that would enable them to escape annihilation and survive to fight another day.

Finding the rebel forces too strong and well organized to suppress, the Roman governor, Tinnius Rufus, withdrew his garrison of legionnaires from Jerusalem to Caesarea. The revolutionaries established their own government in Jerusalem, minting coins that proclaimed 131 as "Year One of the Redemption of Israel."

The Romans reacted to the new uprising as they had to the First Jewish Revolt. Publicius Marcellus, the governor of Syria, was the first to respond. He collected his troops, ordered reinforcements from as far away as

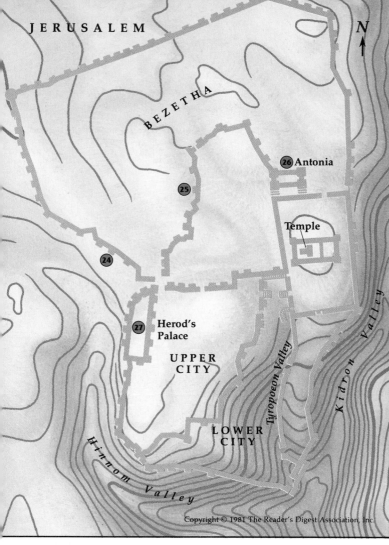

JERUSALEM

BEZETHA

26 Antonia

25

24

Temple

27 Herod's
Palace

UPPER
CITY

Tyropoeon Valley

Kidron Valley

LOWER
CITY

Hinnom Valley

The Arch of Titus was built in Rome during the reign of Domitian (81–96) to commemorate the crushing of the Judean revolt of 66–70 by his father, Vespasian, and his brother, Titus. This frieze shows triumphant soldiers carrying off a seven-branched menorah and other spoils seized from the Temple in Jerusalem.

Egypt, and attempted to stamp out the rebellion before it spread. Details of the subsequent fighting are not recorded, but the outcome was overwhelmingly in Bar Kokhba's favor. Soon nearly all of Judea was in the hands of the rebels. But, as was true of the earlier war, Rome was stung into action by this grave setback to its power and prestige. Hadrian recalled his most skilled general, Julius Severus, from Britain to take command of the Judean campaign.

Having had experience with the guerrilla tactics of the Britons, Severus conducted a cautious campaign. He assembled an exceedingly powerful force—six legions plus detachments from a number of other legions and numerous foreign auxiliaries—and in 134 opened a full-scale offensive against the Jews. Avoiding open battle, Bar Kokhba withdrew into the highlands south of Jerusalem and conducted a savage guerrilla campaign from his strongholds at Tekoa (31, map on page 200), Herodium (32), and Beththter (33). In this harsh and forbidding landscape marked with rocky defiles and hidden caves, the fighting became a series of ambushes and hit-and-run raids countered by plodding but continuous pursuit. Losses were very heavy on both sides.

In the end, relentless Roman power gained the upper hand. By 134 Jerusalem had been recaptured; the ruinous condition of its walls and towers made it impossible to defend effectively. Bar Kokhba and his remaining fol-

lowers retreated to Beththter, where—perhaps finally exhausted and too weak to continue the war of maneuver—the Jewish army made its last stand. It is not known when the siege began or how it progressed, but in about August of 135 the Romans finally broke through the walls and slaughtered the defenders. Simon bar Kokhba was among the fallen.

The remaining rebels had taken refuge in caves overlooking the Dead Sea, north of Masada. Many perished of thirst or starvation; many died at the hands of the Romans; some killed themselves. Possibly a handful survived. By the end of 135 the Bar Kokhba Revolt was over, crushed beyond revival.

Not content with this victory, Hadrian determined to eradicate the slightest possibility of any future Judean uprising. Those Jews who did not manage to flee the land were killed or enslaved. Jerusalem became a Romanized city, completely resettled by Gentiles and with a statue of Hadrian in the temple to Jupiter placed on the site of the former Holy of Holies. The practice of the Jewish religion was proscribed. By imperial decree the name of Judea was changed to Syria-Palestina. While the Jewish settlements and communities in other lands and cities (including Rome itself) gained strength as a result of the influx of refugees from Judea, the Jews became a people without a homeland. So they would remain until the establishment of the modern state of Israel in 1948.

The Spread of Christianity

"Go into all the world," Jesus said to the apostles, "and preach the gospel to the whole creation." That solemn commission was undertaken at the festival of Pentecost, seven weeks after the Crucifixion, when Peter started preaching to "devout men from every nation" who had traveled to Jerusalem (1). Such an occasion—a traditional religious festival held in a remote corner of the Roman empire—must have seemed unimportant to the local authorities. Yet in the perspective of history this Pentecost would stand out as the beginning of a process destined not only to conquer Rome's vast empire but also to shape the future of western civilization.

The first generation of Christian evangelists, as recorded in the New Testament, seems dominated by the tireless Paul and his companions. Yet theirs were not the only important missionary journeys undertaken during the crucial period. Indeed, by the time of Paul's conversion a number of Christian communities had already come into being—not only in the Holy Land but also in Phoenicia, Syria, and parts of Asia Minor. And when Paul later traveled to Rome (2), there were church members waiting to greet him at several stops on the way. Unfortunately, little is known of the founding of these congregations or of any others that may have taken root elsewhere—in North Africa, perhaps, or Mesopotamia—during these formative years. What we know is that by the end of Paul's life, outposts of the new faith were flourishing from the Holy Land north to Syria and across the northern rim of the Mediterranean through Asia Minor and Greece to Rome.

The westward spread of Christianity was aided by a combination of historical and cultural factors, chief among them the Roman empire itself. With the exception of the two Jewish rebellions, the lands within its

borders were at peace for generations. Commerce flourished as merchant ships sailed a Mediterranean free of pirates and as caravans traveled a vast network of well-patrolled roads, some 60,000 miles in all. Travel was far easier than ever before—whether for merchants or missionaries—and the general level of prosperity encouraged the contributions needed to support the evangelists and their fledgling congregations.

Important too was the presence of Jewish synagogues in virtually every major population center in the empire. After several centuries of the Diaspora, there were probably more Jews living outside the Holy Land than in it. Their synagogues were the first places Paul (and, presumably, other early missionaries) visited on arriving in a new city and frequently the first places he made converts.

Still another factor that played a vital role in the rapid spread of Christianity was the Greek language, which was widely used across the empire by Jews and Gentiles alike, thereby doing away with the handicap of a language barrier. It also helped unite the growing network

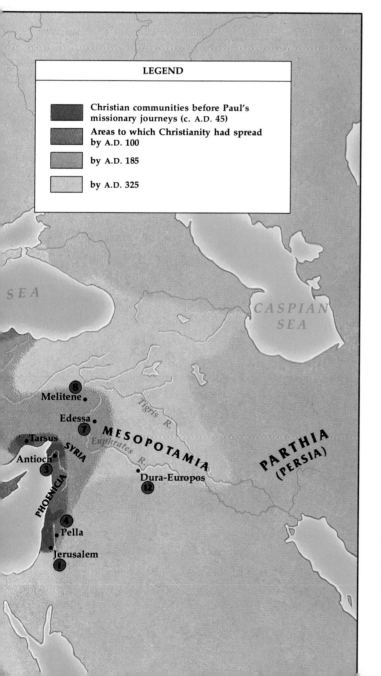

LEGEND

Christian communities before Paul's missionary journeys (c. A.D. 45)

Areas to which Christianity had spread by A.D. 100

by A.D. 185

by A.D. 325

SEA

CASPIAN SEA

Melitene

Tigris R.

Edessa

MESOPOTAMIA

Tarsus

Euphrates R.

Antioch SYRIA

PARTHIA (PERSIA)

Dura-Europos

PHOENICIA

Pella

Jerusalem

of Christian churches, which remained Greek-speaking as far west as Gaul throughout the 1st and 2nd centuries. Of course, none of these factors would have mattered without the zeal of the early Christian missionaries and the inherent appeal of a faith that held out the promise of salvation to all those who truly believed, regardless of their race or nationality or station in life.

The church's history in the decades following Nero's persecution of A.D. 64 is not well documented, though fragmentary evidence provides a hint of the developments that were taking place. A major one was the rapid decline of the Jerusalem church, which had early come under pressure from Jewish authorities there. As hostilities intensified—fueled by bitter disputes over observance of Jewish law—many church members left Jerusalem for Antioch in Syria (3), which was emerging as the dominant center of Gentile Christianity. Finally, at the outbreak of the Jewish revolt in 66, the remaining church members in Jerusalem fled to the safety of Pella (4), east of the Jordan River, and with this the importance of Jerusalem in the church's early history came to an end.

Asia Minor, however, continued to provide fertile soil for church growth. It was one of the most prosperous areas of the empire, with commerce moving incessantly over its cool mountains, across its hot plains, and down its coastal valleys to bustling ports, such as Ephesus (5). With the traders and their caravans went the Christian faith. By the year 100, it is estimated that there were already upward of 300,000 believers throughout the empire—an eightfold increase in 30 years—and of these some 80,000 were concentrated in Asia Minor. In a letter to the emperor Trajan written about 112, Pliny the Younger, governor of Bithynia, noted that "this contagious superstition [has] spread" throughout the province, leaving the ancient temples almost deserted. Trajan counseled moderation in dealing with the Christians, but the correspondence illustrates the tenuous position of the church and the problems its continued growth raised for the Roman government.

Indeed, that growth was creating problems for the church itself. A list of bishops drawn up in 185 by Irenaeus, the bishop of Lyons (6) in Gaul, makes clear just how much expansion had taken place since the end of Paul's ministry. To the east the faith had reached into Mesopotamia, with churches in Edessa (7)—probably the first place where Christianity was made an official religion—and Melitene (8). In North Africa there were two major centers—one in Alexandria (9) and the other in Carthage (10)—both of which assumed leading roles in the development of Christian scholarship and theology. In Europe, finally, the church's frontiers had pushed westward into Spain and northward as far as Cologne (11) in the Rhine valley. "We are but of yesterday," wrote the great theologian Tertullian at the end of the 2nd century, "yet we overspread your empire; your cities, islands, forts, assemblies, camps, palace, senate, forum all swarm with Christians."

Inevitably, this continuing geographical expansion, combined with the relative autonomy of individual churches, gave rise to inconsistencies and conflicts. While all shared the same fundamental beliefs, there de-

The Spread of Christianity (continued)

veloped a bewildering variety of local rites and doctrines. Increasingly it became evident that a more formal structure or mechanism was needed to bind the far-flung congregations together and resolve their differences through recognized channels of authority. It also became evident—though more gradually, and not without vigorous dissent—that Rome was the natural center from which that authority should flow.

There were a number of outstanding Christian centers in the 2nd century—Antioch, Ephesus, Alexandria, and Carthage among them—but none had a stature equal to that of the Roman church. Its location at the heart of the empire had set it apart from the beginning, and the traditions associating it with both Peter and Paul enhanced its claim to primacy. By the end of the 1st century, Clement, the bishop of Rome, had expressed pastoral concern over other churches, asserting his views in a manner reminiscent of Paul's epistles. Early in the 2nd century, when Bishop Ignatius of Antioch was en route to his dramatic martyrdom in Rome, he requested that the church there not try to intervene in his behalf—an indication that church leaders in Rome may have been influential enough to effect government actions. In any event, Rome's role in the expanding Christian world continued to increase, as evidenced late in the 2nd century when Irenaeus of Lyons asserted that each church must agree with the Roman church on matters of policy.

One measure of the church's position was the appearance during the 2nd century of a body of literary and intellectual diatribes against it. These, in turn, inspired vigorous rebuttals by Christian intellectuals who not only defended their faith but counterattacked the emptiness of pagan religion and the immorality of Roman life. Known as the Apologists, they came to prominence in widely separate places—reflecting the fact that Christian communities in many parts of the empire were maturing into important centers of scholarship. Tertullian of Carthage emerged as a leading voice of Christian thought toward the end of the 2nd century and was also the first major church scholar to use what would become the principal language of western Christianity: Latin.

Perhaps the best known of the early literary assaults on Christianity was written by Celsus, a leading Roman political theoretician. He accused Christianity of appealing to the lowest types of people, to "illiterate and bucolic yokels." If Jesus could convince no one during his life, Celsus argued, it was absurd that his followers should hope to convince multitudes now that he was dead.

Celsus was answered in a long and skillful rebuttal by Origen, the brilliant onetime student of the Christian catechetical school in Alexandria. The truly perceptive thinker, said Origen, seeks the hidden truths of the law, the prophets, and the gospels. These Celsus had dismissed "as if they contained nothing of importance," but in fact it was only because he "did not examine their meaning, or attempt to enter into the purpose of the writers." Who, then, is truly the fool, asked Origen. The one who investigates and then decides, or the one who simply refuses to look at the evidence?

Needless to say, the friction between Christian and pagan values was not confined to literary exchanges,

which may have interested Rome's educated elite but hardly touched the lives of ordinary people. Too often, the conflict took a more brutal form. Christians openly condemned gladiatorial combat and other public spectacles and for this were branded as misfits, enemies of the Roman way of life. Rumors were widely circulated that Christian worship included such practices as cannibalism (a reference to the Eucharist), incest (they espoused love toward their "brothers" and "sisters"), and witchcraft (they testified to miraculous cures). Fueled by these lurid tales, popular hostility sometimes flared into bloody anti-Christian riots—with the approval of local officials.

Rome's policy toward Christians was marked by extreme fluctuations throughout the first 300 years of the church's existence. Twice in the 1st century—under Nero in 64 and Domitian in 95—there were officially sponsored persecutions, though how widely spread beyond Rome is not known. Of particular concern to the government was not only the geographical spread of the new religion but its upward movement through the class structure from the lower and middle levels of Roman society to the most worldy and privileged classes. Domitian's anti-Christian campaign may even have reached the royal family: Flavius Clemens, a cousin of the emperor, was executed and his wife exiled for "atheism"—probably meaning Christianity.

During the first half of the 2nd century a moderate policy prevailed, first established by Trajan in his correspondence with Pliny and generally followed in the reigns of Hadrian (117–38) and Antoninus Pius (138–61). Nonetheless, Christianity was still not officially tolerated, and its adherents remained liable at any time to arrest, torture, imprisonment, confiscation of property, banishment to the galley ships or mines, and even execution.

During the latter part of the 2nd century, official attitudes toward Christianity hardened once again. By then the faith was gaining real strength in numbers, partly because of the ideals set by Christians who refused to renounce their faith in the face of persecuion. As the number of such determined believers increased throughout the empire, official hostility intensified. The philosopher-emperor Marcus Aurelius (161–80) was deeply antagonistic toward Christians, and during the reign of this otherwise moderate man assaults on them intensified.

Nevertheless, this renewed wave of persecution was no more successful in stamping out Christianity than earlier attempts had been, and the faith continued to spread. Most Christian communities were centered in homes—"house-churches"—where the congregation gathered, usually on Sunday, to celebrate Jesus' resurrection with prayers, hymns, and study of the Scriptures. The earliest known Christian church building, excavated at Dura-Europos (12) on the Euphrates River in eastern Syria and dating from about 232, was just such a house-church.

The 3rd century continued to produce sporadic but minor anti-Christian outbursts, with little impact on church growth. By midcentury, however, the empire was caught up in a deepening spiral of political and economic chaos: its border areas in the west were being regularly plundered by Germanic tribes, its eastern frontier was

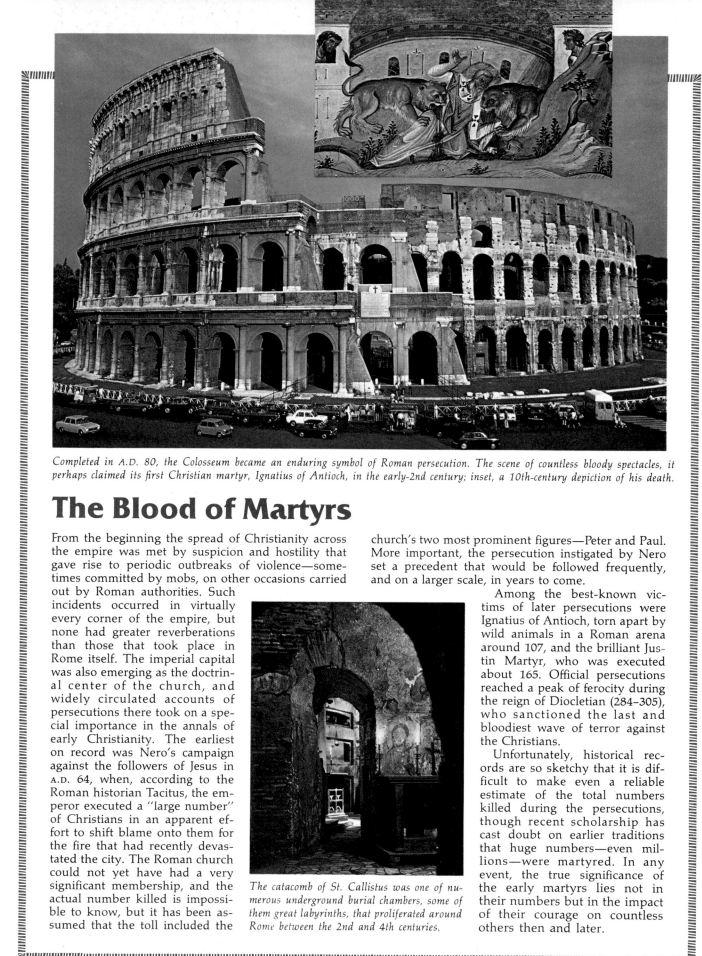

Completed in A.D. 80, the Colosseum became an enduring symbol of Roman persecution. The scene of countless bloody spectacles, it perhaps claimed its first Christian martyr, Ignatius of Antioch, in the early-2nd century; inset, a 10th-century depiction of his death.

The Blood of Martyrs

From the beginning the spread of Christianity across the empire was met by suspicion and hostility that gave rise to periodic outbreaks of violence—sometimes committed by mobs, on other occasions carried out by Roman authorities. Such incidents occurred in virtually every corner of the empire, but none had greater reverberations than those that took place in Rome itself. The imperial capital was also emerging as the doctrinal center of the church, and widely circulated accounts of persecutions there took on a special importance in the annals of early Christianity. The earliest on record was Nero's campaign against the followers of Jesus in A.D. 64, when, according to the Roman historian Tacitus, the emperor executed a "large number" of Christians in an apparent effort to shift blame onto them for the fire that had recently devastated the city. The Roman church could not yet have had a very significant membership, and the actual number killed is impossible to know, but it has been assumed that the toll included the

The catacomb of St. Callistus was one of numerous underground burial chambers, some of them great labyrinths, that proliferated around Rome between the 2nd and 4th centuries.

church's two most prominent figures—Peter and Paul. More important, the persecution instigated by Nero set a precedent that would be followed frequently, and on a larger scale, in years to come.

Among the best-known victims of later persecutions were Ignatius of Antioch, torn apart by wild animals in a Roman arena around 107, and the brilliant Justin Martyr, who was executed about 165. Official persecutions reached a peak of ferocity during the reign of Diocletian (284–305), who sanctioned the last and bloodiest wave of terror against the Christians.

Unfortunately, historical records are so sketchy that it is difficult to make even a reliable estimate of the total numbers killed during the persecutions, though recent scholarship has cast doubt on earlier traditions that huge numbers—even millions—were martyred. In any event, the true significance of the early martyrs lies not in their numbers but in the impact of their courage on countless others then and later.

The Spread of Christianity (continued)

threatened by a newly resurgent Persian empire, and its armies were beset by an epidemic of insubordination and mutiny. One of the steps taken in hopes of halting the decline and rallying the populace around the emperor was to revive public worship of the empire's traditional gods. When large numbers of Christians refused to participate, a brutal campaign to exterminate them was launched by the emperor Decius (249–51) and carried on intermittently by his successors, Gallus and Valerian.

The bloodletting was stopped in 261 by an edict granting equal toleration to all religions. During the next four decades Christian communities appeared as far as Britain in the northwest and beyond the empire's eastern boundary in Mesopotamia. This respite, however, was brought to a sudden end in 303, when the emperor Diocletian launched what was to be the last and most violent attempt to rid the empire of Christianity. A former army officer, Diocletian had taken far-reaching steps to restore order to the empire since coming to power in 284. His most radical move was to divide the sprawling realm in two, delegating control of the western portion to a co-emperor, Maximian. At first Diocletian was tolerant of Christianity (whose following may have included his own wife and daughter). But increasingly he came to view the faith as a threat to his authority. In 303 Diocletian issued a series of decrees ordering, among other things, the destruction of all church buildings and the imprisonment, exile, or execution of those who refused to make sacrifices to the imperial gods.

The campaign inflicted terrible suffering on Christian communities in many parts of the empire, but in the end it was doomed to failure. The sheer numbers of Christians made such an undertaking difficult and costly, and the widespread sympathy for the victims led more and more local officials to moderate their attempts to enforce the persecution.

Both Diocletian and Maximian abdicated in 305, plunging the divided empire into disorder. In 306 the young army commander Constantine was proclaimed emperor of the west by his troops, but six years passed before he took undisputed possession of that title by invading Italy and defeating his principal rival, Maxentius, at the historic battle of Milvian Bridge (13). It was there, according to tradition, that Constantine saw a fiery cross in the sky—an omen of victory that convinced him of the truth and power of Christianity. Not yet a convert, Constantine nonetheless established himself as an active and generous patron of the church. In 313 he and his eastern co-emperor, Licinius, proclaimed freedom for all religions and restored property that had been confiscated from the Christians. A series of other measures followed—providing generous financial support and permitting churches to receive property, exempting Christians from participation in gladiatorial games and pagan sacrifices, designating Sunday a day of rest, and more—all bolstering the church's position.

Constantine's support of Christianity, of course, was not without practical benefits to him. Christians were not yet a majority of the empire's population, but they were numerous, widely dispersed, and cohesive enough to provide a much-needed unifying force. This was especially so in Asia Minor and other eastern areas, which had some of the oldest and most influential Christian communities—and which readily closed ranks behind Constantine when he finally defeated Licinius and reunited the empire in 324.

Fittingly, it was Constantine himself who convened a historic church council the following year at the city of Nicaea (14) in Bithynia. Some 300 bishops gathered there to deal with a stormy controversy over the nature of Christ's divinity that was threatening to splinter the church from within. After several weeks of debate the council arrived at a resolution that would remain at the core of Christian doctrine, the declaration of faith known to later centuries as the Nicene Creed.

The long struggle of survival was over. The Christian faith was widely and firmly planted—indeed, it would outlast the empire that had tried to suppress it and that now openly embraced it. Christianity was still a minority religion concentrated chiefly in the cities of the empire. But it was now secure and in years to come would win the allegiance of a great majority of the populace. The apostles and those that followed had labored long and well, going out "into all the world" to preach their master's gospel, and in the triumph of the church under Constantine could be seen a resounding fulfillment of the mission begun three centuries earlier in Jerusalem.

In this 9th-century illumination, the sign of the cross confirms Constantine's decisive victory in 312 B.C. at the Milvian Bridge against Maxentius, his rival for the imperial throne. According to a famous story handed down from antiquity, Constantine adopted the cross as his army's emblem after it appeared to him in a vision, accompanied by the Latin words In hoc signo vinces—"By this sign you shall conquer."

Gazetteer of the Bible World

The gazetteer that begins on the following page is an alphabetical guide to places in the biblical world. The names of villages, towns, and cities mentioned in the Revised Standard Version of the Bible and in the Apocrypha are listed. There are also entries for places that figured prominently in the history of the Jewish people and in the rise of Christianity but which are not named in the Bible—for example, Machaerus in the Transjordan, where, according to the historian Josephus, John the Baptist was put to death. Countries, regions, and geographical features such as mountains and rivers, however, are not included in this gazetteer.

The spelling of each place-name conforms to the Revised Standard Version. Alternate names appear as separate entries, which include the pertinent biblical citations for that name, and are cross-referenced to the main entry in boldface type. In addition to straight cross-references, boldface also indicates where additional information either directly or indirectly related to that site can be found.

Each place-name is followed by its pronunciation; the key to diacritical marks appears on the bottom of page 210. Where location of an ancient site is known, the modern name is provided. The Arabic words *Tell* and *Khirbet* (abbreviated as T. and Kh.) that precede the modern name mean "mound" and "ruin" respectively. A question mark after the name indicates a degree of un-

certainty about this identification. In some instances, however, the ancient and the current names are the same or so similar that further identification is unnecessary.

The bracketed letter and number after the modern site name are keyed to the grid on the introductory maps on pages 44–45 and 46–47. A-1 through J-7 refer to the northern segment of the Holy Land shown on pages 44–45 and K-1 through T-7 to the southern portion on pages 46–47. The locator on page 44 permits the siting of important places that are off the base map. Of course, not every place in the gazetteer is shown on these maps. In cases where a choice had to be made, the more important or more positively identified has been sited.

Wherever possible, each gazetteer entry gives a general location for the site. A short history of the site as it relates to the Bible follows, together with appropriate biblical references as well as references in other contemporary literature, such as the Amarna Letters of the 14th century B.C. or the Moabite Stone. Less important biblical mentions are listed at the close of the entry.

This gazetteer of the Bible world not only provides the basic geographical and biblical data about each place but the system of cross-referencing invites the reader to explore the possible connections between these ancient sites. The gazetteer was researched and written by Prof. Harry Thomas Frank, the principal adviser and editorial consultant on this volume.

Arabs take their camels across an overgrown viaduct leading to a gate in the ancient, crumbled walls of Caesarea Philippi. This engraving, as well as all but one of the following views, is from an 1880's publication, Picturesque Palestine.

A

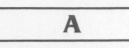

ABDON (ab' dŏn) Kh. Abda [4–B] Levitical city in Asher. Assigned to Gershon, or Gershom, son of Levi (Jos. 19:28, where called Ebron; 21:30; 1 Chr. 6:74).

ABEL (ā' bəl) Another name for **Abel-beth-maacah** (2 Sam. 20:18).

ABEL-BETH-MAACAH (ā' bəl bĕth mā' ə kə) Abil el-Qamh [6–A] Northernmost town in Israel. Rebellious Sheba sought refuge here (2 Sam. 20:14, 15, 18) and was killed. Conquered by Ben-hadad (1 Kg. 15:20; 2 Chr. 16:4). Captured by Tiglath-pileser III in 733 B.C. (2 Kg. 15:29). Called Abel of Beth-maacah in 2 Sam. 20:14, 15; Abel in 2 Sam. 20:18; Abel-maim in 2 Chr. 16:4.

ABEL-KERAMIM (ā' bəl kĕr' ə mĭm) Naur? [7–H] Town in Ammon. Farthest point in Jephthah's victory over the Ammonites (Jg. 11:33).

ABEL-MAIM (ā' bəl mā' im) Another name for **Abel-beth-maacah** (2 Chr. 16:4).

ABEL-MEHOLAH (ā' bəl mĭ hō' lə) T. Abu Sus? [6–E] Town in the Jordan valley. Midianites fled this way after their defeat by Gideon (Jg. 7:22). In Solomon's fifth administrative district (1 Kg. 4:12). Home of Elisha (1 Kg. 19:16), where Elijah cast his mantle over his successor.

ABEL-SHITTIM (ā' bəl shĭt' tĭm) Another name for **Shittim** (Num. 33:49).

ABRONAH (ə brō' nə) Umm Rashrash? [4–T] Watering place in the Arabah. Hebrews camped here between Jotbathah and Ezion-geber (Num. 33:34–35).

ACCO (ăk' ō) T. el-Fukhkhar [3–B] Coastal city north of Mount Carmel. Assigned to Asher, who were unable to drive out the Canaanites (Jg. 1:31). Taken by Alexander the Great c. 332 B.C. Name changed to Ptolemais during reign of Ptolemy II Philadelphus (284–246 B.C.). Annexed by the Syrian Seleucids c. 198 B.C. Near here Simon rescued the Galilean Jews in 164 B.C. (1 Macc. 5:15, 22). Jonathan treacherously seized here by Tryphon in 143 B.C. (1 Macc. 12:48). Captured by Pompey in 64–63 B.C. Visited by Julius Caesar in 47 B.C. Where Herod the Great landed in 39 B.C. to begin conquest of his kingdom. Paul spent a day here when returning from his third missionary journey (Acts 21:7).

ACHSHAPH (ăk' shăf) Kh. el-Harbaj? [3–C] Canaanite town on the Plain of Acco. Its king joined coalition against the Israelites (Jos. 11:1) and was defeated by Joshua at the waters of Merom (Jos. 12:20). Assigned to Asher (Jos. 19:25).

ACHZIB (ăk' zĭb) 1. T. el-Beida? [3–I] Town in the Shephelah. Assigned to Judah (Jos. 15:44). Also mentioned in Gen. 38:5, where called Chezib; Mic. 1:14. 2. ez-Zib [4–B] Greco-Roman Ecdippa. Town on the Phoenician coast. Assigned to Asher (Jos. 19:29), who were unable to drive out the Canaanites (Jg. 1:31). Captured by Sennacherib in 701 B.C. Here Herod the Great's brother, Phasael, and Hyrcanus II, the Hasmonean High Priest, were imprisoned by the Parthians.

ACRABA (ăk' rə bə) Akrabeh [5–G] Village in Samaria mentioned in Jdt. 7:18.

ADADAH (ăd' ə də) Town in the Negeb. Assigned to Judah (Jos. 15:22). Site unidentified but possibly the same as **Aroer 3**.

ADAM (ăd' əm) T. ed-Damiya [6–G] Town at a major ford of the Jordan River north of Jericho. Here waters of the Jordan were stopped to allow the Hebrews to pass into Canaan on dry ground (Jos. 3:16). Also mentioned in Hos. 6:7.

ADAMAH (ăd' ə mə) Qarn Hattin? [5–C] Fortified city in Naphtali (Jos. 19:36).

ADAMI-NEKEB (ăd' ə mī nĕk' ĕb) Border town in Naphtali (Jos. 19:33). Site unidentified.

ADASA (ăd' ə sə) Kh. Addasa [4–H] Town on the Way of Beth-horon. Where Judas Maccabeus defeated Nicanor (1 Macc. 7:40, 45).

ADDAR (ăd' är) Ein Qedeis? [1–O] Place on the border of Judah (Jos. 15:3). Sometimes identified with Hazar-addar of Num. 34:4, which is probably the same as **Hezron** of Jos. 15:3.

ADDON (ăd' ŏn) Unknown place in Babylonia from which exiles returned (Ezra 2:59; Neh. 7:61).

ADIDA (ăd' ə də) Hellenistic name for **Hadid** (1 Macc. 12:38; 13:13).

ADITHAIM (ăd' ə thā' əm) Town in the Shephelah (Jos. 15:36). Site unidentified.

ADMAH (ăd' mə) One of the five Cities of the Plain at the southern end of the Dead Sea. Site unidentified. Attacked by the kings of the north (Gen. 14:1–12). Destroyed with Sodom, Gomorrah, Zeboiim, and Bela (Zoar) (Gen. 19:24–29; Dt. 29:23). Also mentioned in Gen. 10:19; Hos. 11:8.

ADORA (ăd' ə ra) Greco-Roman name for **Adoraim.**

ADORAIM (ăd' ə rā' əm) Dura [3–J] Greco-Roman Adora. Town in Judah; later one of the leading cities of eastern Idumea. Fortified by Rehoboam (2 Chr. 11:9). Where a snowstorm stopped Trypho's advance in 142 B.C. (1 Macc. 13:20–22). Captured by John Hyrcanus in 129 B.C. Rebuilt by Gabinius in 59 B.C. and made an administrative center.

ADRAMYTTIUM (ăd' rə mĭt' ĭ əm) Port in Mysia in the Roman province of Asia. Paul began his journey from Caesarea to Rome in a ship of Adramyttium (Acts 27:2).

ADULLAM (ə dŭl' əm) T. esh-Sheikh Madhkur [3–I] Greco-Roman Odollam. Canaanite royal city in the Shephelah. Scene of Judah-Tamar incident (Gen. 38:1, 12–20). Captured by Joshua in the conquest (Jos. 12:15). Assigned to Judah (Jos. 15:35). Probable location of the cave to which David fled from Saul (1 Sam. 22:1; 2 Sam. 23:13; 1 Chr. 11:15). Fortified by Rehoboam (2 Chr. 11:7). Settled by Jews returning from the Exile (Neh. 11:30). Here Judas Maccabeus retired after defeating Gorgias in 164 B.C. (2 Macc. 12:38).

AENON (ē' nŏn) Place near Salim where John was baptizing (Jn. 3:23). Site unidentified.

AHLAB (ā' lăb) Town near Tyre assigned to Asher, who failed to drive out the Canaanites (Jg. 1:31). Sometimes identified with **Helbah** of Jg. 1:31. Another name for **Mahalab.**

AI (ā' ī) 1. Kh. et-Tell [4–H] Canaanite city in the Saddle of Benjamin. Abraham twice pitched his tent near here (Gen. 12:8; 13:3). Joshua's first attempt to capture it failed (Jos. 7:2–5), but his second attempt was successful (Jos. 8:1–29; 9:3; 10:1). Settled by Jews returning from the Exile (Ezra 2:28; Neh. 7:32). Sometimes identified with Aiath of Is. 10:28 and Aija of Neh. 11:31. 2. Ammonite city mentioned in Jer. 49:3. Site unidentified.

AIATH (ā' yăth) Possibly the same as **Ai** (Is. 10:28).

AIJA (ā' jə) Possibly the same as **Ai** (Neh. 11:31).

AIJALON (ā' jə lŏn) 1. Yalo [3–H] Amorite city in the western foothills commanding an important route into the highlands of Judah. At the battle of Gibeon Joshua commanded the moon to stand still in the valley of Aijalon (Jos. 10:12). Assigned to Dan (Jos. 19:42). When Dan proved unable to drive out the Amorites, Ephraim took Aijalon (Jg. 1:35). Levitical city (Jos. 21:24) and a city of

The Books of the Bible

The original Hebrew Bible consists of 24 books—Torah, or Law (5 books); Prophets (8 books); Writings (11 books). These same books are rearranged and divided into the 39 books of the Protestant Old Testament. The Catholic Old Testament also includes these 39 books, in a different order, plus the seven books indicated in brown in the list below, at right. The Greek Orthodox Old Testament follows the Catholic version with some further additions from this list. These works are called deuterocanonical, meaning that they were added later to the canon of the Holy Scripture. In the Protestant Bible, these books generally constitute a separate section entitled the Apocrypha, which is usually placed between the Old and New Testaments.

The New Testament in Catholic, Protestant, and Orthodox Bibles consists of 27 books. However, the Apocalypse of John is called the Revelation of John in the Protestant version. The abbreviations of the books of the Bible that appear in the gazetteer and in the list of biblical citations used in this book (see page 245) follow *The New Oxford Annotated Bible with the Apocrypha* (Revised Standard Version).

Acts	The Acts	3 Jn.	3 John	S. of S.	Song of Solomon
Am.	Amos	Job	Job	1 Th.	1 Thessalonians
1 Chr.	1 Chronicles	Jon.	Jonah	2 Th.	2 Thessalonians
2 Chr.	2 Chronicles	Jos.	Joshua	1 Tim.	1 Timothy
Col.	Colossians	Jude	Jude	2 Tim.	2 Timothy
1 Cor.	1 Corinthians	1 Kg.	1 Kings	Tit.	Titus
2 Cor.	2 Corinthians	2 Kg.	2 Kings	Zech.	Zechariah
Dan.	Daniel	Lam.	Lamentations	Zeph.	Zephaniah
Dt.	Deuteronomy	Lev.	Leviticus		
Ec.	Ecclesiastes	Lk.	Luke	**THE APOCRYPHA**	
Eph.	Ephesians	Mal.	Malachi	Ad. Est.	Additions to Esther
Est.	Esther	Mic.	Micah	Bar.	Baruch
Ex.	Exodus	Mk.	Mark	Bel	Bel and the Dragon
Ezek.	Ezekiel	Mt.	Matthew	1 Esd.	1 Esdras
Ezra	Ezra	Nah.	Nahum	2 Esd.	2 Esdras
Gal.	Galatians	Neh.	Nehemiah	Jdt.	Judith
Gen.	Genesis	Num.	Numbers	Let. Jer.	Letter of Jeremiah
Hab.	Habakkuk	Ob.	Obadiah	1 Macc.	1 Maccabees
Hag.	Haggai	1 Pet.	1 Peter	2 Macc.	2 Maccabees
Heb.	Hebrews	2 Pet.	2 Peter	3 Macc.	3 Maccabees
Hos.	Hosea	Phil.	Philippians	4 Macc.	4 Maccabees
Is.	Isaiah	Philem.	Philemon	Man.	Prayer of Manasseh
Jas.	James	Pr.	Proverbs	Ps. 151	Psalm 151
Jer.	Jeremiah	Ps.	Psalms	Sir.	Ecclesiasticus (Sirach)
Jg.	Judges	Rev.	Revelation	S. of 3 Y.	Prayer of Azariah and Song of the Three Young Men
Jl.	Joel	Rom.	Romans		
Jn.	John	Ru.	Ruth	Sus.	Susanna
1 Jn.	1 John	1 Sam.	1 Samuel	Tob.	Tobit
2 Jn.	2 John	2 Sam.	2 Samuel	Wis.	Wisdom of Solomon

refuge (1 Chr. 6:69). In Solomon's second administrative district (1 Kg. 4:9, where called Elonbeth-hanan). Fortified by Rehoboam (2 Chr. 11:10). Also mentioned in 1 Sam. 14:31; 2 Chr. 28:18. Sometimes identified with **Elon** of Jos. 19:43. **2.** Place in Zebulun where the judge Elon was buried (Jg. 12:12). Site unidentified.

AIN (ān) **1.** City on the boundary of Canaan (Num. 34:11). Site unidentified. **2.** Another name for **En-rimmon** (Jos. 15:32; 1 Chr. 4:32). **3.** Another name for **Ashan** (Jos. 21:16).

ALEMA (ăl′ ə mə) City in Gilead (1 Macc. 5:26, 35). Possibly the same as **Helam** of 2 Sam. 10:16–17.

ALEMETH (ăl′ ə mĕth) Kh. Almit. Levitical city in Benjamin (1 Chr. 6:60; Jos. 21:18, where called Almon).

ALEXANDRIA Egypt's capital and most important city in Hellenistic and Roman times. Founded by Alexander the Great in 331 B.C. Sailing from Myra in Lycia, Paul was shipwrecked on Malta in a ship of Alexandria (Acts 27:6). Paul also sailed from Malta to Puteoli in a ship of Alexandria (Acts 28:11).

ALLAMMELECH (ə lăm′ ə lĕk) Town in Asher (Jos. 19:26). Site unidentified.

ALMON (ăl′ mən) Another name for **Alemeth** (Jos. 21:18).

ALMON-DIBLATHAIM (ăl′ mən dĭb′ lə thā′ əm) Kh. Deleilat esh-Sherqiya [7–I] City in Moab. Where the Hebrews camped between Dibon-gad and the mountains of Abarim (Num. 33:46–47). Perhaps the same as Beth-diblathaim of Jer. 48:22.

ALUSH (ā′ lŭsh) Place where the Hebrews camped in the Sinai between Dophkah and Rephidim following the Exodus (Num. 33:13). Site unidentified.

AMAD (ā′ măd) Town in Asher (Jos. 19:26). Site unidentified.

AMAM (ā′ măm) City in Judah (Jos. 15:26). Site unidentified.

AMPHIPOLIS (ăm fĭp′ ə lĭs) City in Macedonia. Paul passed through here on his second missionary journey (Acts 17:1).

ANAB (ā' năb) Kh. Anab es-Saghira [3-K] Town in the hill country of Judah. Where Joshua expelled the Anakim (Jos. 11:21). Assigned to Judah (Jos. 15:50).

ANAHARATH (ə nā' ə rāth) T. el-Mukharkhash [5-D] Town in Lower Galilee. Assigned to Issachar (Jos. 19:19).

ANANIAH (ăn' ə nī ə) Another name for **Bethany 1** (Neh. 11:32).

ANATHOTH (ăn' ə thŏth) Ras el-Kharruba [4-H] Levitical city in Benjamin (Jos. 21:18; 1 Chr. 6:60). Home of Jeremiah (Jer. 1:1; 11:21, 23; 29:27; 32:7–9). Settled by Jews returning from the Exile (Ezra 2:23; Neh. 7:27; 11:32; 1 Esd. 5:18). Also mentioned in 2 Sam. 23:27; 1 Kg. 2:26; 1 Chr. 11:28; 12:3; 27:12; Is. 10:30.

ANEM (ā' nəm) Levitical city in Issachar (1 Chr. 6:73). Site unidentified but perhaps the same as **En-gannim 2**.

ANIM (ā' nĭm) Kh. Ghuwein et-Tahta [4-K] City in the hill country of Judah. Assigned to Judah (Jos. 15:50).

ANTIOCH (ăn' tĭ ŏk) **1.** Antakiya. Capital and chief city of Greco-Roman Syria. Founded by Seleucus I Nicator (305–280 B.C.) and named for his father, Antiochus. Earliest great center of Gentile Christianity, where the followers of Jesus were first called Christians (Acts 11:26). Barnabas brought Paul here from Tarsus (Acts 11:25–26). Base for Paul's missionary journeys (Acts 13:1 ff.). Paul opposed Peter (Cephas) here (Gal. 2:11). Also mentioned in Acts 6:5; 11:19–22, 27; 15:22–23, 30, 35; 18:22. **2.** City (of Pisidia) in Asia Minor near border with Phrygia. Visited by Paul on his first missionary journey (Acts 13:14; 14:19, 21; 2 Tim. 3:11).

ANTIPATRIS (ăn tĭp' ə trĭs) Town rebuilt by Herod the Great and named for his father. Roman name for **Aphek 1** (Acts 23:31).

APHAIREMA (əfār' ə mə) Another name for **Ophrah 1** (1 Macc. 11:34).

APHEK (ā' fĕk) **1.** Ras el-Ain [3-G] Hellenistic Pegae, Roman Antipatris, Roman Arethusa? Town at the source of the Yarkon River on the coastal plain where important routes join. Canaanite royal city whose king was slain by Joshua (Jos. 12:18). Here Philistines concentrated their forces for the battle of Ebenezer (1 Sam. 4:1) and for the battle of Mount Gilboa (1 Sam. 29:1). Rebuilt by Herod the Great and named Antipatris in honor of his father; here Paul came by night (Acts 23:31, where called Antipatris) as a prisoner on his way from Jerusalem to Caesarea. **2.** Town on the boundary of the Amorites, regarded by Israel as part of its inheritance (Jos. 13:4). Site unidentified but possibly the same as Afqa, east of Byblos. **3.** T. Kurdana [3-C] Town in western Galilee. Assigned to Asher (Jos. 19:30), who were unable to drive out the Canaanites (Jg. 1:31, where called Aphik). **4.** Kh. el-Asheq? [6-C]

Waters of an affluent of the Jordan River course beneath a stone-arch bridge in northern Galilee.

City in Bashan on route between Beth-shan and Damascus. Where Ahab of Israel defeated the Syrians (1 Kg. 20:26, 30). Elisha prophesied victory for Joash of Israel over the Syrians here (2 Kg. 13:17).

APHEKAH (ə fē' kə) Kh. el-Hadab? [3-J] City in Judah. Assigned to Judah (Jos. 15:53).

APHIK (ā' fik) Another name for **Aphek 3** (Jg. 1:31).

APOLLONIA (ăp' ə lō nĭ ə) City in Macedonia on the Egnatian Way. Paul passed through here on his second missionary journey (Acts 17:1).

AR (är) el-Misna [7-K] Moabite city on the south bank of the Arnon River. Defeated by the Hebrews (Num. 21:28). Given to sons of Lot (Dt. 2:9). Also mentioned in Num. 21:15; Dt. 2:18, 29; Is. 15:1.

ARAB (är' ăb) Kh. er-Rabiya. Village in the hill country of Judah. Assigned to Judah (Jos. 15:52).

ARAD (âr' ăd) **1.** T. el-Milh [4-K] Canaanite city in the Negeb. Its king attacked the Hebrews (Num. 21:1; 33:40) and was defeated by Joshua (Jos. 12:14). **2.** T. Arad [4-K] Kenite settlement mentioned in Jg. 1:16.

ARADUS (ăr' ə dəs) Greco-Roman name for **Arvad** (1 Macc. 15:23).

ARBATTA (är băt' ə) Jews of this city led by Simon to Judea (1 Macc. 5:23). Site unidentified.

ARIEL (âr' ĭ əl) Another name for **Jerusalem** (Is. 29:1, 2, 7).

ARIMATHEA (ăr' ə mə thē' ə) Home of Joseph, who secured Jesus' body and buried it in his own tomb (Mt. 27:57; Mk. 15:43; Lk. 23:50; Jn. 19:38). Another name for **Ramah 4**.

AROER (ə rō' ər) **1.** Kh. Arair [7-J] City on the northern rim of Arnon River gorge in Moab. Taken by the Hebrews in defeat of King Sihon (Jos. 12:2; Dt. 2:36; 4:48). Assigned to Reuben (Jos. 13:9, 16; Dt. 3:12; 1 Chr. 5:8) and to Gad (Num. 32:34). Also mentioned in Jg. 11:26; 2 Sam. 24:5; 2 Kg. 10:33; Jer. 48:19. **2.** Town in Gilead assigned to Gad (Jos. 13:25) but contended by the Ammonites (Jg. 11:33). Site unidentified. **3.** Kh. Arara [4-L] City in the Negeb. One of the places to which David sent booty taken from the Amalekites (1 Sam. 30:28). Possibly the same as **Adadah** of Jos. 15:22.

ARPAD (är' păd) T. er-Refad. City in northern Syria destroyed by the Assyrians (2 Kg. 18:34; 19:13; Is. 10:9; 36:19; 37:13; Jer. 49:23).

ARUBBOTH (ə rŭb' ŏth) Town in Solomon's third administrative district (1 Kg. 4:10). Site unidentified.

ARUMAH (ə rōō' mə) Kh. el-Orma [5-G] Town in the eastern hill country of Samaria. Where Abimelech resided after being driven from Shechem (Jg. 9:31, 41).

ARVAD (är' văd) Ruwad. Greco-Roman Aradus. Island city off the coast of Syria. Mercenaries from here served Tyre (Ezek. 27:8, 11). Informed of Rome's friendship for the Jews (1 Macc. 15:23, where called Aradus). Also mentioned in Gen. 10:18; 1 Chr. 1:16.

ASCALON (ăs' kə lən) Hellenistic name for **Ashkelon** (Jdt. 2:28).

ASHAN (ā' shən) City in the Shephelah. Site unidentified. Assigned to Simeon (Jos. 19:7; 1 Chr. 4:32) and to Judah (Jos. 15:42). Levitical city (1 Chr. 6:59; Jos. 21:16, where called Ain). City to which David sent spoils recovered at Ziklag (1 Sam. 30:30, where called Borashan).

ASHDOD (ăsh' dŏd) Isdud [1-I] Greco-Roman Azotus. City on the southern coastal plain. Assigned to Judah (Jos. 15:46, 47); inhabited by the Anakim (Jos. 11:22). Taken by the Philistines (Jos. 13:3); one of the five major Philistine cities. Captured ark of the covenant taken there (1 Sam. 5:17; 6:17). Walls destroyed by Uzziah of Judah (2 Chr. 26:6). Disaster foretold by prophets (Jer. 25:20; Am. 1:8; Zeph. 2:4; Zech. 9:6). In conflict with Nehemiah (Neh. 4:7; 13:23, 24). Captured by Sargon II (Is. 20:1) c. 712 B.C. Hellenistic capital of the province of Azotus and renamed Azotus. Syrian Greek stronghold against the Hasmoneans (1 Macc. 4:15; 5:68; 10:84; 11:4). Captured by John Hyrcanus (1 Macc. 16:10). Part of Alexander Janneus' kingdom. Conquered by Pompey in 63 B.C. and annexed to Syria. Rebuilt by Gabinius c. 57 B.C. Part of Herod the Great's kingdom. Philip the evangelist passed through here after baptizing the Ethiopian eunuch (Acts 8:40).

ASHKELON (ăsh' kə lən) T. Asqalan [1–I] Hellenistic Ascalon, Roman Askalon. Seaport on the southern coast. Retaken by Ramses II c. 1280 B.C. after revolting against Egypt. Settled by the Philistines in the 12th century B.C.; one of the five major Philistine cities (1 Sam. 6:17; 2 Sam. 1:20). Not captured by the Hebrews in the conquest (Jos. 13:3). Said to have been taken by Judah (Jg. 1:18). Samson killed men from here (Jg. 14:19). Destroyed by Nebuchadnezzar (Jer. 25:20; 47:5–7). Hostile toward the Jews (Zech. 9:5). Friendly with the Maccabees (1 Macc. 10:86; 11:60; and 12:33, where called Askalon). Free city during Herod the Great's time. Also mentioned in Jdt. 2:28, where called Ascalon; Am. 1:8; Zeph. 2:4, 7.

ASHNAH (ăsh' nə) **1.** City in the Shephelah assigned to Judah (Jos. 15:33). Site unidentified. **2.** City in the Shephelah assigned to Judah (Jos. 15:43). Site unidentified.

ASHTAROTH (ăsh' tə rŏth) T. Ashtarah. City in Gilead. Assigned to the half-tribe of Manasseh (Jos. 13:31). Levitical city (1 Chr. 6:71; Jos. 21:27, where called Be-eshterah). Also mentioned in Jos. 9:10; 12:4; 13:12; Dt. 1:4. Possibly the same as **Carnaim.**

ASHTEROTH-KARNAIM (ăsh' tə rŏth kär nā' əm) Probably another name for **Carnaim** (Gen. 14:5).

ASKALON (ăs' kə lən) Roman name for **Ashkelon** (1 Macc. 10:86; 11:60; 12:33).

ASSOS (ăs' ŏs) Port in Mysia in Roman province of Asia. Here Paul, returning from his third missionary journey, boarded ship on way to Jerusalem (Acts 20:13, 14).

ATAROTH (ăt' ə rŏth) **1.** Kh. Attarus [6–J] Town in Moab. Mentioned on the Moabite Stone. Sought by Gad and Reuben (Num. 32:3), but building attributed to Gad (Num. 32:34). **2.** T. el-Mazar? Town on the border of Ephraim (Jos. 16:7). **3.** Town on the border of Ephraim and Benjamin (Jos. 16:2). Perhaps the same as **Ataroth-addar.**

ATAROTH-ADDAR (ăt' ə rŏth ăd' ər) Raddana? Town on the border of Ephraim and Benjamin (Jos. 16:5; 18:13). Possibly the same as **Ataroth 3.**

ATHACH (ā' thăk) City in Judah. One of the places to which David sent booty taken from the Amalekites (1 Sam. 30:30). Site unidentified but perhaps the same as **Ether 2** of Jos. 19:7.

ATHENS Leading city of Attica and cultural center of Greece. Visited by Paul on his second missionary journey (Acts 17:15, 16, 22; 18:1). Also mentioned in 1 Th. 3:1.

ATROTH-BETH-JOAB (ăt' rŏth bĕth jō' ăb) Village near Bethlehem 1 (1 Chr. 2:54). Site unidentified.

ATROTH-SHOPHAN (ăt' rŏth shō' făn) City in Gilead assigned to Gad (Num. 32:35). Site unidentified.

ATTALIA (ăt' ə lī' a) Port on coast of Pamphylia. Paul sailed from here on his way to Antioch at the end of his first missionary journey (Acts 14:25).

AVITH (ā' vĭth) City in Edom; home of Hadad, king of Edom (Gen. 36:35; 1 Chr. 1:46). Site unidentified.

AVVA (ăv' ə) Town probably in northern Syria or Babylonia from which Assyrians sent people into Samaria after the fall of Israel (2 Kg. 17:24). Site unidentified. Called **Ivvah** in 2 Kg. 18:34; 19:13; Is. 37:13.

AVVIM (ăv' ĭm) Kh. Haiyan? City in Benjamin (Jos. 18:23).

AYYAH (ā' yə) Town in Ephraim (1 Chr. 7:28). Site unidentified.

AZEKAH (ə zē' kə) T. ez-Zakariya [3–I] City in the Shephelah commanding important routes into the highlands. After the battle of Gibeon, Joshua pursued Canaanites as far as Azekah (Jos. 10:10, 11). Assigned to Judah (Jos. 15:35). Fortified by Rehoboam (2 Chr. 11:9). Attacked by Nebuchadnezzar in 588 B.C. (Jer. 34:7). Settled by Jews returning from the Exile (Neh. 11:30). Also mentioned in 1 Sam. 17:1.

AZMAVETH (ăz' mə vĕth) Ras Khukeir [4–H] Town in Benjamin. People from here returned from the Exile (Ezra 2:24). Singers from this city celebrated dedication of wall of Jerusalem (Neh. 12:27–29). Called Bethazmaveth in Neh. 7:28; Bethasmoth in 1 Esd. 5:18.

AZMON (ăz' mən) Ein Muweilih? Town on southern border of Judah near the Brook of Egypt (Num. 34:4, 5; Jos. 15:4).

AZNOTH-TABOR (ăz' nŏth tā' bər) Kh. Umm Jubeil? [5–D] Town possibly on southern border of Naphtali (Jos. 19:34).

AZOTUS (ə zō' təs) Greco-Roman name for **Ashdod.**

B

BAAL (bā' əl) Another name for **Baalathbeer** (1 Chr. 4:33.)

BAALAH (bā' ə lə) **1.** Another name for **Kiriath-jearim** (Jos. 15:9–10; 1 Chr. 13:6). **2.** Another name for **Balah** (Jos. 15:29).

BAALATH (bā' ə lăth) Danite settlement in the Shephelah (Jos. 19:44). Site unidentified. Perhaps the Baalath built by Solomon (1 Kg. 9:18; 2 Chr. 8:6).

BAALATH-BEER (bā' ə lăth bĭr) Town in Simeon. Called Be-aloth in Jos. 15:24; Baal in 1 Chr. 4:33. Sometimes identified with **Ramah of the Negeb** of Jos. 19:18.

BAALE-JUDAH (bā' ə lī jōō' də) Another name for **Kiriath-jearim** (2 Sam. 6:2).

BAAL-GAD (bāl găd') Town in the valley west of Mount Hermon. Site unidentified. Northernmost limit of Joshua's conquest (Jos. 11:17; 12:7; 13:5). Also mentioned in Jg. 3:3.

BAAL-HAMON (bāl hā' mən) Unknown site of King Solomon's vineyard (S. of S. 8:11).

BAAL-HAZOR (bāl hā' zôr) Jebel el-Asur? [4–G] Place of sheepshearing in the hill country of Ephraim where Absalom had Amnon killed (2 Sam. 13:23).

BAAL-HERMON (bāl hûr' mən) Hivite city on the border of Manasseh spared in Joshua's conquest (Jg. 3:3; 1 Chr. 5:23). Site unidentified.

As storm clouds gather over the Sea of Galilee, shepherds point to a caravan winding along the shore.

BAAL-MEON (bāl mē' ŏn) Main? [7–I] Town in Moab assigned to Reuben (Num. 32:38; Jos. 13:17) and occupied by the Reubenites (1 Chr. 5:8). Also mentioned in Ezek. 25:9. Called Beth-baal-meon in Jos. 13:17; Beth-meon in Jer. 48:23. Probably the same as Beon of Num. 32:3.

BAAL-PEOR (bāl pē' ôr) Kh. esh-Sheikh Jayil [6–H] Place in Moab. Where the Israelites were punished for worshiping Baal of Peor (Num. 25:3, 5; Dt. 4:3; Ps. 106:28; Hos. 9:10). Probably the same as **Beth-peor.**

BAAL-PERAZIM (bāl pĭrā' zĭm) Place near Jerusalem where David defeated the Philistines (2 Sam. 5:20; 1 Chr. 14:11). Site unidentified.

BAAL-TAMAR (bāl tā' mər) Village possibly in Benjamin where the Hebrews gathered for a successful attack on Gibeah (Jg. 20:33). Site unidentified.

BAAL-ZEPHON (bāl zē' fŏn) Place in Egypt near which the Hebrews passed (Ex. 14:2, 9; Num. 33:7). Site unidentified.

BABEL (bā' bəl) Another name for **Babylon** (Gen. 10:10; 11:9).

BABYLON Ancient city on the east bank of the Euphrates River. Its site is about 20 miles from Baghdad. Capital of the neo-Babylonian empire. Babylonians conquered Jerusalem in 587 B.C. and took many Judahites into exile (2 Kg. 24:12–16; 25:7, 11, 21; 2 Chr. 36:6, 7, 10, 18, 20; Mt. 1:11, 12, 17). Jeremiah prophesied the fall of the city (Jer. 50:1–46; 51:1–64). Captured in 539 B.C. by the Persian king Cyrus, who allowed the Jews to return to Judah. In the New Testament Babylon became a symbol for Rome and its evils (Rev. 14:8; 16:19; 17:5; 18:2, 10, 21; 1 Pet. 5:13). Other frequent mentions of Babylon appear mainly in the books of 2 Kg., Is., Jer., Ezek., Dan.

Upper Beth-horon dominated a major route from Jerusalem and the highlands to the coastal plain.

BAHARUM (bə hâr' əm) Another name for **Bahurim** (1 Chr. 11:33).

BAHURIM (bə hyōōr' ĭm) Ras et-Tmim [4–I] Village east of Jerusalem. Where Paltiel and Michal parted as she was returning to David (2 Sam. 3:16) and where Shimei cursed David as he fled from Absalom (2 Sam. 16:5; 19:16; 1 Kg. 2:8). Jonathan and Ahimaaz hid in a well here while spying for David (2 Sam. 17:18). Also mentioned in 2 Sam. 23:31; 1 Chr. 11:33, where called Baharum.

BALAH (bā' lə) Town in the Negeb assigned to Simeon (Jos. 19:3) but inherited by the people of Judah (Jos. 15:29, where called Baalah). Site unidentified. Called Bilhah in 1 Chr. 4:29.

BALAMON (bāl' ə mən) Place in Samaria near Dothan. Site unidentified. Judith's husband was buried near here (Jdt. 8:3). Probably the same as Balbaim of Jdt. 7:3; Bebai of Jdt. 15:4; Belmain of Jdt. 4:4.

BALBAIM (bāl bā' əm) Probably the same as **Balamon** (Jdt. 7:3).

BAMOTH (bā' mŏth) Another name for **Bamoth-baal** (Num. 21:19–20).

BAMOTH-BAAL (bā' mŏth bāl') Town in Moab. Site unidentified. Where Balak and Balaam made a sacrifice (Num. 22:41). Assigned to Reuben (Jos. 13:17). The Hebrews passed through here in their wanderings (Num. 21:19–20, where called Bamoth).

BASKAMA (bǎs' kə mə) el-Jummeiza [6–C] Town northeast of the Sea of Galilee. Here Trypho killed Jonathan in 143 B.C. (1 Macc. 13:23). Also known as Bascama.

BE-ALOTH (bē' ə lŏth) Another name for **Baalath-beer** (Jos. 15:24).

BEALOTH (bē' ə lŏth) Town in Asher. Site unidentified. In Solomon's ninth administrative district (1 Kg. 4:16).

BEBAI (bē' bī) City whose people helped destroy fleeing Assyrian troops (Jdt. 15:4). Probably the same as **Balamon.**

BEER (bîr) **1.** Place in Moab where the Hebrews dug a well during their wanderings (Num. 21:16). Site unidentified. Perhaps the same as **Beer-elim** of Is. 15:8. **2.** Place to which Jotham fled (Jg. 9:21). Site unidentified.

BEER-ELIM (bîr ē' lĭm) Place mentioned in Isaiah's oracle concerning Moab (Is. 15:8). Site unidentified but perhaps the same as **Beer 1** of Num. 21:16.

BEER-LAHAI-ROI (bîr' lə hī' roi) Oasis in the desert near Kadesh-barnea. Site unidentified. Where an angel comforted Hagar as she fled from Sarah (Gen. 16:14). Isaac's home where Rebekah came to him (Gen. 24:62) and where he dwelt after the death of Abraham (Gen. 25:11).

BEEROTH (bē' ə rŏth) Nebi Samwil? [4–H] Hivite city on the plateau northwest of Jerusalem. Made a treaty with Joshua and was spared in the conquest (Jos. 9:17). Assigned to Benjamin (Jos. 18:25). Rechab and Baanah, assassins of Ishbosheth, were from here (2 Sam. 4:2, 3, 5, 9). Also mentioned in 2 Sam. 23:37; 1 Chr. 11:39; Ezra 2:25; Neh. 7:29; 1 Esd. 5:19. Site unidentified but possibly the same as **Berea** of 1 Macc. 9:4.

BEEROTH BENE-JAAKAN (bîr' ŏth běn' ĭ jā' ə kən) Place where the Hebrews camped on the border of Edom and near which Aaron died (Dt. 10:6). Site unidentified. Called Bene-jaakan in Num. 33:31, 32; Jaakan in 1 Chr. 1:42.

BEER-SHEBA (bîr shē' bə) T. es-Saba [3–K] Major oasis city in the Negeb. Considered the southern limit of Israel, as in the expressions "from Beer-sheba to Dan" (1 Chr. 21:2; 2 Chr. 30:5) and "from Dan to Beer-sheba" (Jg. 20:1; 2 Sam. 17:11; 24:2, 15; 1 Kg. 4:25). During the divided monarchy Judah's borders were "from Geba to Beer-sheba" (2 Kg. 23:8). Abraham and Isaac dug wells here and made treaties with Abimelech of Gerar (Gen. 21:31–33; 26:23, 33). Abraham returned to his home here after nearly sacrificing Isaac (Gen. 22:19). Jacob fled from Beer-sheba to Haran to avoid Esau's wrath (Gen. 28:10). Jacob sacrificed at the important shrine here on his way to Egypt (Gen. 46:1, 5). Assigned to Judah (Jos. 15:28) but given to Simeon (Jos. 19:2). Sons of Samuel judged in Beer-sheba (1 Sam. 8:2). Also mentioned in Gen. 21:14; 2 Sam. 3:10; 17:11; 24:2, 7, 15; 1 Kg. 19:3; 2 Kg. 12:1; 1 Chr. 4:28; 2 Chr. 19:4; 24:1; Neh. 11:27, 30; Am. 5:5; 8:14.

BE-ESHTERAH (bē ěsh' tə rə) Another name for **Ashtaroth** (Jos. 21:27).

BELA (bē' lə) Another name for **Zoar** (Gen. 14:2, 8).

BELMAIN (bēl' mān) Probably the same as **Balamon** (Jdt. 4:4).

BENE-BERAK (běn' ĭ bîr' ăk) el-Kheiriya. Town on the coastal plain. Assigned to Dan (Jos. 19:45).

BENE-JAAKAN (běn' ĭ jā' ə kən) Another name for **Beeroth Bene-jaakan** (Num. 33:31, 32).

BEON (bē' ŏn) Probably the same as **Baal-meon** (Num. 32:3).

BEREA (bĭ rē' ə) Place in Judea where Bacchides camped before the battle of Elasa in 161 B.C. (1 Macc. 9:4). Site unidentified but possibly the same as **Beeroth.**

BERED (bîr' ĕd) Possibly an oasis near Kadesh-barnea (Gen. 16:14). Site unidentified.

BEROEA (bĭ rē' ə) **1.** Verroia. City in Macedonia. Where Paul and Silas came on the second missionary journey (Acts 17:10) and from where Paul went to Athens (Acts 17:15). Also mentioned in Acts 20:4. **2.** Hel-

At Bethany, east of Jerusalem, Jesus raised Lazarus from the dead and was anointed for his own burial.

lenistic name for Aleppo. One of the chief cities in Syria. Where the Seleucid king Antiochus V caused the High Priest Menelaus to be put to death (2 Macc. 13:4).

BEROTHAH (bĭ rō′ thə) City in Syria on the northern limits of the inheritance of Israel (Ezek. 47:16). Site unidentified. Another name for **Berothai.**

BEROTHAI (bĭ rō′ thī) City in Syria from which David took bronze booty (2 Sam. 8:8). Site unidentified. Called Cun in 1 Chr. 18:8; Berothah in Ezek. 47:16.

BETAH (bē′ tə) City in Syria from which David took bronze booty (2 Sam. 8:8). Site unidentified. Called Tibhath in 1 Chr. 18:8.

BETEN (bē′ tən) Kh. Ibtin [3–C] Town in western Galilee. Assigned to Asher (Jos. 19:25).

BETH-ANATH (bĕth ā′ năth) Safed el-Battikh? [5–A] Canaanite city in Upper Galilee. Assigned to Naphtali (Jos. 19:38), who failed to drive out the inhabitants (Jg. 1:33).

BETH-ANOTH (bĕth ā′ nŏth) Kh. Beit Einum [4–J] Village in the southern hill country of Judah. Assigned to Judah (Jos. 15:59). Possibly the same as **Bethany 3** of Jdt. 1:9.

BETHANY (bĕth′ ə nĭ) **1.** el-Azariya [4–I] Village in Benjamin on the eastern slope of the Mount of Olives. Settled by Jews returning from the Exile (Neh. 11:32, where called Ananiah). Home of Mary, Martha, and Lazarus (Lk. 10:38; Jn. 11:1, 18), where Jesus raised Lazarus from the dead. Where Jesus lodged on final journey to Jerusalem for Passover (Jn. 12:1) and retired after cleansing the Temple (Mt. 21:17). Jesus anointed in the house of Simon the Leper (Mt. 26:6; Mk. 14:3). Scene of the Ascension (Lk. 24:50–51). Also mentioned in Mt. 21:17; Mk. 11:1, 11, 12; Lk. 19:29. **2.** Place east of the Jordan River where John the Baptist was baptizing (Jn. 1:28). Site unidentified. **3.** Town near Jerusa-

lem which refused to join Nebuchadnezzar in war against Medes (Jdt. 1:9). Possibly the same as **Beth-anoth** of Jos. 15:59.

BETH-ARABAH (bĕth ăr′ ə bə) Ein el-Gharaba [5–H] Settlement in the Wilderness of Judah on Judah's northern border (Jos. 15:6) and Benjamin's southern border (Jos. 18:18). Also mentioned in Jos. 15:61; 18:22.

BETH-ARBEL (bĕth ăr′ bəl) Irbid? [7–D] Town in Gilead. Destroyed by Shalman (Hos. 10:14), who is generally identified with the Assyrian king Shalmaneser V (726–722 B.C.).

BETH-ASHBEA (bĕth ăsh′ bĭ ə) Town in Judah from which a family of linen workers came (1 Chr. 4:21). Site unidentified.

BETHASMOTH (bə thăz′ mŏth) Another name for **Azmaveth** (1 Esd. 5:18).

BETH-AVEN (bĕth ā′ vən) **1.** T. Maryam? Town in the Saddle of Benjamin. Here Saul defeated the Philistines (1 Sam. 13:5; 14:23). Also mentioned in Jos. 7:2; 18:12. **2.** Another name for **Bethel 1** (Hos. 4:15; 5:8; 10:5).

BETH-AZMAVETH (bĕth ăz′ mə vĕth) Another name for **Azmaveth** (Neh. 7:28).

BETH-BAAL-MEON (bĕth′ bāl mē′ ŏn) Another name for **Baal-meon** (Jos. 13:17).

BETH-BARAH (bĕth bâr′ ə) Town in the Jordan valley seized by the Ephraimites in Gideon's pursuit of the Midianites (Jg. 7:24). Site unidentified.

BETHBASI (bĕth bā′ sī) Kh. Beit Bassa [4–I] Village in the Wilderness of Judea north of Tekoa. Fortified by Jonathan and Simon and unsuccessfully besieged by Bacchides in 158 B.C. (1 Macc. 9:62, 64).

BETH-BIRI (bĕth bĭr′ ī) Another name for **Beth-lebaoth** (1 Chr. 4:31).

BETH-CAR (bĕth kär′) Unknown place beyond which the Hebrews drove the Philistines after defeating them at Mizpah (1 Sam. 7:11).

BETH-DAGON (bĕth dā′ gən) **1.** Village in the Shephelah assigned to Judah (Jos. 15:41). Site unidentified. **2.** Village on the border of Asher (Jos. 19:27). Site unidentified.

BETH-DIBLATHAIM (bĕth′ dĭb lə thā′ əm) Perhaps the same as **Almon-diblathaim** (Jer. 48:22).

BETH-EDEN (bĕth ē′ dən) Aramean kingdom between the Euphrates and Balikh rivers. Amos prophesied the exile of its people (Am. 1:5). Also mentioned in 2 Kg. 19:12; Is. 37:12. Called Eden in Ezek. 27:23.

BETH-EKED (bĕth ē′ kĭd) Beit Qad [5–E] Place between Jezreel and Samaria in the foothills south of the Great Plain. Here Jehu slew the kinsmen of Ahaziah of Judah (2 Kg. 10:12, 14).

BETHEL (bĕth′ əl) **1.** Beitin [4–H] Ancient Canaanite shrine of Luz in the Saddle of Benjamin; later one of the most important of the Israelite shrines. Abraham camped near here (Gen. 12:8; 13:3). Where Jacob dreamed of angels descending and ascending a ladder to heaven (Gen. 28:19). The Lord called himself "the God of Bethel" (Gen. 31:13). Hebrews under Joshua ambushed the men of Ai between that city and Bethel (Jos. 8:9, 12, 17). Taken by Joshua (Jos. 12:16) and assigned to Benjamin (Jos. 18:13, 22) on the border with Joseph (Jos. 16:1, 2). Deborah judged near here (Jg. 4:5). On Samuel's annual circuit (1 Sam. 7:16). Site of one of Jeroboam's infamous altars (1 Kg. 12:29–33; 13:1, 4, 32). Location of Amos' prophetic ministry (Am. 7:10, 13). Fortified by Bacchides in 160 B.C. (1 Macc. 9:50). Also mentioned in Gen. 35:1, 3, 6, 8, 15, 16; Jos. 7:2; 12:9; Jg. 1:22–23; 20:18, 26, 31; 21:2, 19; 1 Sam. 10:3; 13:2; 30:27; 1 Kg. 13:10, 11; 16:34; 2 Kg. 2:2, 3, 23; 10:29; 17:28; 23:4, 15, 17, 19; 1 Chr. 7:28; 2 Chr. 13:19; Ezra 2:28; Neh. 7:32; 11:31; Jer. 48:13; Hos. 12:4; Am. 3:14; 4:4; 5:5, 6; 7:10, 13; Zech. 7:2. Also called Luz in Gen. 28:19; 35:6; 48:3; Jos. 16:2, where near Bethel; 18:13; Jg. 1:23. Called Beth-aven in Hos. 4:15; 5:8; 10:5. **2.** Another name for **Bethuel** (1 Sam. 30:27).

BETH-EMEK (bĕth ē′ mĭk) T. Mimas [4–B] Village on the border of Asher (Jos. 19:27).

BETH-EZEL (bĕth ē′ zəl) Village in southern Judah mentioned in Mic. 1:11. Site unidentified.

BETH-GADER (bĕth gā′ dər) Village in Judah mentioned in 1 Chr. 2:51. Site unidentified.

BETH-GAMUL (bĕth gā′ məl) Kh. el-Jumeil [7–J] Town on the Moabite plateau. Jeremiah pronounced judgment against it (Jer. 48:23).

BETH-GILGAL (bĕth gĭl′ găl) Place mentioned in Neh. 12:29. Site unidentified.

BETH-HACCHEREM (běth' hă kĭr' əm) Kh. Salih? Village in the hill country of Judah near Jerusalem. Signal post mentioned in Jer. 6:1. One of Nehemiah's administrative centers (Neh. 3:14).

BETH-HAGGAN (běth hăg' ən) Place toward which Ahaziah of Judah fled following the murder of Jehoram of Israel by Jehu (2 Kg. 9:27). Sometimes identified with **En-gannim 2** of Jos. 19:21; 21:29.

BETH-HARAM (běth hâr' əm) T. Iktanu [6–H] Stronghold on the Plains of Moab. Part of the kingdom of Sihon of Heshbon assigned to Gad (Jos. 13:27). Called Beth-haran in Num. 32:36.

BETH-HOGLAH (běth hŏg' lə) Deir Hajla [5–H] Town southeast of Jericho. Assigned to Benjamin (Jos. 18:19, 21); on the border with Judah (Jos. 15:6).

BETH-HORON (běth hôr' ən) Site of two adjacent towns: Lower Beth-horon (Beit Ur et-Tahta) [3–H] and Upper Beth-horon (Beit Ur el-Foqa) [4–H] Astride the Way of Beth-horon, a ridge route and one of the most important approaches from the coastal plain to the central highlands and Jerusalem. Near the border of Joseph, Ephraim, and Benjamin (Jos. 16:3, 5; 18:13, 14). Levitical city (Jos. 21:22; 1 Chr. 6:68). Joshua pursued the five Amorite kings "by the way of the ascent of Beth-horon" (Jos. 10:10, 11). Fortified by Solomon (1 Kg. 9:17; 2 Chr. 8:5). Where Judas Maccabeus defeated Seron (1 Macc. 3:16, 24). Where Nicanor camped before the battle of Adasa (1 Macc. 7:39). Fortified by Bacchides in 160 B.C. (1 Macc. 9:50). Also mentioned in 1 Sam. 13:18; 1 Chr. 7:24; 2 Chr. 25:13; Jdt. 4:4.

BETH-JESHIMOTH (běth jĕsh' ə mŏth) T. el-Azeima [6–I] Town on the Plains of Moab. The Hebrews encamped here (Num. 33:49). Taken by the Hebrews (Jos. 12:3). Assigned to Reuben (Jos. 13:20). Also mentioned in Ezek. 25:9.

BETH-LE-APHRAH (běth' lĭ ăf' rə) Town mentioned in Mic. 1:10. Site unidentified.

BETH-LEBAOTH (běth' lĭ bā' ŏth) Town in southern Judah. Site unidentified. Assigned to Simeon (Jos. 19:6). Called Beth-biri in 1 Chr. 4:31; Lebaoth in Jos. 15:32.

BETHLEHEM (běth' lĭ hĕm) **1.** Beit Lahm [4–I] Town in the hills of Judah south of Jerusalem on the ridge route to Hebron. Burial place of Rachel (Gen. 35:19; 48:7, where identified with Ephrath; but see 1 Sam. 10:2, where Rachel's tomb is located in Benjamin). Setting for the book of Ruth (Ru. 1:1, 2, 19, 22; 2:4; 4:11). Home of David, where he was anointed by Samuel (1 Sam. 16:4; 17:12, 15; 20:6, 28). Fortified by Rehoboam (2 Chr. 11:6). Settled by Jews returning from the Exile (Ezra 2:21; Neh. 7:26). Identified by Micah as the place from which the Messiah would come (Mic. 5:2, where identified with Ephrathah). Birthplace of Jesus (Mt. 2:1, 5, 6, 8, 16; Lk. 2:4, 15; Jn. 7:42).

Also mentioned in Jg. 17:7, 8, 9; 19:1, 2, 18; 2 Sam. 2:32; 23:14, 15, 16, 24; 1 Chr. 2:51, 54; 4:4; 11:16, 17, 18, 26; Jer. 41:17. **2.** Beit Lahm [4–C] Town in Lower Galilee. Assigned to Zebulun (Jos. 19:15). Home of Ibzan, one of the minor judges (Jg. 12:8, 10).

BETH-MARCABOTH (běth mär' kə bŏth) Town in the Negeb assigned to Simeon (Jos. 19:5; 1 Chr. 4:31). Site unidentified. Called Madmannah in Jos. 15:31; 1 Chr. 2:49.

BETH-MEON (běth mē' ŏn) Another name for **Baal-meon** (Jer. 48:23).

BETH-NIMRAH (běth nĭm' rə) T. el-Bleibil [6–H] Town on the Plains of Moab near the Jordan River. Assigned to Gad (Num. 32:36; Jos. 13:27). Called Nimrah in Num. 32:3.

BETH-PAZZEZ (běth păz' ĭz) Town assigned to Issachar (Jos. 19:21). Site unidentified.

BETH-PELET (běth pē' lĭt) T. es-Saqati? [3–K] Town in the Negeb. Assigned to Judah (Jos. 15:27). Settled by Jews returning from the Exile (Neh. 11:26).

BETH-PEOR (běth pē' ôr) Town in Moab near Mount Nebo where Moses was buried (Dt. 34:6). Assigned to Reuben (Jos. 13:20). Also mentioned in Dt. 3:29; 4:46. Probably the same as **Baal-peor.**

BETHPHAGE (běth' fə jĭ) Kafr et-Tur? Village on the Mount of Olives east of Jerusalem. From here Jesus sent two disciples to bring a colt for his triumphal entry into Jerusalem (Mt. 21:1; Mk. 11:1; Lk. 19:29).

BETH-REHOB (běth rē' hŏb) Place near Dan (Jg. 18:28–29) on the northernmost limit of Canaan (Num. 13:21 and 2 Sam. 10:8, where called Rehob). Site unidentified. Also mentioned in 2 Sam. 10:6.

BETHSAIDA (běth sā' ə də) el-Araj? [6–C] Fishing village on the northern shore of the Sea of Galilee near which the Jordan River flows into the lake. Home of Apostles Philip, Andrew, and Peter (Jn. 1:44; 12:21). Visited by Jesus (Mk. 6:45), who healed a blind man here (Mk. 8:22). Among the cities upon which Jesus pronounced woe (Mt. 11:21; Lk. 10:13). The feeding of the 5,000 took place near here (Lk. 9:10).

BETH-SHAN (běth shăn') T. el-Husn [5–E] Greco-Roman Scythopolis, Seleucid Nysa-Scythopolis. Canaanite city strategically located at the junction of the Jezreel and Jordan valleys. Assigned to Manasseh, who failed to drive out the Canaanites (Jos. 17:11, 16; and Jg. 1:27, where called Beth-shean). Philistine base where the body of Saul was hanged on the wall (1 Sam. 31:10, 12; 2 Sam. 21:12). In Solomon's fifth administrative district (1 Kg. 4:12, where called Beth-shean). Where Jonathan confronted Trypho (1 Macc. 12:40–41). Captured by Pompey in 63 B.C. and made a free city, which it remained throughout Roman times. One of the largest cities of the Decapolis. Also called Beth-shean in 1 Chr. 7:29; called Scythopolis in 2 Macc. 12:29, 30; Jdt. 3:10.

BETH-SHEAN (běth shē' ən) Another name for **Beth-shan** (Jos. 17:11, 16; Jg. 1:27; 1 Kg. 4:12; 1 Chr. 7:29).

BETH-SHEMESH (běth shĕm' ĭsh) **1.** T. er-Rumeila [3–I] Fortified city in the Sorek valley commanding the Way of Beth-shemesh, one of the major routes from the coastal plain to the Judah highlands and Jerusalem. Assigned to Dan (Jos. 19:41, where called Ir-shemesh), who failed to drive out the Canaanites (Jg. 1:35, where called Har-heres). Later a Levitical city in Judah (Jos. 21:16; 1 Chr. 6:59). Philistines returned the ark of the covenant to Beth-shemesh (1 Sam.

The ruins of Caesarea, Herod the Great's magnificent port city, silently guard the Mediterranean shore.

6:9–20). In Solomon's second administrative district (1 Kg. 4:9). Amaziah of Judah captured in battle near here by Jehoash (Joash), king of Israel (2 Kg. 14:11, 13; 2 Chr. 25:21, 23). Philistines captured it from Ahaz, king of Judah, c. 734 B.C. (2 Chr. 28:18). Also mentioned in Jos. 15:10. **2.** Kh. er-Ruweisi? [5–B] Canaanite town in Upper Galilee. Assigned to Naphtali, who were unable to drive out the Canaanites (Jos. 19:38; Jg. 1:33). **3.** Kh. Sheikh esh-Shamsawi? Town on the boundary of Issachar near the Jordan River (Jos. 19:22).

BETH-SHITTAH (bĕth shĭt′ ə) Place probably in the Transjordan to which the Midianites fled from Gideon (Jg. 7:22). Site unidentified.

BETH-TAPPUAH (bĕth tăp′ yōō ə) Taffuh [3–J] Town in the hill country of Judah near Hebron. Assigned to Judah (Jos. 15:53).

BETHUEL (bĭ thōō′ əl) Town in southern Judah. Site unidentified. Assigned to Simeon (1 Chr. 4:30). David sent part of the booty taken from the Amalekites to the elders there (1 Sam. 30:27, where called Bethel). Another name for Bethul of Jos. 19:4.

BETHULIA (bĭ thōō′ lĭ ə) City in Samaria mentioned in Jdt. 4:6; 6:10, 11, 14; 7:1, 3, 6, 13, 20; 8:3, 11; 10:6; 11:9; 12:7; 13:10; 15:3, 6; 16:21, 23. Site unidentified but possibly the same as **Shechem.**

BETH-ZAITH (bĕth zā′ ĭth) Kh. Beit Zeita. Town in southern Judea north of Hebron. Bacchides came here from Jerusalem after the killing of 60 men seeking peace in 162 B.C. (1 Macc. 7:19).

BETH-ZECHARIAH (bĕth′ zĕk′ ə rī′ ə) T. Beit Sikariya [4–I] Place in southern Judea on the road from Hebron to Jerusalem. Where Judas Maccabeus suffered a major defeat at the hands of the Seleucids (1 Macc. 6:32, 33) and where Eleazar was killed by a war elephant.

BETH-ZUR (bĕth zûr′) Kh. et-Tubeiqa [3–J] Town in southern Judah strategically located on the central ridge route, north of Hebron. Assigned to Judah (Jos. 15:85). Fortified by Rehoboam (2 Chr. 11:7). Settled by Jews returning from the Exile (Neh. 3:16). Judas Maccabeus fought Lysias here (1 Macc. 4:29) and fortified it in 162 B.C. (1 Macc. 4:61; 6:7, 26; 2 Macc. 11:5). Recaptured by the Seleucids after a prolonged siege (1 Macc. 6:31, 49; 2 Macc. 13:9, 22). Fortified by Bacchides in 160 B.C. (1 Macc. 9:52). Place of refuge for renegade Jewish garrison after Bacchides abandoned his other strongholds (1 Macc. 10:12–14). Also mentioned in 1 Chr. 2:45; 1 Macc. 11:65–66; 14:7, 33.

BETOMASTHAIM (bĕt′ ə məs′ thā əm) Place mentioned in Jdt. 15:4. Site unidentified. Called Betomesthaim in Jdt. 4:6.

BETOMESTHAIM (bĕt′ ə mĕs thā əm) Another name for **Betomasthaim** (Jdt. 4:6).

BETONIM (bĕt′ ə nĭm) Kh. Batna [6–G] Town in Moab. Assigned to Gad (Jos. 13:26).

BEZEK (bē′ zĕk) **1.** Kh. Ibziq [5–E] Town on the eastern edge of the hills of Samaria overlooking the Jordan valley. Where Saul rallied the Israelites for a night march to deliver Jabesh-gilead from siege (1 Sam. 11:8). **2.** Town probably in western Judah where the tribes of Judah and Simeon defeated the Canaanites and Perizzites (Jg. 1:4, 5). Site unidentified.

BEZER (bē′ zər) Umm el-Amad? [7–H] City in northern Moab. Mentioned on the Moabite Stone as being captured and rebuilt by Mesha of Moab. Levitical city and a city of refuge in Reuben (Dt. 4:43; Jos. 20:8; 21:36; 1 Chr. 6:78). Probably the same as **Bozrah 3** of Jer. 48:24.

BILEAM (bĭl′ ĭ əm) Levitical city in Manasseh (1 Chr. 6:70). Site unidentified but perhaps the same as **Ibleam.**

BILHAH (bĭl′ hə) Another name for **Balah** (1 Chr. 4:29).

BIZIOTHIAH (bĭz′ ĭ ō thī′ ə) Village in the Negeb assigned to Judah (Jos. 15:28). Site unidentified.

BOCHIM (bō′ kĭm) Place in the Saddle of Benjamin where an angel rebuked the Hebrews (Jg. 2:1, 5). Site unidentified.

BORASHAN (bôr ā′ shən) Another name for **Ashan** (1 Sam. 30:30).

BOSOR (bō′ sôr) City in Gilead where the Jews were rescued by Judas Maccabeus and Jonathan (1 Macc. 5:26, 36). Site unidentified.

BOZKATH (bŏz′ kăth) Village in the Shephelah assigned to Judah (Jos. 15:39). Site unidentified. Also mentioned in 2 Kg. 22:1.

BOZRAH (bŏz′ rə) **1.** Buseirah [7–N] Powerful fortress-city in northern Edom guarding the approaches to the copper mines of the Arabah. Capital of Edomite king Jobab (Gen. 36:33; 1 Chr. 1:44). Symbol of Edom's strength for the prophets (Is. 34:6; 63:1; Jer. 49:13, 22; Am. 1:12). **2.** Busra eski-Sham. City of Bashan at an important route junction south of the Hauran mountains. Judas Maccabeus and Jonathan burned the city and slaughtered its males in rescuing Jews there c. 163 B.C. (1 Macc. 5:26, 28). **3.** Probably another name for **Bezer** of Jer. 48:24.

BUZ (bŭz) Place mentioned in Jer. 25:23. Site unidentified.

C

CABBON (kăb′ ən) Village in the Shephelah assigned to Judah (Jos. 15:40). Site unidentified.

CABUL (kā′ bəl) Kabul [4–C] Village in western Galilee assigned to Asher (Jos. 19:27). Perhaps the administrative center of the land of Cabul mentioned in 1 Kg. 9:13.

CAESAREA (sĕs′ ə rē′ ə) Qaisariya [2–E] Phoenician Strato's Tower. The most important port in Judea in New Testament times. Captured by Pompey in 63 B.C. Given to Cleopatra by Marc Antony. Enlarged by Herod the Great, who renamed it Caesarea in 9 B.C. in honor of Caesar Augustus. Called Caesarea Maritima to distinguish it from other cities named Caesarea. Chief city of Judea under the Romans and residence of Roman governors after A.D. 6. Where Philip the Evangelist preached and lived (Acts 8:40; 21:8). Centurion of Caesarea converted by Peter (Acts 10:1, 24; 11:11). Herod Agrippa I died here (Acts 12:19). Paul sailed from here to Tarsus (Acts 9:30). Where Paul landed after his second missionary journey (Acts 18:22) and where he stayed with Philip on his way to Jerusalem after his third missionary journey (Acts 21:8, 16). Paul taken here from Jerusalem under heavy guard (Acts 23:23, 33). Where Paul was imprisoned and appeared before Roman governors Felix and Festus and Herod Agrippa II (Acts 25:1, 4, 6, 13) and from where he sailed to Rome.

CAESAREA PHILIPPI (sĕs′ ə rē′ ə fĭl′ ə pī) Banias [6–A] Canaanite Paneas, Roman Neronias. Ancient shrine to the god Pan at the southwestern foot of Mount Hermon. Where Antiochus III defeated Ptolemy V and brought Judea under Seleucid rule c. 200 B.C. City rebuilt by Philip the Tetrarch and renamed Caesarea Philippi (to distinguish it from Caesarea Maritima). Jesus and his disciples withdrew here (Mt. 16:13; Mk. 8:27).

CALAH (kā′ lə) Nimrud. City near the junction of the Tigris and Upper Zab rivers in Mesopotamia. One of the cities of Assyria (Gen. 10:11, 12).

CALNEH (kăl′ nē) City in Mesopotamia mentioned in Am. 6:2. Site unidentified. Called Calno in Is. 10:9; Canneh in Ezek. 27:23.

CALNO (kăl′ nō) Another name for **Calneh** (Is. 10:9).

CANA (kā′ nə) Kh. Qana? [5–C] Village in Lower Galilee. Here Jesus performed his first miracle by turning water into wine at a wedding feast (Jn. 2:1, 11). Home of Nathaniel (Jn. 21:2). Also mentioned in Jn. 4:46. Also known as Kanah.

CANATHA (kĕ′ năth ə) Greco-Roman name for **Kenath.**

CANNEH (kăn′ ē) Another name for **Calneh** (Ezek. 27:23).

CAPERNAUM (kə pûr′ nĭ əm) T. Hum [6–C] Fishing village on the northwestern shore of the Sea of Galilee. Center of Jesus' Galilean ministry (Mt. 4:13). Site of many miracles of Jesus (Mk. 2:1; Mt. 8:5 and Lk. 7:1; Mt. 17:24; Mk. 1:21 and Lk. 4:31; Jn. 4:46; 6:17). Jesus taught in the synagogue here (Jn. 6:59). Jesus pronounced woe upon Capernaum (Mt. 11:23; Lk. 10:15). Also mentioned in Mk. 9:33; Lk. 4:23; Jn. 2:12; 6:24.

CAPHARSALAMA (kăf' ər säl' ə mə) Kh. Salama? [4–H] Village northwest of Jerusalem on the Way of Beth-horon. Where Judas Maccabeus ambushed and defeated the forces of Nicanor in 162 B.C. (1 Macc. 7:31).

CARCHEMISH (kär' kə mĭsh) Jerablus. Important city in northern Syria on the western bank of the Euphrates River. Where Nebuchadnezzar of Babylon defeated Pharaoh Neco II of Egypt in 605 B.C. after Neco came to the rescue of the Assyrians (2 Chr. 35:20; Jer. 46:2; 1 Esd. 1:25). Also mentioned in Is. 10:9.

CARMEL (kär' məl) Kh. el-Kirmil [4–J] Village in the hills of Judah southeast of Hebron. Assigned to Judah (Jos. 15:55). Saul erected a victory monument here after defeating the Amalekites (1 Sam. 15:12). Where David's servants confronted Nabal and where he later sent for Nabal's widow, Abigail (1 Sam. 25:2, 5, 7, 40; 27:3; 30:5; 2 Sam. 2:2; 3:3). Also mentioned in 2 Sam. 23:35; 1 Chr. 11:37.

CARNAIM (kär nā' əm) Sheikh Sa'd. Town in Gilead. Burned with its defenders by Judas Maccabeus and Jonathan while rescuing Jews there (1 Macc. 5:26, 43–44; 2 Macc. 12:21, 26). Probably another name for Karnaim of Am. 6:13 and Ashteroth-Karnaim of Gen. 14:5. Possibly the same as **Ashtaroth.**

CASIPHIA (kə sĭf' ĭə) Unknown place in Babylonia mentioned in Ezra 8:17.

CASPIN (kăs' pən) Khisfin [7–C] Fortified city east of the Sea of Galilee. Captured by Judas Maccabeus, who slaughtered its inhabitants c. 163 B.C. (2 Macc. 12:13). Called Chaspho in 1 Macc. 5:26, 36.

CAUDA (kô' də) Small island south of Crete near which Paul sailed on his way to Rome (Acts 27:16).

CENCHREAE (sĕng' krə ē) Kechriais. Seaport of Corinth on eastern side of the Isthmus of Corinth. Where Paul cut his hair as part of his Nazirite vow before sailing for Syria on his second missionary journey (Acts 18:18). Also mentioned in Rom. 16:1.

CHAPHENATHA (kə fĕn' ə thə) Place near Jerusalem fortified by Jonathan (1 Macc. 12:37). Site unidentified.

CHARAX (kâr' ăks) Town in Gilead with a Jewish community in the time of Judas Maccabeus (2 Macc. 12:17). Site unidentified.

CHASPHO (kăs' fō) Another name for **Caspin** (1 Macc. 5:26, 36).

CHELOUS (kĕl' əs) City in southern Judah mentioned in Jdt. 1:9. Site unidentified.

CHEPHAR-AMMONI (kē' fər ăm' ə nī) Kafr Ana? Village in the Saddle of Benjamin. Assigned to Benjamin (Jos. 18:24).

CHEPHIRAH (kĭ fī' rə) Kh. el-Kefira [3–H] Hivite city on the plateau northeast of Jerusalem. Made a treaty with Joshua and was spared destruction in the conquest (Jos. 9:17). Assigned to Benjamin (Jos. 18:26). Settled by Jews returning from the Exile (Ezra 2:25; Neh. 7:29; 1 Esd. 5:19).

CHERUB (kĕr' əb) Unknown place in Babylonia from which the exiles returned (Ezra 2:59; Neh. 7:61).

CHESALON (kĕs' ə lŏn) Kesla. Town on the western edge of the hills of Judah near the Way of Beth-shemesh. Assigned to Judah (Jos. 15:10).

CHESIL (kē' səl) Town in the Negeb assigned to Judah (Jos. 15:30). Site unidentified.

CHESULLOTH (kĭ sŭl' ŏth) Iksal [5–D] Hellenistic Exaloth. Town in the Chesulloth valley in Lower Galilee. Assigned to Issachar (Jos. 19:18); on border with Zebulun (Jos. 19:12, where called Chisloth-tabor).

CHEZIB (kē' zĭb) Another name for **Achzib 1** (Gen. 38:5).

CHILMAD (kĭl' măd) City in Mesopotamia mentioned in Ezek. 27:23. Site unidentified.

CHINNERETH (kĭn' ə rĕth) Kh. el-Ureima [6–C] Roman Gennesaret. Fortified city on the Way of the Sea on the northwestern shore of the Sea of Galilee. Allied with Jabin of Hazor against Joshua (Jos. 11:2). Assigned to Naphtali (Jos. 19:35). Captured by Ben-hadad (1 Kg. 15:20). Also mentioned in Dt. 3:17. Called Chinneroth in Jos. 11:2; 1 Kg. 15:20; called Gennesaret in Mt. 14:34; Mk. 6:53.

CHINNEROTH (kĭn' ə rŏth) Another name for **Chinnereth** (Jos. 11:2; 1 Kg. 15:20).

CHISLOTH-TABOR (kĭs' lŏth tā' bər) Another name for **Chesulloth** (Jos. 19:12).

CHITLISH (kĭt' lĭsh) Town in the Shephelah assigned to Judah (Jos. 15:40). Site unidentified.

CHOBA (kō' bə) el-Marmala? Village in the Jordan valley. Fortified against Holofernes (Jdt. 4:4). Also mentioned in Jdt. 15:4.

CHORAZIN (kō rā' zĭn) Kh. Keraza [6–C] Village on a bluff north of the Sea of Galilee. One of the cities upon which Jesus pronounced woe (Mt. 11:21; Lk. 10:13).

CHUSI (kū' sī) Kh. Quza? [4–G] Village in Samaria mentioned in Jdt. 7:18.

CITY OF DAVID Another name for **Jerusalem.**

CITY OF MOAB City in Moab where Balak went to meet Balaam (Num. 22:36). Site unidentified.

CITY OF PALMS Another name for **Jericho.**

CITY OF SALT Kh. Qumran [5–I] Greco-Roman Qumran. Settlement in the Wilderness of Judah on the northwest shore of the Dead Sea. Assigned to Judah (Jos. 15:62). Rebuilt in the late 2nd century B.C. by a Jewish sect, identified by many scholars as Essenes. Dead Sea Scrolls found here. Destroyed by the Romans in the First Jewish Revolt (A.D. 66–70); held by Jewish rebels in the Second (Bar Kokhba) Jewish Revolt (132–35).

CNIDUS (nī' dəs) City in the region of Caria on the southwest coast of Asia Minor. Strong winds off Cnidus forced Paul's ship to sail past Crete on his voyage to Rome (Acts 27:7). Also mentioned in 1 Macc. 15:23.

COLOSSAE (kə lŏs' ī) City in the Lycus valley in Phrygia in Asia Minor. Paul addressed a letter to the church there (Col. 1:2).

CORINTH Great commercial center on the Isthmus of Corinth. Leading city of Greece in New Testament times. Capital of the Roman province of Achaia. Site of Paul's lengthy ministry on his second missionary journey (Acts 18:1) where he wrote 1 and 2 Thessalonians. Paul addressed letters to the church there (1 Cor. 1:2; 2 Cor. 1:1, 23). Also mentioned in Acts 19:1; 2 Tim. 4:20.

COS (kôs) City and island in the Aegean Sea off the southwest coast of Asia Minor. Paul passed here on his way to Judea at the end of his third missionary journey (Acts 21:1). Also mentioned in 1 Macc. 15:23.

COZEBA (kō zē' bə) Village in Judah mentioned in 1 Chr. 4:22. Site unidentified.

CUN (kŭn) Another name for **Berothai** (1 Chr. 18:8).

CUTH (kŏŏth) T. Ibrahim. City in Babylonia. Men of Cuth were among the foreigners brought to Samaria by the Assyrians after the fall of Israel in 721 B.C. (2 Kg. 17:30). Called Cuthah in 2 Kg. 17:24.

CUTHAH (kŏŏth' ə) Another name for **Cuth** (2 Kg. 17:24).

CYAMON (sī' ə mən) Place mentioned in Jdt. 7:3. Site unidentified.

CYRENE (sī rē' nī) Cirene. Important Greek commercial center in North Africa. Capital of the Roman province of Cyrenaica. A man from here, Simon of Cyrene, was compelled to carry Jesus' cross (Mt. 27:32; Mk. 15:21; Lk. 23:26). Men from here attended Peter's Pentecost sermon in Jerusalem (Acts 2:10) and preached to Greeks at Antioch (Acts 11:20). Also mentioned in Acts 13:1; 1 Macc. 15:23.

Everything—including a crocodile hanging from the rafters—is on sale at this Damascus bazaar.

D

DABBESHETH (dăb' ə shĕth) T. esh-Shammam? [4–D] Town on the western Great Plain. On the border between Issachar and Zebulun (Jos. 19:11).

DABERATH (dăb' ə răth) Daburiya [5–D] Town at the northwestern foot of Mount Tabor. Levitical city in Issachar on the border with Zebulun (Jos. 19:12; 21:28; 1 Chr. 6:72). Called Rabbith in Jos. 19:20.

DAMASCUS Major commercial center on the main routes between Mesopotamia, Egypt, and Arabia. Chief city of Syria. Home of Abraham's chief steward (Gen. 15:2). Capital of one of the Aramean kingdoms (1 Kg. 19:15; 2 Kg. 8:7, 9; 2 Chr. 16:2; 24:23; 28:5, 23; Is. 7:8; 17:3). David defeated the Syrians here (2 Sam. 8:5, 6; 1 Chr. 18:5, 6). Allied with Judah against Israel (1 Kg. 15:18). Conquered by Tiglath-pileser III in 732 B.C. (2 Kg. 16:9–12; Is. 8:4). Conquered by the Babylonians in the 7th century B.C., by the Persians in the 6th century B.C., and by Alexander the Great in 332 B.C. Under rule of the Nabateans after 85 B.C. Jewish community here had early Christian disciples (Acts 9:2, 10, 19, 22, 27; 22:5; 26:12, 20). Paul converted near here and brought blinded into the city (Acts 9:3, 8; 22:6–11). Also mentioned in Gen. 14:15; 1 Kg. 11:24; 20:34; 2 Kg. 5:12; 14:28; S. of S. 7:4; Is. 10:9; 17:1; Jer. 49:23–27; Ezek. 27:18; 47:16, 17, 18; 48:1; Am. 1:3, 5; 5:27; Zech. 9:1; 2 Cor. 11:32; Gal. 1:17.

DAN (dăn) T. el-Qadi [6–A] Hellenistic Antiochia. Canaanite city of Laish (Jg. 18:7, 14, 27, 29) in the Huleh valley near one of the sources of the Jordan River. Here Abraham ambushed the kings of the north (Gen. 14:14). Captured by the migrating Danites, who renamed it Dan (Jos. 19:47, where called Leshem; Jg. 18:29). Site of one of Jeroboam's infamous shrines (1 Kg. 12:29–30; 2 Kg. 10:29). Captured by Ben-hadad (1 Kg. 15:20; 2 Chr. 16:4). Considered the northern limit of Israel, as in the expressions "from Dan to Beer-sheba" (Jg. 20:1; 2 Sam. 3:10; 17:11; 24:2, 15; 1 Kg. 4:25) and "from Beer-sheba to Dan" (1 Chr. 21:2; 2 Chr. 30:5). Also mentioned in Dt. 34:1; 2 Sam. 24:6; 2 Chr. 2:14; Jer. 4:15; 8:16.

DANNAH (dăn' ə) Village in the southern hill country of Judah assigned to Judah (Jos. 15:49). Site unidentified.

DAPHNE (dăf' nĭ) Place near Antioch in Syria where the temple to Apollo is located. The High Priest Onias sought refuge here (2 Macc. 4:33).

DATHEMA (dăth' ə mə) Stronghold in Gilead where Jews took refuge in the time of Judas Maccabeus (1 Macc. 5:9). Site unidentified.

DEBIR (dē' bər) **1.** T. Rabud? [3–J] Canaanite royal city in the hills of southern Judah. Destroyed by the Hebrews in the conquest (Jos. 11:21; 15:15–16; Jg. 1:11, where also called Kiriath-sepher). Levitical city (Jos. 21:15; 1 Chr. 6:58). Also mentioned in Jos. 10:38, 39; 12:13; 15:49. **2.** Place on Judah's northern border (Jos. 15:7). Site unidentified. **3.** Another name for **Lodebar** (Jos. 13:26).

DERBE (dûr' bĭ) Kerti Huyuk. Town on the Lycaonian plateau in Asia Minor. Paul stopped here on his first and second missionary journeys (Acts 14:6, 20; 16:1). Also mentioned in Acts 20:4.

DESSAU (dĕs' ô) Village in Judea where Jews led by Simon fought the forces of Nicanor in 161 B.C. (2 Macc. 14:16). Site unidentified.

DIBON (dī' bŏn) **1.** Dhiban [7–J] City on the King's Highway north of the Arnon River in Moab. One of the chief cities of the Moabites. Captured by the Hebrews from King Sihon (Num. 21:30). Sought by Gad and Reuben (Num. 32:3), but building attributed to Gad (Num. 32:34). Assigned to Reuben (Jos. 13:17). Symbol of Moabite power for the prophets (Is. 15:2, 9; Jer. 48:18, 22). Where the Moabite Stone of King Mesha was found in 1868. Also mentioned in Jos. 13:9. Called Dibon-gad in Num. 33:45, 46. **2.** Town in the Negeb. Site unidentified. Settled by Jews returning from the Exile (Neh. 11:25).

DIBON-GAD (dī' bŏn găd) Another name for **Dibon 1** (Num. 33:45, 46).

DILEAN (dĭl' ĭ ən) Village in the Shephelah assigned to Judah (Jos. 15:38). Site unidentified.

DIMNAH (dĭm' nə) Another name for **Rimmon** (Jos. 21:35).

DIMONAH (dī mō' nə) Town in the Negeb assigned to Judah (Jos. 15:22). Site unidentified.

DINHABAH (dĭn' hə bə) City in Edom. Capital of King Bela the son of Beor (Gen. 36:32; 1 Chr. 1:43). Site unidentified.

DIZAHAB (dĭz' ə hăb) Place in the wilderness east of the Arabah. Site unidentified. Associated with the last words of Moses (Dt. 1:1). Called Mezahab in Gen. 36:39; 1 Chr. 1:50.

DOK (dŏk) Jebel Quruntul [5–H] Mountaintop fortress northwest of Jericho. Where Simon and two of his sons were murdered by Simon's son-in-law, Ptolemy, in 134 B.C. (1 Macc. 16:15).

DOPHKAH (dŏf' kə) Serabit el-Khadim? Place in the Sinai near the Wilderness of Sin. Hebrews stopped here on their Exodus journey (Num. 33:12, 13).

DOR (dôr) Kh. el-Burj [3–D] Hellenistic Dora. Canaanite city on the Plain of Dor south of Mount Carmel. Port in Greco-Roman times. Joined Hazor in coalition defeated by Joshua (Jos. 12:23). Assigned to Manasseh, who failed to drive out the Canaanites (Jos. 17:11; Jg. 1:27). Considered to be a part of Ephraim on the border with Manasseh (1 Chr. 7:29). Besieged by Antiochus VII c. 138 B.C. (1 Macc. 15:11, 13, 25). Made a free city by Pompey in A.D. 63. Also mentioned in Jos. 12:23. Called Naphath in Jos. 17:11; Naphath-dor in 1 Kg. 4:11; Naphoth-dor in Jos. 11:2.

DOTHAN (dō' thən) T. Duthan [4–E] City on the Plain of Dothan in northern Samaria. Here Joseph's brothers sold him to caravaners going to Egypt (Gen. 37:17). Syrians besieged the city hoping to capture Elisha in the late 9th century B.C. (2 Kg. 6:13). Holofernes camped near here (Jdt. 3:9; 4:6; 7:3). Also mentioned in Jdt. 7:18; 8:3.

DUMAH (dōō' mə) 1. Kh. Doma ed-Deir [3–J] Town in the hills of southern Judah. Assigned to Judah (Jos. 15:52). 2. Place mentioned in Is. 21:11. Site unidentified.

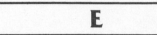

E

EBENEZER (ĕb' ə nē' zər) Majdel Yaba? [3–G] Place on the eastern edge of the coastal plain near Aphek. Where the Israelites camped before their battle with the Philistines in which the ark of the covenant was captured (1 Sam. 4:1; 5:1).

EBEZ (ĕb' ĕz) City in Issachar mentioned in Jos. 19:20. Site unidentified.

EBRON (ĕb' rən) Another name for **Abdon** (Jos. 19:28).

ECBATANA (ĕk băt' ə nə) Hamadan. Capital of Media. Captured by Cyrus the Great and became his summer capital. Record of Cyrus' decree allowing the rebuilding of the Temple in Jerusalem found here (Ezra 6:2). Antiochus IV retreated here c. 165 B.C. after being defeated (2 Macc. 9:3). Home of Tobit (Tob. 3:7; 6:5; 7:1, 8; 14:12, 14). Also mentioned in 2 Esd. 6:2; Jdt. 1:1, 2, 14.

ECDIPPA (ĕk dĭp' ə) Hellenistic name for **Achzib 2.**

EDEN (ē' dən) Another name for **Beth-eden** (Ezek. 27:23).

EDER (ē' dər) Village in the Negeb assigned to Judah (Jos. 15:21). Site unidentified.

EDER, TOWER OF (ē' dər) Place on the central ridge route between Bethlehem and Hebron where Jacob camped after the death of Rachel (Gen. 35:21). Site unidentified.

EDREI (ĕd' rī ī) 1. Dera. City in Bashan. Home of King Og (Dt. 1:4). 2. City in Upper Galilee assigned to Naphtali (Jos. 19:37). Site unidentified.

EGLAIM (ĕg' lĭ əm) Town in Moab mentioned in Is. 15:8. Site unidentified.

EGLATH-SHELISHIYAH (ĕg' lăth shĭ lĭsh' ə yə) Town in Moab mentioned in Is. 15:5; Jer. 48:34. Site unidentified.

EGLON (ĕg' lŏn) T. el-Hesi? [2–J] Canaanite royal city in the northwestern Negeb at the edge of the coastal plain. On a branch of the Way of the Sea. Part of Amorite coalition against the Gibeonites (Jos. 10:3). King from here killed by Joshua (Jos. 10:23, 37; 12:12), who also destroyed the city (Jos. 10:34). Assigned to Judah (Jos. 15:39).

Hot-water springs at the En-gedi oasis have drawn visitors to the Dead Sea shore since biblical times.

EKRON (ĕk' rən) Kh. el-Muqanna? [2–I] Hellenistic Accaron. City on the southern coastal plain. One of the five chief cities of the Philistines (Jos. 13:3). Assigned to Judah (Jos. 15:11, 45–46) and to Dan (Jos. 19:43). Captured ark of the covenant returned from there to the Israelites (1 Sam. 5:10; 6:16–17). Captured by Shishak c. 918. Ahaziah of Israel consulted Baal-zebub, god of Ekron (2 Kg. 1:2, 3, 6, 16). Condemned by the prophets (Jer. 25:20; Am. 1:8; Zeph. 2:4; Zech. 9:5, 7). Given to Jonathan by Alexander Balas c. 147 B.C. (1 Macc. 10:89). Also mentioned in Jg. 1:18; 1 Sam. 7:14; 17:52.

ELAM (ē' ləm) Town in Judah west of Bethzur (Ezra 2:31; Neh. 7:34; 1 Esd. 5:22). Site unidentified.

ELASA (ĕl' ə sə) Kh. el-Ashshi [4–H] Village on the plateau north of Ramah. Judas Maccabeus camped here in 161 B.C. before a battle against Bacchides' forces (1 Macc. 9:5), where he was killed.

ELATH (ē' lăth) Town sometimes identified with **Ezion-geber** (Dt. 2:8; 2 Kg. 14:22; 16:6).

ELEALEH (ĕl' ĭ ā' lə) el-Al [7–H] City in Moab northeast of Heshbon. Assigned to Reuben, who rebuilt it (Num. 32:3, 37). Later retaken by the Moabites (Is. 15:4; 16:9; Jer. 48:34).

ELIM (ē' lĭm) Wadi Gharandel? Oasis in the Sinai. First place where the Hebrews found fresh water in their Exodus journey (Ex. 15:27; 16:1; Num. 33:9–10).

ELKOSH (ĕl' kŏsh) Home of the prophet Nahum (Nah. 1:1). Site unidentified.

ELON (ē' lŏn) Village in the Sorek valley assigned to Dan (Jos. 19:43). Site unidenti-

fied but perhaps the **Elonbeth-hanan** of 1 Kg. 4:9. Sometimes also identified with **Aijalon 1.**

ELONBETH-HANAN (ē' lən bĕth hā' nən) Village in Solomon's second administrative district (1 Kg. 4:9). Site unidentified but perhaps the same as **Elon** of Jos. 19:43.

ELOTH (ē' lŏth) Another name for **Elath** (1 Kg. 9:26; 2 Chr. 8:17; 26:2).

EL-PARAN (ĕl pâr' ən) Place near the Gulf of Aqabah. Site unidentified. Southernmost limit of raid of Chedorlaomer in which Lot was taken captive (Gen. 14:6).

ELTEKE (ĕl' tə kə) Another name for **Eltekeh** (Jos. 21:23).

ELTEKEH (ĕl' tə kə) T. esh-Shallaf? [2–H] Town on the coastal plain. Assigned to Dan (Jos. 19:44), who failed to drive out the Philistines. Levitical city in Dan (Jos. 21:23, where called Elteke). Where Sennacherib defeated Egyptian-Ethiopian army in 701 B.C.

ELTEKON (ĕl' tə kŏn) Village in the hill country of Judah assigned to Judah (Jos. 15:59). Site unidentified.

ELTOLAD (ĕl' tō' lăd) City in the south of Judah assigned to Judah (Jos. 15:30) and to Simeon (Jos. 19:4). Site unidentified. Called Tolad in 1 Chr. 4:29.

EMEK-KEZIZ (ē' mĭk kē' zĭz) City in the vicinity of Jericho assigned to Benjamin (Jos. 18:21). Site unidentified.

EMMAUS (ĕ mā' əs) 1. Imwas [3–H] Town commanding a vital route junction at the eastern end of the Valley of Aijalon. Here Judas Maccabeus defeated Gorgias (1 Macc. 3:40, 57; 4:3). Fortified by Bacchides in 160 B.C. (1 Macc. 9:50). Destroyed by Varus, the Roman governor of Syria, in 4 B.C. 2. el-Qubeiba? [4–H] Village northwest of Jerusalem. The resurrected Jesus appeared to two men going to Emmaus (Lk. 24:13). 3. Roman name for **Mozah**.

ENAIM (ī nā' əm) Another name for **Enam** (Gen. 38:14, 21).

ENAM (ē' nəm) Village in the Shephelah near Azekah. Site unidentified. Assigned to Judah (Jos. 15:34). Called Enaim in Gen. 38:14, 21.

ENDOR (ĕn' dôr) Kh. Safsafa [5–D] Village on the lower northern slope of Mount Moreh. In the territory of Issachar but held by Manasseh (Jos. 17:11). Saul consulted a medium here the night before the battle of Mount Gilboa (1 Sam. 28:7). Also mentioned in Ps. 83:10.

EN-EGLAIM (ĕn ĕg' lĭ əm) Place on the shore of the Dead Sea mentioned in Ezek. 47:10. Site unidentified.

EN-GANNIM (ĕn găn' ĭm) 1. Village in the Shephelah near Beth-shemesh. Assigned to

Judah (Jos. 15:34). Site unidentified. **2.** Jenin [4–E] Greco-Roman Ginae. Town south of the Jezreel valley at an important pass into the hills of Samaria. Levitical city in Issachar (Jos. 19:21; 21:29). Perhaps the same as Anem of 1 Chr. 6:73 and **Beth-haggan** of 2 Kg. 9:27.

EN-GEDI (ĕn gĕd′ ī) Ein Jidi [5–J] Oasis created by a hot-water spring on the western shore of the Dead Sea. One of the wilderness sites assigned to Judah (Jos. 15:62). Near here David sought refuge from Saul (1 Sam. 23:29; 24:1). Renowned for its vegetation and beauty (S. of S. 1:14; Sir. 24:14). Also mentioned in Ezek. 47:10. Called Hazazon-tamar in Gen. 14:7; 2 Chr. 20:2.

EN-HADDAH (ĕn hăd′ ə) el-Hadatha [5–D] City in Lower Galilee. Assigned to Issachar (Jos. 19:21).

EN-HAKKORE (ĕn hăk′ ə rī) Spring at **Lehi** (Jg. 15:19).

EN-HAZOR (ĕn hā′ zôr) Fortified city in Upper Galilee assigned to Naphtali (Jos. 19:37). Site unidentified.

ENMISHPAT (ĕn mĭsh′ păt) Another name for **Kadesh 2** (Gen. 14:7).

EN-RIMMON (ĕn rĭm′ ən) Kh. Umm er-Ramamin [3–K] Village in southern Judah. Assigned to Simeon (Jos. 19:7; 1 Chr. 4:32, where identified as two separate villages, Ain and Rimmon) and to Judah (Jos. 15:32). Settled by Jews returning from the Exile (Neh. 11:29).

EN-ROGEL (ĕn rō′ gəl) Bir Ayyub. Spring in the Kidron valley southeast of Jerusalem. On the border between Benjamin and Judah (Jos. 15:7; 18:16). Two of David's spies stayed here on a mission to observe Absalom (2 Sam. 17:17). Where Adonijah performed sacrifices without King David's knowledge (1 Kg. 1:9).

EN-SHEMESH (ĕn shĕm′ ĭsh) Ein Hod. Spring on the edge of the Wilderness of Judah east of Jerusalem. On the border between Benjamin and Judah (Jos. 15:7; 18:17).

EN-TAPPUAH (ĕn tăp′ yŏŏ ə) Another name for **Tappuah 1** (Jos. 17:7).

EPHES-DAMMIM (ē′ fĭz dăm′ ĭm) Place in the Shephelah near Azekah and Socoh. Site unidentified. Where the Philistines gathered before facing Saul's army in the confrontation in which David killed Goliath (1 Sam. 17:1; 1 Chr. 11:13, where called Pas-dammim).

EPHESUS (ĕf′ ə səs) Important port on the western coast of Asia Minor. Capital of Roman province of Asia. Famous for Temple of Artemis, one of the wonders of the ancient world. Center of Paul's missionary activity in western Asia Minor where he taught for more than two years (Acts 19:1) or for three years (Acts 20:31). Paul driven from here by a riot instigated by the silver-smiths of the city (Acts 19:26; 20:1; 1 Cor. 15:32). Paul addressed a letter to the church there (see book of the Ephesians). One of the seven churches of the Revelation (Rev. 1:11; 2:1). Also mentioned in Acts 18:19, 21, 24; 19:17, 26, 28, 34, 35; 20:16, 17; 1 Cor. 16:8; 1 Tim. 1:3; 2 Tim. 1:18; 4:12.

EPHRAIM (ē′ frĭ əm) Another name for **Ophrah 1** (2 Sam. 13:23; Jn. 11:54).

EPHRATH (ĕf′ rəth) City identified with **Bethlehem 1** (Gen. 35:16, 19; 48:7).

EPHRATHAH (ĕf′ rə thə) City identified with **Bethlehem 1** (Ru. 4:11; Mic. 5:2).

EPHRON (ē′ frŏn) **1.** Strong city on the road from Carnaim to Scythopolis. Site unidentified. Captured by Judas Maccabeus, who killed all the male inhabitants and razed the city c. 163 B.C. (1 Macc. 5:46; 2 Macc. 12:27). **2.** Another name for **Ophrah 1** (2 Chr. 13:19).

ERECH (ĭr′ ĕk) Warka. One of the oldest and most important cities of Sumer in southern Mesopotamia. In the kingdom of Nimrod (Gen. 10:10). Men from Erech were among foreigners who settled in Samaria and Judea, or "the province Beyond the River" (Ezra 4:9).

ESBUS (ĕz′ bŭz) Roman name for **Heshbon.**

ESEK (ē′ sĕk) Well dug by Isaac's servants near Gerar (Gen. 26:20). Site unidentified.

ESHAN (ē′ shən) Village in the hills of southern Judah assigned to Judah (Jos. 15:52). Site unidentified.

ESHTAOL (ĕsh′ tĭ əl) Ishwa [3–H] Town in the Shephelah. Assigned to Dan (Jos. 19:41) and to Judah (Jos. 15:33). Samson buried near here (Jg. 16:31). Also mentioned in Jg. 13:25; 18:2, 8, 11.

ESHTEMOA (ĕsh′ tə mō ə) es-Samu [4–K] City in the hill country of Judah. Levitical city and a city of refuge (Jos. 15:50, where called Eshtemoh; 21:14; 1 Chr. 6:57). Place to which David sent booty taken from the Amalekites (1 Sam. 30:28).

ESHTEMOH (ĕsh′ tə mō) Another name for **Eshtemoa** (Jos. 15:50).

ETAM (ē′ təm) **1.** Kh. el-Khokh? [4–I] Town in central Judah near Bethlehem. Fortified by Rehoboam (2 Chr. 11:6). **2.** Village in southern Judah assigned to Simeon (1 Chr. 4:32). Site unidentified.

ETAM, ROCK OF (ē′ təm) Place where Samson went after burning the fields of the Philistines in the Sorek valley (Jg. 15:8, 11). Site unidentified.

ETHAM (ē′ thəm) Place on the edge of the wilderness in eastern Egypt. Site unidentified. The first place beyond Succoth to which the Hebrews came in their Exodus journey (Ex. 13:20; Num. 33:6–8).

ETHER (ē′ thər) **1.** City assigned to Judah (Jos. 15:42). Site unidentified. **2.** City assigned to Simeon (Jos. 19:7). Site unidentified, but perhaps the same as **Athach** of 1 Sam. 30:30.

ETH-KAZIN (ĕth kā′ zĭn) Town in Zebulun (Jos. 19:13). Site unidentified.

EZEM (ē′ zəm) Town in the Negeb assigned to Judah (Jos. 15:29) and to Simeon (Jos. 19:3; 1 Chr. 4:29). Site unidentified.

EZION-GEBER (ē′ zĭ ən gē′ bər) T. el-Kheleifa [4–T] Hellenistic Berenice. Port at the head of the Gulf of Aqabah. Place in the wilderness wanderings of the Hebrews (Num. 33:35, 36; Dt. 2:8). Here Solomon based his Red Sea merchant fleet (1 Kg. 9:26; 2 Chr. 8:17). Jehoshaphat's merchant fleet built here (2 Chr. 20:36). Sometimes identified with **Elath.**

F/G

FAIR HAVENS Harbor on the southern coast of Crete. Where it was unsafe for Paul's ship to spend the winter on his voyage to Rome (Acts 27:8).

FORUM OF APPIUS (ăp′ ĭ əs) Station on the Appian Way 43 miles south of Rome. Where Christians from Rome came to greet Paul (Acts 28:15).

GABA (găb′ ə) Kh. el-Harathiya? [3–D] Greco-Roman town at the western entrance to the Great Plain. Given by Augustus to Herod the Great, who rebuilt it as a military colony c. 23 B.C.

GADARA (găd′ ə rə) Umm Qeis [6–D] City in Gilead southeast of the Sea of Galilee. Conquered by Antiochus III in 198 B.C., who turned it into a Hellenistic city. One of the cities of the Decapolis. Taken by Alexander Janneus in c. 84 B.C. Made a free city by Pompey in 63 B.C. but later became part of the kingdom of Herod the Great. Near here Jesus healed two demoniacs (Mt. 8:28), but see Mk. 5:1 and Lk. 8:26, 37 where a similar story is located near **Gerasa.**

GALLIM (găl′ ĭm) Town in Benjamin. Site unidentified. Home of Palti, to whom Saul gave Michal, David's wife (1 Sam. 25:44). Assyrian army passed through here on its way to Jerusalem (Is. 10:30).

GAMAD (gā′ măd) Place mentioned in Ezek. 27:11. Site unidentified.

GAMALA (gā′ mă lə) es-Salam [7–C] Fortress east of the Sea of Galilee. Captured by Alexander Janneus in c. 84 B.C. Taken by Vespasian in A.D. 67 in the First Jewish Revolt.

GATH (găth) T. es-Safi? [2–I] City on the southern coastal plain. Canaanite city not captured in the conquest (Jos. 11:22). Inhabited by men of great stature (2 Sam. 21:20,

22; 1 Chr. 20:6, 8). One of the five major Philistine cities (Jos. 13:3; 1 Sam. 6:17). Ark brought here by the Philistines (1 Sam. 5:8). Home of Goliath (1 Sam. 17:4, 23). Where David sought refuge (1 Sam. 21:10, 12; 27:2–4). Destroyed by Hazael of Damascus (2 Kg. 12:17). Conquered by Uzziah of Judah (2 Chr. 26:6). Also mentioned in 1 Sam. 7:14; 17:52; 27:11; 2 Sam. 1:20; 15:18; 1 Kg. 2:39–41; 1 Chr. 7:21; 8:13; 18:1; 2 Chr. 11:8; Am. 6:2; Mic. 1:10. Called Metheg-ammah in 2 Sam. 8:1.

GATH-HEPHER (găth hē' fər) Kh. ez-Zurra [5–D] Village in the hills of Lower Galilee. Assigned to Zebulun (Jos. 19:13). Home of the prophet Jonah, son of Amittai (2 Kg. 14:25).

GATH-RIMMON (găth rĭm' ən) **1.** T. Jerisha? [2–G] City on the central coastal plain. Levitical city in Dan (Jos. 19:45; 21:24; 1 Chr. 6:69). **2.** Levitical city in Manasseh (Jos. 21:25). Sometimes identified with **Bileam.**

GAZA (gā' zə) el-Ghazza [See locator] Important Canaanite commercial city on the southern coastal plain along the Way of the Sea. Assigned to Judah (Jos. 15:47; Jg. 1:18), who failed to drive out the inhabitants. Destroyed by the Sea Peoples in the 12th century B.C. (Dt. 2:23). One of the five major Philistine cities (Jos. 13:3; 1 Sam. 6:17). Where Samson visited a harlot (Jg. 16:1) and was later blinded (Jg. 16:21). Captured by Tiglath-pileser III in 734 B.C. Captured by Sargon II in 720 B.C. Taken by Nebuchadnezzar c. 600 B.C. Condemned by the prophets (Jer. 25:20; 47:1, 5; Am. 1:6, 7; Zeph. 2:4; Zech. 9:5). Made part of the Persian empire in 525 B.C. Besieged and taken by Alexander the Great in 332 B.C. Fell to Jonathan (1 Macc. 11:61, 62) and destroyed by Alexander Janneus in 96 B.C. Rebuilt by Gabinius in 57 B.C. Philip the evangelist met the Ethiopian eunuch on the way to Gaza (Acts 8:26). Also mentioned in Gen. 10:19; Jos. 10:41; 11:22; Jg. 6:4; 1 Kg. 4:24; 2 Kg. 18:8.

GAZARA (gā' ză rə) Greco-Roman name for **Gezer** (1 Macc. 4:15; 7:45; 9:52; 13:43, 51; 14:34).

GEBA (gē' bə) **1.** Jeba [4–H] Strategic town near the Wadi Suweinit commanding the Michmash pass in the Saddle of Benjamin. Levitical city in Benjamin (Jos. 18:24; 21:17; 1 Chr. 6:60; 8:6). Where Saul and Jonathan fought the Philistines successfully (1 Sam. 13:3, 16; 14:5). On the northern border of the kingdom of Judah (2 Kg. 23:8; Zech. 14:10). Fortified by Asa of Judah (1 Kg. 15:22; 2 Chr. 16:6). Settled by Jews returning from the Exile (Ezra 2:26; Neh. 7:30; 11:31; 12:29; 1 Esd. 5:20). Also mentioned in Is. 10:29. Called Gibeath-elohim in 1 Sam. 10:5. **2.** Place near Dothan where Holofernes camped (Jdt. 3:10). Site unidentified.

GEBAL (gē' bəl) Jebeil. Important Phoenician port. Famous for ships built of cedars of Lebanon. Men from here cut timber for Solomon's ships and prepared stones for the Temple (1 Kg. 5:18). Also mentioned in Jos. 13:5; Ezek. 27:9.

GEBIM (gē' bĭm) Place in the Saddle of Benjamin on the route of Assyrian army attacking Jerusalem (Is. 10:31). Site unidentified.

GEDER (gē' dər) Town in the Shephelah conquered by Joshua (Jos. 12:13). Site unidentified.

GEDERAH (gĭ dĭr' ə) **1.** Town in the Shephelah assigned to Judah (Jos. 15:36). Site unidentified. Also mentioned in 1 Chr. 4:23; 12:4. **2.** Village in Benjamin. Site unidentified. Home of Jozabad, one of David's mighty men who joined him at Ziklag (1 Chr. 12:4).

GEDEROTH (gĭ dĭr' ŏth) Town in the Shephelah, perhaps near the Sorek valley. Site unidentified. Assigned to Judah (Jos. 15:41). Conquered by the Philistines (2 Chr. 28:18.).

GEDEROTHAIM (gĭ dĭr' ə thā ĭm) Village in the Shephelah assigned to Judah (Jos. 15:36). Site unidentified.

GEDOR (gē' dôr) **1.** Kh. Jedur [3–I] Town in the hill country of Judah. Assigned to Judah (Jos. 15:58). Also mentioned in 1 Chr. 4:39. **2.** Place in Benjamin mentioned in 1 Chr. 12:7. Site unidentified.

GELILOTH (gĭ lī' lŏth) Place in Judah mentioned in Jos. 18:17. Site unidentified but possibly the same as Gilgal 4 of Jos. 15:7.

GENNESARET (gĕ nĕs' ə rət) Roman name for **Chinnereth** (Mt. 14:34; Mk. 6:53).

GERAR (gĭr' är) T. Abu Hureira [1–K] Canaanite city in the northern Negeb. Abraham and Isaac dwelt here and made treaties with King Abimelech (Gen. 20:1; 26:1, 17, 20, 26). Also mentioned in Gen. 10:19; 2 Chr. 14:13, 14.

GERASA (gĕr' ə sə) Jerash [7–F] Hellenistic Antioch-on-the-Chrysorrhoas. Greek city in Gilead founded as a city by Antiochus IV. Captured by Alexander Janneus c. 82 B.C. Taken by Pompey in 63 B.C. One of the cities of the Decapolis. Near here Jesus healed a demoniac (Mk. 5:1; Lk. 8:26), but see Mt. 8:28 where a similar story is located near **Gadara.**

GEZER (gē' zər) T. Jazer [3–H] Greco-Roman Gazara. Strategically located Canaanite city in the northern Shephelah commanding major approaches to the highlands north of Jerusalem. Mentioned in the inscriptions of Thutmose III (15th century B.C.), in the Amarna Letters (14th century B.C.), and on the Merneptah, or Israel, Stele (c. 1230 B.C.). King of Gezer killed by invading Israelites (Jos. 10:33; 12:12; Jg. 1:29). Levitical city of Ephraim (Jos. 16:3; 21:21), who failed to drive out the Canaanites (Jg. 1:29). Where David fought the Philistines (2 Sam. 5:25; 1 Chr. 14:16; 20:4). Given by Egyptian Pharaoh as part of his daughter's dowry to Solomon, who rebuilt it (1 Kg. 9:15, 16, 17). Taken by Tiglath-pileser III in 734 B.C. Fortified by Bacchides (1 Macc. 4:15; 7:45; 9:52, where called Gazara). Captured in 142 B.C.

by Simon, who settled Jews here (1 Macc. 13:43, 51; 14:34, where called Gazara). Where John was commander (1 Macc. 13:53) when Simon was murdered at Dok in 134 B.C.

GIAH (gī' ə) Village probably in eastern Benjamin along the route of Abner's flight from Gibeon (2 Sam. 2:24). Site unidentified.

GIBBETHON (gĭb' ə thŏn) T. el-Melat [2–H] City along the Way of the Sea at the edge of the hills in the northern Shephelah. Levitical city of Dan (Jos. 19:44; 21:23). Became a Philistine city (1 Kg. 15:27). Where Baasha killed King Nadab of Israel in 900 B.C. (1 Kg. 15:27, 28). Omri was besieging the city when Zimri killed King Elah, Baasha's son (1 Kg. 16:15).

GIBEAH (gĭb' ĭ ə) **1.** T. el-Ful [4–H] Town on the ridge route in the central hills of Benjamin north of Jerusalem. Assigned to Benjamin (Jos. 18:28). Figured in intertribal warfare among Hebrews (Jg. 19:12–16; 20:4–43). Home of Saul, first king of Israel (1 Sam. 10:26; 11:4; 15:34; 22:6; 23:19; 26:1; Is. 10:29). Home of one of David's mighty men (2 Sam. 23:29) and of the mother of King Abijah (Abijam) of Judah (2 Chr. 13:2). Also mentioned in Jos. 24:33; 1 Sam. 10:10; 13:2, 15; 14:2; 14:16; Hos. 5:8; 9:9; 10:9. **2.** Village in the hill country of Judah assigned to Judah (Jos. 15:57). Site unidentified.

GIBEATH-ELOHIM (gĭb' ĭ ăth ĕl' ō hĭm) Another name for **Geba 1** (1 Sam. 10:5).

GIBEATH-HAARALOTH (gĭb' ĭ ăth hā är' ə lŏth) Place in the southern Jordan valley near Gilgal. Site unidentified. Where the Israelites were circumcised after entering Canaan (Jos. 5:3).

GIBEON (gĭb' ĭ ən) el-Jib [4–H] Greco-Roman Gabao. City northwest of Jerusalem. Member of the Hivite coalition that tricked Joshua into a treaty and were spared destruction (Jos. 9:3, 17; 10:1; 11:19). Where the sun stood still while Joshua won the battle (Jos. 10:2–12, 41). Levitical city in Benjamin (Jos. 18:25; 21:17; 1 Chr. 8:29; 9:35). Where forces of Joab met those of Abner (2 Sam. 2:12, 13, 16, 24; 3:30). Where David fought the Philistines (2 Sam. 5:25, where called Geba; 1 Chr. 14:16). Where Joab killed Amasa (2 Sam. 20:8). Sons and grandsons of Saul were hanged here (2 Sam. 21:1–9). Solomon sacrificed at the high place at Gibeon and had his famous dream here (1 Kg. 3:4–5; 9:2). Site of the tabernacle and place of sacrifice (1 Chr. 16:39; 21:29; 2 Chr. 1:3, 13). Men from here helped Nehemiah rebuild the walls of Jerusalem (Neh. 3:7; 7:25). Site of the pool of Gibeon (Jer. 41:12). Also mentioned in 1 Chr. 12:4; Is. 28:21; Jer. 28:1; 41:16.

GIDOM (gī' dəm) Unknown place in Benjamin mentioned in Jg. 20:45.

GILGAL (gĭl' găl) **1.** Kh. el-Mafjar? [5–H] Ancient shrine in the southern Jordan valley

David is said to have hanged Ishbosheth's murderers by this pool at Hebron. The shrine marking the patriarchal tombs dominates the view at right.

near Jericho. Where the Hebrews camped after crossing the Jordan River into Canaan (Jos. 4:19; Mic. 6:5) and set up 12 memorial stones taken from the dry riverbed (Jos. 4:20; Jg. 3:19). Hebrews were circumcised nearby while camped at Gilgal (Jos. 5:9). Where Joshua had his military headquarters (Jos. 9:6; 10:6, 7, 9, 15, 43; 14:6). On Samuel's annual circuit (1 Sam. 7:16), and he sacrificed here (1 Sam. 10:8). Saul anointed king here (1 Sam. 11:14–15). Here Samuel rebuked Saul (1 Sam. 13:8, 12, 15; 15:12, 21) and killed Agag (1 Sam. 15:33). Also mentioned in Jos. 5:10; Jg. 2:1; 1 Sam. 13:4, 7; 15:12, 21; 2 Sam. 19:15, 40; Hos. 4:15; 9:15; 12:11; Am. 4:4; 5:5. **2.** Jiljuliah [4–G] Village in the hill country of Judah north of Bethel. From here Elijah and Elisha went down to the Jordan valley and Elijah was taken up into heaven (2 Kg. 2:1; 4:38). **3.** Place near Mount Gerizim mentioned in Dt. 11:30. Site unidentified. **4.** Place mentioned in Jos. 15:7. Site unidentified but possibly the same as Geliloth of Jos. 18:17.

GILO (gī′ lō) Another name for **Giloh** (2 Sam. 23:34).

GILOH (gī′ lō) Village in southern Judah assigned to Judah (Jos. 15:51). Site unidentified. Also mentioned in 2 Sam. 15:12; 23:34, where called Gilo.

GIMZO (gĭm′ zō) Jimzu [3–H] Town in the Shephelah near Lod. Captured by the Philistines during the reign of Ahaz of Judah, 735–715 B.C. (2 Chr. 28:18).

GITTAIM (gĭt′ ĭ əm) Village on the coastal plain, possibly near Lod. Site unidentified. Here men from Beeroth sought refuge (2 Sam. 4:3). Settled by Jews returning from the Exile (Neh. 11:33).

GOLAN (gō′ lən) Sahm el-Jaulan? [See locator] City in Bashan. Levitical city in Manasseh and a city of refuge (Dt. 4:43; Jos. 20:8; 21:27; 1 Chr. 6:71).

GOMORRAH (gə môr′ ə) City in the Valley of Siddim, possibly in the southern Dead Sea area. Site unidentified. Attacked by Chedorlaomer (Gen. 14:2, 8, 10, 11). Destroyed for its wickedness (Gen. 13:10; 18:20; 19:24, 28; Dt. 29:23; Is. 1:9, 10; 13:19; Jer. 23:14; 49:18; 50:40; Am. 4:11). Symbol of evil (Dt. 32:32; Jer. 23:14; 49:18; 50:40; Am. 4:11; Zeph. 2:9; Mt. 10:15; Rom. 9:29; 2 Pet. 2:6; Jude:7). Also mentioned in Gen. 10:19.

GOPHNA (gŏf′ nə) Hellenistic name for **Ophni.**

GORTYNA (gôr tĭ nə) City in central Crete to which Lucius, the Roman consul, sent a letter on behalf of the Jews in 138 B.C. (1 Macc. 15:23).

GOSHEN (gō′ shən) Town in the hill country of southern Judah assigned to Judah (Jos. 15:51). Site unidentified.

GOZAN (gō′ zăn) Place in Assyria to which Israelites were deported (2 Kg. 17:6; 18:11; 1 Chr. 5:26, where identified with the river Gozan). Destroyed by the Assyrians (2 Kg. 19:12; Is. 37:12).

GUDGODAH (gŭd gō′ da) Place where the Hebrews stopped in their wilderness wanderings (Dt. 10:7). Site unidentified. Called **Hor-haggidgad** in Num. 33:32, 33.

GURBAAL (gûr′ bāl) Where Uzziah fought the Arabs (2 Chr. 26:7). Site unidentified. Possibly the same as **Jagur** of Jos. 15:21.

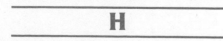

H

HADASHAH (hə dăsh′ ə) Village in the southern Shephelah assigned to Judah (Jos. 15:37). Site unidentified.

HADID (hā′ dĭd) el-Haditha [3–H] Hellenistic Adida. Town in the northern Shephelah.

Settled by Jews returning from the Exile (Ezra 2:33; Neh. 7:37; 11:34). Fortified by Simon, who also camped here c. 143 B.C. (1 Macc. 12:38 and 13:13, where called Adida).

HA-ELEPH (hā ē′ lĭf) Town north of Jerusalem assigned to Benjamin (Jos. 18:28). Site unidentified.

HAHIROTH (hə hī′ rŏth) Another name for **Pi-hahiroth** (Num. 33:8).

HALAH (hā′ lə) City in Assyria to which Israelites were deported following the fall of Samaria (2 Kg. 17:6; 18:11; 1 Chr. 5:26; Ob. 20). Site unidentified but possibly on the Habor River.

HALHUL (hăl′ hŭl) Halhul [3–J] Town in the hills of Judah north of Hebron. Assigned to Judah (Jos. 15:58).

HALICARNASSUS (hăl′ ə kär năs′ əs) Greek city in Caria in southwestern Asia Minor to which Lucius, the Roman consul, sent a letter on behalf of the Jews in 138 B.C. (1 Macc. 15:23).

HAMATH (hā′ măth) Hama. City on the Orontes River in Syria. Capital of the Aramean kingdom of Hamath. King Toi of Hamath congratulated David on his victories (2 Sam. 8:9; 1 Chr. 18:9). People from here settled in Samaria after the fall of Israel in 721 B.C. (2 Kg. 17:24). Also mentioned in 2 Kg. 14:28; 17:30; 18:34; 19:13; 1 Chr. 18:3; Is. 11:11; 36:19; 37:13; Jer. 49:23; Am. 6:2; Zech. 9:2.

HAMMATH (hăm′ ăth) **1.** Hammam Tabariya [6–C] Hellenistic Ammathus. Fortified town on the western shore of the Sea of Galilee. Levitical city in Naphtali (Jos. 19:35; 21:32, where called Hammoth-dor). Possibly the same as Hammon 2 (1 Chr. 6:76). **2.** Town of the Kenites (1 Chr. 2:55). Site unidentified.

HAMMON (hăm′ ən) **1.** Umm el-Awamid [4–A] Town on the coast of Upper Galilee north of Achzib. Assigned to Asher (Jos. 19:28). **2.** Levitical city in Naphtali (1 Chr. 6:76). Site unidentified but possibly the same as **Hammath 1.**

HAMMOTH-DOR (hăm' əth dôr') Another name for **Hammath 1** (Jos. 21:32).

HAMONAH (hə mō' nə) City mentioned in Ezek. 39:16. Site unidentified.

HANES (hā' nĭz) City in Upper Egypt mentioned in Is. 30:4. Site unidentified.

HANNATHON (hăn' ə thŏn) T. el-Bedeiwiya [4–C] Hellenistic Asochis. Town in Lower Galilee. Mentioned in Amarna Letters (14th century B.C.). Assigned to Zebulun (Jos. 19:14).

HAPHARAIM (hăf' ə rā' əm) et-Taiyiba. Town in southeastern Lower Galilee. Assigned to Issachar (Jos. 19:19). Conquered by Shishak c. 918 B.C.

HARAN (hâr' ən) Harran. Important commercial city and caravan center in northwestern Mesopotamia. Here Terah, Abraham's father, settled with his family and later died (Gen. 11:31, 32). Abraham set out from here for Canaan (Gen. 12:4, 5). Jacob went toward there to avoid Esau's wrath (Gen. 27:43; 28:10). Also mentioned in Gen. 12:5; 29:4; 2 Kg. 19:12; Is. 37:12; Ezek. 27:23; Acts 7:2, 4.

HAR-HERES (här hĭr' ĭz) Another name for **Beth-shemesh 1** (Jg. 1:35).

HAROD (hâr' ŏd) Ein Jalud [5–D] Spring near Mount Moreh where Gideon camped (Jg. 7:1). Also mentioned in 2 Sam. 23:25; 1 Chr. 11:27.

HAROSHETH-HA-GOIIM (hə rō' shĕth hə goi' ĭm) T. el-Amr? [3–C] Canaanite town in Lower Galilee. Home of Sisera, the commander of King Jabin's army (Jg. 4:2, 13), who was defeated by Barak (Jg. 4:16).

HASHMONAH (hăsh mō' nə) Place in the Sinai where the Hebrews camped in their wilderness wanderings following the Exodus (Num. 33:29-30). Site unidentified.

HAVVOTH-JAIR (hăv' ŏth jā' ər) Collection of villages (possibly 30 or 60) in Gilead and Bashan. Sites unidentified. Possibly taken by Manasseh (Num. 32:41; Dt. 3:14). Also mentioned in Jg. 10:4; 1 Chr. 2:23. Called "towns of Jair" in Jos. 13:30; "villages of Jair" in 1 Kg. 4:13.

HAZAR-ADDAR (hā' zər ăd' ər) Sometimes identified with **Addar** (Num. 34:4). Probably another name for **Hezron** of Jos. 15:3.

HAZAR-ENAN (hā' zər ē' nən) Town on the northeastern frontier of Canaan below Mount Hermon (Num. 34:9). Site unidentified. Called Hazar-enon in Ezek. 47:17, 18; 48:1.

HAZAR-ENON (hā' zər ē' nŏn) Another name for **Hazar-enan** (Ezek. 47:17, 18; 48:1).

HAZAR-GADDAH (hā' zər găd' ə) Town in southern Judah assigned to Judah (Jos. 15:27). Site unidentified.

HAZARMAVETH (hā' zər mā' vĭth) Unknown place or region in southern Arabia (Gen. 10:26; 1 Chr. 1:20).

HAZAR-SHUAL (hā' zər shoo' əl) Town in the Negeb. Site unidentified. Assigned to Judah (Jos. 15:28) and to Simeon (Jos. 19:3; 1 Chr. 4:28). Settled by Jews returning from the Exile (Neh. 11:27).

HAZAR-SUSAH (hā' zər soo' sə) Town in the Negeb assigned to Simeon (Jos. 19:5). Site unidentified. Another name for Hazarsusim of 1 Chr. 4:31.

HAZAR-SUSIM (hā' zər soo' sĭm) Another name for **Hazar-susah** (1 Chr. 4:31).

HAZAZON-TAMAR (hăz' ə zŏn tā' mər) Possibly a city in the Arabah south of the Dead Sea. Amorite city subdued by Chedorlaomer (Gen. 14:7). Also called **En-gedi** in 2 Chr. 20:2.

HAZER-HATTICON (hā' zər hăt' ə kŏn) Place mentioned in Ezek. 47:16. Site unidentified.

HAZEROTH (hə zīr' ŏth) Place in eastern Sinai where the Hebrews camped during the Exodus (Num. 11:35; 33:17) and where Miriam and Aaron spoke against Moses because of his Cushite wife: Site unidentified. Also mentioned in Dt. 1:1.

HAZOR (hā' zôr) **1.** T. el-Qedah [6–B] Canaanite royal city dominating the Way of the Sea north of the Sea of Galilee. Mentioned in the Egyptian Execration Texts (19th–18th century B.C.), the Mesopotamian Mari Letters (18th century B.C.), the Amarna

Letters (14th century B.C.), as well as inscriptions of Pharaohs Thutmose III and Amenhotep II (15th century B.C.) and Seti I (14th–13th century B.C.). Jabin, king of Hazor, was defeated by Joshua, who burned the city (Jos. 11:1, 10–13; 12:19). Assigned to Naphtali (Jos. 19:36). Where Barak defeated Sisera, commander of Hazor's army (Jg. 4:2, 17). Fortified by Solomon (1 Kg. 9:15). Rebuilt by Ahab, who had the water tunnel dug here. Destroyed by Tiglath-pileser III in 733 B.C. (2 Kg. 15:29). Also mentioned in 1 Sam. 12:9. **2.** Kh. Hazzur? Village north of Jerusalem. Settled by Jews returning from the Exile (Neh. 11:33). **3.** Town in the Negeb assigned to Judah (Jos. 15:23). Site unidentified. **4.** Place or region in northern Arabia. Site unidentified. Attacked by Nebuchadnezzar in 598 B.C. (Jer. 49:28, 30, 33). **5.** Another name for **Kerioth-hezron** (Jos. 15:25).

HAZOR-HADATTAH (hā' zôr hə dăt' ə) Village in the Negeb near Beer-sheba assigned to Judah (Jos. 15:25). Site unidentified.

HEBRON (hē' brən) el-Khalil [3–J] Canaanite royal city in the hill country of Judah. Chief city of the region. Dwelling place of Abraham (Gen. 13:18), where he buried Sarah in the cave of Machpelah (Gen. 23:2, 19). Here Moses' spies saw the Anakim, whom Joshua later destroyed (Num. 13:22; Jos. 11:21). Built seven years before Zoan in Egypt (Num. 13:22). Joined alliance against Joshua but destroyed by him (Jos. 10:3, 5, 23, 36, 39; 12:10). Given to Caleb (Jos. 14:13, 14; Jg. 1:20). Levitical city and a city of refuge (Jos. 21:13; 1 Chr. 6:55, 57). Place to which Samson carried the gates of Gaza (Jg. 16:3). David sent Amalekite booty to elders here (1 Sam. 30:31). Where David was anointed king of Judah and ruled seven years (2 Sam. 2:1, 3, 11; 1 Chr. 11:1, 3; 29:27). Center of Absalom's revolt (2 Sam. 15:7, 9, 10). Fortified by Rehoboam (2 Chr. 11:10). Idumean town captured and burned by Judas Macca-

The historic Jordan River meanders through its hot, below-sea-level valley before emptying into the Dead Sea.

beus in 163 B.C. (1 Macc. 5:65). Where Herod the Great rebuilt the cave of Machpelah. Destroyed by the Romans in the First Jewish Revolt (A.D. 66–70). Also mentioned in Gen. 37:14; 2 Sam. 2:32. Called Kiriath-arba in Gen. 23:2; 35:27; Jos. 14:15; 15:13, 54; 20:7; 21:11; Jg. 1:10; Neh. 11:25.

HELAM (hē' ləm) City in northern Gilead where David fought the Syrians (2 Sam. 10:16–17). Possibly the same as Alema of 1 Macc. 5:26, 35.

HELBAH (hĕl' bə) Town near Tyre assigned to Asher, who failed to drive out the Canaanites (Jg. 1:31). Sometimes identified with Ahlab of Jg. 1:31. Probably the same as **Mahalab** of Jos. 19:29.

HELBON (hĕl' bŏn) Halbun? Town in the mountains of Lebanon mentioned in Ezek. 27:18.

HELEPH (hē' lĕf) Town in Lower Galilee assigned to Naphtali (Jos. 19:33). Site unidentified.

HELIOPOLIS (hē' lĭ ŏp' ə lĭs) Hellenistic name for **On** (Jer. 43:13).

HELKATH (hĕl' kăth) T. el-Qassis? [4–D] Town at the western end of the Great Plain north of Mount Carmel. Levitical city in Asher (Jos. 19:25; 21:31; 1 Chr. 6:75, where called Hukok).

HEPHER (hē' fər) T. el-Ifshar? [3–E] City on the Plain of Sharon. Its king was defeated by Joshua (Jos. 12:17). In Solomon's third administrative district (1 Kg. 4:10).

HERODIUM (hĭ rō' dĭ əm) Kh. el-Fureidis [4–I] Mountaintop fortress built by Herod the Great in the Wilderness of Judea near Tekoa. Near here Herod defeated hostile Jews while fleeing to Masada and then Egypt. Where Herod was buried. One of the last places taken by the Romans after the capture of Jerusalem at the end of the First Jewish Revolt (A.D. 66–70). Held by Jewish rebels in the Second (Bar Kokhba) Jewish Revolt (132–135). Later a Roman outpost; then a Byzantine monastery.

HESHBON (hĕsh' bŏn) Hisban [7–H] Hellenistic Esebon, Roman Esbus. Important city on the King's Highway in northern Moab. City of Amorite king Sihon defeated by Moses and the Hebrews (Num. 21:25–34; Dt. 1:4; 2:24, 26, 30; 3:2, 6; 4:46; 29:7; Jos. 9:10; 12:2, 5; 13:10, 21; Jg. 11:19, 26; Neh. 9:22). Assigned to Reuben (Num. 32:3, 37; Jos. 13:17, 21) and to Gad (Jos. 13:26). Levitical city (Jos. 21:39; 1 Chr. 6:81). Recovered by Moab (Is. 15:4; 16:8, 9; Jer. 4:2, 34, 45). Also mentioned in S. of S. 7:4; Jer. 49:3.

HESHMON (hĕsh' mŏn) Town in southwestern Judah assigned to Judah (Jos. 15:27). Site unidentified.

HEZRON (hĕz' rən) Town in the Wilderness of Zin on the southernmost border of Judah. Assigned to Judah (Jos. 15:3). Probably the same as **Addar** of Jos. 15:3. Sometimes identified with Hazar-addar of Num. 34:4.

HIERAPOLIS (hī' ə răp' ə lĭs) Important city in the Lycus valley in southwestern Asia Minor where Epaphras ministered (Col. 4:13).

HILEN (hī' lən) Another name for **Holon** (1 Chr. 6:58).

HIPPUS (hĭp' əs) Qalaat el-Husn [6–C] City of the Decapolis east of the Sea of Galilee.

HOLON (hō' lŏn) **1.** Village in the southern hill country of Judah. Site unidentified. Levitical city in Judah (Jos. 15:51; 21:15; 1 Chr. 6:58, where called Hilen). **2.** Town in Moab mentioned in Jer. 48:21. Site unidentified.

HOREM (hŏr' ĕm) Town in Upper Galilee assigned to Naphtali (Jos. 19:38). Site unidentified.

HORESH (hŏr' ĕsh) Kh. Khureisa? Place in the Wilderness of Ziph in southeastern Judah to which David fled from Saul (1 Sam. 23:15–19).

HOR-HAGGIDGAD (hŏr' hə gĭd' găd) Place where the Hebrews camped in their wilderness wanderings following the Exodus (Num. 33:32, 33). Site unidentified but perhaps near the southern Arabah north of Ezion-geber. Called Gudgodah in Dt. 10:7.

HORMAH (hŏr' mə) Kh. el-Mishash [3–K] Town in the Negeb. Assigned to Judah (Jos. 15:30) and to Simeon (Jos. 19:4; 1 Chr. 4:30). Called Canaanite Zephath in Jg. 1:17. Also mentioned in Num. 14:45; 21:3; Dt. 1:44; Jos. 12:14; 1 Sam. 30:30.

HORONAIM (hŏr' ə nā' əm) el-Iraq? [7–L] Hellenistic Oronaim. City in southern Moab on an important road that connected the southeastern shore of the Dead Sea with the King's Highway. Condemned by the prophets (Is. 15:5; Jer. 48:3, 5, 34). According to the Moabite Stone, it was captured by King Mesha of Moab. Taken by Alexander Janneus and annexed to the Hasmonean kingdom c. 88 B.C. Promised to King Aretas of the Nabateans by Hyrcanus II.

HOSAH (hō' zə) Town in Asher (Jos. 19:29). Site unidentified but perhaps in western Upper Galilee.

HUKKOK (hŭk' ŏk) Town in Napthali (Jos. 19:34). Site unidentified but perhaps in Lower Galilee near Chinnereth.

HUKOK (hŭk' ŏk) Another name for **Helkath** (1 Chr. 6:75).

HUMTAH (hŭm' tə) Village assigned to Judah (Jos. 15:54). Site unidentified.

HYRCANIA (hûr kā' nĭ ə) Kh. Mird [5–I] Fortress in the Wilderness of Judea east of Bethlehem. Built by John Hyrcanus (134–104 B.C.). Destroyed by Gabinius c. 57 B.C. and rebuilt by Herod the Great as a state prison.

I

IBLEAM (ĭb' lĭ əm) Kh. Balama [4–E] City south of the Great Plain by the Ascent of Gur. Conquered by Thutmose III in the 15th century B.C. In the territory of Issachar but given to Manasseh, who failed to drive out the Canaanites (Jos. 17:11; Jg. 1:27). Near where Ahaziah of Judah was fatally wounded by Jehu's men in 842 B.C. (2 Kg. 9:27). Perhaps the same as Bileam of 1 Chr. 6:70 and also Gath-rimmon of Jos. 21:25.

ICONIUM (ī kō' nĭ əm) Konya. City in Galatia in central Asia Minor. Paul and Barnabas taught in the synagogue here on Paul's first missionary journey but fled the city to avoid stoning (Acts 13:51; 14:1, 19; 2 Tim. 3:11). Later they returned to found a church here (Acts 14:21; 16:2).

IDALAH (ĭd' ə lə) Village in Lower Galilee assigned to Zebulun (Jos. 19:15). Site unidentified but possibly southwest of Nazareth.

IIM (ī' ĭm) Village in the south of Judah (Jos. 15:29). Site unidentified.

IJON (ī' jŏn) Town on the northern limit of Israel west of Mount Hermon. Site unidentified. Conquered by Ben-hadad of Syria c. 878 B.C. as a part of his alliance with Asa of Judah (1 Kg. 15:20; 2 Chr. 16:4). Taken by Tiglath-pileser III in 733 B.C. (2 Kg. 15:29).

IMMER (ĭm' ər) Unknown place in Babylonia from which Jews returned after the Exile (Ezra 2:59; Neh. 7:61; 1 Esd. 5:36).

IPHTAH (ĭf' tə) Village in the southern Shephelah assigned to Judah (Jos. 15:43). Site unidentified.

IRNAHASH (ĭr nā' hăsh) Deir Nakhkhas? [3–I] Town in the southern Shephelah mentioned in 1 Chr. 4:12.

IRPEEL (ĭr' pĭ əl) Town north of Jerusalem assigned to Benjamin (Jos. 18:27). Site unidentified.

IR-SHEMESH (ĭr shĕm' ĭsh) Another name for **Beth-shemesh 1** (Jos. 19:41).

ISANA (ĭ sā' nə) Greco-Roman name for **Jeshanah.**

ITHLAH (ĭth' lə) Village in the Sorek valley assigned to Dan (Jos. 19:42). Site unidentified.

ITHNAN (ĭth' năn) Village in eastern Judah near Ziph assigned to Judah (Jos. 15:23). Site unidentified.

IVVAH (ĭv' ə) Town probably in northern Syria or Babylonia destroyed by Sennacherib, 704–681 B.C. (2 Kg. 18:34; 19:13; Is. 37:13). Site unidentified. Called Avva in 2 Kg. 17:24.

IYE-ABARIM (ī′ yə āb′ ə rīm) el-Medeiyina? [7–M] Place on the edge of the wilderness east of Moab near the Zered. Where the Hebrews camped in their wilderness wanderings following the Exodus (Num. 21:11; 33:44, 45, where called Iyim).

IYIM (ī′ yīm) Another name for **Iye-abarim** (Num. 33:45).

J

JAAKAN (jā′ ə kən) Another name for **Beeroth Bene-jaakan** (1 Chr. 1:42).

JABESH (jā′ bĭsh) Another name for **Jabesh-gilead** (1 Sam. 11:1–10; 31:12, 13; 1 Chr. 10:12).

JABESH-GILEAD (jā′ bĭsh gĭl′ ĭ əd) T. el-Maqlub [6–E] City in the Wadi Yabis in Gilead. Hebrews there massacred by other Hebrews who saved 400 virgins for the Benjaminites (Jg. 21:8–14). Delivered from the Ammonites by Saul (1 Sam. 11:1–10, where also called Jabesh). Men of the city took the body of Saul and his sons from Beth-shan and buried them at Jabesh-gilead (1 Sam. 31:11; 12 and 13, where called Jabesh; 2 Sam. 2:4; 1 Chr. 10:12, where called Jabesh). David blessed the men of the city for honoring Saul (2 Sam. 2:5) and later took the bones of Saul and Jonathan from here and reburied them at Zela (2 Sam. 21:12).

JABEZ (jā′ bĭz) Village in the hill country of Judah (1 Chr. 2:55). Site unidentified.

JABNEEL (jăb′ nĭ əl) **1.** Yibna [2–H] Greco-Roman Jamnia. Town on the coastal plain. Assigned to Judah (Jos. 15:11). Captured by Uzziah from the Philistines in the mid-8th century b.c. (2 Chr. 26:6, where called Jabneh). Name changed to Jamnia in the Apocrypha. Base for Seleucid armies in the Maccabean Wars (1 Macc. 4:16; 5:58). Burned along with the port of Jamnia by Judas Maccabeus in 164 b.c. (2 Macc. 12:8–9). Captured by Hyrcanus. Part of Alexander Janneus′ kingdom. Taken by Pompey in 63 b.c. and rebuilt by Gabinius c. 57 b.c. Part of Herod the Great′s kingdom, it eventually became the property of the Emperor Tiberius. Occupied by Vespasian in the First Jewish Revolt (a.d. 66–70). Became center of the Sanhedrin after the fall of Jerusalem in a.d. 70. Canon of the Old Testament discussed here c. 90. Also mentioned in Jdt. 2:28; 2 Macc. 12:40. **2.** T. en-Naam [5–D] Village assigned to Naphtali (Jos. 19:33).

JABNEH (jăb′ nə) Another name for **Jabneel 1** (2 Chr. 26:6).

JAGUR (jā′ gər) T. Ghurr? [4–K] Village in southern Judah assigned to Judah (Jos. 15:21). Possibly the same as **Gurbaal** of 2 Chr. 26:7.

JAHAZ (jā′ hăz) Kh. el-Medeiyina [7–J] City in eastern Moab. Where the Hebrews defeated the Amorite king Sihon (Num. 21:23; Dt. 2:32; Jg. 11:20). Assigned to Reuben (Jos. 13:18). Levitical city (Jos. 21:36; 1 Chr. 6:78). Conquered by Moabites (Is. 15:4; Jer. 48:21, where called Jahzah; 48:34). Mentioned on the Moabite Stone as an Israelite base against King Mesha of Moab.

JAMNIA (jăm′ nĭ ə) Greco-Roman name for **Jabneel 1.**

JAMNIA, PORT OF (jăm′ nĭ ə) Minet Rubin [1–H] Greco-Roman Iamnitarum Portus. Harbor of Jamnia on the Mediterranean coast. Judas Maccabeus burned the ships in the harbor here (1 Macc. 12:8, 9).

JANIM (jăn′ ĭm) Village in the hill country of Judah near Hebron assigned to Judah (Jos. 15:53). Site unidentified.

JANOAH (jə nō′ ə) **1.** Yanuh [4–B] Town in Upper Galilee destroyed by Tiglath-pileser III in 733 b.c. (2 Kg. 15:29). **2.** Kh. Yanun [5–G] Town in Samaria on the border of Ephraim (Jos. 16:6, 7).

JAPHIA (jə fī′ ə) Yafa [4–D] Village in Lower Galilee near Nazareth assigned to Zebulun (Jos. 19:13). Fortified by Josephus in the First Jewish Revolt (a.d. 66–70).

JARMUTH (jär′ mŭth) **1.** Kh. Yarmuk [3–I] Canaanite royal city in the Shephelah. Its king and his allies defeated by Joshua (Jos. 10:3, 5, 23; 12:11). Assigned to Judah (Jos. 15:35). Settled by Jews returning from the Exile (Neh. 11:29). **2.** Levitical city in Issachar (Jos. 21:29). Site unidentified but possibly the same as Ramoth of 1 Chr. 6:73 and Remeth of Jos. 19:21.

JATTIR (jăt′ ər) Kh. Attir [4–K] Levitical city and a city of refuge in the southern hill country of Judah (Jos. 15:48; 21:14; 1 Chr. 6:57). David sent Amalekite booty to the elders here (1 Sam. 30:27).

JAZER (jā′ zər) Kh. es-Sar? [7–H] Amorite city in Gilead captured by Hebrews (Num. 21:24, 32). Levitical city in Gad (Num. 32:1, 3, 35; Jos. 13:25; 21:39; 1 Chr. 6:81). Captured by Moabites (Is. 16:8–9; Jer. 48:32). Taken by Judas Maccabeus in 163 b.c. (1 Macc. 5:8). Also mentioned in 2 Sam. 24:5; 1 Chr. 26:31.

JEBUS (jē′ bəs) Canaanite name for **Jerusalem** (Jos. 18:28; Jg. 19:10; 1 Chr. 11:4, 5).

JEHUD (jē′ hŭd) Place in Dan (Jos. 19:45). Site unidentified.

JEKABZEEL (jĭ kăb′ zĭ əl) Another name for **Kabzeel** (Neh. 11:25).

JERICHO (jĕr′ ə kō) **1.** T. es-Sultan [5–H] Ancient oasis city at a major spring in the lower Jordan valley. First city in Canaan to be destroyed by Joshua in the conquest (Jos. 2:1–3; 3:16; 4:13, 19; 6:1, 2, 26). Here Ehud murdered King Eglon (Jg. 3:13, where called the city of Palms). Here David′s disgraced servants waited until their beards grew again (2 Sam. 10:5; 1 Chr. 19:5). Rebuilt by Hiel of Bethel in the 9th century b.c. (1 Kg. 16:34). Scene of activity of Elijah and Elisha (2 Kg. 2:4–5, 15, 18). Judahites captured in war with Israel returned here c. 735 b.c. (2 Chr. 28:15). Zedekiah captured by Nebuchadnezzar near here (2 Kg. 25:5; Jer. 39:5; 52:8) and city destroyed by Babylonians in 587 b.c. Settled by Jews returning from the Exile (Ezra 2:34; Neh. 7:36; 1 Esd. 5:22). People from here helped rebuild the walls of Jerusalem (Neh. 3:2). Part of Persian province of Yehud. Old Testament site abandoned in Hellenistic period. Also mentioned in Num. 22:1; 26:3, 63; 31:12; 33:48, 50; 34:15; 35:1; 36:13; Dt. 32:49; 34:1, 3; Jos. 5:10, 13; 7:2; 8:2; 9:3; 10:1, 28, 30; 12:9; 13:32; 16:1, 7; 18:12, 21; 20:8; 24:11; 1 Chr. 6:78; Heb. 11:30; 2 Macc. 12:15. Called city of Palms in Dt. 34:3; Jg. 1:16; 2 Chr. 28:15. **2.** T. Abu el-Alayiq [5–H] City on the Wadi Qilt guarding the road to Jerusalem. Syrian commander Bacchides built a fortress here in 160 b.c. (1 Macc. 9:50). Simon killed near here (1 Macc. 16:11,14). Pompey destroyed two forts here in 63 b.c. One of Gabinius′

The Dome of the Rock dominates Jerusalem in this prospect from the slopes of the Mount of Olives.

administrative centers, 57–55 B.C. Herod the Great died in palace he built here. Damaged in riots following Herod's death. Restored by Archelaus (4 B.C.–A.D. 6). Jesus healed a blind man here (Mt. 20:29; Mk. 10:46; Lk. 18:35) and called Zacchaeus down from a tree (Lk. 19:1). Good Samaritan helped traveler en route here (Lk. 10:30). Destroyed in First Jewish Revolt (A.D. 66–70).

JERUSALEM el-Quds [4–I] Canaanite Jebus, Roman Aelia Capitolina. Fortified city in the hill country on the border between Benjamin and Judah. Most important biblical city. Mentioned in Egyptian Execration Texts (19th–18th century B.C.), Amarna Letters (14th century B.C.), and Assyrian annals of Sennacherib (6th century B.C.). Coalition of Amorite kings, led by king of Jerusalem, defeated by Joshua at Gibeon (Jos. 10:1, 3, 5, 23; 12:10). Assigned to Benjamin, who failed to drive out the Jebusites (Jos. 15:8; 18:28; Jg. 1:21; 19:10). Captured by David, who made it the capital of his kingdom (2 Sam. 5:5–6; 1 Chr. 11:4, 5, and 7, where also called Jebus and city of David) and brought the ark of the covenant here to make the city the focus of national religion (2 Sam. 6:10, 12, 16 and 1 Chr. 15:1, 3, and 29, where again also called city of David). Temple built here by Solomon on land bought by David (2 Sam. 24:16; 1 Kg. 8:1, where also called Zion; 1 Chr. 6:10; 2 Chr. 3:1; 5:2, where also called city of David and Zion). Capital of Judah after the division of the monarchy following Solomon's death. Treasures of the city given to Shishak c. 918 B.C. (1 Kg. 14:25; 2 Chr. 12:2–9). Plundered by Jehoash of Israel (2 Kg. 14:13; 2 Chr. 25:23). Fortifications strengthened by Hezekiah (2 Chr. 32:2). Besieged by Sennacherib in 701 B.C. (2 Kg. 19:10; 2 Chr. 32:2, 22; Is. 36:2, 7, 20; 37:10, 22, 32). Plundered in 597 B.C. (2 Chr. 36:10) and destroyed by Babylonians in 587 B.C. (2 Kg. 24:10; 25:10; 2 Chr. 36:19). Second Temple dedicated in 515 B.C. (Ezra 6:18). Walls rebuilt by Nehemiah c. 445 B.C. (Neh. 2:11–13, 17, 20; 3:8, 9, 12; 4:7–8). Capital of Persian province of Yehud. Captured by Ptolemy I of Egypt in 301 B.C. Taken by Antiochus III of Syria in 198 B.C. Temple taken and rededicated by Judas Maccabeus in 164 B.C. (1 Macc. 4:37 and 60, where called Mount Zion). Capital of Hasmonean kingdom (141–63 B.C.). Taken by Pompey in 63 B.C. Seized by Parthians in 40 B.C. Captured by combined Roman and Jewish army under Sosius and Herod the Great in 37 B.C. City and Temple rebuilt on magnificent scale by Herod. Jesus of Nazareth crucified here c. A.D. 29 (Mt. 16:21; Mk. 10:33; Lk. 18:31). Destroyed by Titus in A.D. 70. Rebuilt by Hadrian, who called it Aelia Capitolina after A.D. 134. Probably the Salem of Gen. 14:18; Ps. 76:2; Heb. 7:1, 2. Called Jebus in Jos. 18:28; Jg. 19:10; 1 Chr. 11:4, 5. Called Ariel in Is. 29:1, 2, 7. Also called city of David, Zion, or Mount Zion. Jerusalem is the most frequently mentioned site in both the Old and New Testaments and the Apocrypha. After its first mention in Jos., the name appears in all subsequent books of the Old Testament, with the following exceptions: Ru., Job, Pr., Hos., Jon.,

Nah., Hab., and Hag. Jerusalem appears in all four Gospels of the New Testament and in Acts, Rom., 1 Cor., Gal., Heb., and Rev. The name appears in 11 of the 18 books of the Apocrypha, namely 1 Esd., 2 Esd., Tob., Jdt., Ad. Est., Sir., Bar., and 1–4 Macc.

JESHANAH (jĕsh' ə nə) Burj el-Isana [4–G] Greco-Roman "Isana. Town in the hills of Samaria on the central ridge route. Captured in the 10th century B.C. by Abijah (Abijam) of Judah from Jeroboam of Israel (2 Chr. 13:19). Here Herod the Great defeated Antigonus' general, Pappus, in 37 B.C. Also mentioned in 1 Sam. 7:12.

JESHUA (jĕsh' ōō ə) T. es-Sawa? [4–K] Village in the Negeb near Beer-sheba settled by Jews returning from the Exile (Neh. 11:26).

JEZREEL (jĕz' rī əl) **1.** Zirin [5–D] City on the plain north of Mount Gilboa at a point where the valley falls away sharply to the east yielding a spectacular panoramic view. Assigned to Issachar (Jos. 19:18). Where Saul's army camped before the battle of Gilboa (1 Sam. 29:1). Part of Solomon's tenth administrative district (1 Kg. 4:12). Site of the winter palace of the Omride kings from the time of Ahab (1 Kg. 18:45, 46). Naboth's vineyard was here (1 Kg. 21:1). Where Joram of Israel went to recover from battle wounds and was visited by Ahaziah of Judah (2 Kg. 8:29; 9:15; 2 Chr. 22:6). Jezebel and other Omrides murdered here (2 Kg. 9:30, 36; 10:11). Heads of 70 princes of Israel sent to Jehu at Jezreel (2 Kg. 10:6–7). Also mentioned in 1 Sam. 29:11; 2 Sam. 2:9; 4:4; 1 Kg. 21:23; Hos. 1:4. **2.** Town assigned to Judah (Jos. 15:56). Site unidentified. Ahinoam, one of David's wives, came from here (1 Sam. 25:43; 27:3; 30:5; 2 Sam. 2:2; 3:2).

JOGBEHAH (jŏg' bə hə) Kh. el-Jubeihat [7–G] City in Ammon near the King's Highway. Assigned to Gad (Num. 32:35). In the

vicinity of Gideon's attack on fleeing Midianites (Jg. 8:11).

JOKDEAM (jŏk' dĭ əm) Village in the hill country of Judah south of Hebron assigned to Judah (Jos. 15:56). Site unidentified.

JOKMEAM (jŏk' mĭ əm) **1.** T. es-Simadi? [5–G] Town in the Wadi Farah near the junction with the Jordan River. Levitical city in Ephraim (1 Chr. 6:68). **2.** Another name for **Jokneam** (1 Kg. 4:12).

JOKNEAM (jŏk' nĭ əm) T. Qeimun [4–D] Canaanite royal city northwest of Megiddo commanding a major pass through the Carmel range. Conquered by Thutmose III in the 15th century B.C. Taken by Joshua (Jos. 12:22). Levitical city on the border with Zebulun (Jos. 19:11; 21:34). In Solomon's fifth administrative district (1 Kg. 4:12, where called Jokmeam; 1 Chr. 6:53).

JOKTHEEL (jŏk' thĭ əl) **1.** Village in the southern Shephelah assigned to Judah (Jos. 15:38). Site unidentified. **2.** Name given to **Sela** by Amaziah of Judah (2 Kg. 14:7).

JOPPA (jŏp' ə) Yafa [2–G] Rocky harbor on the central coast. Chief port for Judah in Old Testament times. Captured by Thutmose III in the 15th century B.C. Mentioned in the Amarna Letters (14th century B.C.). Assigned to Dan (Jos. 19:46), who failed to drive out the Philistines. Wood for Solomon's palace and Temple floated from Lebanon to Joppa (2 Chr. 2:16). Occupied by Sennacherib in 701 B.C. Where Jonah boarded a ship bound for Tarshish (Jon. 1:3). Wood for rebuilding the Temple after the Exile floated from Lebanon to Joppa (Ezra 3:7; 1 Esd. 5:55). Captured by Alexander the Great in 332 B.C. and damaged in fighting after his death. Part of Egyptian Ptolemaic kingdom c. 301–198 B.C. and of Syrian Seleucid empire, 198–143 B.C. Judas

Waves dash against the coast at Jaffa (ancient Joppa), the chief port of Judah in Old Testament times.

227

Maccabeus burned ships here in 164 B.C. (2 Macc. 12:3, 4, 7). Captured in 147 B.C. by Jonathan (1 Macc. 10:75–76), who met Ptolemy VI here (1 Macc. 11:6). Garrisoned by Simon in 143 B.C. and incorporated into Hasmonean state (1 Macc. 12:33; 13:11; 14:5, 34; 15:28, 35). Made independent by Pompey in 63 B.C. Returned to Jews by Julius Caesar in 47 B.C. Captured by Herod the Great in 37 B.C. Given to Cleopatra by Antony and returned to Herod by Augustus in 30 B.C. Here Peter raised Tabitha from the dead and stayed in the house of Simon the tanner (Acts 9:36, 38, 42, 43; 10:5) and here he had a vision (Acts 11:5, 13) before being summoned by Cornelius to Caesarea (Acts 10:23, 32). Destroyed by Vespasian in A.D. 67 during the First Jewish Revolt. Also mentioned in 2 Macc. 4:21.

JORKEAM (jôr′ kĭ əm) Place in Judah mentioned in 1 Chr. 2:44. Site unidentified.

JOTAPATA (jŏt′ ə pāta) Greco-Roman name for **Jotbah.**

JOTBAH (jŏt′ bə) Kh. Jefat [4–C] Greco-Roman Jotapata. Town in the hills of Lower Galilee. Captured by Tiglath-pileser III in 733 B.C. Home of Meshullemeth, mother of King Amon of Judah (2 Kg. 21:19). Fortified by Josephus, who withstood a 47-day siege before surrendering to Vespasian in A.D. 67.

JOTBATHAH (jŏt′ bə thə) Bir Taba [4–S] Oasis in the Arabah where the Hebrews camped in their wilderness wanderings after the Exodus (Num. 33:33–34; Dt. 10:7).

JUTTAH (jŭt′ ə) Yatta [3–J] Town in the hill country of Judah assigned to Judah (Jos. 15:55). Levitical city (Jos. 21:16).

K

KABZEEL (kăb′ zĭ əl) Kh. Gharra? [4–K] Town in the eastern Negeb. Assigned to Judah (Jos. 15:21). Settled by Jews returning from the Exile (Neh. 11:25, where called Jekabzeel). Birthplace of Benaiah (2 Sam. 23:20; 1 Chr. 11:22).

KADESH (kā′ dĭsh) 1. T. Nebi Mend. City on the Orontes River in Syria. Mentioned in 2 Sam. 24:6. 2. Another name for **Kadesh-barnea** (Gen. 14:7, where also called Enmishpat; 16:14; 20:1; Num. 13:26; 20:1, 14, 16, 22; 27:14; 33:36, 37; Dt. 1:46; Jg. 11:16, 17; Ps. 29:8).

KADESH-BARNEA (kā′ dĭsh bär′ nĭ ə) Ein el-Qudeirat [1–O] Major oasis in the southwestern Negeb on the southern limit of Canaan (Num. 34:4; Jos. 15:3). Where the Hebrews stayed in their wilderness wanderings following the Exodus (Dt. 1:19, 46, where called Kadesh) and from which spies were sent into Canaan. Place from which the Hebrews set out for the Plains of Moab (Num. 20:14, 16; 33:36 and 37, where called Kadesh; Jg. 11:16, 17). Also mentioned in

Dt. 1:2; 2:14; 9:23; Jos. 10:41; 14:6, 7. Called Massah in Dt. 6:16; 9:22. Called Kadesh in Gen. 14:7, where also called Enmishpat; 16:14; 20:1; Num. 13:26; 20:1, 14, 16, 22; 27:14; 33:36, 37; Ps. 29:8. Called Massah and Meribah in Ex. 17:7; called Meribah in Num. 20:13, 24; 27:14; Dt. 33:8, where mentioned with Massah; Ps. 81:7; 95:8, where mentioned with Massah; 106:32. Called Meribath-kadesh in Dt. 32:51; Ezek. 47:19; 48:28.

KAIN (kān) Kh. Yaqin. Village in the southern hill country of Judah near Hebron. Assigned to Judah (Jos. 15:57).

KAMON (kā′ mən) Qamm? [6–D] Town in Gilead. Jair, one of the minor judges, was buried here (Jg. 10:5).

KANAH (kā′ nə) Qana [4–A] Town in Upper Galilee. Assigned to Asher (Jos. 19:28).

KARKA (kär′ kə) Ein el-Qeseima? [1–N] Place in the southwestern Negeb in the vicinity of Kadesh-barnea. On the southern border of Judah (Jos. 15:3).

KARKOR (kär′ kôr) Place possibly in eastern Gilead where Gideon defeated the Midianites (Jg. 8:10). Site unidentified.

KARNAIM (kär nā′ əm) Probably another name for **Carnaim** (Am. 6:13).

KARTAH (kär′ tə) Levitical city in Zebulun (Jos. 21:34). Site unidentified.

KARTAN (kär′ tăn) Levitical city in Naphtali (Jos. 21:32). Probably the same as Kiriathaim of 1 Chr. 6:76.

KATTATH (kăt′ ăth) Town assigned to Zebulun (Jos. 19:15). Site unidentified but probably the same as **Kitron** of Jg. 1:30.

KEDEMOTH (kĕd′ ə mŏth) Qasr ez-Zaferan? City in eastern Moab. Levitical city in Reuben (Jos. 13:18; 21:37; 1 Chr. 6:79). Also mentioned in Dt. 2:26.

KEDESH (kē′ dĕsh) 1. T. Kedesh [6–A] Greco-Roman Cadasa. Canaanite town in Upper Galilee on the main route from the Huleh valley to the coast. King of Kedesh defeated by Joshua (Jos. 12:22). Assigned to Naphtali (Jos. 19:37). Levitical city and a city of refuge (Jos. 20:7; 21:32). Home of Barak where the Hebrews assembled for their battle with Sisera (Jg. 4:6, 9, 10). Captured in 733 B.C. by Tiglath-pileser III, who deported its inhabitants to Assyria (2 Kg. 15:29). Where Jonathan defeated Demetrius (1 Macc. 11:63, 73). Also mentioned in Jos. 12:22. 2. Levitical city in Issachar (1 Chr. 6:72). Site unidentified but probably the same as **Kishion** of Jos. 19:20; 21:28. 3. Town on southern border of Judah (Jos. 15:23). Perhaps the same as **Kadesh-Barnea.**

KEDESH-NAPHTALI (kē′ dĕsh năf′ tə lī) T. Qedosh [6–C] Town on the western shore of the Sea of Galilee (Jg. 4:6).

KEDRON (kē′ drən) Qatra [2–H] Town on the coastal plain. Fortified by Antiochus VII as a base for attacking Judea (1 Macc. 15:39, 41; 16:9).

KEHELATHAH (kē′ ə lā′ thə) Place in the Sinai where the Hebrews camped in their wilderness wanderings following the Exodus (Num. 33:22–23). Site unidentified.

KEILAH (kē ī′ lə) Kh. Qeila [3–I] Walled town in the Shephelah. Mentioned in the Amarna Letters (14th century B.C.). Assigned to Judah (Jos. 15:44). Delivered by David from Philistine attack, but its inhabitants were loyal to Saul (1 Sam. 23:1–13). Settled by Jews returning from the Exile (Neh. 3:17, 18).

KENATH (kē′ năth) Qanawat. Greco-Roman Canatha. Town east of the Jordan conquered by Nobah of the tribe of Manasseh, who renamed it Nobah (Num. 32:42). Retaken by the Arameans (1 Chr. 2:23). City of the Decapolis founded by Pompey in 64 B.C. As Canatha, site of Herod the Great's defeat by the Nabateans.

KERIOTH (kĕr′ ĭ ŏth) el-Qereiyat [6–J] Stronghold on the tableland of Moab. Mentioned in Jer. 48:24; Am. 2:2; and also on the Moabite Stone.

KERIOTH-HEZRON (kĕr′ ĭ ŏth hĕz′ rən) Kh. el-Qaryatein? [4–K] Town in the Negeb. Assigned to Judah (Jos. 15:25, where called **Hazor).**

KINAH (kī′ nə) Town in southeastern Judah assigned to Judah (Jos. 15:22). Site unidentified.

KIR (kĭr) 1. Place in Mesopotamia mentioned in 2 Kg. 16:9; Is. 22:6; Am. 9:7. Site unidentified. 2. Another name for **Kir-hareseth** (Is. 15:1).

KIR-HARESETH (kĭr hăr′ ə sĕth) el-Kerak [7–L] Fortress-city on a high plateau east of the Dead Sea in western Moab. Capital of Moab. Unsuccessfully besieged by combined forces of Israel, Judah, and Edom with disastrous consequences for the attacking armies (2 Kg. 3:25). Mentioned on the Moabite Stone. Condemned by the prophets (Is. 15:1, where called Kir; 16:7; 16:11 and Jer. 48:31, 36, where called Kir-heres). Perhaps the same as **Mizpeh 2** of 1 Sam. 22:3.

KIR-HERES (kĭr hĭr′ ĭz) Another name for **Kir-hareseth** (Is. 16:11; Jer. 48:31, 36).

KIRIATHAIM (kĭr′ ĭ ə thā′ əm) Levitical city in Naphtali (1 Chr. 6:76). Probably the same as Kartan of Jos. 21:32.

KIRIATH-ARBA (kĭr′ ĭ āth är′ bə) Ancient name for **Hebron** (Gen. 23:2; 35:27; Jos. 14:15; 15:13, 54; 20:7; 21:11; Jg. 1:10; Neh. 11:25).

KIRIATHARIM (kĭr′ ĭ āth âr′ ĭm) Another name for **Kiriath-jearim** (Ezra 2:25).

KIRIATH-BAAL (kĭr′ ĭ ăth bā′ əl) Another name for **Kiriath-jearim** (Jos. 15:60; 18:14).

KIRIATH-HUZOTH (kĭr′ ĭ ăth hū′ zŏth) City in Moab (Num. 22:39). Site unidentified.

KIRIATH-JEARIM (kĭr′ ĭ ăth jē′ ə rĭm) Deir el-Azar [3-H] Town on the Way of Beth-shemesh in the hill country of Judah west of Jerusalem. Hivite town in the Gibeonite confederation (Jos. 9:17). On the border of Judah and Benjamin (Jos. 15:9-10, where called Baalah; 15:60; 18:14, where called Kiriath-baal; 18:15, 28). Ark of the covenant placed here after being returned by the Philistines (1 Sam. 6:21; 7:1-2) and then taken from here to Jerusalem (2 Sam. 6:2, where called Baale-judah; 1 Chr. 13:5-6, where called Baalah; 2 Chr. 1:4; Ps. 132:6, where called Jaar). Settled by Jews returning from the Exile (Ezra 2:25, where called Kiriath-arim; Neh. 7:29). Also mentioned in Jg. 18:12; Jer. 26:20.

KIRIATH-SANNAH (kĭr′ ĭ ăth săn′ ə) Another name for **Debir 1** (Jos. 15:49).

KIRIATH-SEPHER (kĭr′ ĭ ăth sē′ fər) Older name for **Debir 1** (Jos. 15:15; Jg. 1:11).

KISHION (kĭsh′ ĭ ən) el-Khirba? Town between Mount Moreh and Mount Tabor. Levitical city in Issachar (Jos. 19:20; 21:28). Probably the same as Kedesh 2 of 1 Chr. 6:72.

KITRON (kĭt′ rŏn) Town assigned to Zebulun, who failed to drive out the Canaanites (Jg. 1:30). Site unidentified but probably the same as Kattath of Jos. 19:15.

L

LABAN (lā′ bən) Place in the Sinai mentioned in Dt. 1:1. Site unidentified.

LACHISH (lā′ kĭsh) T. ed-Duweir [2-J] Major fortress-city in the Shephelah. Mentioned in the Amarna Letters (14th century B.C.). Where the king of Lachish, member of the Amorite confederation, was defeated by Joshua (Jos. 10:3, 5, 23, 31-35; 12:11). Assigned to Judah (Jos. 15:39). Fortified by either David or Solomon. Refortified by Rehoboam (2 Chr. 11:9) and probably strengthened by Asa of Judah. King Amaziah of Judah assassinated here in 783 B.C. (2 Kg. 14:19; 2 Chr. 25:27). Defenses strengthened by Hezekiah, but city fell to Sennacherib of Assyria in 701 B.C. after a siege, depicted on a relief found at Nineveh. Refortified (probably by Manasseh) but destroyed by Nebuchadnezzar in 588 B.C. Settled by Jews returning from the Exile (Neh. 11:30). Also mentioned in 2 Kg. 18:14, 17; 19:8; 2 Chr. 32:9; Is. 36:2; 37:8; Jer. 34:7; Mic. 1:13.

LAHMAM (lā′ măm) Kh. el-Lahm? [2-J] Village in the Shephelah. Assigned to Judah (Jos. 15:40).

Jebel Musa, "Mountain of Moses," thought to be Mount Sinai, towers over a wilderness oasis.

LAISH (lā′ ĭsh) Canaanite name for **Dan** (Jg. 18:7, 14, 27, 29).

LAISHAH (lā′ əsh ə) el-Issawiya? Village in Benjamin. Mentioned in Is. 10:30.

LAKKUM (lăk′ əm) Kh. el-Mansurah [6-D] Town in the hills of Lower Galilee southwest of the Sea of Galilee. Assigned to Naphtali (Jos. 19:33).

LAODICEA (lā ŏd′ ə sē′ ə) Eskihisar. City in the Lycus valley in southwestern Asia Minor. Church here mentioned in Col. 2:1; 4:13, 15, 16. One of the seven churches of the Revelation (Rev. 1:11; 3:14).

LASEA (lə sē′ ə) City on the southern coast of Crete near Fair Havens (Acts 27:8).

LASHA (lā′ shə) Place on the border of Canaan (Gen. 10:19). Site unidentified.

LASHARON (lə shâr′ ən) City whose king was defeated by Joshua (Jos. 12:18). Site unidentified.

LEBAOTH (lĭ bā′ ŏth) Another name for **Beth-lebaoth** (Jos. 15:32).

LEBONAH (lĭ bō′ nə) el-Lubban [4-G] Village near the Ascent of Lebonah on the central ridge route in the hill country of Ephraim (Jg. 21:19).

LECAH (lē′ kə) Village probably in Judah (1 Chr. 4:21). Site unidentified.

LEHEM (lē′ hĕm) Place probably in Judah (1 Chr. 4:22). Site unidentified.

LEHI (lē′ hī) Village in the hill country of Judah. Site unidentified. Raided by the Philistines (Jg. 15:9). Here Samson slew the Philistines with the jawbone of an ass (Jg. 15:14, 17, where called Ramath-lehi). At a spring here God provided water for Samson (Jg. 15:19, where also called En-hakkore). Also mentioned in 2 Sam. 23:11.

LESHEM (lē′ shəm) Another name for **Laish** (Jos. 19:47), Canaanite **Dan**.

LIBNAH (lĭb′ nə) **1.** T. el-Beida? [3-I] Canaanite royal city in the Shephelah assigned to Judah (Jos. 15:42). Destroyed by Joshua (Jos. 10:29, 31-32, 39; 12:15). Levitical city in Judah (Jos. 21:13; 1 Chr. 6:57). Revolted against Judah (2 Kg. 8:22; 2 Chr. 21:10). Attacked by Sennacherib in 701 B.C. (2 Kg. 19:8; Is. 37:8). Also mentioned in Jer. 52:1. **2.** Place in the Sinai where the Hebrews camped in their wilderness wanderings following the Exodus (Num. 33:20-21). Site unidentified.

LOD (lŏd) el-Ludd [2-H] Hellenistic Lydda, Roman Diosopolis. Important town and route junction on the coastal plain along the Way of the Sea. Mentioned as Canaanite town by Thutmose III (15th century B.C.). Built by the Benjaminites (1 Chr. 8:12). Settled by Jews returning from the Exile (Ezra 2:33; Neh. 7:37; 11:35). Given by Demetrius II to Jonathan in 145 B.C. (1 Macc. 11:34). Rights of Jews there restored by Julius Caesar in 47 B.C. Inhabitants sold into slavery by Cassius c. 45 B.C. Peter healed a cripple here (Acts 9:32, 35, where called Lydda). Burned by Cestius Gallus in A.D. 66 and occupied by Vespasian in 68.

LODEBAR (lō dē′ bər) Umm ed-Dabar? [6-D] City in northwest Gilead assigned to Gad (Jos. 13:26, where called Debir). Where Mephibosheth lived after the death of Saul and from which David brought him to Jerusalem (2 Sam. 9:4, 5). Machir of Lodebar supplied David with provisions during Absalom's revolt (2 Sam. 17:27). Also mentioned in Am. 6:13.

LUZ (lŭz) **1.** Canaanite name for **Bethel 1** (Gen. 28:19; 35:6; 48:3; Jos. 18:13; Jg. 1:23) or site nearby (Jos. 16:2). **2.** City built in the land of the Hittites (Jg. 1:26). Site unidentified.

LYDDA (lĭd′ ə) Hellenistic name for **Lod** (Acts 9:32, 35, 38).

M

MAARATH (mā′ ə răth) Village in the hill country of Judah. Assigned to Judah (Jos. 15:59). Sometimes identified with Maroth of Mic. 1:12.

MACHAERUS (mə kĭr′ əs) Kh. el-Mukawer [6-J] Mountaintop fortress east of the Dead Sea. Built by Alexander Janneus in 57 B.C. Destroyed by Gabinius in 56 B.C. Rebuilt by Herod the Great. Where Herod Antipas had John the Baptist put to death c. A.D. 26. Held by Jewish rebels in the First Jewish Revolt, until captured by the Romans in A.D. 73.

MACHBENAH (mǎk bē′ nə) Village in Judah mentioned in 1 Chr. 2:49. Site unidentified.

MADMANNAH (măd măn′ ə) Another name

for **Beth-marcaboth** (Jos. 15:31; 1 Chr. 2:49).

MADMEN (măd' měn) Kh. Dimna? [7–K] Town in Moab mentioned in Jer. 48:2.

MADMENAH (măd mē' nə) Village north of Jerusalem in the line of the Assyrian advance against that city in 701 B.C. (Is. 10:31). Site unidentified.

MADON (mā' dŏn) T. el-Khirbeh? [5–B] Canaanite city in Galilee. Joined Jabin of Hazor in unsuccessful coalition against Joshua (Jos. 11:1; 12:19).

MAGBISH (măg' bĭsh) Kh. el-Makhbiya? Town in Judah. Settled by Jews returning from the Exile (Ezra 2:30).

MAGDALA (măg' də lə) Majdal [5–C] Greco-Roman Taricheae. Town with fishing industry on western shore of the Sea of Galilee. Home of Mary Magdalene (Mt. 27:56, 61; 28:1; Mk. 15:40, 47; 16:1, 9; Lk. 8:2; 24:10; Jn. 19:25; 20:1, 18). Held by Jewish rebels in the First Jewish Revolt, until captured by the Romans in A.D. 67.

MAHALAB (mā' ə lăb) Kh. el-Mahalib? Town near Tyre. Assigned to Asher (Jos. 19:29). Captured by Sennacherib in 701 B.C. Another name for Ahlab. Probably the same as **Helbah** of Jg. 1:31.

MAHANAIM (mā' ə nā' əm) T. edh-Dhahab el-Garbi? [6–F] City on the Jabbok River in Gilead. Mentioned in assignment of territory to both Gad and Manasseh (Jos. 13:26, 30). Levitical city in Gad (Jos. 21:38; 1 Chr. 6:80). Near here Jacob wrestled with a divine being (Gen. 32:2). Ishbosheth established his government here after the death of Saul (2 Sam. 2:8, 12, 29) and was murdered here. David fled here from Jerusalem during Absalom's rebellion (2 Sam. 17:24) and heard of the victory of his army over his son. Administrative center of Solomon's seventh district (1 Kg. 4:14). Also mentioned in Gen. 32:2.

MAHANEH-DAN (mā' ə nə dăn') Place near Kiriath-jearim where the Danites camped (Jg. 18:12). Site unidentified.

MAKAZ (mā' kăz) Kh. el-Mukheizin? Village on the edge of the southern coastal plain near Ekron. In Solomon's second administrative district (1 Kg. 4:9).

MAKHELOTH (măk hē' lŏth) Place in the Sinai where the Hebrews camped in their wilderness wanderings following the Exodus (Num. 33:25–26). Site unidentified.

MAKKEDAH (mə kē' də) Canaanite city in the Shephelah. Site unidentified. The five kings of the Amorite coalition were found hiding in a cave here and were put to death by Joshua (Jos. 10:16, 17, 21). City taken and all the inhabitants killed (Jos. 10:28, 29). Assigned to Judah (Jos. 15:41). Also mentioned in Jos. 10:10; 12:16.

MALLUS (măl' əs) City on the Pyramus River in Cilicia in southeastern Asia Minor. Along with Tarsus revolted against Antiochus IV in 170 B.C. (2 Macc. 4:30).

MAMRE (măm' rĭ) Ramat el-Khalil. Place near Hebron. Where Abraham built an altar and dwelt for some time (Gen. 13:18; 14:13; 18:1). Isaac dwelt here (Gen. 35:27). Also mentioned in Gen. 23:17, 19; 25:9; 49:30; 50:13.

MANAHATH (măn' ə hăth) el-Malhah. Village in the hill country southwest of Jerusalem. Benjaminites from Geba were carried into exile here (1 Chr. 8:6).

MAON (mā' ŏn) Kh. Main [4–J] Town in the hill country of Judah. Assigned to Judah (Jos. 15:55). Near the Wilderness of Maon where David was almost caught by Saul (1 Sam. 23:24, 25). Home of Nabal and his wife, Abigail (1 Sam. 25:2), whom David later married.

MARAH (mâr' ə) Oasis in the Wilderness of Shur in the northwest Sinai. Site unidentified. Where the Hebrews found bitter water on their first encampment after the Exodus (Ex. 15:23; Num. 33:8, 9, where the Wilderness of Shur is identified with the Wilderness of Etham).

MAREAL (mâr' ĭ əl) T. el-Ghalta? Village in the Great Plain north of Megiddo. Assigned to Zebulun (Jos. 19:11).

MARESHAH (mə rē' shə) T. Sandahannah [2–J] Greco-Roman Marisa. Canaanite city in the Shephelah. Mentioned in the Amarna Letters (14th century B.C.). Assigned to Judah (Jos. 15:44). Fortified by Rehoboam (2 Chr. 11:8). Here King Asa of Judah defeated Zerah the Ethiopian (2 Chr. 14:9–10). Home of the prophet Eliezer (2 Chr. 20:37). Leading city of western Idumea during the Exile. Sidonian colony c. 250 B.C. Attacked by Judas Maccabeus in 163 B.C. (1 Macc. 5:66 and 2 Macc. 12:35, where called Marisa) and conquered by John Hyrcanus c. 126 B.C. Taken by Pompey in 63 B.C. Destroyed by Parthians in 40 B.C. Also mentioned in 1 Chr. 2:42; 4:21; Mic. 1:15.

MARISA (măr' ə sə) Greco-Roman name of **Mareshah** (1 Macc. 5:66; 2 Macc. 12:35).

MAROTH (mâr' ŏth) Village in Judah mentioned in Mic. 1:12. Sometimes identified with Maarath of Jos. 15:59.

MASADA (mə sā' də) es-Sebba [5–K] Mountaintop fortress above the western shore of the Dead Sea south of En-gedi and across from the Lisan peninsula. According to Josephus, originally fortified by "the high priest Jonathan," identified either with Judas Maccabeus' brother (mid-2nd century B.C.) or Alexander Janneus (103–76 B.C.). Where Herod the Great left his family when he fled to Rome in 40 B.C. Rebuilt by Herod, who added the palace-villa. Last stronghold of Jewish rebels in the First Jewish Revolt until finally taken by the Romans in A.D. 73.

MASHAL (mā' shəl) Another name for **Mishal** (1 Chr. 6:74).

MASREKAH (măs' rə kə) Town in Edom mentioned in Gen. 36:36; 1 Chr. 1:47. Site unidentified.

MASSAH (măs' ə) Another name for **Kadesh-barnea** (Ex. 17:7; Dt. 6:16; 9:22; 33:8; Ps. 95:8).

MATTANAH (măt' ə nə) Place in Moab where the Hebrews camped in their wilderness wanderings following the Exodus (Num. 21:18–19). Site unidentified.

MEARAH (mē âr' ə) Place probably near Sidon not conquered by the Hebrews (Jos. 13:4). Site unidentified.

MECONAH (mĭ kō' nə) Town in southern Judah settled by Jews returning from the Exile (Neh. 11:28). Site unidentified.

MEDEBA (mĕd' ə bə) Madeba [7–I] Town on the tableland of northern Moab on the King's Highway. Taken from Sihon by the Hebrews (Num. 21:30) and assigned to Reuben (Jos. 13:9, 16). Ammonite center in the wars with Joab of Israel (1 Chr. 19:7). Mentioned on the Moabite Stone. Condemned by Isaiah (Is. 15:2). Besieged and taken by John Hyrcanus c. 128 B.C. Also mentioned in 1 Macc. 9:36.

MEGIDDO (mə gĭd' ō) T. el-Mutesellim [4–D] Canaanite royal city strategically located on the Way of the Sea at the northern end of the Wadi Ara where it enters the

Buildings cut from living rock made the Nabatean capital at Petra a wonder of the ancient world.

Great Plain. Most important city of the area. Mentioned in the Amarna Letters (14th century B.C.) and the inscriptions of Thutmose III (15th century B.C.), Seti I (14th-13th century B.C.), and Shishak (10th century B.C.). Conquered by Thutmose III, it became a major Egyptian base. Its king defeated by Joshua (Jos. 12:21). Assigned to Manasseh, but city not taken (Jos. 17:11; Jg. 1:27; 1 Chr. 7:29). Near here Barak defeated Sisera (Jg. 5:19). Administrative center for Solomon's fifth district (1 Kg. 4:12). Fortified by Solomon (1 Kg. 9:15). Captured by Shishak c. 918 B.C. Stable complex built by Ahab of Israel for his chariot corps in the 9th century B.C. Where King Ahaziah died after being wounded by Jehu's men (2 Kg. 9:27). Destroyed by Tiglath-pileser III in 733 B.C. Capital of Assyrian province of Magiddu. Where King Josiah was mortally wounded in battle against Pharaoh Neco in 609 B.C. (2 Kg. 23:29-30; 2 Chr. 35:22). Possibly the Armageddon ("Hill of Megiddo") of Rev. 16:16. Also mentioned in Zech. 12:11.

MEMPHIS (mĕm' fĭs) Major city and religious center in Egypt near the apex of the Nile Delta. Capital of Egypt (3rd-10th Dynasty, c. 2664-2134 B.C.). Also mentioned in Is. 19:13; Jer. 2:16; 44:1; 46:14, 19; Ezek. 30:13; Hos. 9:6.

MEPHAATH (mĕf' ĭ ăth) T. Jawah? Town in Ammon assigned to Reuben (Jos. 13:18). Levitical city in Reuben (Jos. 21:37; 1 Chr. 6:79). In Moabite possession in 7th-6th century B.C. (Jer. 48:21).

MERIBAH (mĕr' ə bə) Another name for **Kadesh-barnea** (Ex. 17:7; Num. 20:13, 24; 27:14; Dt. 33:8; Ps. 81:7; 95:8; 106:32).

MERIBATH-KADESH (mĕr' ə băth kā' dĭsh) Another name for **Kadesh-barnea** (Dt. 32:51; Ezek. 47:19; 48:28).

MEROZ (mĭr' ŏz) Town cursed in Jg. 5:23 for its failure to help Deborah and Barak against Sisera. Site unidentified.

MESALOTH (mĕs' ə lŏth) Village in Galilee taken by Bacchides in 161 B.C. (1 Macc. 9:2). Site unidentified.

METHEG-AMMAH (mē' thĕg ăm' ə) Another name for **Gath** (2 Sam. 8:1).

MEZAD-HASHAVYAHU (mē' zəd hăs' hăv yā' hoō) [2-H] Fort on the southern coast west of Jabneel. Built in the 7th century B.C. probably by Josiah. Ancient name unknown.

MEZAHAB (mĕz' ə hăb) Another name for **Dizahab** (Gen. 36:39; 1 Chr. 1:50).

MICHMASH (mĭk' măsh) Mukhmas [4-H] Hellenistic Machmas. Strategic town at the western end of the Wadi Suweinit in the Saddle of Benjamin. Here Saul gathered an army (1 Sam. 13:2). Philistines encamped here to prepare for battle with the Hebrews (1 Sam. 13:5, 11, 16, 23). Saul's son Jonathan sought out the Philistines here (1 Sam.

14:5), killing several. Saul and his army joined Jonathan here and defeated the Philistines in the ensuing battle (1 Sam. 14:31). Taken in 701 B.C. by the Assyrians advancing on Jerusalem (Is. 10:28). Settled by Jews returning from the Exile (Ezra 2:27; Neh. 7:31; 1 Esd. 5:21). Here Jonathan set up a Hasmonean opposition government before taking over Jerusalem (1 Macc. 9:73). Also mentioned in Neh. 11:31. Name spelled Michmas in Ezra 2:27; Neh. 7:31; 1 Esd. 5:21.

MICHMETHATH (mĭk' mə thăth) Kh. Makhna el-Foqa? [4-F] Village in Samaria on the central ridge route south of Shechem. On the border between Ephraim and Manasseh (Jos. 16:6; 17:7).

MIDDIN (mĭd' ən) Kh. Abu Tabaq? [5-I] Village in the Wilderness of Judah. Assigned to Judah (Jos. 15:61).

MIGDAL-EL (mĭg' dəl ĕl') Village in Upper Galilee assigned to Naphtali (Jos. 19:38). Site unidentified.

MIGDAL-GAD (mĭg' dəl găd') Kh. el-Majdala? [2-J] Village in the southern Shephelah assigned to Judah (Jos. 15:37).

MIGDOL (mĭg' dōl) Town east of the Delta in northern Egypt. Hebrews passed through here in the Exodus (Ex. 14:2; Num. 33:7). Where Jews lived in exile (Jer. 44:1; 46:14). Also mentioned in Ezek. 29:10; 30:6.

MIGRON (mĭg' rŏn) Village in Benjamin where Saul observed movements of the Philistine army (1 Sam. 14:2). On route taken by Assyrians advancing on Jerusalem (Is. 10:28). Site unidentified.

MILETUS (mī lē' təs) Important port on the western coast of Asia Minor. Here Paul met with the Ephesian elders on his third missionary journey (Acts 20:15, 17). Also mentioned in 2 Tim. 4:20.

MINNITH (mĭn' ĭth) Town in Ammon near which Jephthah defeated the Ammonites (Jg. 11:33). Site unidentified.

MISHAL (mī' shəl) Town in Lower Galilee. Conquered by Thutmose III in the 15th century B.C. Levitical city in Asher (Jos. 19:26; 21:30; 1 Chr. 6:74, where called Mashal). Site unidentified.

MISREPHOTH-MAIM (mĭz' rə fōth mā' əm) Place near Sidon to which Joshua pursued fleeing Canaanites following battle of the Waters of Merom (Jos. 11:8; 13:6). Site unidentified.

MITHKAH (mĭth' kə) Place in the Sinai where the Hebrews camped following the Exodus (Num. 33:28-29). Site unidentified.

MITYLENE (mĭt' ə lē' nĭ) Port and main city of the island of Lesbos in the Aegean Sea. On Paul's route returning from his third missionary journey (Acts 20:14).

MIZPAH (mĭz' pə) **1.** T. en-Nasba? [4-H] Fortress-city on the central ridge route north of Jerusalem. Assigned to Benjamin (Jos. 18:26, where called Mizpeh). Benjaminites punished here for the outrage of Gibeah (Jg. 20:1, 3; 21:1, 5, 8). Fortified by Asa of Judah as border stronghold against Israel (1 Kg. 15:22; 2 Chr. 16:6). Administrative center of Judah following fall of Jerusalem in 587 B.C. Gedaliah murdered here (2 Kg. 25:23, 25; Jer. 40-41). Here Judas Maccabeus gathered his army before the battle of Emmaus in 166 B.C. (1 Macc. 3:46). Also mentioned in 1 Sam. 7:5-7, 11, 12, 16; 10:17; Neh. 3:7, 15, 19. **2.** Kh. Jalad? [7-G] Town in Gilead. Where Laban caught up with the fleeing Jacob and made a covenant with him (Gen. 31:49). Where the Israelites gathered and made Jephthah their leader (Jg. 10:17; 11:11). After passing here, Jephthah made a vow before the Lord and here his daughter met him, forcing him to sacrifice her in fulfilling that vow (Jg. 11:29, 34). Assigned to Gad (Jos. 13:26, where called Ramath-mizpeh). Hos. 5:1 probably refers to this place.

MIZPEH (mĭz' pə) **1.** T. es-Safieh? Village in the Shephelah assigned to Judah (Jos. 15:38). **2.** Place in Moab to which David brought his parents to the Moabite king for safety (1 Sam. 22:3). Perhaps the same as **Kir-hareseth. 3.** Another name for **Mizpah 1** (Jos. 18:26).

MODEIN (mō' dēn) el-Arbain [3-H] Village in the southwestern foothills of Samaria near Lod. Home of Mattathias Hasmoneas where Maccabean revolt began in 167 B.C. (1 Macc. 2:1, 15, 23). Judas Maccabeus attacked Antiochus V and Lysias here (2 Macc. 13:14). Where John Hyrcanus and Judas camped before the battle of Kedron in 137 B.C. (1 Macc. 16:4). Site of the Hasmonean family tombs (1 Macc. 2:70; 9:19; 13:25, 30).

MOLADAH (mōl' ə də) Kh. el-Waten? [3-K] Town in the Negeb near Beer-sheba. Assigned to Judah (Jos. 15:26) and to Simeon (Jos. 19:2; 1 Chr. 4:28). Settled by Jews returning from the Exile (Neh. 11:26).

MOREH (môr' ə) Place in Canaan at Shechem. Site of "oak of Moreh," where God repeated his promise to Abraham, who built an altar here (Gen. 12:6). Also mentioned in Dt. 11:30. Site unidentified.

MORESHETH (môr' ə shĕth) Another name for **Moresheth-gath** (Jer. 26:18; Mic. 1:1).

MORESHETH-GATH (môr' ə shĕth găth) T. el-Judeida? [3-I] City in the Shephelah. Home of the prophet Micah (Jer. 26:18 and Mic. 1:1, where called Moresheth). Also mentioned in Mic. 1:14.

MOSERAH (mō' zə rə) Place in the Sinai where Aaron is said to have died (Dt. 10:6; but see Num. 33:38). Site unidentified. Called Moseroth in Num. 33:30-31.

MOSEROTH (mō' zə rŏth). Another name for **Moserah** (Num. 33:30-31).

MOZAH (mō' zə) Kh. Beit Mizza? Roman Emmaus. Village in the hills west of Jerusalem. Assigned to Benjamin (Jos. 18:26). Made into a military colony after the First Jewish Revolt (A.D. 66–70) and renamed Emmaus (not to be confused with **Emmaus 1** or **Emmaus 2**).

MYNDOS (mĭn' dəs) Gumushli. City in southwestern Asia Minor. Roman consul Lucius sent a letter here on behalf of the Jews in 138 B.C. (1 Macc. 15:23).

MYRA (mī' rə) Major city of Lycia near the southwestern coast of Asia Minor. At Myra's port (Andriaca) the centurion taking Paul to Rome found a ship of Alexandria bound for Italy (Acts 27:5).

N

NAAMAH (nā' ə mə) **1.** Kh. Fered? [2–H] Village in the Shephelah assigned to Judah (Jos. 15:41). **2.** Home of Zophar the Naamathite (Job 2:11; 11:1; 20:1; 42:9). Site unidentified but probably east of the Jordan River.

NAARAH (nā' ə rə) T. el-Jisr [5–H] Hellenistic Neara, Roman Noaran. Village in the lower Jordan valley northwest of Jericho. Near the plenteous spring of Ain Duq. In Ephraim on border with Benjamin (Jos. 16:7; 1 Chr. 7:28, where called Naaran). Water from here used by Archelaus (4 B.C.–A.D. 6), son of Herod the Great, to expand the date palm groves on plain of Jericho.

NAARAN, (nā' ə răn) Another name for **Naarah** (1 Chr. 7:28).

NADABATH (năd' ə băth) Kh. et-Teim? [7–I] Place near Medeba east of the Jordan River. Here Jonathan and Simon avenged the murder of their brother John in 160 B.C. (1 Macc. 9:37).

NAHALAL (nā' ə lăl) T. en-Nahl? [3–C] Town in southwestern Lower Galilee assigned to Zebulun (Jos. 19:15), who were unable to drive out the Canaanites (Jg. 1:30, where called Nahalol). Levitical city (Jos. 21:35).

NAHALIEL (nə hā' lĭ əl) Place in Moab where the Hebrews camped in their wilderness wanderings following the Exodus (Num. 21:19). Site unidentified.

NAHALOL (nā' ə lŏl) Another name for **Nahalal** (Jg. 1:30).

NAHOR (nā' hôr) City in Mesopotamia, possibly the birthplace of the Patriarch Abraham (Gen. 24:10; 29:5). Site unidentified.

NAIN (nān) Nein [5–D] Village on the northwest slope of Mount Moreh in Lower Galilee. Here Jesus went with his disciples and, near the gate of the city, raised a widow's son from the dead (Lk. 7:11).

NAIOTH (nā' yŏth) Dwelling place of prophets in or near Ramah in Samaria. Here David fled to Samuel and here Saul was taken with prophesying (1 Sam. 19:18, 19, 22, 23; 20:1). Site unidentified.

NAPHATH (nā' făth) Probably another name for **Naphath-dor** (Jos. 17:11).

NAPHATH-DOR (nā' făth dôr') Perhaps a region of Dor (Jos. 12:23). Probably another name for **Naphath**; also another name for **Dor** (1 Kg. 4:11).

NAPHOTH-DOR (nā' fŏth dôr') Another name for **Dor** (Jos. 11:2).

NARBATA (när băt' ə) Possibly another name for **Arbatta** or **Arubboth**.

NAZARETH (năz' ə rĭth) en-Nasira [4–D] Village in a basin in the hills of Lower Galilee. Home of Joseph and Mary where an angel foretold Jesus' birth (Lk. 1:26; 2:4). Where Jesus grew up (Mt. 2:23; Mk. 1:9; Lk. 2:39, 51; 4:16) From here he departed to be baptized by John the Baptist (Mk. 1:9). From here he went to dwell in Capernaum by the sea (Mt. 4:13). Jesus rejected in synagogue here and people sought to kill him (Lk. 4:16). Also mentioned in Jn. 1:46. Jesus called Jesus of Nazareth in Mt. 21:11; 26:71; Mk. 1:24; 10:47; 16:6; Lk. 4:34; 18:37; 24:19; Jn. 1:45; 18:5, 7; 19:19; Acts 2:22; 3:6; 4:10; 6:14; 10:38; 22:8; 26:9.

NEAH (nē' ə) Place on the border of Zebulun (Jos. 19:13). Site unidentified.

NEAPOLIS (nē ăp' ə lĭs) Major seaport in eastern Macedonia serving the city of Philippi. Where Paul landed in Europe on his second missionary journey (Acts 16:11).

NEARA (nē' ə rə) Hellenistic name for **Naarah.**

NEBALLAT (nĭ băl' ət) Beit Nabala [3–G] Village in the hills northeast of Lod overlooking the central coastal plain. Settled by Jews returning from the Exile (Neh. 11:34).

NEBO (nē' bō) **1.** Kh. el-Mekhaiyet [6–I] Town in northwestern Moab near which Hebrews camped (Num. 33:47). Assigned to Reuben (Num. 32:3, 38; 1 Chr. 5:8). Condemned by prophets (Is. 15:2; Jer. 48:1, 22). Mentioned on the Moabite Stone as being captured by Mesha. **2.** Nuba? [3–J] Village in Judah settled by Jews returning from the Exile (Ezra 2:29; Neh. 7:33). Some from here married foreign wives (Ezra 10:43; 1 Esd. 9:35).

NEIEL (nē ī' əl) Kh. Yanin [4–C] Village in the foothills of northwestern Lower Galilee. Assigned to Asher (Jos. 19:27).

NEPHTOAH (nĕf tō' ə) Lifta. Village at a spring northwest of Jerusalem. Called Waters of Nephtoah in Jos. 15:9; 18:15.

NETAIM (nĭ tā' əm) Place in Judah where royal potters lived (1 Chr. 4:23). Site unidentified.

NETOPHAH (nĭ tō' fə) Kh. Bedd Faluh? [4–I] Village on the edge of the Wilderness of Judah southeast of Bethlehem 1. Home of three of David's mighty men (2 Sam. 23:28, 29; 1 Chr. 11:30; 27:13, 15) and of others (2 Kg. 25:23; 1 Chr. 2:54; 9:16; Neh. 12:28; Jer. 40:8). Settled by Jews returning from the Exile (Ezra 2:22; Neh. 7:26; 1 Esd. 5:18).

NEZIB (nē' zĭb) Kh. Beit Nasib. Village in the eastern Shephelah. Assigned to Judah (Jos. 15:43).

NIBSHAN (nĭb' shăn) Kh. el-Maqari? [5–I] Village in the Wilderness of Judah northwest of the Dead Sea. Assigned to Judah (Jos. 15:62).

NICOPOLIS (nĭ kŏp' ə lĭs) City of Epirus in western Greece. Founded by Augustus to commemorate the victory at Actium (31 B.C.), which is close by. Mentioned in Tit. 3:12.

Women balancing jars on their head pass through the vale of Nazareth, home to Jesus in his early years.

NIMRAH (nĭm′ rə) Another name for **Beth-nimrah** (Num. 32:3).

NINEVEH (nĭn′ ə və) T. Nebi Yunus and T. Quyunjiq. City on the Tigris in central Mesopotamia. One of the cities founded by Nimrod (Gen. 10:11). Made the capital of Assyria by Sennacherib in late-8th century B.C. Sennacherib went there after his unsuccessful attack on Judah in 701 B.C. (2 Kg. 19:36; Is. 37:37) and was murdered there by his sons. Condemned by prophets (Nah. 1:1; 2:8; 3:7; Zeph. 2:13). City to which Jonah was sent (Jon. 1:2; 3:2, 3–7; 4:11; Mt. 12:41; Lk. 11:30, 32). Israelites taken into exile here (Tob. 1:3, 10, 17, 19, 22; 11:1, 16; 14:4, 8, 10, 15). Destroyed by the Medes, the Scythians, and the Babylonians in 612 B.C. Also mentioned in Jdt. 1:1; 2:21.

NOB (nŏb) el-Isawiya? [4–H] Village on the eastern slope of Mount Scopus northeast of Jerusalem. "The city of the priests" (1 Sam. 22:19) after the loss of the ark and the destruction of Shiloh. Where David fled from Saul and received the bread of the Presence and Goliath's sword (1 Sam. 21:1; 22:9, 11). Saul took revenge upon priests of Nob (1 Sam. 22:19). Settled by Jews returning from the Exile (Neh. 11:32). Also mentioned in Is. 10:32.

NOBAH (nō′ bə) 1. Another name for **Kenath** (Num. 32:42). 2. Town in eastern Gilead near Jogbehah. Gideon passed along the caravan route east of here to attack the Midianites (Jg. 8:11). Site unidentified.

NOHAH (nō′ hə) Place in Benjamin (Jg. 20:43). Site unidentified.

NYSA (nĭs′ ə) Additional Seleucid name for Scythopolis **(Beth-shan).**

O

OBOTH (ō′ bŏth) Place in Moab where the Hebrews camped in their wilderness wanderings following the Exodus (Num. 21:10–11; 33:43–44). Site unidentified.

OCINA (ō sī′ nə) Town on the coast of Phoenicia south of Tyre mentioned in Jdt. 2:28. Site unidentified.

ODOLLAM (ō dŭl′ əm) Greco-Roman name for **Adullam.**

ON (ŏn) T. Husn. Hellenistic Heliopolis. One of the more important centers of sun worship in Egypt. North of modern Cairo. Mentioned in Gen. 41:45, 50; 46:20; Jer. 43:13, where called Heliopolis; Ezek. 30:17.

ONO (ō′ nō) Kafr Ana [2–G] Town on the central coastal plain. Mentioned in Thutmose III's list of conquered Canaanite towns (15th century B.C.). Settled and fortified by the Benjaminites (1 Chr. 8:12). Settled by Jews returning from the Exile (Ezra 2:33; Neh. 7:37; 11:35; 1 Esd. 5:22). Sanbal-lat of Samaria offered to meet Nehemiah in a village near here (Neh. 6:2).

OPHNI (ŏf′ nī) Jifna [4–H] Hellenistic Gophna. Village in the hills of Samaria. Assigned to Benjamin (Jos. 18:24).

OPHRAH (ŏf′ rə) 1. et-Taiyiba [4–H] Hellenistic Aphairema. Town in the hill country northeast of Jerusalem. Assigned to Benjamin (Jos. 18:23). Philistines raided here (1 Sam. 13:17). Where Absalom had Amnon murdered (2 Sam. 13:23, where called Ephraim). Captured from Jeroboam of Israel by Abijah of Judah (2 Chr. 13:19, where called Ephron). Given to Jonathan by Demetrius I and confirmed by Demetrius II (1 Macc. 11:34, where called Aphairema). Avoiding hostility in Jerusalem, Jesus withdrew here (Jn. 11:54, where called Ephraim). 2. et-Taiyiba? [5–D] Town in Lower Galilee. Home of Gideon (Jg. 6:11, 24; 8:27), who was buried here (Jg. 8:32). Home of Abimelech (Jg. 9:5).

ORTHOSIA (ôr thō′ zĭ ə) City north of Tripolis on the Syrian coast. Site unidentified. Where Trypho fled after his defeat by Antiochus VII in 137 B.C. (1 Macc. 15:37).

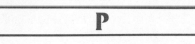

P

PAI (pā′ ī) Another name for **Pau** (1 Chr. 1:50).

PANEAS (pā′ nē əs) Canaanite name for **Caesarea Philippi.**

PAPHOS (pā′ fŏs) Baffo. City on the southwestern coast of Cyprus. Seat of Roman government in mid-1st century A.D. Where Paul on his first missionary journey confronted Bar-Jesus in the presence of the Roman governor (Acts 13:6). Paul sailed from here to Perga (Acts 13:13).

PAPYRON (pə pī′ rŏn) Ein-Hajle? [5–H] Village or marshy area near the mouth of the Jordan River north of the Dead Sea. Where Aristobulus II defeated Hyrcanus II and his Nabatean allies in 64 B.C.

PARAH (pâr′ ə) Kh. el-Farah [4–H] Village at the bountiful spring of Ein Farah in the hills northeast of Jerusalem. Assigned to Benjamin (Jos. 18:23).

PAS-DAMMIM (păs dăm′ ĭm) Another name for **Ephes-dammim** (1 Chr. 11:13).

PATARA (păt′ ə rə) Major port in Lycia in southwestern Asia Minor. On his third missionary journey Paul boarded a ship here bound for Tyre (Acts 21:1).

PAU (pā′ ū) City in Edom (Gen. 36:39). Site unidentified. Called Pai in 1 Chr. 1:50.

PEGAE (pēg′ ā) Hellenistic name for **Aphek 1.**

PEHEL (pēh′ ĕl) Canaanite name for **Pella.**

PELLA (pĕl′ ə) Kh. Fahil [6–E] Canaanite Pehel. City in the Jordan valley southeast of Beth-shan. Mentioned in the Egyptian Execration Texts (19th century B.C.), the inscriptions of Thutmose III (15th century B.C.), the Amarna Letters (14th century B.C.), and inscriptions of Seti I and Ramses II (14th–13th century B.C.). Destroyed in the Canaanite period. Refounded after conquests of Alexander the Great in 332 B.C. and named for his birthplace in Macedonia. Destroyed by Alexander Janneus early in 1st century B.C. Rebuilt by Pompey in 63 B.C. City of the Decapolis. Where Christians of Jerusalem fled at outset of the First Jewish Revolt (A.D. 66–70).

PELUSIUM (pĭ lōō′ shĭ əm) T. Farama. Important border fortress on the northeast frontier of the Nile Delta in Egypt. Condemned by Ezekiel (Ezek. 30:15, 16).

PENIEL (pĕn′ ĭ əl) Another name for **Penuel** (Gen. 32:30).

PENUEL (pĭ nōō′ əl) Tulul edh-Dhahab [6–F] City on the Jabbok River in Gilead. Where Jacob wrestled with a divine being and received the name "Israel" (Gen. 32:30, where called Peniel; 32:31). Attacked by Gideon after people here refused him food when he was pursuing the Midianites (Jg. 8:8, 9, 17). Fortified by Jeroboam I (1 Kg. 12:25).

PEREZ-UZZA (pĭr′ əz ŭz′ ə) Another name for **Perez-uzzah** (1 Chr. 13:11).

PEREZ-UZZAH (pĭr′ əz ŭz′ ə) Place between Kiriath-jearim and Jerusalem where Uzzah died when he touched the ark of the covenant (2 Sam. 6:8). Site unidentified. Called Perez-uzza in 1 Chr. 13:11.

PERGA (pûr′ gə) Murtana. Leading city of Pamphylia in south-central Asia Minor. Visited twice by Paul on his first missionary journey (Acts 13:13–14; 14:25).

PERGAMUM (pûr′ gə məm) Bergama. Greco-Roman city in Mysia in western Asia Minor. One of the seven churches of the Revelation was here (Rev. 1:11; 2:12).

PERSEPOLIS (pər sĕp′ ə lĭs) Takht-i Jamshid. Ancient city in Persia built by Darius the Great (521–485 B.C.) and his son Xerxes (485–465 B.C.). Plundered and burned by Alexander the Great in 330 B.C. Antiochus IV failed in attempt to rob temples here in 164 B.C. (2 Macc. 9:2).

PETHOR (pē′ thôr) City near the junction of the Sajur and Euphrates rivers. Home of Balaam, who cursed the Hebrews in Moab (Num. 22:5; Dt. 23:4).

PETRA (pē′ trə) Rekem [6–P] Capital city of the Nabateans on the plateau of Edom southeast of the Dead Sea. Trade center controlling caravan routes. Attacked by Antigonus in 312 B.C. King Aretas led army here to aid Hyrcanus in 65 B.C. Annexed by Rome in A.D. 106.

PHARATHON (fär' ə thŏn) Hellenistic name for **Pirathon** (1 Macc. 9:50).

PHASAELIS (fə sā' lĭs) Kh. Fasayil [5–G] Town in the lower Jordan valley north of Jericho. Founded by Herod the Great, who named it for his deceased older brother.

PHASELIS (fə sē' lĭs) Port in Lycia in southwestern Asia Minor to which the Roman consul Lucius sent a letter on behalf of the Jews in 138 B.C. (1 Macc. 15:23).

PHILADELPHIA (fĭl' ə dĕl' fĭ ə) **1.** Alashehir. City in Lydia in western Asia Minor. One of the seven churches of the Revelation was here (Rev. 1:11; 3:7). **2.** Greco-Roman name for **Rabbah 1.**

PHILIPPI (fĭl' ə pī) Filibedjik. City on the Via Egnatia and a leading city of Macedonia. Where Octavian and Marc Antony defeated Brutus and Cassius in 42 B.C. Roman colony. Visited by Paul on his second and third missionary journeys (Acts 16:12; 20:6). Paul wrote a letter to the church there (Phil. 1:1). Also mentioned in 1 Th. 2:2.

PHILOTERIA (fĭl ə tər ē' ə) Kh. el-Kerak [6–D] Town on the southwestern shore of the Sea of Galilee near where the Jordan River resumes its course south. Founded by Ptolemy II (283–245 B.C.). Captured by Antiochus III in 198 B.C. Conquered by Alexander Janneus.

PHOENIX (fē' nĭks) Loutro? Harbor in south-central Crete. Paul's ship was headed there when it was blown into the open sea (Acts 27:12).

PIBESETH (pī bē' zĭth) T. Bastah. City on the Nile in Egypt. Condemned by Ezekiel (Ezek. 30:17).

PI-HAHIROTH (pī' hə hī' rŏth) Place in the Egyptian Delta. Site unidentified. The Hebrews camped here in their Exodus journey (Ex. 14:2, 9; Num. 33:7). Called Hahiroth in Num. 33:8.

PINON (pī' nŏn) Another name for **Punon** (Gen. 36:41; 1 Chr. 1:52).

PIRATHON (pĭr' ə thŏn) Farata [4–F] Hellenistic Pharathon. Town in the hills of Samaria. Home of the judge Abdon in Ephraim (Jg. 12:15). Home of Benaiah, one of David's mighty men (2 Sam. 23:30; 1 Chr. 11:31; 27:14). Fortified by Bacchides in 160 B.C. (1 Macc. 9:50, where called Pharathon).

PITHOM (pī' thəm) T. er-Retabeh? An Egyptian royal store city in the eastern Nile Delta built by enslaved Hebrews (Ex. 1:11).

PTOLEMAIS (tŏl' ə mā' ĭs) Greco-Roman name for **Acco.**

PUNON (pū' nŏn) Feinan [6–O] Town in the copper mining area of Edom. Prosperous c. 2200–1800 B.C. but much reduced and then abandoned until 13th century B.C. The Hebrews camped here in their wilderness wanderings following the Exodus (Num. 33:42–43). Abandoned in the 7th century B.C., the mines were reopened by the Nabateans, exploited by the Romans, and continued to be worked until medieval times. Called Pinon in Gen. 36:41; 1 Chr. 1:52.

PUTEOLI (pū tē' ə lī) Pozzuoli. Port on the Bay of Naples where Paul landed in Italy (Acts 28:13).

Q/R

QUMRAN (kŏŏm' rän) Greco-Roman name for the settlement on the site of **City of Salt.**

RABBAH (răb' ə) **1.** Amman [See locator] Greco-Roman Philadelphia. City along the King's Highway at the edge of the desert in Ammon. Chief city and capital of Ammon. On the border of Gad (Jos. 13:25) but not conquered by Hebrews under Joshua. Besieged by Joab and taken by David (2 Sam. 11:1, 12:26–29; 1 Chr. 20:1). Shobi of Rabbah aided David during Absalom's revolt (2 Sam. 17:27). Condemned by prophets (Jer. 49:2, 3; Ezek. 21:20; 25:5; Am. 1:14). Renamed Philadelphia by Ptolemy II Philadelphus (284–246 B.C.). Successfully withstood siege by Alexander Janneus. City of the Decapolis. Also mentioned in Dt. 3:11; 2 Sam. 17:27. **2.** Kh. Bir el-Hilu? Village in the western hill country of Judah. Assigned to Judah (Jos. 15:60).

RABBITH (răb' ĭth) Another name for **Daberath** (Jos. 19:20).

RAGES (rā' jēz) Rey. Town in Persia mentioned in Tob. 1:14; 4:1, 20; 5:5; 6:12; 9:2.

RAKKATH (răk' ĭth) Kh. el-Quneitira [6–C] Fortified town on the western shore of the Sea of Galilee. Assigned to Naphtali (Jos. 19:35).

RAKKON (răk' ŏn) Village in Dan (Jos. 19:46). Site unidentified.

RAMAH (rā' mə) **1.** er-Ram [4–H] Town along the central ridge route on the plateau north of Jerusalem. Assigned to Benjamin (Jos. 18:25). Fortified by Baasha, king of Israel, but dismantled by Asa, king of Judah, who used the materials to fortify Geba and Mizpah (1 Kg. 15:17, 22; 2 Chr. 16:1, 5–6). Captives from fallen Jerusalem assembled here by the Babylonians for deportation (Jer. 40:1). Where Rachel was buried (Jer. 31:15; Mt. 2:18; but see Gen. 35:19). Settled by Jews returning from the Exile (Ezra 2:26; Neh. 7:30; 11:33; 1 Esd. 5:20). Also mentioned in Jg. 19:13; Is. 10:29; Hos. 5:8. **2.** Town on the northern border of Asher near Tyre (Jos. 19:29). Site unidentified. **3.** Kh. Zeitun er-Rama [5–B] Fortified town in the hills of Lower Galilee. Assigned to Naphtali (Jos. 19:36). **4.** Rentis [3–G] Greco-Roman **Arimathea.** Town in southwestern Samaria. Home of Samuel (1 Sam. 1:1, where called Ramathaim-zophim; 1:19; 2:11; 7:17; 8:4), where he was buried (1 Sam. 25:1; 28:3). Here Deborah judged under the palm (Jg. 4:5). Also mentioned in 1 Sam. 16:13; 19:18; 20:1. Called **Rathamin** in 1 Macc. 11:34. **5.** Another name for **Ramoth-gilead** (2 Kg. 8:29; 2 Chr. 22:6).

RAMAH OF THE NEGEB (rā' mə) Town in Judah. Site unidentified. Assigned to Simeon (Jos. 19:8, where identified with Baalath-beer). One of the towns to which David sent booty taken from the Amalekites (1 Sam. 30:27, where called Ramoth of the Negeb).

RAMAT MATRED (răm' ăt măt' rēd) [2–N] Agricultural settlement in the Negeb dating from the time of Solomon. Destroyed by Shishak c. 918 B.C. Ancient name unknown.

RAMAT RAHEL (răm' ăt räh' ĕl) Place in the hill country of Judah south of Jerusalem. Military fortress and site of the palace of Jehoiakim (609–598 B.C.). Ancient name unknown but thought by some to be the same as **Beth-haccherem.**

RAMATHAIM-ZOPHIM (răm' ə thā' əm zō' fĭm) Another name for **Ramah 4** (1 Sam. 1:1).

RAMATH-MIZPEH (rā' mĭth mĭz' pə) Another name for **Mizpah 2** (Jos. 13:26).

RAMESES (răm' ə sēz) San el-Hagar. Hellenistic Tanis. One of the Egyptian royal store cities in the eastern Nile Delta. Where Israelites began their Exodus from Egypt (Ex. 12:37; Num. 33:3, 5). Called Zoan in Num. 13:22; Ps. 78:12, 43; Is. 19:11, 13; 30:4; Ezek. 30:14. Also known as Raamses. Identified with Avaris, the Hyksos capital.

RAMOTH (rā' mŏth) Levitical city in Issachar (1 Chr. 6:73). Called Remeth in Jos.

A stone arch marks the narrow entrance to the secluded valley in which the Nabateans built Petra.

The ancient Phoenician port of Sidon, seen here from across its bay, furnished carpenters for Solomon's building projects. Paul stopped here en route to Rome.

19:21. Sometimes identified with **Jarmuth 2** of Jos. 21:29.

RAMOTH-GILEAD (rā' məth gĭl' ĭ əd) T. Ramith. City of northern Gilead strategically located on the frontier with Bashan. Levitical city and a city of refuge in Gad (Dt. 4:43; Jos. 20:8; 21:38; 1 Chr. 6:80, where called Ramoth in Gilead). Chief town of Solomon's sixth district (1 Kg. 4:13). Captured by Syria in the 9th century B.C. King Ahab was killed here during war with Syria for possession of city (1 Kg. 22:3, 4, 6, 12, 15, 20, 29; 2 Chr. 18:2, 3, 5, 11, 14, 19, 28). Here King Joram (Jehoram) was wounded fighting the Syrians (2 Kg. 8:28–29; 2 Chr. 22:5). Elisha had Jehu anointed here in 842 B.C. and from here Jehu launched his revolt (2 Kg. 9:1, 4, 14). Called Ramah in 2 Kg. 8:29; 2 Chr. 22:6.

RAPHIA (rə fī' ə) T. Rafah. City on the southern coastal plain along the Way of the Sea near the frontier with Egypt. Where Sargon II defeated the Egyptians in 720 B.C. Ptolemy IV defeated Antiochus III here in 217 B.C. (3 Macc. 1:1). Taken by Alexander Janneus in 97 B.C. but made a Greek city once more by Gabinius c. 55 B.C.

RAPHON (rā' fŏn) er-Rafeh. City in Batanea east of the Sea of Galilee. Sometimes listed as a city of the Decapolis. Judas Maccabeus defeated Timothy here in 163 B.C. (1 Macc. 5:37).

RATHAMIN (răth' ə mĭn) Within the area given by Demetrius II to Jonathan in 145 B.C. (1 Macc. 11:34). Another name for **Ramah 4.**

REHOB (rē' hŏb) **1.** T. Bir el-Gharbi [4–C] Town on the Plain of Acco. Assigned to Asher (Jos. 19:30), who failed to drive out the Canaanites (Jg. 1:31). Levitical city (Jos. 21:31; 1 Chr. 6:75). **2.** T. el-Balat? Town in Upper Galilee assigned to Asher (Jos. 19:28). **3.** Another name for **Beth-Rehob** (Num. 13:21; 2 Sam. 10:8). **4.** T. es-Sarem [5–E] Canaanite royal city below Mount Gilboa where the Jezreel valley meets the Jordan River. Conquered by Shishak c. 918 B.C.

REHOBOTH (rĭ hō' bŏth) **1.** Kh. Ruheibe? [1–M] Place in the Valley of Gerar. Here Isaac dug a well (Gen. 26:22). **2.** Home of Edomite king Shaul (Gen. 36:37; 1 Chr. 1:48). Site unidentified.

REHOBOTH-IR (rĭ hō' bŏth ĭr') City in Assyria mentioned in Gen. 10:11. Site unidentified.

REKEM (rē' kəm) Town assigned to Benjamin (Jos. 18:27). Site unidentified.

REMETH (rē' mĭth) Another name for **Ramoth** (Jos. 19:21).

REPHIDIM (rĕf' ə dĭm) Place in the southern Sinai where the Hebrews camped following the Exodus (Ex. 17:1; 19:2; Num. 33:14, 15). Here Joshua defeated the Amalekites (Ex. 17:8).

RESEN (rē' zən) City in Assyria mentioned in Gen. 10:12. Site unidentified.

REZEPH (rē' zĕf) Resafa? Town southeast of Aleppo. Destroyed by the Assyrians (2 Kg. 19:12; Is. 37:12).

RHEGIUM (rē' jĭ əm) Reggio. Port on the southwestern tip of Italy on the Strait of Messina. Paul's ship stopped here (Acts 28:13) as he was journeying to Rome.

RHODES Port on the northeastern shore of the island of Rhodes. Where Paul's ship stopped on his return from his third missionary journey (Acts 21:1). Also mentioned in Ezek. 27:15; 1 Macc. 15:23.

RIBLAH (rĭb' lə) **1.** Ribla. City in Syria south of Kadesh. Important military base for both the Egyptians and the Babylonians. Where Pharaoh Neco deposed King Jehoahaz of Judah in 609 B.C. and replaced him with Jehoiakim (2 Kg. 23:33). Where Nebuchadnezzar had Zedekiah, the last king of Judah, blinded after witnessing the slaying of his sons (2 Kg. 25:6; Jer. 39:5, 6; 52:9, 10). Where the chief priest of the Temple and other high officials of Judah were killed following the fall of Jerusalem in 587 B.C. (2

Kg. 25:20, 21; Jer. 52:26, 27). Also mentioned in Ezek. 6:14. **2.** Unidentified place near the northeastern boundary of Canaan (Num. 34:11).

RIMMON (rĭm' ən) **1.** Rummana [5–C] Town in Lower Galilee. Assigned to Zebulun (Jos. 19:13). Levitical city (1 Chr. 6:77, where called Rimmono; Jos. 21:35, where called Dimnah). **2.** Another name for **En-rimmon** (Jos. 15:32; 1 Chr. 4:32; Zech. 14:10).

RIMMONO (rĭ mō' nō) Another name for **Rimmon 1** (Chr. 6:77).

RIMMON-PEREZ (rĭm' ən pĭr' ĭz) Place in the Sinai where the Hebrews camped following the Exodus (Num. 33:19–20). Site unidentified.

RISSAH (rĭs' ə) Place in the Sinai where the Hebrews camped following the Exodus (Num. 33:21–22). Site unidentified.

RITHMAH (rĭth' mə) Place in the Sinai where the Hebrews camped following the Exodus (Num. 33:18–19). Site unidentified.

ROGELIM (rō' gə lĭm) Bersinya? [7–E] City in northern Gilead. Home of Barzillai, who aided David at Mahanaim as he fled from Absalom (2 Sam. 17:27; 19:31).

ROME City on the Tiber River in west-central Italy. Capital of the Roman empire. Antiochus IV (175–164 B.C.) was a hostage here (1 Macc. 1:10) after his father's defeat by the Romans at the battle of Magnesia in 190 B.C. His nephew Demetrius I (162–150 B.C.) set sail from here (1 Macc. 7:1) and landed in Syria, where he became king of the Seleucids. In the mid-2nd century B.C. Judas Maccabeus and his brother Jonathan sent messengers here seeking an alliance with the Romans (1 Macc. 8:17, 19, 24, 26, 28; 12:1, 3, 16). Aristobulus banished here after the fall of Jerusalem in 63 B.C. and again in 56 B.C., after escaping to Judea and leading a new uprising. Where Herod the Great came in 40 B.C. to seek favor with Antony and was declared king of Judea. Herod's sons

Archelaus, Antipas, and Philip journeyed here in 4 B.C. to have his will ratified by Augustus. Herod Agrippa I, Herod's grandson, was educated here and became protégé of emperors Caligula (A.D. 37–41) and Claudius (A.D. 41–54), who made him king of all the territories once ruled by Herod the Great. Paul sent a letter to the church there between A.D. 54 and 58 (Rom. 1:7, 15). Where Paul was held under house arrest (Acts 28:14, 16). Early center of Christianity and scene of persecution and martyrdom of Christians beginning in A.D. 64 under the Roman emperor Nero. Traditional site of martyrdom of Apostles Peter and Paul. Ignatius of Antioch and Justin Martyr among other prominent Christians martyred here in the 2nd century A.D. Also mentioned in 1 Macc. 14:16, 24; 15:15; Acts 2:10; 18:2; 19:21; 23:11; 2 Tim. 1:17.

RUMAH (rōō' mə) Kh. er-Ruma [4–C] Town in Lower Galilee. Home of Zebidah, mother of King Jehoiakim of Judah (2 Kg. 23:36).

S

SALAMIS (săl' ə mĭs) Port on the east coast of Cyprus and chief city of the island before Roman rule. Paul stopped here on his first missionary journey (Acts 13:5).

SALECAH (săl' ə kə) Salkhad. City in eastern Bashan belonging to King Og (Dt. 3:10; Jos. 12:5). Assigned to Gad (1 Chr. 5:11). Also mentioned in Jos. 13:11.

SALEM (sā' ləm) Probably another name for **Jerusalem** (Gen. 14:18; Ps. 76:2; Heb. 7:1, 2).

SALIM (sā' lĭm) Salim? [5–F] Place in east-central Samaria. John the Baptist was baptizing here (Jn. 3:23).

SAMARIA (sə mâr' ĭ ə) Sebastiya [4–F] Roman Sebaste. Major city in Samaria. Founded by King Omri in 9th century B.C. as capital of Israel (1 Kg. 16:24). Besieged by Ben-hadad of Syria c. 855 B.C. (1 Kg. 20:1, 10, 17; 2 Kg. 6:24). Where King Ahab built the "ivory house" mentioned in 1 Kg. 22:39 and Am. 3:15, and where he was buried (1 Kg. 22:37). Seventy sons of Ahab beheaded here during Jehu's revolt in 842 B.C. (2 Kg. 10:1). Condemned by prophets (Is. 10:9–11; Hos. 7:1; 8:5, 6; 10:5; 13:16; Am. 3:9; 4:1; 6:1; 8:14; Mic. 1:1, 5, 6). Destroyed by Sargon II of Assyria in 721 B.C. after a three-year siege (2 Kg. 17:5, 6; 18:9, 10) and its people deported to Assyria and Media (2 Kg. 17:6). Along with other cities of Samaria, settled by foreigners (2 Kg. 17:24, 26). Probably capital of Samaria after the Exile. Revolted against Alexander the Great. Taken and resettled by 6,000 Macedonian mercenaries c. 331 B.C. Captured by John Hyrcanus in 107 B.C. Greek city reestablished by Pompey in 63 B.C. Expanded and entirely rebuilt by Herod the Great, who renamed it Sebaste. Frequently mentioned in 1 Kg. 16:28–22:51; 2 Kg.

1:2–21:13; 2 Chr. 18:2–28:15; also mentioned in Is. 7:9; 8:4; 9:9; 36:19; Jer. 23:13; 31:5; 41:5; Am. 3:12.

SAMPSAMES (sămp' sə mēz) Possibly the port of Samsun on the Black Sea coast of Asia Minor. The Roman consul Lucius sent a letter there on behalf of the Jews in 138 B.C. (1 Macc. 15:23).

SANSANNAH (săn săn' ə) Kh. esh-Shamsaniyat [3–K] Town in the Negeb assigned to Judah (Jos. 15:31). Possibly the same as **Hazar-susah** or Hazar-susim in the parallel lists of Jos. 19:5 and 1 Chr. 4:31.

SARDIS (sär' dĭs) Chief city of Lydia in western Asia Minor. Site of one of the seven churches of the Revelation (Rev. 1:11; 3:1, 4). Perhaps the same as **Sepharad** of Ob. 20.

SARID (sâr' ĭd) T. Shadud [4–D] Town in the Great Plain. Assigned to Zebulun (Jos. 19:10, 12).

SCYTHOPOLIS (sĭth ŏp' ə lĭs) Greco-Roman name for **Beth-shan** (Jdt. 3:10; 2 Macc. 12:29, 30).

SEBAM (sē' băm) Another name for **Sibmah** (Num. 32:3).

SEBASTE (sĭ băs' tē) Herod the Great's name for **Samaria.**

SECACAH (sĭ kā' kə) Kh. es-Samra? [5–I] Settlement in the Wilderness of Judah southwest of Qumran. Assigned to Judah (Jos. 15:61).

SELA (sē' lə) es-Sela? [7–N] Fortress-city and capital of Edom. Taken by Amaziah of Judah, who renamed it Joktheel (2 Kg. 14:7). Also mentioned in Jg. 1:36; Is. 16:1; 42:11.

SELEUCIA (sĭ lōō' shə) Saluqiya. Port of Syrian Antioch. Paul sailed from here to begin his first missionary journey (Acts 13:4). Also mentioned in 1 Macc. 11:8. Also known as Seleucia Pieria, to distinguish it from other cities called Seleucia.

SEPHAR (sē' fər) Place mentioned in Gen. 10:30. Site unidentified but perhaps in southern Arabia.

SEPHARAD (sēf' ə răd) Place where exiles from Jerusalem lived following the conquest of Judah by the Babylonians (Ob. 20). Site unidentified but perhaps the same as **Sardis.**

SEPHARVAIM (sēf' ər vā' əm) City in northern Syria or Assyria. Site unidentified. People from here were brought to Samaria following the fall of Israel in 721 B.C. (2 Kg. 17:24, 31; 18:34; 19:13; Is. 36:19; 37:13). Perhaps another name for **Sibraim** of Ezek. 47:16.

SEPPHORIS (sēf' ŏr əs) Saffuriya [4–C] City in western Lower Galilee. Administrative capital of Galilee in time of Alexander Jan-

neus in the 1st century B.C. One of Gabinius' five administrative centers, 57–55 B.C. Garrisoned by Cestius Gallus in A.D. 66. First town to capitulate to Vespasian during the First Jewish Revolt (A.D. 66–70).

SHAALABBIN (shā' ə lăb' ən) Another name for **Shaalbim** (Jos. 19:42).

SHAALBIM (shā ăl' bĭm) Selbit. Town in the northern Shephelah. Assigned to Dan (Jos. 19:42, where called Shaalabbin), who failed to drive out the Amorites (Jg. 1:35). In Solomon's second administrative district (1 Kg. 4:9). Possibly the same as Shaalbon of 2 Sam. 23:32; 1 Chr. 11:33.

SHAALBON (shā ăl' bŏn) Possibly another name for **Shaalbim** (2 Sam. 23:32; 1 Chr. 11:33).

SHAARAIM (shā' ə rā' əm) 1. Kh. esh-Sharia? Town in the Shephelah assigned to Judah (Jos. 15:36). Israelites pursued the Philistines past here following David's victory over Goliath (1 Sam. 17:52). 2. Another name for **Sharuhen** (1 Chr. 4:31).

SHAHAZUMAH (shā' ə zōō' mə) Town in Lower Galilee on the border of Issachar (Jos. 19:22). Site unidentified.

SHAMIR (shā' mər) 1. el-Birah? Village in the southern hill country of Judah. Assigned to Judah (Jos. 15:48). 2. Village in the hill country of Ephraim. Site unidentified. Home of the minor judge Tola (Jg. 10:1, 2).

SHAPHIR (shā' fər) Unknown place mentioned in Mic. 1:11.

SHARUHEN (shə rōō' ən) T. el-Farah [1–K] Town on the southern coastal plain. Fortified by the Hyksos following their expulsion from Egypt c. 1550 B.C. Assigned to Simeon (Jos. 19:6). Taken by Shishak c. 918 B.C. Called Shilhim in Jos. 15:32; Shaaraim in 1 Chr. 4:31.

SHEBARIM (shĕb' ə rĭm) Place in the Saddle of Benjamin to which the men of Ai chased the Hebrews (Jos. 7:5). Site unidentified.

SHECHEM (shĕk' əm) T. Balata [4–F] Major Canaanite city and religious center at the eastern end of the pass between Mount Ebal and Mount Gerizim in central Samaria. Mentioned in the Egyptian Execration Texts (19th century B.C.) and the Amarna Letters (14th century B.C.). Important Hyksos settlement c. 1750–1550 B.C. First city to which Abraham came in Canaan (Gen. 12:6). Jacob came here on his return from Paddan-aram (Gen. 33:18). Attacked by Simeon and Levi (Gen. 34:26). Where Jacob buried his household idols (Gen. 35:4). Joseph sought his brothers here (Gen. 37:12–14). Joseph's body brought from Egypt and buried here (Jos. 24:32; Acts 7:16). Assigned to Manasseh (Num. 26:31; Jos. 17:2, 7) and to Ephraim (1 Chr. 7:28). City of refuge (Jos. 20:7; 21:21; 1 Chr. 6:67; 7:28). Scene of Joshua's assembly (Jos. 24:1, 25). Birthplace of Abimelech, who failed to make himself king here and subsequently burned the city (Jg. 8:31; 9:1-41, 49, 57). Where the elders of the northern tribes failed to anoint Rehoboam as king and instead picked Jeroboam as ruler of the independent northern kingdom of Israel (1 Kg. 12:1, 25; 2 Chr. 10:1). Jeroboam made the city the first capital of Israel (1 Kg. 12:25), but the government soon moved to Tirzah. Devastated by the Assyrians under Shalmaneser c. 724 B.C. Samaritan center after the Exile. Destroyed by John Hyrcanus in 107 B.C. Also mentioned in Jg. 9:46, 47, 49, 57; 21:19; Ps. 60:6; 108:7; Jer. 41:5; Hos. 6:9. Thought by some to be the same as **Bethulia.**

SHEMA (shē' mə) Village in the Negeb assigned to Judah (Jos. 15:26). Site unidentified.

SHEPHAM (shē' fəm) Unknown place on the northeastern boundary of Canaan (Num. 34:10, 11).

SHIHOR-LIBNATH (shī' hôr lĭb' nãth) Place on the border of Asher (Jos. 19:26). Site unidentified but possibly on the plain of Dor.

SHIKKERON (shĭk' ə rŏn) T. el-Ful [2-H] Village on the coastal plain near the Sorek valley. On the border of Judah (Jos. 15:11).

SHILHIM (shĭl' hĭm) Another name for **Sharuhen** (Jos. 15:32).

SHILOH (shī' lō) Kh. Seilun [4-G] Town in central Samaria east of the central ridge route (Jg. 21:19). The most important Hebrew religious center from the time of Joshua to the time of Samuel (c. 1250-1050 B.C.) because it was the home of the ark of the covenant (Jos. 18:1; Jg. 18:31; 1 Sam. 4:3, 4). Here Joshua assigned the tribal areas to the Hebrews (Jos. 18:8, 9, 10) and named the Levitical cities (Jos. 21:2). Place of assembly for the tribes (Jos. 22:9, 12) and site of an annual religious festival, where once Benjaminites abducted girls as they danced in the vineyards (Jg. 21:19, 21). Where Samuel was dedicated to the Lord (1 Sam. 1:24) and

served under Eli at the shrine; where the Lord appeared to him (1 Sam. 3:21). The ark was taken from here to Ebenezer (1 Sam. 4:3, 4), where it was captured by the Philistines in battle. Also mentioned in Jos. 19:51; Jg. 21:12; 1 Sam. 1:9; 2:14; 4:12; 14:3; 1 Kg. 2:27; 14:2, 4; Ps. 78:60; Jer. 7:12, 14; 26:6, 9; 41:5.

SHIMRON (shĭm' rŏn) Kh. Sammuniya [4-D] Canaanite royal city in Lower Galilee on the northern edge of the Great Plain. Its king joined the coalition of Jabin of Hazor against Joshua (Jos. 11:1). Assigned to Zebulun (Jos. 19:15). Called Shimron-meron in Jos. 12:20.

SHIMRON-MERON (shĭm' rŏn mĭr' ŏn) Another name for **Shimron** (Jos. 12:20).

SHION (shī' ən) Village in Lower Galilee assigned to Issachar (Jos. 19:19). Site unidentified.

SHITTIM (shĭt' ĭm) T. el-Hammam [6-H] Town on the Plains of Moab across the Jordan River from Jericho. Hebrews camped here before invading Canaan (Num. 25:1; 33:49, where called Abel-shittim; Jos. 3:1). Joshua sent spies from here to Jericho (Jos. 2:1). Also mentioned in Hos. 5:2; Jl. 3:18; Mic. 6:5.

SHUNEM (shŏŏ' nəm) Sulam [5-D] Town at the western foot of Mount Moreh. Conquered by Thutmose III in the 15th century B.C. Mentioned in the Amarna Letters (14th century B.C.). Assigned to Issachar (Jos. 19:18). Where the Philistines camped before the battle of Mount Gilboa, in which Saul died (1 Sam. 28:4). Captured by Shishak c. 918 B.C. Home of wealthy woman (2 Kg. 4:8) whose child was revived by Elisha.

SIBMAH (sĭb' mə) Town on the plateau east of the Plains of Moab, probably between Heshbon and Nebo. Taken from King Sihon by the Hebrews and assigned to Reuben (Num. 32:3, where called Sebam; 32:38; Jos. 13:19). Mentioned in prophecies against Moab (Is. 16:8-9; Jer. 48:32).

SIBRAIM (sĭb rā' əm) City on the northern boundary of Israel between Damascus and Hamath (Ezek. 47:16). Perhaps another name for **Sepharvaim.**

SICYON (sĭsh' ĭ ən) City northwest of Corinth. The Roman consul Lucius sent a letter here on behalf of the Jews in 138 B.C. (1 Macc. 15:23).

SIDE (sī' dĭ) Port in Pamphylia in southern Asia Minor. The Roman consul Lucius sent a letter here on behalf of the Jews in 138 B.C. (1 Macc. 15:23).

SIDON (sī' dən) Saida. Major Phoenician port north of Tyre. Mentioned in the Ugaritic Texts (15th-14th century B.C.), in the Amarna Letters (14th century B.C.), the writings of the Egyptian Wen Amon (11th century B.C.), and Homer's *Odyssey*. Paid tribute to Tiglath-pileser I (c. 1116-1078 B.C.), Ashurnasirpal II (884-860 B.C.), Shalmaneser III (859-825 B.C.), Tiglath-pileser III (745-727 B.C.), and Shalmaneser V (726-722 B.C.). David, Solomon, and exiles returning from Babylonia employed Sidonian carpenters in their building projects. Condemned by prophets (Is. 23:2, 4, 12; Jer. 25:22; 27:3; 47:4; Ezek. 28:21-22; Jl. 3:4). Captured by Sennacherib in 701 B.C. and destroyed by Esarhaddon in 677 B.C. Sidon furnished ships and crews for Persian king Xerxes I at the battle of Salamis against the Greeks in 480 B.C. Burned by Artaxerxes in 351 B.C. and taken by Alexander the Great in 333 B.C. Taken by Antiochus III in 198 B.C. Jews of Galilee rescued from Sidonian oppressors by Judas Maccabeus' brother Simon in 163 B.C. (1 Macc. 5:15). Independence recognized by Pompey in 64 B.C. Julius Caesar favored the Jews there in 47 B.C. One of the many cities outside Judea beautified by Herod the Great. Paul stopped here on his journey to Rome (Acts 27:3). Also mentioned in Gen. 10:15, 19; 49:13; Jos. 11:8; 19:28, where called Great Sidon; Jg. 1:31; 10:6; 18:28; 2 Sam. 24:6; 1 Kg. 17:9; Ezek. 27:8; Zech. 9:2; Mt. 11:21, 22; 15:21; Mk. 3:8; 7:24, 31; Lk. 4:26, where called land of Sidon; 6:17; 10:13, 14; Acts 20:20.

SIPHMOTH (sĭf' mŏth) Town in southern Judah to which David sent booty recovered from the Amalekites (1 Sam. 30:28). Site unidentified.

SIRAH (sī' rə) Watering place north of Hebron where Joab sent for Abner in order to murder him (2 Sam. 3:26). Site unidentified.

SMYRNA (smûr' nə) Izmir. One of the most important commercial centers of western Asia Minor in Greco-Roman times. Site of one of the seven churches of the Revelation (Rev. 1:11; 2:8).

SOCO (sō' kō) Another name for **Socoh 1** (2 Chr. 11:7; 28:18).

SOCOH (sō' kō) **1.** Kh. Abbad [3-I] Town in the Shephelah at the western end of the Valley of Elah, between Adullam and Azekah. Assigned to Judah (Jos. 15:35). Philis-

Arab Nablus occupies a site near Shechem, ancient religious center between Mounts Ebal and Gerizim.

237

tines camped nearby before David's fight with Goliath (1 Sam. 17:1). Fortified by Rehoboam but retaken by the Philistines (2 Chr. 11:7 and 28:18, where called Soco). **2.** Kh. Shuweika [3–J] Town in the southern hill country of Judah near Debir. Assigned to Judah (Jos. 15:48). **3.** T. er-Ras Shuweika [3–F] Canaanite town at the edge of the Plain of Sharon at important junction along the Way of the Sea. Captured by Thutmose III and Amenhotep II in the 15th century B.C. and by Shishak c. 918 B.C. In Solomon's third administrative district (1 Kg. 4:10).

SODOM (sŏd' əm) City in the Valley of Siddim, possibly east of southern Dead Sea. Site unidentified. Lot went in the direction of Sodom (Gen. 13:10, 12). Attacked by coalition of kings from the north, who were pursued and defeated by Abraham in order to rescue Lot (Gen. 14:2, 8–14). Destroyed because of its wickedness (Gen. 19:24, 28). Other frequent mentions appear in Gen. 10:19–19:4; also mentioned in Dt. 29:23; 32:32; Is. 1:9–10; 3:9; 13:19; Jer. 23:14; 49:18; 50:40; Lam. 4:6; Ezek. 16:46, 48, 49, 53, 55, 56; Am. 4:11; Zeph. 2:9; Mt. 10:15; 11:23–24; Lk. 10:12; 17:29; Rom. 9:29; 2 Pet. 2:6; Jude 1:7; Rev. 11:8.

SPARTA Capital of Laconia in the Peloponnese. Military city-state in ancient Greece. Member of Achaean League but alone of Greek cities granted independent status by the Romans. Jonathan sent a letter to Spartans seeking friendship and alliance (1 Macc. 12:2, 5, 6, 20, 21). Sparta grieved by Jonathan's death (1 Macc. 14:16, 20). The Roman consul Lucius sent a letter there on behalf of the Jews in 138 B.C. (1 Macc. 15:23).

STRATO'S TOWER Phoenician roadstead at site of **Caesarea.**

SUCCOTH (sŭk' əth) **1.** T. Deir Alla? [6–F] Town in the central Jordan valley near mouth of Jabbok River. Festival site before coming of the Hebrews. Where Jacob built booths on his return from Paddan-aram (Gen. 33:17). Taken from King Sihon and assigned to Gad (Jos. 13:27). Punished by Gideon for refusal to aid him as he pursued the Midianites (Jg. 8:5–6, 8, 14–16). Between here and Zarethan, Hiram cast bronze vessels for Solomon's Temple (1 Kg. 7:46; 2 Chr. 4:17). Also mentioned in Ps. 60:6 and 108:7, where called Vale of Succoth. **2.** T. el-Maskhutah? City east of Egypt's Delta. Possibly a border fortress. First place to which the Hebrews came in their Exodus journey after leaving Rameses, or Raamses (Ex. 12:37; 13:20; Num. 33:5–6).

SUR (sŏŏr) Coastal city mentioned in Jdt. 2:28. Site unidentified.

SUSA (sŏŏ' sə) Shush. City in Elam east of Mesopotamia. Royal city of Persia under Darius I (522–486 B.C.) and his successors (Neh. 1:1; Est. 1:2, 5; 2:3, 5, 8; 3:15; 8:14; 9:6, 11, 12; Dan. 8:2). Where Alexander the Great had more than 10,000 of his soldiers

Tiberias, the capital dedicated in A.D. 18 by Herod Antipas, sits on the shore of the Sea of Galilee.

marry native women in 324 B.C. Also mentioned in Ezra 4:9; Est. 4:8, 16; 8:15; 9:13, 14, 15, 18.

SYCHAR (sī' kär) Askar [4-F] City in Samaria. Here Jesus talked with a Samaritan woman (Jn. 4:5).

SYENE (sī ē' nĭ) Aswan. Town in Upper Egypt near the first cataract of the Nile. Marked the southern boundary of Egypt proper in biblical times (Ezek. 29:10; 30:6). Also mentioned in Is. 49:12.

SYRACUSE Greco-Roman port and chief city of Sicily. Paul's ship stopped here for three days on his journey to Rome (Acts 28:12).

T

TAANACH (tā' ə nāk) T. Tinnik [4–E] Canaanite royal city on the southern edge of the Great Plain. Mentioned in city lists of Thutmose III and other Egyptian and Canaanite documents of the 15th and 14th centuries B.C. King of Taanach listed among those defeated by Joshua (Jos. 12:21) and city assigned to Manasseh in Issachar's area (Jos. 17:11; 1 Chr. 7:29), who failed to drive out the inhabitants (Jg. 1:27). Levitical city (Jos. 21:25). Site of the battle between Sisera and Barak (Jg. 5:19). In Solomon's fifth administrative district (1 Kg. 4:12). Destroyed by Shishak c. 918 B.C.

TAANATH-SHILOH (tā' ə nāth shī' lō) Kh. Tana el-Foqa [5–F] Village in the hills of eastern Samaria. Assigned to Ephraim (Jos. 16:6).

TABBATH (tāb' əth) Ras Abu Tabat? [6–F] Place in the mountains of western Gilead. Where Gideon pursued the Midianites (Jg. 7:22).

TABERAH (tāb' ə rə) Place in Sinai where the Hebrews camped following the Exodus. Site unidentified. When they provoked the Lord with their complaints, he destroyed part of the camp with fire (Num. 11:3; Dt. 9:22).

TABOR (tā' bər) Levitical city in Zebulun mentioned in 1 Chr. 6:77. Site unidentified but probably near Mount Tabor.

TADMOR (tăd' môr) **1.** City built in the wilderness by Solomon (2 Chr. 8:4). Possibly the same as **Tamar. 2.** Palmyra. Oasis and major commercial center in the northern Syrian desert.

TAHATH (tā' hāth) Place in the Sinai where the Hebrews camped following the Exodus (Num. 33:26, 27). Site unidentified.

TAHPANHES (tā' pə nēz) T. Dafanna. Hellenistic Daphnae. City on the eastern edge of the Delta in Lower Egypt. Where Jeremiah was taken by the Judahites fleeing the Babylonians (Jer. 43:7–9; 44:1; 46:14). Also mentioned in Jer. 2:16; Jdt. 1:9.

TAMAR (tā' mər) Ein Husb [5–N] City in the Arabah south of the Dead Sea. On border between Judah and Edom (Ezek. 47:18, 19; 48:28). Built by Solomon (1 Kg. 9:18). Probably the same as **Tadmor 1** of 2 Chr. 8:4. Thought by some to be the **Hazazontamar** of Gen. 14:7.

TAPPUAH (tăp' yŏŏ ə) **1.** Sheikh Abu Zarad [4–G] Town in central Samaria. King of Tappuah among those defeated by Joshua (Jos. 12:17). Assigned to Ephraim (Jos. 16:8; 17:8), but "the land of Tappuah" was assigned to Manasseh (Jos. 17:7, where called En-tappuah; 17:8). Brutally assaulted by Menahem of Israel (2 Kg. 15:16). Fortified by Bacchides in 160 B.C. (if the Tephon of 1 Macc. 9:50 is the same as Tappuah). **2.** City in the Shephelah assigned to Judah (Jos. 15:34). Site unidentified.

TARALAH (tăr' ə lə) Kh. Irha? Village in the hill country of Benjamin north of Jerusalem. Assigned to Benjamin (Jos. 18:27).

TARICHEAE (tăr' ĭ kə a) Greco-Roman name for **Magdala.**

TARSHISH (tăr' shĭsh) Fabled port probably in Mediterranean area (Gen. 10:4; Is. 23:1) or perhaps along the Red Sea or Indian Ocean (1 Kg. 10:22; 22:48; 2 Chr. 9:21; 20:36; Ps. 72:10). Where Jonah was going when swallowed by a fish (Jon. 1:3; 4:2). Also mentioned in 1 Chr. 1:7; Ps. 48:7; Is. 2:16; 23:6, 10, 14; 60:9 66:19; Jer. 10:9; Ezek. 27:12, 25; 38:13.

TARSUS Chief city of Cilicia in southeastern Asia Minor on a major route from Mesopotamia and Syria. Destroyed by Sea Peoples in 13th–12th century B.C. Captured by Shalmaneser III in 832 B.C., as recorded on the Black Obelisk, and by Sennacherib in 698 B.C. Cyrus the Younger of Persia passed through here in 401 B.C. Held by Alexander the Great in 333 B.C. and by Antiochus IV in 170 B.C. (2 Macc. 4:30). Capital of Roman province of Cilicia after 67 B.C. Where Cleopatra visited Antony on her famous golden barge in 41 B.C. Birthplace and home of Paul (Acts 9:11, 30; 11:25; 21:39; 22:3).

TEKOA (tĭ kō' ə) Kh. et-Tequ [4–I] Town on the edge of the Wilderness of Judah south of Bethlehem 1 at the western end of the Ascent of Ziz. Where Joab sent for a wise woman, who persuaded David to allow Absalom to return to Jerusalem (2 Sam. 14:2, 4, 9). Fortified by Rehoboam (2 Chr. 11:6). Near here Jehoshaphat defeated a coalition of the Ammonites, Moabites, and Meunites (2 Chr. 20:20). Home of the prophet Amos (Am. 1:1). Perhaps fortified by Bacchides in 160 B.C. (if the Tephon of 1 Macc. 9:50 is the same as Tekoa). Served first as a Jewish and later as a Roman base in the First Jewish Revolt (A.D. 66–70). Also mentioned in 2 Sam. 23:26; 1 Chr. 11:28; 27:9; Jer. 6:1.

TEL-ABIB (tĕl' ə bĭb') Town in Babylonia where exiles from Judah were settled in the early-6th century B.C. (Ezek. 3:15). Site unidentified.

TELAIM (tĭ lā' əm) Town in eastern Judah near Ziph. Site unidentified. Assigned to Judah (Jos. 15:24, where called Telem). Where Saul assembled his forces to fight the Amalekites (1 Sam. 15:4).

TEL-ASSAR (tĕl ăs' ər) City conquered by Assyria (2 Kg. 19:12; Is. 37:12). Site unidentified but perhaps in northern Mesopotamia.

TELEM (tĕ' lĕm) Another name for **Telaim** (Jos. 15:24).

TEL-HARSHA (tĕl här' shə) Unknown town in Babylonia from which exiles returned (Ezra 2:59; Neh. 7:61; 1 Esd. 5:36).

TEL-MELAH (tĕl mē' lə) Unknown town in Babylonia from which exiles returned (Ezra 2:59; Neh. 7:61; 1 Esd. 5:36).

TEPHON (tē' fŏn) Another name for either **Tappuah** or **Tekoa** (1 Macc. 9:50).

TERAH (tĭr' ə) Place in the Sinai where the Hebrews camped following the Exodus (Num. 33:27, 28). Site unidentified.

THAMNA (thăm' nə) Greco-Roman name for **Timnath-Serah.**

THEBES Chief city and major religious center of Upper Egypt. Capital of Egypt during most of the period between c. 2134 B.C. and 663 B.C. Mentioned by prophets, usually as a symbol of destruction (Jer. 46:25; Ezek. 30:14–16; Nah. 3:8).

THEBEZ (thē' bĭz) Tubas [5–F] Town northeast of Shechem where inland routes converge. Here Abimelech was killed (Jg. 9:50; 2 Sam. 11:21).

THESSALONICA Salonika. City in Macedonia on the Via Egnatia. Founded as port and commercial center in the Hellenistic period. Capital of the Roman province of Macedonia. Paul preached here for three weeks on his second missionary journey (Acts 17:1, 11, 13) and later wrote letters to the church there (1 and 2 Th.). Also mentioned in Acts 27:2; Phil. 4:16; 2 Tim. 4:10.

THREE TAVERNS Road junction on the Appian Way south of Rome where Christians from the city came out to greet Paul (Acts 28:15).

THYATIRA (thī' ə tī' rə) Akhisar. City in ancient Lydia in the Lycus valley of western Asia Minor. Refounded as a Greek city under the Seleucids in the 3rd century B.C. and became an important manufacturing center. Lydia, Paul's first convert in Europe (at Philippi), was from here (Acts 16:14). Site of one of the seven churches of the Revelation (Rev. 1:11; 2:18, 24).

TIBERIAS (tī bĭr' ĭ əs) Tabariya [6–C] City on the western shore of the Sea of Galilee. One of the chief cities of Galilee in the Roman period. Built near natural hot springs and dedicated in A.D. 18 by Herod Antipas to succeed Sepphoris as his capital. Named for the emperor Tiberius. Sea of Galilee became known as Sea of Tiberias (Jn. 6:1; 21:1). Also mentioned in Jn. 6:23.

TIBHATH (tĭb' hăth) Another name for **Betah** (1 Chr. 18:8).

TIMNAH (tĭm' nə) **1.** T. el-Batashi [3–I] Town in the Sorek valley of the Shephelah. Assigned to Dan on the border with Judah (Jos. 15:10; 19:43); Danites failed to drive out the Amorites. Where Samson courted a Philistine woman (Jg. 14:1–2, 5). Seized by Philistines in time of King Ahaz of Judah, 735–715 B.C. (2 Chr. 28:18). Taken by Sennacherib in 701 B.C. **2.** Kh. Tibnah [3–I] Village in the hill country of Judah southwest of Jerusalem. Assigned to Judah (Jos. 15:57).

Possibly the same as the Timnah mentioned in Gen. 38:12, 13, 14.

TIMNATH (tĭm' năth) Another name for **Timnath-Serah** (1 Macc. 9:50).

TIMNATH-HERES (tĭm' năth hĭr' ĭz) Another name for **Timnath-Serah** (Jg. 2:9).

TIMNATH-SERAH (tĭm' năth sĭr' ə) Kh. Tibneh [3–G] Greco-Roman Thamna. Village in the hill country of Ephraim in southwestern Samaria on an important road from the coast to Jerusalem. Given to Joshua and where he was buried (Jos. 19:50; 24:30; Jg. 2:9, where called Timnath-heres). Fortified by Bacchides in 160 B.C. (1 Macc. 9:50, where called Timnath). Captured by Vespasian in the First Jewish Revolt (A.D. 66–70).

TIPHSAH (tĭf' sə) Dibse. City on the Euphrates River in Mesopotamia. Northeastern limit of Solomon's kingdom (1 Kg. 4:24).

TIRZAH (tûr' zə) T. el-Farah [5–F] Canaanite royal city at the western end of the Wadi Farah. King of Tirzah defeated by Joshua (Jos. 12:24). Where son of Jeroboam died (1 Kg. 14:17) after capital of Israel had been moved here from Shechem. Probably attacked by Shishak c. 918 B.C. Where King Baasha dwelt (1 Kg. 15:21, 33) and was buried (1 Kg. 16:6). King Elah was murdered here by Zimri (1 Kg. 16:8, 9), who reigned seven days before being overthrown by Omri in 876 B.C. (1 Kg. 16:15, 17). Omri moved the capital from here to Samaria after reigning six years (1 Kg. 16:23). Menahem marched from here in his rebellion against King Shallum of Israel (2 Kg. 15:14, 16). Destroyed by the Assyrians in 721 B.C. Also mentioned in S. of S. 6:4.

TISHBE (tĭsh' bĭ) Listib? [6–E] Village in the Wadi Yabis in western Gilead near the Jordan valley. Home of Elijah (1 Kg. 17:1), who was known as Elijah the Tishbite (1 Kg. 17:1; 21:17, 28; 2 Kg. 1:3, 8; 9:36).

TOCHEN (tō' kən) Village in the Negeb assigned to Simeon (1 Chr. 4:32). Site unidentified.

TOLAD (tō' lăd) Another name for **Eltolad** (1 Chr. 4:29).

TRIPOLIS (trĭp' ə lĭs) Tarabulus. Port on the Syrian coast. Important city in Hellenistic times. Where Greek mercenaries serving in the Persian army seized boats after the battle of Issus in 333 B.C. Where Demetrius I killed Antiochus V and Lysias in 161 B.C. (2 Macc. 14:1). Made a free city by Pompey c. 63 B.C. Beautified by Herod the Great.

TROAS (trō' ăs) Greco-Roman port in Mysia on the northwestern coast of Asia Minor. Founded in the Hellenistic period by one of Alexander the Great's generals. Major city of the area in Roman times. Where Paul had a vision, which caused him to cross over to Macedonia on his second missionary journey (Acts 16:8, 11). Paul visited here on his third missionary journey (Acts 20:5,

6); some think 2 Cor. 2:12 suggests another visit to Troas on his third missionary journey. Also mentioned in 2 Tim. 4:13.

TYRE (tīr) es-Sur [4–A] Phoenician city on an island off the Syrian coast north of the Ladder of Tyre. One of the most important commercial centers for Mediterranean trade from c. 13th century B.C. until Roman times. Mentioned in the Amarna Letters (14th century B.C.). King Hiram of Tyre sent craftsmen and materials to Jerusalem for David's palace (2 Sam. 5:11; 1 Chr. 14:1) and supplied Solomon with craftsmen and materials for his extensive building plan (1 Kg. 5:1; 9:11; 2 Chr. 2:3, 11, 14). Hiram of Tyre cast the bronze objects for Solomon's Temple (1 Kg. 7:13, 14). Sailors from here manned Solomon's Red Sea fleet. Denounced by psalmists and prophets (Ps. 45:12; 83:7; Is. 23:1–17; Jer. 25:22; 27:3; 47:4; Ezek. 26:2–7, 15; 27:2, 3, 32; 28:2, 12; 29:18; Jl. 3:4; Am. 1:9, 10; Zech. 9:2, 3). Paid tribute to Assyrian kings Ashurnasirpal II c. 875 B.C. and Shalmaneser III in 841 B.C. Successfully resisted Assyrian sieges by Tiglath-pileser III and Shalmaneser V in 8th century B.C. and a 13-year Babylonian siege by Nebuchadnezzar in the 6th century B.C. Alexander the Great built a mole to the offshore island to facilitate his conquest of the city in 332 B.C. Free city under Pompey c. 63 B.C. Jewish athletes competing here gave donations to build ships rather than offer them to Hercules (2 Macc. 4:18). Where Paul stayed seven days on his return to Jerusalem from his third missionary journey (Acts 21:3, 7). Also mentioned in Jos. 19:29; 2 Sam. 24:7; 1 Kg. 9:12; Neh. 13:16; Ps. 87:4; 1 Macc. 5:15; 2 Macc. 4:32, 44; Mt. 11:21, 22; 15:21; Mk. 3:8; 7:24, 31; Lk. 6:17; 10:13, 14; Acts 12:20.

A steep road climbs the precipitous slopes of the dramatic coastal headland called Ladder of Tyre.

U/Y

UMMAH (ŭm' ə) Probably another name for **Acco** (Jos. 19:30).

UPHAZ (ū' făz) Unknown faraway place from which gold was obtained (Jer. 10:9; Dan. 10:5).

UR (ûr) el-Muqeiyar. City in Sumer in lower Mesopotamia. One of the earliest cities in the world. Ur of the Chaldeans was home of Abraham (Gen. 11:28, 31; 15:7; Neh. 9:7). Also mentioned in 1 Chr. 11:35.

UZZEN-SHEERAH (ŭz' ən shē' rə) Village near Upper and Lower Beth-horon. Site unidentified. Built by Sheerah, daughter of Ephraim (1 Chr. 7:24).

YIRON (yĭr' ən) Yarun [5–B] Fortified city in Upper Galilee assigned to Naphtali (Jos. 19:38).

Z

ZAANAN (zā' ə năn) Probably another name for **Zenan** (Mic. 1:11).

ZAANANNIM (zā' ə năn' ĭm) Shajarat el-Kalb? Place in eastern Lower Galilee. Boundary of Naphtali (Jos. 19:33). Where Sisera was killed by Jael, wife of Heber the Kenite (Jg. 4:11).

ZAIR (zā' ər) Place south or southwest of the Dead Sea where King Joram (Jehoram) of Judah fought the Edomites in a night battle in an unsuccessful attempt to suppress an Edomite rebellion in the mid-8th century B.C. (2 Kg. 8:21). Site unidentified.

ZALMONAH (zăl mō' nə) es-Salmana? [6–N] Place where the Hebrews camped on the Way to the Arabah after leaving Mount Hor in their wilderness wanderings following the Exodus (Num. 33:41, 42).

ZANOAH (zə nō' ə) **1.** Kh. Zanu [3–I] Village in the central Shephelah assigned to Judah (Jos. 15:34). Settled by Jews returning from the Exile (Neh. 3:13; 11:30). **2.** Kh. Zanuta? [4–K] Village in the southern hill country of Judah. Assigned to Judah (Jos. 15:56).

ZAPHON (zā' fŏn) Kh. Buwaby [6–F] City in the central Jordan valley assigned to Gad (Jos. 13:27). Mentioned in the Amarna Letters (14th century B.C.). Where the Ephraimites confronted Jephthah after his victory over the Ammonites (Jg. 12:1).

ZAREPHATH (zăr' ə făth) Sarafand. Phoenician town on the coast between Sidon and Tyre. Elijah stayed here with a widow and brought her son back to life (1 Kg. 17: 9, 10; Lk. 4:26). Also mentioned in Ob. 20.

ZARETHAN (zăr' ə thăn) T. es-Saidiya? [6–F] City in the central Jordan valley. Place

near Adam where the Jordan River stopped, allowing the Hebrews to cross downstream on dry ground (Jos. 3:16). In Solomon's fifth administrative district (1 Kg. 4:12). Between here and Succoth, Hiram of Tyre cast the bronze vessels for Solomon's Temple (1 Kg. 7:46; 2 Chr. 4:17, where called Zeredah). Perhaps the same as **Zererah** of Jg. 7:22.

ZEBOIIM (zĭ boi' əm) City in the Valley of Siddim in the southern Dead Sea area. Site unidentified. Attacked by the kings of the north (Gen. 14:2, 8). Also mentioned in Gen. 10:19; Hos. 11:8.

ZEBOIM (zĭ bō' əm) **1.** Town on or near the central coastal plain settled by Jews returning from the Exile (Neh. 11:34). Site unidentified. **2.** Wadi Abu Daba. Place northeast of Jerusalem in Benjamin. On the route taken by one company of Philistine raiders (1 Sam. 13:18).

ZEDAD (zē' dăd) Sadad. Place between Riblah and Tadmor. On the northern border of Canaan (Num. 34:8; Ezek. 47:15).

ZELA (zē' lə) Village north and probably west of Jerusalem. Site unidentified. Assigned to Benjamin (Jos. 18:28). Where the bones of Saul and Jonathan were finally buried (2 Sam. 21:14).

ZELZAH (zĕl' zə) Place in Benjamin north of Jerusalem. Site unidentified. Where Rachel's tomb was located and to which Samuel sent Saul after anointing him (1 Sam. 10:2). But see Gen. 35:19 and 48:7, concerning Rachel's tomb.

ZEMARAIM (zĕm' ə rā' əm) Ras et-Tahuna? [4–H] Town in the southeastern hills of Samaria assigned to Benjamin (Jos. 18:22).

ZEMER (zē' mər) Sumra. City in northwestern Syria mentioned in Ezek. 27:8.

ZENAN (zē' nən) Araq el-Kharba [2–J] Town in the Shephelah. Assigned to Judah (Jos. 15:37). Perhaps the same as Zenan of Mic. 1:11.

ZEPHATH (zē' făth) Canaanite name for **Hormah** (Jg. 1:17).

ZER (zûr) Fortified city in Lower Galilee assigned to Naphtali (Jos. 19:35). Site unidentified.

ZEREDAH (zĕr' ə də) **1.** Deir Ghassana [3–G] Town in Ephraim. Home of Jeroboam, 922–901 B.C. (1 Kg. 11:26). **2.** Another name for **Zarethan** (2 Chr. 4:17).

ZERERAH (zĕr' ə rə) Place in Gilead on the route of the Midianites fleeing before Gideon (Jg. 7:22). Site unidentified but perhaps the same as **Zarethan.**

ZERETH-SHAHAR (zĭr' ĭth shā' här) ez-Zarat? [6–J] Moabite town on the eastern shore of the Dead Sea at the site of natural hot springs. Assigned to Reuben (Jos. 13:19). Herod the Great carried there for treatment in his old age.

ZIDDIM (zĭd′ ĭm) Fortified town in Lower Galilee assigned to Naphtali (Jos. 19:35). Site unidentified.

ZIKLAG (zĭk′ lăg) T. esh-Sharia? [2–K] Town in the Negeb. Assigned to Simeon (Jos. 19:5; 1 Chr. 4:30) but held by Philistines; later assigned to Judah (Jos. 15:31). Given to David by Achish of Gath (1 Sam. 27:6). David's base for raiding in the Negeb (1 Chr. 12:1, 20). Amalekites burned and looted here (1 Sam. 30:1, 14). David routed the Amalekites and sent booty from here to various towns in Judah (1 Sam. 30:26). Where David lamented for the slain Saul and Jonathan (2 Sam. 1:1; 4:10). Settled by Jews returning from the Exile (Neh. 11:28).

ZION Another name for **Jerusalem.**

ZIOR (zī′ ôr) Village in the hill country of Judah near Hebron assigned to Judah (Jos. 15:54). Site unidentified.

ZIPH (zĭf) **1.** Kh. ez-Zeifa [5–L] Village in the Negeb. Assigned to Judah (Jos. 15:24). **2.** T. Zif [4–J] Town in Judah southeast of Hebron. Assigned to Judah (Jos. 15:55). Inhabitants told Saul that David was hiding in the nearby wilderness (1 Sam. 23:14, 24; 26:2; Ps. 53:6). Fortified by Rehoboam (2 Chr. 11:8).

ZIPHRON (zĭf′ rŏn) Unknown place on the northern boundary of Canaan (Num. 34:9).

ZOAN (zō′ ăn) Another name for Rameses, or Raamses (Num. 13:22; Ps. 78:12, 43; Is. 19:11, 13; 30:4; Ezek. 30:14).

ZOAR (zō′ ăr) es-Safi [6–M] One of the five Cities of the Plain south of the Dead Sea. Attacked by the kings of the north (Gen. 14:2 and 8, where called Bela). Lot fled here (Gen. 19:22, 23) to escape the destruction of Sodom and Gomorrah. Moabite refugees fled here (Is. 15:5; Jer. 48:4, 34). Captured by Alexander Janneus during the Maccabean wars but promised to King Aretas IV of the Nabateans by Hyrcanus II. Site of extensive Roman date palm and balsam plantations. Also mentioned in Gen. 13:10; 19:30; Dt. 34:3.

ZORAH (zôr′ ə) Sara [3–I] Town in the Shephelah on a ridge overlooking the Sorek valley from the north. Assigned to Dan (Jos. 19:41; Jg. 18:2, 8, 11) but later a part of Judah (Jos. 15:33). Birthplace of Samson (Jg. 13:2, 25), who was buried nearby (Jg. 16:31). Fortified by Rehoboam (2 Chr. 11:10). Settled by Jews returning from the Exile (Neh. 11:29).

Snowcapped Mount Hermon, at 9,232 feet the high point of the Holy Land, towers over a village nestled in its foothills.

A Chronology of Biblical Times

	EGYPT	HOLY LAND	LOWER MESOPOTAMIA	
3000	Narmer unifies Upper and Lower Egypt.		Rise of Sumerian city-states: Sumer, Akkad, Ur.	
	Old Kingdom, c. 2664-2180; pyramids at Giza built during 4th dynasty, c. 2614-2502.	Byblos, Phoenician city-state, trades with Egypt.	Early Sumerian dynasties, c. 2850-2360.	
2500				
	Middle Kingdom, c. 2052-1786.		Sargon unites Mesopotamia; creates Akkadian empire, c. 2360-2180. Gutians invade Mesopotamia.	
2000		Abraham arrives in land of Canaan; Isaac, Jacob, Joseph.	Third dynasty of Ur, c. 2060-1950; ziggurat of Ur built. Invading Amorites establish dynasty in Babylon, 1830.	
1800	Hyksos rule, c. 1700-1550.		Hammurabi reunifies Mesopotamia, issues Babylonian law code.	
1600				
	New Kingdom, c. 1554-1075. Thutmose III, c. 1490-1436; wins battle of Megiddo, c. 1469; takes north Syria from Mitanni.		Kassites rule Babylonia.	
1400	Akhenaton, c. 1366-1349, worships one god; succeeded by Tutankhamen, c. 1348-1339. Seti I, c. 1305-1290, Ramses II, c. 1290-1224, extend border of Egypt northward.	Moses leads Exodus of Jews from Egypt. Joshua invades Canaan. Rise of Phoenician city-states, c. 1200.	Emergence of Assyria.	
1200	Ramses III, c. 1183-1152, defeats Sea Peoples.	Philistines settle coastal plain. Period of Judges. Saul named first king of Israel, c. 1020.	Tiglath-pileser I establishes Assyrian empire.	
1000		David rules Judah, c. 1000-993; captures Jerusalem and rules united kingdom of Israel, c. 993-961. Solomon, c. 961-922. Beginning of divided monarchy, c. 922.		
	Libyan dynasty, c. 935-725. Shishak, c. 935-914.		Period of Assyrian weakness.	
900		House of Omri rules Israel, 876-842. Revolt of Jehu, 842. Shalmaneser III, invades Syria, Israel. Renaissance of Israel under Jeroboam II, 786-746, and Judah under Uzziah, 783-742.	Shalmaneser III, c. 859-825, attempts to extend empire; his rule ends in revolt.	
800		Assyrians capture Samaria, end of kingdom of Israel, 721. Sennacherib attacks Judah, 701.	Tiglath-pileser III restores Assyrian power, 745.	
700	Assyria conquers Egypt, c. 664; Saite dynasty, c. 664-525.	Babylonians take Jerusalem, end of kingdom of Judah, 587.	Chaldean dynasty rules in Babylon, 626-539. Babylonians conquer Nineveh, 612; end of Assyrian empire.	
600	Cambyses of Persia conquers Egypt, first Persian period, 525-404.	Edict of Cyrus, 538; Jews return to Holy Land, Nehemiah builds Temple, Ezra brings the Law.	Persians conquer Babylonians, 539.	
500				
400	Second Persian period, 341-332. Alexander conquers Egypt, founds Alexandria, 332. Ptolemies begin Egyptian rule.	Alexander conquers Tyre en route to Egypt, 332.	Alexander the Great defeats Persians at Issus, 333; Gaugamela, 331; end of Persian empire. Upon return from India, Alexander dies at Babylon, 323.	
300		Four Syrian wars, 276-217; power struggle between Seleucids and Ptolemies to control Syria and Phoenicia. Battle of Paneas, 198; Seleucid rule of Holy Land.	Alexander's generals divide empire, Seleucids rule Mesopotamia.	
200	Antiochus IV invades Egypt, 168; checked by Romans.	Beginning of Maccabean revolt, 167. John Hyrcanus II, High Priest, 134-104. Hasmoneans rule Judea, 104-37. Pompey captures Jerusalem, extends Roman rule to Holy Land, 63.		
100	Julius Caesar secures throne for Cleopatra, 48.	Parthians invade, put Antigonus II on throne, 40-37. Herod the Great, 37-4. Life of Jesus, c. 7 B.C.–c. A.D. 29.		
0		Pontius Pilate, governor of Judea, 26-36. Paul begins missionary journeys, c. 44; taken to Rome, 60, where he is martyred. First Jewish Revolt against Rome, 66-73.		
100		Second (Bar Kokhba) Jewish Revolt against Rome, 132-135; ends in complete Roman victory, Jews dispersed.		

Pyramids at Giza

Hammurabi receives the law

Assyrian war chariot

Alexander the Great

Cleopatra

UPPER MESOPOTAMIA AND ASIA MINOR	GREECE AND AEGEAN	ROME AND WESTERN MEDITERRANEAN	
			3000
Troy founded.			2500
Hittites settle in Anatolia.	Rise of Minoan sea empire on Crete.		2000
Hittite war chariot	*Cretan snake goddess*		1800
			1600
Hurrians form kingdom of Mitanni.	Volcano destroys civilization on Crete, c. 1470; possible source of Atlantis legend.		1400
Battle of Kadesh, c. 1286; Hittites, Egypt divide Syria. Sack of Troy, c. 1250.	Sea Peoples destroy Mycenaean civilization.		1200
			1000
		Rome's legendary founders: Romulus and Remus	900
Battle of Qarqar, 853; coalition of kings check Assyrian drive southwest.	*Mycenaean gold mask*	Phoenicians found Carthage on North African coast, 814.	800
	First Olympic games, 776. *Greek discus thrower*	Legendary founding of Rome, 753.	700
Medes rule Upper Mesopotamia, 625-550.		Etruscan kings dominate Rome.	600
Lydian kingdom at its height. Cyrus of Persia conquers Medes, 550; Lydians, 547; Persians rule Asia Minor.		Roman republic founded, 509.	500
	Greeks defeat Persians at Marathon, 490; Thermopylae, Salamis, 480. Golden Age of Greece.		400
	Antigonids rule Asia Minor, Macedonia.		300
		First Punic War between Rome and Carthage, 264-241. Hannibal crosses Alps at start of Second Punic War, 218-201.	200
Rome defeats Antiochus III the Great at Magnesia, 190.	Rome conquers Macedonia, 168.	Carthage destroyed by Rome at end of Third Punic War, 149-146.	
		Julius Caesar conquers Gaul, Britain, 58-51. Caesar, Crassus, Pompey form first triumvirate, 60. Caesar assassinated, 44. Second triumvirate, 43.	100
	Octavian defeats Antony and Cleopatra at naval battle of Actium, 31.	Reign of Octavian as Augustus Caesar, 27 B.C.- A.D. 14. Reigns of Tiberias, 14-37; Caligula, 37-41; Claudius, 41-54.	0
Roman warship at Actium		Reign of Nero, 54-68; Christians persecuted after Roman fire, 64. Reigns of Vespasian, 69-79; Titus 79-81. Persecution of Christians reaches peak during reign of Diocletian, 284-305. Constantine wins battle of Milvian Bridge, 312; issues Edict of Milan, 313.	100

Bibliography

Aharoni, Yohanan. *The Land of the Bible: A Historical Geography*, trans. A.F. Rainey. London: Burns and Oates Limited, 1966.

Aharoni, Yohanan, and Michael Avi-Yonah, *The Macmillan Bible Atlas*, rev. ed. New York: Macmillan Publishing Co., Inc., 1977.

Albright, William Foxwell. *From the Stone Age to Christianity: Monotheism and the Historical Process*, 2nd ed. Garden City, NY: Doubleday & Company, Inc., 1957.

Alon, Azaria. *The Natural History of the Land of the Bible*. Garden City, NY: Doubleday & Company, Inc., 1978.

Atlas of Israel, 2nd ed. Jerusalem: Survey of Israel, Ministry of Labour; and Amsterdam: Elsevier Publishing Company, 1970.

Avi-Yonah, Michael. *The Holy Land: From the Persian to the Arab Conquest (536 B.C.–A.D. 640): A Historical Geography*, rev. ed. Grand Rapids, MI: Baker Book House Company, 1977.

Baly, Denis. *The Geography of the Bible*, rev. ed. New York: Harper & Row, Publishers, Inc., 1974.

Baly, Denis, and A.D. Tushingham. *Atlas of the Biblical World*. New York: The World Publishing Company, 1971.

Bermant, Chaim, and Michael Weitzman. *Ebla: A Revelation in Archaeology*. New York: Quadrangle/The New York Times Book Co., Inc., 1979.

Bright, John. *A History of Israel*, 2nd ed. Philadelphia: The Westminster Press, 1972.

Bruce, F.F. *New Testament History*. Garden City, NY: Doubleday & Company, Inc., 1971.

The Cambridge Ancient History Series. Vol. 1, Pt. 2–Vol. 10, *Augustan Empire (44 B.C.–A.D. 70)*. London: Cambridge University Press.

Cansdale, George. *All the Animals of the Bible Lands*. Grand Rapids, MI: Zondervan Publishing House, 1970.

Cornfield, Gaalyah. *Archaeology of the Bible; Book by Book*. New York: Harper & Row, Publishers, Inc., 1976.

Daniel-Rops, Henri. *Daily Life in the Time of Jesus*, trans. Patrick O'Brian. New York: Hawthorn Books, Inc., 1962.

Daniel-Rops, Henri. *Jesus and His Times*, trans. Ruby Millar. New York: E.P. Dutton & Co., Inc., 1954.

Encyclopaedia Judaica, 17 vols. and Yearbooks. Jerusalem: Keter Publishing House Jerusalem Ltd., 1972.

Finegan, Jack. *The Archaeology of the New Testament: The Life of Jesus and the Beginning of the Early Church*. Princeton, NJ: Princeton University Press, 1969.

Frank, Harry Thomas. *Bible Archaeology and Faith*. Nashville, TN: Abingdon Press, 1971.

Frank, Harry Thomas. *Discovering the Biblical World*. Maplewood, NJ: Hammond Incorporated, 1975.

Grollenberg, L.H. *Atlas of the Bible*, trans. and ed. Joyce M.H. Reid and H.H. Rowley. London and Edinburgh: Thomas Nelson and Sons Ltd., 1956.

The Interpreter's Dictionary of the Bible: An Illustrated Encyclopedia, 4 vols. Nashville, TN: Abingdon Press, 1962. Supplementary Volume, 1976.

Josephus. *Works of Josephus*, 9 vols. (Loeb Classical Library), ed. E.H. Warmington. Cambridge, MA: Harvard University Press.

Keller, Werner. *The Bible as History: A Confirmation of the Book of Books*, rev. ed., trans. William Neil. New York: William Morrow and Company, 1964.

Kenyon, Kathleen M. *Beginning in Archaeology*, rev. ed. New York: Frederick A. Praeger, 1961.

Kenyon, Kathleen M. *Royal Cities of the Old Testament*. New York: Schocken Books, 1971.

Lapp, Paul W. *Biblical Archaeology and History*. Cleveland: The World Publishing Company, 1969.

Magnusson, Magnus. *BC The Archaeology of the Bible Lands*. London: The Bodley Head Ltd., and the British Broadcasting Corporation, 1977.

May, Herbert G., ed. *Oxford Bible Atlas*, 2nd ed. Oxford, England: Oxford University Press, 1974.

May, Herbert G., and Bruce M. Metzger, eds. *The New Oxford Annotated Bible with the Apocrypha*, RSV. New York: Oxford University Press, Inc., 1977.

Moorey, P.R.S. *Biblical Lands* (The Making of the Past Series). Oxford, England: Elsevier International Projects Ltd., 1975.

Nelson's Complete Concordance of the Revised Standard Version Bible, 2nd ed. Nashville, TN: Thomas Nelson Inc., Publishers, 1972.

New Catholic Encyclopedia, 17 vols. New York: McGraw-Hill Book Company, 1967.

Paul, Shalom M., and William G. Dever, eds. *Biblical Archaeology*. New York: Quadrangle/The New York Times Book Co., 1974.

Pritchard, James B. *The Ancient Near East in Pictures: Relating to the Old Testament*, 2nd. ed. Princeton, NJ: Princeton University Press, 1969.

Pritchard, James B., ed. *Ancient Near Eastern Texts: Relating to the Old Testament*, 3rd ed. Princeton, NJ: Princeton University Press, 1969.

Reicke, Bo. *The New Testament Era: The World of the Bible From 500 B.C. to A.D. 100*, trans. David E. Green. Philadelphia: Fortress Press, 1974.

Rowley, H.H. *Dictionary of Bible Place Names*. Greenwood, SC: The Attic Press, Inc., 1970.

Schürer, Emil. *The History of the Jewish People in the Age of Jesus Christ (175 B.C.–A.D. 135)*, rev. ed., ed. Geza Vermes and Fergus Millar. Edinburgh: T. & T. Clark Ltd., 1973.

Smith, George Adam. *The Historical Geography of the Holy Land*. New York: Harper & Row Publishers, Incorporated, 1966.

Thomas, D. Winton, ed. *Documents From Old Testament Times*. New York: Harper & Row Publishers, 1961.

Wright, G. Ernest. *Biblical Archaeology*, rev. ed. Philadelphia: The Westminster Press, 1962.

Wright, G. Ernest. *Shechem: The Biography of a Biblical City*. New York: McGraw-Hill Book Company, 1965.

Wright, George Ernest, and Floyd Vivian Filson, eds. *The Westminster Historical Atlas to the Bible*, rev. ed. Philadelphia: The Westminster Press, 1956.

Yadin, Yigael. *The Art of Warfare in Biblical Lands: In the Light of Archaeological Study*. New York: McGraw-Hill Book Company, Inc., 1963.

Yadin, Yigael. *Hazor: The Rediscovery of a Great Citadel of the Bible*. New York: Random House, 1975.

Yadin, Yigael. *Masada: Herod's Fortress and the Zealots' Last Stand*. New York: Random House, 1971.

Credits

Biblical Citations

This list provides the chapter and verse of biblical citations used in the text. Boldface numbers indicate the page, followed by the first few words of each biblical quote used on that page and the source. In a few cases the citations are given in the text and are therefore not repeated here. All quotes, unless otherwise noted, are from the Revised Standard Version. A list of abbreviations of the books of the Bible is on page 211.

Page 5. To your descendants . . . Gen. 12:7; a good land . . . Dt. 8:7; defeated the whole land . . . Jos. 10:40; fishers of men . . . Mk. 1:17; Ur of the Chaldeans . . . Gen. 11:31; **7.** We came to the . . . Num. 13:27; **10.** In the beginning . . . Gen. 1:1-2; A river flowed . . . Gen. 2:10; which flows around [Havilah] . . . Gen. 2:11; which flows around [Cush] . . . Gen. 2:13; **11.** And as men migrated . . . Gen. 11:2; Ur of the Chaldeans . . . Gen. 11:31; **18.** wild ass of a man . . . Gen 16:12; the wolf shall dwell . . . Is. 11:6; **20.** like the growling . . . Pr. 19:12; like a lion . . . 1 Macc. 3:4; Beware of false prophets . . . Mt. 7:15; I will make Jerusalem . . . Jer. 9:11; go and tell . . . Lk. 13:32; like a leopard . . . Hos. 13:7; **21.** the heavens were opened . . . Mt. 3:16; neither sow nor . . . Lk. 12:24; I will fall upon . . . Hos. 13:8; a she-bear robbed . . . Pr. 17:12; as if a man fled . . . Am. 5:19; You brood of . . . Mt. 3:7; above all cattle . . . Gen. 3:14; Can you draw . . . Job 41:1; Can you fill . . . Job 41:7; Who can penetrate . . . Job 41:13; His back is made . . . Job 41:15; He makes the deep . . . Job 41:31; **25.** thirty pieces of silver . . . Mt. 26:15; **30.** Go up and down . . . Jos. 18:8; **38.** Thou didst set the . . . Ps. 104:5-8; the place which thou . . . Ps. 104:8; **56.** Cities of the Plain (King James Version) . . . Gen. 13:12; **57.** to go into the land . . . Gen. 11:31; Go from your country . . . Gen. 12:1-2; **59.** with Bethel on the west . . . Gen. 12:8; very rich in cattle . . . Gen. 13:2; moved his tent . . . Gen. 13:12; to Hobah . . . Gen. 14:15; who has delivered . . . Gen. 14:20; like the smoke . . . Gen. 19:28; Take your son . . . Gen. 22:2; **61.** reaped in the same . . . Gen. 26:12; was a quiet man . . . Gen. 25:27; house of God . . . Gen. 28:17; If Esau comes . . . Gen. 32:8; Your name shall . . . Gen. 32:28; **62.** went into a land . . . Gen. 36:6; God has taken . . . Gen. 30:23; Israel loved Joseph . . . Gen. 37:3; Go now, see . . . Gen. 37:14; I have heard . . . Gen. 42:2; in the best . . . Gen. 47:6; Behold, your father . . . Gen. 48:1; When Jacob finished . . . Gen. 49:33; multiplied and grew . . . Ex. 1:7; **66.** Now there arose . . . Ex. 1:8; about 600,000 men . . . Ex. 12:37; Red Sea . . . Ex. 13:18, 15:22; in front of Pi-ha-hiroth . . . Ex. 14:2; by the sea . . . Ex. 14:2; When Pharaoh let . . . Ex. 13:17; **71.** Go up into . . . Num. 13:17; Rehob, near the entrance . . . Num. 13:21; seemed to ourselves . . . Num. 13:33; flows with milk . . . Num. 13:27; Lord is not . . . Num. 14:42; as bees do . . . Dt. 1:44; **72.** by

stages . . . Ex. 17:1; **73.** flowing with milk . . . Ex. 3:8; they carried it . . . Num. 13:23; **74.** wept for Moses . . . Dt. 34:8; **75.** city of palms . . . Jg. 1:16, 3:13; **77.** the house of the Lord . . . Jos. 6:24; sojourner as well as homeborn . . . Jos. 8:33; **80.** hewers of wood . . . Jos. 9:27; until the nation took . . . Jos. 10:13; So Joshua defeated . . . Jos. 10:40; **82.** old and advanced in years . . . Jos. 13:1; allot the land . . . Jos. 13:6; **83.** In those days . . . Jg. 21:25; the city of palms . . . Jg. 3:13; his cool roof chamber . . . Jg. 3:20; by the waters of Megiddo . . . Jg. 5:19; From heaven fought . . . Jg. 5:20; **85.** A sword for the Lord . . . Jg. 7:20; a snare to Gideon . . . Jg. 8:27; came out to meet . . . Jg. 11:34; Shibboleth . . . Jg. 12:6; Sibboleth . . . Jg. 12:6; smote them hip . . . Jg. 15:8; the ropes which . . . Jg. 15:14; **86.** the top of the hill . . . Jg. 16:3; vexed to death . . . Jg. 16:16; A razor has never . . . Jg. 16:17; than those whom . . . Jg. 16:30; judged Israel . . . Jg. 10:2; in the hill country of Ephraim . . . Jg. 10:1; killed six hundred . . . Jg. 3:31; caravans ceased . . . Jg. 5:6; **87.** there was no smith . . . 1 Sam. 13:19; **89.** The glory has departed . . . 1 Sam. 4:22; a deathly panic . . . 1 Sam. 5:11; all Israel . . . 1 Sam. 3:20; the Lord thundered . . . 1 Sam. 7:10; now appoint for us . . . 1 Sam. 8:5; from his shoulders . . . 1 Sam. 9:2; **90.** I will send . . . 1 Sam. 9:16; you shall reign . . . 1 Sam. 10:1; Long live the king! . . . 1 Sam. 10:24; men of valor . . . 1 Sam. 10:26; and his anger . . . 1 Sam. 11:6; Whoever does not come . . . 1 Sam. 11:7; as one man . . . 1 Sam. 11:7; until the heat . . . 1 Sam. 11:11; like the sand . . . 1 Sam. 13:5; a man after . . . 1 Sam. 13:14; surging hither and thither . . . 1 Sam. 14:16; **91.** wherever he turned . . . 1 Sam. 14:47; Because you have rejected . . . 1 Sam. 15:23; Surely the bitterness . . . 1 Sam. 15:32-33; As your sword . . . 1 Sam. 15:33; **92.** evil spirit . . . 1 Sam. 16:15; Saul was refreshed . . . 1 Sam. 16:23; whose height was . . . 1 Sam. 17:4; was like a weaver's beam . . . 1 Sam. 17:7; All the men . . . 1 Sam. 17:24; And the women sang . . . 1 Sam. 18:7; an evil spirit from . . . 1 Sam. 18:10; and he raved . . . 1 Sam. 18:10; Saul was David's enemy . . . 1 Sam. 18:29; If you do not save . . . 1 Sam. 19:11; prophesying . . . 1 Sam. 19:20; well disposed . . . 1 Sam. 20:12; **94.** every one who was in distress . . . 1 Sam. 22:2; stronghold . . . 1 Sam. 22:4; Saul went on one side . . . 1 Sam. 23:26; As the Lord lives . . . 1 Sam. 26:10; he sought for . . . 1 Sam. 27:4; smote the land . . . 1 Sam. 27:9; **95.** from twilight until . . . 1 Sam. 30:17; he was afraid . . . 1 Sam. 28:5; and tomorrow you . . . 1 Sam. 28:19; fields of disaster (Professor Frank's translation), *but see* fields of offering (King James Version) . . . 2 Sam. 1:21; come and thrust me . . . 1 Sam. 31:4; Saul took his own sword . . . 1 Sam. 31:4; to carry the good news . . . 1 Chr. 10:9; Then David took hold . . . 2 Sam. 1:11-12; Thy glory, O Israel . . . 2 Sam. 1:19; **96.** Gilead and the Ashurites . . . 2 Sam. 2:9; king over the house . . . 2 Sam. 2:4; pool of Gibeon . . . 2 Sam. 2:13; arise and play . . . 2 Sam. 2:14; Turn aside from . . . 2 Sam. 2:22; Shall the sword devour . . . 2 Sam. 2:26; And Joab and his men . . . 2 Sam. 2:32; long war

(Continued on next page.)

between . . . 2 Sam. 3:1; went in peace . . . 2 Sam. 3:21; Behold, we are . . . 2 Sam. 5:1; **97.** pool of Gibeon . . . 2 Sam. 2:13; **98.** King David . . . 2 Sam. 5:3; You will not come . . . 2 Sam. 5:6; city of David . . . 2 Sam. 5:7; like a bursting flood . . . 2 Sam. 5:20; was not willing to . . . 2 Sam. 6:10; as one of the vulgar . . . 2 Sam. 6:20; **100.** so Absalom stole . . . 2 Sam. 15:6; Absalom is king at Hebron . . . 2 Sam. 15:10; expert in war . . . 2 Sam. 17:8; swallowed up . . . 2 Sam. 17:16; saddled his ass . . . 2 Sam. 17:23; Deal gently for my sake . . . 2 Sam. 18:5; We have no portion . . . 2 Sam. 20:1; **101.** died in a good old . . . 1 Chr. 29:28; **102.** So the kingdom was established . . . 1 Kg. 2:46; silver . . . was not considered . . . 1 Kg. 10:21; **104.** came to test him . . . 1 Kg. 10:1; she gave the king . . . 1 Kg. 10:10; gave to the queen . . . 1 Kg. 10:13; **105.** all Israel . . . 1 Kg. 4:7; **106.** For the Lord has . . . Ps. 132:13; built the city round . . . 1 Chr. 11:8; houses for himself . . . 1 Chr. 15:1; **110.** all Israel . . . 1 Kg. 12:1; My father chastised you . . . 1 Kg. 12:11; What portion have we . . . 1 Kg. 12:16; all Israel . . . 1 Kg. 12:20; **111.** war between Rehoboam . . . 1 Kg. 14:30; **114.** the fortified cities . . . 2 Chr. 12:4; **116.** and they shall . . . Ezek. 28:7; **118.** Tibni the son of Ginath . . . 1 Kg. 16:21; ivory house . . . 1 Kg. 22:39; **120.** For three years . . . 1 Kg. 22:1; between the scale armor . . . 1 Kg. 22:34; **121.** and the dogs licked . . . 1 Kg. 22:38; **122.** limping with two . . . 1 Kg. 18:21; As the Lord . . . 1 Kg. 17:1; by the brook . . . 1 Kg. 17:3; illness was so severe . . . 1 Kg. 17:17; Go, show yourself . . . 1 Kg. 18:1; Is it you, you . . . 1 Kg. 18:17; because you have forsaken . . . 1 Kg. 18:18; who eat at Jezebel's table . . . 1 Kg. 18:19; a little cloud . . . 1 Kg. 18:44; ran before Ahab . . . 1 Kg. 18:46; **123.** forty days and forty . . . 1 Kg. 19:8; a still small voice . . . 1 Kg. 19:12; And him who escapes . . . 1 Kg. 19:17; eat Jezebel within . . . 1 Kg. 21:23; You shall not come . . . 2 Kg. 1:4; if you see me as . . . 2 Kg. 2:10; The spirit of Elijah . . . 2 Kg. 2:15; **124.** Shall I recover . . . 2 Kg. 8:8; Is it peace . . . 2 Kg. 9:22; What peace can . . . 2 Kg. 9:22; **125.** Is it peace . . . 2 Kg. 9:31-33; Throw her down . . . 2 Kg. 9:33; all that remained . . . 2 Kg. 10:11; Ahab served Baal . . . 2 Kg. 10:18; My father, my father! . . . 2 Kg. 13:14; **126.** fifty horsemen . . . 2 Kg. 13:7; like the dust at threshing . . . 2 Kg. 13:7; set his face . . . 2 Kg. 12:17; **130.** vulture . . . Hos. 8:1; For lo, I will . . . Am. 9:9; A vulture is over . . . Hos. 8:1; **131.** shields, spears, helmets . . . 2 Chr. 26:14; mighty men of valor . . . 2 Chr. 26:12; against the Arabs . . . 2 Chr. 26:7; spread even to the border . . . 2 Chr. 26:8; **132.** he ripped up . . . 2 Kg. 15:16; the son of Tabeel . . . Is. 7:6; his heart and the heart . . . Is. 7:2; **133.** Take heed . . . Is. 7:4; smoldering stumps . . . Is. 7:4; **138.** afflicted him instead . . . 2 Chr. 28:20; **139.** the protection of Pharaoh . . . Is. 30:3; **141.** Make your peace . . . Is. 36:16; **142.** vermilion . . . Jer. 22:14; With the burial . . . Jer. 22:19; **143.** How lonely sits . . . Lam. 1:1; left some of the . . . 2 Kg. 25:12; **144.** gather wine . . . Jer. 40:10; remnant of Judah . . . Jer. 40:15; **145.** waters of Babylon . . . Ps. 137:1; Build houses and live . . . Jer. 29:5-6; By the waters of . . . Ps. 137:1; **148.** Who stirred up . . . Is. 41:2; prince of Judah . . . Ezra 1:8; each to his own town . . . Ezra 2:1; Is it time . . . Hag. 1:4; **149.** this house of God . . . Ezra 6:7; **150.** You see the trouble . . . Neh. 2:17; Yes, what they are . . . Neh. 4:3; spears, shields, bows . . . Neh. 4:16; **151.** weeping and casting . . . Ezra 10:1; It is so . . . Ezra 10:12; **152.** He advanced to . . . 1 Macc. 1:3; **153.** ends of the earth . . . 1 Macc. 1:3; **154.** They all put on . . . 1 Macc. 1:9; **156.** abomination of desolation (Professor Frank's translation), *but see* abomination that makes desolate . . . Dan. 11:31, 12:11; wise in counsel . . . 1 Macc. 2:65; has been a mighty . . . 1 Macc. 2:66; He was like a lion . . . 1 Macc. 3:4; and used it in battle . . . 1 Macc. 3:12; to wipe out . . . 1 Macc. 3:35; Behold, our enemies are . . . 1 Macc. 4:36; **157.** Judas detailed men to . . . 1 Macc. 4:41; When the sun shone . . . 1 Macc. 6:39; **158.** Far be it from . . . 1 Macc. 9:10; And all Israel made . . . 1 Macc. 9:20-21; to recruit troops . . . 1 Macc. 10:6; **159.** and the people began . . . 1 Macc. 13:42; **160.** and opened a way . . . 1 Macc. 14:5; tilled their land in . . . 1 Macc. 14:8; **172.** Now when Jesus was born . . . Mt. 2:1; When Quirinius was . . . Lk. 2:2; wise men from the East . . . Mt. 2:1; shepherds out in . . . Lk. 2:8; will turn many . . . Lk. 1:16; was sent from God . . . Lk. 1:26; He will be great . . . Lk. 1:32; into the hill country . . . Lk. 1:39; Blessed are you . . . Lk. 1:42; My soul magnifies . . . Lk. 1:46; **174.** Lord, now lettest . . . Lk. 2:29; wise men from . . . Mt. 2:1; king of the Jews . . . Mt. 2:2; opening their treasures . . . Mt. 2:11; Rise, take the . . . Mt. 2:20; and dwelt in . . . Mt. 2:23; grew and became

strong . . . Lk. 2:40; listening to them . . . Lk. 2:46; Did you not know . . . Lk. 2:49; **175.** And she gave . . . Lk. 2:7; **178.** appeared in the . . . Mk. 1:4; man sent from God . . . Jn. 1:6; was not the light . . . Jn. 1:8; Bethany beyond . . . Jn. 1:28; was led up by . . . Mt. 4:1; set him on . . . Mt. 4:5; The time is fulfilled . . . Mk. 1:15; Follow me . . . Mk. 1:17; at home . . . Mk. 2:1; the whole city . . . Mk. 1:33; Blessed are the poor . . . Mt. 5:3; The scribes and . . . Mt. 23:2-3; **180.** Follow me . . . Mk. 1:17; appointed seventy others . . . Lk. 10:1; shake off the dust . . . Lk. 9:5; he welcomed them . . . Lk. 9:11; **181.** went up on the . . . Mt. 14:23; for the wind . . . Mt. 14:24; walking on the sea . . . Mt. 14:25; the country of the Gadarenes . . . Mt. 8:28; And a storm of . . . Lk. 8:23; rebuked the wind . . . Lk. 8:24; the region of Tyre . . . Mk. 7:24; through the region of the Decapolis . . . Mk. 7:31; great crowds came . . . Mt. 15:30; Jeremiah or one . . . Mt. 16:14; You are the Christ . . . Mt. 16:16; a high mountain apart . . . Mt. 17:1; This is my beloved . . . Mt. 17:5; Get away from . . . Lk. 13:31; that fox . . . Lk. 13:32; Nevertheless, I must . . . Lk. 13:33; **182.** Three times in the year . . . Ex. 23:14; among robbers, who . . . Lk. 10:30; Our fathers worshiped . . . Jn. 4:20; true worshipers will . . . Jn. 4:23; feast of the Jews . . . Jn. 5:1; **183.** the lilies of the field . . . Mt. 6:28; the region of Judea . . . Mk. 10:1; the wilderness, to a . . . Jn. 11:54; The poor you always . . . Jn. 12:8; Hosanna! Blessed is . . . Mk. 11:9; For the days shall . . . Lk. 19:43-44; **186.** Hosanna . . . Mk. 11:9; looked round at . . . Mk. 11:11; overturned the tables . . . Mk. 11:15; Is it not written . . . Mk. 11:17; Neither will I . . . Mk. 11:33; Render to Caesar . . . Mk. 12:17; love your neighbor . . . Mk. 12:31; as was his custom . . . Lk. 22:39; **187.** then, arraying him . . . Lk. 23:11; the chief priests . . . Lk. 23:13; Peace be with you. . . . Jn. 20:19; **188.** suddenly a sound came . . . Acts 2:2-4; Whether it is right . . . Acts 4:19-20; let them alone . . . Acts 5:38-39; a city of Samaria . . . Acts 8:5; toward the south . . . Acts 8:26; As a sheep . . . Acts 8:32, *see also* Is. 53:7; passing on he preached . . . Acts 8:40; went here and there . . . Acts 9:32; full of good works . . . Acts 9:36; **189.** like a great sheet . . . Acts 10:11; What God has cleansed . . . Acts 10:15; to hear all that . . . Acts 10:33; Truly I perceive that . . . Acts 10:34-35; the gift of the . . . Acts 10:45; exhorted them all . . . Acts 11:23; **190.** was ravaging the church . . . Acts 8:3; I advanced in Judaism . . . Gal. 1:14; still breathing threats . . . Acts 9:1; Saul, Saul . . . Acts 9:4; I am Jesus . . . Acts 9:5-6; without sight . . . Acts 9:9; something like scales . . . Acts 9:18; into Arabia . . . Gal. 1:17; preaching boldly . . . Acts 9:29; and in Antioch the disciples . . . Acts 11:26; with the sword . . . Acts 12:2; was sleeping between two . . . Acts 12:6; **191.** proclaimed the word . . . Acts 13:5; through the whole island . . . Acts 13:6; a Jewish false prophet . . . Acts 13:6; Immediately mist and . . . Acts 13:11; Paul and his company . . . Acts 13:13; bodily ailment . . . Gal. 4:13; in danger from rivers . . . 2 Cor. 11:26; any word of exhortation . . . Acts 13:15; I have set you . . . Acts 13:47, *see also* Is. 49:6; stirred up persecution . . . Acts 13:50; to the Jew first . . . Rom. 1:16; for a long time . . . Acts 14:3; to molest them . . . Acts 14:5; The gods have come . . . Acts 14:11; to continue in the . . . Acts 14:22; my persecutions . . . 2 Tim. 3:11; when they had spoken . . . Acts 14:25; **192.** Three times I have . . . 2 Cor. 11:25; and declared all that . . . Acts 14:27; who belonged to . . . Acts 15:5; abstain from what . . . Acts 15:29; yoke upon the . . . Acts 15:10; and see how they are . . . Acts 15:36; and had not gone . . . Acts 15:38; having been forbidden . . . Acts 16:6; the Spirit of Jesus . . . Acts 16:7; strengthening all . . . Acts 18:23; Come over to . . . Acts 16:9; who had a spirit . . . Acts 16:16; singing hymns . . . Acts 16:25; as was his custom . . . Acts 17:2; **193.** received the word . . . Acts 17:11; strange things . . . Acts 17:20; because Claudius had . . . Acts 18:2; if God wills . . . Acts 18:21; After spending some time . . . Acts 18:23; **194.** straightforward about . . . Gal. 2:14; I live by faith . . . Gal. 2:20-21; a wide door . . . 1 Cor. 16:9; beasts at Ephesus . . . 1 Cor. 15:32; the daily pressure . . . 2 Cor. 11:28; **195.** Great is Artemis . . . Acts 19:28; **198.** When we came into Macedonia . . . 2 Cor. 7:5; taken up dead . . . Acts 20:9; Do not be alarmed . . . 20:10; I am ready not only . . . Acts 21:13; God had done . . . Acts 21:19; **199.** I appeal to Caesar . . . Acts 25:11; You have appealed to . . . Acts 25:12; But soon a tempestuous . . . Acts 27:14-15; the sailors suspected . . . Acts 27:27; On seeing them . . . Acts 28:15; at his own expense . . . Acts 28:30-31; **204.** Go into all . . . Mk. 16:15; devout men from . . . Acts 2:5; **208.** into all the world . . . Mk. 16:15.

Index

*Numbers in **boldface** refer to captions to illustrations.*

A

Ezion-geber, 67, 68, **71,**
  72–74
  rebuilding of, 120
  Shishak's attack on, 115
  Solomon and, 102, 106
  Syrian control of, 133
  trade routes and, 150
  Uzziah's capture of, 131
Ezra, 145, 150–151

F

Fair Havens, 199
Farming. *See* Agriculture.
Feifeh, 60
Fertile Crescent, 50–57
  Babylonians and, **146**
  clothing of, **12–17**
Festivals, Jewish, 182
Festus, Porcius, 198–199
Fishing in Galilee, **180**
Flavius Clemens, 206
Flocks, 62, **63**
Flood, Great, **10,** 11
Florence Baptistery, **175**
Flowers, **22–23**
Footwear, **12, 16**
Fortified cities. *See* Walls,
  city.
4th Dynasty (Egypt), 55
Fox, **20**
Frankincense, 22, 174
Freedmen, synagogue of,
  188

G

Gaba, 165, 168
Gabinius, 166
Gabriel, 172
Gad, 74, 82
Gadara, 166, 168, 176
Gadarenes, Jesus and, 179,
  181
Gaius (of Macedonia), 195
Galatia, 191, 192, 194
Galilee, 55
  Assyrian conquest of,
    136–138
  Deborah and, 83
  Hasmoneans and, 160
  Herod Antipas and, 176,
    177
  Herod the Great and,
    167–169
  Jesus in, 172–175,
    178–182, 187
  Jezreel valley and, **124**
  Joshua and, 80–81
  Maccabees and, 157, 159
  rebellion in, 176
  road to, **184**
  Romans and, 165, 166,
    201
  Vespasian's invasion of,
    201

Galilee, Sea of, **32, 40,** 174
  Alexander Janneus and,
    161
  fishing in, **180**
  formation of, 38, **39**
  Jesus at, 178–180
  Romans and, 177
Galil-ha-goiim, 138
Gamala, 161, 201
Gamaliel, 188
Gath, 87, 89, 92, 113, 131
  Assyrian defeat of, 138
  David in, 92, 94, 98
  Syrian capture of, 126
Gaugamela, 153
  elephant of, **19**
Gaul, 163, 205
Gaza, 57, 87, 89
  Alexander at, 152
  Alexander Janneus and,
    161
  Assyrians and, 136, 138,
    139
  Babylonian victory at,
    143
  coin of, **25**
  commerce and, 149–150
  Egyptians and, 114, 115,
    154
  Philip (deacon) at, 188
  Romans and, 165, 176
  Samson and, 86
  Tell el-Hesi and, 34, 36
Gazara, 158, 160, 165
Gazelle, **19**
Geba, 89, 90, 111
  Assyrian attack on, 140
Gedaliah, 144
Gederoth, 133
Geneva Bible, 29
Gennesaret, 180, 181
Gentiles, 188, 189
  Court of, 186
  Paul and, 191–199
Geology, 38–39
Gerar, 59, 61
Gerasa, 165
Gerizim, Mount, 62, 77, 182
  revolt at, 201
German language, Bible
  and, 27
Germans, 163, 206
Geshem, 150
Geshur, 100
Gessius Florus, 201
Gethsemane, garden of,
  184, 186
Gezer, 98, 102, 111
  archaeology and, 35, 136
  walls of, 115
Ghor Plain, **39**
Gibbethon, 110, 118
  Assyrian capture of, 138
Gibeah, 90, 92, 143
Gibeon, 77, 80, 100
  David at, 96
  Shishak's invasion and,
    114

water system at, 96, **97**
Gideon, 83–85
Gihon River, 10
Gihon spring, 10, **107,** 139
Gilboa, Mount, **95, 124**
  Moreh hill viewed from,
    41
Gilead, 61, 76, 85, 86, 120
  Assyrians in, 136, 138
  David and, 100
  Hazael's attack on, 126
  Jeroboam II and, 128
  Maccabees and, 157
Gilgal, 76, 80, 83, 123
  David at, 100
  Samuel and, 89
  Saul at, 90, 91
Gilgamesh epic, 10–11
Gimzo, 133
Ginae, 182, 183
Ginath, 118
Gischala, 201
Giza, pyramids of, **55**
Goat, **18**
Gold coin, **25**
Golden Gate, **32,** 186, 188
Golgotha, **184,** 187
Goliath, 92
Gomorrah, 59, 60
Gophna Hills, 156, 157, 158
Gorgias, 156
Goshen, 62, 66
Gospel, 172
  early spread of, 188–189
  Paul and, 191–199
Gracchus, Gaius, 163
Grapes, 22, 71, **72,** 73
Great Bible, 27–29
Great Plain, 113
Great Rift Valley, 38, **39**
Great Sea (Mediterranean
  Sea), 66
Greece, 154, 155
  coins of, **25**
  dress and, 16
  Paul in, 193, 198
  Roman conquest of, 162
  Syria and, 155, 156
  trade with, 149
Greek language, 26, 205
Gulf of Aqabah, **71,** 74, 102
Gur, 125
Gurbaal, 131
Gutians, 57

H

Hadrian, **107,** 202, 203, 206
Hagar, 59, 61
Haggai, 148–149
Hajlah ford, 178
Hamath, 61, 71
  Maccabees in, 159
  revolt of, 138
Hammurabi, 57
Hamor, 62
Hanging Gardens of

Babylon, **147**
Hannah, 89
Hannathon, 136
Hannibal, 155, 162
Hanukkah, 157, 183
Haran, 57, 59, 61, 142
Harod, 85
Harosheth-ha-goiim, 83
Hasidim, 156, 157
Hasmoneans, 160–161
  palace of, **184**
  Romans and, 160, 164
  See also Maccabees.
Hasmoneas, Mattathias,
  156
Hattin, 180
Havilah, 10
Hazael, 123, 124, 126
Hazor, 56, **78,** 102, 111
  archaeology and, 34, 35
  Assyrian destruction of,
    136
  commerce and, 149
  conquest of, 80–81
  damage to, 126
  earthquake at, 128
  Maccabees at, 159
  prosperity in, 128
  rebuilding of, 118, **120**
  road at, **41**
  sanctuary at, **80**
Heber, 83
Hebrew language, Bible
  and, 26
Hebrews, 10, 64–98
  animals of, 18
  clothing of, **12,** 14, 16
  coins of, 24, **25**
  Exodus of, 64, 66–68
  invasion of Canaan by,
    76–81
  Judges of, 83–86
  Philistines and, 87–88
  plants of, **22–23**
  tribes of, 82
  wanderings of, 71–74
  See also Israel (kingdom);
    Jews; Judah (king-
    dom); Judea.
Hebron, 59, 62, 66, 71, 80
  Absalom in, 100
  David in, 96, 97
  Edomites and, 150
  Herod and, 169
  Jeroboam and, 113
  Jewish resettlement and,
    148
  Maccabees and, 157
  Samson and, 86
Helena (Constantine's
  mother), 68
Hellenizers, 155, 156, 158,
  159, 194
Hellespont, 152
Hereth, Forest of, 94
Hermon, Mount, 39, **41,**
  136, 154, 174
  headwaters at, **40**